As Much as I Dare

'Arnold Wesker . . . the unique outsider in the British Theatre . . .'
Ronald Bryden

ARNOLD WESKER, FRSL, born in London 1932, is the author of 34 plays mainly for the stage, three books of short stories, two collections of essays and a book for young people. His plays include *The Kitchen* (1957), *The Wesker Trilogy* (1958/60, comprising *Chicken Soup With Barley, Roots, I'm Talking About Jerusalem*), *Chips With Everything* (1962), *The Four Seasons* (1965), *Love Letters on Blue Paper* (1976), *Shylock* (1976), *Caritas* (1980), *Annie Wobbler* (1982), *When God Wanted a Son* (1986), *Wild Spring* (1992).

His work is continually performed worldwide, translated and published in 16 languages, winning prizes here and abroad. In 1989 and 1995 Wesker received an honorary degree and honorary Fellowship from the Universities of East Anglia and London.

He has directed his plays in Havana, Stockholm, Munich, Aarhus, London, Oslo, Madison, and Rome.

to
my grandchildren
Natasha and Werner
and
those to come

As Much as I Dare

An Autobiography
(1932–1959)

Arnold Wesker

ARROW

This edition published by Arrow Books Limited 1995

1 3 5 7 9 10 8 6 4 2

First published in the United Kingdom in 1994 by
Century
Random House UK Ltd, 20 Vauxhall Bridge Road, London, SW1V 2SA

Arrow Books Ltd
Random House UK Ltd, 20 Vauxhall Bridge Road, London, SW1V 2SA

Random House Australia (Pty) Limited
20 Alfred Street, Milsons Point, Sydney
New South Wales 2061, Australia

Random House New Zealand Limited
18 Poland Road, Glenfield
Auckland 10, New Zealand

Random House South Africa (Pty) Limited
PO Box 337, Bergvlei, South Africa

Random House UK Limited Reg. No. 954009

A CIP catalogue record for this book is available
from the British Library

Papers used by Random House UK Limited are natural, recyclable products made from wood grown in sustainable forests. The manufacturing processes conform to the environmental regulations of the country of origin.

ISBN 0 09 935901 4

Typeset by SX Composing Ltd, Rayleigh, Essex
Printed and bound in the United Kingdom by
Cox & Wyman Ltd, Reading, Berks.

Publisher's note

Every effort has been made to contact the authors of copyright material reproduced in this volume. Apologies are offered in advance for any unauthorised usage.

Author's note

In the quoted fiction real life has been used only as a starting point for fictitious and dramatic work. Though a real person may have inspired the creation of a character it does not follow that the person is to be identified with the character in any other way.

Acknowledgements

These are the people without whom this book would never have been put together in so short a time – eighteen months: my assistant, Jan Morris (and her patient young sons, Jonathan and Justin, coping with an absent mother), who typed, checked, rechecked, and encouraged. My dear friend, Mikki Groom, who researched sheets and sheets of queries, encouraged along the way, too. And my editor, Mark Booth, who not only persuaded me to consider what I'd initially thought beyond me, but who taught me the function of an editor: someone who points to that which one instantly recognises is irrelevant, suspect, overblown, distracting, verbose – simply mediocre writing. I'm grateful more than these sparse words convey.

All writers of such works depend upon the generous spirit of permission which I here also acknowledge to:

first, my sister for agreeing that the writings – diaries and letters – of our parents be included; cousins Thelma, Norma and Maurice for permission to print excerpts from their father's letters; cousin June who's helplessly hooked assembling the vast family tree from which I filched and found my way beginning with great-grand-parents; friends and colleagues Alastair Sutherland, Sydney Greenspan, John Smith, John Osborne, Lindsay Anderson (who sadly died a few weeks after writing me his blessing), D.A.N. Jones, Anne Jellicoe, Richard Eyre, Stanley Kalms who permitted me to quote from either their essays or letters or both; to Valerie Grover for permission to quote from the letters and writings of her late husband, Robert Copping; to Cape and Penguin Books, my publishers, for permission to quote from my plays and stories.

'I'm not very good at being old. Some people are like that; only a certain period in their life suits them. Some are lovely children and rotten adults. Me, I was good at being young . . .'

Boomy from *The Old Ones*

Contents

Prologue

I sometimes feel I've never been truly alive, corporally existed, all systems go, nerve ends exposed. Rather, I've just drifted through, an observer sent to report for someone, never actually part of what I've been experiencing.

To become entangled in relationships, action, merely enabled me to make that report, function adequately; but . . . somehow . . . I was never here.

In such a state everyone I know becomes a stranger.

It is a depressing sensation because I want to be here, to belong.

Introduction to paperback edition

Here is the hazard of autobiography – we are handling a life still fluid. Much happens to change its course, alter views of it. Despite those changes I considered it a mistake to tamper with the mood in which the whole was written.

Inevitably a handful of people mentioned have been upset for a variety of reasons. Protestations have ranged from the foolish to the genuinely pained. It is impossible to write of a life without bringing into it those who touch that life. Most complainants simply looked up the index to see if they were mentioned and so were oblivious to the overall tenor of the work. They must not be surprised if I have scant sympathy for their niggles. Others I've written to.

It is, at the time of writing, only eight months since first publication. In that time four mentioned in the book have died; two playwrights, John Osborne and Robert Bolt; Kathleen Tynan, widow and biographer of theatre critic, Kenneth Tynan; and film director, Jack Clayton. Lindsay Anderson, the film director to whom I owed my beginning, died while writing the book.

The hardback edition was vast and daunting. It pleased those who enjoy long novels. Reviews have been widespread and the attention given – gratifying. I hope cuts have not destroyed the careful orchestration of the original but rather resulted in a refinement attracting a wider public that has so much else of value competing for its attention.

Never has any work I've written so drained me as did the writing of *Dare*. I would not have imagined it possible to be left reeling somnambulistically with little thought in my head and few wishes driving my spirit. As though I'd rubbed myself out. Most odd.

Or perhaps odder still that I'm surprised.

Blaendigeddi
1 May 1995

Introduction

The internal contradiction of autobiography is that it demands organisation of the unorganisable, explanation of the inexplicable. Experience is the sum total of minute detail. I try to arrange feelings in an orderly manner saying, for example, that my love for Esther was a kind of Rosebud throughout my life; but stumbling upon a youthful diary reveals aspects of her character that irritated me. Monday I desired her passionately, Tuesday she drove me to distraction. Contradictions, but a recognisable truth about relationships.

What does the title mean? *As Much as I Dare*. All that I dared and did not dare in life? As much as I dare reveal of what *was* dared? As much as I dare reveal of the life of others? As much castigation as I dare heap upon those in high places who have behaved dishonestly, treacherously, in a cowardly way? We are talking here both of other people's privacy and reputations, and of the sticky urge to revenge, the temptation to perpetrate professional animosities at a time when I am still in need of professional support. Not wise!

Perhaps the beginning of any autobiography should declare what it will *not* declare, to obviate the reader being drawn along by false expectations. This then will be a book of *some* private confession but not a tell-all; it will contain little theatre gossip and only a touch of malice – the reader must look to the more theatrical mentality for that. It is not possible to protect all the feelings of those close to me but respect will be maintained and, if anyone comes off badly, it will be me.

I am interested mainly in those details of a life which I *think* informed the plays and stories. Inevitably much will be quoted from them and – I prepare the reader – from letters and diaries, sometimes to reveal how, through imaginative restructuring, life was transmogrified into literature, sometimes because the works themselves carry autobiographical details which take up the story, and sometimes because, in the letters and diaries, more is remembered with greater clarity than I can muster.

Artists reveal many things about themselves through their work. Not only what they've done but what they would *like* to have done; not only what, through their characters, they *declare* they think but also, shielding behind those characters, what they dare not think; not only who they are but the kind of person they would like to be, or, often, the kind of person they *fear* they *may* be! Almost everything I am – what I fear, think, feel – is touched on, hinted at, blatantly stated in what I write. To understand, for example, my view of myself as a writer look to *Annie Wobbler*.

> I think I began writing when I wanted to affect others the way writers affect me. I think.

My deepest fear is there, too:

> Of being afflicted with a sense of futility. Of violence and certitudes. Of failing my son. Of being disliked . . . mediocre. Somewhere within us all is a body waiting to give up, don't you think?

Why should I think my life more interesting than any chance body passed in the street? The answer is I don't. It isn't. Not necessarily.

Fame and achievement invite curiosity. Autobiographies are written to satisfy that curiosity and answer the simple questions: what forces and influences came together over the years to shape the personality and mind responsible for those performances, those political acts, those paintings, plays, musical compositions – that life?

Contemplating whether to write this autobiography – assembling and looking through old files, making notes, hazarding these first pages, fixing the landmarks – I had to weigh up the material alongside my ability to handle it, uncertain whether it was the book I wanted to take on just now. Was I in the right state of mind?

Author's pen and ink drawing of his study in Wales

I live alone. That sounds more dramatic than the reality. Mostly I enjoy living alone but – to explain briefly: four years ago while directing *The Merry Wives of Windsor* in Oslo I fell in love with a Norwegian friend of eleven years' standing, Mona Levin. Though I didn't fall out of love with Dusty, our thirty-five-year-old marriage went reeling. The repercussion is distressing. As I write I know neither the love affair can be sustained – pain has been created, I carry too much history; nor can I return home – a sense of something unfulfilled would haunt. Dusty, the 'blonde bombshell', lives in the London house, I live in the Welsh cottage. My younger son, Daniel, a photographer, is marrying a German teacher of art in Leipzig where he will live; my daughter, Tanya Jo, conducts English conversation in České Budějovice, the town in the Czech Republic where the first-ever foreign production of one of my plays – *Roots* – took place in 1958. She plans a career in therapy. My second daughter, Elsa, by a Swedish journalist, is married to a Cossack dancer and lives between Moscow and Stockholm studying

Russian and anthropology, working sometimes for the Swedish Embassy.

You, Lindsay Joe, my first, my eldest, are head of music for the commercial radio station Kiss FM. You refuse to talk to me because of the break-up, nor will you allow me to see my grandson, Werner, now aged three. My children are my only real passion. The unimaginable has happened. I miss you, I miss them. It causes me heartache but, more, I fear for you, that when I am dead you will grieve with a deep guilt. Your grandmother constantly warned your father: 'Don't talk to me and behave in a way you'll regret when I'm gone.' Though never as good as I should have been, I was not a bad son. Yet I still regret. On the other hand you've given me a gorgeous granddaughter, Natasha, progeny of your first partner, the young black playwright, Jacqueline Roudet – pseudonym for Magdalene St Luce.

My professional fortunes have struggled through the normal vicissitudes early fame brings. The volumes of writing – ephemeral or not – are gratifyingly numerous, evidence that I have worked! I am not Britain's favourite theatre son at this moment and, thank God, I have made a healthy number of enemies – or should it be 'a number of healthy enemies'? But, though unloved, I have not dried up, and I suppose my name has its place in the world's theatre.

So, I will begin. Not sure I'll finish, but I'm hooked. What on earth *did* happen? Those letters, my mother's papers, the stories, the poems, the early diaries – I'm in there somewhere. This will be the nearest I get to therapy. They tell me it will be a painful journey.

I have already wept.

Chapter One

Toe in the water

Can we be trusted to remember clearly, record accurately, reflect honestly?

I would prefer to be my biographer than autobiographer. All manner of fears tempt us to the extremes of either arrogance or self-deprecation. I hover between modest hesitancies: 'My work seemed to find approval with the public'; and defiant assertions: 'I am gifted with genius.' Genius? There is in the notion of genius a quality God-like rather than human, or God-inspired; genius as a vehicle carrying something that is not really his. Or hers. I don't feel this. Nothing God-like flows through me. Very human, my blood. For me the experience of writing is one of hewing clumsily marshalled thoughts and material I do not instantly comprehend, with tools I do not naturally know how to handle, a prose I must forge slowly, slowly, over long periods. God seems to have a scant role in my wrestlings. I feel out there on my own, with no help. It cannot be said, therefore, 'I am gifted with genius.'

And I suffer from nostalgia like some people suffer from heartburn. They instantly turn food into painful acids, I instantly turn hours into painful past – not necessarily because the past was painful but painful for being past.

Images, events, faces – I recall much that is concretely visual, but what were my feelings aged seven, thirteen, seventeen? An early image is of my paternal grandfather tapping his way with a white stick from Rothschild's Buildings in Flower and Dean Street to Fashion Street, the parallel street where we lived in Stepney, London E1. He was half blind. I was about six years old. Did I love him? I see vividly my paternal grandmother curled crippled in bed from arthritis and remember approaching her with anticipation,

1

hoping she would reach under her pillow for a farthing or a half-penny. Did I love her? We didn't know each other long enough!

So many possible beginnings – streets, smells, sounds, family life, family history, social background. I've wept but am intrigued. A lot has happened. In one corner – creative output and professional blunders; in another – the joys, miseries and mistakes of a private life. Rich, full and floundering days.

First image – a school photograph. The Jewish Infants School, Commercial Street, London E1. A teacher and thirty-two children – twenty-one girls, eleven boys – face the camera. Only eight of the girls and four of the boys risk a smile. The floor is wooden parquet. A clock on the wall, roman numerals, tells the time is 2.20 p.m. I'm sitting in the front row, cross-legged, hands resting on my ankles. My eyes are wide with mischief and feigned innocence. The right side of my face seems swollen. I have not been socked. My tongue is in my cheek.

Earliest memories – my father Joe's sisters. He had four: Rae, Sara, Billie and Ann. I loved them and they cared for me. Rae died in 1976 and her ashes are buried in a Jewish cemetery full of burial stones with evocative names like Sara Bella Peterkovsky, Morris Shmercovich, Rae Rutkowski, Sophie Sprintz, Jenny Smolask, Abraham Vegoda, Mark and Leah Glick. Sara was a trade-union organiser of the Tailor and Garment Workers' Union. She died in 1971, her ashes lie under a tree in my sister's garden in Norfolk. Annie died in 1992 and her ashes are buried under a red rhodo-dendron in the garden where I live in Wales. Billie, when I started writing this book, was in a home suffering out her last senile dementia years. She died around page 300 on 8 October 1993. In 1979 I recorded a conversation with Aunt Annie in which I probed her about my mother as a young woman. 'Ach!' she said, 'what do you want to remember for? It'd be too painful.' Why? What was there about my mother as a young woman that would pain me? Aunt Annie was evasive.

'You had blond hair up till the age of two or three . . . your teeth grew crooked . . . you never *wore* your overcoat, you always tied it round your neck by the sleeves. And you never pulled your gloves off proper-like, you pulled them off with your teeth. I used to yell at you, "If you do that again I won't knit you any more!" . . . You never listened. You were a dead-end kid. Always getting yourself lost. The policeman was always bringing you home. We used to be terrified of leaving you alone in case you fell out of the window. You were very capable of climbing on the ledge and we were three storeys up. Whenever you got into trouble with the kids in the playground I'd hear you call "Aunty Aaaaaaaneeeeee" . . .' She laughed. 'Well, what else can I remember? You go back a bloody hell of a long way, you know! I remember this . . .' She was a laugher my Aunt Ann, even up to her last days when I used to visit her in The Jewish Home in Finchley; despite the bitter melancholia that afflicted her at the end, she would find something to say that made her laugh. 'I remember this – when you were born, the Boba [Yiddish for 'grandmother'] took one look at you and said: "Well, he's either going to be a great man or a murderer!"' How she laughed. 'And Della used to mother you . . .'

Della, my sister, eight years older than me, mothered me but dropped me on my head when I was about eighteen months old. The scar is still visible. She was cradling me between her legs as she'd seen our mother do it, her hands under my head. I wriggled, slipped out of her control. Over my squalling she cried: 'I was holding his head, I was holding his head.' When I questioned her in 1979 she reminded me that I was unmanageable as a child. 'You broke the bars of your cot to get out. The truth is no one could control you except me. *We* had a good relationship. You'd listen to me . . .' In later years she corrected the myth of me being dropped on my head. 'You slipped between my legs but I caught you. *You* were OK but I was sobbing.'

'Where did my scar come from, then?'

'I don't know. You had a growth I think, and the doctor cut it away and left a scar . . .' I prefer the story of being dropped on my head. It seems to account for much.

My hair didn't stay blond for long. On 16 May 1982, six days before my fiftieth birthday, a woman named Rosie Saunders wrote to me from London NW8. Her handwriting was all capitals:

. . . I AM A WOMAN IN MY SIXTIES BEING BORN & BROUGHT UP IN THE EAST END & ONLY COMING TO MARYLEBONE WHEN WE WERE BOMBED OUT IN 1941. I FIRST SAW YOU HOLDING THE HAND OF YOUR LITTLE SISTER, WAITING FOR YOUR DAD IN A WORKSHOP IN FASHION ST E1. MY FATHER WHOSE NAME WAS FISHEL & WHO WAS A MEMBER OF THE NUTGW [National Union of Tailor and Garment Workers] IN GT GARDEN ST WAS ASKED BY YOUR AUNT SARA WESKER IF HE COULD POSSIBLY TAKE A PLAIN MACHINER TO MAKE LININGS, AS HE WAS OUT OF WORK WITH TWO SMALL CHIL-DREN & NEEDED MONEY BADLY. MY DAD AGREED & ASKED HIS GUVNER WHOSE NAME WAS SYD TO GIVE HIM A CHANCE. I WAS WORKING THERE TOO, & RE-MEMBER YOUR DAD MOST VIVIDLY. HE WAS A VERY DARK THIN MAN WHO SPOKE INTELLIGENTLY, BUT VERY QUIETLY. HE WORKED ONLY 3 WEEKS WITH US AS HE DIDN'T LIKE THE WORK AND ATMOSPHERE. MY DAD GAVE YOU & YOUR SISTER A PENNY EACH ON THE FRIDAY NIGHT WHILE YOU WERE WAITING FOR YOUR DAD. YOU HAD BLACK CURLY HAIR, & THROUGHOUT YOUR SUCCESSES I HAVE OFTEN THOUGHT BACK TO THOSE DAYS . . .

Aunt Ann went on to remind me of what I already knew, that my mother gave birth to a second child, who would have been my brother, some time near the end of January 1925. 'But when he was six weeks they took him to The London Hospital where he died from meningitis. My father looked after the funeral arrangements.' Going through my mother's papers I discovered a small envelope on which she had written 'Mervin Wesker. My son who died 1.3.25.' Inside was a sad little card with a black surround. Aunt Ann had got it wrong. It was The Queen's Hospital for Children. Connaught Ward. They had spelt the name as Whesker. 'You know what your mother named him? – this is how bloody daft we all were in those days – she named him Mervin Lenin!'

I asked about my grandfather.

'Your Zeyda [Yiddish for 'grandfather'] was a military tailor when he was a conscript in Russia. Out of the military he was a general tailor. Helped to found one of the first unions. But his heart was not in tailoring, his heart was in singing. His father died when he was young so he *had* to go in for tailoring. My father handed down his good singing voice to Sara and Joe and Rae. Not me. I can't crack a note. He was a Talmudic scholar, my father. Apart from having a lovely voice he was a Talmudic scholar. It meant a lot to him.'

My mother, Leah Wesker, née Perlmutter, born in Gyergószentmiklos, Transylvania, on 24 July 1898, one of eleven children, arrived in this country aged eleven. The first of the strong women. On 2 March 1948, when she was fifty, she wrote a short letter which she never sent. I leave in her grammar and spelling to convey its flavour. Later excerpts from her letters and diaries will be corrected.

My Dearest Children

Nothing worst than to be lonely.

I have always been left alone. I am not malow-drematic as my daughter would say.

That was always my weakness, I could never stand lonelyness.

From childehood, onwards, I always's liked to be with lots of people. My husband has left me maney a times, during the aile years, of my marrege, & that what made me go back with him, each time, was my being alone. There is no reason to be upset just now, my Arnold has only gone for one week, to my daughter, but I can't bare parting from my children.

It is raining & misrible & I have just come home from work, & I feel terrible depresed, I always's do, escpecly today.

I will feel much better when I gett a telegram, that theiy are arived saftly.

My father, Joe, hated his work as a tailor's machinist. He was more often at home than at work, preferring to bury his head in a book. Like my father I would sometimes prefer to be reading than writing. A fantasy I play with is: if I become rich I'll study for a degree in philosophy, or Jewish history, or the history of ideas.

My mother was tiny, about four feet eight inches. Her nieces and nephews – and in later years her grandchildren – measured their maturity comparing their height to hers. She was pretty and fiery, her temper reserved for ugly behaviour – from the irresponsibility of my father to the callous indifference of exploiting employers, from rudeness to arrogance, from brutal hands to brutal words. But her smile was gentle. She was tender and she loved.

My father was not much taller; dark and handsome with a high forehead and thoughtful brown eyes. His threshold of tolerance of fools was low. Born with a natural intelligence he could detect the sloppy thought, the careless, shallow utterance. He loved company and conversation, and, though he too was tender like my mother, his need was more to be loved than to love.

I know why Aunty Annie talked of pain and was evasive about the early years of my mother and father. One of my earliest memories of them is a quarrel which ended as a comic tragedy. My father fled down the flight of stairs of our tenement with my mother chasing, brandishing an enamel wash basin, and him shouting up from the street where neighbours had gathered: 'She's mad your mother, she's mad.'

Both my parents began autobiographies. Joe started his in a red exercise book with a white label announcing that its owner attended 'The County Secondary School, Clapton, Laura Place, Lower Clapton Road, E5'. In it are the first forty-four pages of his attempt. Though he had numbered in hopeful anticipation up to page 228, he only ever wrote as far as page 122.

I leave, in the first few lines, his spelling and syntax.

Of me The Dummy and my Family

Sitting at my work in the shop one day my attention was drawn to the dummy that we all try the work on.

The rhythm of the mashins and my constant looking at the dummy rocked me of in a kind sleepy dase.

And to my surprise the dummy began to take the shape of a human it began to speak softly at first so softly I could hardly hear it.

And then louder and still louder and it seemed to raise its eyebrows and with a challenge asked 'your life. What of . . .' My life? I had never thought and now I began to take my mind back way back to the time when I was a little boy.

My mother wrote hundreds of letters and copious diary sheets. Many of the letters were never posted, many of her diary sheets she tore up, fearing that the bitterness and accusations they contained would hurt her children. A great deal remains, however, facts I'd forgotten, confused political thoughts, heartbreaking self-recriminations for a marriage she felt she had failed, for a life wasted. Among her papers are the letters she wrote to Dusty and me when we worked in Paris in 1956, and the first sixteen sheets of an autobiography begun in competition with my father when she discovered he had started to write his. The title was to have been:

It Was The Year 1910

the year she arrived in England with the youngest two of her brothers. She began to write it on 23 August 1956.

I must start from the beginning of my life. I have written many a bit and pieces, of my thoughts, and about my relationship with my husband and children, but I burnt it all up. It did not sound good as it was in the middle of my life, and to know what I mean and to make it more clear I must start at the beginning.

I am now fifty-nine years of age and would I have had the education in a proper school and to the right age as children go to, and going to high schools, I might have been in a good position. I might have been even a writer because as old as I am I have an inclination to write. I am for ever jogging down one thing and another only I always tore them or burn them . . .

Among my mother's papers are a mass of extraordinary doodles – reproduced here as end papers. Together with her writings they speak of a genuine and powerful creative urge that is dark and sweet and playful. Though with no dark side, my father was also sweet and playful. How could two sweet people make each other so miserable? Their tragedy, my inheritance.

Chapter Two

State of mind

I'm anxious about states of mind. It's a legitimate question: what was his state of mind when he began to write his autobiography? It matters. At the height of a career? Self-satisfied? Restless with discontent? Warm with approbation? Frazzled and smouldering with neglect? Luminous and creative? Pale and blocked?

I was never an angry young man, none of us were, a silly, journalistic misnomer. On the contrary we were all very happy young men and women (let's not forget Doris Lessing, Anne Jellicoe, Shelagh Delaney). Who would *not* have been happy? Discovered, paid, applauded, made internationally famous overnight! But at this moment I have five new plays unperformed and rejected by theatres in this country, and two major, well-reviewed plays not seen in London: *Shylock* and *The Wedding Feast*.

I smoulder, I'm bewildered, I'm hurt and frustrated. I feel like a leper, conscious of a furtive, embarrassed moving away, a shunning. That's my state of mind. Of course by the time this book appears in the shops the situation may have changed. It is a feature of a playwright's life that fortunes alter overnight. Tomorrow's post may bring a letter from the National Theatre requesting the rights for a revival of *The Kitchen* or – a play never seen in this country as I wrote it – *Their Very Own and Golden City*. Shone upon from such heights the leprosy would fade. Meanwhile the non-appearance of so much work clots, though fortunately, so far, has failed to stem, the flow of inspiration. There exists a myth that misery drives creation (was God *so* unhappy?) It is not *my* myth. I need joy in order to write. Yet despite rejection and the joy souring, I do somehow find the energy, even the delight, to shape new works.

It is the queerest of sensations, this literary leprosy. Chilling.

And difficult to talk about. Shunned, what face does one wear? How must one form one's features? I write at least a play or long story or major adaptation every year, the press has been generous with space given at regular intervals and yet I sense within the profession a kind of nervous terror of me. What is this plague which I fail to recognise but obviously marks me like Cain? I search around as one does for stains on a shirt, shit clogged in a shoe, a torn pocket. Does my breath smell? Are my armpits unwashed? I don't remember murdering anyone. I've fulfilled all professional commitments, turned up on time, stabbed no one in the back, directed and made stars of actors I've chosen against advice, guided an actress to win a prize, helped students with their theses, praised colleagues, given time to friends, family and strangers, answered all mail – promptly! What could be my crime? It's like not being there. Invisible man. As though I am air through which the profession walks. Who did I offend? Who began the whisper? What could be so awful in my writing to earn such neglect? For neglect I feel. That is my state of mind.

On the other hand I'm intrigued. Sometimes amused. Richard Eyre for example. A kindly and courteous man who gazes down on one as though he was the local vicar consoling bereavement. He has promptly and unstintingly read and said no to six new plays, including one for children, replying in short notes with no reasons offered (except on one occasion), simply the observation that 'it is not for us'. He never fails to sign off in the most friendly manner and more than once has added 'stay in touch'. I began to feel guilty placing him in a situation where he would have once again to write 'not for us'. Did he sigh every time he heard from me?

Dear Arnold

I don't sigh every time I hear from you, in fact I am rather pleased to hear from you, although I never escape a feeling of re- morse when I send back a play of yours with a disappointing answer.

Please continue to send me your work. As you know I very much

10

appreciate the fact that we are able to maintain a relationship in spite of my disappointing response to your work recently. I am sorry you are having financial problems and send you all the best wishes in the world.

Yours – Richard

No doubts there about genuine concern but I will never know what it is he thinks he's read, or why 'it's not for us'. Nor will I ever understand who 'us' is. It made me smile after a while, that phrase, 'not for us', and my own short replies teased a little, though I'm not sure he ever divined the tease. Turning down a Rabelaisian love story adapted from my original film script *Lady Othello* he suggested it might have a better chance in the provinces. I was uncertain what the implications of that suggestion were – that there is a 'provincial' play and a 'metropolitan' one? That couldn't be. *His* career had developed in provincial theatres – Nottingham among others, where he had premiered one of the most powerful plays ever: Trevor Griffith's *The Comedians*. I wrote, tongue in cheek:

> I'm sorry that *Lady Othello* hasn't found favour with your eyes. Perhaps you're right about it needing to have its beginnings in a good rep., rather like with the Griffith masterpiece *The Comedians* and my *Trilogy* which began in Coventry's Belgrade. Thanks for the tip.

It's difficult, we must concede, for Eyre to head a theatre that is not only the nation's but, in a way, the world's. London remains the centre of world theatre. A success in that beautiful city is a virtual guarantee of worldwide performance. But rejection is humiliating for the playwright who has an international reputation. Worse, to magnify the embarrassment of rejection, Eyre's view will never be the one considered mistaken. It is in the nature of being an artistic director that he or she is presumed right. The playwright always will be presumed to have written a dud play, and any protest will be distorted or dismissed as sour grapes. Nothing can alter that. It's the relationship of teacher and pupil, parent and child, critic and artist; the one is cloaked with authority, the other positioned for ineluctable submission.

A friend sent me a cutting from *The Times* about Mozart.

> Mozart's inability to believe that he might be a failure, even when his concerts were a disaster, was an essential part of his genius, according to psychologists.
>
> . . . Failure or defeat were not part of his vocabulary and the idea that fate might be against him, even when he suffered a series of setbacks, was inconceivable . . .
>
> In 1790, after giving a disastrous concert in Frankfurt, Mozart wrote to his wife: 'My concert . . . was a splendid success from the point of view of honour and glory but a failure as far as money was concerned. Unfortunately some prince was giving a "déjeuner" and the Hessian troops were holding a grand manoeuvre. But . . . I was in such good form . . . they implored me to give another concert next Sunday.'

I read back over neglected and rejected work and all my nerve ends register meaning and quality. I have respected my material. The one concept of art for which I have little patience is 'art as a means of self-expression'. What engages my interest in other writers is their quality of intellect, their poetic insights applied to understanding their material. I am worried by writers who straitjacket their material into personal mannerisms or instantly recognisable tricks of dialogue which are then mistaken for their 'voice' or their 'style'. I'm not such a one. Believing in the power and significance of my material I allow it to dictate its own inherent style.

Time, as has been said through all time, will tell. My state of mind, however, oscillates between gloomy suicidal doubts and a deep Mozartian faith that the work will come into its own.

Add to all this my current emotional life torn between two women, bereft of my children, one of whom scorns me, the rest – scattered. Once there was a family – with ups and downs, inevitably – but essentially happy, with rhythms and an eventful history. Now there is none.

All these things stick to me like barnacles on a wreck. And yet, and yet – although there is much in this chilly landscape that will warm the hearts of my lovely enemies – those for whom I can never do right especially the more right I do – I am afraid I cannot satiate their fireside hopes with tales of total collapse. No nervous breakdown. Forgive me, I'm a survivor. This has often worried me, not to have been afflicted with a nervous breakdown. There is something about a collapse of being that betokens evidence of true sensitivity. Those of us who survive must be, I reason in my darkest moments, unfeeling. Somewhere in me is a play about a man who, in distress, confronts a psychiatrist, and with a crippling sense of guilt confesses: 'I've never had a nervous breakdown! Why? Something must be wrong if I can cope with life. Good men break down, why not me?'

For the truth is that though rejected I swim, and while I swim I don't drown, I'm not sinking. Nor is the rejection total; plays continue to be performed around the world, the Penguin volumes sell endlessly, I have been commissioned to record my life, and who knows what might not be revived by the time this book appears in print. A centre holds.

Postscript to Chapter Two

Well, the landscape *did* change!

Towards the end of writing the first draft of this book a production of *The Kitchen* was mounted at the Royal Court theatre directed by Stephen Daldry – his inaugural production as its new artistic director! I had been nagging the National since the time of Peter Hall, and Max Stafford-Clark since the beginning of his artistic directorship of the Court over ten years ago, to mount the play. 'Finally,' said Stephen, 'we brought it from the back burner to the front one!'

I have not read the reviews or all the profiles but I'm told they are 'a playwright's dream'. Suddenly, my position is changed: producers have emerged interested in other work. There is a buzz around my name. Respect has returned. I can write letters knowing there will be no surprised exclamation: 'Good Lor! He's still alive!' The acclaim is as eerie as the wilderness. I don't really believe it. The buzzing may quickly fade. This renewed attention may be a flash of sunlight from a sliver of broken glass in the gutter. If a new work is performed in the wake of *The Kitchen*'s success the critics may feel, having disgorged such abundance of praise, that they have earned the right to slap it down. We blossom in fields of mad threshing machines careering who-knows-where, but at least we blossom. That's gratifying. And I must confess, the way this unexpected success has been greeted by others reveals huge reserves of goodwill I had not been aware existed.

Should I, therefore, have omitted this chapter? The fluctuations of fortune are part of a life. With luck and a little care I might live another twenty years during which time the cycle of ravage and repair will continue. Besides, the state of mind described is what shaped the bulk of this tome. What quality of frustration seeps through is not, I hope, flavoured with bitter malevolence. I have debated with colleagues, that's all, just as in the pages which follow I have debated with my life.

Postscript to the 'Postscript to Chapter Two'

I was right. A flash of sunlight from the gutter. What happened? Full houses, audiences queuing for returns from four in the afternoon, producers emerged with money and venue for an extended ten week season, the talk of the town – and yet? The transfer did not happen. Complex explanations – always. Potential royalties staunched. The buzz faded. Silence returned.

Chapter Three

Fashion Street

Born 24 May 1932, Empire Day, no middle name, just Arnold, from the Germanic word meaning 'eagle strength'.

My mother gave birth at Mother Levy's, the Jewish maternity home in Underwood Street off the Whitechapel Road. One day in the mid eighties I returned from abroad to a message from a Dr Sachs who, Dusty told me, wanted to speak with me because he'd just read *Say Goodbye, You May Never See Them Again*, my text to John Allin's primitive paintings of the East End, and was certain he had been the doctor who'd delivered me – an old man, alert and delighted that he'd traced one of his 'children'. 'You know,' he told me, 'I also have a son who's a writer.' Was he about to request I read his writer-son's works? 'Of course,' he continued, 'he's really a doctor but he wrote a book, you should read it, you'd like it, it's called *Awakenings . . .*' Which is how I came to the works of Dr Oliver Sachs.

The address on my birth certificate is 447a Hackney Road, Bethnal Green (Registrar A.F. Brady), but we were not there many weeks. Della lists a number of places we moved to – Wilkes Street, Grey Eagle Street – before settling finally in Fashion Street. Why did we move so often, I wonder? I think of Leah and Joe with their baby boy and the beautiful, ever-so-sensible girl of eight going from rented rooms to rented rooms, wandering-Jew-like. Though Fashion Street was not rented furnished. Everything in it was ours. I described it to John Allin for *Say Goodbye*. He painted the front room with its sloping ceilings, not in the right proportions and not with the actual furniture, but still – the only 'record'.

Fashion Street, backing on to Itchy Park over which towers the rediscovered magnificent Hawksmoor Christ Church of Spitalfields,

15

is one of the horizontal streets joining Brick Lane to Commercial Street. Parallel to the south was Flower and Dean Street (known as 'the Flowery' and put in the past tense because it no longer exists) where my grandparents and aunts lived in Charlotte de Roths-child's Dwellings built by Rothschild's '4% Industrial Dwellings Company' founded to provide homes for Jewish artisans; to the north is Fournier Street, two eighteenth-century rows of fine Huguenot houses, very fashionable now. An alley called Fashion Court joined Fashion Street and Flower and Dean Street. At the Flower and Dean end was a plaque with these words:

> In Fashion Court lived Abe Glickstein, founder of The Harlem Globe Trotters.

Fashion Street was put together in 1654 under the name of Fossan Street which by 1676 had been Chinese-whispered into Fashion Street. We lived on the top floor at number 43 and so had use of a landing which we turned into a kitchen, leaving free a bedroom *and* a living room. The living room had sloping attic-type ceilings, a taste for which I've held to ever since. I loved, for example, the little attic room where I lived-in working as a kitchen porter for the Bell Hotel, Norwich. Sloping ceilings there. My study in the Highgate house, which it broke my heart to sell after twenty-five years, had sloping ceilings, as did the study in the new Crouch End house, a feature that persuaded Dusty to make a bid for it.

Grieving a lost house – an aside

Traumatic to leave a house where the children grew up and the rooms rock with memories. Twenty-seven Bishops Road had to be sold because royalties were drying up, the bank overdraft had soared out of control. I was the last one to sleep there, on the floor of my sloping-ceilinged study. Just me, a mattress, and the stereo, to play music into the night, and a huge oak desk once owned by Ernst Jones, Freud's biographer (I'd bought it from his son, the novelist, Mervyn Jones). A melancholy last night. But within months an arch had been knocked into the wall dividing two attic rooms in the Ashley Road house and I had my sloping-ceilinged study back again, longer and larger. Seven years on, my tongue slips Freudian, calling 'Ashley Road' 'Bishops Road'. Perhaps that's where I still live. The Crouch End house is Dusty's, she found it and put it together. I never really felt it was mine. Nor did I mind too much. It was time to step back and let her create the ambience she wanted. Besides, this house in the Black Mountains contains the other half of me and is where, since 1968, most of my work has been written. Dusty was always restless here. 'I was brought up in the country,' she used to say. 'I don't need it. I love the city. Or the sea.' We could never afford sea *and* mountain though I frequently urged her to look for a house on the coast, and had it contained an attic with sloping ceilings we'd have exchanged this for that. Why not? I loved the sea, too. But she never looked. We each buried our hearts in different settings.

Fashion Street – continued

The East End is a trap, inviting sentimentality and cosy longing for 'the good old days'. I loved them, wrote about them with love, hoarded the past as though it were food for a time of famine, but not my family. They remembered those days as days of misery. A distinction must be made, between being romantic and being senti-mental. To look back romantically is to look back with love. Sentimentality is looking back with dishonesty.

I love street names: Fashion Street, Weaver Street, The Old Lady of Thread-a-needle Street – who *was* the old lady of 'Thread-a-needle Street'? Flower and Dean Street, Whitechapel Road, Black Lion Yard. Whoever owned black lions? Wentworth Street, Old Montague Street, Thrawl Street. What did they mean? Who named them? Foggy, narrow streets. Little sky could get through. I don't think I can remember summer in them. But I remember these things: gas lamps and a man on a bike going round with a long pole with a hook on the end of it which he'd slip into a ring at the bottom of a chain and pull – light! Yellow-lit streets! And Blooms, the kosher restaurant, queueing for salt-beef sandwiches. Tight, close streets. I used to stand across the road in Fashion Street and call up: 'Mum! Throw me down a penny!' And down it would come, odd coppers screwed up in a piece of paper. Once I was left in the care of my sister and her friend, Frances, and they went out for a minute, only a minute, and whoosh! I was dressed and out! Out on the streets, round the corner to my friends. Panic! Fournier Street, Charlotte de Rothschild's Dwellings, Itchy Park, Old Jewry. Nowhere was far away.

Charlotte de Rothschild's Dwellings sounded posh but were tenements with no bathrooms, no hot water and poky living space. But it was an interesting concept – flats surrounding a playground, a private space which even though it looked like Sing Sing prison was a safe area enclosed by family and friends. Protection! Privacy for working-class families! In those days remarkable.

And tramps. Annie Wobbler – part tramp part char lady. She used to 'do' for us in Fashion Street. When I was seventeen she became a portrait in one of my earliest literary attempts: *East End Sketches*.

> Annie was old. Annie was shaggy as well. Shaggy because of her rags and age, shaggy because of her thought, and so old because of her shaggy thought.

There we were, an attic with two rooms and a gas stove on the landing and we had this 'help' who called my parents 'the madam' and 'the master' and me and my sister 'little mistress' and 'little master'. We invented her past. Because her manner was haughty and her speech 'refained' we imagined she'd once been a maid for aristocracy. By the time she reached us she had become eccentric, wore a mass of skirts and petticoats with all manner of things hidden in them: tin mug, cutlery, paper bags; and on her head a hat with a stuffed bird in place. I once pulled it off her head. She was bald. How she cried. Made me cry, too. And what was there for her to keep clean? Some stone stairs, a few squares of linoleum – an excuse for my mother to give her a sixpence or a mug of tea with bread and butter. Annie's memory lingered. In 1982 I finally captured her in the first of my one-woman plays, *Annie Wobbler*. She slept rough in Itchy Park.

I once asked my mother what she could remember of Fashion Street. She said: 'I don't *want* to remember. I don't think I'll ever remember anything about Fashion Street. Nowhere in my life have I regretted to live anywhere than in Fashion Street.'

But in Fashion Street began my first essay into theatre. Tucked away in the dark beneath a conical duvet, talking up through a megaphone made from newspaper, pretending I was 'The Man in Black' introducing a horror play for radio – there it began. A seven-year-old playing the entertainer, fantasies unlimited. 'Tonight's story will be . . .' and off I would go. I have no recollection of what I invented, lurid imitations no doubt, but a beginning. Nor do I have any recollection of my parents' response. I recall no screaming to 'stop that', 'get out of bed', 'don't be stupid'. As always I was indulged. But that scene – the seven-year-old, solitary, huddled in darkness, dramatising little nothings to amuse himself – was the first step into a life of theatre. Paper funnel – darkness – tented duvet: my first empty stage.

I have recurring dreams about the East End. When they pulled down Rothschild's Dwellings I dreamt about them being built again but there was an orchestra in the playground, a big one, a philharmonic, and trees, and I was playing games with friends.

The first draft of *Chicken Soup with Barley* inevitably had Act I set in an attic tenement flat modelled on Fashion Street. The date was 4 October 1936, the day when the East Enders took over the streets to prevent Sir Oswald Mosley and his Blackshirts from marching provocatively through a Jewish area. The Kahn family – my family in essence – were preparing to take part. John Dexter, the director, confronted the problem of trying to recreate the excitement and movement of that day of agitation. Difficult from an upstairs attic! Couldn't I, he asked, set it in a basement? This would allow us to have a grille showing the pavement past which legs could be seen and heard running to the scene of action. We would only need two stage managers running round and round to give the illusion of dozens. I didn't have to think long about Dexter's clever idea. We hadn't lived in the basement but a basement existed in each of the Fashion Street blocks, and though most were used as workshops – a furrier had his workshop in the basement of 43 – there was no reason why there couldn't have been living quarters. I rewrote. It made all the difference.

So the four of us lived in two rooms. The landing – big enough for a gas stove, kitchen cabinet and deal stool – was utilised as the kitchen. The smaller room, tiny, space only for two narrow beds and a chest of drawers, was assigned to Della and me. The front room, not much bigger, was dining room, living room, parents' bedroom, morning room, meeting room, games room, music room, library, all in one, full of life most of the time. I remember: a fire-guard of crisscross crinkled wire with a brass rim. The wires slipped out of shape. It was satisfying to slip strips back into their crinkle, rather as I put books in order on the shelves of bookshops where it's none of my business. That fender is a strong visual memory. I'd lean over it with a slice of bread at the end of a three-pronged toasting fork or a long bread knife to make myself, and whoever, toast. I loved creeping out of bed to be with company, propping myself on the brass rim, warming myself in front of the coal fire, hating to be in bed, away from people and talk. That's why my aunts remember me as white-faced – I never slept! I had an appetite for company, a curiosity to know what was going on.

The table was square and deal-topped, the chairs were pressed bentwood. In a corner under one sloping ceiling was another table, round, whose top was never screwed tight to the stem, and wobbled. On it sat a wind-up gramophone, a small black contraption with a lid, through whose sound box crackled my first classical music; nothing difficult, Rossini overtures, Puccini arias, Russian and Yiddish folk songs, Paul Robeson. I recall a set of records on dark blue Decca labels we played over and over: *The Gypsy Princess* by the Czech composer Emmereich Kálman. Under the window was a divan which opened as a double bed; its system of swivel-hinging fascinated me. My father slept in it. My mother slept with either Della or with me. Sometimes I'd sleep with my sister to give my mother a decent sleep on her own. I suppose she must occasionally have slept with my father but I have only one memory of it, many years later, when I caught them making love in the Clapton flat. On either side of the fireplace were built-in cupboards, one floor-to-ceiling, the other low – with shelves of books above. I think there was a glass cabinet in the room. The smaller room was perhaps eight by six foot; the larger about twelve by ten and covered with linoleum.

Linoleum! Now there's a smell from childhood. And fun buying it. In rolls. The salesman would throw them expertly forward to unwind, and we'd choose. Never able to lay expensive linoleum – which would last – we bought cheap. Holes spread fast. Expensive is cheap, cheap is expensive – the first law of housekeeping! It was in the Fashion Street flat that I developed a curious delight in scrubbing floors. My mother had willing home help in her only son who loved the scrubbing and sudding.

Annie Wobbler, part-time tramp, part-time cleaning woman, is finishing scrubbing the 'kitchen'. Her actions are meticulous . . . : rag into pail, slop water around area to be cleaned. Rub huge Lifebuoy soap on to huge scrubbing brush. Scrub! Wring out rag, make a length, draw length down bit by bit to gather soapy area, squeeze out, draw length down again and so on. Final dry-up with wrung cloth. She enjoys the actions. The ritual satisfies her.

Annie Wobbler, stage directions

The ritual satisfied me too.

We kept as clean as possible. No bathroom but plenty of water. Fill enamel bowl with cold from tap over a sink one flight down, place on the deal stool, add hot water boiled on gas stove, stand over bowl and wash. In the first years I was bathed in a tin bath in the front room before the fire, towels warming on that brass fender. I have a memory of being bathed in the presence of my first girl-friend, aged about five, Rosalind Yenish, who sat by the fire singing 'They Gave Him a Gun To Play With' – a 1938 song by Tommie Conroy and Hamish Kennedy played by Joe Loss and his band.

We kept ourselves clean but the fight against bugs was endless. The big enemy! They'd get into mattresses and behind wallpaper. Burning-out sessions were exciting. Candles lit, battalions scorched, dropped on to newspaper laid on the floor, screwed up and flushed down the lavatory. My mother was vigilant and furious. Little round things they were, full of blood. For the privilege of living in those two rooms we paid 11/6d in rent which I was frequently sent to pay in the rent office at the Brick Lane end of Fashion Street, up a flight of stairs to a man behind a grille.

Everything we needed was minutes away. Opposite the rent office a little greengrocer from whom we bought coal by the bucket – 7lbs in each. I can see that grocer's face and his action of shovelling coal into a brass scoop on scales. We bought two buckets at a time. Schwartz the printer was next door, not that we ever needed anything printed; and Greenberg (or was it Rosenberg?) the button-maker was on our block at number 43, not that we frequently needed buttons either! I'd sometimes drink a cup of tea at Monty's Café a few doors away, and I loved errands to Katie's packed and caverned grocery shop on the corner of Flower and Dean Street, Brick Lane end. Rinkoff the baker was in Thrawl Street, and Petti-coat Lane only a hop, skip and jump away.

My parents may have fought in Fashion Street, Leah may have screamed Yiddish insults and curses at Joe but I remember a happy childhood in that flat. Of course I don't remember the pram-and-cot days. Della remembers those and told me that aged six weeks I was sent to my father who'd retreated to his mother's flat in the Flowery, where I was looked after by my grandmother. Not much breast-feeding, then! Once back in Fashion Street I was put in a cot but left alone for long, frustrating periods – accounting for the broken bars. I would like, romantically, to claim that as a metaphor for all that followed in my life; but perhaps most of us break one set of bars only to find ourselves confined by others.

Fashion Street seemed to me constantly filled with visiting uncles, aunts, and cousins. Uncle Harry's daughters, Norma and Thelma, spent their time trying out my tiny mother's high-heeled shoes. Party branch meetings were held there; games of solo with their inevitable aftermath of inquest and reproach; a game for two that I quickly learned and played frequently into adulthood – Clubyash, otherwise known as 'Five Hundred', with its exotically named tricks: 'yuss', the jack of trumps worth twenty points, 'menele', the nine of trumps worth fourteen points, 'bella', queen and king of trumps worth twenty points, 'shtoch', the last trick worth twenty points. A run of three was a bonus twenty points, a run of four, fifty. Played with thirty-two cards, seven to ace.

Solo required the greatest skill and provoked the most heated of arguments – a dramatic event in our household, full of tension and humour. It had to be the event around which I wrote the last scene in *Chicken Soup with Barley*. When John Dexter sent the play to Kenneth Tynan to read he responded warmly but with two major warnings: he didn't think it would be possible to stretch the play over a period of twenty years – from the 1936 Mosley riots, to the Soviet suppression of the Hungarian uprising in 1956; nor did he think the game of solo would work. Dexter replied he would prove the *Observer* critic wrong, and did so. In the original script the characters were given solo-type lines of the sort I heard as a child bandied around the solo table. By the time we came to rehearsals it was obvious to Dexter that precise calls needed to correspond precisely with the lines. I worked out a hand that is now part of the printed text.

Ralph

It was from Fashion Street that Della married Ralph Saltiel in the old Bevis Marks synagogue. She was seventeen, he was nineteen –

ten years older than me, and my mentor. We were an Ashkanazi family, Ralph's family were Sephardic, probably leaving Spain under the expulsion in 1492, landing in England in 1732. Ralph, whose parents were Cockney-speaking Jewish market traders with a stall in Petticoat Lane, was a carpenter/joiner, a young communist, literate, intelligent, with ambitions to be a writer. During the 1939/45 war he was conscripted into the RAF, Air Sea Rescue Service, building boats, stationed in India and Ceylon – now Sri Lanka. He wrote stories with titles like 'Dumb Tor', 'Portrait of an Airman Returning Home', 'Interlude with Beauty'; poems entitled 'Possessed', 'Barbarians', 'Kandy Road: '44'; pages and pages of notes about the books he read: Virginia Woolf's *Orlando*, John Dover Wilson's *Life in Shakespeare's England*, Freud's *Totem and Taboo*, Plutarch's *Lives*. The Jewish working-class intellectual is a dying breed. They worked as tailors, taxi-drivers, electricians and bakers; they read political economy and the classics from Chaucer to Hemingway; they demonstrated, went on rambles, visited each other's homes for gramophone recitals of classical music played on 78-rpm records and wind-up gramophones, and planned tomorrow's brave new world into the early hours of the morning.

Della and Ralph treated me like an equal and laid down my early reading. When Ralph was abroad with the RAF we corresponded. Long letters which I kept, as I do everything, until in a fit of 'cleaning out the cupboards' my mother threw them down the chute. Ralph didn't keep any of the letters I sent him either. A pity. Much of who I then was, what I thought and felt, is lost to me. Ralph nurtured me and I loved him, as I still do, and in May 1945, just approaching my thirteenth birthday, I wrote – from no creative spark, just to please and impress him – my first poem. 'The Breeze'.

I keep getting this urge, you see, to write poetry, it's a very strong urge and I become filled with a special kind of – kind of – how can it be described? An incorporeal expectation. A bit like being on heat. And out it comes, this poetry, this selection of words and images I *think* is poetry. And it's shit. And a pain. Such a pain. You've no idea the pain it is to begin with this heat, this fever, this sense that an astonishing assembly is about to take place and all that assembles is shit!

Annabella Wharton – *Annie Wobbler*

I continue to write poetry undeterred that most of it is still shit, hoping one day there might, just might be enough for a slim volume.

Leah and Joe, in their own words

Leah and Joe, parents; Della (Adela on the birth certificate), my sister. Four of us. Mervin was born in between but after a few weeks had died of meningitis. Imagine, I nearly had an elder brother named Lenin! Della, who had a mania for tidying up around her, told me of a childhood image she retains: a velveteen cloth laid over an open drawer 'like a coffin', her only memory of his death. 'I can't remember anything else, only that Zeyda [my father's father] took care of the funeral arrangements. "He would have been blind had he lived," he said. "It was a happy release."'

Neither Leah nor Joe were born into such a neat unit. On my father's side were the four Wesker sisters; on my mother's side were the four Perlmutter sisters and six brothers:

How my older sisters and brothers were educated I don't know. As I was the youngest of the girls, and two younger brothers than myself, we three had the most education in England. No, it would not be true to say that I had my education in England. I had none at all anywhere. I only learnt to write and read, and that I didn't learn thoroughly . . . up till nine years of age I only remember a private tutor who just taught me how to read and write in Hungary – Hungarian, German and Jewish.

My mother and father were very religious. My father was a Rabbi and a shoichet [a ritual slaughterer of meat and fowl]. He was one of those Talmuds. His father was one who wrote, or rather rewrote, the Ten Commandments, which is the highest honour in Jewish religion.

She means he rewrote the scrolls of the Torah, the Five Books of Moses, which rested in the ark – considered the most sacred part of a synagogue – and which faded from constant handling, rolling and unrolling, and so required 'rescribing'.

There is one thing I would like to know, how and where did my father learn other languages than Jewish? In those days orthodox Jewish people were forbidden to know or speak none other languages than Jewish, and my father could speak and write Hungarian and German . . . I believe though that my father, as religious he was, he was also progressive for education because all my brothers and sisters were educated. I don't know how but they were somehow or other, and that way I remember that I too was taught this little that I know.

My father was not fanatic, and as we lived in a small village where there was no school, only those that could afford paid for a private tutor to teach us. But unfortunately my education was stopped when I was nine years of age.

. . . my mother, she was a little woman like myself but as far as I remember she was quiet and liked singing. Not the ways I would sing, only quietly, folk songs . . .

I remember she had big black eyes. . . . and she was called the peace maker. . . .

As far as I remember our house was jolly. That is while my mother was alive. I used to like very much when Friday night came and the long table was laid to supper with fourteen candles lit, and we were bathed and dressed in our best, and waited for our father to come from singing, and blessed us all before sitting down to the table. Twelve of us sat down, ten of us, sisters and brothers, and my two parents and we always had a poor or displaced person for supper. Sometimes we had two or three people. My father used to bring them with him when he came from synagogue. After supper the whole household used to sing . . .

One day my mother was brought into the house by my father

holding her under one arm and the coachman under her other. That day they went to town to buy or rather to do some shopping. I don't know what they bought. Still, coming back from town something happened on the way with the sledge as it was winter, and my mother and father were supposed to be falling out from the sledge. I say they were supposed to, because I don't remember. I only repeat what my eldest sisters and brothers were saying. I only remembered how she looked when they brought her in, and before we managed to get a doctor she died. And then from then on I left education. The tutor that was teaching us, or rather me, had to leave as my father scattered all of us.

. . . My father got married again, then I was sent to another sister, a married sister. She got married after my mother died . . . And she was so poor, this sister, she had children of her own, that she couldn't look after me. I heard that my father wanted to come to England and he was taking Harry to England [Perly and Barney were already there] and I carried on very much to my sister until she had to leave me to go home where my father lived with my step-mother, and I said, 'I want to go to England as well.'

Leah's diaries – 23 August and 3 October 1956

I learn about my paternal grandparents from my father's auto-biography:

My first recollections of my childhood are from the age of 5.

I was born in Russia, both of my Parents are Russian Jews. My father I first remember as a young man of 27, rather on the small side slightly broad shoulders, a head of black hair, a very wide fore-head, a well shaped straight nose and a very brown beard.

He was a military tailor.

My mother was tall and dark with long tresses of black hair very sharp and Mongol features, a woman of a strong character and will power who was passionately fond of her children.

My father was born in a little village near Shklov called Chary, and, as all boys of his age, spent his boyhood in the study of the Talmud and was very good at the subject. Dad lost his father at a very early age with the result that he had to earn his living and also keep his mother at the same time.

But for all that he still managed to carry on with his studies which he kept up till he was called up for the Russian army.

And I remember him telling us children that he did not want to serve in the army of the Czar so he set about to find ways and means how to avoid it till some one told him that if he sucked sugar dipped in paraffin he could get rejected on medical grounds.

Being a young man and raised in a small village in Russia he knew no better, so he carried on sucking sugar dipped in paraffin for three months feeling confident he would get rejected. But can you imagine the shock he got when three months later he got before the medical board and the doctor told him in honest to goodness Russian that his cough he got through sucking the sugar will remain with him all his life and passed him A1.

And so my father had to serve 3 years & 8 months in the Czar's army.

My mother was a woman of a different calibre, of different intellect.

Born in the town of Chkla her mother was nurse in the town's hospital. She was nurse, not a trained nurse, she helped the assistant doctor known in Russia as a 'flesher'(?)

Mother was always more determined, more practical in her ideas, in her ways and in her mode & ways of life. We, my 4 sisters and myself, always said that mother was born 50 years too soon. She would have made a good revolutionary now.

My parents were first-cousins having met at the age of 10. Whether they fell in love or not I don't know. But my father married mother at 24 years of age when he came home to his village after serving 3 years and 8 months in the army.

Soon after their wedding they moved to the Ukraine to a town in the name of Ekaterinoslav known after the revolution as Dneiper-petrovsk. The town was one of the few where the Jews were allowed to live and there in that town I and my sisters were born. Rae and I were twins, then Sara, Bella, Ann and another brother whose name was Sam, but he died at the age of 1 year & 8 months through sheer negligence of my father and the lack of medical attention . . .

My father's autobiography took him up to his arrival in England. His father had travelled ahead to join a sister and her family in Swansea. His mother, her son and four daughters followed. Their ship docked in Hays Wharf, London. Next day a relative collected them and took them to Swansea where after a year's schooling, my father was encouraged to become a travelling salesman among the miners. He was not a success.

> . . . the more I tried the more hopeless the whole thing became to me. It became hopeless because of two things. Firstly I could not sell my wares, I did not have it in me I was not a salesman I could not knock at the door and make a miner's wife buy my wares, I just did not have it in me . . .
>
> I do not remember how long I was out of work but in the end I found a job with a picture frame maker. I worked 12 months with no prospects in view but it was an experience of a kind . . . and having learned very little I left.
>
> By that time my father started making trousers at home and my sister and I stayed at home to help him. For me it meant that I was to learn a trade. As for myself I did not know what I wanted. I did not know whether I wanted to learn a trade or not. One thing I did know that things are happening but I did not know what! After a few weeks holiday I began to learn how to make trousers.
>
> Our workshop was in the front room of the house we lived in. It was a small room and in it we had a machine two tables a gas stove and some stools. It was very compact and tight but we worked in it my father my sister and a girl and myself.

My father was embarked on a trade he was to hate, and avoid as often as he could. It drove my mother to distraction. I loved him but despaired of him, and now that I've lived with his autobiography – there is much more, telling of his childhood in Russia – now that I've lived close to his early youth and felt this trickle of talent and intelligence struggling to find fulfilment, like a stream in search of a river, I regret, as children regret, not having had sufficient curiosity about his longings. He was made for more – a little Charlie Chaplin of a man who sang Russian and Yiddish songs in an untrained, strained but rich tenor voice. My mother was admired, esteemed, he was charming and indulged.

My father's sisters, Ann and Sara, have other memories. I got them talking into a cassette in 1970. Sara, one of the first women to have a serious role as a trade-union organiser, for the Tailor and Garment Workers' Union, had been brought shockingly low by a stroke. Ann was looking after her. Poor Aunt Ann. A rotten life, first looking after her arthritic mother and then her debilitated sister.

They talked about the time I was evacuated in 1939. I didn't want to go, I hated the idea of leaving home. Sara, by now a collapsed little thing, barely able to move because of her stroke, stuttered into the recorder:

> Your face was white like sheets, no matter what we offered you to eat and drink you wouldn't, you didn't want to go . . . Your mother said you've got to go with Della. You were in an awful state . . . Your mother brought you to our house. We washed you and changed you and you sat on the sofa near the window and you wouldn't eat a thing . . .

Della

The tape reminded me that we, my sister and I, were brought up by these spinster aunts for our first years. Joe left Leah for a period of two years and she in turn left us with his mother, our grandmother, while she went out to work. Even when they were back together again they would leave us in Rothschild's Buildings in order to earn a living. The aunts loved my sister.

ANN   . . . she was very, very clean as a child. Very clean . . . if she had a speck on her pinafore we had to take it off and give her a clean one. She was very very clean and you could take her anywhere. At the age of three or four you could take Della out to tea in the afternoon up West and not be afraid that she's going to show you up or do anything, you know, to make you feel what a rotten child . . . she was so clean and so well behaved . . .

SARA   And I always remember we took her Saturday afternoon to tea in Tottenham Court Road, Maison Lyons . . . she sat down and then the band started to play so she got up, didn't ask anybody and she danced round. Then she sat down, had her tea and she said, 'Ooh, that was lovely.' But she kept everybody looking at her as she was dancing round. She always was beautifully dressed because from our dresses we used to make her frocks . . . she was lovely. She was a lovely child. She was very pretty, she wasn't like you – big lobus [rascal]!

Della was not pretty. She was beautiful. Hair long, black, ebony sheen, high cheekbones, dark, serious eyes. The kind of Jewish beauty gentiles romanticised – Hebrew pride and mystery! In Yiddish there is a word to describe a person of dignity, honour and moral courage: *mensch*. Literally it means 'man'. In essence it means someone to be trusted at all levels. I feel the matriarchs must have been like Della, a mensch who protected my childhood and wellbeing, patiently bearing the brunt of my parents' quarrelling which was at its height during impressionable years, thus affecting her more.

I wonder, she has always been a bad timekeeper – is this the result of parental strife? She has improved in these last years but it is a curious flaw. As some are tone deaf she appeared to be time blind – unable to gauge the hours required to prepare for departure and arrival. Fiercely jealous of her rights and freedoms she seemed to view time passing as infringement of them. Time as a dictator. She would not be hurried. Not to be hurried was a way of asserting independence, defying the dictator. She came finally never to wear a watch. Those bought for her she lost. These days we set dates half an hour earlier than needed.

As a teenager she was a young communist expelled from school for selling the Young Communist League newspaper, *Challenge*. Easter 1940. She had returned home from Ely, where we were evacuated, for the holidays. May Day fell after she was due to return. She wanted to stay in London to celebrate it. Her headmistress forbade her. Della told her with the weight of teenage moral earnestness: 'I'm afraid I must stay.' When she returned the headmistress warned her she had to promise to stop selling *Challenge* or else leave. My honest sister replied: 'I *can't* give you my word.' She was expelled and sent home to London. A week later one of her school teachers turned up in Fashion Street – Miss Lily Bronowski, sister of Professor Jacob Bronowski who later anchored the first of those mammoth TV explorations: *The Ascent of Man*. She and a Miss Noakes, both Communist Party members, had secured a place for Della in Parliament Hill Fields School. The school had agreed to pay her fare from the East End. Della kept the fare money and cycled every day. She didn't pass her matriculation – failed in French – but she won a school certificate. In an essay about ambition she wrote:

> Ambition is a curse as is everything which is done to excess. My ambition is to go to university but as my parents can't afford it I have decided to devote myself to the cause of the working class. To quote Lenin:
>
> > 'A man's dearest possession is life, and since it is given to him to live but once, he must so live it that dying he can say all my life and all my strength has been given to the greatest cause in the world, the liberation of mankind.'

She began by working for the London District of the Young Communist League, followed by an assortment of jobs in the course of which she acquired the skills of a book-keeper, useful in later years when she and Ralph ran a joinery business, the 'liberation of mankind' being – energetic, imaginative and kindly though they both remained – beyond their capabilities!

Are there separate, distinguishable Wesker and Perlmutter traits? I think of the matter-of-factness of Aunts Billie, Sara and Rae. Ann and Joe were softer. Perhaps that's how the difference between the two families could be described: hard and soft. Or perhaps it was coolness and sentiment. The Perlmutters would embrace you and coo. The Weskers had no time for any of that 'nonsense'. They *were* full of love, thoughtfulness, and generosity; it was just not their nature to illustrate it. Aunts Ann and Billie laughed a lot, Sara and Rae smiled, but none of them possessed a sense of fun.

Unlike the Perlmutters who had a great sense of fun. And playfulness. They told jokes, laughed at each other's foibles, mocked a little, sometimes confused exuberance for silliness. The valedictory monologue from *Love Letters on Blue Paper* records that even in the days when she was dying my mother could laugh. When I checked on her in bed, she could see my sadness and tried to joke it away. 'I might go any time. Suddenly. Plonk! Finished! What can you do?' And her doodles. What playfulness is in them!

The one Perlmutter quality with which both Della and I are afflicted – I use that word carefully – is unworldliness. Honourable, generous, just, intelligent – yet the Perlmutters were deeply, deeply unworldly, even the successful businessman, Uncle Perly.

Before every family decision Della asked: 'And what about Arnold?' Though emotional, she inherited more Wesker traits than me, she was less demonstrative, more contained. I was more Perlmutter. I put it in the past tense because with age we have both shifted a little, towards the centre!

My aunts were less ecstatic about *me*. The cassette winds on:

ANN   You were a real dead-end kid. You wouldn't have
       your . . . you wouldn't have your dinners in school
       because you didn't like onions. [Laughs] 'I don't like

onjuns.' So you went through a period where you used to come in to me for your lunch. And Della came in one lunch time, she'd been looking for you, and you said to her, 'Tell Mummy I'm having dinner by Aunty Ann.' [Laughs]

SARA   Never 'Aunts', never 'Aunty Sara' or 'Boba' [Yiddish for 'Grandmother']. 'Aunty Ann!'

ANN   Well, they were used to seeing me . . . Arnold, after seeing me at home about three times . . . you once said to me, 'Are you the Mummy now?'

ARNOLD   What other things can you remember about me in the East End?

SARA   You used to come in and ask Mamma for money.

ARNOLD   I remember that. She had a purse under her pillow.

SARA   You used to . . . she used to keep that money under . . . whenever Arnold came he always got a halfpenny or a penny.

ARNOLD   Or a farthing.

ANN   No, no . . .

ARNOLD   I remember the farthings.

ANN   . . . no no, by the time you were a child, at that age, you didn't see farthings.

SARA   No, a halfpenny you used to get.

ANN   You could get something for a halfpenny in those days. Well I remember when I was at school a man used to stand outside the gates and sell home-boiled sweets for a farthing. He used to wrap it up in a white paper, he used to do a roaring trade with the kids . . . number one I never liked sweets, number two I never, I never knew what it was like to have money to buy sweets after school . . . He used to stand outside, and

34

he had the barrow and he had a huge white paper round him and the kids used to cluster . . .

ARNOLD   Did I used to bring my friends in?

TOGETHER   Yes.

ANN   You used to be friends with an Indian boy.

ARNOLD   [Suddenly remembering] Called Sabu. Sabu!

ANN   Well . . . whatever his name is . . . he once asked you to go to the mission with him, so you said to him, 'I can't do that, I'm a Yiddish boy,' so he said [starts to laugh] he said to you, 'That's nothing, everybody goes.' You always looked after lame dogs, Arnold. You played with them because nobody else would play with them.

Sara, known as Ketzel – kitten; tiny-framed, exotically beautiful with those Mongol features my father described their mother as possessing, an astute organiser and a fiery speaker. My mother disliked Aunt Sara for what she saw as cold indifference to her strained relationship with my father.

SARAH   I hate her!

HYMIE   Don't be a silly girl. Cissie is a good trade-union organiser.

SARAH   She's a cow! Not a bit of warmth, not a bit! What's the good of being a socialist if you're not warm?

HYMIE   But Cissie has *never* liked Harry.

SARAH   Not a bit of warmth. Everything cold and calculated. People like that can't teach love and brotherhood.

PRINCE   Love comes later, Sarah.

SARAH   Love comes now. You have to start with love. How
          can you talk about socialism otherwise?
                    Chicken Soup with Barley, Act I Scene 2

It was true. Aunt Sara for her part had little patience with my
mother's emotional distress over her brother, Joe, against whom
Leah had been warned by the Wesker sisters. Sara had even less
patience with her brother, though she was constantly finding him
jobs.

Sara was a communist, invited many times to the Soviet Union
where, as though they were her recalcitrant union members, she
chastised them for unsanitary lavatories and inept organisation. But
she did love and of course, like all the party members of the early
days, excused them and saw nothing. Once, when some of her
clothes were stolen, her union counterparts were so embarrassed
they loaded her with presents of silk.

The Garment Workers' Union, whose leadership was anti-communist, retired the thorn in their side in February 1965 after
twenty-seven years, with good wishes, a bouquet, and a cheque for
£210 handed to her at a farewell ceremony which I attended with
the union's founder and general secretary, J.L. Fine, her former
boss, at the Bonnington Hotel in Southampton Row. A press
photograph shows her sad and lost. Nor did she have a husband to
fall back on. She once fell in love, with a comrade, Mick Mindel.
Della remembers calling into the aunts' flat and finding Sara crying.
She'd heard, not from Mick, that he was going to marry someone
else. She was heartbroken and looked no further. Mick melted
down to be her union colleague and wove into the family's fabric. I
saw him frequently in Rothschild's Dwellings unaware of the heartache. Politics, the improvement of working conditions for her
members, these became her passions. When they were taken from
her she foundered and never recovered. Within a few years she had
a stroke. We watched her dying at Whipps Cross Hospital in
Epping Forest. By September 1971 she was dead.

Aunt Rae said: 'She gave up as soon as she retired. Sat in an arm-chair and never moved again. You know they offered her a job, a small job, at party headquarters? She said no. At the time your Uncle Sammy said, and I didn't believe him then but I'm beginning to think he's right now, he said it was Russia that finished her off. She never recovered from the Khrushchev revelations. And then she became just like Joe, just like your father. You used to say some-thing to him and he'd say, "Uch! leave me alone." I used to tell Sara to get up, move about, do things, she'd say, "Uch! I can't be bothered." Exactly the same.'

Aunty Rae and my father were the eldest and twins. 'But if you're interested, I came first,' she told me.

'A Time of Dying' – a story

Aunt Ann, the chuckler, she was also the victim, or rather – as the novelist, Bernice Reubens, names them – the elected one. Her nature was sweet, her instinct forgiving and indulgent; she more than the other sisters relented and found sympathy for my father's lapse of character, but for her sweet and obliging nature she paid the price – nursing arthritic mother and then stricken sister. As the sages warn: no good deed goes unpunished.

Her life haunts me, especially when I look at that photograph of the four sisters, young and full of expectations. One day she gave up, let go of life, sat in her flat and did the minimum required, sometimes not even that. She used to make crocheted bed-cover-ings for members of the family. A day came when, having made hundreds of squares for her great-nephew, Miles, and sewn up all bar about thirty, she stopped. The last crocheted squares remained unattached. She also stopped watering her plants, stopped taking buses to visit us, stopped washing herself. At one moment on a cer-tain day her spirit wound down to a halt. We looked after her the best we could – I rang her every other day, brought her to our houses, took her food. Nothing helped. She had collapsed into her-self, ceased all effort, held a book in her hand out of habit but didn't read it.

I saw my father in her just as Aunt Rae, my father's twin sister, had seen my father in the paralysed Sara. Rae never gave up. She was a plodder who one day just died. Aunt Billie, who used to yell impatiently at poor Ann in the same way Rae yelled at Sara to move, get up, *do* things, also never gave up until struck down with senile dementia. Three out of five gave up. Is that a Wesker trait, too? I fear it constantly, this struggle raging within me between the capitulating, worldly Weskers and the defiant, unworldly Perlmutters.

Yet – the women! It's the women who surge strong and clear. I came from and was nurtured by a family of women – mother, grandmother, aunts, cousins, sister. By October 1941, when Della was that breathtaking Jewish beauty of seventeen who spoke posh and said 'hwhen, hwhich, and hwhether' and I was nine, she married handsome, articulate, Cockney Ralph who was nineteen. Her caring and attention were transferred to him. Leah took over.

Leah

My Lord, Ladies and Gentlemen. I had a mother – yes, even old women may once have had mothers – I had a mother, a strong and tiny thing she was who gave me two pieces of advice. 'Talk,' she said, 'always say it. Something is remembered.' And once, when I was rude and she was upset, I told her, 'But I was only joking.' 'There are no jokes. Nobody,' she said, 'makes jokes.'

Whatever Happened to Betty Lemon

For my mother's funeral service at the East Ham cemetery in Marlow Road, Tuesday, 12 October 1976, I wrote a valediction which you, Lindsay Joe, her third grandson, read out. I couldn't. We knew I wouldn't get past the first sentence, didn't we? Remember?

It's not that we are distressed she is dead, so much as grieved she's not alive . . .

. . . in what lay her strength? It was a strength of a particularly
Jewish character, a strength comprising of an ancient, healthy fear
that madmen are knocking at the gate, lurking everywhere ready to
pounce, and so one must be on guard, be careful; together with a
sense of humour that mocked that fear and brushed it away with a
third quality: a powerful belief that the madmen must be countered
and that there were honourable and good people enough to do it.

In her was combined the protective Jewish mother and the international idealist. A mixture which sometimes lay uneasily side by
side, producing paradoxes and contradictions and frequent tensions,
but a mixture which, through its strange diplomacy, kept an arguing
family together.

Her priorities were very set and they consisted in loyalties –
parent to child, child to parent, brother to sister, sister to brother,
husband to wife, wife to husband – whatever she thought of either!
A promise is a promise, blood is blood, a bond is a bond. And to
those she kept us, and for those she gathered us round her. And,
also, we were gathered to her.

But she was not an angel and we would betray her real humanity
if we pretended she was. She was stubborn, self-willed, often just
wrong in her understanding of the world, and frequently burning
with that unbearable Jewish female reproach – making us guilty of
what we'd not committed though she *may* have been right in thinking us capable of it!

Her grandchildren will miss their pocket money and her quiet
prompting to take an interest in politics; her caring and affectionate
in-laws will miss her suspicions that the chicken wasn't kosher; her
nieces and nephews will miss having someone to tease; her brothers
will miss her anxieties for them; her friends will miss her friendship,
and all of us will miss her strength and that lovely, lovely sweetness
which made her adorable and adored.

My mother's death affected me profoundly. As she was dying I was
in Stockholm with Dusty watching the world premiere of *Shylock*.
Della rang the theatre and spoke with the actor, Jan Olaf Strandberger, then the artistic director of Stockholm's Royal Dramatic
Theatre, and told him not to tell me until the first night was over.

Next morning Dusty and I were at the opening of an exhibition I had set up of the John Allin folio of prints, *Stepney Streets*. Strandberger came in with the press representative, Berit Gullberg, and, unseen by me, called Dusty aside to give her the news. Dusty knew she had to tell me without any preambles or drama. She approached immediately and gently whispered into my ear, 'Mummy's dead.' We walked back to the hotel, not speaking. She held my hand tightly. I wept as we walked.

Over the next weeks I assembled my mother's papers and placed them in a box file labelled LEAH. Della kept back books of her diary, fearing their bitter thoughts would distress me. But there, amid the clutter, were other things, more interesting, gems of her personality – her doodles. When, to help me write this autobiography, Della handed over the diaries, I found more scattered throughout the sheets. Startling shapes. Not really doodles but amazing line meanderings in which, now I look at them more closely, I can see their power.

She knew she was dying. It bewildered her. Her bewilderment distressed me. Her last diary entry – 19th September 1976 – nineteen days before she died, reads:

I came home thinking that this time I'll be brave and not mind being home alone. But a big mistake. I cannot live alone. I like people and want people. I don't feel good being alone. I must take Arnold's advice to give up my flat and go to live with Della. I have not very long to live so I'll go to live with Della and another time with Arnold, and so I live with my children, half drawn here, there, they come, sometimes I go to them, so on and on. They cannot be with me all the time. After all they have their own problems, or having no time. However, I want to put down where and what I go or do. So many things I want to write but I cannot write. However I'll try to describe my latest being not well. I forgot what I suffered with. I laid a day in bed but I am better now. I stayed with Della. She wanted that I should stay longer but I came home. I am not well enough to stay by myself. I am really not well enough to stop by myself. Not so bad day time, but at night not. The time is 10.30. I am still writing.

But nothing followed.

She vomited all the time, was constipated, had no appetite. During those last days – living with us when not at Della's – she'd eat little, complain of pain in her gums, vomit while I held her head and say: 'When? When? When will it be over, done, finished with?' She couldn't understand. 'I've never been so ill. Never!' She'd be angry but she'd make jokes. To my daughter, Tanya Jo, who was visiting her bedside one day, she said: 'What they say about those men from Transylvania – it's true.' She knew Tanya enjoyed coming from the land of vampires. On her good days when she could eat and not feel nauseous, she'd sit up, hold out her hand and cross her fingers. 'Don't say anything,' she'd caution, 'just hope!' And as I fed her the umpteen prescribed pills she'd mock her plight: 'Well, I'm a good pill-taker at least.' Once when the doctor came and she was particularly flat out, collapsed utterly into her pillow, he asked in that breezy voice doctors reserve for the dying, 'And how are you today?' She replied with gentle self-mockery, holding her aching gums: 'Oh, very well, thank you!'

One image stands out. I'm sitting by her bed. She's propped up against cushions. In her hand she holds up a little mirror. After looking for a while she laments: 'How could I become such a face, how?' And she clutches the side of her head and rocks it as though trying to shake her mind and memory back into place. Then she stops, and says simply: 'I want no fuss, you know what I mean? No fuss. It's got to come sometime or other, sooner or later.'

It was an emotional time. I wept round every corner. Everything about her became unbearably dear to me, as though my unhappiness gave each detail of memory an extra meaning. I had to keep driving to her flat to look for mail, reassure the neighbours, collect her pension, and even driving up to the council estate, just the act of swerving the car into the kerb, an action I'd done a hundred times before, caused me to swallow hard because I associated it with driving to see her. There she'd be, writing her diary, watching television, cooking or just standing in front of the gas stove hoping the warmth from the upper grill would ease the pain in her gums. I was covering ground I knew she'd never cover again. That quadrangle of old neighbours looking out of their windows, waiting, now became a place of loneliness filled with a sense of time past. I felt an overwhelming ache to be young again with her, to watch her cooking for my friends, hear her telling me off for late hours while at the same time joining in whatever it was that kept the hour late.

Of course she'd make those emotional times worse by talking as though dying was the most natural thing in the world. Which it is, we know. Only it never seems so. 'I don't mind,' she'd say. 'Only peace, let there be peace in the world, and friendship in the family. Stay together. Don't be sad. I don't really mind.'

As the pain in her gums increased she needed to be kept on Palfium drugs. Morphine-based. She'd get high, lose her memory, construct strange or unfinished sentences. 'I'll soon tell you, I'll soon tell you all about it.' About what? God knows! She never finished. Once I went into her room and found her sitting up and clutching at something in the air, as though reaching out for a person, and she said, 'Suddenly, just then, I felt that really I was alone.' In the end none of the pills helped. I just sat close to her and cradled her in my arms, holding her hands. 'Ah, warmth, warmth!' she'd say. 'There's nothing like warmth.'

'Snuggle down into bed,' I'd say, 'that'll make you warm.'

'Not warm like this,' she'd say as I held her.

One day, before we left for Stockholm, I went into her room – I'd go there first thing as soon as I got up – and found her sitting with her hands behind her head, her eyes bright. 'I feel so excited about something,' she said. 'I want something to happen, some event, some special event.' I took her downstairs, walking in front of her, holding her hand, high up, to steady her. She descended, slowly, sedately. 'The bride!' she said, and smiled at the inevitability of things. Self-mockery never left her.

But she *was* judgemental, and family, friends, and comrades felt her disapproval. Not all her assessments were accurate. She often judged based on a tone of voice, the melody, which sometimes carries the real message of what a person is saying. Nevertheless in the way she looked at you – and I find myself looking at people with the same suspicion, disbelief, and contempt *her* eyes carried – she inspired a certain respect spiced with fear.

And she was intemperate, unable to refrain from the damning comment or observation which diplomacy and sound human relationships require. I have inherited her intemperate nature. A sliver has splintered off from her, embedded itself in me like an awkward curse, and so I have learned not to trust myself in confrontations. Like her, my nervous system contains one raw, exposed nerve end which identifies, like a scanner, thugs and cretins, braggarts and bullies, those who wish me ill, engage in tiresome competition, sacrifice me to their opportunism. It crackles, this maternal Geiger counter, at the mere hint of minds crippled by stupidity clutching bureaucracy for support; throbs when it encounters those stubbornly clinging to positions they no longer believe in or have mistakenly adopted but have not the courage to relinquish, those defeated by their mistakes, poisoned with discontent for what they know themselves unable to be, searching for what can be brought down to appease their failures. My mother made me sensitive to such people, bequeathed me a nerve end honed over centuries, flashing danger signals at a loaded word here, a hint of sneer in the voice there, be they from fellow-artists, politicians, journalists, television interviewers, guests round a dinner table, chance encounters at parties, members of an audience to whom I've just lectured and who have bristled at something I've said. Anyone anywhere! My nerve end recognises them in an instant, perhaps as they don't recognise themselves, and something snaps in my equanimity.

Poor Anyone Anywhere! He, She, They instantly become for me the personification of that which makes the world an ugly place. Every frustrating, demoralising experience suffered at the hands of humankind gathers like a furious storm and settles in this one person. Like quarrelling couples, one incident can fetch up the bile of an entire hateful married life. 'You,' I want to say to them, 'are what makes life depressing. History and literature teaches that you and your Lilliputianism are everywhere and have been since Adam!'

For certain I would have been a useless negotiator to free hostages. 'Illiterate thugs!' I would want to cry at the brutal guards. 'Bigots!' I would want to scream at religious fundamentalists demanding respect for their beliefs at the point of a gun. Every religion or political party, every profession gives birth to its opportunists, to its murderous nothings of history – those who know how to work the system. 'Opportunists!' I would want to rage at those round the negotiating table cloaking their country's cruelties in holiness. 'Demagogues!' at those who commit their murderous idiocies in the name of 'The People'. 'Mumbo-jumbo!' at those surrendering their lives in prayer before a God who makes no sense in a wayward world of horrendous earthquakes, hurricanes, floods and heartbreaking famine. 'God works in mysterious ways!' 'Conveniently mysterious indeed!' I would want to explode. Reason drains from me like blood out of a grievous wound. Emotion floods my calm. Fury and contempt take over. Stupidity knows itself. My kind of screaming threatens it. The nervous finger of the inferiority complex is too near the trigger. I would never have made a politician, could never have been a diplomat.

All inherited from my mother, an unsophisticated woman who could see danger as it was brewing long before even the brewer knew. And though, of course, I really do know, as diplomats know, that the fool must be told he has a just cause, that 'patience, patience, patience' is the only answer, yet I do not possess the diplomat's quality of patience. My mother had it not. I have it not! Appoint me plenipotentiary to nowhere. Someone must be left behind to scream.

There is no doubt in my mind – my mother was a writer. I hadn't realised it before but confronted with her notebooks and letters – so many letters are in the hands of others, and sheets upon sheets are torn from her diaries – I can see it. Her instinct when overwhelmed with emotion for one reason or another – it could be joy as well as pain as well as a thought to be recorded – was to reach for her pen and tell it.

On 13 June 1960 she wrote a kind of will.

I make my wish. When I die I want both Della and Arnold to sit shiva [mourning] after me in this house, and if my brothers want to sit shiva here with Della and Arnold that also would be my wish. I want Ralph to leave Della alone here, not to bother her with work. He can together with Dusty and their aunties to look after them for one week, and I wish you all be in peace. You can play cards as long as you are all here for a whole week together.

I beg my nearest friends to help clear my clothes and anything that's left of their father's, to give back this flat clean. Della and Arnold share everything what you want. Not much left you [even] if you wanted!

Arnold, if Della would like the settee I would like her to have it as at the moment you seem to make a few pounds and you can easily buy others. Della usually waits until Ralph makes it. That is if you, Dear Della, want to accept it. You can have it upholstered.

And be well. I beg you to live in peace and in harmony and help each other when necessary. You are only two of you. Stick together until death. Don't let children or outsiders come between you. There is nothing so close as brothers and sisters when they like each other and they are close. Please do that.

I have joined the United Synagogue. That will cover I hope my funeral, and there is insurance money. After all this is finished, my darlings, don't mourn very long for me. See that you go away at least for a week to recuperate. Especially Della will need it, as she isn't out so much as you are, Arnold. Please my Darling Arnold don't you cry either much or long after me.

You were both wonderful. I love you all.

Mummy   XXXXXXX

She died in my sister's house. Cause – arteriosclerosis of the liver. Her last request was for a plate of mashed potatoes. Della asked grandson Adam to sit with her while she made it. By the time she returned it was too late. He said it was a peaceful end. I deeply regret not being with her in her last moments. She lives on in four of the plays and three of the stories and her final days are recorded in my diary from which I culled the long speech given to Professor Maurice Stapleton in *Love Letters on Blue Paper*. It was my farewell to her.

Ralph, her son-in-law, composed the words carved into her gravestone which we laid down the customary year after her burial, on 23 October 1977.

Leah Wesker
Née Perlmutter
Daughter of Jacob
28 July 1898 – 8 Oct. 1976

Lived – passionately
Fought for right – endlessly
Loved family and friends – deeply

Mourned by her
children   Della and Ralph
                   Arnold and Dusty
grandchildren Miles, Adam, Lindsay,
                   Tanya, Jake, Daniel
brothers   Perly, Barney, Layosh, Oscar

and all who knew her

Two other artists in the family

Three of my mother's brothers remained in Transylvania and survived the Nazi occupation, mainly, I was told, because the

Rumanian government had secured the right to do what they liked with their Jews who consequently were in the advantageous position of being able to bribe for their lives. Having discovered that Jews were a saleable commodity the Rumanians later sold them – those who wanted to leave – to Israel for handy dollars. All the brothers except one, Layosh – a sweet, innocent and dedicated communist – emigrated to Israel after the war, where they bred countless cousins. In 1960 I took my mother to visit the brothers she had not seen for fifty years, and nieces and nephews she had *never* seen. There they were, lined up at Lod airport, waiting to greet us. They laughed, glanced, joked and argued in exactly the same timbres and rhythms. Mirror images of my English uncles and cousins. It was emotional and comical. My mother assumed the role of elder sister at once despite not *being* the elder sister; she was simply English and carried that air of sophistication which fifty years of peace and metropolitan life endows even to the unworldly. Nothing was new, except the landscape and the smells of blossom and petrol.

That's not quite true, how could it be! Two of the uncles – the elderly, ultra-orthodox Isidore married to his second wife, Koto, and Oscar married to Zelma, were both possessed of – uncharacteristic in the London branch of the family – insanely jealous streaks which surfaced once they'd passed the age of fifty. Isidore used to lock his wife up in the evenings to protect her from the gaze of men; Oscar was so convinced his wife was eyeing the man across the road that he moved house. Isidore lost a grandson killed in the '67 war, and a son called Jossi, murdered by his wife in Rumania with a carving knife. An unsaleable Jew, obviously! What dark passions there.

The Israeli branch of the Perlmutters, though lovely, were slightly crazier – the result no doubt of living in Rumania during the occupation and then emigrating to a country war-tense from birth. Israeli Jews are not like diaspora Jews, they're tougher, rougher, more cynical.

There are two other Perlmutter artists: a writer and a painter.

About Zoltan, the painter, born to Oscar in the 1920s, there is a story.

On that first trip to Israel with my mother, Zoltan was the black sheep of the family, a wastrel who – to the despair of his wife and parents – wanted to paint. Many years later he came to London loaded with jewellery, cameras, a huge car, money enough to afford a flat in Hampstead as well as one in Antwerp. He'd made it! Well, almost. Fortune had come to him, though not real fame. He had achieved exhibitions in many cities in Europe and now hoped to conquer London with an exhibition in a not particularly salubrious venue. The family dutifully viewed his paintings, and many bought them – in particular our wealthy Uncle Perly who gave an exhibition in his house for all his business friends. I was uncertain about the work. It seemed garish, facile. But an energy seemed to drive it and confused my judgement, an energy I later came to recognise as spurious. Zoltan asked me to put him in touch with a good gallery. I knew none. It was not my world. But I did know a leading art critic, David Sylvester, who happened to be an admirer of my plays. I begged of him a favour to view Zoltan's work. David, bon viveur as well as art critic and curator, generously agreed. It was an embarrassing evening which he handled with courtesy and grace.

I assembled a collection of Zoltan's paintings upstairs in the study of Bishops Road. Zoltan remained downstairs, rigid with angst, smoking non-stop. He looked like everyone's stereotype image of the artist – long, flowing grey hair, a pointed beard, mischievously smiling Perlmutter eyes – though not on this occasion – coloured waistcoat and generally flamboyant dress. David looked at a few of the canvases and I could tell at once that I should have trusted my instinct and not wasted his time. He searched for, and offered, the best approbation he could extract from his vocabulary of contempt, one which turned out to be a huge insult to my own profession. 'Has your cousin thought of designing for the theatre?'

How then did Zoltan achieve a doubtful fame and a very considerable fortune? He confided – through a kind of scam. Near where he'd lived in Israel was an art gallery to which he had constantly offered work and been rejected. He conceived a plan: borrowed a sum of money, persuaded the gallery to hang his paintings, and gave the money to trusted friends to buy them. Somehow – and I'm not in possession of the fine details – it worked. He went from success to success, invented his own reputation.

We saw a lot of him at one time. He left his Israeli wife, linked up with a Hungarian beauty, enjoyed the high life, and was involved in a shooting incident in a Cornish gambling club where a gambler went berserk and shot dead some while others, including my cousin and his Hungarian beauty, crawled under tables to avoid the bullets. They were not successful. Each hosted a bullet. Not fatal but not comfortable.

The other Perlmutter artist is a writer, Andrei Codrescu, living in New Orleans, known nationwide for his cryptic contributions to a National Public Radio show, *All Things Considered*. He teaches writing and literature at Baton Rouge in Louisiana State University, and edits a magazine called *Exquisite Corpse: a journal of Books & Ideas*. One of his books, *Road Scholar* – travels through the States – was filmed and screened on Channel 4. In a recent letter Andrei recounted my mother's visit to Rumania in the early sixties:

> Have I ever told you about the time your mother visited us in Sibiu? She was quite enchanted by what she saw as working socialism, including our dingy apartment in the basement of a workers' 'building block'. My mother said, 'If you think this is so great why don't you move here and we move into your place in London?' At least that's how the exchange came down via my mother, who was convinced, by the way, that you lived in a palace in London studded with innumerable white telephones. (Big deal these *white* telephones, pure symbols of capitalist luxury.)

I asked him, for the purpose of this autobiography, to explain exactly how we were related. He faxed back:

It's the first time I have a sense that I actually come from some people . . . I always thought my mother and I were a solo act . . . My mother's side remains obscure. She hated her mother and she made sure the world started with her . . .

As for my father, Julius, son of Oscar, he married my mother, Eva Geller. I was their only son. My father divorced my mother when I was only six months old. He emigrated to Israel in the early 1960s and died there at the age of forty-six, I think . . . I hope to see his grave some day. He married a blonde Russian woman named Olga who smoked from a cigar holder over mega-bosoms framed by a major decolletage but they had no children, and then had a third wife, a very sexy, red-haired Hungarian girl named Lola whom I remember very well because she was always warm and smelled delicious; they had a son together, my half-brother, who was a juvenile delinquent and spent time in the poky . . . (I hear now that he boasts of having a famous brother in America: I expect him any day to show up and contribute to the crime wave in New Orleans . . .)

My name *is* Perlmutter. I changed it first to STEIU in Rumania in order to publish poetry (too Jewish for publication) but it was also too close to STEIN (looked the same handwritten in fact) so I changed it again to CODRESCU which was close enough to CODREANU, Rumania's greatest Jew hater. How is that for unselfconscious anti-semitism? When I realised what I'd done I kept it anyway, vowing to eventually make CODREANU only a footnote in *my* history. How am I doing? As for me, CODRESCU, I'm married to Alice Henderson, and we both have two children: LUCIAN (b.1970) and TRISTIAN (b.1978) – and they are both CODRESCUS, the first of their line.

I envy his style. I struggle with prose like a man trying to remember the tune.

The death of cousin Annie

One of my earliest childhood memories, when I was seven, was the death of lovely cousin Annie, knocked down and killed by a bus on the Balls Pond Road in Dalston during the blackout in the war, and how the news was brought to us. She was one of four children born to my mother's second eldest brother, Barney (Bernard). The others were Billie, Tom, and Bert. The boys were larky, Jewish Cockneys, full of street-corner scepticism about the gullible working class on whose doors they knocked to sell whatever they could lay their hands on. Smooth talkers, charmers, on-the-knocker lads. 'Keep laughing,' they'd say on parting; life was so absurd it had to be laughed at. They loved both my parents whose bitter, absurd fights they attempted to laugh away. Laughter – a Perlmutter trait.

Bert and Tom once took my father dancing to the Lyceum off the Strand, attempting to get him drunk. 'But he drank *us* under the table!' They told the story endlessly. And they were shit-stirrers. They'd sit in our attic flat in Fashion Street at family get-togethers and deliberately raise political issues, knowing that sooner or later the right-wingers would be at loggerheads with the left-wingers. Bert and Tom's sister Billie was a good cousin to me. In my early teens I was like the Ancient Mariner, stopping anyone who would listen to yesterday's scribblings – Billie listened, patient with my awful poetry, and encouraging. She and her brothers adored their sister, Annie. We all did. A pretty young woman, constantly smiling with delight at life, enjoying her world of family. I loved her because she indulged my mischievous ways. '*There's* nice!' she cooed. I hear her emphasising 'there's'. '*There's* nice!'

Almost opposite Fashion Street in Brick Lane was the Mayfair Cinema (later renamed the Odeon, and when the Asians moved in, the Naz) where I nagged to be taken as often as possible and where, I surmise, the seeds of what talent I possess for drama were sown. One afternoon, 21 November 1941, two years into the Second World War, I was with my mother in the Mayfair watching George Brent, Basil Rathbone and Ilona Massay in *International Lady* (the B movie was *Roar of the Press*) when my father appeared in the aisle, bending and peering along the rows this way and that way looking for us. Leah knew from the urgency of his whispered summons that something was wrong. I trailed behind her as she hurried

with him out into the glare of the afternoon light demanding to
know what happened. He would not say at once, thoughtfully wanting to get her into the familiar and reassuring setting of our own
flat, where she could react in privacy, away from public gaze. The
storming little woman was insistent, fearing, no doubt, that it was
bad.news about her other child, Della. My father managed to get
her across Brick Lane but she couldn't bear not knowing and
stopped him on the corner of Fashion Street. I see that scene before
me, vividly. I know where each was standing – she with her back to
the wall near a little greengrocer's shop, he with his back to the
kerb. I'm looking from one to the other.

'What is it? What's happened?' she demanded angrily, as though
whatever it was, he was responsible. He told her simply 'Annie's
dead.' My mother screamed. Her favourite niece. I can remember
nothing else, neither how my father was told nor what we did next.

Annie had worked for Ever Ready batteries as a clerk. She had
wanted to improve her lot and was attending evening classes to
learn shorthand. On the way to her class the previous night, the city
blacked out against bombers, foggy, too, as well as dark, Annie misjudged the speed of an approaching trolley bus, walked into it and
was cruelly battered. She lasted twelve hours in hospital. Uncle Barney and his wife, Esther, never really recovered. Aunt Esther
became strange and in some way held the rest of the family to
blame for the tragedy. They all moved to Cornwall as though from
the stench of death, and though we have stayed in touch it has been
only through sporadic encounters. Cousin June, Uncle Perly's girl,
named her daughter after Annie. Jews never name their offspring
after the living, only the dead.

Family, friends, other people's lives – all fed what I wrote. I confess, I have a thin imagination. Little that I can invent is more
extraordinary than lives lived. Barney and Esther, for example.
Being older than my mother he'd come to England earlier and had
bummed around working as allsorts. At one time during the First
World War he was in the British Army, fighting against his
brother, Layosh, who was in uniform for the Germans. He ended

up lumberjacking in Poland, where he married Esther under the canopy in the snow while the rest of the villagers shone them through the ceremony holding flaming torches. Romantic! Aunty Esther had a sister living in America. They couldn't decide where to emigrate – England with Barney's family or America with hers. They tossed a coin. Barney won. It was England. Perhaps that's why Aunt Esther developed her melancholy resentment of us after the death of her daughter. It wouldn't have happened in America!

Chapter Four

The milieu

My parents met at work, tailoring machinists both, sang together in the choir of a Socialist Zionist organisation called Poale Zion, and married on 27 November 1923. The following 27 August, nine months to the day, Della was born.

The East End was a ferment of activity. Lives collided in sweat shops, political groups, workers' cultural associations, youth clubs, street corners. Jews dominated that area and that generation before me lived vociferously, argumentatively, emotionally, with a kind of desperation. Fear of pogroms lay dormant. There were no illiterate peasants to get drunk and go on a rampage but every street corner had a pub – it was never known what drunken angers of frustration would emerge from it. Jews have a healthy belief that life is given to be lived here and now on this earth. Deep in Jewish perception is a scepticism about the hereafter. They know that promises of paradise encourage unscrupulous priests to bamboozle the gullible for their own ends – no fooling the Jews! Besides, they possessed huge appetites for living and a desire to experience to the full all that their bountiful God had provided. England was free like nowhere else, all energies were released – the good and bad: exploiter and exploited, rich and poor, the literate and the philistine.

I resist the temptation to collate a history of the Jewish East End and its swarming social and political activity. The waves of Jewish immigration from Russia and Eastern Europe which flooded France, Great Britain, the United States and Latin America is a remarkable story. Two good books chart the British tales of immigrants: *Point Of Arrival* by Chaim Bermant, and the scholarly, fascinating *East End Jewish Radicals, 1875–1914* by Professor William Fishman, a book which ends where my family history began, recording the birth of the Tailor and Garment Workers' Union, the London branch of which Aunt Sara became a luminary.

My earliest memories in the tiny tenement flat in Rothschild's Buildings are of Aunt Sara relating union stories, frequently about Mr Fine, her superior in the union, with whom she was always quarrelling. 'So Fine said this . . . and I said to Fine . . .' A shadowy figure who I came finally to meet when he retired and I was invited to be an honoured guest at his farewell dinner, but whose real place in the scheme of things I only understood on reading the Fishman book.

J.L. Fine was the union leader who, in 1912, persuaded the garment workers to hold out long enough to win a strike that enabled him to form a united tailoring workers' union. An even more extraordinary aspect of that strike, as Fishman's history records, is the role played by one Rudolph Rocker, a German anarchist, a gentile, who came to London and taught himself Yiddish in order to help organise the Jewish immigrant workers he found to be living in conditions of hardship and depression. Rocker's protégé was J.L. Fine. When Fine was about to concede victory to the master tailors, Rocker urged him to hold out another day. He did. The Tailor and Garment Workers' Union came into existence and Aunt Sara, many years later, became one of its most colourful, respected and, by some, feared organisers.

Nor was Rocker the only charismatic character in the East End. The animated political and cultural climate into which my parents were thrust, which nurtured them and, through them, subsequently me, was formed by a host of personalities, and organisations lovingly documented in the books of Fishman and Bermant. But one they could not have known centred round a modest little organisation whose vague, heroic language must have settled in my mother's consciousness and prepared her for membership of the Communist Party – though the modest little organisation's founder, Mrs Violet English, would have been horrified at the thought. My mother and her brother, Perly, together with his girlfriend, Betsy O'Solky – Aunt Betty, that is – went on rambles and

met with like-minded youngsters in different venues they called
The Rooms, one in the East End, another somewhere in a forest
glade in Taplow, Buckinghamshire, where they sang and planned
the future. They were the 'Guild of the Citizens of To-Morrow'.
The foreword to their recruiting pamphlet rings stirringly for these
young immigrants of the Guild, which had branches in nineteen
cities from Belfast to Ipswich, Gateshead-on-Tyne to Southampton,
and Scarborough to Southend.

> For years to come men and women in all countries will be occupied
> with problems of reconstruction. It is fully recognised that all that
> has become worn out in the old basis of society must be replaced by
> new and firmer material, and the whole world acknowledges that
> the new material is to be found in the younger generation alone.
> Children and young people are more plastic than adults and can be
> more readily taught to stem the old currents of competition and
> rivalry and turn them into the nobler channels of co-operation and
> service . . .

Look at them round the Guild Flag, lovely young faces with the
world standing equally before them all. My mother took the Guild's
ideals one way via Socialist Zionism into the Communist Party,
sweated labour and poverty. Her brother Perly with his wife Betty
took them in another direction, via hard work into wealth and Zionist causes.

I would love to dwell on this swarming life in the East End, the
interaction of groups, the coming together and splintering of political organisations, seeds laid here which sprouted there, the crossing
of barriers, the interaction of lives, intellectual and cultural cross-
fertilisation. It all fascinates me. Barnardo and Booth began there.
The Whitechapel Library and Art Gallery belong to the same
period as Toynbee Hall. Jack London came to the East End in 1902
and lived in a doss house in Thrawl Street, where Rinkoff's the
baker baked one of my birthday cakes. On the other side of the road
the barber, plank across the chair to make little boys high enough to

be reached with scissors. Dora Gaitskell came from those streets to become a Labour leader's wife; and Solomon, a pianist; Lew (Lord) Grade grew up in Brick Lane and founded a TV empire – ATV; Sidney (Lord) Bernstein's father owned silent movie houses there; Lionel Bart, Georgia Brown (real name Lily Potts), Bernard Kops ran around in the area. Comedian Bud Flanagan, band leader Joe Loss, the poet Isaac Rosenberg, the painters Mark Gertler and David Bomberg all flowered in that maze of teeming streets.

There was even a spread-over into New York. A dashing young actor named Jacob Adler led a Yiddish theatre in Princelet Street where someone called 'Fire!' after a gas lamp exploded, causing a stampede which killed seventeen members of the audience. Adler was given money to take himself and his unholy profession to New York, where he set up another Yiddish theatre employing the talents of such as Edward G. Robinson, who later became a big Hollywood movie star. Out of Adler's theatre grew The Group Theatre which nurtured the talents of writers like Clifford Odets. Adler had two daughters, Cecilia and Stella. From Stella Adler and Lee Strasberg came the method school of acting, touching the talents of Marlon Brando, Lee J. Cobb, Pacino, De Niro, Hoffman ... I know, I know, the line gets thinner the further away it's stretched, but the line and the link exist unmistakably.

'Like most women she'd married the wrong man' – from The Visit

They say there are more interesting women in the world than men and – I don't know about the world – the *world*, I mean there's millions and millions in the *world* so we shouldn't generalise, but – in my experience, the women I meet, from all sorts of backgrounds, professions, countries, some have been married, some are single parents, some work hard at home, some at the top of their profession – nearly all of them tell me: they can't find a man! Not a really kind, gentle, tender, intelligent, imaginative, interesting, supportive, thoughtful, respectful, educated, courageous, chivalrous, witty, thrilling, thrilling, thrilling man.

Perhaps we're asking too much!

Melanie – *Letter to a Daughter*

My mother and father were not made for each other. There are some who say none of us are made for each other. We meet, and after the halcyon days of love and roses simply become used to each other. Or we don't. My parents didn't.

> Mr Lander, to whom each fresh example of feminine resentment was a source of renewed bewilderment, used these gatherings to continue his ruminations upon wives and the female temperament. Pretending to talk to his son alone he'd affect, nevertheless, the public tone for the benefit of his friends and with obvious relish locked in his complaints, he'd rhetorise: 'I'm not saying all men are lovely but, I don't know, men forgive each other more readily. Your mother, hard-working, devoted, 100-per-cent dependable, can forgive no one anything; not God for the world, not her parents for making her woman, not me for being a man, not even herself – for putting up with everything. Have you noticed? You come in and say what a lovely day it is outside and she's got so much into the habit of expecting catastrophe that she clicks her tongue and says, "I knew it would be." "But Selma," I say, "a *lovely* day, I said *lovely* day." "Don't talk to me about lovely days," she says, "have I got pleasures? Blessing? A new gas stove?" No logic. No concentration. You'd think she's a fool the way she talks, your mother, but she's no fool. She has only one fault. Me! I'm the crack in her make-up. She doesn't like me. It's no joke living with a woman who doesn't want you near her and holds you responsible for war, famine and pestilence.'

> *The Man Who Would Never Write Like Balzac*

The mined waters of love and marriage have taken up much of my writing: my parents' sad and acrimonious relationship recorded in *Chicken Soup with Barley*; the explosive denouement in *The Kitchen*, when the married mistress of the central character, Peter, finally declines his invitation to go off with him; Dobson, the cynical friend in *I'm Talking about Jerusalem*, relates the saga of two disastrous marriages; *The Four Seasons* – given entirely to the re-creation of a passionate love that goes wrong. The failure of marriage, the impossibility of sustained love, the changing needs of couples who cannot help but grow apart – it's all there in plays like *Yardsale, The Mistress, One More Ride on the Merry-Go-Round, Lady Othello*. Even the central thesis of *When God Wanted a Son* – that anti-semitism is deep-rooted, here for ever in the bloodstream of human society – is explored through the tension of a broken marriage.

Does all that stem from the experience of growing up with parents who quarrelled? Well, to be Jewish about it, yes and no. Which is a way of saying maybe. Or – no life is that simple. Della reminds me that I was a disruptive and obstinate child. She attributes this to their quarrelling. 'They were inconsistent, they confused you.' She believes there is a pattern to my life which repeats the inconsistencies. I don't accept this. Contradiction and paradox ravage me like they do most people but I take responsibility for who I am and believe my parents' fighting contributed to only a part of the pattern. After all, each had a sense of humour. Didn't I inherit that? Both were playful – I inherited that too.

Mother and I played out a running fantasy that she was not really my mother, I was adopted, my real mother was a gypsy who had abandoned me. We would tell this story to strangers and each new friend I made. Sometimes we would forget to untell it and for all I know there are some who still think me born of gypsies! We were a good act together.

'Do you love me?'
'Yes.'
'How much?'
'Sixpence.'
'Is that all?'
'Two and sixpence, then.'
'Only two and sixpence?'

'I love you all the world.'

'No more?'

'All the world, all the world, all the world, all the world, all the world . . .'

Playfulness, as I think about her more and more, was her essential quality. She was judgemental, she reproached, but she was happiest being playful. It's there in her tone of voice as I hear it after all these years on the tape – she makes light of things, mocks, laughs a lot. We shared a sense of the ridiculous, detected and laughed together at other people's ponderous sense of importance. In a letter she wrote when I was in Paris working in a kitchen and had told her of the boss's son who hated me and had called me 'a foreigner', she advised: 'Tell him you're *not* a foreigner, you're English!' Inheriting her playfulness and sixth sense for detecting humbug has landed me – as it landed her – in a lot of trouble. I learned from her not to keep my mouth shut even though she constantly warned me to so do, do, do . . . 'Please, Arnold, do. Not as I do but as I teach you to do.' From her I learned not to take myself seriously. I take my work, social and political issues, and my children seriously but not who I am – unless confronted with fools and minimalisers. And her playfulness, her merriment, her bold joy is there, forever captured – I see it now – in her doodles which are the other side of her sad and depressed diary entries.

With my father, who was often called by his Yiddish name 'Yossel', I used to wrestle and box. Neither of us were adept, it was more a comedy act. I was in my early teens.

'I'll knock your block off!' he'd threaten.

'Knock whose block off?' I'd taunt.

'Your block off.'

'Try it.'

'Don't tempt me.'

'I'm tempting you.'

'Sohelpme if you don't leave off . . .'

We also sang together. With his lovely tenor voice he was constantly asked to sing 'Stenka Razin', sometimes called 'Volga Volga!'

about the Russian folk hero. The plea would go up, 'Sing "Volga Volga!", Yossel, "Volga Volga!"'. Others would join in and it would start off a singsong consisting of Yiddish and revolutionary songs, many of them to be sung, harmonised, in my plays. I sang 'Stenka Razin' to the children and now to my granddaughter. I'd sing it to my grandson if you'd let me, Lindsay Joe.

> *Silver sheen when dawn is breaking*
> *Gold and crimson glow at noon*
> *Hush at depths when twilight cometh*
> *Gold and silver is thy croon.*

Did I remember the words correctly? They don't seem to make sense now. What does 'Gold and silver is thy croon' mean? Should it be 'Cold and silver is thy croon'? Or is my sister right when she says the line is 'Gold and silver are thy hues'? The rest made perfect sense.

> *Volga Volga mighty Volga*
> *Thou art beautiful and strong*
> *List O list you now to Razin*
> *Listen to my cossack song.*
>
> *I have fought and bled for freedom*
> *Earthly loves I have but three,*
> *She my Volga she my mistress*
> *And the sweet cause of liberty.*

The last two lines were repeated in harmony. My sister insists the last line of the second verse is not 'Listen to my cossack song' but 'Listen to my *peasant* song'. She's wrong of course.

As well as being called upon to sing, Joe would be asked to give an impersonation of Charlie Chaplin's walk. He was so thin his trousers hung about him like the movie clown. On reaching my teens I could haul him over my shoulders and twist him round and round to make him giddy and unsteady, the easier to box him. He loved being in the midst of people, and loved being loved. There were times we enjoyed each other so much that it would irritate my mother.

Curious the way laughter can sometimes annoy a woman. Dusty was another – she would stiffen if I laughed too loud and long. I wonder why this is, this female frowning upon the gaiety of their spouse? Perhaps it's rooted in their need to be the provider of all things, and if joy and laughter stem from a source other than theirs they freeze with reproach.

One of my theories about art is that it deals with what I call 'secondary truths' as opposed to 'primary' or 'absolute truths'. There is no *absolute* truth about the nature of love, women, happiness, the nature of anything. The poets write different songs about each, and each is right for some of us, and for some of us at different times, and for some of us only some of the time.

You know, when I was born I was born with a great laughter in me. Can you believe that? A great laughter, like a blessing. And some people loved and some hated it. It was a sort of challenge, a test against which people measured themselves as human beings; and I could never understand, not at all, the extremes of their love or their hatred. Have you ever been with a beautiful woman, a really breathtaking beauty, and watched or felt the passionate waves of devotion and loathing she attracts, and noticed how the people around feel the irresistible need to say sly, unpleasant things to show they're not intimidated by her beauty? So it was with my laughter.

And she, who had no need to measure herself against anything or anyone because she was endowed with her own loveliness, her own intelligence – she too began to measure herself against that laughter. And why? Because it belonged to me you see; I was born with it, she couldn't bear that it hadn't been bestowed by her and so she began to measure herself against me and challenge all that was mine.

Adam – *The Four Seasons*

Why did they marry then, Leah and Joe? The view of aunts Ann and Sara was that my mother hoped she could change him. They claimed they had warned her of his indolent and irresponsible ways. She had ignored them – on her head be it! It went wrong from the start. He left her within the first months of their marriage. A 1973 diary records a conversation with my sister:

29 November 1973

Had a long talk with Della yesterday . . . she had said: 'I could tell you a lot.' Made a lunch date and had barley soup with her (Somali Road, her house) . . .

I began by asking exactly what had happened. She said:

'I remember, very vividly, a time when I was playing in Rothschild's Buildings and suddenly I saw daddy who I hadn't seen for a long time, and that I was pleased to see him and obviously he was pleased to see me. I think what had happened was that mummy had gone to the Jewish Board of Guardians for help and they'd asked "what was your husband doing?" and so she was pressed to claim the maintenance money the court had awarded her. She pressed and he didn't pay and so he went to prison and only then did the Board of Guardians give her money . . . When you were born daddy left us for about eighteen months . . .' This surprised me.

'You mean we were both without him for eighteen months?'

'No, no. We saw him at Boba's . . .' She thought and tried to reconstruct from her memory. This, perhaps not in this order, but more or less, is what she recounted.

'We lived in Hackney Road when you were born in Mother Levy's, and when mummy got back from confinement daddy had gone. In the next eighteen months we moved to Wilkes Street which is just off Fournier Street, and then to Grey Eagle Street which is just behind Wilkes Street. I can remember mummy gave us to Boba and the aunts for periods. Daddy was staying there so we saw him. But I suppose, in all, they were separated for about a year . . . You see he just hated his work, he couldn't bring himself to do it, even for the family, and mummy felt it was his responsibility and fought him to do it so he just fled . . . Aunty Annie used to complain that all the responsibility was falling on her. I can remember Aunty Rae choking on a sandwich because she felt they oughtn't give in to daddy. On the other hand they all felt he'd married some-one less intelligent and so they didn't have all that much sympathy for mummy . . . Yes, it all affected me terribly. It's not that mummy took it out on me, on the contrary, she never behaved like that at all, compared to other mothers she was loving and tolerant and under-standing, but she was always involving me. "Look at your father, ask him if he got the sack or he just walked out . . ." She actually re-sented me taking his part or going to the aunts and Boba, so I felt my loyalties were split all the time. I couldn't show daddy as much affection as I wanted to . . . I don't know why it didn't affect you in the same way . . . don't forget you had me, we had a very good re-lationship really . . .'

I suggested to Della that going to Spitalfields Central Foundation Girls' School and having a political circle of friends she had perhaps developed a more sensitive and delicate personality. I was very much a street urchin. And if I had her then she, we both, had the aunts to cushion us also. She continued:

'I mean you can't remember the awful rows . . . I can remember once returning home seeing a crowd gathered outside number 43 . . . and once you were so frightened you crawled under the table. Of course daddy was no angel. He got me out of bed one evening and dressed me and took me to a party at the clothing factory, a party with all the "yoikletas" [gentiles], the girls, and he told me "don't tell your mother". But mummy had brought me up to be absolutely truthful, it was the most important thing she forced on to me, and so I had to tell her when she asked me and then I felt guilty for betraying daddy . . . you talk about her "queenly feelings", well, that may be so, but I think she had the one great failing of never being able to understand the other person's situation when it was to do with her, and what was worse she didn't think it was necessary to do so . . . Really she was a very irrational woman; it may have been true that daddy didn't go to work some times but she didn't under-stand about politics in those days. It was the depression and all that, and she didn't ever consider it likely that it was for economic reasons he got the sack. No! it was always his fault. Just like now it's the reverse, it's always the employer's fault. I'm not blaming her for what happened, it's just that neither of them were good for each other. I mean he would always ask me to respect mummy as "the mother" but things had gone so far that she never ever asked me to respect him as "the father". Even in families where the father was a bastard the mother always called for respect for him.'

Yet I remember, in later years in Weald Square, mum would tell me I had to respect him. I pointed that out to Della and she agreed that in the later years mum had risen to the challenge of being a wife and had looked after him, even with affection.

'We were so poor. You've no idea how poor we were. Much poorer than others. Even the poorest had furniture. But mummy had to pawn our furniture. She had to pawn her wedding ring too . . . And yet, I suppose that it's to their credit, both, as well as ours, that we've come through as reasonably good people. Not without ill effects, of course. When I get into a depression it's not just a passing thing. I mean I don't just feel it as a passing thing, to me it seems there's no good in anything . . .'

'Me too,' I joined her. 'About once every quarter something happens and for Dusty it lasts 24 hours but for me it seems the ultimate sign of how rotten everything is and I can't shake it off for days . . . But it seems to me that we've inherited daddy's intelligence, mummy's instincts, intuition, and a mixture of each one's special brand of gaiety. And they *were* gay, and good humoured, both of them, weren't they?'

Della agreed and I think we both would have liked to cry.

'My God, Arnold, how long is it since we've sat and talked like this?' she said. We had sat for about three hours.

Letters dating back to 1925 written from my mother's brother, Harry, to their brother, Perly, further testify to my good-natured dad's ungovernable waywardness. I shall quote some of those letters but first, about the brothers.

Mother's brothers

Barney, the eldest, I have already described. He was never quite together after the death of his daughter, Annie. An eccentric character nevertheless, cared for by his children with love and watchful eyes. He had been all sorts, but had turned to tailoring, then selling, schooled by his door-knocker-salesman sons. Born a Perlmutter flirt, even into old age, he could charm the 'dears at the doors'. But Uncle Barney didn't impinge on my life as much as Harry and Perly about whom, oddly, I never wrote – which says something, incidentally, about the drive of literary process needing an incident or image to fire it. *Said the Old Man to the Young Man* was inspired by one of Uncle Barney's visits to London for Rosh Hashona – he wanted to greet the Jewish New Year in his old synagogue in Dalston. My nephew, Miles, was supposed to pick him up from there and return him for the meal, made by my sister, to break the Yom Kippur fast. Arrangements had been misunderstood and the old man was kept waiting in the rain by the young man. Out of which grew the story. Harry and Perly lived full, eventful lives but nothing filtered through to me with impact sufficient to spark off that fire.

Harry appears briefly as Hymie in *Chicken Soup with Barley* and as himself in 'A Time of Dying'. He'd married the taller, hard-working beauty, Ray Goldstein, who lived in Nathaniel Dwellings in Flower and Dean Street, the street of my grandparents. A slim, handsome man, who grew podgy in middle age. From his early years he involved himself in Jewish left-wing politics, becoming, in the early 1930s, one of the first members of the British Communist Party, followed later by my mother and father. His biggest regret, it affected him like an ever-open wound, was that he had not been educated. He was more kindly than perceptive, struggling hard to articulate like a political thinker but failing. You could hear his voice imagining it was the real thing – a brilliant orator's before the multitude. It wasn't. He was long-winded and pedantic, an unworldly Perlmutter. But he was kind from every pore of his being, and I was deeply fond of him. He was my mother's favourite.

She had saved him from drowning in the river which ran through Harumcort ('Three Wells') in Transylvania. When Aunty Ray was dying he was filled with remorse for his political fights with her. 'I blame myself for everything,' he said. They once came for a holiday here in Wales and one evening I defended something Aunty Ray had said. A raw nerve end within him was pricked and he broke through his normal kindness to rage at me, screaming:

'Don't think I can't use big words. You're not the only one who knows big words.' How bitterly he resented having had no education, and I'd not realised it until then.

He launched small business after small business, propped up by his patient brother, Perly. Each one failed. Unlike many communists from that East End era who had learned well the workings of evil capitalism and had become high financiers, Uncle Harry knew only that capitalism was evil, not how it worked.

I loved his ill-fated little stationery and printing businesses, offices full of staplers, date stamps, name stamps, paper clips, carbon papers, pink rubber finger grips, white pads. Who knows but that my first excitement for ink on paper was not stirred by his storerooms of office equipment? A kind man upon whom I could always rely for pocket money and attention.

While the dying Aunty Ray was being steered in pain from the kitchen to her bedroom I said to cousin Norma: 'The trouble with our family is they're all kind. Good-natured and kind. We grew up without any experience or understanding of the nature of evil. It's a serious defect, like being colour blind or tone deaf. I bet everyone in our family has made huge mistakes because of it.'

Perly, on the other hand, the youngest, was the one who despite not having a real education created a successful enterprise manufacturing gas thermostats. My mother described to me an almost mystical experience she had with him.

You know my brother, Perly, he was here three years before we came and he was five years old and he went to a school right from the beginning, from his infants. He got his schooling right through from five years old until sixteen years old. He could have studied, he could have gone on studying for whatever he wanted, really. He had to come out from the school because he wasn't English-born. But while taking the exams he used to get very ill because he was a very good scholar, very clever. He got through all his exams and he got excited I suppose, or worried, and he used to get ill, he used to have a temperature when he had to do the exams. One night I came into the room where he was sleeping and his eyes were glistening they were so light, like lit-up, really like a lit-up lamp, the whole room wasn't lit but it was light from his eyes when I came in and saw him. And I'll never forget that.

Perly and Betty lived in Surrey. Trips to their house with its long garden, on the Cheam Common Road, were an exciting outing. From Manor House on the Piccadilly Line to Leicester Square, then the Northern Line to Morden. It took for ever to get there, and coming out at Morden station was like arriving into a new world – open, suburban, rich. There was still one more leg to the trip, by bus. Like Harry, Perly was kind; unlike Harry, he had the where-withal to be more generous. And generous he was to most in the family – his children, brothers, his sister, nieces and nephews – the rich one of the family to whom we all looked up. Certainly I was helped by him through bad times. Nor did he ever pull rank, flaunt wealth; on the contrary he was modest, even apologetic for his golden touch. When he sold out to Elliot Automation he couldn't bear not running his own outfit and had to start up again, again achieving success until Parkinson's debilitated him. His death was the end of a family era. Impossible ever to have imagined that it could happen.

In 1925, six months after his marriage, Uncle Perly contracted TB. While in the Croydon Sanatorium his sister and brother wrote him letters. They tell not only of my father's neglect to pay my mother's court-order maintenance – in fact that's only a brief item in passing – they also convey a flavour of the days in which my sister was born: daily life, observations, quaint expressions of concern, asides which bring personalities to life and communicate their values. Only one letter from my mother survives but selected paragraphs from Harry's are worth quoting.

I am writing this in the workshop in between my cutting. I was very busy of the weekend with arranging one or two things that I had no time [to] write. Although you are not pleased to be confined to bed, yet I am pleased they are doing so. Which only proves that they are tackling the case properly. You mustn't mind that, as I suppose it is for the best. Anyhow, how did you get on Derby Day at Epsom. Did you pull a few pounds. I expect you did as I know you had the winners just one minute I am going to cut a pair of trousers. Hello, are you impatient I have cut two pair trousers and taken a private on . . .

I am still in very unstable circumstances. I am still unable to give back that money I owe you. I hope you don't mind and at first chance I will send it on to Betty so cheerio . . .

I must apologise as usual for being late with my answer. That is just what I am doing the whole of this season apologising again and again to my customers until they lose confidence in me, and they refuse to give me work. But never mind don't take my troubles to heart as they are not the worse and I am finding a way out and have managed to get Ray to borrow the money necessary to fix power machines which will help me to be able to get people in to work easier. You must remember that I am telling to you in confidence as to where I am getting the money. Don't mention as to whereabouts of the money in any letter that you write to me, as Ray reads all the letters. Anyhow I know that I am taking a great risk and responsibility but I mean to fight through until next season then I shall know that I am prepared and ready to grasp the opportunities that the next season might offer me. I think this will be enough about my dear self . . .

To tell you the truth that I feel at the moment that I wouldn't object of being confined to bed for about two weeks. I feel that every bone is aching me. That is all from hard work and worry. Never mind old chap, do as I am doing, be contented with the thought that what you are doing at present, will bear fruit in the future. Somehow us unfortunate three will be able to look back at old times and smile with success . . .

When I suggested that we could form a partnership I had in mind that you would not be fit for machining or for any indoor work. Travelling would be just a suitable job, always out in the open air, of course taking it very easy. Apart from this suggestion there are numerous of others, as you suggested, living in the country. Would not a little tobacco shop be ideal. One I think could easily be obtained at a very low premium. There are plenty of country places where from time to time the village or the town where the inhabitants increase year by year, new houses are being built and all the more enterprising it gets. Sometimes such places when you are able to get a shop, one with a good business view, can grow with the growing enterprise. Then there are lots of others.

You ask me to write in detail how I am getting on, at present very unsatisfactory. I have lost the season. Not only have I lost the season, but I am struggling to pay my expenses. That is all because I did not have anybody to work for me when the work was pouring down on me. At present it is very quiet. Although I am fixed up and can more easily get work people, I have now trouble in getting work. No doubt all beginners have to go through the same process. I have not lost hope, I am still confident, and I am certain I will strike lucky one day. I am making myself known amongst the shops and some day they will think of me, or I will worry them to death until I get work . . .

Leah is going to Southend on Thursday with Della, from the nursery, and I am very glad, as it will make a change for her. Last week she received £1-0-0 from Joe, although not the full amount that's all better than what she had when he was at home. When the amount runs up to 45/– she will be able to summons for it . . .

Anyhow don't take my troubles too seriously, as I still hope some day to make good. I don't give in until I will make good . . .

One of my mother's last doodles was in colour – yellow flowers in a grey vase speckled yellow. When Harry died she was shattered. Mother loved this gentle brother most of all and survived him less than a year. Seven months before she died she scribbled one of her last diary notes.

14.3.76
.I am very sad and lonely. I will never survive from my shock or come to my original health again. I don't think I will be happy again at any time, that is if I live.

Mother's friend, Arthur

My mother worked sometimes as a tailor's machinist, which she hated; sometimes as a cook, which she preferred. Actually an assistant cook, and only in one kitchen – Cohen's bakery and restaurant which flourished in Wentworth Street. I was happy when she worked there, for two reasons: food at home became more various, not that she stole it but was able to buy it for a song, and there were always leftovers which Mrs Cohen handed on. And Arthur! the chef of whom my mother was fond, secretly in love with, I believed, though she denies it in her diaries. He was the kindliest of men and I knew that if ever I called on her at work he'd reach into his pocket for a penny. Della's memory is different. He bought her her first ever silk stockings, with a heel and seam, but she resented him.

'I could see,' she told me, 'that she was very happy with him but it came just as things were calming between Mummy and Daddy.' My mother's diary entry is sweet and sad, the other side of her strident political self.

4.12.61
Today I have torn out all the pages I wrote during this last year nearly. If I can't write better things I must not write at all. I have torn out 10 pages, it's nearly broke 'my heart' but I feel much better now and I am going to sleep peacefully. Good night all.

Arthur used to say if you are desperate and you want to write something down or to someone, write it, and then tear it out. He was such a genuine friend. Honest and respectful. There was a real platonic friendship. I only known him for the time I worked at Mrs Cohen, and I did not work there more than 6 months it was during the war, there was such a scarem darem time, I don't know what I was thinking of. Joe was not home much those days, he used to go a lot to his parents. I was always alone, had to make my own life, he had a life of his own. So was Arthur lonely. He used to confide in me about his own life.

He came from middle-class family, from Yorkshire. He was a school master and his parents wanted him [to marry] but they were against him marrying someone whom he loved. And she that girl had a child from him. But it seems that after she had that child that is while he was in London to try and bring her to London to get married she found someone else and left the child to his parents to be brought up.

Before he left York he had a terrible row with his father and he would not return back. He lost his job to teach. Not knowing what to do he got work as a kitchen porter. I believe he worked somewhere else before he worked for Cohen. Then I thought I was so right by telling him about my troubles, and so he asked me if I would like to come and see 'Fantasia' with him. He liked classics. He talked about music and theatre. He listened to my politics but didn't agree with me. He was terribly anti-communist. And I used to go a few times for a ride. Elephant and Castle there was a little Italian tea place we used to go in and have a cup of tea. I would never have anything to eat as I never like eating in any of these places. I didn't let him spend anything at all on me. I insisted that I pay myself for anything I have, and he always used to say, Leah you are a very intelligent woman and good woman, Joe ought to appreciate you. And then I would say he is not bad at all, he loves me. Only I put all the blame on his mother. His mother, even she wasn't to blame. Only that is beside the point. I will write later on about Joe's mother.

However this was Arthur. Just a friend whom we kept company now and again. It was for a very short time as not long afterwards he joined the army. We corresponded for a while and then lost touch as I could not keep up correspondent with him. Joe began to be really ill and we moved from East 1 to East 5. I heard from friends that he got wounded, lost all his hair, eyebrows . . . and was very ill. I ought to get in touch with him but I also heard from people who knew him, and they think he died.

I believe he must have died otherwise he would get in touch with me, and if he does not it means that he does not want to probably, either he is embarrassed or maybe he is back in York, and maybe married. Whatever his reasons ' :now he would if he could. And now that Joe is dead I would not like to renew friendship with him. I am 10 years older than him but at that time I looked very very young. Younger than he looked. Although he knew my age. However there is no point about Arthur, I would not want Arthur or anyone else for a friend or even husband. It's only that I talked about tearing up writings that he came to my mind. That happens to be very good advice, write and tear up and you will feel good.

Now I hurry. Race through images. My father used to put a cube of sugar in his mouth and drink tea through it, cooled, from a saucer, unless he wanted to warm his hands and then he'd fold his palms around the hot cup and slowly sip . . . I went to the cinema three times a week, fell in love with Deanna Durbin, modelled my cool style on Spencer Tracy . . . two things I considered flashy and attractive – going downstairs sideways and raising my left eyebrow . . . aunts Ann and Sara called me 'junior' . . . Aunt Rae enrolled me in Toynbee Hall's art class because I expressed an interest in, and showed an aptitude for drawing – somewhere is a drawing of Karl Marx, as well as the drawing of my father – I didn't attend more than three classes – over these last years I've toyed with rough sketches of the rooms we've lived and worked in – I'd like to learn how to draw and wield a brush, apply colour . . . as a young reader I chose books from the Whitechapel Library whose pages were more laden with dialogue than prose, which bored me, though not, thankfully, beyond the age of ten. My favourite comic into my early teens was *The Wizard*, especially its story of Wilson, the hermit athlete who was more fleet of foot than the cheetah, could leap higher than the kangaroo, and swim faster than the istiophorus pla-typterus.

Whatever happened to my Fashion Street friends? Sammy

Lyons who taught me to swim in Goulston Street baths? Martin Landau who became apprenticed to a silversmith? Vervel Schwartz, the printer's son next door? I met Alan Tapper in later years but where is he now? Lily Peltz who became Terry – is she still selling in Petticoat Lane? Rosalind Yenish – ended up marrying a jeweller with a shop in Mare Street, Hackney; but what became of Sabu, the first of the Asians who now flood Brick Lane with leather shops and Indian restaurants? He was a Sikh, I remember now. Wasn't there an incident when some other boys ripped off his turban, beneath which were plaits, and he cried?

The streets were full of characters: eschatologists on the Whitechapel Road, screaming families in Fashion Street; fantastic 'Prince' Monolulu the tipster, an apparition straight out of Tarzan's jungle, headdressed in feathers, a tartan scarf round his waist, a waistcoat of cabalistic signs, flouncing bets in Petticoat Lane – 'I gotta horse! I gotta horse!'; a Jewish tailor's machinist with whom Mother once worked who strode regularly between the East and West End, long flowing grey hair, a suit with an open-necked shirt, an umbrella elegantly employed as a walking stick, lean and urgent, looking more like a musician stretching his legs, the first bohemian I ever saw, spoke to no one; Mendel, pushing his pram in which was a gramophone playing cracked Yiddish records for pennies; cursing Yetta selling bagels from a basket on the pavement in front of Bloom's kosher restaurant – an ill-tempered lady wrapped in shawls; the barber for whom I sat on the indispensable plank across a chair in his shop in Hanbury Street, Commercial Street end, near Christchurch Hall – where George Bernard Shaw in the 1880s addressed the Bryant and May matchmaker girls on strike – who had a daughter choked to death on a fish bone; I spent hours watching Mr Greenberg (or was it Rosenberg?) making buttons to order with his pull-down machine – you brought your material, he matched you a button; and at the Commercial Street end of Fashion Street was the light engineering factory – precision spindles mesmerisingly shaving steel in white oil, I smell it when I lift the bonnet of a car; my father often took me to Curly's Café on the Whitechapel Road, a haunt of the boxing fraternity, walls covered with photos of Jewish boxers – Harry Mizler, 1934 British Lightweight Champion; Harry Mason, British Lightweight Champion 1925; Jack 'Kid' Berg, 1930 Welterweight Champion of the World; Heavyweight Champion, Max Baer – *The Art of Boxing* was written in 1785 by David Mendoza who billed himself 'Mendoza The Jew' and was the first boxer ever to receive royal patronage; the treat in Curly's Café was thick slices of buttered toast with strong tea, John Allin painted for the *Stepney Streets* folio a version of Curly's Café which he combined with the eel-and-pie cafés of his own childhood; boating in Victoria Park with a picnic was a day's outing, never the seaside, occasionally rowing on the Serpentine in Hyde Park; Lyons Corner House with its red plush interiors and gypsy bands – baked beans on toast was my favourite with chocolate eclair to follow, junk-food addict from the start; high days were May Day when I was carried shoulder-high through crowds of thrilled and good-natured demonstrators to hear Harry Pollitt or Willie Gallagher fire the multitude with dreams and laughter; the Walls ice cream man came round pedalling a tricycle that pushed an ice box before it, no bells, just his yodelling cry; there were trams in those days which I loved riding, especially the route that took us underground from Aldwych up into the light of Kingsway; my clothes were bought on the 'never never', mainly from Wickhams of Stepney Green, often through Uncle Harry who was an agent for them – and how many times, I now wonder, did he pay the week's dues for my mother? One Christmas, wanting to be like the other boys, I hopefully hung a stocking on the rail of my iron bedstead and found it filled next morning with an orange put there by my sister, full of anxiety that her little brother would wake to nothing; we all went to the Rivoli cinema to hear and cheer cousin Cissie sing 'When They Begin the Beguine' in a singing competition and applauded wildly when she came second; my mother was constantly yelling at me for washing with clothes on, leaving a tidemark where my face was clean and my neck wasn't; I learned only a little Hebrew in the Machzike Hadas synagogue on the corner of Fournier Street, the one built as a

Huguenot Church in 1743 and used variously as a missionary centre, a Methodist Church, and now, since 1975, a mosque; I swam in the Thames by the Tower of London and played leapfrog on to the black old cannons from the Elizabethan wars; I recall thick fogs called peasoupers, wagons of beer barrels drawn by huge dray horses, the water troughs from which they drank, the smell of their steaming shit in the middle of the road collected for sale to gardeners in the Home Counties, the warm smell of the steam iron in the sweat shops where my parents worked and where I sometimes visited them after school, the smell of chicken hairs being burned over a gas stove, of dust and stale sweat in the Underground during the blitz, of tea cloths boiling in an enamel bowl. I cracked my fingers, told lies, thought baked beans on toast was living it up, always wanted to wear glasses, loved bubbles of soap made for me between thumb and forefinger then blew them for my children, knitted, nagged to stay up late, was happy and afraid of nothing. My first ambition was to be a coal miner, I can't remember why. Sex began aged six.

Sex at six

Well, hardly hard core.

Rosalind Yenish looked like Shirley Temple. She lived in the street next door, Fournier Street, full of houses I thought were just slums like ours but when my eyes were taught how to look I understood were beautiful Georgian residences built by the rich Huguenot weaving community. Rosalind, as I've recorded, sat and watched me being bathed in the tin bath before the fire and sang 'They Gave Him a Gun To Play With'. What I'm about to relate may seem illogical, and indeed I don't know if it happened before or after the tin-bath vigils, but one day Rosalind and I agreed to 'show me yours and I'll show you mine'. Why was this necessary if young Yenish had already watched me being bathed? I don't know.

Either I thought unilateral viewing was unfair, or perhaps my mother bathed me discreetly and nothing was on view to inflame Rosalind's curiosity, or the event took place *before* the bathings. Whatever, the venue decided upon for this thrilling exchange of visions was the second-floor lavatory of number 43 – one short, one long, one short flight down. We locked ourselves inside and it was agreed she would be the first to pull down her knickers. I have no recollection of what I felt on seeing this gentle hairless mound, I only know that my sister came by just then and a first opportunity to flash my confused little thing was lost amidst embarrassed scoldings. I shall make no attempt to trace the impact of this 'coitus interruptus' upon the rest of my sex life, which must be left for others to judge.

The next incident opened dark corridors. A school friend from Deal Street School – why do I think his name was David Miller? – had parents who owned a pub somewhere near Aldgate East Underground, the Petticoat Lane end, a huge Victorian edifice with turret windows at the top. One day, I was seven or eight, he took me up into one of the turret attic rooms – I dimly remember a narrow winding staircase and a small room full of boxes, though I can't remember if only the two of us or a third school friend was there. He pulled out a box and handed me postcards with drawings and photographs of strange goings-on. I understood none of it and can only remember one drawing – or was it a sepia photograph? – of a maid in an upper-class house, on her knees, apparently cleaning ashes from the fireplace but with her skirt hoisted, her knickers down, and a man, her employer, spanking her bare bottom.

Looking up teachers' skirts, exchanging sightings with sweet Rosalind, stealing kisses from Lily Peltz – who I don't think much fancied me – all this was mischief, curiosity, pre-pubescent larking around. Erotic cards, though I couldn't connect them either with experience or with any recognisable longing, secret or otherwise, was quite, quite different. They led to nothing but I remembered them, and, though I have no awful confessions to make of a debauched or bizarre life-of-the-flesh resulting from this childhood experience, yet from that small beginning I discovered arousal from reading and gazing at erotica.

My sexual development is easy to describe and fairly conventional. There were touchings, neckings, and homosexual skirmishes. I lost my virginity around the age of 15 to Cissie Rickless (whose story is to come). How and where I can't remember. We met in 1947 at a mildly left-wing Zionist Youth camp, run by Habonim (Hebrew for 'The Builders'), in the Wye Valley. She was older than me by a few months, and we immediately sparked off one another and believed ourselves to be in love. I called her 'Shifra' which I assumed, probably erroneously, was the Hebrew equivalent of 'Cecilia'. No one else ever called her by that name. On our return home – she up north, me down south – we exchanged love letters and I sent her my poetry. Love and high emotion are difficult to sustain across two hundred miles. The 'passion' ended in epistolic violence within months. I recall only one lyrical moment in our relationship. I spent some days with her in her parents' home in Manchester, from where we went on a climb through the Peaks. At one hilltop she bid me 'close your eyes'. I did so. She undid the buttons of my shirt, bared my chest, unbuttoned her blouse and pressed her breasts against me. I cherished this moment and attempted to recreate it in *The Four Seasons*.

It would have been a daring and first such moment on the English stage had Diane Cilento the courage to play it with Alan Bates as I'd written it. Stage directions called for nothing lurid, just the two standing in profile, no passionate embrace, merely a gentle touching of flesh. Cilento refused to expose her breasts in profile to the audience. Nor to Alan Bates. She would pull her blouse off her shoulders halfway down her arms only if her back was to the audience. Even her nipples were crisscrossed with Elastoplast to be hidden from the gaze of Bates, who by this time would have preferred to gaze upon not one part of her either stripped or clothed. The two ended up not talking to one another during the run of this intense love story. It was the first of my plays which appeared on stage not as I had conceived it.

Masturbation was unknown to me until the age of around twelve. The kids in the playground of Weald Square made lewd incomprehensible references accompanied by lewd incomprehensible hand movements which struck me as absurd and represented I knew not what. But from twelve on I had need of that activity fairly regularly – indifferent to tales of blindness – adolescence into late teens and early manhood being filled with girls I thought I loved but who mostly didn't respond, or if they did it was not for long. Those were the years of unrequited love and rejection slips. I lacked promise . . . there was no future in me . . . I was too intellectual . . . too pretty . . . too flippant . . . laughed too much. ('You smile too much,' said Kathleen Tynan after I'd given a lecture to open the annual conference of the International Theatre Institute in Montreal's Expo '67. *Too* much?) Home life was no hindrance – I had a mother who brought tea to me and a procession of girlfriends in bed. Perhaps I was too romantic – candlelight, moonlight, stars, poetry against a background of music before, during and after. Who understands why they are loved or not!

With experience came confidence and I felt no need to prove staying powers. Lovemaking was not a macho act for me, pleasure given was as satisfying as pleasure received. Cunnilingus and laughter, I became addicted – not at the same time, you understand! The gyrations of the act, the screams, the huffing and puffing were comic as well as erotic. I enjoyed both. Only one weakness – curiosity. 'I've never looked at a woman without measuring the possibility of what could be between us,' wrote Charlie Chaplin. Many men recognise that. I certainly do. Mostly I simply measure; but there were times, too many perhaps, when I argued with myself: how can you deny this woman's uniqueness, her spirit, her smell, her intelligence, the heightened never-to-be-repeated moment, the explosion of passion, how? It made for an intense, tempestuous life.

Sex in my plays

In 1978 an actress observed that there was no sex or violence in any of my writings. It was true – apart from the violent ending of *The Kitchen*, the beating up of an old woman in *The Old Ones* and references to 'love in the afternoon' in *Roots*. My 'blue period' began.

I characterise pornography as erotica without art. Blue movies arouse but finally offend by tattiness, absence of subtlety, wooden acting, impoverished plot, character, and text. Perhaps most offensive is the singular motive: to film the boring, repetitive poke. The question I considered was this: if stimulating people to think and feel, laugh and cry, even to take action in their lives, is a valid function of art, can stimulating one of the most vital and driving of human urges – the sexual urge – be denied? Or if your view is of art as a record, a bearing of witness, can the passion, pain, beauty, ludicrousness, the diverse, perverse variousness of desire and its fulfilment be avoided in the literary chronicling of human behaviour? In two works I attempted to treat of sex as I treated of political disillusion, self-discovery, love, old age, and confrontation with death. One, an original film script, *Lady Othello*, was bought by Goldcrest Films, though not made, for reasons I'll explain in a moment. The other, a play full of laughter and bawdiness, lived and died after a three-week run in Leicester's Phoenix Theatre. To both there is a story.

One More Ride on the Merry-Go-Round, written first, in 1978, is about a fifty-year-old Cambridge professor of philosophy separated from his wife whom he describes to his young American girlfriend and colleague as having been without interest or passion. The first act opens with the sounds of orgasm – they belong to the professor and his young American lecturer. The second act also opens with the sounds of orgasm – this time belonging to his wife with her young boyfriend, a successful publisher. The wife is not at all as the professor has described her. Both have become, on separating, what each wanted the other to be when married. Fast, Rabelaisian and, I think, funny – the play is about the inhibiting factor in marriage, the difficulty of living full and useful lives in wedlock. But its characters are literate – they express complex thoughts and uncomfortable observations. Wittily. Which is confusing.

I had learned over the years that critics and audiences see in a play what they have been conditioned to expect from a playwright. When Shelagh Delaney refused to repeat herself by not writing *Taste of Honey* as her second play, but attempted something braver with *Lion in Love*, she was scolded. Alan Bennett moved out of line with a play called *Enjoy* and was told to behave himself. Michael Frayn attempted something new with *Here* and all those who had laughed with him in his previous successes stayed away. Part of the reason *The Four Seasons* received mixed reviews was that I had been typecast as a playwright of what was imagined to be 'social realism', a meaningless label founded on a misreading of the first five plays. A love story was not considered my provenance. Yet from a certain point of view *The Four Seasons* was more my province than the first five plays which had to be got out of the way before arriving at what I really wanted to write – a play about love.

Not wishing to repeat the experiences of being criticised for writing that which it was deemed I had no right to write, and enjoying the prospect of a theatrical hoax, I decided to offer *One More Ride on the Merry-Go-Round* under a pseudonym. (In later years Doris Lessing was to do the same, more successfully, with a novel called *The Diaries of a Good Neighbour* offered under the pseudonym of Jane Somers – the book is now called *The Diaries of Jane Somers*, a marvellously wrought work which her own publisher turned down!)

I called myself Neil Gray and wrote a mini-biographical sketch claiming to be a professor of philosophy who had written a few radio plays, nothing serious. I was married, had four daughters, my father had been a miner killed in a pit disaster, I called myself Neil Gray after Simon Gray and Neil Simon, both of whose wit and style I admired – this was my first attempt at full-length drama. My agent offered it around. The Royal Court under Stuart Burge were interested but wanted to meet the author. I refused, saying they could meet him only after a contract was signed. They lost interest.

The RSC admired it but those were the days before they thought in commercial terms – they advised it be offered to a commercial management. It was sent to a commercial management, Michael Codron, who returned it saying what a lot of nonsense and the author should learn from his heroes that there was a craft to writing a play. No one picked it up until Charles Marowitz, one-time assistant to Peter Brook during his season 'The Theatre of Cruelty', who had run the Open Space theatre where he produced anarchic versions of Shakespeare, read it and enthused. It was, he told my agent, the most literate comedy he'd read in the last ten years. By this time I was tired of anonymity and decided to come clean. Marowitz was not told the name of the author but was brought to his house by the agent. *One More Ride on the Merry-Go-Round* is also the title of a song sung by a glorious American singer, completely unknown in this country, called Jane Olivor. Her song was playing as Charles came through the front door opened by you, Lindsay Joe, remember? Charles would have recognised Dusty but he didn't know you. He sat in the lounge wondering where he was. The song came to an end – curtain up. I appeared.

'I bet you didn't believe you'd see *me*, did you, Charles?'

'I still don't believe I'm seeing you,' he replied. I was the last person he imagined could write such a play.

We worked on the text together during the next weeks, after which he tried, without success, to persuade producers to let him direct it. Charles faded away to his old home in the States where he found a greater openness for the kind of work he wanted to give himself to. I continued offering the play around, at one time changing the author's name to a woman's, hoping to arouse greater interest. Not even that worked, nor I imagine would it have worked had I changed my name to one that was recognisably black or Asian. Whatever had made the first plays difficult to lift off the page and command instant acceptance was still seeping through this pseudonymous one. I dropped the fake name and the play was finally picked up by the Leicester theatre and played in a set that never managed to get completed, with the wrong actor in the lead.

The role of the philosopher required a cross between the doomed intelligence of a Paul Scofield and the sophisticated flippancy of a Noël Coward. No national critic bothered to attend the first night but it was gratifying to see how well the play worked with audiences, who were on the edge of their seats with interest and laughter. The play has not been heard of since. I am perplexed.

Lady Othello is a love story set in New York between a white English professor – Jewish – and a black New York mature student – Catholic. It contains explicit but comic self-mocking lovemaking scenes. Goldcrest, in the form of an enthusiastic young producer called Susie Richards, who kept ringing me to say she couldn't stop reading the script which 'turns me on every time I read it', hung on for months looking for the right director. They found him, Joseph Losey, one of the 'Hollywood ten' who had to flee during the McCarthy era. He had made *For King and Country*, directed a couple of film adaptations by Harold Pinter, and a film of Mozart's opera *Don Giovanni*. But I didn't want Losey. His films suggested he lacked the sense of humour *Lady Othello* required. Further, I'd heard from my friend, Tom Wiseman, whose novel *The Gentle Englishwoman* Losey had directed with Glenda Jackson, that he was a bullying monster. It was unheard of that a mere writer should turn down a director with an international reputation. Susie's enthusiasm diminished and she faded away over a series of silences which grew longer and longer. Shortly afterwards Goldcrest declared itself bankrupt. I don't think I was the cause. Other producers have raved and passed on. The film remains unmade. I adapted it for the stage. The play remains unperformed. It is a sad, bawdy, and humorous work carefully wrought. I am perplexed.

Perhaps, as with emotion in my plays, the sex was too raw. Or too irreverent. The British warm to lavatory humour, like Joe Orton's, or the asinine 'Carry On' films, or to cheap mockery. The combination of humour and intellect seems to have died with Shaw. Tom Stoppard is the exception. But this boy, with a tongue in his cheek, fails to please. An image, misunderstood from the start, has frozen. He awaits a little warm cherishing to melt it.

First fumblings

I return to adolescence. There was only one sexual experience that was out of the ordinary. I can relate it because Audrey is dead. Little Audrey the hairdresser who laughed and laughed and who loved me dearly but not I her.

'Be my mistress,' I said to her. I must have been about eighteen, she sixteen.

'I don't want to be your mistress,' she said, 'I want to be your wife.' Loving me didn't prevent her bestowing her favours upon our circle of friends. She was a naturally sexual being who enjoyed initiating young men into the pleasures of the flesh. Warm-hearted, mischievous, audacious, and good-natured, she was petted and spoilt by everyone, male and female alike, when she came to our homes to wash and perm our mothers and aunts.

Squibbs, a friend who will take shape later on, was part of our circle. One day the three of us found ourselves in my room in Weald Square (Clapton, where we moved to from Stepney), contemplating a wild experiment – the two of us making love to Audrey. I can't recall how the moment began, what led up to it. Did we talk about it? Did she invite us? Such an invitation would not have been beyond her. Did the moment simply 'fade in'? The novelist, Lisa Appignanesi, once considered exploring those seconds leading up to the first kiss. What happens to make two people turn to one another and know they can share that most intimate of embraces – the touching of lips? What combination of word, glance, touch, friendship, fused to sanction between Audrey, Squibbs and myself the intimacy of a sweet threesome? No shame. No guilt. No sense of the forbidden or even the unusual. It seemed the most natural thing in the world. If only the rest of our lives had been as simple and innocent.

Homosexual skirmishes were all, except one, advances made to me. The first tampering, aged six or seven, was from my cousin, Ralph, when he returned from that part of the Turkish Empire known as Palestine and lived with us in Fashion Street. He tried to rub me up. I pulled away. He never tried again. A distant relative of the other Ralph, my brother-in-law, at a family event, took me into a room, had a feel and gave me half a crown to pay for my silence. I was perhaps eleven and didn't really comprehend what was being done to me, something not allowed, I knew, but no traumas followed. Perlmutter-like, I was innocent and obliging, the kind who carried up a neighbour's shopping.

On another occasion, outside Weald Square on the Upper Clapton Road, a young Jewish man stopped me and asked did I know of a gun shop in the area. Anyone less innocent would have run, or told him to buzz off – one didn't say 'fuck off' in those days, at least not in my community. Some of the yobs on the LCC estate might. (From Jill Tweedie's autobiography I learned, by the way, that 'yob' is 'boy' spelt backwards.) When I think of my foolishness I blush. I actually paused, scratched my head and thought about where a gun shop might be. I'd never seen a gun shop. Anywhere. Ever.

Somehow he manoeuvred the conversation around to self-defence and his prowess at judo. He demonstrated some grips, an interesting chap as well as friendly. I invited him up to our third-floor flat for a cup of tea – my mother was used to the waifs and strays I brought through the front door – and took him into my room where he demonstrated more jujitsu holds but this time with a difference. He held my hands behind my back and rubbed himself up against them. It was not a friendship I encouraged.

The homosexual relationship that developed was with a Czech Jewish refugee who came to Upton House School after the war. Sam Braun, the ugliest, sweetest and cleverest of all my peers. I was fifteen, he a year older. He wore heavy-lensed glasses, was stocky, thick-lipped, orthodox and touchy. His accent and cleverness attracted, inevitably, bullying. I defended him. We became friends, exchanged poems we'd written, and talked each other through mathematical problems. He often stayed the night in Weald Square. I had a double bed. We slept together. When he made his first advance to my turned back I pretended to be asleep. When I allowed him to make me come I was angry. But he released the pleasures of being touched, and I found it difficult to resist his advances. I was not homosexual, however. Nothing about men attracted or stirred me. Even now, with few exceptions, I don't enjoy male company. My rhythms swing more comfortably with women. The affair soon ended and was written out of my system in a long short story called 'The Two Friends'. Sam became Steve, the Jew in him became Irish – I must have reasoned that one outsider was as good as another. It's interesting to read this story – or it would be were it not so badly written and so I can't take myself beyond the first few pages – it contains clues to myself as a teenager. I called myself Ronald, that anagram for Arnold used in the Trilogy!

> Ronald could mix with the boys; he could swear back at them when they were funny, he could overrule their mimicking with sarcasm, he could return their pranks and shout loud when they shouted . . .

'Cuss their cockiness' would have been more succinct than 'swear back at them when they were funny'; 'override their mimicry' not 'overrule their mimicking'; 'match their pranks' not 'return their pranks'.

> . . . he spoke well, with a lovely musical sound that made him be chosen to read the poetry in the literature classes every time . . .

I'd forgotten that.

> Ronald once wrote in an essay, 'We are a school of smart-alecs, the only ones who aren't are the masters.' He had to write that out five hundred times . . .

Was that true? And if the samples of verse quoted in the story really belonged to 'Steve' then Sam Braun wrote better poetry than I did!

The experience left me with just one tiny twitch of curiosity which I exercised upon younger, thirteen-year-old cousin Maurice, who I once touched up when he slept overnight. Neither of us was enthusiastic.

The last experience is an example of the observer in me. I am often slow to react or even to react at all to what is happening around me, so curious am I to see where it will lead. This characteristic applies variously from watching a building being demolished to seeing a bad television movie through to its depressing end. You're a bit like that, Lindsay Joe. I remember attending one of your school football matches and was amused at the way you stood around watching the ball as though it had dropped out of the skies and possessed a life of its own over which you could not possibly have control. Observers, both of us.

I was nineteen, hitchhiking from London back to an RAF camp, Moreton-in-Marsh, I think, or Wellesbourne Mountford. It was the last lift. A middle-aged man picked me up. We spoke little. I was not by any stretch of the imagination a young man of the world, a fact no doubt apparent to one and all from the earnestness of my questions and the innocence of my answers. Halfway there he laid a hand on my knee. I didn't remove it, it seemed a harmless gesture. Nor did I want to offend him by doubting his intentions. But that I made no move he interpreted as silent acquiescence. His hand travelled. Soon both curiosity and pleasure in being touched permitted the rest, made easier by my abhorrence of scenes – a Fashion Street reflex from the days when my parents quarrelled in full view of neighbours, and I was acutely embarrassed. Which explains why I rarely quarrel. To have shouted and raged more often might have avoided trouble and been worth the public scene. I never quarrelled with Dusty. If something upset me I entered an icy silence sometimes lasting weeks. And so I allowed this man, who was driving me through the night, to move where he wanted and stroke me to come in his hands. He left me standing at the RAF camp gates sheepish and amazed at myself and the strange goings-on in other people's lives.

These incidents aside I am, as already confessed, a woman's

man, yet paradoxically I never know if a woman wants me. She has to be obvious with statement or action. Only on rare occasions has a mutual desire been silently understood and led somewhere. For the rest, though I flirt – more mischievously than lasciviously – I rarely dare presume the first advance.

Attitudes to sex are complex. One of those secondary truths it is difficult to articulate in the current education debate about the teaching of sex in schools, even if you place it in the context of love and marriage, is the paradox of finding it is possible to be in love with someone you don't desire, and desire someone you don't love, though woe betide he or she who marries only for the fuck – what do you talk about after it? My life has succumbed to infidelities of which I'm neither proud nor ashamed, relationships of give and take with their beginnings, middles, and endings – some, inevitably, wretched – but rich in much that I cherish. I deeply regret the unhappiness caused but I was who I was, and almost succeeded in maintaining the right balance between a passion for family and a passion for other women; always – until the last one – conducting life responsibly, happily, lovingly, with wife and children as priority. Falling in love with ML changed all that. I write this book amid the resulting ruins.

The war

At the outbreak of war on 3 September 1939 most children were evacuated with their school. Not me. My sister was too anxious to let me be separated from her. She arranged that I be shipped off with the Spitalfields Central Foundation Girls School and sent to Ely in the Fens. My mother told a story of how, as some of the children were assembled in Liverpool Street station, belted overcoats, caps, gas masks in cardboard boxes slung over our shoulders, unmanageable cases in our hands, excited by the adventure of it all, a teacher said to the aching parents: 'Well, say goodbye, you may never see them again!' It became the title of a book of primitive

paintings by John Allin for which I assembled text: each of us talking about our different childhoods in different parts of the East
End.

Why do I have no wish to detail the war, the years from aged
seven to thirteen? Only a succession of images and sounds come to
me: the heart-churning sound of the air-raid siren, its heaving wail,
its up-down-up-down warning that German bombers were coming
to kill us. It was a frightening sound that whirred from a low base
note mounting to a shrill rising and falling threat to move fast or
else. For years afterwards my heart jumped at any sound that resembled it. The end of a raid was signalled by a steady drone on
one note. *All – clearrrrrrrrrrrrrrrrrrrr.* Della reminded me that in
the first days of the war we were sent to Adelaide, just outside Ely.

'We were three of us, this new girl, poor girl, she was in first
term, and we all slept in the same bed on our first night away from
home. She was on one side of me, you on the other and I was plonk
in the middle; and she cried and you cried and I cried because you
cried and that's how we fell asleep. Don't you remember? And I
said to Broni [her maths teacher] next day, "If you don't get us out
of that place, if you don't find us a new place, I'll go home, I'll run
away home." And of course she did. You were with the Carvers,
very kind they were, and you looked so well there. You looked
healthy, a bit of colour, you were neat and clean and even learned a
bit of politeness. Don't you remember?'

I told her I remembered looking through a window and seeing
the stars for the first time, and spiders; that I learned to ride a bike
in Ely, and that the Carvers rapped me over the knuckles if I didn't
put my knife and fork down after each mouthful.

'You were sexually precocious,' she said. 'Used to tell me stories
about the Carvers being on top of each other. "What are they
doing?" you used to ask me. "Why is he jumping on her?"'

I told her I remembered a picnic on the banks of a river because
she was going back to London.

'I felt very guilty at leaving you; shouldn't have done it, you were
only eight.'

Jack Carver was a lay preacher. They took me with them to church. When I visited them in 1992 their first exclamation was: 'That's him! He hasn't changed a bit!' I asked what they remembered of me. 'You made us laugh,' they said. 'You told us stories to make us laugh.'

I was evacuated all over the place because I hated being away from home and nagged to come back each time I was sent somewhere. After the kindly Carvers of Ely I was sent to Buckingham where my foster mother – whose name, I think, was Mrs Webb – instructed me to tell my real mother, the foreigner, to go back where she came from – meaning Transylvania. My mother smiled her self-mocking smile when I related this to her. 'You should tell her that it would be very difficult to go back where I came from.' Meaning the womb. After Buckingham came Barnstaple, joining Aunty Ray and cousins Norma, Thelma, and Maurice. Memorable because I had my first experience there of acting in public – a story to come. And in between was the Blitz. Somehow I managed to be home for its worst days. It happened like this.

It was imagined that London, particularly the East End with its docks, harbours, and railway installations, would be bombed at once. Anti-aircraft guns were placed in open spaces such as Victoria Park where we once went boating. Barrage balloons drifted up into the air hoping to deter the planes whose wings might become entangled in their ropes. We hung and pinned black curtains to keep out the light. Air-raid wardens – my father was one of them – with steel helmets and official long, ungainly blue coats wandered the streets shouting, 'Put that light out,' and we all scrambled to check our windows. Fingers of searchlight probed the night sky slowly waving, circling, warning the enemy to stay away. They did. For a year. Which is why most of us evacuees returned home and I was able to witness the first bombing raid on Friday, 5 September 1940, when the German Luftwaffe sent over sixty-eight bombers, followed next day by another two hundred. The next night droned with the throbbing engines of three hundred and twenty bombers and six hundred fighters. It was like that for fifty-seven nights in succession. Fires raged, houses, buildings and monuments were blown to pieces, helpless fire engines screamed through the streets against crazy odds. Twelve thousand people were killed, huge areas of the city were flattened. Lives, homes, and history lost for the cause of Aryan supremacy.

Across the road from Fashion Street was the Spitalfields Fruit Exchange to which growers and importers brought their produce of fruit and vegetables for sale to early-morning greengrocers stocking up for the day. Beneath the Victorian iron arcades of the Exchange were catacombs converted into air-raid shelters. At seven o'clock, or earlier, each evening we'd take up our bed space and settle for the night. A community established itself there. I remember a cafeteria, ping-pong tables, card games; and in the morning the streets sprawling with hose pipes, the pavements wet, the smell of burnt wood, smoke in the air, the aftermath bustle of disaster and chaos. We lived part of our lives underground, the shelter became another room of our Fashion Street flat. I'm appalled to remember it as fun, especially when we shifted from the Fruit Exchange to become part of the teeming thousands bedding down on iron bunks in the London Underground, which meant we kids could ride at random up and down the line.

And what adventure playgrounds the bombed warehouses turned into. Dangerous sites with gaping holes in the floors over which we swung, Tarzan-like, on ropes suspended from charred beams. A favourite haunt was the remaining winding, narrow stair-case of the shattered Whitechapel Church tower. It led up to nowhere but a sheer drop to the rubble below.

On 2 November the bombing stopped.

The respite did not last long and bombing was resumed on 6 November. On 29 November came the great raid on the City which was to be called the second fire of London. Gas mains were set alight, water mains blown up. The Thames was at low tide and little water could be pumped from the river. The fires started by the one wave of bombers illuminated London for the next and sent up a glow like the midnight sun. Many fires were out of control and burned through the night and for much of the day, crackling here, dancing there, or leaping with a roar into the skies. Sirens sounded nightly and the raids continued into the new year. Whitechapel station was hit, Charrington's brewery, Crossman's brewery. Incendiaries and high explosives peppered the London Hospital.

'They did what they liked with us,' said one woman living near the West India Docks . . .

Point of Arrival, Chaim Bermant

By May 1941 the Blitz was over. Freedom from the piercing screech of siren, the crack of ack-ack guns, the rumble of bombs. For three years. And then, on 10 June 1944, four days after D-Day – the allied invasion of German-occupied France – came the first doodlebug, an unmanned robot filled with high explosives which flew low. You first heard its drone, then the engine cut out, it glided in silence, fell. Drone, shutdown, silence, explosion. Hundreds were fired at us. Fighters were sent up to catch them over the sea. Guns tried to explode them at the coast. We all hoped the engine would cut out immediately over us, that meant it would drift on elsewhere. Thus we each hoped for our neighbour's death.

A greater terror was to come – the V2 rocket. The last, cruel gasp of a defeated enemy. No engine drone, no warning, just a brief, fierce whistling through the air followed by an instant murderous explosion. No time to wish our neighbours dead, only to pity them. They began arriving in September 1944 and continued into the spring of 1945. The last one fell on 27 March. The German scientist whose brilliance invented them was a man called Braun. The Americans appropriated him to help them send a rocket to the moon.

Evacuation to Llantrisant in South Wales was to avoid the doodlebugs and V2s. I enjoyed this period most of all. We were billeted in the night. The next day there was a knock at the door. 'Would the evacuee like to come out and play?' It was in Llantrisant where I first smoked, aged twelve, and fell in love with Pat Lewis. A girl called Rusty fell in love with me. We all necked in the hut of the immaculate bowling green and in the old ruin at the top of a hill called the Billy Whint where I loved climbing. The blackout ended during my time there. Suddenly the windows came alive at night. The village sparkled. I remember the fun of lit candles inside empty tins on a string. We ran and spun them round, creating a spectacle of candlelight in the dark evenings.

The war in Europe was over on 8 May – VE Day; the war against Japan ended on 15 August – VJ Day. There were parties in the streets. Della and I celebrated with cousins in Hyde Park. There's a faded photograph of us all, arms round each other's waists, kicking our legs can-can-like in the air. Survivors!

Comparisons

We understand by comparisons. Noel Annan writes in *Our Age*:

> How did one get accepted as a member of Our Age? . . . far more came from another aristocracy – the intellectual families that inter-married in the nineteenth century and were in full flower between the wars. These families produced a disproportionately large number of eminent men and women and a fair share of those of not outstanding ability but who occupied top posts in academic and cultural life. There was the Macaulay-Cripps-Hobhouse-Babington-Booth-Beatrice Webb clan; a great-niece of Beatrice Webb was to marry Victor Rothschild. There was the Arnold-Trevelyan-Huxley-Darwin-Wedgwood clan which contained members of the Keynes, Vaughan-Williams, Sidgwick, Cornford and Barlow families. Or the Fry-Hodgkin-Haldane-Mitchison-Butler-Faber-Adam Smith connection. Or the Stephen-Venn-Elliott-Strachey-Barnes-Shuckburgh strain, and so on. These intellectuals were not an intelligentsia burning to overthrow institutions. Whereas in the nineteenth century their grandfathers disliked the jaunty Palmerston, and still more imperialism, by the mid-twenties they had become more seducible by upper-class graces. Nevertheless, they threw up their share of left-

wing activists. J.B.S. Haldane and his sister Naomi Mitchison; John Strachey and his sister Amabel William Ellis; Vanessa Bell's sons, Julian and Quentin; and John Cornford who, like Julian Bell, was killed in the Spanish Civil War. Dozens of their children became the radicals of the thirties.

My mother's attempt at autobiography seems war-ravaged by comparison.

When I look back I was very ignorant about life and how to arrange my life in the right way. I didn't know the economics of house holding or keeping. I didn't know the value of money. I am sorry to say I don't now, it is very true as I am getting for 60 years of age. And even when I had my two younger brothers here and I thought we can all leave my sister who brought us up, and set a home up for ourselves. By that time I was about 17 or 18 years of age, my brothers 16 and 14 years or there about. Actually we must have all been older than that, with one or two years, because before we set our own home we lived in lodgings here and there. When I think what a fool I have been I would like to kick myself. We all went out to work and I kept home. If only I had known how to keep house we would all have had money and would not suffer poverty as we did.

The Annan passage conjures up an image of gorgeous shrubbery and mighty oaks, a dazzling landscape; my mother's excerpt projects a barren landscape, lonely, in which sparse roots struggle to break surface. The comparison between the two passages is not made merely to highlight privilege and deprivation; my shortcomings and inadequacies can in many ways be traced back to those barren beginnings etched out by my mother, and I may not have come from those illustrious families catalogued by Annan, or benefited from their connections, but I did find myself in a milieu that encouraged me to read the books produced by brilliant members of those families: Roger Fry's *Art and Design*, Lytton Strachey's *Eminent Victorians*, the novels of Virginia Woolf (a Stephen). Nevertheless the differences will always hold me in thrall. How often, taking friends from abroad on an East End tour, I've stood before number 43 Fashion Street and incredulously marvelled: I was born *here*? And on the other hand, meeting with or reading about other lives, I've regretted – why wasn't I born *there*?

I'm terrified all the time of being 'found out', of confronting 'the real thing', of stretching the thinly imposed skin beyond what it can sustain. Somewhere within me I share my mother's incomprehension that plays I had written others were prepared to put money into, and still others were prepared to see, and even become stirred enough to applaud. From her diary of 11 June 1959 (she had been listening to Semperini's *Serenade for Piano and Orchestra* on the radio, it helped put her in a good mood):

> I can say I have really enjoyed listening to this programme and believe that this is due because I feel a little happier and more content for three reasons. Joe seems to be and looks much better. He is really not always, but sometimes I feel a little hopeful. Then Della and Ralph have settled and they know where they are going. Thank goodness they have a house to go to. I hope and wish that they will be happy and have work to be able to keep the house up. And Arnold has success with his plays that he wrote and he has a little money. I do hope that he gets a regular job.

And so my unworldly mother, to whom it was all strange and incomprehensible, never ceased worrying about me. She could see the progress from a basement flat in Upper Clapton to a larger one in Finsbury Park, and then into the huge Victorian house in Bishops Road, but gnawing away in her Jewish heart was the old Jewish fear that 'they' – whoever 'they' were – would get her son in the end for having dared show his head above that barren landscape, for presuming to drift next door to the lush, landscaped gardens of colour and glory. This may seem surprising. Were not Jewish parents, mothers especially, ambitious for their children? The answer is that Jews are like most groups: divided roughly between those who, due to a long history of struggle and persecution, have limited expectations in life, and those who belong to the illustrious families of trade, profession and scholarship – the equivalent of the 'Arnold-Trevelyan-Huxley-Darwin-Wedgwood clan which contained members of the Keynes, Vaughan-Williams, Sidgwick, Cornford and Barlow families.'

The history of Jewish communities is infinitely more complex than such a simple division implies, but it's sufficiently true for me to place my parents in the group that had limited expectations. To 'get on' meant, for them, to command a reasonably secure trade. Obtaining the wherewithal to support us through university in order to achieve a profession was not merely a remote possibility, it was a nonexistent one. Uncle Sammy, the taxi driver, a man of genuine rough intelligence – who was so embarrassed by his passion for his wife, Aunt Billie, that he needed to cloak it with clumsy humour, calling her 'the old cow' – *did* have expectations for his son. He saved up taxi tips and put my cousin Bryan through law school, whereas my mother was content just to think of me as a woodworker, or an electrician.

SARAH   . . . What are *you* doing, Ronnie?

RONNIE   An evening in. I want to write a novel tonight.

SARAH   What, all in one night? Ronnie, do you think you'll ever publish anything? I mean, don't you have to be famous or be able to write or something? There must be such a lot of people writing novels.

RONNIE   Not socialist novels. Faith, Mother, faith! I am one of the sons of the working class, one of its own artists.

HARRY   You mean a political writer like Winston Churchill?

SARAH   What, does he write *novels* as well? I thought he was only a politician.

RONNIE   Well, he's both – *and* he paints pictures.

SARAH   A painter? He paints pictures? Landscapes and things?

RONNIE   Of course! And in his spare time he—

SARAH   What, he has spare time also?

RONNIE   In his spare time he builds walls at the bottom of his garden.

SARAH   A bricklayer! Ronnie, I told you you should take up a trade . . .

Chicken Soup with Barley, Act II Scene 2

Note Ronnie's 'tongue-in-cheek' line: 'Faith, Mother, faith! I am one of the sons of the working class, one of its own artists.' He has ambition but must mock his own seriousness. As the writer I contribute to the deflation by following it with a comic exchange. This interests me: Jewish self-mockery or English self-deflation? Both, probably, because I'm a very English Jew, and that worries me – they're not the most dynamic of Jewish communities, the English lot, fearing to be caught serious in case thought solemn. They aspire to appear cool, not too loud, not too driven, too anxious, too ambitious, too 'clever-by-half' – a dreadful expression – though they can't but help be all those things.

It is important for me to be clear about this. It's not easy because I'm dealing with a paradox. While, like most Jews, revering the value of education, my parents nevertheless had modest expectations of it being within their family's grasp. Formal, academic education, that is. Books and the exchange of ideas through conversation and debate – these were possible because cheap. And so emphasis and encouragement was given to what was possible. University was not. Not in their unworldly assessment of things. And this is what I inherited: a view that books in the house and animated conversation would be sufficient to inspire my children to go to university. My parents didn't drive their children, I in turn didn't drive mine. Oh, I had expectations of them but I considered it wrong to push them, and I succumbed to the misguided principle of comprehensive education. No special schools for *my* progeny. On the contrary, theirs was such a unique background – a house constantly full of interesting personalities from all over the world, first nights, first-night parties, trips abroad, exposure to the worlds of art and intellect, the opening of endless horizons – that a counterbalance was imperative. And what could that be? Contact with other, less privileged lives. They were in possession, I reasoned, of a wealth of experience it was their responsibility to share. Our lifestyle in Bishops Road – a ferment of activity and open house (my construction of a lifestyle experienced in Fashion Street where, albeit on a humbler scale, open house prevailed and activity also fermented) – liberated the imagination and generous spirit of my children who, in turn, would be able to open up worlds upon worlds for their school friends. Highgate Comprehensive, with its large intake of ethnic and working-class kids, was just what my children needed to offset life in Bishops Road. Wrong!

You, Lindsay Joe, were driven to waste learning time defending yourself from physical attacks which distracted you from study, remember? And your sister, Tanya Jo, had to suffer the inanities of teachers who spitefully said such things as 'Just because you're Arnold Wesker's daughter don't imagine that . . .' By the time Daniel arrived you both had established a defence system behind which his charm could operate unthreatened. In 1975 I wrote a long essay for a lecture tour of Italy called *Words – as Definitions of Experience*. It began with a story.

One day my eldest son, aged thirteen then, was standing outside his school talking to some friends. It's a local school with a 70% immigrant and working-class population. He's a big boy who – it was three years ago – had very long hair and those irritatingly happy, intelligent eyes. Two older boys from the school approached him. One kicked him in the backside. He ignored the kick. 'Get stuffed!' said the other boy to him. 'All right, I will,' replied my obliging son, and he continued to ignore the two fourth-formers. 'Get stuffed!' said the other boy again. My son assured him, confidently, that as he'd promised, he *would* 'get stuffed'. The boy drew back his arm and with a heavy-ringed fist smashed into my son's right eye. 'Good God!' said my son, reeling back, unable to believe anyone could do that or that it could happen to him. And then he came home.

His bewilderment is perhaps what distressed me most. It seemed to him to have no logic, no reason, no point, he couldn't account for it.

He was not equipped with those concepts of human behaviour which might have enabled him to place their actions within a pattern of behaviour he recognised, enough for him to have worked out some effective or self-reassuring response. Words contain within them concepts of human behaviour. He was not equipped with such words.

The essay went on to argue for a new subject on the curriculum: Words. In the course of five years would it not be possible, I argued, to assemble a basic vocabulary of fifty conceptual words without which no child should leave school? The word 'intimidate' might have helped Lindsay Joe understand what had invited the vicious thump to his eye. A certain kind of brutal mentality is intimidated by what it senses to be a threatening intelligence or a colourful personality. Although my *son* had received the thump, it was not the thumpers who were intimidating him but he who was intimidating them.

Nor were my three able to resist peer pressure on modes of speech. Dropped 'aitches', boring, impoverished catch phrases, an urgency to belong dominated their attention. It will be asked: should I have been distressed? Surprised? Well, yes. *I* never succumbed at school. It never occurred to me not to speak in the 'posh' tones inherited from my sister. In Fashion Street days I remember the grocer asking my mother, 'Is he your son? He doesn't talk like your son . . .' Nor would I have dreamt of changing my views, values, arguments to fit in with peers – a stance which earned me a cloth of hostilities and admiration I've worn throughout life.

And here's the fourth most important thing I have to tell you: select your peers. In fact perhaps it's *the* most important thing I have to tell you because if you get this wrong then anything else I tell you will go down the drain.

Select your peers. Don't go with the herd. Don't look to be one of the gang. I know there's great comfort in a gang, in belonging, in being accepted but – resist it! A gang consists of people who are living their lives through each other. Ask me – I know! I was part of a gang. Always busy being what I thought would please the others, picking up their bad habits, thinking their thoughts, sharing their stupid prejudices, laughing at their mindless hatreds. We never questioned each other, we just stroked and confirmed each other's nonsense. 'Right!' we'd say. 'You've said it! Good for you! You've hit the nail on the head.' We thought we were strong but we were all terrified of stepping out of line. Not one of us was independent. Not one of us had an opinion that was our own. And we intimidated each other. If one of us dared to say 'I don't agree! I don't think we should' out would come that dreary old cry: 'Who does she think she is? Who – does she think – she is!'

I think I hate that cry more than any other in the whole wide world. If anyone cries it out to you, Marike, you tell them: she thinks she's an individual! She thinks she can think her own thoughts! She thinks she can rise above the herd! You tell them that.

Letter to a Daughter

Where was this Jewish drive which would have ensured my children went to the best schools and on to university? I didn't possess it because my parents didn't possess it, and, to deal plainly with myself, my intelligence was not functioning at full throttle in the days when their education was an issue. Not functioning at all in fact. To my children I apologise. Though of course that's not the full picture. Now young adults, they have made good lives for themselves. Lindsay prospers more than Daniel and Tanya at this moment, and that he does confuses the issue even more, for he, like me, didn't go to university or college while Tanya and Daniel, belatedly, did; one to achieve a degree in 'theatre and women's studies', the other in photography.

Nor was my parents' lack of ambition for me the only reason I didn't go to university. The truth is I did not possess an academic mind. I was good at what I was good at, what interested me, and even then only *in the way* it interested me. By which I mean I had no memory for facts. I was not university material.

Crime and punishment

> For the man who is small must think
> Small acts of goodness are of no benefit –
> And does not do them; and small acts of meanness
> Do not harm – and does not abstain from them.
> So he can tell himself the river moves
> The river on – it is unalterable – and sleeps.
> Combing his hair each day but not his heart.
>
> 'A Singing Prayer', Christopher Logue

Domestic chores, classical records, books, family games, family rows, debate, open fires, open house – the man takes shape in the child's environment. The good and the not so good. The 'not so good' – and how fearfully I dare confess it – is a thin line of thin sin, or, to be charitable to myself since heaven and posterity may not be, mild misdemeanour. But before confession, one really noble act by way of atonement.

Aunt Sara, returning from her visits to the Soviet Union in the late thirties, brought back some twenty or so beautiful stamps. I had a small collection. They became its jewels. One day I came to know – don't ask me how, I just did – that we had no money in the house. I took my collection to a stamp shop from where I must once have bought stamps or how else could I have known to go there, and offered the contents of my album: a schoolboy's worthless collection except for the Soviet 'gems'. They gave me £3 10s which I was thrilled to hand to my mother. Fish and chips that evening, a taste

I've never lost, from Alf's on the corner of Brick Lane and Hope-town Street. I remember exactly where the stamp shop is, in the prettiest of Edwardian architecture off Kingsway, Sicilian Arcade. This nine-year-old seemed able to find his way from Stepney to anywhere in the Metropolis. When I played truant from school and persuaded my friend, Martin Landau, to play hooky with me, we found our way to the South Kensington Science Museum, the other side of the world.

In what stead will that noble deed stand me before heaven's gates alongside the shabby acts of life, those thin sins, mild misdemeanours? Mild except one, for which not even confession will wipe away shame.

I possessed this naughty skill to thieve. It began round the solo table when I would slide away from a player's winnings a halfpenny here, a penny there, my fingers creeping artfully over the edge of the table when the players were in the midst of quarrelling over who let the caller win a 'mizzere', or when there was a pause for tea and biscuits. I organised raids on Woolworths at the corner of Commercial Street and Whitechapel. In those days the sweet counters were partitioned by glass held at right angles by metal clips. Sometimes the clips slipped, or were loose, enabling us to snatch at the odd sweet hanging out. At the end of the raid we'd meet to share spoils. I think I pinched a few books from the book-shop where I worked, but only a few. For an aspiring writer to indulge in full-scale book theft would have been a betrayal of colleagues. So, mostly mischief. No criminal trait. Essentially honest and trustworthy – though I do have a weakness for looking in drawers in strange houses in pursuit of the owner's personality, a temptation, rest assured, dear host, I resist much of the time. Only one brief period seriously blots my past and makes me squirm at the shabbiness of it. It happened during conscription in the RAF.

RAF Patrington, post-eight-weeks square-bashing, April 1951 (I can date it accurately because of a letter from cousin Bryan addressed to 'Dish Washer and Tea Maker in Chief, Our little Naafi, Patrington'). I was given the job along with one or two others of selling cakes and tea during morning and afternoon break. A tradition existed of charging halfpennies or pennies more than the real cost, and pocketing the difference. Those inheriting the job inherited the skulduggery. I could have withdrawn once the racket was apparent, or reported it. I did neither and became guilty of one of the ugliest petty deceits – cheating mates who were no doubt as impecunious as I was. There is no excuse for the lapse and it is only small consolation that nothing else as shabby blots my life. Ever since, I have been scrupulous in money matters to the point of foolishness. Bills are paid promptly, and on one occasion someone else's debt – John Allin's.

John was not the most principled of my acquaintances. A year into our relationship he began complaining about his awkward bank manager. Impetuously I recommended him to mine in the Finsbury Park branch of NatWest who immediately accepted him as a client, no questions asked. John drew out the total of his agreed overdraft, £500, and was never in touch with the bank again. I felt so guilty having recommended him that I paid half what he owed before they wrote him off as a bad debt.

Had my mother found out I stole sweets from Woolworths she would have walloped me. I was far from being a beaten child but occasionally I drove my parents beyond endurance and was slapped on my legs and bottom – never the face or about the head. Physical chastisement did not come naturally to our family. Uncle Harry slapped my face once and bitterly regretted it. So too did Uncle Sammy, the taxi driver, who I exasperated by pulling and releasing his braces while he was eating his supper of eggs and chips. When it was my turn to be a parent I slapped you, Lindsay Joe, aged about eight. You'd kicked your mother. She called up in distress and I stormed downstairs from the study and struck you a number of times about the thigh, and then crept away and wept. You fled to your room. When I recovered and moved upstairs to make friends I passed a note you'd pinned beneath a windowsill. 'It's too late for you to apologise now.' Remember, Lindsay Joe?

My mother put a premium on honesty. As a communist she

might publicly blame society for criminality among the poor but privately would not have accepted poverty as an excuse for crime in her own family. Self-respect was high on her list of priorities. Such a view, considered from one angle, could be thought insulting to the poor. 'It is acceptable for you who are impoverished to steal, self-respect has no need to apply to you, but for my children it *must* apply.'

Chapter Five

Schools

Good. He should realise though that people older than himself
should be able to guide him.

Sylvia Webb, Geography mistress,
school report from Upton House Secondary School,
18 July 1947

I was unschooled. I've suggested exams were failed for want of an
academic mind. Perhaps I do myself an injustice. The war disrupted education. Without interruption an academic seam might
have sweated through. I will never know. Scant memories remain of
early schools, only their names: The Jewish Infants, Commercial
Street, Dean Street, and Christ Church Elementary. I remember no
teachers, no incidents, and though the faces on the first school
photographs are familiar, I mean I can *see* those kids running
around, yet I remember nothing of friendship with them – except
for two. The boy sitting to my right, named Alan Tapper, whose
mother always hoisted her skirt before she reached the lavatory. I
think he became a Labour councillor for Stepney, or stood to be
elected. And a girl called Shirley – Shirley who? Why do I think her
surname began with a 'B'? – first left, third row down, who lived in
Lolseworth Buildings, a tenement block in Thrawl Street – the
street where (I thought) Jack London dossed out – and whose
father, a builder's labourer, murdered her mother and mistakenly
laid her to rest in lime he imagined would destroy all trace of the
body. It was the wrong lime. He'd bought preserving lime. The
body stayed around. That flat was boarded up for years afterwards.
Christ Church School is perhaps the most vivid in memory

because it backed on to Fashion Street. I could look at the play-ground from our back window, and wave to the back window from the playground. John Allin painted it for *Say Goodbye*. The school is very much in existence today, filled with Asian children, but in those days it was mostly Jews – and presumably my Indian friend, Sabu. At the top of one of the school's drainpipes is a Magen-David, Star of David, the Jewish emblem, which announced at the height of Jewish immigration that in this school were teachers who spoke Yiddish. The only friend I remember from Christ Church is Lily Peltz. I was crazy about her. She looked like Barbara Stanwyck. Her parents owned a stall in Petticoat Lane selling – was it blouses or handbags? – which she subsequently took over. I used to see her in later life when taking friends 'down the Lane'. A striking woman who hated the name 'Lily' and insisted on being called 'Terry'. We ended up living near each other in Hackney but shared no social times thereafter. Lives!

But where did Rosalind Yenish fit in – my first sexual ex-perience, aged six? Did she go to Christ Church School? I know she lived in Fournier Street but I can't see her in a classroom. I remem-ber so little of school days in Stepney, not even the occasion when the photograph was taken. All I remember is being given spoonfuls of malt; half-pint bottles of milk which we sucked through a straw; rest periods when we were expected to sleep on canvas beds during the afternoon; and lying on my back on that parquet floor during PE times with a coloured team-band – red? yellow? blue? green? – across my chest, looking up the skirts of the teacher.

And who taught me to read? I must have learned to read from someone. It can only have been in those schools, but I have no memory of the process of learning. I certainly remember White-chapel Library and the books borrowed from there. Brer Rabbit and the William books. I missed out on Beatrix Potter but I know I read *The Wind in the Willows* about half a dozen times, and wept over it.

I do however remember the main school I attended when, in 1942, aged ten, we moved from Stepney to Hackney. In those days there existed five kinds of schools. The private school which had to be paid for and could be attended regardless of intelligence; the grammar school to which you went having achieved the highest examination marks possible at the end of elementary schooling, and your teachers thought you brilliant; the secondary modern school, to which you were sent because, although you may not have been brilliant, you were very clever indeed. But if you failed your examinations and it was obvious you possessed no power of thought or, as Hazlitt phrased it, no 'power of abstraction', but were fit to be merely a labourer, perhaps a skilled labourer, and therefore could be apprenticed to a carpenter or electrician, then you would finish your education in the elementary school up to the age of fourteen. I had a year more to do at one of them before taking the equivalent of the eleven plus – Northwold Road Elementary, a vast Victorian, dark-bricked building.

There was however, and for this the system must be credited, another category of child who may have failed examinations but had manifested an intelligence, a spark, a 'something' which might benefit from exposure to a more demanding curriculum than that offered by the elementary school. Not a professor, scientist, or prime minister – grammar school! Not a bureaucrat or school teacher – secondary modern school! Not a manual labourer – elementary school! But perhaps a clerk! A shop assistant! A very minor bureaucrat! If the teacher in elementary school recognised such qualities then the child could be recommended to – a central school! I failed my examinations but manifested a 'something' and was recommended. To Upton House Central School on Urswick Road, Hackney, E9 I went with my bad memory, an inability to spell (which even now only the spell check in my word processor hides), a hazy comprehension of how the English language was constructed (I still cannot name the parts of grammar), and an appetite for books. And *there* was Mr Walsh!

Well, I say 'there was Mr Walsh' but I'm not certain of that. I can't remember my first year at Upton House, only that it was a Victorian building, L-shaped, and had once been a borstal. Classrooms were at ground level, the assembly hall and playground were large, and this oddball educational establishment proudly possessed a laboratory and a small indoor swimming pool. I remember names: Captain Allard, the headmaster; Mr Thomas (sweet Mr Thomas) for French; Miss Webb (who opened her legs to the class) for geometry, typing and shorthand; Miss Hood (beleaguered and lanky) for singing; Mr Cox (ex-RAF, warmly stern, timed our laughter) for arithmetic, algebra, book-keeping and physical training; Mr Loader (important character in the wings of a drama soon to be related) for Jewish religious knowledge; Mr Jones (*were* we educated by the Welsh?) for history; Mr Walsh (wonderful Walsh) for English. Two whose names I can't remember – the science master who had an eternal drip on the end of his very pointed nose; and the master for geometry who had a hole between his two front teeth which made his *s*'s whistle. Was his name Mr Hook?

Science bored me, or rather the science master was depressingly boring. I've since made up for it researching science for my plays. I understand the structure of DNA! History, dramatically unfolding, captured my imagination then as now. I derived great satisfaction drawing maps for geography. But surprisingly it was maths, especially geometry, in which I excelled. Aside from the fun of drawing shapes with ruler and set square, the logic, the symmetry, the order intrigued me. I found the proof of theories to be exhilarating. It's true that for second-year exams I cheated, came second in geometry, and *had* to be good from then on. Nevertheless it was a subject I delighted in. If drama can be described as the unfolding of·events which culminate in an explosion of light then it's not surprising that both geometry and history turned out to be subjects holding my attention. As for the subjects designed to turn me into a clerk/bookkeeper, I mastered only one – typing. The outlines of Pitman's shorthand slipped through memory though I enjoyed keeping neat columns of figures for book-keeping, but it is for typing that I'll be forever grateful to Upton House. I *wanted* to type, and touch-type I can. My fingers fly over the keyboard, especially on a word processor which enables mistakes to be swiftly corrected. As in life, if your sins can be easily forgiven you sin with greater confidence.

My greatest debt of gratitude, however, goes not to Miss Webb for teaching me to type, but to Mr Walsh, Bill Walsh, for fanning the flames of my imagination while cooling my cockiness and mocking my spelling. Dear Mr Walsh, who suffered from a clinging collar like a starched noose which his fingers were forever struggling to separate from his neck, a kind of nervous tic to accompany the seductive sarcasm he laid upon everyone, even those for whom he had hope and affection, like myself. His great virtue, at least the one I will always be indebted to him for, was his readiness to distinguish between formal knowledge and an unusual imagination. I received low marks for spelling, punctuation, and grammar (he wanted me to be in no doubt about my failings) and high marks for imagination. I see him, a short, very English man, pulling at his collar, standing in tweeds before the blackboard chalking up our errors, going through the current batch of derisory English compositions. I reconstruct, with some licence!

The spelling of the English language is without logic. You must not expect it to make sense. 'Thick' ends with 'k', 'stick' ends with 'k'. 'Enigmatic' however, as the otherwise talented Wesker seems with illogical logic to suppose, does *not* end in 'k'. Nor does 'pneumatic'! However, 'pneumatic', for reasons to which Wesker was oblivious and for which few others can account, further confuses us by unreasonably beginning with 'p'. Of course there *is* a reason why it begins with 'p', because it derives from the Greek word 'pneumatikos' in which you *will* find a 'k', to do with wind, and breathing . . . But this wish to make sense out of that which makes no sense will, if you let it, forever inhibit your learning of spelling. English spelling is a task of memory . . .

Perhaps his personality is best glimpsed through his comments on my dreadful English compositions. From one called 'A Hot Day':

. . . Through clamy, narrow, heavy eyes I saw teeming walls and boiling pavements, motion-less leaves on motion-less boughs, and a tired dog squashed by an agravated driver . . .

A pencil line slashes through the misspelt *aggravated*. A circle rounds the misspelt *clammy* with a comment in the margin, 'means cold and wet when spelt correctly'. Of my childish imaginings: '. . . I saw teeming walls and boiling pavements . . .' he asked the question: 'teeming with what? boiling with what?' I wrote:

> . . . Swaying crowds, pushing, shoving . . .

His comment: 'not a very hot day'. I wrote:

> . . . and not caring who saw their breasts through the open dress or their pants above the top rim of their trousers . . .

His comment: 'lack of morals rather than due to heat'. Nevertheless he gave me 16/20. For an essay entitled 'On seeing ourselves as others see us' he only gave me 13/20, writing in the margin; 'Poor stuff not at all like you . . . not at all like the Wesker that was.' Over my last sentence beginning: 'I have no time to finish . . .' he couldn't resist writing: 'thank goodness'. Looking at the exercise book marked 3A I see another high mark, another 19/20, this time for something called 'Recollections of Early Childhood'. There it is, the beginning of this autobiography, more or less the same memories except for images of a black cat with a missing ear, and 'the white-haired old lady down-stairs who used to kiss me when I came home from evacuation . . .' And the murder:

> A dead body was found in a corner there once. I shall never forget that. I came home from school one day and heard my mother talking about a Mrs X that used to live upstairs us. 'Been found dead in Crumpling Alley.' Of course I was instantly excited at the word dead and rushed down to see what was what . . .

Walsh underlined and queried 'upstairs us' but wrote 'V good' at the end.

The English composition book for the fourth year contains the zenith of my schooldays' achievement. Twenty out of twenty for a poem called 'Snow', and 10/10 for a prose poem called 'Snow Sculpture'. It also contains a tongue-in-cheek essay on a topic for which I obviously had no feeling, 'Spring Flowers'.

> I like spring flowers. I like them because my mother's brother's sister-in-law, who gives me one pound for a birthday present, also likes them. There is however one sad difference; she likes buttercups but I do not, and I like daisies but she does not . . .

'A serious subject is always worth treating seriously' admonished my English teacher.

And yet for all his fond nurturing it could be said Bill Walsh misled me. Indulging my unconventional interpretation of essay titles lured me into wild flourishes of composition which I foolishly imagined the Cambridge examiners would recognise, as Walsh did, to be the embryonic signs of literary genius. I was wrong then and frequently have been since. What burns brightly, blinds. Even burns! Writing where my fancy took me may have given the heart of generous Walsh a warm glow, but such a free spirit was obviously intolerable for the solid examiners of Cambridge. I achieved a mere pass in English, and when a subdued Mr Walsh had, with surprise and apology, to inform me of the result I had difficulty restraining tears.

As soon as *Roots* was published in its first, slim Penguin edition I sent him a copy expressing my gratitude. He responded:

> Thank you for your kind words – I still find that boys with a feeling for English – though perhaps lacking your sublime discontent, which is going, I hope, to make you famous – still fail their examinations, while the clods somehow pass.

Two curious changes took place while I was at Upton House. The first was my handwriting – I wanted to improve it. There was a boy in my class called Edmunds who was brilliant in every subject, rarely falling short of 90% for anything. He had the most attractive of scripts. I coveted penmanship like his. Mr Thomas wielded a flowing pen and I asked him to write me an alphabet which he was delighted to do and which I practised copying daily. My handwriting never flowed like his or Edmunds but it improved.

The second change while at Upton House was to do with how I held my pen. My sister is not only left-handed, she holds her pen between her forefinger and middle finger. I imitated her, thinking it made me look interesting. It worked. Everyone was interested. They'd watch me write and then ask questions. Often it irritated them that I was different, and to begin with I didn't mind that, either. But then I did. I chastised myself for pretension. The moment I was struck with the thought that I was being pretentious, I ceased. Though why I dropped that pretension and not others – such as the way I wore my clothes – God knows! I think I was the first person to wear a shirt *over* a roll-necked pullover.

I don't suppose I've seen more than half a dozen football matches in my life – large crowds depress me. They're supposed to be exhilarating, and in later years as the Aldermaston marches grew from a few hundred to hundreds of thousands, I was exhilarated by those, but in general the experience of surging humanity in the grip of a passion carries too many murderous overtones for me to feel comfortable with them. On two occasions, though, I played truant from Upton House – along with half the school – to watch the Moscow Dynamos play Spurs and then Arsenal. I was not a football fan but a fan of the Soviet Union. One game took place in a fog. We couldn't see the game and the players could hardly see each other. Why didn't they call it off halfway through?

Two of my closest friends were Mickey Cohen and Malcom Brodinsky (later changed to Brogan to help him get on in the world). Cohen introduced me to the big-band jazz sounds of Stan Kenton and Woody Herman. We took a cycling holiday together. Joined the Youth Hostels Association, pored over maps, plotted a leisurely route through Maidenhead, the Berkshire and Marlborough Downs, visiting the Giant of Cerne carved in the hillside, circling south and back up via Winchester and the Surrey Downs. We were fourteen. Our parents had no fear for our safety. It just rained most of the time.

The names of my fifth-form classmates are written on the back of our end-of-school photograph: Foreman, Turner, Edmunds, French, Smith, Litman, Towner, Errington, Baker, Kiddgel, Smith (again), Isaacs, Jones, Nichol. We all got on well, though no doubt some viewed me as 'the smart alec' – after all, I read books and had opinions! I know myself to have been good-natured and a defender of the weak against bullies but the intemperate nature inherited from my mother, further inflamed by an articulate, fiery tongue, led me down calamitous paths.

Expulsion

With experience and hindsight I now understand that the tensions between Miss Webb, Sylvia Webb, and myself were sexually based. She was dark-haired and pretty with flashing eyes that smiled wickedly as they looked down at your work upon which she was commenting; when she looked up it often would be with her face turned away and her eyes coyly glancing at you out of their corners. There was something sad and yearning in her history as it came down to us – rumour ranged between a soldier husband stationed overseas or a pilot killed on a bombing mission – and such was her sensuality even her thick legs were alluring.

Shorthand and typing were her proficiencies. For geography I suspected she kept only a few pages ahead of us. There were no hooligan elements in our class but she was forced constantly to be alert to ribaldry, which she handled with a mixture of abrupt anger and soft, flirtatious appeal. She knew when to smile away the un-preventable, such as the time a boy called Waterman, the nearest we got to a wild element, roguish more than delinquent, blew up a condom (french letters they were called in those days, God knows why) and swore it was a balloon, Miss. One of only two women in a staff room of men in a school pulsating with young blades on the horny verge of manhood, she must have felt like a doe at bay and, when she wasn't asserting or defending, her eyes looked out as though pleading with us to help her define herself.

I don't remember her as very bright, by which I suppose I mean she had no intellect in the way Walsh had, or Cox – with whom she flirted and who consequently seemed in a permanent state of alarm – and so my interest in literature and politics was, for her, a challenge she felt compelled to meet in other ways: pulling rank, bludgeoning with authority. I wanted relationships of equality leading to friendships such as I had with Mr Walsh. Miss Webb was my first lesson that friendship is not easy between men and women, the tensions of sex hover. We were doomed to clash in a battle of wills sooner or later. What I cannot remember is whether the orgasm came before or after the clash. First, the clash.

Typing classes began in our last year. The fifth form. It was 1947. I was fifteen. The schedule for learning to type was odd. Classes were conducted as extramural activity during one of two hours after normal school time: 4.30 to 5.30, or 5.30 to 6.30. Because I was soon adept on the keyboard I felt relaxed, even casual, about the amount of effort I needed to expend. There came an evening in November when, for a reason I can't recall, I didn't want to attend a 4.30/5.30 session. Seconds before the hour began I told Miss Webb I needed to have a haircut and asked would it be all right if I skipped this lesson? She could have acknowledged that I was well advanced in typing and simply requested a note the following day to confirm my story, there the affair would have ended. Why didn't she do just that? Why don't most of us often do 'just that'? A mood, a spirit, an old grudge, a whim, a sense of threat, a smell of danger, a scent of blood – the moment can turn on a grain of sand, 'just that' is not done and battle commences.

She asked did I have a note requesting that I be allowed off class? No, but I promised one would be brought in next day. Not good enough. Take your seat, Wesker, and start working. I was lying and she was being unreasonable – or was she reasonably seeing through my lie? Such reasoning would not have occurred to me at the time. The battle of wills was on. I refused to take my seat, reiterating the urgency of this haircut for a family event; a note signed by my mother would be brought next day. Miss Webb demanded I sit down to work. I informed her I would sit down but not work. 'Do that,' she said, 'and I'll consider what action to take.' Or some such words. So I sat down, arms defiantly folded in front of my black Imperial typewriter, refusing to work. She turned her attention to the rest of the class, giving out instructions for the next stages of practice. The typewriters clicked, the atmosphere rose in tension, my classmates, who no doubt were divided in their sympathies – I collected hostilities from an early age – watched what for them must have seemed quite gladiatorial, my reputation being disputatious and articulate. After some fifteen minutes she said I could go and she would report me next day to Captain Allard, the headmaster.

I left. God knows why I wanted the evening off – to go to the cinema, to be with a friend, listen to a radio programme? I only know that I chose the wrong evening to lie about needing a haircut. It was a Thursday. Half-day closing! But my mother signed a note – I could talk her into most things. What could it have said? Did I get someone to cut my hair? Did we invent another explanation? Did we face the truth about having mistaken the day? I can't remember. The note was handed in on Friday morning, school day began, the curriculum unfolded: Friday morning assembly, followed by religious instruction with Mr Loader (the Jews to one class, Catholics to another, the rest to remain in the hall), followed by science with Mr Drip-On-The-End-Of-His-Nose (perhaps his name will come to me before I finish this book). No public denouncement came from the Head during main assembly; no word from our form master; silence from Miss Webb. But something was afoot, vibrations in the air, a sense of impending wrath, of prearranged action, planned punishment – which materialised five minutes into the science lesson.

It is a vivid memory. The science lab was a long room. Tables ran down the centre. We sat on high stools either side facing the blackboard and the science master who taught from a raised stage area. Science equipment and space for experiments were on both sides of the long walls. Stairs from the ground floor brought us facing one lab door at the other end away from the blackboard. A second door, at the blackboard end, took us into a corridor which led us back again to the staircase.

That morning I was sitting halfway down the lab on the left facing the blackboard. A voice boomed out: 'Wesker! Pack up your books and get out!' An angry Captain Allard, who limped from war wounds, stood behind us. All heads turned first to him, then to me. I rose, outwardly cool, inwardly trembling, in the region of my legs especially, handed in my science books, exited by the door near the blackboard, walked back along the corridor and proceeded to descend the staircase, passing a watchful headmaster who must have been uncertain what I would do. Perhaps he expected me to become abject and apologise. I had no intention of saying a word. As I passed him – he was halfway down the staircase and was able to look down at me – he said:

'Well, you know what you can do. You can either apologise to Miss Webb or go.'

'I'm going,' I said, bravely as though to the gallows, though I was none too sure my shaking legs would carry me anywhere.

One by one I knocked on classroom doors and handed back textbooks to sad, bewildered and commiserating masters, saying, 'I've been expelled.' I wish I could remember what each said. I think Bill Walsh said something which intimated he was angry with and contemptuous of Sylvia Webb. Cox was sympathetic and stiff-upper-lipped. I was tearful. I walked up Urswick Road to catch the 653 trolley bus outside the Hackney baths (across the road was the gas company showrooms, I see it all) and by mid-morning was home in Weald Square where I found my father, out of work as usual, on his knees scrubbing the linoleum floor – his contribution to domestic chores and penalty for being out of work. When I told him I had been expelled and explained the story he jumped to immediate solidarity and declared at once that the first step to take in this crisis was to ring George Sinfield.

There were few problems confronting our family – domestic, academic, political – which could not be solved by consulting our very own oracle, George Sinfield, industrial correspondent for the *Daily Worker*, our one contact with the huge, remote but important world beyond the LCC estate. Ours was a tight, narrow circle of friends and family all in roughly the same economic situation, with no one knowing anyone of the slightest influence. I suppose that would not have been true of Aunt Sara, who brushed with well-known Labour leaders like Manny Shinwell and Ian Mikardo, and whose friends were Harry Politt, secretary of the British Communist Party, and Phil Piratin, one of those Jewish street urchins who dragged himself up by his bootlaces to become the only other communist Member of Parliament alongside Willy Gallagher, the Scottish MP for Lanarkshire, and who ended up a wealthy banker. (The East End produced a number of Cockney Jewish party activists who later became successful bankers, financial consultants, and property dealers. As communists they knew how to make a capitalist system work for them!) Nor would it have been true of Uncle Solly, who worked as a sub-editor on the *Daily Mirror*; nor of wealthy Uncle Perly – in fact in later life both uncles used their contacts to help me get a job. But the professional lives of Sara, Solly, and Perly remained shadowy for us, so we clung to our very own influential link, poor George Sinfield, who we rang for advice at the drop of a hat. We knew George through Della. When, in August 1940, she had turned sixteen and opted not to pursue her studies, knowing our parents couldn't afford to keep her, she began a working life in the London offices of the Young Communist League and later became book-keeper for the *Daily Worker*, where she got to know George, who subsequently became a family friend.

What on earth could George do about me being expelled? I'm not even certain my father or I ever got around to phoning him for advice – his name was invoked like a nervous tic at the first sign of trouble. The sequence of events that remain clear are my mother returning from work, her concern, her reproach, the discussion about what next to do and then – the rat-a-tat-tat on the front door.

Before us stood Mr Loader, teacher of Monday- and Friday-morning religious instruction. Mr Loader, who had married the daughter of Ciro's the bulging sweet shop in the parade of shops across the Upper Clapton Road, was also a part-time maths teacher at Upton House who looked like every anti-semite's image of a Jew – small, fat, thick-lipped, shoulders hunched as though in apology to be living; the opposite of my mother's just-as-Jewish stern, dignified, upright defiance apologising to no one for her right to live. We invited him in for tea and cake. He explained.

Captain Allard did not want to expel me but one of his staff had been defied and he had to uphold her authority. Mr Loader was asked to be his envoy, visit the Wesker home and mediate. An apology would suffice. Apologise and the incident would be forgiven, forgotten. The diplomatic ploy grated like scratched iron. The Weskers were Jewish, Mr Loader was Jewish. Peace$=J^2$. Poor Allard! How was he to know each Jew felt themselves in possession of a different truth. The tradition of arguing the meaning of Talmud bequeathed Jews – whom the Bible tells us were a stiff-necked people to begin with – a fractious temperament, even to those who had never quarrelled over the multiplicity of tiny meanings embedded between the lines of Talmudic wisdom. Jews quarrelled! It's what happens when you know yourself to be born in the image of God! (I've often suspected that such fractiousness accounts for the endless splintering of left-wing groups which seem to attract the stiff-necked, righteous, Talmudic, hair-splitting Jewish temperament.) And so, Allard, imagining he had set like with like, had unwittingly set like with very unlike – Mr Loader and Mrs Wesker.

Mrs Wesker, not wishing to see her son shamed by expulsion and thinking an apology would cost me no part of dignity, was in the process of persuading me to return and apologise when Mr Loader overstepped the mark and supported his case with the one argument calculated to make my mother grow tall with indignation, which she did when he obsequiously said: 'You know, we are Jews, foreigners, and sometimes in a foreign land it becomes necessary to eat humble pie.' Foreigners? The Weskers? Humble pie? Her voice rose in anger and she showed him the door. He left, undaunted, un-apologetic, and for all I know uncomprehendingly, urging us not to be hasty, to think about it. I can't remember what happened next, what prompted the decision, but I returned to school.

In Captain Allard's room I was brought together with Sylvia Webb and lectured about honour and good behaviour. I still re-fused to apologise but with great magnanimity Miss Webb declared she did not want an apology, just a promise that I would work hard and behave in future. Since I worked reasonably hard – at least on those subjects I enjoyed – and didn't see myself as a chronic mis-behaver, such a promise was not difficult to make.

The incident was closed. Not, however, my relationship with Miss Webb. We had eyes for each other and both regretted this unneces-sary interruption.

Dear Miss Webb

There is no tale following of secret assignations, exchanged kisses in school corridors, or even whispered endearments. But she was a deeply sensuous woman who sighed and stretched, arched her back to thrust forward her breasts, crossed her legs in wide sweeps, hugged her tibia, and occasionally sat on top of a school desk with her knees touching and her feet apart exposing thigh, stocking-top and suspender for brief, captivating moments. I don't think her in-tention was anything as vulgar as prick-teasing, more an instinct to command attention and a quality of loyal affection through which to control us; a way of telling us she was ours if in return we would quietly be hers. For the most part we were, and on one occasion she bestowed a favour that made me alone completely hers. I say 'me alone', perhaps it was a moment others shared but held back from confiding. I think not, however.

It took place during an end-of-term exam for maths – arithmetic or algebra perhaps. I was fifteen. Sylvia Webb – late thirties? – was our invigilator. Not a difficult paper. I was a good mathematician and able to finish ahead of time. She sat at her table sideways, facing the classroom window to the playground, her left half towards us, reading, looking up every so often to check no one was cheating. As I worked we exchanged looks now and then until she entered a period of what seemed to be deep concentration in what she was reading. Still sideways, her legs thrust forward, she was engaged in one of the most erotic actions I have ever witnessed. In the way the thoughtful professor might rub a forehead, the contemplative woman brush her lips with a finger, the hesitant snooker player scratch the back of his neck with a cue end, so Miss Sylvia Webb nonchalantly stroked the inside of her thigh. But not in one place only. No. Slowly, slowly but inexorably, she was moving up so that her skirt pulled back; not pulled back far enough to reveal flesh – that would have amounted to crude, unacceptable flashing – but enough to allow her hand to move higher still so that it could be imagined it *did* touch flesh and, who knows, soft other places.

It took all my concentration to finish the exam, fortunate that I *was* a good mathematician. Halfway through her meandering she looked directly at me and smiled. It was then I knew *she* knew what she was doing, nothing nonchalant about her explorations at all. She was intent on exciting me, and excite me she did. Somewhere between an algebraic equation or multiplicity of fractions – I came. No moans, of course. A wriggling, no doubt, a cough, perhaps, a sinking sigh which could be thought the solution of the knottiest of mathematical theories, or at most a clasping of my face as though confronting the algebraic conundrum of the century, whatever – Miss Webb had roused me to orgasm and reawakened a modest penchant for voyeurism which had begun in a turret room above a Victorian pub, about which more later.

I fed lonely nights on that vision for many years afterwards, and even when not lonely have often wondered about the wicked-eyed mistress of Imperial's keyboard. Did her airman laddie return? Was she a widow ever after? Did she marry again and have children? Once, in Hay on Wye, among the bookshops, in the mid seventies or thereabouts, I was sure it was her. An old woman, stout, but those unmistakable eyes searching for confirmation of their owner's existence. It is one of my regrets that I did not approach her and ask: 'Miss Webb?' But I think she recognised me and, if she did not want to face old times, then I would respect that.

Should this story have been written up in the chapter allotted to sex? No. Miss Webb was part of my schooling. I owe her a place under the heading naming her vocation. Being able to touch-type must have contributed to the quantity, if not the quality, I dared write. I hereby acknowledge my debt to her.

But I am not yet finished with Upton House. There are the stories to do with the boy, Nichol.

Education through books

'There's no better education than life.' Life, I've often thought, is not what educates but what one needs educating to comprehend. No, my education was not found on the street corner – a suspect, sentimental claim, that; it came from the conversations to which I was exposed and the books I stumbled upon, was encouraged to read. Joe was an avid reader, he picked up everything and anything that was to hand – travel or thriller, classic or polemic.

If asked which books 'educated' me it would not be difficult to re-member between the ages of seventeen and twenty that I had been absorbed by D.H. Lawrence. Putting a date to others strains memory. I have to scan bookshelves. Lewis Mumford's *The Culture of Cities* – is that what prompted me to use cities as a metaphor for the experience of Centre Fortytwo? Was it Howard Spring's *Fame is the Spur* with its span of decades which gave me the courage to write *Their Very Own and Golden City*, a saga covering sixty years? Herbert Read's *The Meaning of Art*: what part did that play in my foolish Perlmutter faith that art is a natural human activity central to the wellbeing of civilised society? I know I've read Lytton Stra-chey's *Eminent Victorians* and Peter Quennell's biographies of

Byron, but when? When did I read Silone's *Fontamara*, Colette's *Cheri*, Wilder's *The Bridge of San Luis Rey*, Waugh's *Brideshead Revisited*? Waugh is the only writer one of whose books grated so offensively on my nerves that I was driven to tear it up halfway through. But which one? And how old was I? Yet I wept over *Brideshead*.

Of this I'm certain: my beginnings were formed by *Morte d'Arthur*, *The Wind in the Willows*, Arthur Ransome, *The Three Musketeers*, and the poetry of Louis MacNeice – especially *Autumn Journal*. At Upton House I formed my own group of Musketeers of whom, naturally, I was D'Artagnan, and *The Tales of Arthur*, which I pored over endlessly, account for more of me than I care to acknowledge. Or perhaps I *should* acknowledge their influence: chivalry, the pursuit of justice, the quest for the holy grail, the shattered dream of equals who once shared a round table. Aren't my plays often about people driven by dreams which shatter? The huge doubt that gnaws at my ageing is whether I was ever a knight on a white horse or just poor old daft Don Quixote tilting at windmills!

From thirteen to sixteen I was learning political history and forming basic socialist values from the novels of Upton Sinclair and Jack London, with Sinclair Lewis, Howard Spring, Howard Fast and A.J. Cronin tucked in between. By the time I reached late teens Dostoevsky, the Brontës, Turgenev, De Maupassant, Gorky and Hemingway were reaching out to me from my family's bookshelves and teaching me that man was very complex, sad and devious indeed. I stumbled across Thomas Hardy and E.M. Forster during conscription in the RAF but, ashamedly, had to wait until my thirties and the dubious responsibilities of fame to discover Austen, Henry James, George Eliot, Balzac, Ruskin and Carlyle, at which point I believe my writing to have deepened and matured. To write an essay I would often dip into a Ruskin lecture and refresh myself upon his style and clarity of argument. Would that I had his power of thought.

Books! Voyages of discovery! In those days, when I travelled the globe through literature, meshed in its pages with other lives and relationships, wrestled intoxicated over new thoughts written by inspired writers, I would panic in case another book was not leaning by to be snatched up and read as soon as the current one was finished. Heady days!

But which books made those special, searing impressions? I once planned to write a play on the life of Jesus, thinking to recreate him as the natural and inevitable product of the Jewish personality he must have been. Were the seeds for that planted by reading Renan's *Life of Jesus* and George Moore's *The Brook Kerith*? That plan still races round my head but I need a period of three years to pace myself for the research required, and to have three years free of worry requires a commercial success I seem incapable of producing. In 1962, when most critics had praised *Chips with Everything* and given me the only commercial success of my career, there was one voice which dissented, Bamber Gascoigne writing in *The Spectator*. I had previously given an interview in which I'd announced my hope. Gascoigne picked it up. At the end of his none too complimentary review he added: 'I hear Mr Wesker is contemplating a play on the life of Jesus, no doubt another stage in his autobiography!' The wit was irresistible. I rang him up to ask would he lunch with me. We became instant friends.

No date exists for the experience of reading Edmund Wilson's *To the Finland Station* but an experience it was. Here, for the first time, I encountered the notion that ideas had a history. More than that, they were dramatic! Ideas and history unfold, are to do with cause and effect, with change, development, the shaping of lives, all that is thrilling about the intellectual and emotional energy driving human beings. There is often a confusion among critics who imagine that my plays and stories are about ideas. They're not, they're about human beings *animated by ideas*. There's a difference. To the extent *I* was animated by history and ideas so such characters interested me. A character's life is a history; characters can't *not* think; the richest thought is fuelled by ideas.

Bill Walsh introduced us to a splendid, rather daring collection for its day called *The Albatross Book of Living Verse – English and*

American Poetry from the thirteenth century to the present day, edited
by Louis Untermeyer. When I found a copy in a bookshop some
years later I had to buy it. Just flicking its pages at random, lighting
upon first lines, provokes memories of exhilarating hours. Look at
them, they marked my adolescence:

> *Glory be to God for dappled things . . .*
> *It is an ancient Mariner . . .*
> *When I consider how my light is spent . . .*
> *What passing-bells for those who die as cattle? . . .*
> *Every one suddenly burst out singing . . .*
> *I will arise and go now, and go to Innisfree . . .*
> *'Twas brillig, and the slithy toves . . .*
> *Come to me in the silence of the night . . .*
> *I met a traveller from an antique land . . .*
> *Had we but world enough, and time . . .*

> > *Proud men*
> > *Eternally*
> > *Go about*
> > *Slander me,*
> > *Call me the 'Calliope',*
> > *Sizz . . .*
> > *Fizz . . .*

Gerard Manley Hopkins, Coleridge, Milton, Wilfred Owen, Sieg-
fried Sassoon, Yeats, Lewis Carroll, Christina Georgina Rossetti,
Shelley, Andrew Marvell, Vachel Lindsay. Like a roll call of
honour.

Reading aloud is a favourite weakness. I read Salinger's *The
Catcher in the Rye* to Dusty in bed and we laughed night after night
before making love. I subsidise capricious earnings with readings
from the *One Woman Plays*. There was the memorable time I read
to my mother from *Autumn Journal* by Louis MacNeice, a poet
whose spirit nourished me perhaps like few others. The volume

lived on my sister's shelves in its brown and yellow dust-jacket, tall and slim, printed in what I think is Times Roman, a typeface favoured in those days by Faber for its poets. When torn apart by the essays in *The God That Failed*, when brought low by the Soviet suppression of the Hungarian uprising, when in despair with fortune and my promise unfulfilled, the last stanza of *Autumn Journal* would bubble, bubble up, as my Shylock says, '. . . like a little lost spring . . . for dying men to drink, for survivors from dark and terrible times . . .' I would read it again and again, and one day, high on an umpteenth reading, I felt driven to read it aloud to someone, there and then! My mother was cleaning out the flat, no one else around. I took the broom from her hand, sat her down – as I often did, stopping her in the midst of work usually to read something *I* had just written, and she was a good listener even though she didn't always know what to say – and I read:

> *Sleep, my body, sleep, my ghost,*
>   *Sleep, my parents and grandparents,*
> *And all those I have loved most . . .*

> *. . . The New Year comes with bombs, it is too late*
>   *To dose the dead with honourable intentions:*
> *If you have honour to spare, employ it on the living;*
>   *The dead are dead as 1938.*
> *Sleep to the noise of running water*
>   *To-morrow to be crossed, however deep;*
> *This is no river of the dead or Lethe,*
>   *To-night we sleep*
> *On the banks of Rubicon – the die is cast;*
>   *There will be time to audit*
> *The accounts later, there will be sunlight later*
>   *And the equation will come out at last.*

When I finished she looked up, her eyes shining with pleasure and pride. 'Now that,' she said, '*that* you should try and get published!' Grace and taste had my mother.

A great disservice to literature is committed when 'top twenty' lists are proclaimed. George Steiner who, it will be recognised, is a source for much that I know about literary criticism, writes of F.R. Leavis that in his major work, *The Great Tradition*, he 'reshaped the inner landscape of taste'. Steiner, before criticising, argues in defence of Leavis's stringent insights into those writers he wishes to judge and elect to the high table or dismiss to queue for crumbs of attention. Steiner's description of Leavis's attitudes to writing is clear, salutary:

> His refusal of elegance is the expression of a deep, underlying Puritanism. Leavis detests the kind of 'fine' writing which by flash of phrase or lyric surge of argument obscures thinness of meaning or unsoundness of logic. He distrusts as spurious frivolity all that would embroider on the naked march of thought.

I'm grateful to be put on my toes as both writer and reader but I wonder is not the concept of 'The Top Twenty' a pernicious one? Assembled by a lesser intellect than Leavis's the list becomes like borrowed jewels to reflect the glorious intelligence of the compiler rather than an exercise to establish literary standards. What about those *odd* books, the enthusiasms of one's eccentric friends who might eccentrically pick out Leavis's *The Great Tradition*? I delight in other people's enthusiasms, anything from a favourite landscape to a favourite piece of music, from a long-loved friend to a long-loved painting, from a passion for a private collection to a passion for an oft-thumbed book. The great works stride around in the marketplace challenging us to compare them, and so we do. But there are minor works, small gems, which have their place in hidden corners, calling for no comparisons, existing alone in their own worlds, happy to wait and be discovered by those who wander off the beaten track. Mr Leavis must forgive those of us who slip away from the main stage, who will not be deprived of Helen Thomas's *As it Was and World Without End*, endless copies of which I used to buy for any and everyone, or Elliot Paul's *A Narrow Street*, Arthur Morrison's *A Child of the Jago*, Sinclair Lewis's *Main Street*, André Gide's *Narrow is the Gate*, Jack London's *Iron Heel* . . . the list of smaller-scaled works glittering around the huge jewels of world literature is endless, and I dare not begin to list the fine writing of my contemporaries from Latin America, the United States, Europe and this United Kingdom.

Books have moulded me. In Thornton Wilder's *The Bridge of San Luis Rey* one of two brothers discovers that of two people who love, one always loves less. Relationships faltered anxiously after stumbling across perceptions like that. Fitzgerald's *Tender is the Night* charts the slow decline of the strong at the hands of the weak. I am not certain I could have written *The Four Seasons* without it. Nor do I think I'd have considered *Chicken Soup*, a play spanning twenty years, had I not immersed myself in those thick sagas by A.J. Cronin – *Hatter's Castle*, *The Citadel*, *The Stars Look Down* – which tell, if I remember correctly, of young working-class people ending successful and jaded.

Through literature I learned, early on, that the impact of art is not immediate but cumulative. Literature's truths assume greater significance as one lives and lives on. Its powers take time to effect, the light hangs around until one's own moment of darkness comes. Through books in general I discovered the diversity of minds, the kaleidoscope of personality, the plethora of contradictory truths which must live side by side, the cycles of human stupidity and courage, the richness of human ingenuity. The flaw in this edifice of edification – and here I dare confess a dark suspicion about a major flaw in my psyche – is that the discovery came to me as God comes to sinners, or Catholicism to the convert – I became more Catholic than the Pope. In discovering that books, the best of them, were a defence against ignorance – which left people vulnerable to the seductive certitudes of dogma – I paradoxically elevated their glories to a dogma. I became certain of the inefficacy of certainty. I made a gospel of books which I believed questioned gospels. Relatives, friends, and workmates must have found my passion unbearable, but there it sounds, echoing across the pages of my plays through characters who are imbued with it – *Roots*, *Shylock*, *The Old Ones* . . .

I'm here once and once only. And when I'm gone I'll not care one bit about any of you but you're going to care about and remember me. You, each one of you, are nothing in this society. Nothing! You are poor, used, nothings who will mostly end up unhappy, frustrated and thoroughly defeated. You think you're in control, that no one can shove you around, that you're God almighty free Englishmen but you're not. You can bash each other and pinch sweets and knock old women on the head but the great world goes on and ignores you or knows and cares little for you just as you boast that you know and care little for it. What, what is there you can do? Can you take a yacht round the world? Can you fly to wherever you want? Can you speak another language, split on atom, transplant a heart, live where you like, climb a mountain? You won't even find the job you want, most of you. So get that straight, firm, in your heads. It's a big world in which control rests with other people, not you. Not you.

Good. You're listening. It makes a change. I don't say any of these things happily. Do you think I like how we're forced to live with each other? But someone must warn you. Who knows, one of you might even listen. One of you might rise to the challenge and have done with his tiny ambitions of petty kingships and turn it on himself and find his real strengths. And it will only be one of you – the rest will end up on the scrapheap of dead-end jobs with dead-eyed wives.

You hate me, don't you? I can see from your eyes and clenched mouths that you hate every part of me; the sound of my voice, what I say, the way I dress, the life you imagine I lead. I'm sorry about that. Hate's a sterile emotion. Useless! It'll take you round in circles while others go straight for what they want. Still, I suppose that's the diet most of you will live with from now on. Hate. Sad. BUT HERE! Here is a book. Books! Take them. Use them. Other men may build an alien world out there you never dreamed of. Defend yourself! Books! Centuries of other people's knowledge, experience. Add it to yours, measure it with yours. They're your only key to freedom and happiness. Books! There is no other. I promise you. There – is – no – other!

Rosa – The Old Ones

I was not born into a family or milieu where the trained mind was taken for granted. Only one cousin, Bryan, went to university, to study law – a Wesker, not a Perlmutter! Even in his retirement and blindness he's studying for a degree in liberal studies. And I regret it – this lack of formal education – I feel naked, exposed, vulnerable. With it I might have found a way of carrying education with grace instead of patchwork enthusiasm, and been more bearable to those around me. Instead I am what they call an 'autodidact'. It has an heroic ring but I miss what I imagine would have been the rigorous intellectual demands of university. Friends who experienced the halls of academe declare what talent I have would have been destroyed there. I can't believe that, too many brilliant writers and poets went to university. It's a lack which John Dexter always felt and, he once told me, was made to feel at the Royal Court where everyone went through either Oxford or Cambridge. 'They were always a little contemptuous of you and me,' he revealed one day during rehearsals of *Shylock*. Maybe. I never felt it, but then perhaps I was too giddy and exhilarated at being considered at all. Since then being an artist has felt equal to anything or anyone coming from anywhere. What higher state could there possibly be? Royalty, politicians, millionaires – no one makes me feel lesser. (Not helpful in life, that. People need you to defer to their view of themselves!) Nevertheless, though I'm not without a certain pride for having educated myself, I feel a lack.

Like most Jews I'm manic about the need for education and the value of knowledge. We fear ignorance as a cesspit breeding inferiority complexes out of which creeps mob hatred of what is unknown. Willy Goldman, author of 'East-End My Cradle', a book that confirmed my youthful belief that my milieu might provide material for writing, observed in an interview: 'People with warped lives will forgive you anything but being different from themselves.' I read, listen, converse, but I'm not blessed with the ease of erudition. I shall always feel like a novice, a convert, an alien. Neither clarity nor power of thought comes easily to me, sometimes not at all. The joy of writing certain of the plays was the need to research for them. *Their Very Own and Golden City* led to a history of architecture. *The Friends* involved reading about the scientific 'revolutions' that led up to DNA. Through *Shylock* I discovered the Renaissance. Preparing for *Caritas* I had to read English medieval history and studies in Catholic mysticism. Even so, there are certain people I sense not to engage with, I smell their learning, their feats of memory, their fluency, their power to marshal argument, as dogs smell one another knowing they can trot or not trot alongside them.

One other, just as important area of education – radio. In my aunts' Charlotte de Rothschild's Dwellings there crackled and hissed a battery set that sent me to sleep reassuringly. My possessive love affair with the BBC began there. By the time we reached Weald Square I was an avid listener, organising my poor mother's life around my radiophonic appetite. Come Thursday we would buy the *Radio Times* which I combed from beginning to end, marking out all the plays, concerts, lectures, documentaries that promised exhilarating listening. Dates with friends were sometimes agreements to share a radio adaptation of a Chris Fry play, a Beethoven concert, a lecture on new trends in Italian cinema. BBC radio and Penguin Books – my university. Whenever I read fine writing I feel I'm a writer of substance; when it's bad then it seems to me all I have written is mediocre.

The boy, Nichol

I was confronted with my first dark image of human behaviour in the school playground of Upton House, an image I have still to use in a play. It's one of two stories to do with this classmate whose first name has fled memory. The first story makes me wince, revealing a side of my character partly to respect partly despair of.

In my father's collection of books were two or three that contained faintly salacious passages. I think the word 'fuck' appeared in one; in another was a tantalisingly erotic love scene, timid by today's standards, but then, for boys of fourteen, enough to create pubescent trembling. Nichol desperately wanted to possess those books. They were not mine to give away, but what he was offering was tempting beyond my powers of resistance, and I suspect was not his to give away, either: a small sackful of cigarette cards. Someone in his family had collected them over the years, all sorts, all sizes. Only now do I comprehend their value. Or perhaps they had none in those days, perhaps it's only in the last ten years or so that they have accrued a collector's worth. There were thousands of them and I spent many delightfully absorbed hours sorting them into sets.

There were the familiar ones: cars, aeroplanes, exotic flowers, soldiers through the ages, British kings, film stars and so on. But there were also specials, like 'Ancient Warriors', 'Treasure Trove', 'Characters from Dickens', 'Characters from Shakespeare'. I can't remember them all. Today they can be bought mounted in special frames. There were cards from other countries belonging to double-sized packets, long packets; one set, I remember, carried lurid drawings of the atrocities of war. I don't think it would be an exaggeration to say that had I hung on to them they would have now been worth in the region of a couple of thousand pounds. But I didn't hang on to them. It will not be believed what I did. Yes, I hung on to some of the sets, perhaps a dozen or so, but the remainder I dispensed like alms, as Lord Hereford is purported to have done with gold sovereigns from the top of the hill I can see from my window – he threw them, so local mythology goes, to be hunted like treasure trove by farm labourers. So I sat at our third-floor window in Weald Square and scattered down cigarette cards on to the grass area below among the disused air-raid shelters in which we hid during the doodlebug and rocket era of the war, enjoying the sight of neighbouring kids racing here and there to grab at the fluttering things. Hundreds and hundreds rained down with majestic carelessness, earning me a spurious reputation for benevolence. Perlmutter idiocy, more like!

The second Nichol story is darker. And simpler. He was a bully was Nichol. One day, queuing up for school lunch, he withdrew from his pocket a stick of liquorice, a hard brown twig of a thing, and insisted everyone take a lick. I didn't like liquorice and politely declined. He thumped me.

I want to begin a play with that image. Just that. Few words, just the offer, the declination, the thump. It was my first lesson about that deep need to have others share your passions. Nothing wrong with that, providing it's only a wish to share pleasure. Too often it is a need to share bigotry and prejudice, to be admired. Refusal, contradiction is a threat – 'If you do not want to share what I offer then you are criticising what it is I am offering, and thereby criticising me.' It begins with liquorice and moves to religious belief, political opinion, taste, territory – bigot, chauvinist, xenophobic, fundamentalist. For certain personalities, what they like and believe is an extension of who they are; contradict them and you touch nerve centres of irrational violence which cannot be contained, only defended against.

> . . . I'm referring to the men of *real* inferiority, men who suspect their own stupidity. That's where violence comes from. The anger of self-knowledge. Self-knowledge that he's a pig and then – everything intimidates him: a tone of voice, a way of dressing, a passion for literature, a passion for music, for anything! He hates it! One little speck of colour on a man's personality unleashes such venom, such venom . . .
>
> Boomy – *The Old Ones*

Chapter Six

The boy still – games and pranks

'You were a real dead-end kid,' said Ann. Was I really? It is impossible to recreate that nine-year-old. Interweave memories with what the aunts remember, place them in the larger weave alongside photographs and something is captured, but what? A flavour, an elusive shadow, a sewn-together cloth that's tattered with time and you're not quite sure what patch belongs where or even if these are the right remnants.

I look at the photograph taken on the occasion of the marriage of Aunt Rae to her cousin, Solly Lipson. There we are on the steps of Brondesbury Registry Office – the three other aunts, Annie, Billie, Sara; my sister, Della, with her Spitalfields Foundation school hat and uniform; the bride and groom; and me! I'm about six or seven. It's obvious I've been making a nuisance of myself. Uncle Solly holds me firmly by the right arm, Aunt Rae's hand grips my shoulder. My white socks are down to the ankles, one lower than the other; my knobbly knees are grubby, the shoes look worn at the tips, my general appearance is crumpled. It's the eyes that are the giveaway. I'm looking out of the corner of them to the right, they're full of mischief, I'm waiting like a young hound to be released and do more damage. The photograph makes me smile. It is a moment more than itself, it tells of the second before and hints at what might have followed. Della must have received special permission to be there. My parents aren't there because my mother barely got on with her sisters-in-law, and my father being a black sheep was rarely invited to anything anywhere!

There's another photograph, part of a set, taken by an East End photographer who photographed us all – Jerome. My arms are folded, leaning on a table or a ledge. Jerome has asked me to look in different directions. One is in profile, the second is full face. I look at the images. They touch me.

Immodest though it sounds, it is a sweet face. I may not be much loved now but I can see why I was loved and indulged then. Those eyes tell that whatever wildness drove the 'dead-end kid' was tempered by gentleness and affection. More, they tell of having *received* gentleness and affection. I look at that boy, who I so long to meet again, and can tell, feel, something of his life and family, but why can't I feel *him*? Why can't I *feel* him? I would love to encounter that boy christened 'eagle strength'.

These are the things I might find him doing, though I don't know when, exactly, or with whom: playing games in the enclosed playground of Rothschild's Buildings – marbles, rounders, hoops, small wooden spinning tops whipped with a thin strand of leather tied to the end of a stick, soap bubbles blown out of clay pipes. With a debonair flourish I spin cigarette cards in crafty curves to cover my opponents'. I'm throwing hazel nuts into matzo boxes with holes in them. I'm amusing myself blowing bubbles from a film of soap spread between forefinger and thumb – a skill shared with my children and granddaughter. (I'd share it with my grandson if you'd let me, Lindsay Joe.) I'm sliding on metal studs which some shoes have nailed in their soles to make them last longer. I'm skipping – in those days boys as well as girls skipped, and jumped over ropes in a game called 'higher and higher'.

I nagged for things seen in toy shops, or toy departments or stationery shops like Strakers on the corner of Brick Lane and Whitechapel: a conductor's set, once. And once I remember using all my powers of persuasion, pointing out what wonders of sculpture would appear if only my mother bought me a box of coloured plasticine. And Monopoly, a game of capitalism played endlessly and excitedly by a bolshevik family of squabbling business failures who satiated their avariciousness over a board game rather than in the property market. Surprising, really, for I learned at a tender age the simple truth that if you bought the slums of Old Kent Road and Whitechapel – brown – and Pentonville Road, Euston Road, and the Angel Islington – light blue – you made your fortune faster than those struggling with the high cost of building Bond Street, Regent Street, and Oxford Street – green – Park Lane and Mayfair – dark blue – who could then be bankrupted and bought for a song. My father astonished us one day by returning in his ARP tin helmet and long, dark blue coat from an all-night session of fire-spotting duty, with hundreds of Monopoly notes 'rescued' from a bombed-out shop. Used them for years.

If you 'made out' with someone today it would signify you had made love with them; to 'make out' in my childhood meant to break off friendship. 'I'm making out with you,' you'd say to a friend you no longer wanted as a friend, repeatedly sliding the inside of your left forefinger away from you in your curved right forefinger. Minutes later, making up because you'd been offered a placatory sweet, you'd link and shake little fingers. Primitive rituals going back to God knows when.

With cousin Bryan I played 'twopenny ha'penny football': a penny each as the player and a halfpenny for the ball. The aim was, using the edge of a comb, to knock your penny against the ball and get it into the goal. It required an elementary billiard-ball skill to hit the halfpenny at an angle.

Was it with Bryan that I set up and tickled a crystal set with heavy earphones to catch radio sounds?

In addition to the sophisticated games of solo and clubyash I'd find me playing the card games of Newmarket and sevens; the solitary game of patience, and a variation called Kings. Never bridge. In later life whist, poker, rummy, and kaluki but not bridge. Nor did I play a good game of chess. I was a sneaky draughts player but could never plan far enough ahead for chess. What a curious reflection of male/female relationships that game is – the Queen, who must protect the King, can move backwards and forwards horizontally and diagonally at will, while the King, the object of everyone's evil schemes and attacks, can only limp around, crippled, one space at a time.

There was another street game which I can't make sense of in my memory. It involves leaping on to the backs of friends bent double, hands hugging each other's haunches, the front one pushing against the wall. What on earth were we doing? I thrilled to the 'chariot fight', however. Two boys would crisscross and clutch each others hands from behind; a third would bend, holding on to the linked arms; a fourth would straddle, sometimes stand on, the third's back and 'the chariot' lurched into battle with another, the aim being to haul the rider off his perch. It's a childhood memory I used in *Their Very Own and Golden City* as an image of youth riding bravely into a future they could not know would fail their dreams.

At cricket and football I was more stylish than skilful. To be honest – I was hopeless! I'd burst into a run after the ball, get there before an opponent, stand over it as though I knew what I was doing, and then dribble it either straight into my opponent's feet or trip over it, landing on my face crying 'Foul!' Nor could I ski. Friends in Czechoslovakia took me to the gentlest of slopes, clamped me into absurd, unmanageable lengths of lethal wood, and in each hand stuck sticks I had no idea how to use. Fortunately I remembered film footage of professional skiers. I stylishly imitated their crouched stance. And was off! I just didn't know how to stop.

A good moment, this, to dare another confession: the young Byron complex. My teens were full of romantic flourishes – like racing for the football, crouching like I knew how over skis, walking coolly away from cricket stumps rubbing the ball on my trouser leg, standing like Adonis on the edge of a diving board – the swallow in my mind's eye – uttering French words with an impressive French accent. But just as my French sentences collapsed with no grammar to hold them up, so my swallow dive more resembled a plummeting cabbage, my spin balls usually spun a foot wide of the wicket, and I frequently managed to kick the football with the inside of my heel. But young Byron I was – when I was not being D'Artagnan, Lenin or Spencer Tracy.

I do however remember being a good captain. I could organise, lead, encourage those whose skills I recognised were superior to mine; I'm afraid I was frequently the instigator of the raids upon the Woolworths sweet supply, the initiator of truant expeditions, the leader of dangerous escapades like swinging on ropes across collapsed floors in bombed-out warehouses. Later, during Upton House days, there developed an annual winter battle between us and the roughnecks from nearby Berger Road School, by the Berger paint factory. It began mildly when one lunchtime someone rushed into the playground excitedly announcing that a snowball fight was taking place on a nearby bombed site and our boys were outnumbered. A group of us rushed to the spot. High-spirited snowballing was in progress. It was fun. The fun intensified as we began to be systematic and I organised the building of stockpiles of balls in strategic places so that heavily equipped front lines could storm at the enemy without having to pause, bend down, and mould a white shell every second. The other side quickly learned. I think the battles occurred on three winters – our winter sports – growing in both sophistication and urgency until one day one of our side sustained a cut eye. The enemy – a yob elementary school, what could you expect! – had begun putting stones inside the pressed flakes. The headmaster intervened. My army command came to an end.

A car ran me down, once, in Fashion Street, as I was playing a game of 'Tin-can-copper', like this: a tin was thrown down the street, I had to run for it, slowly walk backwards, the others hid, I had to search for them. As soon as I saw someone I'd rush back to the tin and bang it on the road calling, 'Tin-can-copper I see Martin hiding in number 39!' While hunting, the hiders would have to reach the can before I could return to it. If successful they'd bang and shout, 'Tin-can-copper – home!' One day I walked backwards into a car. It was moving slowly but, not believing I would continue walking backwards, didn't stop. How didn't I hear it? It bumped me on to its bonnet and I rolled over into the road. Everyone called for my mother, who took me into the passage of number 43 and, in front of my friends, pulled down my trousers searching for bruises and broken bones. I was unharmed, merely mortified.

During the Fashion Street days I built a balsawood raft and sailed it alone across an Emergency Water Supply tank – bricked pools of filthy water established throughout London from which to pump out incendiary fires in case the mains supply had been put out of action. Many children drowned in them. I was caught by a policeman who invited me to show him where I lived – he was going to tell on me. During the walk to Fashion Street I sweet-talked him out of reporting me to my parents. He left me in front of number 43 with a stern warning about the dangers of life which, to my shame and downfall, I heeded not.

One of the first most stupid acts I ever committed established a pattern of stupid acts which I have repeated throughout my life. It was a playground craze I brought into the Weald Square flat, lasting a brief period during the Upton House days. We brought to school old keys, thin tubes of metal with a hole in the teeth end and an elliptical eye at the handle end, filled the hole with the sulphurous tips of red matchsticks, wedged in a nail, tied string through the eye, and twirled it round to fly as high as possible into the air. On landing the nail would be rammed into the key's barrel, causing a satisfying little explosion. Aged about thirteen and unscientific I attempted this in one of the Weald Square rooms: matchstick tips into barrel, swing key up – not too high or it would hit the ceiling – descend, but no explosion. Insufficient powder in the barrel, obviously. Break off more tips, fill the key's hole, swing, descend. Still no explosion. I kept filling the hole and swinging it up until, frustrated, I held the key between my thumb and forefinger and banged the nail in with the back end of a black wire hairbrush, determined to have my fireworks. I had my fireworks all right, a nice little explosion which took off the end of a forefinger and thumb, part of an eyebrow, and some eyelashes. There's still a space among the right lashes as evidence.

The incident is significant. Intelligence spans a spectrum of colours and hues. The most intelligent are well hued; others, like me, are not so well hued. Whatever hue of intelligence was needed to tell me that banging a barrelful of red matchstick tips would result in a painful explosion, I seemed deficient in. The deficiency has led me to climb ladders that can't carry me, wash wine glasses in water that is too hot, defy gravity by piling books too high, garden with spectacles hanging round my neck so that I choke on an over-hanging branch or lose a lens. Friends and relatives will no doubt remember more. I suspect it's also a deficiency that leads me to make the incorrect decision about a route from A to B. If there is a wrong turning to take on the motorway, I will take it.

I wonder, as I write about this deficiency, this lack of the in-telligence hue which enables us to make the right decision or judgement about a certain area in the conduct of life, whether it is the same lack that disables me from knowing about people. I heard on the radio an employer tell of how he can judge a person from a mere telephone conversation. I can judge no one until I've had a re-lationship with them – either social, professional, or amorous. People reveal themselves to me through their behaviour. Not the most efficacious way to make friends and fortune. I may sense something not quite right about a person but always doubt my initial judgement, fearing to be wrong, so I start off giving everyone the benefit of the doubt. Not wise. Not comfortable. To begin a re-lationship at 100 per cent means it can only ever progress downhill as the disappointments accumulate. Better the person blessed with confidence enough to credit newcomers with no attributes whatso-ever; their relationships can only improve as each surprising quality unfolds to reveal another. I am not blessed. The required hue is missing. It is presumably the same lack detected in me by the radio and TV director, Margaret Windham, who had directed *Caritas* and *Bluey* on radio: 'Your trouble is, Arnold, you remain loyal to third-rate talents.' I blow off thumbs, lose my way, misjudge the heat of water and the hearts of people. It has not made for the most successful of lives.

The problem with me and games is that though I enjoy winning, winning is not important to me. They say we reveal ourselves in the way we play games. If so then this autobiographical revelation tells I am not competitive. You're not like that either, are you, Lindsay Joe? Do you remember how it upset you if ever we played a game

139

and I lost? Lovable, endearing, that. We're all determined, though, in our family. Hard workers with high standards in what we pursue, but competitive we are not. I think this absence of a competitive spirit has been a source of hostility and resentment: how dare I be so confident that I feel no need to compete?

> I used to drive a car, believe it or believe it not, and there was never a journey without meeting some little smart-arse at the lights who'd grin at me through his window and rev his engine. He wanted to be the first off on the yellow, see! What did you do, Lady Lemon? You revved to make him *think* you were competing and when the lights changed you stayed stock still. Made the little smart-arse really smart.
>
> Let 'em win! Let the relentless silly buggers win!
>
> *Whatever Happened to Betty Lemon*

Health

An incident took place in my late teens which shaped my attitude towards medical matters and pain, and led to my arriving three days away from death's door. Very little went wrong with the Fashion Street 'dead-end kid'. I survived chickenpox, swallowed the eye of my teddy bear, and later a shilling piece which my mother never believed. An X-ray taken in the London Hospital revealed nothing and confirmed for her that I'd spent it, despite the logic of the doctor's suggestion that it might have 'passed through'. I seemed constantly to be having my teeth out or filled, due no doubt to the dreadful boiled sweets I sucked and impatiently crunched. Two front teeth emerged at angles, uncertain whether to retreat or protrude, but somehow sensibly grew straight without the aid of a brace. I developed impetigo and had to be tied down in a hospital bed to prevent my fingers digging out the scabs. And once I went to a convalescent home – convalescing from what, I've no idea – in

Broadstairs near a beauty spot I always thought to be 'The Devil's Sponge Hole' until later years identified as a dramatic flaw in the landscape known as 'The Devil's Punchbowl'. It was a vile place, the convalescent home. The taste and smell of cabbage made me sick. I was not only forced to eat the cabbage which I vomited up, but forced to eat the vomit, too! I seemed not to have got it right with authority from the start!

When it was time to have my tonsils out my mother had to chase me round the table before she could grab and haul me off. Even before leaving I had to be slapped into submission, more as a game than a beating.

'You coming to the hospital?'

'No!' Wallop!

'You coming to the hospital?'

'No!' Wallop!

'You still not coming to the hospital?'

'I'm still not coming to the hospital!' Wallop, wallop!

Light slaps, till I agreed, probably more tired of the game than cowed. A minor operation, but one that gave me my first and only hallucination. I used to lie in bed praying to see a ghost. My prayers were answered. Feverish from the fright of hospital and brutal instruments I woke up in the middle of the night and stared ahead at a chest of drawers, seated upon which, like grey stone busts, were the head and shoulders of the doctor and nurse. He hovers in my memory attired more like a priest, but the matron is clearly there with a flat-topped matron's hat, both staring fiercely at me. I was petrified, in the literal sense, unable to move a muscle or make a sound. All I could do was close my eyes again. A hue of intelligence was at work on that occasion, telling me that if I closed my eyes the images would disappear. So confident was I that I dared open them again after some seconds. The images had gone. I was able to go back to sleep.

So, an illness-free childhood, apart from weak ankles which I constantly ricked and had to encase in elastic bandages. Even my eyesight remained till just gone forty, despite that I always wanted to wear glasses, imagining they would make me look more intelligent. An illness-free life in fact, apart from this one threat I am about to relate, when Old Nick nearly came close enough to bestow his kiss.

Around the age of seventeen a pain developed in my chest. I took little notice until aunts Ann and Sara nagged me to have myself X-rayed at the London Hospital. The doctor who hung up the black and white negatives in front of a lamp to explain what had been found was an ashen-faced, weary man weighed down by the parade of pain and misery he had to witness and respond to day after day. 'This,' he pointed out, 'is the duodenum. In it you have an ulcer. It's called a duodenal ulcer.' Those or some such words rang like bells of doom made more awesome by his sepulchral tones. My response makes me blush as I recall it. Remember, I was not only young Byron, I also wanted to be an actor; my sense of the dramatic was ever present if unsubtle; I wrote heavyweight poetry with titles like 'Loneliness', 'Metamorphosis', 'So Sad a Day My Love', 'Death'; and first lines like 'From these mad miasmatic eyes . . .' , 'Through the black of nights and thoughts . . .' , 'Death . . . is man's last answer to existence . . .'

As the gaunt and probably underpaid medic listed what I had from now on to eat and not eat for the rest of my life (milk dishes – fine, fried fish and chips – forbidden) I rolled the Latin around in my imagination: duodenal ulcer, duodenal ulcer! The affliction ravaging my insides could be nothing but fatal. The moment obviously called for Byronic heroism.

'Doctor,' I said, my voice low and humble, 'you will . . . you will . . . you will tell me if . . .' The look in my eyes and the pleading ring of my delivery of the word 'if' left him in no doubt how the line ended.

'Yes,' he said, successfully hiding his amusement and responding generously to my melodramatics, 'I will!'

When, years later, I discovered that anybody who was both anybody or nobody suffered from this rudimentary pain, especially Jews with their neurosis about everything, I vowed never again to take pain too seriously. A hypochondriac would I not be – though these days I enjoy wringing wry humour out of the physical disintegration that accompanies ageing.

So there came a day in 1963, shortly following the arduous, adrenalin-pumping Fortytwo festivals, when I developed a pain in my back to which I paid scant attention – a passing strain from a too-sudden exertion I'd forgotten about. The pain increased and I thought it prudent to offer it up to my (then) doctor, one of the old kind about whom my Norfolk mother-in-law would explain: 'You know what they say about him – if you've got a headache you're all right, but if you've got something more you've had it!' It was true. I had something more and nearly 'had it'.

At first he prescribed painkillers, taking his diagnosis from my dismissive description of, and explanation for, the stabbings in the back. When the pain persisted he took a guess it might be a virus and prescribed antibiotics. The pain sharpened and I found myself beginning to stoop, but still imagined it would pass, and continued going into the Centre Fortytwo offices in 20 Fitzroy Square, attending meeting after meeting, trying to raise funds and interest in the organisation's future. Friends recommended osteopathy. If, as I told everyone, I had pulled a muscle then it had to be clicked back into place again. One osteopath manipulated my torso into such contortions of pain that my arm jerked and I nearly fisted him flat. Another, observing the pain I was in, advised me to come back when it had passed. I took his advice, but the pain never passed.

About this time a lunch date had been made with J.B. Priestley and his wife, Jacquetta Hawkes, at their Albany flat in Piccadilly to persuade him to sign the Fortytwo Appeal. I was flat on my back, too ill to keep the date. Instead we invited them to Bishops Road, promising that Dusty would bring lunch up into my bedroom. They graciously agreed. There they sat, poor dears, in front of the window, food on their laps, eating and conversing with this wild-eyed young colleague rendered prone with pain caused by he knew not what, confusing their sympathies between his hurt and his dream to convert the Roundhouse in Chalk Farm into a pulsating centre for art aimed at a popular audience. None of us could know I was delirious from toxic poisoning, though J.B. might have guessed when I asked him:

'Tell me, J.B. I've calculated that if there are 75,000 English-speaking amateur companies around the world paying £10 per performance, and if only a third of them perform just one of my five plays once in the course of five years I'd earn £250,000 – that's £50,000 a year for amateur rights alone, which would do nicely, but am I right? I mean – what are *your* earnings from amateur royalties?' I think he smiled a canny Yorkshireman's smile and gave a canny Yorkshireman's reply. 'Not bad, not bad, aye, lad, not bad.' I never made anything resembling that amount of money from my amateur royalties, not even up to this day thirty years and twenty-eight plays later, though I've no doubt J.B. did, for he was an intelligent man with a popular touch which seems to have eluded me. He signed the appeal.

Next morning I woke in a state never before encountered. I had sweated so much that not only my pyjamas but the sheets were wet. Not merely damp. Wringable. 'I think,' I told Dusty, 'something is serious. You'd better call the doctor, useless though he is. Even he must see something's not right.' He came and fortunately had the wit and humility to see something was indeed not right.

'I'll call the local butcher,' he said. Ho! Ho!

A marvellous surgeon sped up from the Whittington Hospital, gave me a brief inspection, asked a few questions, darkened with rage when I told him about osteopaths, and said, 'I'll call the ambulance now and operate in two hours.' He drained the poison from me that had spread throughout my body from a couple of abscesses which had blossomed gloriously in the region of the kidneys. 'Three more days and you'd have been dead,' he informed me. Mr Stidolph was his name. He saved my life and I will forever be grateful to him.

And then there was hair. Or rather, then there was *not* hair. Baldness. Uncle Perly went bald, and Uncle Barney, and Barney's boy, Boomy, and my two sons. It began while working as a chef in

Paris. I went for a haircut and was proffered one of the most chilling remarks ever made to me: 'Monsieur, vos cheveux sont malades!' Men and hair. It seems to matter, or did then. Lindsay and Daniel, my sons, appear not to mind. Nor has it affected their sense of themselves as attractive young men, but I must have been deeply affrighted, for following the French barber's casual doomsday observation I suffered recurring nightmares in which I was pulling out tufts of hair. My two sons are bald, but *grâce à* Leonard, a barber in Jermyn Street to whom Noël Coward and John Dexter went in the sixties and who advised me to wash my hair every day, massaging the scalp, I've succeeded in hanging on to enough to appease my poor vanity. Years later I discovered 'popping'.

On a visit to New York we were invited to a Sunday matinée concert conducted by Leonard Bernstein who called us backstage to his dressing room, large and full of people. Bernstein sat at his piano being photographed and talking with his manager. Finally he came and sat by us to chat but even then combined it with another activity. A woman threw a cloth round him, as at a barber, and began to massage his head – that famous head full of wavy grey hair. At a certain moment she stopped and engaged in the most curious of actions. She twisted a lock around her forefinger, paused, then gave a sharp jerk which produced a clicking sound. When she'd done this a number of times I couldn't contain myself and had to ask what on earth she was doing. Bernstein replied: 'I'm glad you asked. She's popping my hair.'

'What's popping?'

'I'm glad you asked. Now,' it was Bernstein the teacher, '*you* think the difference between men and women is tits and all that. Well, let me tell you, it's not. It's this.' He presented the back of his very hairy hand and pinched the skin. 'You see this? Between the bone and the skin there's gristle. Hair can grow because blood flows easily. That's what there is on a woman's head. Between her scalp and skin is gristle. She never goes bald. See this?' He clenched his fist and presented a knuckle. 'No hair! Why? Because there's no gristle. That's what a man's head is like. No gristle. And if the skin gets too tight on the bone blood can't flow, hair can't grow. This lady behind me, when she pulls, is pulling the skin off the bone and allowing the blood to rush through, nourishing the roots, which is how I keep my hair.'

'Doesn't it hurt?' I asked.

'When you don't hear the "pop" – it hurts.'

I offer up silent prayers to be so far unafflicted by any serious illness – though why I tempt fate this way I can't say. It is still possible to drop dead from a heart attack, my cholesterol used to be high. Do you remember, Lindsay Joe, I had to take all the children to the Whittington for blood tests – cholesterol was thought to be hereditary. You laughed about it and passed out. Remember?

The moral of the abscess tale is: avoid falling in love with a cherished image of yourself. My first love was the doomed, ulcerated Byronic young man bravely facing his death; my second love was the Byronic debonair insouciant whom nothing ill could befall. Well, all befell, sooner or later! Poison within and without.

But not upon the Fashion Street kid. All health to him, slums or no slums. Have I finished with Fashion Street now? Not quite.

Mrs Levy

Poor old Mrs Levy was brought over from, I think, Poland by her husband who soon died and left her with an assortment of goods and chattels overcrowding her dingy basement flat in Nathaniel Buildings, opposite my grandmother's Charlotte de Rothschild's Dwellings in Flower and Dean Street. Was Mrs Levy 'old'? Aged nine one never knows. She was penniless and unable to speak English. My mother adopted her and drew her to the attention of the Jewish Welfare, arranging for her to collect food and clothes from the Soup Kitchen For The Jewish Poor – a building painted by John Allin for the *Stepney Streets* folio – which still stands in Brune Street, E1, though doesn't function.

I often shopped for Mrs Levy, in the beginning with my mother then off my own volition. When we knocked she opened the door a fraction, peering out in fear. She was yellow from no sunlight. Her room was squalid. Cases, pieces of European furniture, cluttered surfaces – one in particular with unopened tins of soup. It was here I encountered for the first time, poised on a mantelpiece alongside empty pipe boxes, a stuffed bird in a glass case. Intriguing for a child. How did it get in there so whole and lifelike? Had it ever been real? Aged nine who knew of taxidermy? The diminutive, timid old lady – she couldn't have been more than forty – slept in a bed of sheets which seemed never to have been changed. Hardly a room lived in, rather more one in which objects had been dumped, waiting to be taken somewhere else. That was it! Mrs Levy and her belongings were in a state of transit.

My mother was an ever-hopeful and meticulous football pools player.

Things I must do with my £75,000

1. Buy a house large enough for my daughter, my son, their families and me to live in so that we are all together.
2. Present them with the money they need to live their lives.
3. Give my brothers Hymie, Stanley and Martin £3000 each.
4. Give my friend Lottie £1000. And also Maurice, Jackie, Gertie.
5. Spend £20 on a holiday in a little seaside village.
6. Buy myself a pair of fur-lined boots for winter.
7. Pay back £10 to Steve Isaacs.

And so on. A long list of numbered items with each detail carefully written out, and changes seriously made to the order and relative importance of certain articles of clothing.

Now she carefully scrutinised her list and made one more correction. In between items 4 and 5, that is to say after giving £1000 to Lottie, Maurice, Jackie and Gertie and before allotting £20 for her holiday, she wrote:

5. Put aside £5000 to help Mrs Levy.

Then she folded up her list and laid it aside.

'Pools' – a short story

My mother never won the pools. Mrs Levy didn't receive her £5000 nor my uncles their £3000.

I can't remember when we stopped visiting Mrs Levy. I don't know how she died. Unlike my grandparents she had no children or relatives to care for her; nor was her plight helped by her stubbornness – fear mixed with pride mixed with simple-mindedness.

Boba and Zeyda

I've not written much about grandparents, memories of them are thin. The Zeyda was half blind. I can just recall him tapping his way with a white stick from Flower and Dean Street round the corner to where we lived in Fashion Street. Unlike the rest of the Wesker family he liked my mother and enjoyed visiting us. She made him matzo-brile – crumpled matzo softened up by hot water then soaked in whipped eggs and fried in butter. Sugared or salted, I make it for myself even to this day. I only ever knew my grandmother when she was bedridden with arthritis. I remember her kindness, the purse under the pillow, her coughing and phlegm, a smell of sennapods kept on the kitchen windowsill. That kitchen! That flat! That building! All more vivid than she is in memory.

In a way Charlotte de Rothschild's Dwellings was a handsomely conceived block. Though without hot water or bathrooms it let in light and provided an enclosed, protected space for play. Because I spent half my childhood in that flat its details are clear. Tiny but packed – divan under the window looking out to the playground, chest of drawers at right angles, two armchairs by a fire, a pull-out table in the middle, chairs around it, the Boba's bed in an alcove, a cabinet with records and books and over it a shelf carrying the crackling radio, a cupboard for crockery on top, tins, jars and boxes

of food beneath, and a certain tin, always full of sweets and chocolate, the first thing I made for on entering their flat. In later years I
built them shelves for their records. When they were offered a flat
in Chingford I helped them move and built more shelves for their
books. The kitchen was tiny – a sink, a gas stove, a kitchen cabinet,
a fireplace, an open storage area for kitchen utensils above and coal
beneath, covered by a curtain. I'd earn ha'pennies shopping for
them. My second home, my second library, my concert hall. I
dream a recurring dream of return – I'm either in my aunts' kitchen
or running a restaurant!

When the Boba died and the aunts had gathered to mourn I
wanted to cheer them up. I offered a daft 'performance' with crockery to my grieving aunts – a gravity-defying balancing act, or was it
a hopeless juggling act? Whatever, I failed lamentably. There was a
crash. I went crimson with shame. The aunts scolded, except Ann
the chuckler whose ashes lie in my garden: 'Ah, leave him alone.
Look, you're making him cry. He was only trying to cheer us up!'
May she rest in peace.

A boy-beneath a lorry

What significance resides in another image – a boy beneath a lorry?
What precursor of reactions to come? I was on an errand and had
run to the top of Fashion Street, the greengrocer end (where now
there's a large Asian textile shop called Marks and Menders!). To
my right, in Brick Lane, was a lorry. A small, agitated crowd had
gathered around the bonnet where the driver had only just, it
seemed, arrived to find a young boy on his back, his leg pinned by a
front wheel, writhing. That's all I saw. My reaction was this: I
looked, was upset, instantly turned to run back, ran a few steps,
stopped, went back as though to continue on my errand perhaps
not believing what I'd seen, turned and turned again. Disaster,
shock, confusion, paralysis! I have no memory beyond that: not of

continuing the errand nor of returning home to report what I'd seen, nor of hanging around to see how the child fared.

Did I continue living my life this way, running from disaster to paralysis? Occasionally, yes. Mostly I'd like to think not. My old girlfriend, Audrey, died of cancer, and though she expressed a wish that I shouldn't visit her to witness how the advanced state of illness had robbed her of youth and prettiness, yet I should have insisted. I retained guilts for that, which I tried to wash away along with others in a radio play called *Bluey*. These days, as I write, Aunt Billie, the last of my father's sisters, is in a home withering from senile dementia. She was a dear aunt, a stern Wesker but unhesitatingly kind and forgiving. I can't bring myself to visit her. I know it will upset me and be of no comfort to her. I also know I should. On the other hand I was the only one in the family who regularly visited and cared about Aunt Ann, hoovering and cleaning out her flat and frequently taking home soiled underwear which I washed by hand rather than give it to Dusty. What is beyond my help and comfort I leave be, and only face unhappiness I feel able to alleviate. Perhaps there is no link between my reaction to the boy beneath the lorry and the rest of my life. No patterns, just a chaos of responses.

Chapter Seven

Stepney to Hackney

My mother continuously applied to be given an LCC flat. Her friend, Lily, had been moved from Bacon Street, near the arches end of Brick Lane, to a council flat – Millington House, number 30, in Stoke Newington Church Street adjacent to Green Lanes, opposite Clissold Park – a move from darkness into light. My mother wanted the same for us. Della remembers her being offered council flats, handsome and well equipped with modern facilities, which she turned down because the rent was too high. One, near Hackney Marshes, she turned down because there was a kitchen range in the front room – a layout utterly alien to her. Nor were the Marshes a Jewish area. The Upper Clapton Road, on the other hand, stretching from Clapton Pond to Stamford Hill, now the centre of the Chassidic community, was very Jewish. And more, Weald Square, a block in the LCC Northwold Estate facing the Upper Clapton Road – three floors up, no lift, ugly iron railings on the balcony instead of brick – was cheaper. We moved there in December 1942. The Blitz is over. But the war continues. The previous month, November 1942, the British and American forces landed in French North Africa – Morocco and Algeria – the beginning of their thrust east which took them through Sicily up into Italy.

We had our own front door at the end of a landing – which meant neighbours on only three sides instead of four – two bedrooms, a front room, a dining room, a separate kitchen, our own lavatory. No separate bathroom, no hot running water, no central heating – just a coal fire – but we had space. Space, space, space! and, most important for me, I had a room of my own. Ten years old, evacuated into other people's space, sardined into Fashion Street, but now? – the Upper Clapton Road was wide, and pretty

Springfield Park only a ten-minute walk away, with a putting green on which I was to spend hours knocking a golf ball into holes with a primitive golf club hired for about 9d. And beyond the park the River Lea! Rowing boats! Tall grass the other side for hidden hugs and wet kisses, while further up, on Lea Marshes, the seasonal fairs. Della lived in Riverside Road, close to the Lea, further north.

Most important, the extended family was not far away. The Kurtas in Stoke Newington, the Lipsons in Finsbury Park and Highbury, the Perlmutters in Dalston Junction and Kingsland High Road.

The furthest were Uncle Perly and Aunty Bet with cousins June and David. The house in Cheam Common Road would remain a day's outing, the treat, for many years to come.

The ones who lost out were aunts Ann and Sara. They were to remain in Charlotte de Rothschild's Dwellings for another six years until they too were taken out of the dark into the light, from grubby Flower and Dean Street to a ground-floor flat in a dreary suburban house in a quiet suburban road – number 7 Ashley Road – in Chingford. I don't think they had been too worried about remaining in the East End – Sara was near her union offices, and Ann was near her workplace – a tailor's machinist in a clothing factory.

I was to live in 32 Weald Square, with only an eighteen-month break for National Service and a nine-month break working in a Paris kitchen, until marriage in 1958. Sixteen years. Childhood to manhood. In the beginning I played cricket and football in the tarmac playground, at the end I was being photographed in the same playground for *Reynold's News*, hanging out washing. Across that playground, in a block called Woolmer House, lived a young boy whose family arrived after ours, and who was destined to become a multimillionaire in the hi-tech age that was upon us with the advent of the microchip – the Amstrad man, Alan Sugar. We didn't know each other, and later when I wrote to him looking for arts sponsorship he didn't consider our shared domicile sufficient reason for even the courtesy of a reply. The school I was to go to, Upton House Central, was a pale shadow of the upmarket school nearby,

Grocers, a grammar school which schooled another playwright who, five years later, I was to see give a fine performance (or so it seemed to me at the time) as Macbeth in a school production – Harold Pinter.

As the war progresses and I grow older the second front opens and a large map of the world gets pinned up on the wall in the front room of Weald Square, on which I plot the advance of the Allies. The British, French and Americans cross France and Germany from the west; the Russians through Poland, Rumania, Hungary, Yugoslavia, from the east – both sides converging upon Berlin. East and west will meet. The Soviet, French, American and British soldiers will clasp each other in friendship, congratulate each other on winning the war; the Berlin wall will be built as a new chill sets in, and vast amounts of money and resources will be spent re-arming. It is appalling and none of it stops me enjoying life, family and friends and embarking upon puberty, poetry, amateur dramatics and the quest for love.

Battle to move

One year and one month after moving into Weald Square my mother – using the handwriting of a friend – wrote to the LCC asking to be moved again.

> The flat in which I am now living, although clean and roomy, lacks the most necessary convenience, namely a separate bathroom. The bath in the flat is situated in the scullery and should I or any other member of my family desire to use it we have to fill the bath with water by hand, there being no mechanical device for doing so. Thus, this is very hard on me, especially as I am not strong. The stairs, too, are an added inconvenience as this flat is on the third floor.

If you will kindly give this matter your attention and consideration I shall be much obliged.

Yours faithfully,

L. Wesker pp

Who wrote it for her, I wonder? Her request was not granted. Nor was it entirely honest – she was diminutive but strong – which is why, I imagine, there was no second letter. Someone probably put it to her that she should not have accepted the flat without a bath. Lily had one, after all! She had tried her luck.

Years later, however, there was a very good reason for the council to offer her a change of flat – my father fell ill. From the time of his first stroke there issued forth from 32 Weald Square to the housing department of the LCC a barrage of letters appealing for an exchange, mostly worded and typed by me. I didn't win. Leah continued to nurse her husband from a third- floor flat with no bath or hot running water until he died and she replaced his illness with her own. It was only much later, in the spring of 1968, seven years into my career – the LCC had become the Greater London Council – that my unhappy mother was offered and accepted a new flat: number 21 Landor Court, Boleyn Road, N16, first floor, two rooms with kitchen and bathroom, rent 60/6d – including rates, water charges and central heating. My heart sank moving her in; it seemed so much smaller than Weald Square.

Well I am here in 21 Landor Court. I can't say I am very happy at all. I have good reasons not to be happy. The bedroom is filled with a smell of coke burning on the installation of the sink hot water. I cannot go in to sleep. I am sleeping on the divan in the sitting room. I cannot go off to sleep.

Leah's diary, dated 28.5.68

Nine days later she seems a little happier, despite the weather which always affected her.

I don't ever remember such awful miserable rainy day . . . It should
have been a flaming month . . . only the birds seem to believe that it
is nice because they are switing and singing as if it's really their summer even though it's raining cats and dogs and miserable. I must say
this district where I am, particularly this estate, is very romantic. I
may feel a bit lonely – it's actually built in the heart of the slums –
and yet as I sit here writing, waiting for rain to stop and sun to come
about I feel as if I am in a suburb with lots of green trees and birds
are singing. I really don't feel as miserable on such days as to day as
I did in Weald Square. I don't really know why. I can only put it
down to the reason that this flat is all furnished new, and I like it.
Thanks to my children. I have very good children. I do love them.

It worried me in later years that we had foolishly rushed to buy new
furniture when she should have been surrounded by familiar pieces.
She held on to many but there was not enough room. Della and I
divided what couldn't be fitted in. To create an atmosphere of familiarity and family I had two huge blow-ups printed in sepia, of Della
aged twenty, and of me with Tanya Jo as a little girl leaning on my
lap, which hung on her new wall. Nothing really helped. Only now,
having gone through the painful experience of quitting a house saturated with ardent memories, do I understand what it must have
meant for her. Eight years later she was dead.

A *room of my own*

Could it have been more than twelve by eight feet? A box of a
room. Ordinary. The window looked out into Weald Square's playground where children played and washing was hung. I had it from
the start and consider myself privileged.

With a room of my own came the habit of hoarding and order. I
filed my poems, laid out sheets of paper and carbons in drawers,
lined my books in alphabetical order on shelves and windowsills.
Hoarded and hung. A room of my own encouraged a mania for

hanging things – an animal instinct for claiming a space. Actors do it to their dressing rooms. Up go first-night cards; a table becomes littered with paraphernalia from home – a favourite cushion, a scarf draping a cherished mirror, a worn blanket for naps. The hoarding of my fifty years lives in boxes numbered one to sixty-eight, noted on computer sheets, up in the attics of Ashley Road and Blaendi-geddi. Ideally I'd like to build a separate storage room that would accommodate it all: original manuscripts, fifty novels-worth of diary handwritten in notebooks, student theses, Fortytwo's archives, royalty statements, book proofs, copies of *Time Out* dating back to the first edition, letters from agents, letters from translators, letters from organisations inviting me to lecture and donate money, correspondence from all and sundry. And chequebooks. Everything is hoarded including my first ever chequebook, beginning June 1958. (The first cheque, dated 7 June 1958, is for £12.10.0. recorded as 'self for Beck Farm'. Beck Farm was where Dusty's parents lived outside Harleston in Norfolk, where her mother still lives. On 20 June I'm there and begin writing *Roots*.)

These days, despite some of the boxes being full of clutter, I'm still able to find a newspaper cutting, a photo, old accounts. And around the house I know where is, and can reach for, a book, a nail, a coffee bean, tea bag, sticky label, spade, socks, clean towel, toilet roll, cassette tape, Sellotape, printed notepaper, compost, magazine or postage stamp. Or large brown envelopes. I hoard – wrapping paper, string, plastic bags, plastic ice cream containers, foreign stamps, and large brown envelopes.

Most letters are answered on the same day and scripts promised are dispatched immediately. A plastic sleeve contains a follow-up file. In the pc are directories that record: all requests for performing rights; to whom scripts were sent and when; all daily output of letters, faxes, postcards and packages; a bibliography of printed material, and much else. I don't think my instinct for order is anal, since disorder is around, too.

My latest obsession is to record selected telephone messages on to tape. There is no phone in this study, only in the main house which is across a courtyard. Messages accumulate. As these years have been sad I have kept the voices of a distressed wife, concerned friends and relatives, the warm, deep tones of a patient MoJo, as well as professional and domestic calls. It struck me that in the sequence of such messages, through a combination of words with timbre of voice, a kind of life is chronicled.

And all because from the age of ten I was given a room of my own which invited me to keep order. What would have happened without it? What of character? This claim I make of being a free spirit (yes, yes, I know, no one is *really* free), does such confidence begin in a room of one's own? I know only that I basked in the new freedom offered by this LCC flat on the Upper Clapton Road, a room which I laid out, arranged and rearranged countless number of times.

The LCC estate

Northwold Estate was built around 1934. It consisted of twenty-one brick blocks of varying sizes and layouts – some were just a length, others L-shaped, some three-sided, but all the same height with monotonous ambience. A little 'village' of workers' dwellings. When first built, each block had iron railings made from First World War stretchers. Gradually brick replaced them. Even Weald Square. Except *our* part of Weald Square! For a reason unfathomable they stopped building pretty brick balconies on two blocks numbered 1 to 35, and 55 to 74.

The estate was built at the height of the interwar housing boom. Nearly three million houses went up. It was a boom launched by Lloyd George after the 1914–18 conflict, a scheme of 'homes fit for heroes'. I don't know if those who lived in number 32 before us or before them or before even them, were heroes, certainly we were not. But we were grateful.

Our block, because it had iron railings, looked cheaper. They probably were less rent than the others and the reason why my mother opted for them. The bath was in the kitchen covered by a fold-down slab of wood used as a worktop. I loved sitting on it with my back to the wall, knees hunched up, talking with my mother while she cooked. Often I helped, peeling potatoes, rolling out pastry, shelling peas. We rarely used it as a bath, getting hot water into it was such a long-winded rigmarole. To the left of the long iron enamelled tub was a huge black caldron needing to be filled with cold water and heated by a coal fire underneath, a Fred Kano system which heated the end of the bath as well, as I found out when I leaned against it one day and burned my back. In later years we got rid of it and installed a hot-water heater. It didn't help – to combine the cooking place with the place for bathing was the pinch-penny thinking of idiot architects. Instead we got into the routine of travelling to the Hackney Baths where, though unknown to us, John Allin was a bath attendant.

My father mostly used the vapour baths – the 'schwitz', Yiddish for sweat. 'I suppose you're going to the schwitz again,' my mother would taunt him as he rolled his towels and prepared to escape to a place where everything was on offer except opium. And women. He once took me. As with other things in life I overdid it and stayed in too long. The debilitating heat knocked me out and I had to sleep the afternoon away. I remember the incident because that evening for the first time in my life I was going ice skating with friends. A quarrel ensued with my mother who refused to let me go on the illogical assumption that skating on ice hours after a vapour bath would give me influenza or rheumatoid arthritis or some other killer affliction.

The ritual of taking a public bath was pleasing. You bought a ticket and, if required, a small bar of soap. You could also hire a huge rough bath towel. To enter either schwitz or bath you sat on wooden benches waiting to be called – 'Next!' The schwitz to the left, the baths to the right. 'Next!' Inside, a bath had been mopped clean with a long mop soaped in a bucket filled with all the leftover little soaps, and was filling up with water regulated from the outside by the attendant with a brass hand-held 'tap'. You tested it and, when the water was what you could stand, said 'Fine,' locked the door, undressed, and soaked. When the water cooled you called out, 'More hot number seven, please,' and along came the attendant echoing your call to alert you, 'More hot number seven,' and twisted more hot water into your tub until you scalded and cried out, 'Thank you.' If you stayed in too long he'd knock on your door: 'Out number seven, please.' 'Coming,' you'd reply, and when you finally did emerge rosy-cheeked, clean for the week, relaxed and re-lieved – for a lot of masturbation went on between those green walls, one heard the moans – you called, 'Out number seven!'

Hackney Baths contained two swimming pools – I used those too and had my first wristwatch, given me as a barmitzvah present from Uncle Perly, stolen within days of receiving it.

There were criminal kids in Weald Square but no one ever entered a neighbour's flat. It would have been easy to get into ours, all you had to do was put your hand through the letter box and pull out the key at the end of a piece of string. It's true that at night we'd draw the string aside to hang over the brass lock but that's because there was a dark world beyond neighbours.

The juddering clink of the key being hauled up was an exciting sound, as was the clang of footsteps along the balcony. Would they stop at the Gammers' next door or progress on to us? Who was coming? Who was entering? We had no phone to make dates, announce arrivals. All was unexpected.

Neighbours

We were the fifth Jewish family to take possession in Weald Square. The Kieves had moved there in 1935, a floor below in the corner where the L formed. Mr Kieve, a cabinet-maker who, with his heavy cabinet-maker's hands, played the piano with passion, had a hump and was insistently kind, married to a pretty wife who was quietly kind. They had the most gauche of sons, Jeffrey, who transmogrified into a brilliant economist writing a standard text-book called *Urban Land Economics*, which went into five editions, and another, *The Economic and Social History of the Electronic Tele-graph*, an invention that made a quantum leap in communications. Jeff married a beautiful, buxom girl called Millie who wanted to be an actress. He had made her choose – him or acting. She chose him. They went into property management, with success, and reared four children, one of whom is now a well-known illusionist, Paul Kieve, who devised illusions for such shows as *The Invisible Man*, and David Edgar's version of *The Strange Case of Dr Jekyll and Mr Hyde*. Though Millie didn't regret her choice she hankered through the years to act and in later life did just that, forming her own com-pany. She had become close to my mother in the Weald Square years, staying at number 32 over a period of months while I was in the RAF. Her obsession was to play Sarah in *Chicken Soup with Barley*. Cool, clever Jeffrey made a fortune, collected old postcards, and learned how to play bridge. Millie indulged her passion and mounted a production of *Chicken Soup* at the Half-Moon Theatre near Stepney Green station in the summer of 1987. I enjoy the spec-tacle of lives growing from nowhere and nothing into something unexpected.

Below us were the Mansfields, Alf and Kitty, who fought. Or rather he did, the first wife-beater I ever encountered before know-ing such a social malaise existed. Quiet, well spoken, obliging by day, he became a hysterical malcontent by night. His thick-lensed wife was by this time a pathetic soul. They had two distressed and bewildered children, Gerald and Joan. Sad and disturbing Jewish neighbours who one day moved out. Next door to the Mansfields was another Jewish family, the Greenbergs, who have faded com-pletely from memory.

On the ground floor at number 8 were what seemed like hun-dreds of Phillips. Stern father, patient Jewish mother and lots of laughing offspring. When *Chicken Soup with Barley* opened in Coventry we discovered that one of the laughing sons, Henry, and his wife, Phyllis, had moved there and set up, next door to the Bel-grade Theatre, a branch of The City Pram Shop owned by Phyllis's

uncle, whose main shop was in Finsbury Park. Where we were later
to move! We remained friends over many years, buying from their
range as each of our three children was born, and inheriting from
them a splendidly carved Victorian mantelpiece of embossed
knights and fruit prised from the front room of the house they had
just bought. They had contemplated throwing it into the dustcart.
We begged them to hold on to it until – who knows – the day we
might buy a house, which we did – number 27 Bishops Road. It became the focal point of the long room created by knocking down a
wall – Jews, a response to growing up cramped, always knock down
a wall when they move into a new house, a ritual offering to God
for having survived and prospered against the odds. Countless
family photographs exist in front of that glorious monstrosity.
When we sold the house, the mantelpiece had to stay. Losing both
upset me beyond words. I dream that if ever I become rich and
famous I'll buy back number 27 with its heavy, dark-stained, oak
fire-surround.

Above us were a noisy family, I forget their names, who sounded
as though they spent their nights sawing wood and knocking in
nails. My mother frequently had to use the end of a broom to rap
the ceiling for a little peace. A chilled co-existence hung icily between us.

The Burkes were on the ground floor. My relationship with their
son, Pat, began as one of bully and victim but, as with some bullies,
he had a latent sensitivity which I managed to touch and we ended
friends. The old man, however, was a declared anti-semite whose
barbed remarks we ignored because his wife was a gentle soul. It's
possible he had been a wife-beater too. We also ignored the anti-
semitism of the Bridger family who seemed to consist mainly of
thieves and robbers tracking backwards and forwards between jail
and the next house-break. Their anti-semitism was tempered
because we were such friendly and obliging Jews, always able to
loan a quarter of butter, a 2lb packet of sugar or a packet of Typhoo
tea; besides, we had the saving grace of not being rich or too clever,
which always helps avoid trouble. By the time it was discovered

that Jeff Kieve was clever enough for university and I talented enough to get my name in newspapers, we were entrenched neighbourly neighbours who had shared air-raid shelters during bombing raids and walked back through the night after the all-clear, blankets over our shoulders, exchanging sleepy gratitudes for having survived yet again; old-timers who had grieved together over the death of elderly neighbours.

After my father had his first stroke he became friendly with the two anti-semites, Bridger and Burke – who sound like a hopeless music hall act – for no other reason than that they too had been struck down by strokes. What a bizarre trio they formed.

Poor Harry, he's had two strokes. He won't get any better. Paralysed down one side. He can't control his bowels, you know . . . You think *he* likes it? It's ach-a-nebish [what-a-pity] Harry now. It's not easy for him. But he won't do anything to help himself. I don't know, other men get ill but they fight. Harry's never fought. Funny thing. There were three men like this in the flats, all had strokes. And all three of them seemed to look the same. They walked the same, stooped the same, and all needing a shave. They used to sit outside together and talk for hours on end and smoke. Sit and talk and smoke. That was their life. Then one day one of them decided he wanted to live so he gets up and finds himself a job – running a small shoe menders – and he's earning money now. A miracle! Just like that. But the other one – he wanted to die. I used to see him standing outside in the rain, the pouring rain, getting all wet so that he could catch a cold and die. Well, it happened, last week he died. Influenza. He just didn't want to eat. But Harry wasn't like either of them. He didn't want to die but he doesn't seem to care about living. So! What can you do to help a man like that? I make his food and I buy him cigarettes and he's happy. My only dread is that he'll mess himself. When that happens I go mad – I just don't know what I'm doing . . .

Sarah – *Chicken Soup with Barley*, Act III Scene 1

Mrs Bridger seems to have fought with the council in a way my mother didn't know how, because *they* were moved down to a ground-floor flat; perhaps because of the old man's multiple afflictions – he wheezed as well. A family of Morrises took over. We befriended Alan Morris, one of the sons, who had a spark which never quite took fire: there are such souls, engaged in a conflict old as time between what is glimpsed but unattainable because of what is endowed. Says George, the aspirant playwright in the Osborne/Creighton play, *Epitaph for George Dillon*:

> What is worse is having the same symptoms as talent, the pain, the ugly swellings, the lot – but never knowing whether or not the diagnosis is correct . . .

Alan was a fantasist. He imagined he could drive a car before he could and took Leah, of whom he was fond like a surrogate mother, out for a spin, crashing and bruising her. Later he became a driving instructor and, in after years when we met, was upset that we had learned to drive from someone else. 'I'd've taught you for free.' He had wanted to repay debts. 'Your mum was good to me.'

I turned Peeping Tom on a Morris daughter who undressed behind not-quite-drawn curtains. Voyeur schooled in erotic postcards sneak-previewed in a pub turret, I outed my light, stood behind my own not-quite-drawn curtains and waited for revelations of flesh. I once saw young breasts. Nothing more. And tired quickly from the vigil, partly from shame, partly from impatience.

The neighbours who seared their way into my imagination and became an image of the British working class, blighting, almost irrationally, my perception of them, were the Gammers who lived next door. Mrs Gammer, Lil, was a tall, thin thirty-year-old Cockney with slightly protruding front teeth and a ginger hue about her, whose husband, Bill – Lil and Bill, another music-hall act – shorter in height, and coiled dangerously to snap and hurt, was away in the merchant navy. He had left her a son, Michael. I see her standing outside her door, leaning over the iron balcony looking down from the third floor at the goings-on in the playground – kids hurling football advice at one another, the traffic of neighbours coming and going, of passers-through from Rossington Street to other parts of the estate; a woman waiting, longing, distant. Of course my mother befriended her as she was to befriend Alan Morris and as she had befriended Mrs Levy and others, mostly old Jewish waifs and strays. Lil had to be looked after because her husband was at war for us. She was invited in for meals, sometimes meals and cakes were taken in to her.

Humanity is divided in many ways: rich and poor, sick and healthy, wise and foolish, good and bad, we know them; but perhaps one of the saddest divisions is between givers and takers. My mother belonged to the givers – I think all the Perlmutters were givers – and of the wise and foolish probably belonged to the foolish. The Gammers were neither givers nor foolish. Though our family looked after Lil and young Michael during the last years of the war, she hardly ever returned hospitality. I remember borrowings – neighbours were always borrowing when rations ran out – and I remember we were allowed in her flat for brief periods to exchange gossip, but there was no genuine, warm reciprocity. When her sailor-husband returned to take up civilian life as a bus driver the couple became cooler and even released occasional sour odours of anti-semitism of the kind never overtly expressed, merely hinted at in ways we have come to recognise: 'You people, you always stick together, keep yourselves apart – you can't be surprised if . . .'

In the beginning, though, I sensed none of this corner-of-the-mouth anti-semitism. Young and abandoned Lil Gammer, whose lithe shape I caught through her thin cotton dress, hung around my pubescence. I fantasised being seduced by her. At the same time my mother, torn between her duty as a good communist to love and admire the working class, and her inherited loathing of them as perpetrators of pogroms, quietly complained through the years of the Gammers' tawdry neighbourliness, which confused her loyalties and communicated to me a sense of them as the personification of English, gentile coldness – undemonstrative, tight-lipped, contained, asking for little, giving little, and contemptuous of foreigners. My mother's effusiveness embarrassed them. Our topics of animated conversation, our passionate arguments, the classical music from radio or gramophone heard through thin walls – not too loudly, we were always considerate – the numerous friends and families whose steps went past their door to ours, all must have seemed an incomprehensible irritant to them, inflaming their view of the undesirability of aliens in their midst. We were very alien, and good-natured with it – which made it worse.

One day my mother reported a story about bus driver Bill Gammer which clearly, sharply, and for me, ineradicably, encapsulated their mentality.

. . . Listen, I'll tell you a story. Next door to me, next door where I live is a bus driver. Comes from Hoxton. He's my age, married, and got two kids. He says good morning to me, I ask him how he is, I give his children sweets. That's our relationship. Somehow he seems frightened to say too much, you know? God forbid I might ask him for something. So we make no demands on each other.

Then one day the busmen go on strike. He's out for five weeks. Every morning I say to him, 'Keep going, mate, you'll win!' Every morning I give him words of encouragement, I say I understand his cause. I've got to get up earlier to get to work but I don't mind – we're neighbours – we're workers together – he's pleased.

Then one Sunday there's a peace march. I don't believe they do much good but I go, because in this world a man's got to show he can have his say. The next morning he comes up to me and he says, now listen to this, he says, 'Did you go on that peace march yesterday?' So I says, yes, I did go on that peace march yesterday. So then he turns round to me and he says, 'You know what? A bomb should've been dropped on the lot of them! It's a pity,' he says, 'that they had children with them 'cos a bomb should have been dropped on the lot!' And you know what was upsetting him? The march was holding up the traffic, the buses couldn't move so fast!

Now, I don't want him to say I'm right. I don't want him to agree with what I did – but what depresses me is that he didn't stop to think that this man helped me in my cause so maybe, only maybe, there's something in his cause – I'll talk about it. No! The buses were held up so drop a bomb, he says, on the lot! And you should have seen the hate in his eyes, as if I'd murdered his child. Like an animal he looked. And the horror is this – that there's a wall, a big wall between me and millions of people like him. And I think – where will it end? What do you do about it? And I look around me, at the kitchen, at the factories, at the enormous bloody buildings going up with all those offices and all those people in them, and I think – Christ! I think, Christ, Christ, Christ!

Paul – *The Kitchen*

When I think of the British working class, I can't help it, I think of the Gammers – uneducated, intolerant, bloodless, shiftily unreliable.

This ambivalence towards the working class bubbles forth like danger signals throughout the plays. *Chicken Soup with Barley* (1958), *Chips with Everything* (1962), *Their Very Own and Golden City* (1964), *Shylock* (1976), and elsewhere. By the time of *The Friends* (1970) it had grown into a full-frontal confession. In this play I continued an experiment begun in *Chips with Everything* of interleaving long speeches, described as 'contrapuntal duologues', between characters. Here Manfred talks to one character while Crispin talks to others. I will cut Crispin so that Manfred's words can be read as a continuous speech:

. . . Hate them . . . The working class! Hate them! It's coming, Macey. Despise them! I can hear myself, it's coming. Hate them! The working class, my class, offend me. Their cowardly acquiescence, their rotten ordinariness – everything about them – hate them! There! . . . Those endless dreary episodes of 'ordinary life' on television . . . And there sits the ordinary man, watching himself, pleased and familiar, not even spellbound, just dumbly recognising . . . 'Eh,' he says, 'that's me that is. Gladys, come and look, just like you and me and Jack and Gwen and Kate and bloody ordinary Sammy in the pub. No need to change then, is there? We're good enough to make tele about.' . . . And then his children watch; and slowly they begin living a copy, not of their parents' real life, but the watered-down version other people have made of their parents' real life on the tele . . . Isn't that extraordinary? . . . But look what happens next, Macey . . . Along comes a new generation of writers and they begin writing new episodes about the children – whose ordinariness has doubled because all they've had to look up to was the pale reflection of their parents which the last generation of writers put on the screen . . . And soon, Macey, you'll see, there'll be stories about *their* children and their children's children, and the characters on the screen will become more and more feeble . . . and the more banal their utterances the more like real life it will seem until one day the screen will just be blank, an electronic fog, and they'll sit there and accept it and say nothing . . . We're all poisoned by this hatred, aren't we? . . . A real cancer, this one, growing from faint beginnings, little suspicions, all those people we loved . . . Sad, like disappointed lovers, all that love, gangrenous, inside us . . . I try to ignore it, start afresh, find the world extraordinary . . . but I've no energy, no appetites for new loves . . . Some men could, some men could stay perplexed and wondering all their life and still survive. All their life . . . amazed! . . . Each moment – surprised! . . . And finally – joyous! Joyous to be witness to it all. Lovely men they were, Macey, not sour and thorny like us, but eager, capable – splendid outrages. Terrible . . . Waste . . . That's what I really wanted to say . . . We're too old to pretend.

There is no doubt in my mind that this deep ambivalence had its roots in that relationship with our neighbours, the Gammers, and fed itself through various encounters at school, in the building trade where I worked as a chippy's mate, and a plumber's mate, later on in the air force, and later still in the kitchens of Norwich, London and Paris. Perhaps, then, it was no wonder that in June 1970 playwright John McGrath, reviewing *The Friends* for the short-lived weekly *Black Dwarf*, ended:

What he [Wesker] must do is not confuse anybody, including himself, into thinking that he is in any way a socialist, or that this play relates in any way to any possible form of socialist theatre.

A long correspondence followed. I accused him of 'old-style Stalinist decree-making', of 'stale jargon and jaded spites'. He lamented
I did not respond to his 'blunt thesis' with 'an equally blunt anti-
thesis and, who knows, even the functioning of some kind of
dialectic'. Somewhere in my replies I repeated the accusation that
Simone, the upper-class character in *The Friends*, hurls at her self-
pitying working-class friends.

> In your haste to mobilise support you've given blessings and
> applause to the most bigoted, the most loud-mouthed, the most re-
> actionary instincts in the people . . . And now, I will neither wear
> cloth caps nor walk in rags nor dress in battle dress to prove I share
> his cause; nor will I share his tastes and claim the values of his class
> to prove I too stand for liberty and love and the sharing between all
> men of the good things this good earth and man's ingenuity can
> give. Now shoot me for that!

I have thought long about that speech and much else that has
accumulated over the years, and have come to suspect that perhaps
McGrath was right!

> Was I ever really a socialist? I *called* myself one in those days
> because in those days there was no other name for what I believed.
> But – sssh! Don't let on. I never joined! Wasn't a joiner. Couldn't
> accept majority decisions. Never really liked the majority. Not like
> Sir James. He loved them . . .
>
> They say yesterday's whores are today's nuns. (Beat) Or is it:
> today's nuns were yesterday's whores? (Beat) Or perhaps it's: today's
> whores are tomorrow's nuns? (Beat) Can't bear people who say
> things like that . . .
>
> . . . If only they'd known my father. He wasn't one of the world's
> joiners, either. 'Ach!' he'd say. 'They all talk rubbish and make me
> sick.' Dalston Junction was full of people who talked rubbish and
> made him sick. 'Separate them into individuals,' he said, 'they're
> nicer. Collect them together and you have collective madness.'

Probably inherited my dislike of the majority from him. Lovely man. Everything hurt him.

Whatever Happened to Betty Lemon

Apart from teenage months as a member of the Young Communist League I have never been a member of a political party. On the other hand I considered myself a *new* kind of socialist, new in that I winced when people addressed each other as 'comrade'; not only because such terminology like much other terminology of the old left had become jargon – as Ada in *Chicken Soup with Barley* points out; not only because the clenched fist salute struck me as infantile – gesture in place of thought – and hollow, too, for it was brandished by those who dispatched irritant dissenters to the gulags; but because I was dimly aware that the old left was corrupted by more than a cynical abuse of power or by Stalinist psychopathy, it was corrupted by an internal ideology which laid the blame for all ills upon the state. The heroine of *Roots*, Beatie Bryant, knew this.

Do you think when the really talented people in the country get to work they get to work for us? Hell if they do? Do you think they don't know we 'ont make the effort? The writers don't write thinkin' we can understand, nor the painters don't paint expectin' us to be interested – that they don't, nor don't the composers give out music thinkin' we can appreciate it. 'Blast,' they say, 'the masses is too stupid for us to come down to them. Blast,' they say, 'if they don't make no effort why should we bother?' So you know who come along? The slop singers and the pop writers and the film makers and the women's magazines and the Sunday papers and the picture-strip love stories – thaas who come along, and you don't hev to make no effort for them, it come easy. 'We know where the money lie,' they say, 'hell we do! The workers have got it so let's give them what they want. If they want slop songs and film idols we'll give 'em that then. If they want words of one syllable, we'll give 'em that then. If they want the third-rate, blast! We'll give 'em that then. Anything's good enough for them 'cos they don't ask for no more!' The whole stinkin' commercial world insults us and we don't care a damn. Well Ronnie's right – it's our own bloody fault. We want the third-rate – we got it! We got it! We got it! We . . .

It was not accepted left-wing dogma for the underprivileged to take blame upon themselves. Is this what McGrath saw? Nothing is simple. My experience is rich with working-class encounters I cherish forming the mirror's other side.

An unpleasant incident

I'd like to stay with *The Friends* and relate an incident which illustrates a curious, aberrant metamorphosis that can occur as a character evolves during rehearsals of a play, an incident not unrelated to the previous passage.

Added to the task of controlling character, the process of acting inevitably gives rise within the actor to conflicts which the actor must expend energy taming before he or she can concentrate on the difficult challenge of becoming another person. The actor's craft is complex, its exercise terrifying. The terror resides in vulnerability to the accusation of 'acting'. A paradox! The actor is acutely aware that society normally uses the name of his profession as an insult: 'Oh ignore him, he's just acting.' 'Just acting' is the actor's *raison d'être*. He asks an audience to forget that acting is to pretend to be what and who you are not – which is rightly frowned upon in everyday encounters. What is despised in a person *off*stage the actor asks us to praise *on*stage. The terror is understandable.

Once the terror of this initial conflict is overcome there is the frustrating awareness of high talent measured alongside limitations – the George Dillon nightmare; then, possibly, a conflict with the director over how to play the character. But perhaps the greatest conflict, which I believe should be resolved *before* the actor accepts to play a role, is one that sometimes exists between him and the character he's asked to play. Not that he must admire the personality of Adolf Hitler if that is the role he accepts, but he has to be comfortable with the character's truth: is Adolf Hitler's evil truthfully recreated?

It must have happened elsewhere than in my plays that an actor thought he or she admired the truth – a truth of good or a truth of evil – of the character they had accepted to play and then discovered in the course of rehearsals that they felt antipathetic towards their character. The belated discovery of such lack of sympathy wreaks havoc with an actor's performance.

I had just such an experience during rehearsals of *The Friends* – my first production in this country (the Roundhouse, 1970) – having previously only directed *The Four Seasons* in Havana and the world premiere of *The Friends* in Stockholm. It was a production I lost control of.

A fine cast was assembled: Susan Engel, Ian Holm, Roy Marsden, Anna Cropper, Lynn Farleigh, John Bluthal, Victor Henry. It was Victor Henry, an actor whose brilliance came in occasional flashes, usually when there was no other actor to compete with, who was the catalyst of one of my most profoundly depressing experiences in theatre. He's dead now so I can reveal he was the first person I met who suggested to me the possibility that evil existed in the world. His strength fed on the diminishment of those he felt a threat. His delight was in destruction. But he was more complex than that, for he was also a side-splittingly funny raconteur who overflowed with that sentimental, ephemeral, green-room love bestowed upon those he deemed no threat or challenge.

I first witnessed his erratic talent during the early rehearsals of *Their Very Own and Golden City* – the play I had scored for two groups of actors to play the characters as young and as old, an idea which was dropped by the director, Bill Gaskill, in favour of *one* group of actors playing the characters both young and old. Victor had been electrifying as the young Andrew Cobham and I chased him eagerly for months to cast him as Roland in *The Friends*. What I hadn't known was that when the actors had been told they were not going to be needed to play young in *The Golden City* Victor had smashed up furniture in the rehearsal room. Neither had others, who knew, warned me of his history of violence.

Victor came from Yorkshire, one of that generation of working-class actors who strutted cockily through the profession scorning everyone middle or upper class, and dismissing with contempt anything of intellect or genuine emotion with which they couldn't cope. I had invited the cast to spend a week with me here in the Welsh cottage, hoping beautiful surroundings and time spent together would cement a group who were, after all, to perform in a play called *The Friends*. It developed into a hothouse holiday during which Victor sensed me as the personification of all he hated, not least the fact that I was Jewish. One night, John Bluthal came in a state of distress and fear across the courtyard to where I slept in the study, having heard a drunken Victor attempting (unsuccessfully) to embroil another actor (who subsequently dropped out) in a plot to 'get that Jew upstairs' – where Bluthal was sleeping. Until then I had seen only one sign that Victor possessed an infantile streak – anti-semitism *is*, like nationalism, essentially infantile. There had been a moving evening when everyone performed their party piece and that soft, relaxed atmosphere of bonhomie I had planned and hoped for spread among us like mulled wine as we all sat round the log fire sharing our talents. Suddenly, someone began to sing:

> *Wheer wor' ta bahn w'en Ah saw thee,*
> *On Ilkla Moor baht 'at . . .*

One by one we joined in except – out of a drunken nowhere came Victor's voice, doom-laden, warning: 'Doan't sing that. That song can only be sung on't coach going ter football match.' I didn't think he could be serious and led everyone into the second verse.

> *Tha's bin a-courtin' Mary Jane*
> *On Ilkla Moor baht 'at . . .*

172

But Victor *was* serious and repeated: 'I've told thee, that song can only be sung on't coach going ter football match.' I can't remember what I replied, only that it was an observation so wittily withering that it surprised even me! I am persuaded that from that moment Victor decided to sabotage *The Friends.* He failed to learn his lines, turned up late for rehearsals, ate nothing but tomatoes and returned drunk from lunch breaks. I have an abhorrence of the drunk. Peasants became drunk and staged pogroms. The fear was handed down from my parents' generation to mine. We avoided the pub.

Victor interfered and commented on the performance of other actors and conducted himself with a quiet, menacing sarcasm hinting at physical violence which I confess terrified me. The failure was mine. I should have got rid of him within the first weeks of rehearsal. It would have been a simple matter; he had transgressed all that is normally expected from a professional actor. I didn't, partly because I worried about disturbing the unity, albeit tense, of the ensemble; and partly because of an arrogance afflicting many directors who foolishly and erroneously believe that sooner or later they will discover how to control the anarchic spirit in their cast. There was *one* moment when I fiercely turned on Victor, raging at his shallow opinions and shabby professional behaviour, at which point – like most bullies riddled with sentimentality as woodwork is riddled with woodworm – he crumpled into apology and agreement: 'I'm glad you've said what you've said because look here,' his hands framed a bulge in his trouser pocket, 'that's a gun there that is.'

I believed neither the existence of a gun nor that he would turn in a performance. Early on, fearing calamity, I instructed the understudy – friend and poet, Roger Frith – to learn the part of Roland. A wise move, for prior to the opening Victor feigned an epileptic fit. Roger, word perfect, stepped in, but performances never flowed as intended. Victor had the gall to turn up for the first-night party, where I greeted him with a contempt he could not mistake, and sheepishly explained with asinine nudge-nudge folk wisdom how sometimes it's necessary to bring people down to size.

Such as he and I are born to be enemies. The idea that conflict in life is rooted in failure to communicate is one of the most fatuous notions to grow out of the sixties. People communicate only too well. Hostilities and conflicts flourish between those who have clearly and unequivocally communicated their hatred of one another.

I arrive at the point of this anecdote. Contributing to Victor's instinctive antipathy towards me was the nature of the character he had to play in *The Friends*.

The play finds them at a moment where one of their number is dying and they are all profoundly dissatisfied with their lives and what they feel to be their spurious achievement. Manfred characterises them:

> Our trouble, Crispin, us lot, the once-upon-a-time bright lads from up north, is that we've no scholarship. Bits and pieces of information, a charming earthiness, intelligence and cheek, but – no scholarship. Look at these books here – Renan, Taine, Kirkegaarde, Wittgenstein, Spengler, Plato, Jung, Homer, Vico, Adorno, Lukács, Heine, Bloch – you've not heard of half of them, have you? And half of them, two-thirds, I'll never read. Do you know, new knowledge disrupts me. Because there's no solid rock of learning in this thin, undernourished brain of mine, so each fresh discovery of a fact or an idea doesn't replace, it undermines the last; it's got no measurement by which to judge itself, no perspective by which to evaluate its truth or its worth; it can take no proper place in that lovely long view of history scalloped out by bloody scholarship, because each new concern renders the last one unimportant. No bloody scholarship, us . . .

Not only did working-class Victor have to listen to such sentiments but his own character, Roland, one of those 'once-upon-a-time lads from up north' who had become rich and successful designing for, and running, a chain of 'interior design' shops, had lines like:

> There were times when to pick our noses and put our feet on chairs and swear in front of girls and find it thrilling when they swore

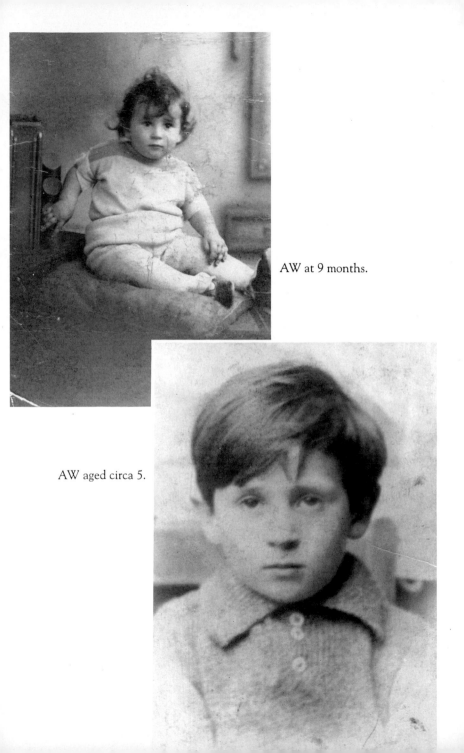

AW at 9 months.

AW aged circa 5.

LEFT Leah with her father, Jacob, and brothers, Barney and Harry.

BELOW LEFT Grandmother (the 'Boba') Rochele

BELOW Grandfather (Zeyda) Mendel.

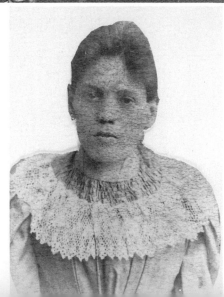

Leah, aged circa 17.

Joe 1928.

Leah, circa 20.

Guild of Citizens of Tomorrow (Leah extreme right, brother Perly and his wife, Betty).

Family in Russia – Sara centre, mid 1920s.

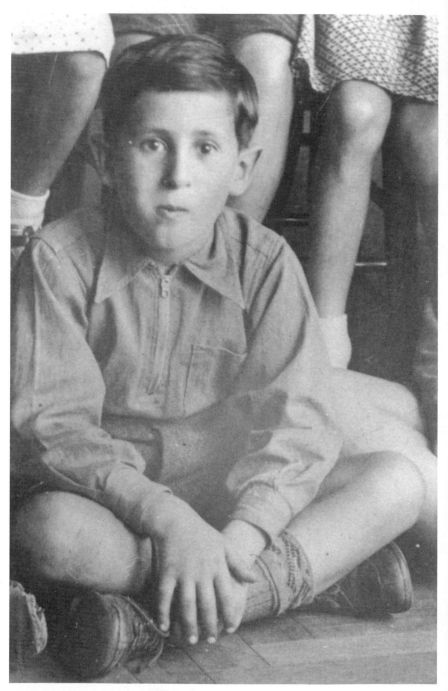

AW, aged 7 – tongue in cheek.

AW and Wesker Aunts at Solly and Rae's wedding. Circa 1938.

BELOW LEFT Leah's brother, Barnard (Barney), his wife, Esther, sons Bert and Tom, daughter, Billie. BELOW RIGHT Leah's brother, Harry, and his wife, Ray.

Leah, aged circa 35.

Joe, aged circa 34.

straight back was all delight. Such defiance, so sweet, so full of its own kind of dignity. But it's such a minor kind of dignity I feel, now; such an ephemeral delight, such a tiresome sort of defiance. There's no – no nobility in it. We're such an odious lot, us; not noble at all. No, no – majesty.

How it must have pained Victor Henry to utter such a self-portrait when he himself was a once-upon-a-time bright lad from up north with no scholarship, no solid rock of learning who repeatedly quoted what seemed like the only Aristotle he had ever read, a line about acting: 'Aristotle used to say . . .' I can't remember what.

His life ended when a car smashed into a lamppost which fell on to his head, leaving him in a vegetable state for many years, prostrate on his back in a hospital up north until he died. He takes his place alongside the Gammers deep within my psyche. Unlike the Gammers he had wit and was possessed of a kind of passion, albeit contaminated by that most insidious of all psychological states – the inferiority complex. I do not recall him with pleasure.

Chapter Eight

Jewishness – melody and the PLO

I begin this section at 5.15 in the afternoon of 13 September 1993, a day everyone is calling historic, the day Israel's Prime Minister, Yitzak Rabin, shakes hands with the PLO's chairman, Yasser Arafat, on the south lawn of the White House in Washington DC. 'There is,' says Rabin, 'a time for war, a time for peace. Enough of blood and tears, enough!' I have always been fascinated by the melody of what is being spoken. In the way some people utter a word is often contained other meanings, more than what is actually said. In a cry can be a lifetime's history. So it was with Rabin's second 'enough': two notes, different for each syllable, the second note rising in tone. Had they been the same, or had the second note gone down instead of up he would have been communicating something different. In taking the second syllable up he identified the last forty-five years of Arab/Israeli conflict as a waste and madness that need not have happened.

I recall two moments: the first, forty-five years ago, also an historic event – 26 April 1947 – the day on which the independence of the state of Israel was declared; I was twenty-eight days away from being fifteen years old. The second, a recent news item on Radio 4's *The World at One*. On the day of independence I was part of a gathering of left-wing young Zionists who danced a 'hora' on the pavement outside the Kingsway Hall in Holborn where a celebratory meeting had taken place. The hora is a circular dance; all have their arms on their neighbours' shoulders, take three steps to the left, a skip to the left, a skip to the right, three steps, skip, skip, skip, left, right. Exuberant, rhythmic, a dance of joy and release that exhilarates and warms with a sense of unity and achievement. Not Kundera's dance which he feared induces the illusion of undying love between one and all rising with its dancers into clouds of fantasy and wish-fulfilment; not a dance that declares all is over, ends have been won, the future is golden from here on; more a dance that celebrates yesterday's efforts without the delusion that there will be no more problems from here on. I loved that dance, and all the other Israeli dances learned during the four or so years I was a member of Habonim. And as we talked, high-spirited outside the Kingsway Hall, I remember saying to my friends, with what I later came to understand was not only mine but a ubiquitous Jewish irony: 'They'll have all the Jews in one place now. Makes it easier for them to get rid of us!' No doubt I was dismissed in the euphoria of the hour.

Second moment. The Washington signing was a period in which everyone was surprised off-balance by the suddenness and momentum of what was unfolding. *The World at One*, in the swift, breathtaking run-up days, interviewed everyone they could lay hands on, among them a spokesman for an Islamic extremist movement – Hamas perhaps. He said something terrifying for the logic of its madness and might be, I fear, a harbinger of the cruel times to come. Supporting the view that Arafat had sold them short, was a traitor and a dead man, he threatened that the struggle to eliminate the state of Israel would continue, for, he said – and these are his exact words: 'we hold life cheaply' and therefore it would be no problem for them to call upon thousands to throw themselves into death's way 'because we know there's a better life to come'. He had no care who or how many will die in the attempt to destroy the Jewish state. 'Virgins as fair as chorals and rubies', as the Koran promises, will be worth it. We cannot be surprised perhaps if the old soldier, Rabin, had no smile on his face.

Coming from a family I loved, many of whom were communists, it was inevitable that I would consider myself one as well; but political understanding came more from reading literature than political economy. I struggled with Marx but even what I comprehended I found difficult to retain. When it comes to fact and theory my head turns into a colander, everything drains away. It is so to this day which is why I've turned down many invitations to debate Oxford and Cambridge University motions – I can neither marshall facts nor think on my feet, at least not at a level I would consider worth exposing to public debate. My teens were not shaped by a political party but by a Zionist youth organisation called Habonim – Hebrew for 'the builders'.

This might confuse some readers for whom the notion of a Zionist is still synonymous with racist, despite the repeal in 1991 of the infamous UN resolution 3379 of 10 November 1975 equating Zionism with racism. When this absurd resolution was first mooted I was astounded. It was like equating Christianity with a form of witchcraft. The idea that Zionism was a racist philosophy must be counted one of the most successful PR jobs in the history of that profession. How was it done I wondered, and created a fantastic scenario to explain it to myself:

One day, in a land of desert, oil, and excitable men – the women nowhere to be seen – a group of clever, sweet-natured but excitable men called Palestinians gathered in an expensive hotel in a state of confusion and despair. Many years ago, under the foolish leadership of foolish leaders they had lost an opportunity to live for the first time in a land of their own because they had wanted all of the land and had not been prepared to share it with another group of people known as Jews – whose women were *every*where to be seen – and who were also living in that land. The Palestinians had terrorised to no avail, wars had been fought on their behalf to no avail. Something was not going right. They called in a man from an important public relations firm, and their chairman, a cloth-shrouded semite sporting a permanent three-day-old stubble, named Yasser Arafat, presented their problem. 'We have a problem,' he said. 'The Jews accepted partition of the land, the Arabs did not. We, the PLO, were not in existence at the time and the Arab countries who went to war with the new Jewish state were undemocratic states ruled by despots. The Jews were mostly socialists living in communist-type settlements feeding the nation with their produce, providing an intellectual élite for running the country, and nurturing its artists and academics; living a lifestyle in which men and women played an equal role and shared equal status. This left us looking like medieval retrogrades; it also threatened to elevate the position of women in our society and for this we were neither happy nor prepared. In addition we Arabs had been a conquering nation subjugating large parts of the Middle East while the Jews have spent two thousand years being victims! They even survived the Nazi holocaust! It doesn't look too good for us. Twenty years after the UN Resolution 111 was passed partitioning Palestine, our organisation was created to do something about it. Cairo – 1968! If the Arab nations couldn't get rid of the Jews perhaps an organisation calling itself the Palestine Liberation Organisation would be more effective. After all, everyone loves a liberation movement. But we're failing. It hasn't worked. Jews have all the sympathy. We're short on it. That's our problem. What can we do?'

The PR man rose and solemnly addressed the central committee members. 'Your problem is an image problem.'

'An image problem?' They were at once animated. 'An image problem? How can that be? We are a proud and lovely people with a proud and lovely history.'

'Proud and lovely is not enough,' said the PR man, 'and the history is ancient.' He paused for dramatic effect and dramatic effect is what he achieved. 'You must become Jews.' They were amazed. He explained. 'Not *really* become Jews, but become *as* Jews. First thing you've got to change is the world's perception of the Arab mentality. Away with medieval thinking, you must become left-wing, that way you'll have at least two super-powers behind you and many havens in Europe to work from. But most important of all – you must stop calling Jews, Jews; and you must persuade the rest of the world to stop calling Jews, Jews. *You* must become Jews, the new Jews of the Middle East. Too many people have love and pity for the Jews, and even those who don't have pity or love for them can't voice it for fear of outrage and accusations of being racist. *That's* your main hurdle, my friends, you must find another name for the Jews.'

There was a long, long silence before the PR man presented

them with his idea, but when it came the room echoed with gasps of amazed admiration for the sheer audacity of it. 'You must call them Zionists,' their new genius said – and we must hope they paid him or her handsomely – though I'd like to think it wasn't a her. 'You must call them Zionists and what's more you must mount a campaign that will make *them* be perceived as racist.'

'How the hell will we achieve that?' a leading committee member cried in helpless tones. 'The Jews have been living with all races since the diaspora, they have contributed massively to the business, intellectual, and artistic life of everyone everywhere. Who's going to accept the notion of the Jew as racist, for God's sake? You're crazy! Let's fire this man before he even starts.'

'I *would* be crazy,' said the PLO's PR genius elect, 'if I was talking about Jews. But remember – I am not! I am talking about Zionists. And haven't the Zionists created an Arab refugee problem? And if you persist with your policy of keeping your brethren in squalid refugee camps for long enough their numbers will grow from thousands to millions and you will be able to point an accusing finger and say, look what the Zionists have done to our race – *ipso facto* they are racists!'

'No one in the outside world will listen to you for one moment,' said the foolish, doubting leading member of the PLO central committee. The eyes of the PR man narrowed with confident, calm arrogance.

'Not only will the outside world believe you,' he promised, 'but I guarantee that one day you will be able to achieve the passing of a United Nations resolution condemning Israel as a racist nation.' At which the PLO sceptic burst into a roar of contemptuous laughter and one by one the other members of the central committee joined in, except their chairman, Yasser Arafat, who took out his pen and gave it to the PR man. Both signed his contract of engagement. This chairman was not chairman without good reason.

I don't expect this 'fantastic scenario' to be loved by everyone. I gamble it having earned the right. Let me explain. This view of the PLO didn't prevent me from sharing a platform with them at a public meeting one Sunday, 5 February 1989, at the Hampstead Town Hall, shortly after Arafat announced his preparedness to recognise the state of Israel. I didn't trust Arafat but what was there to lose? Fesial Aweida from head office and Ms Karma Nebulsi of the London office of the PLO joined with Col. Ran Cohen, a Knesset member representing the Citizen's Rights Party, Dr David Cesarani, scholar and co-chairperson of British Friends of Peace Now, and myself. We were given ten minutes each to make our statements before facing questions from the floor. I read out my carefully considered lines.

... it is at once apparent what should *not* be addressed: the rights and wrongs of the 1947 partitioning of Palestine, and the tit-for-tat blame and counter-blame for massacre or cruel oppression.

Israeli nationhood is a fact of reality, and the aspiration to Palestinian nationhood is a fact of reality. Neither will ever, ever, ever go away ...

... the need to belong to a nation is a deeply rooted one and it behoves us on the one hand to acknowledge it and on the other to help it come about in peace and move as swiftly as possible into maturity and prosperity. The alternative is struggle and poverty and stunted development leading to a national inferiority complex. And there is nothing more dangerous than a national inferiority complex. It becomes a breeding ground for fanaticism ...

... I am not enamoured of Mr Arafat. I don't like demagogues and I'm suspicious of politicians who pull at heartstrings, dress up in uniforms like fancy dress, and grin all the time with flashing eyes. Along with Reagan and the queen of soft-voice melodrama, Mrs Thatcher, he blazes across the TV screen as a bad actor. Nor does the bellicose Mr Shamir impress, full of loud emotional blackmail, wielding the Holocaust in front of world jury as though the Jew as victim can do no wrong. But Arafat has placed himself in the firing line and that commands respect and support.

I share the fears, doubts and anxieties of other Jews. Is there, I can hear them asking with justification, an Arab playwright penning such cautions and criticisms in the Arab press? One of the strongest intellectual traits revered among Jews is the spirit of nonconformity, of questioning the status quo, of challenging authority. I could not trust anyone incapable of disobedience *when it was necessary*. I would not be able to negotiate with people who were terrified of dissent. This is both alien and anathema to me.

But the dialogue must begin . . .

We were four and a half years away from the Washington handshake between Rabin and Arafat.

Habonim – the builders

In the way that youth drifts around streets, mingles at bus stops, has friends who have friends who know girls who have friends from nearby schools, I got to know a group of girls from a nearby school called Laura Place. The 'girls in brown'. These were the girls who – through a friend who had mingled – had heard of the dashingly handsome young man called Harold Pinter who performed *Macbeth* in the posher boys' school called Grocers.

Ruth Star, Bibi Datner, and Pauline Abrahams. These were the girls I got to know. My heart fluttered for a while over Pauline, but she married my second cousin, Tony. I have a drawing of her somewhere. She died young of cancer. Bibi gave birth to an autistic child and became caught up raising funds to research a cure. I heard, just a few months ago, that Ruth too had recently died of cancer. The news threw me into a bout of melancholy. Pauline and Bibi were traditionally dark-haired, Ruth had on her shoulders a rare Jewish head of blond hair. They were a lovely, generous-spirited, laughing trio and were all members of Habonim, which they had no difficulty persuading me to join.

There does not exist, as erroneously imagined, a philosophy called Zionism; not philosophy in the traditional sense of the discipline – a body of thought concerned with the meaning, purpose, or conduct of life. A Zionist, very simply, is someone who believes the Jews should have a land of their own. As soon as Yasser Arafat conceded the right of Israel's existence as a Jewish homeland he became a Zionist.

Within the Zionist framework of the early days were many different ideologies working to root themselves into the fledgling Jewish nation: centre socialists – Ma'apam; left-wing socialists – Hashomer Hatzir; socialists who were not doctrinaire but merely wanted to live a communal life and turn the desert into banana groves – that was Habonim; and communists.

To confuse the notion of a Zionist even more are the existence of varying shades of religious Jews also part of the Zionist movement, and many Jews who live and work in Israel who do not think of themselves as Zionist at all. There is even a sect of Jews who refuse to recognise the state of Israel, declaring there can be no Jewish state until the Messiah arrives who will take with him all the Jews back into the land of Israel.

Habonim was established in the UK the year I was born, 1932. Its aim was to inspire and train young Jews for emigration to Palestine where they would work on a kibbutz and help irrigate, farm, build and transform the land ready for the day when it would become a Jewish state. I joined around late 1945, early 1946, aged thirteen, and remained a member for about three or four years, until I left school. I might seriously have contemplated emigrating to Israel but was not serious for long.

Being a teenage member of Habonim for three years or so is the closest I came to being a member of any Jewish community. I was not a member of a synagogue, though family weddings, barmitzvahs, the deaths of aunts, uncles, parents flowed as family cycles do ('We're the next to go,' said Ralph over the grave of one of my uncles) and so I passed much time in many temples of worship, but I am a non-believer, taking the irreverent view that Abraham invented God to keep his tribe, 'this arrogant, anarchic herd of heathens' (*Shylock*), in check.

Habonim, which produced other personalities like Professor (now Lord) Maurice Peston, and film director, Mike Leigh, was scathingly regarded by the hard-headed, fiercely political left-wingers of Hashomer as nothing more than a Jewish boy-scout movement. True, we learned the art of camping and how to tie a reef knot, for which I am ever grateful, but it was more than that. Habonim provided me with some of the happiest days of my life – companionship, soul mates, gaiety, a sense of purpose, and a deeper awareness of what it meant to be Jewish. I still possess the Habonim handbook – very out of date, I'm sure – a yellow-coloured paperback with the Habonim symbol on the front: a 'beth', בֿ , the second letter of the Hebrew alphabet, for 'bonim', הבונים (builders). Underneath is a quotation:

Call us not thy children. Rather thy builders.

On the inside cover is a letter to builders masculine and builders feminine – 'Dear Bonim and Bonot'. The second paragraph reads:

The handbook is only a beginning, for it is mainly by your own efforts that you will acquire the knowledge that will enable you to understand the position of our people in the world, the Jewish achievement in Eretz Israel and the part we are playing in the struggle for freedom.

They meant 'freedom' for all people, including the Palestinian Arab working class who were perceived mostly as victims of oppressive sheiks or absentee landlords. In 1943 Western Palestine had a population of just over 1,500,000 people. Of these, roughly one million were Arabs and 500,000 were Jews. The 500,000 would bring socialism and democracy to the oppressed million.

The Movement instils in its members the spirit of friendliness towards all races and creeds and kindliness towards all living creatures.

That is how we thought and debated.

Looking through the handbook, mouthing the Hebrew words for

'meeting' – asefat; 'sit' – yashov; 'silence' – sheket, instantly brings back days of singing, dancing and camp, a three-year chunk that was 'yesterday'. We met in huge Edwardian and Victorian houses, first in Cazenove Road then in Queensdown Road opposite the Hackney Downs where some years later two Jewish boys were chased and knifed to death by a gang of mindless fascist thugs. Mild Zionists we were, enjoying each other perhaps more than the ideology. And so when, in 1968, during the weeks of a Japanese festival organised in my honour under the title 'Wesker '68', participating in a public debate and questioned about all aspects of my life and writing, I was asked: 'Is it true, Mr Wesker, that you were a member of a Zionist organisation and if so can you explain why?' I almost couldn't comprehend the question. Those days I was oblivious to the burgeoning attempt to give Zionism a bad name but the melody of my inquisitor sounded ominously McCarthyite. My tongue moved quickly into my cheek and I responded to the question's melody:

'Yes, I was a member of a Zionist youth organisation called Habonim which I joined because I enjoyed singing Israeli songs and dancing Israeli dances and the girls were pretty and eager to share kisses.'

The reply, though aiming to dismiss the man who'd imagined he'd unearthed a ghastly past, was not without some truth. Pauline, Bibi and Ruth were very pretty indeed, and it was in Habonim that I met Esther Lander with whom I fell seriously in love and whose image and persona have never completely left me. I certainly threw myself into the singing and dancing. Habonim had its own choir under the direction Yehuda Goodman who forged his devoted corps into a brilliant ensemble of sounds and harmonies, inspiring us to sing out loud and clear, hearts exposed. The result was not sentimental – he hated that – but hard, crisp, disciplined.

As well as the singing – we sang at the end of group meetings, and the dancing – we danced at the drop of a hat, there was the camping – we camped at weekends and fortnightly each year in the Wye Valley near Monmouth, and the necking parties – we necked at the flash of an eye. It could not be said that I was an earnest Zionist. Transforming swamp and desert into orange grove and banana plantation was not for me, beautiful and heroic though the image loomed. Instead, Wizzie became merely a personality known throughout the movement for energy, organising skills, and tongue-in-cheek humour.

Wizzie? Wizzie? Who, the reader is asking, is Wizzie? I – am Wizzie. It became my nickname. Being a mere five foot four I was fondly nicknamed at school – as we were all nicknamed by each other, sometimes not so fondly – 'Wee Willie Wesker'. The 'Wee' and the 'Wesker' were dropped. 'Willie' remained. When I met up with Bibi, Ruth and Pauline they declared 'Willie' a misnomer. 'Willie whizzes about the place,' they noted, 'he should be called "Wizzie".' 'Wizzie' I became.

You used to call me 'Wiz', Lindsay Joe, in the days when we were friends. I have two tapes of pop songs you assembled for me. One labelled: 'Invigorating Music for Innovative Playwrights', the other 'Nice Songs for Wiz'. Tanya Jo calls me 'Wiz'. And Dusty of course. Not Danny though. 'Dad' for him.

Movement days were nourishing days. I found my first real circle and fed on their friendship. We cared about each other, confided in and advised one another. We even loved one another's parents! One of my girlfriends, Rhoda Leigh, had a young and frisky mum, manageress of a Richard Shop, who when I was going with her daughter, an inch taller than me, consoled us with the observation that 'it makes no difference lying down'. We spent a lot of time lying down, clamped together in their sitting room with our clothes on, listening to De Falla's *Nights in the Gardens of Spain*, necking and heaving our way from one dry fuck – as squeezed urgent passion with clothes on was called in those days – to another without either of us achieving a single orgasm. Not one I recognised anyway!

Friendship was shaped at camps where we cooked on open fires, sang round the flames, danced in the grass, argued politics in our tents. We handed on books we'd read, listened to records in each other's houses – mainly my sister's house using her large mahogany wind-up box. I still have those 78s, Beethoven's 8th, Mendelssohn's Violin Concerto, Dvořák's 'New World', Schubert's 'Unfinished'. Nothing sophisticated, no chamber music, no Schoenberg, certainly no Britten, just luscious, stirring, romantic top-of-the-pops. Because she introduced it to me I bought my sister Rimsky-Korsakov's *Scheherazade* from a record shop called Dunkley's on the Lower Clapton Road, paying for it with octagonal three penny pieces at the rate of sixpence a week.

An event I enjoyed putting together and one which began shaping my sense of the dramatic was called a 'messibah': a cultural evening in which a theme would be chosen and readings of prose and poetry assembled with linking passages written by whoever's evening it was. They would select friends to read the different parts, usually by candlelight behind a long trestle table at which the rest of us gazed, punctuated by specially selected music ground out on a gramophone to create atmosphere, enhance mood. Sometimes an instrument would be played – piano, violin, recorder; or if some-one had a good voice their singing would colour the moment.

I learned from these dramatic presentations two things about music and drama: that music could be a magnifier of thin sub-stance, potent and dangerous, with the power to suggest that what was happening on stage possessed significance the text didn't sub-stantiate. There was a period at the RSC when every production ended with music and dance, meretriciously leaving an audience with the impression it had enjoyed itself even when all that had gone before had been abysmal. In the handful of plays I have directed, mostly my own, music is rarely used unless called for in the text. Two productions of *The Four Seasons* – one in New York, the other in Prague – employed music between the scenes. Fatal. I didn't see the New York production, which bombed, but they sent me a tape of the music and I understood why. It was 'poetic'. *The Four Seasons* is a lyrical play musically structured and with height-ened language. The challenge is to act against the heightened language not drown it with heightened acting; to find the music *in* the structure not smother it with extraneous melodies. The Prague production was the most bizarre. Its director not only felt the need for music but for music that was jazz! For two pianos! Which had to be on stage! Visible! Competing with actors! The production struck me as shrill and dishonest. While pianists competed with actors the director competed with the play, using music like a crutch as though the text was inadequate and needed support. The occasion, however, provided me with one unforgettable moment: I emerged with friends from the theatre into the Prague streets swathed in fog. I do not understand how it was known I was approaching through the mist, but as we stepped carefully towards the restaurant a woman, like an apparition, floated towards us out of the dimness with her arm outstretched, in her hand a rose. 'This, Mr Wesker,' she said, 'is for your beautiful play.' And she disappeared.

The play had reached her despite the two jazz-thumping pianos, but her rose didn't dissuade me from the dangers of opium-like music as background to stage productions. It was romantic for youth-movement days, but I soon adopted a puritanical approach to my craft: everything has to be earned, laughter, tears, anger, nostalgia, emotion of any kind on stage. I will not call upon music to help make an audience feel what my characters in their human condition cannot make them feel.

By the same puritanical token I must resist infusing those movement days with a degree of romantic intensity they did not possess. The memories that linger are joyous ones, innocent and fearless, but early poems reveal depression and self-doubt. I know it is the nature of poetry mostly to record gloom but those awful verses tell something of an adolescent state of mind. On the other hand – I did crazy things. The girls once dared me to dress as a woman and go out into the streets. How could I resist? Flowered dress, stockings, high heels, scarfed hair – the girls made me up – and they all travelled with me on a 653 trolley bus from Lower Clapton to Stamford Hill.

And how do I account for *this*? Yom Kippur, the day of atonement, provided us with a ritual. We fasted and instantly sinned.

The fasting was genuine, not a morsel for twenty-four hours. We'd all gather in Finsbury Park to walk, talk and fantasise about food. A shared experience. Then an hour before sunset each would go to their house and reassemble, usually in Weald Square, armed with food that would take us through the day's three meals we had denied ourselves, starting with bacon and eggs! My parents, not being kosher, had no objection to the bacon, not in those days anyway. As she grew older, though never keeping a strictly kosher house, my mother would only buy meat and chicken from kosher butchers – about whom she would complain for the high prices they charged. One Yom Kippur, appetites high from fasting, a group of us gathered to break fast in Weald Square. There came a moment. My cousin Bryan reached out across the table with a cup and saucer, asking me to refill it with tea. I poured. And poured. And poured. And despite his cries of 'Whoa, whoa! Enough! Enough!' I carried on pouring till the hot tea overflowed into the saucer, burned him and he was forced to let it drop into the middle of the table. I simply couldn't stop. 'Sometimes a mishegass [madness] gets into him . . . grrr!' growled my exasperated mother.

Another joyous tradition we young Zionists established, which today is unthinkable, was singing in the Underground on our way home from choir practice. We would rehearse in a large house in Eton Avenue, Swiss Cottage (change at Baker Street and King's Cross for Manor House). And then, adrenaline high, our heads still ringing with chords, we would sing in the train the choral harmonies we had been rehearsing that evening. Strange Hebrew words, strange sonances.

What on earth did the other passengers think of us? At the time it seemed we were sharing our talents with the world but I suspect motives were mixed: to enjoy ourselves, certainly; perhaps to share our exotic music; without doubt to shock a little. There was a bravado, a chutzpah in our presumptuous 'entertainment' of a gentile audience who had not asked to be entertained. We sang conscious that we were thrusting our alien difference before London Underground passengers who rarely witnessed anything like it – the concert hall brought into their carriage – ever so faintly delighting in the slight discomfort we might be causing with our voices in full throat. Not very English though transparently good-natured – surely we would be loved, at least by those who were not embarrassed. Now no one sings on the Underground except smelly, maudlin drunks. Pity. Singing creates a natural high. My voice croaks these days but my granddaughter still enjoys the songs I sing her. Recently I was amazed to hear of a conference for the tone deaf. That pleases me, teachers who exist to teach the tone deaf how to sing together. It's a terrible affliction not to be able to sing. Children are often embarrassed when their parents break into song. Mine were no exception. 'Daaa-aad!' I resisted and admonished them. 'Never stop anyone singing. Singing is a deep expression of joy. Stop them singing you stop up their joy.'

This bus does not sing – an aside

The *Sunday Times* book section of 24 April 1994 carries a most extraordinary review: of John Osborne's collected prose called *Damn You, England*. The novelist/journalist Keith Waterhouse wrote it. A well-written piece – the kind of relaxed journalism I envy – applauding the collection, and containing at the end a paragraph based upon which an entire study could be written about the nature of the English. Or rather a certain type of English nature. On the surface it is to do with contempt for foreigners, a smug notion that anything not English is faintly ridiculous. But to observe that is to beg the question: *why* should the English feel this? Or a certain type of English. What does it betray of their own personality? It intrigues me. I wish I had collected all such passages in a file called 'The English'.

The thing about the things Osborne has been banging on about for 40 years is that they're all so awfully true to awful life. Never mind:

England hasn't come down yet. One segment of this greatly entertaining collection is about a production of *Look Back in Anger* at a
Moscow Youth Festival in the late 1950s. I happened to be in
Moscow at the time, and Osborne misses one story. The city was
crammed with the youth of all nations and coaches crisscrossed the
Moscow boulevards jam-packed with fresh-faced young men and
women flaunting national costume and yodelling national songs.
Into view sailed the English contingent, silent, sports-jacketed, a
banner draped along the length of the coach, its wording doubtless
instigated by Osborne or Richardson or both: THIS BUS DOES
NOT SING. It made you proud to be damned English.

I'm left speechless at that last sentence. What is there about not
singing to make one proud? It's not even English! The great choirs
of the northern towns – Leeds, Bradford, Huddersfield – of the
miners, of the glorious English cathedrals; the folk-song tradition
that has informed so much of the best English music; and what of
English music itself? From the Tallis forty-part motet to Elgar's
Dream of Gerontius and the Britten operas. To enable his contempt
to score easy points Waterhouse tars all the singing as 'yodelling'.
Why? You can imagine that story being told in the local and all the
crusty, bloodless cronies slapping their thighs with cosy approbation. That's the foreigner all right. He sings! He bloody sings!
What's he got to sing about? He's a bloody foreigner!

Mr Waterhouse would have snarled at our singing Hebrew songs
in the Underground. But I trust he'd not have imagined it was
yodelling.

The Israel Experience

In 1960 I was invited to spend Passover in one of the most beautiful
of kibbutzim, En Hashofet, mainly American-populated and built
by Hashomer Hatzair, the left wing of the Zionist movement. My

host was the poet Dov Vardi. The setting was idyllic – trees, shrubbery, buildings well designed and laid out in a human scale with a new centrepiece: an incomplete, but useable, large concert hall doubling as a theatre. The kibbutz buzzed with hospitality, flowed with relatives and friends. Young children patiently endured the constant caressing of visiting grandparents starved of those grandparental rights to which they'd so looked forward and which their earnest, idealistic children had incomprehensibly denied them. On Passover evening – not conducted as a religious ceremony: eating the bitter herb, relating the story of Moses taking the Jews out of Egypt and bondage into freedom – everyone was dressed fresh and clean, the kibbutznics distinguishable in their white shirts and shorts from the ties and dresses of their guests. Tables of white cloths were bedecked with candles and flowers. Members served us. There was a heart-warming mixture of the casual and the gracious, and when the meal was over the entertainment began. A quartet from Amsterdam played chamber music. A visiting ballet troupe danced. I think there were also individual musicians and singers. When the professionals had finished the kibbutz members cleared the vast hall and we danced and made our own music. My Habonim days stood me in good stead.

Why then, after forty-eight hours, did I want to get out? Here was being enacted almost every socialist principle I ever believed in: communal ownership of the land, everyone employed in what they were best at, art an integral and important part of the community's life. And it was moving, even exhilarating to find myself in a land where I was not made to feel a foreigner. What was wrong? An event occurred next day in the dining room and I understood.

Hashomer was a stridently left-wing grouping, non-religious but puritanical – no make-up, no female permitted dress that emphasised sexuality, sophistication a form of dishonesty. Sitting with my hosts at supper I noticed a beautiful young woman pushing a trolley and collecting dirty dishes. Not only were her eyebrows plucked and shaped, she was wearing a tight skirt hugging hips which swayed sensuously as she walked. I asked my hosts: 'If you frown upon make-up and suggestive dress how do you explain that young woman?' Looks were exchanged, a tone of voice adopted, and I knew – I was in Main Street. It seems she was brought over from Europe, an orphan, and welcomed into the kibbutz but never really settled. That is to say she lacked any political awareness or intellectual curiosity. Her only reading material were women's magazines, never literature, and she disturbed the men! Time and again her case had been discussed in committee but after each deliberation, to the credit of the kibbutz, they couldn't find sufficient reason to expel her. She was their responsibility. Her saving grace was her interest in dance. They sent her to town where she improved her technique and in turn taught the kibbutz youngsters.

I was born with an instinctive aversion to Main Street mentality. It exists in all classes of society – working, middle, upper classes. It is a state of mind that wrinkles its nose at spirit and colour and is frequently identified in left-wing circles. I fled. It was not simply the tight-arsed response to her that worried me; that, after all, had to be set against the magnificent achievement of the kibbutz itself. It was the intellectual claustrophobia that accompanies Main Street mentality. More, I discovered to my mortification that I did not want to share my belongings with anyone. I was a far more possessive creature than I had imagined. I wanted *my* house, *my* record player, *my* very own inviolable space. I did not want to be benignly granted by another body – democratically elected or not – what belonged to me. That for which I worked I wanted acknowledged as mine by right of legitimate acquisition, struggled and paid for in time, energy, risk and talent.

The Two Roots of Judaism

In 1949, when I was seventeen, I wrote an essay under the pseudonym of Jon Smith for a competition organised by the *New Statesman* – 'Faith and Reason':

We are men of passions, filled with emotions we cannot always understand, harbouring hates and desires which confound and vanities that disgust us. Cowardly reactions in some situations contradict strange dignities and courage in others. We are complex creatures.

Complex creatures. I began with that discovery at an early age and it has never left me. The essay argued neither for faith nor reason but for 'behaviour', and, with the bravado of adolescence, hinted at a scholarship I did not possess.

Faith, the need to submit to something we imagine is bigger than ourselves, is an effort to supplement our inadequacy. It is a faith because it does not explain but comforts . . . all the great theological and philosophical works [are] an attempt to explain the mystery of life . . . This is reason . . . But because I do not believe the inadequacy can ever be supplemented or the mystery explained I am concerned neither with religion as a faith nor science as an explanation. It is sufficient that the inadequacy never leaves me rest and that the mystery fills me with awe and keeps me sufferably humble enough to enjoy its beauties. With what, then, am I concerned? Let me say it is with THE CONDUCT OF LIFE.

My credo in capital letters, supported only by the eclectic reading of an autodidact, nailed at an early age to the heavy doors of life. I concluded:

I offer no panacea, no one in his right senses will. He will be humble and start right at the very bottom, where I start – with the man at his elbow, and he will treat him with respect no matter what or who that man is and then he will teach his children that respect.

To the optimistic brother, Manny, in *The Old Ones*, written twenty-two years later, I gave a quotation to hurl at his pessimistic brother with whom he is constantly battling, each using as armoury quotations from the classics – sometimes the same classics!:

Boomy! You listening? I'm reading from Martin Buber again. 'Rabbi Leib, son of Sarah, used to say about those rabbis who only *expound* the Torah that: A man should see to it that all his actions are a Torah and that he himself becomes so entirely a Torah that one can learn from his life.'

When the essay was written I had not read Buber, or any of the learned rabbis. From whom did I inherit this view that *how* people conduct their lives is more important than what they *say*?

George Steiner posed one of his provocative questions at a colloquium on 'The Impact of the Jewish Nature on Jewish Writing' – such colloquiums appear at regular intervals around the world like the footprints of a Yeti which no one is certain exists but which it is endlessly fascinating to contemplate; March 1984:

> Is it at all natural for a Jew to be a writer . . . We have an enormous tradition against it . . . I believe it is natural for a Jew to be a scholar . . .

He named Kafka, Proust, Hofmansthal, Pasternak as writers who

> always felt deeply ill at ease with their being writers . . . a very secondary and sad solution . . .

Only commentary on Torah was to be taken seriously – thoughts which will

> . . . become part of the living eternity of Judaism which is Midrash, the continued argument, the rethinking of what was given us in the Torah . . . if you could add to that one opinion, one question, one insight, you are inside Judaism, living Judaism for ever . . .

There is much to argue with in Steiner's lecture and much I found familiar and disturbing. In later years I too began to feel ambivalent about that part of art which is artificial, and found myself turning again and again to the extended essay or lecture in an attempt to understand what it was I imagined I had created. More, I was interested in philosophical speculation for its own sake unrelated to my plays and stories, hoping to add 'that one opinion, one question, one insight' . . . Jonathan Miller, interviewed in *The Independent* (12 February 1993) complained about his role as a director:

> There's a terrible, ghastly moment at the end of *Jude the Obscure*, when Jude is dying in Oxford, never having got into the university, and he hears the applause and the noise of the people receiving their degrees in the Sheldonian. Well, that's the sort of feeling I have at the moment, as I reach the end of my life. I can hear the din of the real action going on in the area of the brain's sciences, and I'm outside it . . . It's terribly sad.

I am a bit like Jude, regretting never having gone to university, and, like Jonathan, wondering are my plays and stories the work of a writer who would rather have been a scholar? Was this Jewish reverence for the power of intellect handed down to me in ways I failed to recognise? Was the simply argued essay 'Faith and Reason' the direction I should have taken? When I compare the intellectual experience to the theatrical one it is often like moving from the adult world to kindergarten.

And so, when invited in 1982 to deliver a paper to a Rockefeller Foundation conference in Bellagio on 'The survival and transformation of Jewish culture and religious values in literature written since the Second World War' I indulged my taste for intellectual speculation and at the same time grappled with the nature of Judaism. At least a nature of Judaism which would explain me to myself, perhaps identify a quality in my work which made it sit uncomfortably in the English tradition. The paper was called 'The Two Roots of Judaism'. It posed the following dilemma.

Many Jews, not only artists and intellectuals but artisan and businessmen, claimed a profound and undeniable sense of Jewishness unsupported either by a substantial knowledge of Jewish culture or by religious faith. Impossible! cry the orthodox. Adherence to the prescribed rituals and laws of the Torah are what has kept the race alive and given it its identity. Only those who observe the rituals and have faith in the thirteen principles of Maimonides – and of course only those who descend from Jewish mothers – can claim the mantle of Jewishness.

I ignored the number of Jewish kings and princes who married foreign daughters for political expediency – such as the devout Jehoshaphat who, as a political manoeuvre against the growing menace of the Arameans and Assyrians, married his son Jehoram to Athaliah, the daughter of Jezebel no less! Instead I quoted from Isaiah I:11-18:

> To what purpose is the multitude of your sacrifices unto me? saith the Lord. I am full of the burnt offerings of rams, and the fat of fed beasts; and I delight not in the blood of bullocks, or of lambs or of he-goats ... Your hands are full of blood. Wash you, make you clean; put away the evil doings from before mine eyes; cease to do evil; learn to do well; seek judgement, relieve the oppressed, judge the fatherless, plead for the widow. Come now, and let us reason together ...

In Isaiah could be found one of the roots of Jewishness: *let us reason together*. It is a Jewish trait to believe in the power of reason and is both their strength and downfall. From Isaiah to my mother. 'Come, sit down, have some tea, be calm, talk to me, discuss, say it, be reasonable ...'

I then turned to Genesis.

> So God created man in his own image, in the image of God created he him: male and female created he them.

What a strange concept. *In his own image*. What could it mean? That God was of supreme importance for creating humankind or – and here begins a Jewish heresy to which 'we hold life cheaply' is anathema – that humankind was more important because it was created in God's image? From this simple but glorious declaration in Genesis, I concluded, stemmed the two roots of Judaism. Conflicting roots – between those who revered God more than people because he created them, and those who revered people more than God because they were created in his image.

I believe the bias of the majority of Jews is towards the rational. Of course in some of us there is the one and a touch of the other, but . . . most modern Jewish writers and intellectuals are the inheritors of the first: that reverence for, and greater preoccupation with, man and his ways rather than with God and the rituals surrounding the glorification of his name. And that inheritance includes the tradition of prophecy, the spirit of justice and tolerance, and the Jewish energy for action; and by prophecy I do not mean futurology, the visionary forecasts of doom-laden or beautiful times to come, which is Messianic prophecy and something quite different; I mean prophecy as criticism, chastisement, warning. How this spirit was handed down, what paths it took even unto the agnostic son and daughter is something for which I cannot account. I know only that it travelled through the ages, that it touched many of us, that we drew strength from it, that we warmed more to such dictums as that of Moses Mendelssohn's that Judaism only judges action and not religious opinions, and that it made us feel we could justly lay claim to the identity: Jew.

Father Quest

How has this Jewishness affected my family? Jewish orthodoxy decrees that Dusty, the mother, not being Jewish, our children are not Jewish. Neither of the boys – Daniel, nor you, Lindsay Joe – feels particularly Jewish. Tanya Jo does, fiercely, and resents the orthodox stricture disqualifying her from claiming what her head wants and her heart feels. Elsa doesn't feel Jewish though she's dark and beautiful like Tanya and stands out among her blonde friends. I think she enjoys having a Jewish father and appearing the odd one out of her group. Dusty herself adopted my family and they, her. She claims Jewishness through a strong, thirty-five-year association and avows she is more comfortable with Jewish than gentile men. I don't think I will ever turn to religion – it is not in me to have faith in what cannot be evidenced, but Della said to me not long ago: 'Anything I can do that identifies my jewishness I will do.' For that reason she wants to be buried in a Jewish cemetery, whereas I've arranged to be cremated and for my ashes to be buried here in these hills beneath a tree – which kind I have not yet chosen.

There is one last strand in all this which I must come to terms with. I raged at my father but loved him. I loved him but feared becoming like him. I feared becoming like him but miss him. Loss! And so I have searched for a father-figure. When Lindsay Anderson recognised qualities in my play and promoted it I felt I'd found someone who would look after and nurture me. It didn't happen. Someone else entered my life and stayed there intermittently who I must have felt met my need for a father-figure, Sidney Bernstein, head of Granada TV. He commissioned me to write a play for television.

When I was sentenced to an embarrassing month in prison for membership of Committee of 100 (embarrassing because it was such a short and silly sentence), Sidney sent Dusty a cheque for £100 'to help out in a time of need'. I never worked for him again but felt his paternalistic warmth from a distance and on the odd occasions we met socially. When he died he left me £1000 in his will. I was moved, honoured and surprised. Something was there, perhaps I should have cultivated it. Cultivating such relationships doesn't come easy to me, however.

Another, similar, is Arnold Goodman – Lord Goodman – someone who, like Sidney, I've known over a period of thirty years and respected and who, I think, was fondly respectful of me. Civilised, cultured, warm, wise and wry. He once guaranteed a bank overdraft for some thousands to bridge a gap while waiting for a film

advance. He didn't want it but I insisted that my original manuscripts be lodged with him. I had the feeling he was looking for a
son.

The one without whom I'd have sunk, more a friendship than a
fathership, was Bob Gavron, printer and publisher. He belongs to
our earliest days, a name suggested when I was in search of support
for Fortytwo. Curly-haired, clever in every part of his being, he
turned a printing enterprise into a public company worth hundreds
of millions with – so it seemed to me – a corner of his attention.
The rest of the time he read voraciously, went to theatre and opera,
gathered round him a fine and motley circle of highly intelligent
business people, academics and artists. There's some of Bob in my
portrait of Shylock. His early efforts to be a model boss are recreated in *The Wedding Feast*, a play dedicated to him and his
ex-wife, Nikki. I use the past tense because, though Bob and Arnold
are very much alive, I'm not there any more. I'm here. In the hills.

Though I searched. No, I didn't search, I waited, hoped for. And
I hoped for such a figure out of the Jewish community, desperately
wanting to be a loved son. I would not write my plays and stories
deliberately to earn that love but I hoped my independent spirit
would be cherished for its own sake, as a recognisably Jewish spirit
– iconoclastic, humane, mixed of irony, humour, pity, a defiant
Jewish survivor's spirit. Shouldn't that kind of courage be indulged?
Max Stafford-Clark is reported to have said once: the trouble with
Arnold's work is it's too Jewish. What on earth could he have
meant? Jewish like O'Casey is Irish? Jewish like Toni Morrison is
black? A few of the plays and stories use, inevitably, Jewish backgrounds and characters; inevitably Jewish values permeate the
themes. But the themes are not Jewish: political disillusion, self-
discovery, love, old age, death – they're universal.

I have been described as, and part of me enjoys being, an outsider. Another part, however, aches to be accepted. There is
nothing I can do, or would do, to make this possible, but that
father, where was that father? Loss. What is not caused by loss, ah!

Chapter Nine

Love and betrayal

Out of Habonim and dreams of building Jerusalem came love and betrayal – Esther Lander and Cissie Rickless. Cissie I called Shifra and will refer to her as such from here on.

Dividing women into sweet and sour, Martha and Mary, wife and whore is resisted, as generalisations should be, but experience suggests the division echoes a truth. It is not the *only* division that can be cleft through womankind, nor is it necessarily a qualitative division, nor is each role fixed forever. The wanton may wake one morning and reach for a gourmet's cookbook; the doe-eyed home-maker may one night contemplate another use for reef knots. The doe and the wanton often live side by side within the one person-ality. Whatever, the distinction is identifiable, recognisable. Ask women about men: emotional babies or chauvinist pigs, mummy's boy or cocksure, saints or sinners.

Pleasure in female company began with teens; not simply desire – in for a cuddle then back with the boys – but a deliberate pre-ference to share time and experiences. It is not easy to talk about relationships with women. There is a kind of woman who cannot stand me, we know each other at a glance. Others, well, sexuality is never far away but I'm attracted to women for who they are, what they do and how they think. My interest is apparent. I'm neither patronising nor timid nor competitive nor absurdly flattering. Some men, especially in this age when women have achieved a degree of equality (though Rabbi Julia Neuberger lectures on how many of those gains are now lost), assume an embarrassing, deferential stance they *imagine* is the way equals should behave. Their huge efforts belie their acclamations, their humble eyes invite whispered derision, their gestures bring down abuse, and the wiping upon

201

them of high-heeled feet. Or it's patronising: 'Look,' they are saying, 'you *are* equal to me, *there's* nice!' Not easy at all, the male/female relationship. Few get it right. I've only sometimes got it right and then for only part of the time. At the moment I'm getting it all wrong. Perhaps it's too late at sixty-two to think of ever getting it right, especially when I started getting it wrong at the tender age of fifteen.

The story of Esther – part one

At thirteen I fell in love with Esther – Rosebud. She was twelve. Two years later I betrayed her for Shifra.

We were both members of Habonim. She was the first girl I fell in love with. Maternal, ample, rosy-cheeked, pouting lips, quick to blush, with – behind glasses – brown eyes which moved mercurially from laughter to thoughtfulness to honest anger to pity. The melody of her words cooed with love and concern. She was buoyant with hope that the world held riches for her. She was saucy, cheeky. In her presence you felt pulsations. She threatened all the time to take the most outrageous, courageous leap into a life promising *such* possibilities. And whoever she would love she would take with her.

I could make her laugh – a quality that has remained with me even into these fractured times. She complained that she was ugly, which called up the Byronic knight in me who allayed her fears and wooed her as I do not think I have ever wooed since. I think I thrilled to her as to a high-diver about to swallow-dive. Those poised are irresistible. And with it all she was luscious, nubile, and I melted away.

In 1947 our Habonim group attended a two-week youth camp in the Wye Valley where I met Shifra. Shifra, miniature adult, father a chemist, lived in Manchester, later revealed to me: 'I took one look at you and decided to net you.' What a woman in the making she was. Tongue like a whip. Will like a great boulder, and intelligence sharp, like a frightened hawk. I was to carry her scars forever.

Campers lived in tents accommodating eight. Boys were separated from girls until the last night when, in the party spirit of last-everythings, those who had been drawn to one another during two intimate weeks of communal living slept together in each other's tents and arms. Little more than innocent petting could take place but I had achieved what I had wooed hard for during those months leading up to camp. Esther and I lay side by side in her tent and we kissed – a sweetly granted sweet favour. She entrusted herself to lie on my chest, confident enough to fall asleep in my right arm which suffered the undignified hazard of all lovers' arms – pins and needles!

Shifra shared the same tent, curled under her blanket on a straw palliasse the other side of me. Out of the shadows along the groundsheet stretched her hand reaching for mine. What had been sparking between us these two weeks now burned like a fuse. It was electrifying. With a dark thrill my hand accepted her hand. Esther awoke, understood what was happening and gently rolled aside. This moment of betrayal marked me for life. I hang on to her memory as Citizen Kane hung to the memory of a name we finally came to know was painted on his childhood sleigh – Rosebud.

I recovered sufficiently to have relationships which sent me thrilled and tumbling and horrendous-poetry-making all over the place. Even play-writing all over the place. I've committed lovestruck follies, and not-so follies, and made a family. Even now my heart is strung between two loves, rendering me paralysed and trussed up here in the hills, unable to move anywhichway. I remember betrayal like shock. In addition to a sense of betrayal is a sense of unfinished business. I can't remember day-to-day life with Esther. We weren't in and out of each other's homes. In fact I don't think I spent as much time in her place as she did in mine. She lived in a Victorian house in Fountain Road, off Cazenove Road off Upper Clapton Road, roads I loved walking through in autumn, kicking feet through mountains of leaves. Esther used to complain about her mother to such an extent that when she died I imagined Esther was pleased, and committed, one wet April in 1950, aged seventeen, an act of unbelievably insensitive folly. While she was sitting shiva (mourning) I got it into my head that what she longed for was a friend to share not her grief – hadn't she often wished her mother dead? – but her relief.

Some months previously I had performed with the Query Players a modern-dress version of *The Merchant of Venice*, playing Launcelot Gobbo on roller-skates. Never having been on roller-skates I had to learn. Wouldn't it amuse Esther, my foolish head reasoned, to see me staggering about on these crazy four wheels filled with tiny ballbearings like uncontrollable pellets of ice? I lumbered through the gate and fell on to her front door. She half opened it, a sad face with red eyes which, as soon as I saw them, announced my blunder. She gauged my mood and intention, said simply: 'Go away, Wizzie,' then closed the door on me. I was mortified. On absurd skates which had developed a life of their own, my face red with hot blushes and shame, I fled. Well, hardly fled. Novices can't 'flee' on such treacherous wheels. Comedian on stage, dressed to amuse, no one laughing at his jokes – there is no greater fool. Inept skater, inept lover – I had misjudged her feelings.

Somehow the friendship was sustained, with me persisting in the belief that she was the love of my life. When I left school my first job, as a furniture-maker's apprentice, was in Norton Folgate, near Liverpool Street station. The Spitalfields Central Foundation Girls School was nearby. Esther used to get the bus from the Stoke Newington end of Northwold Road – was it a 641 trolley? – to Liverpool Street. I was at work a few minutes ahead of her and stood day after day, watching for the bus that would carry her by, hoping to catch a glimpse, a smile, a wave. She sat at a right-hand window in case we coincided. It didn't always happen, which is why when it did it was such a physical experience. Love turns the smallest gesture into an event.

We grew, in late teens, to become part of a circle of friends who shared not only Zionist aspirations but a social life – rambles, birthday parties, poker schools, cinema. A group of us once decided to see three films in a day. *Fantasia* was one of them, I can't remember the other two. *Fantasia* stays in my memory because I've seen it fourteen times, each time taking younger members of the family to share its fantastic imaginings, though what impact would it make today, I wonder?

Shifra

Shifra was from a completely different world. The daughter of a chemist in Manchester, lean, wiry, a kind of tomboy with knobbly knees like a young colt, determinedly unfeminine. Her spirit hovered between reason and abandon, the tempestuous and the rational. Her Mancunian accent was marked. We eyed each other throughout the two weeks of camp activity – singing, dancing, play-acting, political debate. She commanded attention with assured intelligence, mesmerising strength and a winning sardonic sense of humour which matched the tongue in my cheek. A faded photograph of her, part of a group, shows her as an almost demonic beauty. No, not beauty. She was not that. It was a striking face, dark-skinned and intense-eyed. Esther was cosy, Shifra was exciting.

I may have suffered every adolescent's bouts of despair but felt nothing was beyond my reach. I was aware of a driving power within. Shifra had it too, we recognised it in each other – pubescent dynamism circling one another, sparks of dangerous energy flowing between us, waiting to touch. Which they did, that last night of camp.

We were both strong personalities, each had a sense of how we should live and be loved. What forces were at work to splinter those passionate adolescents? Here's some of the truth – I was a Perlmutter and unworldly, Shifra was born very knowing; cleverer than me and tougher. Tougher meant she had no compunction destroying what was in her path. If one day you're going to build the General Motors building in New York and become a millionairess you need a facility to shed cumbersome compunction.

Her personality surfaces through her letters, which are undated so have to be sleuthed through. I'm not certain I have them in their right order but this is what seems to have happened. We met in the summer of 1947 and corresponded from the end of camp till Christmas when she came to London for a movement conference and a Hebrew seminar. The first letters must have palpitated with young passion. I have only two of them, one a scribbled outburst:

I am called Cecilia Rickless & I say:-
    I love you, yes I do
    It's a sin to tell a lie!
    Tho' not to write on Shabbat! [Sabbath]

The other penned in a greeny-blue ink:

Dear Arnold, are you in bed? Good. Well, snuggle down, my love, & list while I talk to you and smooth your brow. The night is dark and the moon is yellow, the candle flickers and the stars scintillate. All is still and silence rules the hour. My hand is cool, your forehead smooth, your face is in the shadow, my free hand is clasped in yours. Amity herself is envious and as I lay my head on the pillow, cheek by cheek, I talk to you & the whisper of my voice drifts gently round the room and loses itself in the impenetrable dark. List, my love. You're fifteen, now, Arnold, what have you done with the last fifteen years, heh, and what are you going to do with the next fifteen? Ten & five years hence what will you have accomplished? You'll be a man, then, thirty years old & probably with a wife & family – unless you're on a kibbutz in which case you'll have the prospect of just another ten years prior to going to Aliyah [emigration].

But your head lolls & your eyelids they close, your frame it relaxes & your arm around me tightens.

It's cold sitting on the bed, dear one. Kiss me, my sweet & let me return the caress. X there. Whisper 'sweet nothings' in my ear & lose yourself to the land of dreams.

Go, my Arnold, sleep, sleep, sleep, sleep
    sleep, sleep
        sleep
            sleep
                sleep
                    sleep
                        sleep
                            sleep
                                . . . .

Blush, blush to think we ever wrote such feathery sentiments, but we did, most of us. Unbelievably, by the time those fifteen years had passed, Shifra had her degree from the London School of Economics, married and divorced a dentist in Canada, and entered the world of property speculation; I had married, fathered my first son and daughter, and written five stage plays.

Between camp and Christmas, as well as exchanging love letters, I sent her my poetry, and then hitchhiked up to Manchester where I received overwhelming northern hospitality from her family. We spent a day in Blackpool, sat to have two silhouettes scissor-cut – I still have the one of her, and a small horn of hard shell she bought me. And that memorable afternoon among the Edale Peaks. We climbed Loose Hill. I was wearing corduroy shorts on which I marked each hundred feet. It was at the top she offered her bared breast to mine. I gave a shout of joy, grabbed her hand and ran her down the slope we'd just laboriously climbed, '. . . with boulders all round us ready to show us the way down . . .' , leaping dangerously over dangerous stones and me thinking, 'Fool! You have weak ankles! You'll rick one of them!' But what did love ever sensibly care about? Near the bottom we fell and rolled and rolled and created a moment each of us will remember to the grave. Lives are peaked with such highs.

Something happened. Her ardour cooled. She demanded her letters, the cream of her epistolic passion, to be returned. I was blackmailed.

... I want my letters back. Listen carefully, Arnold. I've asked you for them repeatedly – I ask again. I have a very large number of your poems. You want copies of them, or the originals. I've been meaning to send you them as soon as pos. – meaning it for ages & you know it but as somehow I've never got round to it I've decided you shan't have them now until I receive my letters. If you'd rather have my letters to your poems, why then keep 'em, but think hard first which are most valuable to you. You might be able to sell your poems one day – you'll never be able to get any honour from my letters. Your poems mean little to me, my letters mean more ...

I succumbed, made the wrong choice, my poems for her letters. Only now do I realise which were probably more interesting.

Other letters hint at something awful she's discovered about me which led to the cooling of her love. It's never mentioned, but someone else is – her brother. I paled beside her beloved Barney.

... It's very hard to make myself plain. You see, I've had this feeling of disappointment since I found out a particular thing about you but having Barney home and seeing him makes me not want to write to you. He's so fine & good & honest & ... oh a whole host of things, that I feel I just want to finish with someone I can't even trust. I'm 'fraid this letter's harsh but I hope it makes you stop liking me 'cos then I'll know that a) your affection is as shallow as I surmised & b) that two or three harsh letters in succession can alter your feelings ...

Then, it hurt. Now I see the absence of logic. Either I'd done something awful, or she'll know me by the way I respond to 'three harsh letters'. Which is it? Her emotions become erratic. A later letter is full of remorse:

Dear, dear Arnold, I'm very sorry for being awful, honestly I really am. Making a sort of bargain with you about my letters and your poems was a horrible thing for me to do, once again I say I'm sorry. In future I shant use you as an outlet for all my annoyances – you deserve something better & so, d'you know what I'm going to do, heh? I'm going to give you the opportunity of writing your next letter to me in one of two ways. Namely:- cool and unforgiving – it would be quite justified – & telling me you want to end our correspondence or b) A love letter, in the real sense of the phrase.

The choice is yours. Think carefully . . .

Are you looking forward to seeing me . . . Your knife is being done – at least it's at the place just now & it'll be ready in about a month's time so I'll either send it or bring it with me – whichever you prefer.

Arnold, oh I do wish you'd hold me in your arms, tell me you loved me & cover me in kisses. Shall you kiss me when I come down at Christmass . . .

I LOVE YOU

ANSWER SOON, WILL YOU, PLEASE?

Ta-ta my love, you have my love – had it for ages but just let it slip thro' your fingers & took it for granted – once again I give it to you. Shifra.

PLEASE TELL ME JUST WHY YOU SENT MY LETTERS BACK TO ME, THE REAL REASON.

I have no memory of what I wrote to Shifra, she later informed me my letters were all put carefully away in a little box, which is where now, I wonder? What she next writes betrays anxiety about what my feelings for her now are. She wants to be certain, when she comes down at Christmas, of her reception.

Then arrives the letter which leads to the BIG blowup.

I know I haven't written for some time but I was waiting to hear just how you'd gone on at school. Having heard, & by a miracle found some time, I'm writing to you.

Look, I wrote you a very sloppy letter last Saturday sympathising with your trouble at school. Let me say now that everything has turned out all right for you, that I did not mean anything endearing I might have said in it. I'm sorry if this is somewhat harsh but there is now no reason to pretend to feel a feeling for you that I haven't got. I had a very bad 'pash' on you for a short while & the dregs of such an infatuation is friendship – of a description – but it has entirely worn off. I told you so quite plainly but a pleading letter from you, followed very quickly by an account of your bother at school, made me feel that for the time being I ought to keep up our correspondence.

I'm sorry but I think I owe it to you to be honest. Let me say now, once & for all, that I do not love you, that I never have loved you – 'cept for a very brief space of time – & that I never am likely to love you. I have never loved any man. I'm very fond of you because you gave me some very pleasant hours & because you gave me sympathy at a time when I needed it & pleasant companionship at other times.

I doubt if I shall ever forget you & I feel sure that, tho' we may not correspond, if we were to meet we would find a bond of friendship between us. Who knows where we may not crop up against one another during the course of our lives & I feel sure that when we do an easy sense of companionship will exist between us tho' we may not have had any sort of contact for a number of years.

Being in the same movement will ensure that we do not entirely lose contact. I'd rather not write more than once in a blue moon if at all. Now you're writing to Valerie [Rossovsky] that won't matter tho', & indeed I advise you to cultivate your acquaintanceship with her, she's a very nice girl, has her faults but so have we all, anyway if you feel you'd like to adopt her as your 'girl' don't let me or my memory hinder you – 'fact I'd encourage you to write to her, have done from the beginning.

You are under absolutely no obligation to answer this letter either immediately or, indeed at all. So, with these few words, I'll close a brief & very foolish paragraph of my life.

Before I take my leave, Arnold, I'd like to say that you've done nothing to make me annoyed or anything, it's just that I don't like you that way, infatuations wear off, & I think this one has, after 3 months practically worn itself out.

Well, hoping you're not offended or anything so silly, I'll say
Shalom [written in modern Hebrew script] Shifra.

I dearly would love my reply before me. Many years later, when I met Valerie Rossovsky, her bosom friend, in Israel she hinted at a school-girl lesbian relationship between them with Shifra as the dominant one. My response must have been penned in fury and blood for it drew blood and fury. On 17 November came the letter 'bomb', from 'SCHOOL', in an envelope on which was written, for the postman to read:

ANY FURTHER LETTERS FROM YOU – UNLESS MARKED 'UNAVOIDABLE' – WILL BE CONSIGNED TO THE FLAMES.
  GOODBYE AND MAY YOUR LIFE BE LIVED – that is all I have to say – Shifra.
  OURS COULD HAVE BEEN A FRIENDSHIP – 'TWAS A PITY – from your point of view your letter reflects just how conceited and artificial you are. It wouldn't be so bad had you something to be conceited over.

What on earth had I written? There are no clues, only insults.

ARNOLD
I've just recieved your letter & am answering not out of courtesy but to tell you, quite definitely that a) your letter disgusted me both from the point of view of subject matter & of bad grammar plus infantile spelling . . .

I have no doubts she was right about both my grammar and infantile spelling though even I knew that *i* comes before *e* except after *c*.

. . . b) to tell you that you will recieve copies of any poems you wish but no more & c) you will definitely never get your letters back.
  Not, let me assure you, that they mean anything to me but just because, not feeling any real affection for you, I feel myself under absolutely no obligation to give you what is mine, just because you want them.

Different reasoning from that offered when demanding the return of *her* letters. She was not so much a woman for all seasons as one armed with arguments to suit the occasion. Not unfamiliar with hindsight.

> Let me assure you that in years to come I shall read them with great pleasure & enjoyment & I see no reason whatever why I should forgo such enjoyment – especially after the rude tone of your last letter.

Then followed the ferocious damning of my poems.

> ... I have not only analysed your poems but have had them analysed by an authority & the verdict – muddled thought – very 'amateurish' expression of theme – lack of any style – and unoriginal subject matter.
>
> Very often I have spent an hour or so reading your stuff, trying to think where I'd heard it before & then tracing it to other poets who had the same thoughts but couched in better terms.
>
> Your high-sounding sentences analysed from a literary point of view mean nothing. Your pretensions to self-honesty are so stressed that one wonders whom you are trying to convince, the reader or yourself. In fact, your whole make-up appears to be composed of nothing but pretension, affectation and delusions – self and otherwise.
>
> I am not alone in these observations ...

No, she wasn't. I rather agreed, though perhaps not at that precise moment.

> ... & despising you, for that's what it amounts to, for a backboneless character, it is not surprising that I put an end to what I still consider to have been a foolish affair, on my part anyway.
>
> What you think doesn't bother me, and I wish to hear no more either of or from you ... to think I ever necked with you – for as such I *now* classify it – makes me realise just what a fool I was ...

Guilt sets in again. Her next letter – this one is dated 1.12.47 and also written from school (where did she find the time?) – reminds me I was so hurt I was thinking of leaving the movement – after all, broken hearts are more important than a homeland for broken Jews!

> Arnold, please, for your own sake as much as for mine, don't leave the movement. The point is that the fact that I consider your poetry, at the moment, not to be all that could be desired does not mean I don't believe you have it in you to write something really good when you become more mentally & physically mature . . .

What did physical maturity have to do with writing poetry?

> It's only thro' practice now that when you do reach years of maturity you'll be able to translate your feeling adequately . . . discourage-ment can be encouragement. Some of my criticisms were admittedly very harsh & callous but I honestly believed you needed them, if only to improve your work. I could, I admit, have waited till Xmas & then gently brought it up by word of mouth. I'm sorry. Arnold I do feel that when I am in London in approximately 3 weeks hence we should try & find some time in which to be alone & really have a good 'yach' [jaw] & clear a few things up. I doubt if you'll do this, Arnold, but please understand that it's *I* who's asking *you* as a personal favour . . .
>   . . . I may say I did not dream that you cared sufficiently for me to, on the basis of my nastiness, propose to leave a movement whose aims, aspirations & ideals I knew you to believe in . . . please withhold your decision till I see you . . . don't refuse to see me if only because I should hate to feel that, apart from my having lost a friend, I have caused, directly or indirectly, you to leave Habonim a movement which I firmly believe has a great deal to offer to you & which I feel you are capable of giving a great deal to . . .
>   By the way a party from the M/C peleg [branch] decided to go on a ramble last Thursday, Lizzie's wedding day, to Edale & district. I was naturally asked and inquired what part of the district. I learnt that the destination was Loose Hill & so needless to say I refused.

Do me a favour will you and look at your corduroys a sec? How high was Loose? I think it began with 15 – but can't think of any more. You scratched it on didn't you . . .

Clever young woman to reach out to a passionate moment she knew we both treasured.

I send her a birthday present of *The Rubáiyát of Omar Khayyám*. She writes thanking me and reminding me:

. . . Let me impress on you that after the way my family treated you at M/C it would be your duty and no more to receive me with hospitality . . .

She was right. Her family, particularly her father, had been effusively kind. Arrangements are made. She visits me in Weald Square, we go places, we make love, creep into each other's legs beneath the safety of raincoats in the dark of cinemas. She enjoys meeting my mother and father, Della and Ralph, cousin Bryan, friend Sam. But not all of our time together is happy. There's a moment after we'd slept together in Weald Square, when she slaps my face. One of her letters recalls the incident:

. . . I had no wish to slap your face, if you remember you challenged me to, I was not the slightest bit angry with you tho' somewhat with myself . . . When you got up to slap me back & did it so gently – tho' maybe not intentionally so – I felt like bursting out laughing. I thought however how hurt you'd be & not being sufficiently childish as to want to deliberately hurt you I restrained myself.

Why the slap? I think because she'd been reading my letters to Valerie and I had angrily said something that angered her. 'I feel I could hit you for that,' she said. 'Go ahead,' I challenged, not imagining she would do it. Silly me. Of course she would. I rose to hit her back, but never having struck anybody, let alone a woman, I didn't know how. I was deficient in 'thrashing energy', it's not in me to inflict physical pain, which is why I was gentle. The moment, which took place in my bedroom, is vivid in memory. My hand rose and once in the air seemed uncertain where to go, how to behave, which is why it merely floated down. And she *did* laugh. I can't remember what I did. I'd like to think I smiled, at least.

From then on letters are exchanged intermittently. We settle into a friendship. She comes on holiday with her nephew to Wacton; shares with me news that she's failed her higher exams, flunked French, decides not to leave school and go to work but to return and try again. By September 1949 she's smoking and drinking. *Circa* September 1950 she's riding a motorbike, a Royal Enfield 125. Her letters remind me of forgotten moments and actions, such as that I'd signed on to be a film extra. No work was ever offered. She's thrilled that I've won a bronze medal for elocution from LAMDA (London School of Music and Drama – I later win a silver one, too!) and that I've passed the entrance test to RADA. One letter dated 8 February 1950 is sad and saturated with what she seems to feel is a lost past:

. . . It was snowing this morning, & now the sun is shining brilliantly & I feel, in some inexplicable way, that the weather has a great deal to do with my sudden urge to write to you. Can you understand, wise one? I can't.

I have your letter in front of me – written I see on Christmas day. Tell me Arnold, did you type it because the typewriter was there & you felt in the mood for using it, or because you wanted to insult me in a beautifully subtle way? You're so unpredictable – & so very far away from me – that I can't guess.

Unfortunately every time we see one another we seem to get further & further away from each other, in spite of your unfailing courteous and sweet behaviour. I think I must be a pig at heart, and a rather stupid one too – although I wouldn't admit it to anyone but you. You must teach me how to behave some time Arnold, unless the task seems too formidable.

While clearing out some old papers I found our silhouettes & decided to send them both to you. Keep either or both, but, if you decide you only want one or, possibly, neither, may I have the other please?

How's work going Arnold, are you any happier in your job? and home . . . are your parents employed again or are you still supporting the family? Tell me, do you still belong to a dramatic society or have you joined any other clubs? Writing – are you still? Conscription – have you made any enquiries about the navy or taken it for granted that because ma & pa Wesker are aliens you'll be automatically refused? Reading – are you, if so what sort?

You see, there are dozens of things I want to know, providing of course you've no objection to letting me share them. Have you?

Incidentally, Arnold, how is D & R's baby? Now don't look so accusingly at me, I *know* I wrote a nasty, unnecessary & uncalled for letter, so don't start telling me off & scolding me. Besides, it doesn't suit you to look so stern. I'm sorry Arnold . . .

As for me, well, I'm in one of my 'up' periods – comparatively satisfied & more 'settled' than when I last saw you. In spite of the fact that I honestly haven't thought about you for ages, this last couple of days I've found myself thinking about our [bike] ride together at Norfolk – remember? Everything else I want to forget but those couple of hours I think we were both very contented – probably I more than you, since you had the heavy job of dragging me home clinging to your shoulders.

I'm near the end of the sheet, & since I'm not really sure about the reception this letter's going to receive it might be as well to end now, hmm? Please write – soon. Shifra.

She had learnt how to spell 'receive'.

By the time National Service begins she's in London at LSE. (A letter from Bryan records that she came with my mother to see me off at King's Cross Station for RAF Padgate, where life began for new conscripts. Mother was so upset at parting that Shifra took her off for a drink.) I write telling her that I'd failed to get into air crew, she commiserates and enthuses about a new book she's read called *Lust for Life* by Irving Stone.

. . . It's actually Van Gogh's life story. I've no idea about your taste in art or even whether you like art at all, but I suggest that irrespective of your opinion of his work, you read this book. I have only just finished it and I was possessed all the way through by the feeling that this book had a message for you . . .

It did. A mixed one. I went on to read all of Irving Stone's books and fear his style seeped into my early prose, calamitously. He was a hugely successful populariser of famous lives – Gauguin, Jack London, Eugene Debs, Clarence Darrow. Kirk Douglas played Van Gogh in a film of *Lust for Life*. In the mid eighties Dusty and I enjoyed a glorious, long-dreamed-of voyage on the *QE2* in return for which I had to 'entertain' passengers with a couple of lecture/readings. Irving Stone was another of the passenger 'entertainers'. He gave what was obviously an often-delivered talk on the detailed scholarly research that went into his books. It was a defensive lecture rooted in years of criticism from critics who did not take him as seriously as he would have liked. I believed the research, regretted the style.

In that same letter Shifra begins to be nice about my poetry.

. . . Keep away from prose for awhile but for God's sake push on with the poetry. I don't normally say this sort of thing so I hope you will believe me when I say that in this last poem I have of yours 'Rose one night in a sweat of thought . . .' you have written a masterpiece, and God knows I'm not using that word loosely . . . Carry on, I have great confidence that one day you will become a poet of no mean dimensions . . .

Of course it was not a masterpiece, merely another dreadful attempt to hit poetic heights completely beyond my reach. It doesn't stop Shifra from attempting to sell some of my efforts.

. . . Have sent your poems (some of them) away & awaiting letters of acceptance accompanied by cheques . . .

No acceptance. No cheques. But her comments and advice must have made me feel good. And she liked my new girlfriend.

> . . . I'd like to see you get away from the military theme – I know it's important to you – & get down to something dealing with the more fundamental & permanent emotions – Love, Jealousy, Hate, Greed etc . . .
>   . . . Rhoda is a nice girl . . .
>   . . . Object to your very recently acquired habit of calling me Cissie – Shifra to you as it was . . . world without end . . .

As it Was and World Without End – the title of a discovery, Helen Thomas's book about her life with Edward, which I bought as presents for all and sundry, among them Shifra.

The Festival of Britain comes and goes. The love affair with Rhoda comes and goes – a commiserating card from Shifra dates its passing – 27 August (Della's birthday) 1951. I'm demobbed, she can't come to the demob party which cousin Bryan is organising to be held in Aunt Billie's new flat, she urges me to find work in order to pay fees for the Oxford School of Drama or:

> . . . Bulldoze your way into an interview with Mr Justice Karminsky, President of the Jewish Board of Guardians; they have a special department for the purpose. Try the educational assistance fund of the British Legion . . . Don't, I beg you, let the opportunity slip . . .

In the meantime she has become embroiled with my friends, not all of whom are 100 per cent responsible about money she has loaned them. She presses me to get back amounts of £4 from a friend called Ginger, and 15/– from another, Alastair Sutherland. On Wednesday, 15 October 1952, the *Manchester Evening News* carries an article by her which she sends. 'A woman takes a long-term look at equal pay'.

The next letter in my possession is dated quarter of a century later – 16 November 1977, the opening day of *Shylock* (then entitled *The Merchant*) at the Plymouth Theatre, Broadway. I had been ten weeks in New York preparing for the opening, not knowing Shifra was there or anything about the General Motors building. That's not strictly accurate. She had hit the headlines many years earlier as the woman who had beaten a clutch of tough male New York property tycoons by snatching from under their noses the last most valuable plot of real estate in the city. *Shylock* had been written up in *The New York Times*. Shifra read the article and traced me.

767 FIFTH AVENUE
NEW YORK N.Y. 10022

Dear Arnold

You didn't return my call, either because Dusty forgot to give you the message, or you couldn't be bothered. If it's the former you can reach me at my office in the General Motors building (which, incidentally, I built) during weekdays – 355 2887.

If it's the latter, I'm sorry. I called only because I would have loved to wish you Good Luck in person, to meet again and given you a 'mazeltov' hug.

As I recall I was quite helpful to you when you were involved in Theatre in the Round [she means the Roundhouse at Chalk Farm] & needed Sir Max Rayne's help. Max (now Lord Rayne) remains my dearest & closest friend &, since he is now chairman of the National Theatre where, I gather, you have a play opening in due course, I might have been able to do something nice for you.

Truly dear, I am delighted you have so totally met your aspirations. In so far as I, too, have been absurdly successful in the business world, I need nothing from you, & went to some trouble to locate you simply from a wellspring of affection & a feeling that it would be nice, since you are in New York, to touch base.

If my consequence hasn't made me too much of a big shot to call you, yours shouldn't be so out of hand as to stop you calling back either!

Whether I hear from you or not I hope the opening goes well.

Affectionately

Shifra. Benattar (Rickless).

I had every intention of making contact. The letter is strangely sad. She imagines I would no longer want to know her due to my 'consequence'; reminds me of past favours; tempts me with an influential friend – which influence I've no need of and anyway rarely works in London theatrical circles; and reveals no sense that I might be under pressure due to an opening. Anxious and bullying, not a letter written by the girl so bewildered by love she battered our emotions and kicked like a young colt. I rang her and we made a date to meet for lunch the day following the first night which she attended along with an audience who gave the play an ecstatic response.

But *Shylock* could not survive the death of its intended star, Zero Mostel, four days after the first try-out performance in Philadelphia. The director, John Dexter, and I had dragged the production through another set of rehearsals with the understudy, Joseph Leon, taking over the lead. We all thought, after the first-night rapturous applause, that the play had been rescued. Even the hoary old Shubert directors, a mafia trio with hunched shoulders and shifty eyes, thought we had pulled it off. But little works on Broadway without a star, and the all-important *New York Times* critic, Richard Eder, had been in his job only a few weeks and was wet with innocence. I think he wanted the play to succeed but had not yet learned that a critic's advice to book or not to book is contained in the last line. He reviewed the play intelligently, describing what he admired and faulting what he considered flawed, ending: '. . . the evening is stimulating but only sometimes successful.' 'Only sometimes successful' rather than 'the evening is stimulating' is what the punters read. The play's life in New York was terminated, like a struggling newborn having its drip removed, and a defeated playwright lunched with his old girlfriend one day after the opening.

We met in her office on the fifty-eighth or ninth floor. She was proud of her tall skyscraper and its stylish offices. But she was bored. There was little left to do but play the stock market, she told me. Do I remember correctly that she owns a house in Israel and spends a lot of time there? I think she feared forces were gathering against the Jews and that Israel was the only place where we could all survive. Our lunch together, as I recall feeling, was humiliating. Suddenly, after weeks imagining that my financial worries were over – having Zero Mostel in the lead was like inheriting a bank – now I was in great debt.

The previous year was the year of *Stepney Streets*; a handsome folio of eight John Allin prints with a sheet of text from my unpublishable play *The New Play*, limited edition of 250, which I had initiated and for which I'd raised a third of the costs. A hundred had been sold, the remaining hundred and fifty divided between John Allin, John Gorman the printer, and myself. Allin immediately split and sold his, many of mine became birthday or wedding presents, usually pairs of prints. But then I was trying to sell complete folios and had brought with me to the lunch a brochure describing them, hoping Shifra would buy. She agreed to purchase but with an absence of enthusiasm which shamed me. The rich *are* different. Rich ex-girlfriends are painfully different. I should not have done it. What subsequently transpired confirmed I should not have done it – as her only other remaining letter explains. It is dated two months later, 16 January 1978:

Dear Arnold

I received your letter today and owe you an apology for not having been in touch with you before. My schedule since mid December has been absurdly peripatetic – 2 days in London, 9 in Mexico, 6 in Canada & now, this Friday 20th back to London for a day.

What in fact happened is that the day after receiving the call about the lost cheque I called Lord Rayne intending to ask him to issue a replacement cheque to you. When he learned the purpose he offered to give me the set he had purchased, as a Chanukah [New Year] present. Sorry to have done you out of a sale! I think they are charming, although having now seen them they would at £300 have been a bit overpriced.

It is unlikely that I will be in London during February & I take advantage of this opportunity to wish you all you wish yourself for

Love Letters. That volume was among the 4 I received from somebody or other (no note enclosed so didn't know who to thank) for
which I owe you a belated note. I found the writing a delight to read
& the substance of many of the stories hauntingly poignant. How
very blessed you are to have such a gift.

I haven't forgotten my promise to send your letters, poems etc.
I'm slowly starting to go through the massive accumulation of
papers gathered over the decades as part of the packing preparatory
to our move from New York. Since we move in June I have 4
months to get back 29 years!

As soon as I have a visit to London for longer than a day or two,
I'll give you a call. In the meantime seeing you again was delightful
—

Be hugged
Love·
Shifra.

I have not heard from her since. My letters and poems were never
sent. The John Allin prints now sell for around £175 *each* print. She
could have declined the offer of a Chanukah present from Lord
Rayne, it would have made me happier to have once loved her. But
she had responded generously to my stories. I *was* happy to have
once loved her.

The story of Esther – part two

Esther's mother developed breast cancer. Because she lost time at
school looking after her, Esther was not allowed to sit for matriculation. In 1950 her mother died and Esther was put on to a year's
secretarial course. Her first job was with General Electric. From her
first wage packet she bought herself an elegant umbrella. 'I liked the
sound of my high heels tapping the pavement,' she told me, 'and I
walked swinging my new brolly and tapping it along with my high

heels.' Working for a firm of architects she allowed her first ever non-Jewish man to kiss her. But her innocence remained until Israel. Twenty-one years old she went there as a tourist and stayed.

And here looms another life decided by the toss of a coin. She went to the shipping office to cancel her ticket – a young, eager woman, those features restless with expectation, dressed in shorts, unaware that a routine was being played out in the office behind the counter: every time an attractive female came through the doors the young men tossed a coin to decide who'd serve her. The man she was to marry, Nahum Zagel, a sabra (someone born in Israel), won.

Esther returned to London in early 1958 to inform her family. She came to see me. I was at the film school. Dusty was at Butlins – Weald Square was full of her paintings. When I got back my mother met me in the passage.

'Guess who's here?' I paused a long time. Something in her growing smile must have alerted me.

'Esther!'

I told her about Dusty. She told me about Nahum. They were married on 3 June, lived in Haifa, postings to Naples and Sydney with the shipping company. Dusty and I entertained them and their children on a couple of visits they made to London. Esther was around in time to cheer me up when I was on my back struck low with abscess poison. We corresponded from time to time.

From 28 February to 20 March 1984 I was in Israel researching a four-part adaptation of Arthur Koestler's novel, *Thieves in the Night*, about the early Jewish settlers in Palestine. It was to be a German/Israeli co-production. The Israeli end provided me with a wonderful guide, Avner, who drove me around. I was determined to make contact with Esther. A special 110-page diary exists of those days. These extracts continue her story:

Wednesday, 7 March 1984 – Tiberias
Before leaving Haifa I wanted to drop a card in at Esther's house. As there had been no reply to phone calls I assumed they were in London or on holiday somewhere. I wrote my card, Avner asked for

directions and we drove to Haruv 17 stopping on the way at a vantage point to look at a view of the bay. [My card said:]

> I was passing the door so I thought I'd drop in to say hello and look at the sea. No one home. Pity! It would have been good to see you. I'll call again in another ten years' time! Perhaps sooner. I'm here to get background material for a mini TV series based on Koestler's *Thieves in the Night*. So I may return. Are you well? Love Wizzie. PS Pauline Abrahams was cremated the day I left London. 28 February. Cancer.

At number 17 there was no such name. I suggested to Avner that we knock on a door and ask. Perhaps they had moved? Someone might know. The door I chose, at random, was the right one. A woman answered. At the mention of the name Zagel she sent up a sad moan. Two other women came to the door. Their faces were sad. One asked Avner who I was. He said a relative from London. They told us the story. Esther and Nahum were in Jerusalem at the Hadassah Hospital. Their middle son, Boaz, had had an accident during winter manoeuvres. He was in a serious state. One woman took us to her flat in another block where she had the phone number of the hospital. We walked over. She invited us in. The blocks of flats are of the boring square box kind seen all over the world. The interior of this woman's flat, however, was full of ornate things – dolls, blue and white china, ivory elephants. I told her she had a beautiful home and asked was she a collector. No. She'd lived with her husband for five years in Hong Kong and had bought – that's all.

I came away upset. Poor Esther. She will be shattered. I kept putting myself in her place imagining how I'd feel were it one of my sons. But I couldn't maintain my sadness, it would not have been fair on Avner. I asked him was there a high rate of accidents?

'It happens! When you use live ammunition it happens.' It seems the boy was himself responsible and now I wonder if any others were hurt. If they were it will increase Esther's and Nahum's pain and grief . . .

Saturday, 10 March 1984 – Hilton
. . . The operator rang to say Esther had phoned from Beit Levenstein Hospital and to ring her back. I did so immediately. A male

voice said hello. It was Michael the eldest. They were downstairs by a phone box waiting for my call. He passed me on to Esther. Her voice was frail but familiar. She asked how I'd traced them. I told her the story and asked could she speak. The two boys were there and she said she'd go on for as long as she could. 'Are sitting d̶.̶ ̶w̶n̶? she asked me, and began. Boaz had lost his eyes. And he had severe head injuries. 'We don't know how severe. The professors at the Hadassah who were wonderful, everyone was so marvellous, I can't tell you, the professors said it could go any way. The brain was like a black box – the more they knew about it the more they didn't know. One similar case recovered and is now looking after himself and coping. Another after five years became a psychologist. It's difficult to tell just now. But of course you must expect the worst. He's fighting. We can feel he's fighting. His body is trained and his heartbeat is strong. He was in one of the finest units and the terrible thing is he had only just finished his training with others where the comradeship was high and he said he was now worried about where he was going because the level wasn't as disciplined . . .'

I don't think she was clear at this point. She jumped and rambled, unable to put together all the facts she was receiving. She asked what I was doing in the country. I told her. She was able to show great pleasure. 'Oh, how lovely! It's all come round full circle.' Was I coming to Haifa? I said there were no plans. I would ring when I came back from Jerusalem. How was Nahum?

'You know, I have such a wonderful family. The boys have been so supportive. I wish Nahum would cry. He can't. The wind's running out of my sails. At the Hadassah there were other cases – a soldier, a girl of six, we made such friends, it brought out all the best qualities. I'm blessed. You know I'm really blessed with my family. It's a strange thing to say but Boaz was the one it should happen to . . . I . . .'

I could hear she couldn't go on. She gave the phone to Michael.

'I understand,' I told him. 'Tell her I'll phone when I get back from Jerusalem. Either I'll come to the hospital or to Haifa. And tell her I'm grateful she phoned me. I put down the phone and fought back tears. Tears for what? A boy I didn't know! Be sad, yes. But to cry? I had no right. Except that he could have been my son by the first girl I ever loved. And I'm fighting tears still, as I write these lines which I didn't want to write but it's the only way I know how to cope . . .

19 March 1984

. . . Avner drove me to Jerusalem to see Esther, Nahum and Boaz in the Hadassah Hospital. It was a meeting for which I was bracing myself. Avner had to eat before going in. If he doesn't eat at the time he's hungry he becomes tense and nervous 'and I get headaches'. We stopped at a roadside restaurant just before Jerusalem, called The Motza Inn. It looked as though it should have served hamburgers and chips, junk food. The interior was Swiss chalet but there were paintings on the wall, flowers on the table, the Bach Brandenburg Concertos coming through the speakers, the cooking was Moroccan and excellent.

Boaz was in the orthopaedic ward, second floor, room five. I'd brought a copy of *Say Goodbye You May Never See Them Again* and had planned to buy flowers at the hospital. The shop was shut. Room five was two individual rooms with a common 'kitchen'. A man with a yumulka [skull cap] was sitting by a plastic-topped table. Avner asked for Boaz Zagel. I peered into the room on the right. A sewn-up face with eyes that seemed glued shut confronted me. The body was under sheets. A drip fed into the nose. A yellowish plastic something was thrust into the neck by the Adam's apple. His arms were by his sides hidden under the sheets. Esther emerged. She had been sitting in an armchair by his bed. We embraced. She asked, 'Did you see him?' I nodded. She withdrew a photograph. 'Now here's the real Boaz, as he was.' I saw a young man with eyes laughing at the camera. She introduced me to the youngest son, Dan, and pointed to Nahum stretched out on a further bed, sleeping. She was my Esther. A little wrinkled, but those wide round eyes still naive and alert. I saw the girl. I'd expected matronly change but the girl had lingered.

There seemed nowhere to sit. We went into the corridor and sat sideways twisted towards each other, on a black and white striped mattress, a triangular suspended wooden bar with which patients pulled themselves up swinging between us. After more than ten years this is how we met. Avner hovered in the distance, not wishing to intrude. She asked who he was and said she didn't mind him hearing the story. The more the better. Her ebullient nature had surfaced. She'd done some of her crying, had had some of her hysterics, there would be more but now she could be something of herself for me. The story she told was confused, full of anger, bitterness, incomplete because the facts are not fully known yet.

Boaz had volunteered for a unit that was a crack above the paratroopers. Their tasks were special and secret. Esther wouldn't reveal what. She didn't know it all, by far, and should not have known what she did. He hadn't got on with his immediate superior, a religious soldier with a yumulka on his head – which she claims now gives her a hatred for anyone she sees wearing one. 'I've learned to hate so many people.' She talked about a quarrel, 'the only one I've ever had with him'. It seems that he was thrown out of the crack unit, I wasn't sure why – for budget-cut reasons – and she could have said something but had refused to and he was angry with her. He was transferred to somewhere which caused him anxiety because efficiency and discipline were low. There were manoeuvres. He and three or four others were in an area which should have been cleared of mines. It wasn't. He stepped on one. That *seems* to have been the story. No one is sure. No one has told them. There is to be an enquiry.

That was the military débâcle. Next comes the hospital's story. The surgeon who has to tell them the extent of Boaz's damage begins from the bottom upwards. A leg is shattered. They've removed the shrapnel. There seems to be no permanent internal damage. They had to remove his eyes. The brain is damaged but they can't judge the extent. They want to cut off a leg. Nahum insists they save it. Then come details of their efforts to get him into the right ward. He should have remained in intensive care, he's not, he's in the orthopaedic section. They shifted him backwards and forwards between hospitals in this condition. Not all the nurses seemed to know what had to be connected to what. They'd shift his position and accidentally disconnect tubes they would then leave unconnected. Those nurses who worked hard and well were overworked. At one point, during the transfer, Esther lost him! They couldn't find the body! She had hysterics. One day, had they not been there all the time, he'd have died. (Nahum was awake by this time and we were all in the room sitting and talking at the bedside of this patched-up middle son.) Nahum said:

'And what if he'd had no parents, or parents who were too old, or who were ill, or parents who were simple and couldn't fight on his behalf as we could. Oh, I was after blood. I wanted blood but I couldn't find anyone.' He still smiled like a cross between James Dean and Montgomery Clift. But *he* was old. The young man was looking out from the old man's face, he was slim, lithe, but all his hair was gone from the centre and the sides were grey. We embraced. I was so pleased to see him. The male nurse came in when we had sat and were talking. Esther explained who I was. He'd seen *Chips with Everything* at the Cameri Theatre.

'But more important than that,' I said, 'was that I was in love with her before he was.'

'Aha! Competition?'

'No. She rejected me before she met Nahum.'

I apologised for coming empty-handed and brought out the book to give them. Suddenly I realised the other possible significance of the title, *Say Goodbye You May Never See Them Again*. It was too late to do anything about it. I wrote inside what I could. Then Esther showed me something Boaz had written. He'd made a friend in Australia who, somehow or other and against all expectations, turned up in Israel. He brought them a magazine to which Boaz had contributed a couple of poems. The second one read:

> *So much more.*
> *So much more to explore*
> *So much to taste and feel*
> *To see and hear*
> *So much more to experience*
> *So much more to learn*
> *So much more.*

I had only just managed to contain myself. Now I had to flee. When I returned Esther asked was I all right? Was it the poems? I said yes. She made me sit in her chair.

'Do it,' said Nahum, 'sit in the boss's chair. You want a whisky?' He gave me to drink from a leather hip flask one of his sons had brought him home from somewhere as a present. I wasn't listening to details.

So we passed the time chatting till the nurses ushered us out while they changed his dressings and shifted his position. When we went back in Esther and Nahum checked everything and laughed about having to do it after the nurses. At one point Boaz coughed and Esther went round to him to clean some phlegm away. I watched her looking at him. She said to him:

'Oh you *do* smell. You'll have to start cleaning your teeth soon. Do you know who's here? It's Wizzie. From London. Do you remember Wizzie?'

She was looking at the face of her son whom she'd reared and loved and kissed for nineteen years and she was by now beginning to develop a relationship with this new version of him. Having gone past the shock of desecration to the flesh of her flesh she was finding a way to love and find comfort from what remained of him. The stitched-together, unconscious body of her child before her was a new focus, not quite what she could remember but surrogate enough. And what was it she was seeing? A face that now had no eyes and was stitched and black and blue and contained a brain that might never function again. I shall never forget that image of her looking at her prone, oblivious boy. It will stay with me always, and always make me weep.

We left at 4.30. I had my arm round Esther as they walked us to the door. I asked them to walk us to the car. I wanted every minute of them. She put her arm in mine. Nahum walked ahead with Avner.

'I wanted to take you out for dinner and talk about *such* things,' I told her. 'Next time.' Upstairs I had said to her, 'One day I'll tell you the truth.' 'Hurry up,' she said, 'before I'm sixty.' Now I wanted to tell her: there will always be a part of my life incomplete that belongs to her. I wanted to tell her even more: that my greatest wish was to hold her in my arms and complete the embrace I'd betrayed at that camp in the Wye Valley some thirty-five years ago. But the steps to the car were short, and she was telling me other things, and it was not the right moment. I kissed her lips goodbye. Embraced Nahum. They walked away arms around each other. Both were dressed in blue denim jackets and trousers. Young old ones. I was sorry for all the dismissive things I'd once said about him.

I couldn't see Boaz surviving. The thought occurred to me that perhaps the military were saying nothing because Boaz had behaved carelessly and they wanted to spare his parents' feelings. [This turned out not to be so. The mine had gone off because the other young soldiers were carelessly playing around with it.] Perhaps the hospital doctors knew he was a hopeless case and could not release personnel to help cases they knew were hopeless. I was fighting tears all the way back to Tel Aviv . . . Somehow, though angrily, I managed to conduct a newspaper interview for three-quarters of an hour in my hotel room with Immanuel Bar-Kadima, theatre critic from *Yedioth Ahronoth*; somehow I managed to make conversation with Avner and his wife and their two friends . . . I feel utterly shattered. And none of it is important beside that poor boy's destroyed life. I hate my tears. *They* have to live with it, not me.

Boaz was taken off the life support machine some months later. Esther and Nahum had been given time to get used to the loss of a son. I made one other visit and saw Esther's drawings. They were early days. Rushki, her sister, tells me she's added painting to her skills and has greatly improved.

Postscript

Halfway through writing this book Esther phoned Ashley Road. Dusty gave me the message. She was in London with Nahum and their youngest son for a great-nephew's barmitzvah, travel paid for by her very wealthy and generous brother-in-law. She was being treated for breast cancer. That night I immediately dreamt about her: I was in bed and she was sitting at the foot of it and I was telling her I'd been thinking about her. One of those sad, yearning dreams. Next day I found out from Rushki that they were staying at the Durrants Hotel. I rang. They were at breakfast. Nahum came to the phone. 'It's Wizzie.'

'Ah, Mr Wesker! You want Esther. I'll get her.'

That voice. The years rolled back. We talked for about twenty-five minutes. They had house problems, resulting court-case problems. But she was still painting. And the breast cancer? She explained it as 'an accumulation of things'. She gets tired, the chemo- and radio-therapy take their toll. It wasn't stopping her enjoying London however.

'It's pleasant to be spoken to nicely in the shops and have your goods wrapped and put in a bag and not be pushed. Israel is becoming a real Levantine country,' she said, 'loud, noisy, full of blaring music and rudeness . . .' She talked about her 'balm', her youngest son. 'I'd love you to have met him, huge, over six feet tall, and he's sweet, a lovely human being . . .' I asked what he did. 'You wouldn't like what he is doing. He "protects" people.' She wouldn't say more but I suppose she meant he guards a prison camp.

I told her that because of the autobiography I had been living with her for the last year, that she featured prominently in it. Her response was a touching 'thank you'. She confided her fears and complaints. It had been eight years since we'd last met, she was speaking to me as though we were in daily contact. I told her I longed to see her in Wales and hoped one day she would visit me.

'My Wye Valley,' she said. 'You know, there are no places left that aren't crowded.'

'Yes there are,' I replied. 'Canada, for example.'

'And Alaska,' she added. 'One day you and me we'll go off to Alaska for a holiday . . .'

'Ah, Esther, I have such fantasies about you . . . you'll be a presence in my life till the end.'

I had to let her go, finally.

'"God bless" as you used to say,' she said. Strange. I've never ever said 'God bless'! We exchanged telephonic hugs.

'And a kiss to you,' I added. I felt in those last seconds that both of us would like to have been holding tight in each other's arms. February of this year, 1994, she was sixty. In May I will be sixty-two.

Chapter Ten

The School Children's Union

We have been in the future for a long time, I'm afraid, and now must travel back to take up where we left off. It may seem a little crazy, be somewhat disorientating, but I've really only just left school!

I can't remember precisely at what point Robert Copping came into my life. I remember why – the 'School Children's Union', a project similar to one I had argued for when school seemed like a prison, teachers like jailers, and injustice the law of the classroom. Not true, of course, but it seemed to me that individuality, the holding of opinions, the desire to offer them, the offering, the elementary right to protest, question authority – all this was feared by many of the staff, frowned upon, denied. I can remember mooting to school friends the idea of a school children's union as a channel of representation, a means of protection against bullying and unreason. Within a year of leaving school, there in print in a newspaper almost word for word were proposals I'd been outlining. Someone else had set in motion a union for school children – Robert Copping, headmaster of a free school called Horsley Hall in Eccleshall, Staffs. I wrote to him at once. He replied at once. At the impressionable age of sixteen he seemed to me in possession of a brilliantly original mind. True or not he was kind, generous, tender, and influenced me deeply. Both Robert and the personality of Victor Feather, General Secretary of the TUC (1969–73), came together in the character of Victor Marsden in *Love Letters on Blue Paper*.

I know little of Robert's background, or if I knew I've forgotten. He was trained as a biologist, though I don't think he achieved a degree. Perhaps he inherited the capital to found his school. He certainly inherited with his brother a crumbling Victorian house in

Putney called 'Craigleigh', furnished with tattered settees, shaky chairs, cracked enamel pots, all smelling musty and neglected. He was one of nature's survivors – claiming impecuniousness but somehow always able to produce the pennies. Tall, thin, a balding head of spare light ginger hair and a beard at which he constantly tugged as though plucking accompaniment to his fierce commentary on one's life and work which beneath the mocking tone was warm and friendly.

'Don't be a fucking fool, Wizzie, how can that be if the facts are so glaringly other? It stands to reason, old son, that if human beings were of the essence intelligent then the entire world would be in a better state than it manifestly isn't at this moment as a cursory glance at any newspaper headline reveals to even the most stupid of us so get a grip and face what *is* rather than what you'd like to be you tender-hearted numbskull . . .' I invent, more to illustrate a style and force of personality than to record our arguments. We engaged in long conversations and correspondence. I thrilled to his intellectual energy and winced at his severe criticism of my writing.

I was a sixteen-year-old apprentice to a furniture-maker in Norton Folgate, London E1, with a facility to organise learned on active service with Habonim. From the first letter in my possession, dated 17 February 1949, it's obvious Robert was sufficiently impressed to have immediately laid upon me the responsibility of District Organiser (D.O.) for his School Children's Union.

Dear Arnold

Completely disregarding your remarks about not having much time for the next few weeks, I'm sending you a vast quantity of work.

In the first place, as our adult D.O.s in the London area – assuming that by definition you are not adult – are a little timid and uncertain of themselves, I suggest you do their work for them for a little while. The only other two who are officially District Organisers in London are

Charles Esam-Carter   Mrs Cecil Cotton
56/7 Belsize Park   and   19 Shooters Hill Road
London NW3   Blackheath, SE3

though there are about half a dozen more who are willing to give
their services this way. Leave them alone for the time being until
there are branches running smoothly in their areas. They can't be
trusted to do pioneer work.

I'm giving you herewith first a list of Branch Secretaries in the
London area. These I want you to contact as soon as possible: probably it will be best to visit them in their homes of an evening, but if
they are not in leave your name but not the nature of your business.
Don't leave any propaganda unless you deliver it into the hands of
the B.S. himself.

When you see them give them a pep-talk on the lines of the enclosed letter (they will all have received a copy), and explain to them
the following procedure—

I had to inspire them to inspire their classmates, distribute a leaflet
entitled 'The Union Will Stick Up For You', warn the Branch
Secretary that the headmaster was likely to make threats and that
he should only cease activity if the headmaster expressly forbids
him. If the Union is banned the B.S. must contact headquarters in
Staffordshire immediately *by phone, telegram, anything!* – a protest
meeting would be organised . . . and so on. Lenin's call to the
masses! Though Robert would not enjoy the comparison, he was
violently anti-communist as he was anti all forms of authoritarian-
ism. He listed names and addresses of supporters, one of whom ran
'a semi-religious organisation called the White Crusaders, and another called the Robin Hood Rangers', and he advised me, 'don't
disclose you belong to the Y.C.L.!' Ending:

You will see what the various pamphlets are. The ones headed 'The
Union Will Stick Up For You' will want cutting into four. They
aren't central, so it will want doing carefully, but any printer will do
it for a few pence on his guillotine, while you wait.

Keep me posted with your activity. I enclose £1 for your expenses. Take out of it the 6d I owe you. Keep a strict account of what you spend. You will want more 'The Union Will Stick Up For You', and these I'll send. I suggest you also do some missionary work: i.e. give printed leaflets ARE YOU A UNION MEMBER? with the insert 'Do You Want To Be A Branch Secretary' to boys and girls you meet on trains and buses and in the streets.

Do this particularly in the Hampstead area, so that Esam-Carter can have something to get his teeth into.

All the best, and good hunting.

Yours

Robert Copping.

Quaint, comic, and breathtaking. Who were the White Crusaders and what on earth were they crusading about in 1949? I must have sighed at the crazy commands and expectations rather more than I was flattered to be given such responsibility. Most canvassing is depressing – I'd done it for the Young Communist League and the Jewish National Fund. Nevertheless I attempted to distribute leaflets, calling on young people who stood timidly at their thresholds seeming to have regretted their impulsive gesture of union solidarity, devoid of saltpetre enough to set light to their home grates let alone the nation's generation of '49.

If you can bring courage into the hearts of Edward Grant and/or Philip Wood so that we can have some activity in progress in the course of the next few days, so much the better. The Rank Organisation is doing an educational film and wants to take some shots of a protest meeting.

I brought courage to no one. We were not part of the Rank film. This was not a way to form and organise a union – manipulating and cajoling from afar. Certainly not when those to be inspired were mostly below the age of fourteen.

Robert was the first person to introduce me to that English quality envied by the world – pragmatism. This may read strangely about a man who espoused outlandish and, with hindsight, such impossible dreams for young people. Yet it's so. Look how pragmatic he is over the issue of whether or not I should wear my YCL badge while canvassing on behalf of the Union. I had insisted it was a matter of principle. He quickly perceived principle had nothing to do with it.

> The question of wearing or not wearing something like a YCL badge is possibly a question of temperament rather than of principles, but this is how I see it: if I were a Christian and in the custom of wearing a cross round my neck, and if I had to deal with people who had been told that Christianity was a form of cannibalism, I should remove the cross before visiting them for fear that they should be put into such a state of panic that their reason would be upset. If people's reason is upset one just can't talk to them.

English humour and understatement in one. Robert was quintessentially English – fiercely individualistic, jealously guarding personal liberties, possessed of an innate sense of fair play and justice, keenly aware of the absurdity in human behaviour, eccentric and heartily hospitable – but he cared passionately about a world view. Human beings were different, nurtured by strange and separate histories but essentially human.

One of his ideas was the creation of a national newspaper for young people. He produced a specimen issue: *The Invader*. Its contents make compulsive reading.

> . . . If you make adults scared of you by doing crazy things, you'll find you can't get much freedom: we can tell you how to win freedom and at the same time live at peace and friendliness with parents and teachers and all those others who now make up your minds for you.
>
> It's not our job to sell you ideas, but to make suggestions: your common sense will accept or refuse them.
>
> We suggest that you make the most of your chances.
>
> By law, you are forced to spend a lot of hours each week sitting

around in a classroom. While you are there you can do one of three things:

1 You can annoy the teacher in charge. This will provide light entertainment with a certain amount of excitement in it.
2 You can sit and dream (or read a comic under the desk or folded under the textbook).
3 You can learn to the best of your ability.

Most people start by being willing to learn, but often the teaching is so bad that learning is difficult. One or two lessons a week spent ragging is fair enough. An odd period spent in dreaming may be quite a good idea. But to spend a whole week in ragging or dreaming is stupid and pointless.

In the first place it gives adults an excuse for pushing you around.

And it means you are doing nothing while the world is falling to pieces round you. You just can't afford to do nothing.

There's no point in saying: 'What's the use of geometry?' – or Latin or French, or anything else you are given to do. When you're hungry you eat what you can get: some food is better than no food, and some knowledge is better than no knowledge. The more you know the less you have to take on trust. Don't invent excuses for your own slackness.

Make your teachers your servants by making them teach you all they know. Read as widely as you can. Read comics, but read books as well.

Where have I heard that before?

'There's nothing wrong with comics,' he'd cry – he stand up on a chair when he want to preach but don't wanna sound too dramatic ... 'There's nothing wrong with comics only there's something wrong with comics all the time ...'

                                    Beatie Bryant – *Roots*, Act I Scene 1

Robert's passion for young people comes through in the leaflet he wrote called 'Children and The Future'. It begins:

The future contains so many problems that it would hardly seem to matter which, if any, received attention first.

A middle paragraph reads as a principle of faith:

How can we ensure in a world where the majority are irresponsible and ignorant that the children are responsible and filled with knowledge?

The children are good, as good as they have always been. Their intelligence and confidence; their ability to learn and profit by experience are wholly unimpaired. As we are in so poor a position to help them, we must try to provide for them the means for helping themselves. If we train our children to obey rather than to think, to believe rather than to criticise, to respect fools rather than to recognise their foolishness then we shall have our children where we want them and the world on the dust heap.

Adults are scared of children.

They are afraid of their criticism because it is to the point: all adults have failed in one way or another, and no child can believe that failure is necessary.

They are afraid of their courage, because it is dauntless: to one who has decided to submit, bravery is an exasperating reminder.

We call our tiredness 'experience', our failure 'patience', and our fearfulness, 'discretion'.

We are deceiving ourselves. What we call education is a means of defending ourselves against the criticism of our children ...

As a declaration of faith in youth that remains impressive. Robert was not an admirer of *Lord of the Flies*.

So much reflected my own thinking. Robert found in me an eager supporter. The world was no longer a wilderness in which I was a lone outsider wandering between indulgent family and sceptical friends. Here was my cause. Organising skills honed from Habonim, experienced Byronic conferee with an excessive delight in my powers of articulation, yet – there was a flaw. I was utterly devoid of diplomacy or political tact. Over the years I had developed that special, raw nerve end referred to earlier, that intemperate nature inherited from my mother which in later life betrayed me in confrontations. What use could I be to a revolution of minors who were themselves unstable because bewildered? Perhaps I do myself an injustice for I also remember being voted into positions of responsibility and courted for support in resolutions. I must have possessed a *degree* of leadership and persuasiveness.

Arrested for murder

> I remember this – when you were born your grandmother took one look at you and said: 'Well, he's either going to be a great man or a murderer!'

I can't remember whether I first met Robert because he came to London or because I went for a weekend to Horsley Hall in Eccleshall. I shall never forget that weekend. I was arrested for murder.

The school left an impression ramshackle and bohemian which you would expect of a free school. Robert allowed the boys and girls to sleep with each other on condition a condom was used. He reasoned they were going to do that anyway, therefore the most sensible thing was to help them avoid pregnancy. Lessons were conducted by a mixed handful of the bearded and sandalled type hated by George Orwell, the kitchen was casual – a huge deal table stained and covered with unwashed crockery and neglected cornflake boxes. Neglect and casualness – this was a school? Paid for by private inmates? It was all weird and wonderful to me. I warmed to its informal air though understood little of the implication of its learning principles and was in no way qualified to judge or comment on them. A.S. Neil disapproved totally of Robert's views and his learning paradise. That, I remember. The two quarrelled, both privately and in public. Neil feared Horsley Hall would reflect on his own educational innovations.

The absence of even the most inconspicuous discipline resulted not in good humour and a spirit of cooperation all the more lovely for not being enforced, but – as I now understand it – a dreary indifference. We seem to be born neither good nor bad nor a mixture of both but with the *possibility* to be good or bad, sweet or sour, responsible or irresponsible. A permutation of possibilities jockey to produce what is produced – like one's face. It could form in any way – a jumble of genes deals us random features upon which life and weather add their marks. So with our lives. Yet features and lives however randomly assembled need disciplining or they go to pieces. There was none at Horsley Hall. It casually went to pieces. Robert fell in love with one of his students aged sixteen. He ignored his own advice:

> . . . if I had to deal with people who had been told that Christianity was a form of cannibalism, I should remove the cross before visiting them for fear that they should be put into such a state of panic that their reason would be upset.

He was dealing with people who had been 'told' that making love to a sixteen-year-old was 'a form of cannibalism', harmful to their daughter, even though he might be in love and the best person in her life. He had been too casual in assessing the possible outcome of his actions. Her parents sought the court's help in bringing the relationship to an end. They succeeded, the school was tumbled with it. The same casualness led to my being arrested for murder.

It was agreed that one of the teachers would pillion-passenger me on his motorbike to a railway station from where I'd catch a train. I had enough money for that fare and some left over for the Underground home. No more. I can't remember the name of the station, only that no one had worked out how long it would take to reach it in time to catch the train. I missed the last one. Nor had the teacher bothered to wait to ensure that I had caught it. What, I asked the station master who had pointed down the track to show me the train disappearing in the distance, was I to do? If you hurry, he told me, you'll catch a bus that'll get you to – I can't remember *that* station either – where you'll catch the last train to London. There would be no problem, he assured me, because the bus left at such and such a time, the journey was forty-five minutes, the train left fifteen minutes later.

Fine! Though I *did* have a problem. It was this: the station was further north, the ticket would cost more. With the additional bus fare, I did not have enough money. No matter, I reasoned, I'd give them my address and promise to post the fare on. Not unheard of.

Everything went wrong. The bus was delayed. I had mere minutes to rush to the ticket office and explain my plight. The train was waiting at the platform. The ticket man waved me through before I could finish my story, urging me to hurry quick and tell it to the ticket inspector on the train. I ran over the bridge and made it just in time, breathless and, as it turned out, somewhat ill.

The ticket collector was kindly, believed my story, wrote down personal details and sat me in a compartment which blissfully I had to myself until Oxford. At Oxford there came into the carriage four other people: a young man and woman who sat opposite me. They seemed to be students. One, I remember, the young man, was reading a Penguin edition of Shaw's *Pygmalion* and I felt instant affinity with him. A slightly older man (at that age, age was a mystery) took his place in the far opposite corner. The young woman sat opposite, haughty and stern. To my left sat another man of whom I can remember nothing. There was also a change of ticket inspectors. I repeated the story told to the first one, he took details, and left. The train sat in the station for an inordinate time before moving off.

I occupied a window seat, the corridor was to my left. The motorbike ride for which I'd worn only a shirt, trousers, and a jacket, of houndstooth check weave, had left me shivering and feverish. I'd kept the window closed therefore. The inspector returned and asked the young woman sitting opposite me if she'd mind stepping into the corridor for a word with him. She obliged

and returned a changed being. I imagined she'd been asked to cor-
roborate my story in the event of me retracting it. Seemed odd, but
I thought little of it. From time to time she regarded me in the
strangest of ways. I was amused at such severity over an unpaid
ticket.

Some fifteen minutes into the journey she decided to pull down
the window. A huge draught flooded over my temperature. I
suffered for a while and then asked would she mind if I closed it as I
was feeling unwell. Peevishly she allowed me to pull it up but not
close it entirely. Poverty *does* reduce ability to assert one's needs.
Nor was my sense of impotence helped by upper-class demeanour
seeping inexorably out of her being, a quality of molten confidence
which in those days had the power to petrify self-esteem. Besides, I
was too ill to fight. All I could do was muster cheek, pull up my collar in the blatant way of Jews well schooled in guiltmaking, and sink
into myself with that accusative glare: 'If I die be in no doubt who
will be to blame.'

The young man reading *Pygmalion* watched and assessed all that
was bristling between the young upper-class gauleiter and myself,
and when she left briefly to pee, as even royalty must, he rose and
snapped the window up by its leather strap into the 'shut firmly'
mode. He said nothing, just nodded when I muttered a 'thank you'.
The young prude returned, observed the shut window but remained silent. Later I was to understand why: I might have knifed
her.

The train approached Paddington. Everyone rose to move down
the corridor nearer the exit gate. Sensible, I thought, and attempted
to follow. As I stepped out the ticket inspector arrived.

'And where do you think you're going?' he asked.

'To be nearer the exit,' I replied with what I thought was unassailable reason.

'Suppose,' he suggested, 'we sit back in here.' He blocked my way
and manoeuvred me back into the compartment as the train was
pulling into the station. I felt torn between foolish and curious.
What on earth was going to happen? He leaned out of the window,

waved some people towards him, opened the carriage door and announced to one of four tall men, 'This is him.'

The weightiest-looking of the four announced they were station police and ordered me to come along with them to answer some questions. I was utterly bewildered and by now irate. Gathering reserves of what I imagined to be upper-class dignity (like skiing and ballet dancing I'd seen it demonstrated in the movies!) I asked with pathos and affront appropriate to my weakened state: 'Is all this really necessary just to pay for a ticket at the other end?' The copper ignored my performance, experienced amateur actor though I was, and motioned me in the direction to go. I found that little extra puff athletes reach for on the final hurdle and said: 'Well I hope this isn't going to take too long because I'm not feeling very well and I'd like to go home as soon as I can.' Not bad for a seventeen-year-old with no first-hand experience of class authority. In retrospect I know where such chutzpah came from: a mixture of Leah's battling spleen and that centuries-old Jewish belief that gods are created for the service of humankind, to be questioned and told off if dealing unjustly – which belief, of course, nurtured Leah's battling spleen! The weary copper knew nothing about battling spleen, or unjust gods – Jewish or otherwise – and replied tartly if not unreasonably:

'We're also feeling none too well, so if . . .' The following words could have been anything.

We were a comic sight which, touch drama-queen that I sometimes was (am still, no doubt), pleased my sense of the dramatic. We walked the length of the Paddington platform, my interlocutor to my left and his three stalwarts in a semi-circle behind me. I'd no luggage – for one night what need had I of more than a toothbrush? But it *must* have seemed odd. A picture played itself out in my head – what if I made a run for it? The chase, the people moving out of the way, me getting lost in a crowd, turning up next day with money and a grin and my absolutely credible story.

In the station police hut I was asked questions: name, age, address, where I'd been, where was I going, did I have identification . . . For a reason I now can't remember, post-war tic probably, I used to walk around with my birth certificate. I told my story and offered it to the custody of a spare CID foot-slogger to take away and check, presumably with Somerset House. When he returned I asked: 'Well, am I born?' By now they were all relaxed suffi- ciently to smile at adolescent bravado. 'Yes. You're born!'

I asked: 'Am I going to be told what all this is about? It surely can't be because I didn't have the money to pay for a train ticket.'

They explained. 'You've probably heard about the murder over the weekend of the sweet-shop owner in Liverpool . . .?' No, I hadn't. There were no Sunday papers at Horsley Hall. A descrip- tion had been sent out of a man wearing a houndstooth check weave jacket, and the station-master at Oxford thought I fitted the description! What, I wondered – though not aloud – was there about me that had made both the Oxford station-master and my grandmother anxious? I stare hard at photographs – nothing! Eyes bright with scepticism, that's all! Only 'gods' need fear, I'd like to think.

The policeman let me go with apologies and good humour. I asked where was the Underground. A CID man pointed the way. 'And don't forget to buy your ticket!'

That was all I saw of Horsley Hall. The union dream faded away in unpaid union dues, and my enthusiasm to organise drained into the sands of branch-secretaries' adolescent sloth. Robert became a good friend, and for a time I looked after a bedraggled stall that he rented in Bermondsey Market, from which he sold junk-yard leav- ings and where he had made friends with Tommy Steele before he became Tommy Steele. I knew nothing about that relationship until years later, too busy selling nothings from this most abject and pathetic wooden barrow sparsely stocked with cheap castaways Robert had bought at junk auctions – rusty mousetraps, lengths of piping, plastic cups, tins of screws, the detritus of bankrupt petty business ventures and failed lives. I can't remember ever selling enough in a day to pay my wages.

Fortunately my time as a market man was brief. Weeks, I think. Then Robert turned to selling books. He took over a basement in

Holland Place off Kensington Church Street, where on the corner is now Pierre Péchan's Patisserie, and gradually filled it with second-hand books few came to purchase – a sign was put outside that persuaded no one. I spent more time sorting and arranging in subject and alphabetical order than in selling. Not that I minded. Even now, living in the world's largest centre for secondhand books, I find myself in the Hay shops satisfying that urge to rearrange volumes careless browsers have pulled out of order.

Stalin's Idiots

The first World Peace Congress, Paris 1949, was organised by the International Peace Committee, one of those international organisations inspired into existence by the Soviet Communist Party and behind which front of idealism they and party members throughout the Eastern Bloc were more easily able to exercise control. It was to take place in the Salle Pleyel between 25 and 29 April. Picasso designed the emblem – a white dove.

Organisations – those deemed bona fide political, trade union, youth, or 'progressive' – were invited to apply for credentials. A trip to Paris! For a major political and humanitarian event! The School Children's Union was a trade union. *Very* progressive! The war was three years into memory, the Festival of Britain eighteen months away. We were living in the dawn of the Welfare Society – everyone accepted the Beveridge Report and its call upon the state to provide minimum standards of health, education and living. Even full employment was a post-war government commitment – jobs as well as houses for returning heroes. In the euphoria of military victory, against an aggressor whose fighting machines and blond, well-drilled young gods in black jackboots seemed invincible, peace was a cry whose nobleness few could question. Certainly I didn't. At seventeen anything progressive was heroic.

I remember years later, in the late sixties, being host to an old Soviet Yiddish poet (name forgotten) who had been through the gulags and was now unhappily rootless living in Israel. One phrase remained from our conversation. He was explaining how, when G.B. Shaw visited the Soviet Union full of praise for the new society shaping there, this poet had tried to meet with him to reveal the truth of what was really happening in that glorious one-sixth of the world. He failed. Shaw and all those blinded by praise and adulation on their visits were dubbed by this angry old Yiddish poet 'Stalin's Idiots'. In 1949 I was one of Stalin's younger idiots rearing to join the thousands converging on Paris and hold hands with my huge-hearted brothers and sisters from the world over.

But how was I to pay for the package fare, registration fee, and daily living? Robert sanctioned my using the School Children's Union as the umbrella beneath whose shade I could apply for credentials, 'but you'll have to find your own funding, old son', which I did, embarking upon the first appeal in a line of appeals I was to make in a life of good causes – my own being one of them from time to time.

Aunts and uncles were the first to be petitioned for financial support in this Galahad cause ensuring world peace. Half crowns were promised which together with half crowns saved from earnings were still insufficient. I wrote to four celebrities whose reputations as 'progressives' had filtered down to me at grass roots: novelist Ethel Mannin; actress Sybil Thorndike; playwrights Sean O'Casey and George Bernard Shaw.

I can't remember how my letter of appeal was phrased. It can be assumed I didn't say 'Please will you fund a fun trip to Paris.' Peace will have loomed large as a dire cause for which their money was being requested, and no doubt I traded on working-class impecuniosity though I hope I was wise enough to let them know my family shared the burden. Ethel Mannin was abroad in India. Her husband wrote apologising for this but did not step into his wife's place. Sybil Thorndike wrote inviting me to visit her backstage and talk about it. O'Casey, imagining me to be a Cockney, wrote (by hand) from Tingrith, Station Road, Totnes, Devon:

Dear Mr Wesker

Enclosed is a cheque of 10/– made out to yourself for I didn't know whom else to sign it to. All I can afford. I've just sent another 10/– to help a Bristol clergyman to go as a delegate, too.

I'm anything but well-off. I hope GBS responds. It's very doubtful about Miss Mannin although her books sell by tens of thousands. All the best to you cock.

Yours sincerely, Sean O'Casey

How many such letters I've had to write myself!

George Bernard Shaw, who received hundreds of requests for all manner of things from all manner of madmen, had cards specially printed. My letter requesting funds for Paris and Peace must have contained an offer to visit and personally explain myself. Two cards arrived from his home in Ayot St Lawrence dated 1 April 1949. The first, pink, explained why he couldn't help me financially. The second, blue, explained why he couldn't see me.

Pink card:

Mr Bernard Shaw receives daily a mass of appeals from charitable institutions, religious sects and churches, inventors, Utopian writers desirous of establishing international millennial leagues, parents unable to afford secondary education for their children: in short everybody and every enterprise in financial straits of any sort.

All these appeals are founded on the notion that Mr Shaw is a multi-millionaire. The writers apparently do not know that all his income except enough to meet his permanent engagements is confiscated by the Exchequer and re-distributed to those with smaller tax-free incomes or applied to general purposes by which everyone benefits.

Clearly Mr Shaw's correspondents cannot have his income both ways: in cash from himself and in services from the state. He does not complain of this system, having advocated it for more than half a century, and nationalised all his landed property; but now that it is in active and increasing operation it is useless to ask him for money: he has none to spare.

He begs to be excused accordingly. No other reply to appeals is possible.

Blue card:

Mr Bernard Shaw's readers and the spectators at performances of his plays number many thousands. The little time remaining to him at his age is fully occupied with his literary work and the business it involves; and war taxation has set narrow limits to his financial resources. He has therefore to print the following warning.

He cannot deal with individual grievances and requests for money, nor for autographs and photographs. He cannot finance schools and churches. His donations go to undenominational public bodies, and his charities to the Royal Society of Literature.

He cannot engage in private correspondence, nor read long letters.

He cannot advise literary beginnings nor read their unpublished works. They had better study *The Writer's Year Book* (or other books of reference), and join the Society of Authors as associates.

He cannot discuss his published views in private letters.

He cannot receive visitors at his private residence except from his intimate friends.

He begs to be excused accordingly.

That same year I had been cast by the Query Players to play a part long coveted – Marchbanks in *Candida*. I wrote to Shaw again. This time he replied by hand. I'll reveal what he said in the chapter dealing with 'The Unholy Profession'.

It was the generous but cautious Sybil Thorndike who turned up trumps and also provided me with a first glimpse of theatre campery. I went, at the appointed time, to the Duchess Theatre where she was performing in *The Foolish Gentlewoman* by Margery Sharp. I was nervous and awed and recall nothing of our conversation. Only this image remains. At a certain moment, when no doubt I was earnestly describing either the virtues of peace in our time or the importance of creating a School Children's Union, or perhaps slipping in my ambition to be an actor, there came a knock at the door which at the command 'Come in' burst open. Another actress, poised on the threshold, her arms thrown wide, exclaiming, 'Sybil!' Pause. 'Darling!' Sybil 'darling' flung *her* arms and cried back – I think, but can't be 100% certain – 'Edith!' Pause. 'Darling.' Whereupon both fell into each other's embrace and, after a brief, courteous introduction, I was swiftly despatched with my second command to phone, when I'd raised as much as I could, at her flat in Dolphin Mansions up the road from the House of Commons, facing the Thames. Which I did. I was summoned, told to wait at the front door where she reappeared within seconds, thrusting two pound notes into my hands, and good-luck-bon-voyage-and-thank-you-for-fighting-for-peace-on-everybody's-behalf into my spirit. Our only professional contact was when she played the old waitress in a performance of the first act of *The Kitchen*, part of an event at the National Theatre to raise funds for the George Devine Award. (Laurence Olivier played the head waiter, John Osborne the pastry chef, Vanessa Redgrave another of the waitresses.)

So I went to Paris, lived in a tented camp on the outskirts where hunks of bread, a piece of cheese, a cup of coffee, and fruit were sold item by item, and travelled by overground train into this, my first and most thrilling foreign city.

Grapes in Long Acre

Stalin's idiots we may have been, but passion for justice, the fierce defence of individual rights allied to social responsibility, clamouring for equal opportunity, repugnance at human suffering, would have made these idiots of Stalin, had they been within Stalin's reach, Stalin's victims. Good people who with good but careless faith hitched their wagon to a murderous dragon disguised as Pegasus. My militant mother and her intemperate son with their contempt for the stupidity of officials and the arrogance of power would have been rendered instant gulag inmates, for sure.

Heaven was never reached but a community of generous souls grew up around the idea of, and hope for, paradise. Those round my mother were of one sort – homely and concerned with each other's children as well as low wages and the state of the world. Of a different kind were Jack and Joyce Smith, party members but tougher: capable organisers, harder intellects, and childless. Joyce was assigned by the party to become secretary of the British Peace Committee, the next cause to which the rebel applied his political zeal. I had no patience with party politics but 'peace' embraced the world. 'The World' and 'peace' were cosier concepts to handle, who could argue against such deep and universal yearnings? I was happy, humbly, to fill and lick envelopes in number 1 Park Crescent, an astonishing Nash curve of Georgian houses facing Regent's Park, a sight I show visitors to my city.

Jack and Joyce Smith were a handsome couple, older than me by about twenty years. Joyce kept my hot head cool, Jack arranged for my poems to be typed, carbon-copied and stapled to give me a first taste of what book form might feel like. As the son they would have liked they spoilt me with kindness – he the sweeter, she the more stern but striking: she smoked, coughed, had a sexy, sandpapery voice. I fell a little in love with her and learned organisational skills more sophisticated than ever were dreamed of in Habonim. Strong women!

Around this time, we're in 1949, two casual jobs. One in the city, a warehouse where manufacturers of leather coats and jackets came to buy skins. My job, along with others, was to wheel trolleys of skins which the buyers called for from a catalogue, slide the skins off the trolley, slap them on a wooden bench and turn them over for inspection one by one. We were paid a basic wage but the bulk of earnings, which were substantial, came from tips – a job for a number of days which came up every so often, it may have helped towards the Paris trip. The other job, also a fill-in, made a great impression on me. An office in Long Acre – in those days part of the thriving, noisy Covent Garden fruit market – where I manned a phone and wrote down orders from wholesalers of fruit – a revelation of the crazy way the crazy world worked. My employer did nothing but purchase a shipment of fruit on one phone and sell by the crate to wholesalers on another. We ate lots of grapes those days in Weald Square. Were they a present? Did I buy them at cost? Was it part of my pay? I think he was a Greek. Or from Cyprus. I stored him away for twenty-seven years.

> Those books. Look at them. How they remind me what I am, what I've done. Nothing! A merchant! A purchaser of this to sell there. A buyer-up and seller-off. And do you know, I hardly ever see my trade. I have an office, a room of ledgers and a table, and behind it I sit and wait till someone comes in to ask have I wool from Spain, cloth from England, cotton from Syria, wine from Crete. And I say yes, I've a ship due in a week, or a month, and I make a note, and someone goes to the dock, collects the corn, delivers it to an address, and I see nothing. I travel neither to England to check cloth, nor to Syria to check cotton, nor Corfu to see that the olive oil is cleanly corked . . .
>
> Antonio – *Shylock*, Act I Scene 1

Jack and Joyce were far more important in my life but it was the Greek I wrote about, never the Smiths.

Chapter Eleven

Work – carpenter

I left Upton House in the summer of 1948 aged sixteen, having failed to secure school cert. I wanted to be a writer but reasoned thus: writers write whatever they do, wherever they are. I have a responsibility to contribute to the household and must work.

What work would bring me nearest to the creative act, satisfy my urge to 'make' things? Furniture-making, of course! The craft of my fond brother-in-law who is soon to convert a barn in Norfolk and make furniture by hand, including baby Windsor chairs which the Queen Mother will buy for her grandchildren, Charles and Anne. Ralph found me a job apprenticed to an old Jewish craftsman, Mr Goodman, where I expected to settle for life and learn the skill of making antique furniture. His workshop was in a cobbled alley behind Norton Folgate, not far from Liverpool Street station. I see him, thick-set, a rim of hair, bespectacled, blubbery lips. He was a kind and weary man whose sardonic humour tried to make sense of his hopeless struggle against competition from the vast factories mass-producing antique furniture. 'Eny vay, eny how,' he would sigh, reconciling himself to the inevitability of defeat, 'dets dé vay it is.' He acted the caricature Yid and referred enviously to Ralph who worked in *real* wood while he layered veneers over laminated wood.

'Your brudder-in-law handles solyids. Solyid vood. Very nice. I'd also like to be handling solyid voods but you can't do vat you like wi' dem. Plyvood is like its name, pliable. You can bend her dis vay and dat vay, like a voman. *Some* vomans. Some vomans it's not so easy. Some vomans are like solyids, no vay can you bend 'em. Dets how it is. Dets de vay it is.' More or less, uttered while carefully sawing, chipping, nailing, gluing.

I dovetailed small joints for him, and chiselled out mortise and tenon for him. I cut to size thin lengths of quadrant beading and glued them inside drawers for him. I put nail-pins in my mouth and hammered home for him plyboard backs which he veneered. I sandpapered bow-fronted drawers for him which were sent away to be 'distressed'.

But I had made a mistake. No artist-craftsman's life for me. Neither hand nor heart were steady. The bow-saw wobbled. Drawers wiggled at their joints. I sandpapered veneers too thin – the wood showed through. My doves didn't tail, my mortises were chiselled too large for my tenons. I spilled hot glue. Kind Goodman would have patiently seen me through these blunderings but couldn't afford me *and* my mistakes. The competition was too great. At the end of six months I was made redundant. The old man followed soon after. 'Dets de vay it is!'

I wanted to stay with wood and tools, having developed a love of planes, chisels, mallets, marking gauges, spoke-shaves, draw-knives, bow-saws, and scrapers which burnt my thumbs as I drew them clumsily over wood. Tool shops still give me a buzz. An essential part of the conversion of this near-ruin where I now live and work was the creation of a workshop for which was made a huge bench complete with vice and equipped with a basic kit of carpenter's tools. What would I not construct! Other shops affect me that way – stationers and bookshops. All those pencils, pads and paper clips without which the masterpiece can't be written; all those books containing all that knowledge I will one day need! Shops that seduce you into believing you will write gloriously, seated on chairs you have built, inspired and informed by secondhand wisdom.

If I was not made for the fine craft of fabricating distressed Queen Anne chests of drawers, perhaps I could rough-saw rafters, joists and floorboards. Mowlem's, the builders, were my second employers in a trade that became the setting for another guilt, one I have never been able to exorcise.

I became 'mate' for a 'chippie' only a few years older than me called Tom Carter, whose Cockney dialect was so broad my mother had little idea what he was saying. I had to translate for her. Tom was your Tory's archetypal image of the British worker. Our time sheets began at 8 a.m. – the yard left us free to fill them in ourselves – but activity rarely got started before nine. We were assigned to renew window frames in pubs, rehang doors in offices, replace and putty-in smashed glass in school windows. Sometimes we were sent to private houses, and once – I shall never forget – to a small Methodist church off the Kingsland Road. The task was a simple one: prise up floorboards, cut through rotten joist, saw new joist to length, nail joist home, nail back floorboards. Half a day's work! But Tom insisted on playing cricket the length of the church hall. The job took us three days! Multiply sloth like that around the country and it's no wonder that between such practices and managerial reluctance to invest in new machinery British industry declined and lost competitiveness.

My mother liked Tom despite his petty thief's fingers. He flirted with her in his perky Cockney way, a cheerful, warm-hearted bloke who contained within himself those two sides of our ambivalence about the working class. He may have tripled the costs of a job but he was generous-spirited, except over this one guilt-making act I'll come to soon. Leah believed none of his compliments and pushed him off with indulgent, coy smiles. He was, after all, 100% 'solyid' working class.

I don't precisely remember my first encounter with Tom in Mowlem's yard when I was handed over to him as 'your new mate'. He was the first person ever to call me 'china', Cockney rhyming slang: 'china plate' for 'mate'.

TOM	You what they've sent me?
YOUNG HILARY	Afraid so.
TOM	'Fraid so, are you? Well let's 'ope I won't be afraid so. You done this before?
YOUNG HILARY	Not carpenter's mate but building sites plenty.
TOM	You a student?

YOUNG HILARY   Afraid so.

TOM   'Fraid so,' 'fraid so! You better not be 'afraid so' of too many things or you'll be no good to me, china. We climb ladders in this job, swing on roofs, rock in cradles and slide along 'igh rafters. I don't want no crying and no jelly-livers and no 'fraid so's alongside me. You got that?

YOUNG HILARY   You won't have to worry on my account, Mister—

TOM   Tom. You can call me Tom, but that don't mean you can take liberties. I may look only a little older than you and I can see you've got bleedin' clever eyes and I can 'ear your mouth is full of clever books but I'm the chippy on the job and I've got the know-'ow and you see these 'ands? They've got nearly ten years' carpentry in them so what I say goes and that's a thing you and me better get clear from the start. Got that, Mister—

YOUNG HILARY   I think so. And you can call me Hilary.

Bluey – a play for radio

What happened was this. Tom had made friends with a plumber and his mate with whom we were working on a roof job. The old lead had to be peeled off, rafters renewed and guttering replaced. They arranged to syphon off some of the lead (called 'bluey' because it inclined to the colour blue) and sell it, sharing the proceeds between the four of us.

An evening when the job was completed we returned to the site. Tom and I clambered over to the roof. The plumbers stayed on the ground. The long-established routine for throwing discarded materials off roofs entailed shouting 'Below!' before throwing down. I threw a lump of lead over and shouted, 'Below!' a second after instead of before. The plumber looked up and received impact on the side of his face. He went or was taken to hospital. I have no memory of what happened subsequently other than that Tom wanted to share the money from the lead three ways instead of four and I washed my hands of any participation, insisting the plumber was to have the part of the share that was to have been mine. I can't even remember if I visited him in hospital. A vague memory hovers of Tom visiting to report the plumber's recovery, but that may be a subconscious attempt to put myself at ease. I am not.

Work – dusting books

I stayed mere months with Goodman, and mere months with Tom. My mother shared her fears with Uncle Perly who thought and thought and came up with an idea. 'Arnold wants to be a writer? I know a man, Louis Simmonds, runs a bookshop in Fleet Street, with his wife, Rose.' Wonderful! I would be close to books!

Sixteen Fleet Street was a gold mine. The slim space had revolving bookshelves in the centre, every inch used, and in the back a cramped area just big enough to take telephone orders. Two more floors above had their own manageress. Barristers from Inns of Court, journalists from down the road, students from the London School of Economics and a host of office workers sauntered through. Reviewers were sent dozens of books a week which Louis bought and passed on to the public for half price. He was diminutive, Louis, a highly intelligent ex-party member who now cared more for the besieged new state of Israel than the Great Conspiracy Against the Soviet Union. His friend, the dying George Orwell, had no doubt been the one to disabuse him of his bolshevik ecstasies. Louis visited him weekly with parcels of books the great writer had called for.

My main tasks apart from selling were to dust by slapping volumes together and inhaling what flew off, to return order after customers had scattered books around, and to look out for book thieves. They usually carried canvas holdalls.

Reading? Hardly ever. In my lunch break, sometimes. When I did become hooked on a book stuck high on a ladder, a little cough from either Mr or Mrs would send me on my way along the tempting shelves which had to be resisted like women's bums.

For Christmas Louis gave me *carte blanche* to choose my present. I chose two volumes of Sean O'Casey's plays and have them still, which is how it was possible to date precisely when I worked for him. When I think about Louis, time plays tricks, remembers him nicely tart, scathing of my adolescent politics but paternal – after all, he'd once been me! He chain-smoked, a fag hung from his lips all day as he rolled his 'r's and was deferential to his customers, even those he knew were fools certain of details he was certain were incorrect. 'I don't think so, sir, but I *will* check . . .'

Rose, Louis' wife, asked me one day: 'Were you a lonely child?' I was not, far from it. But why? 'Because you whistle all the time. Lonely children whistle.'

Postscript: as the deadline approached for submitting this manuscript, Louis died. 19 April 1994. Aged eighty-seven. From an obituary in *The Guardian* I learned more about my old employer:

> . . . the man who read the manuscript of *Animal Farm* for George Orwell . . . Born Louis Stiglitz, his parents were Jewish immigrants who left their native Poland the day after their wedding . . . A self-educated man, Louis left school at 14 and, at first, worked for his father, a tailor and active fighter for workers' rights in the East End . . .

Ben Okri, I learned, had also worked for Louis at number 16.

It is the year 1950

My eighteenth year. On 9 November I will board the train for RAF Padgate – seen off at the station by my mother and Shifra – to begin a year and a half of National Service. Meanwhile it has been a busy year: working for Louis Simmonds, then Robert, then as a

plumber's mate on St Katherine's Dock, about which period I remember only that I rose at 6.30 a.m. to cycle there and began the
day with a fried breakfast of thick butter-soaked toast, greasy eggs,
bacon, sausage, tomato, and hot strong tea. It's the year I receive
from LAMDA a Silver Medal Honours for Elocution (I'd secured
the Bronze the year before). It's the year I have my first auditions
for RADA, pass, and fail to secure a grant from the LCC. In those
days grants to students needing them were automatically offered by
local authorities on acceptance to a university. Not to students of
the arts, however. For music, dance, painting and acting the LCC
had its own line of defence, a second panel of adjudicators. After all
you can't trust principals of arts colleges, they'll take anyone to
secure the fee.

Nineteen fifty is the year I go on a camping holiday with my
chubby girlfriend, Doris Segal, another hairdresser, like Audrey.
We spend days under canvas in the Lake District where it rains so
hard and constantly that I audaciously suggest we pay a surprise
visit to the Scottish poet, Hugh MacDiarmid, whom I've never met
but who has written encouraging words about my poetry. It's the
year I take on the roles of Telegraph Boy, Doctor, and Lifeguard in
Thornton Wilder's *The Skin of Our Teeth* (the production George
Devine adjudicates), 4 February; also Taplow in *The Browning Version* and 2nd Halberdier in *Harlequinade* by Terence Rattigan, 24
June, programme price Four Pence.

Nineteen fifty is the year I write my first play *And After Today*
for the Query Players, not good; and 'Portrait of a Man', an undis-
guised portrait of my father and his life in these years with my
mother, twenty-four pages long, handwritten, and containing the
seeds of *Chicken Soup with Barley* which will be written seven years
later. Not great prose but it captures some of the atmosphere of
home, an atmosphere upsetting to live through, and yet, I realise
now, I possessed this quality: I could ride it. I could take my parents
in my stride. It's a good phrase, that: 'to take in your stride'. Good
advice to children: don't be judgemental – take your parents in your
stride. Are you hearing me, Lindsay Joe? (Or won't you ever read

this autobiography?) Admire but don't be awed, listen but don't be intimidated, choose your own path but tolerate and forgive flaws. Create no idols to smash, no illusions to grind into the dust. I rode my parents' battles and found love sufficient to help them laugh at themselves. Not always. Their pain, my father's maddening inertia and silly lies, my mother's relentless probing of him, corroded my good humour. It wasn't easy to sustain it twenty-four hours a day. Yet I built a reputation of light and laughter, and flooded the flat with friends and activity. A poker school grew up. We made birthday parties. Relatives visited. Leah and Joe were urged to sing, or I'd recite my latest poem, conduct a symphony, clown, offer them my rendering of 'One Fine Day' which I knew by heart and could hit the top note. I tried to fill the space with gaiety leaving them no room to fight. It didn't always work.

He would sit in a chair, slouched by the fire, his face usually needing a shave – subdued. In a Sunday's quiet she would be making her hair, this little chubby woman standing on a wooden stool in front of the fire, before the mirror. And for an hour she would quietly sometimes, sometimes loudly ask him to explain his soul, what was his very inner soul made of, ask him to describe his reasons for living, for lying, for being mean and artful. 'Look, Jack,' she would say, 'so what have you gained by telling me this lie? All right, so you did go to a shwitz yesterday morning. *I* knew, and the boy knew, but you came home and you said you haven't been. Now Sid says he saw you there. So we know. For certain we know. Just as we know you went to pictures on Friday night when you said you were going to Fanny Cohen's place. *You* said you went one way and *we* saw you get on a bus to go another way. So what have you gained? We always know when you lie because you're not a good liar. We can always tell it. What is it in you that makes you lie? For twenty-five years you have been the same – mean, artful and a liar, and all the time I have lived with you not knowing what it is all about. Just tell me. *You* know. *You* know why you do all these things, no one else knows. I'm asking you Jack, let me be your doctor, let me try and help you. Tell me. What is it that's behind you to make you what you are? What is it that makes you not go to work, that makes you say you've found a job when you haven't. Just tell me, just only tell me.'

And what could he say. He would sit on the chair one leg crossed over the other, his hands between, with his head resting on his chest and the big watery eyes watching the fire. A slouching misery of dead feeling. All was dead within. He would listen to the words coming like a series of dull thuds on his brain knocking him lower and lower into an emptiness of failure. Could he answer why he lied, could he say what it was made him cheat little sixpences from his wife's handbag, could he take that darkness from out of his very stomach and show it to her? Could he take with his two hands and say 'nah (yiddish for 'there'!), this is the weakness of my life'? He would sit on the chair. Just sit with his collar askew and dirty trousers, waiting for it all to end, without life in him, without wanting in him, without even that essential little spark in him.

And watching him she would say: 'Look. Look how he sits. Without a life in him, without a desire to live, to do things, to act, to want . . . Why, Jack, why? What is life to you? What really is your idea of living? Is this what you call a life, this here, this house with the furniture we've got? Don't you know how to live?' She would stop, watch his unanswering face, look at his being trying to hide from her, cowering. And she would answer herself. This time with more anger, with the bitterness of being cheated. '*You* know how to live. And don't you *just* know how to live. When you had a little money how many times did you go up West. Every theatre you went to. Every picture you saw. When you had the money you were always out. You know how to live all right, don't you just know how. It's me who's the fool, me the one to suffer.'

So he accepted this always. Always sitting in silence unable to bite back because he knew she was right. But this knowledge was dead within him. Of course he knew, but what was he to do now except listen, half insensible to meaning as he was insensible to the life which whirled around him and left him, dry on nothing, dead to the core. And in this deadness he tried to excuse himself to himself. Arguing limply within that it was not his fault, that he started off wrong and no one would give him a chance. Arguing that he was ill, a sick man and nobody would believe him. Nobody would understand nobody could know. And in this utter loneliness and misery he sank to self-pity, excusing himself, clearing his conscience so that the way was clear for him to carry on as before.

Shopping with Leah

Shopping with Leah was both an embarrassment and a joy. She complained about prices to greengrocers, butchers, harassed deli-store owners who over the years came to know this tiny, dynamic aggressor suddenly emerging out of the crowds, and occasionally knocked down a price rather than have her hold up the queue. Sometimes I'd walk away, pretend I was someone else's son. Some-times I'd stay put and simply declare out loud:

'She's nothing to do with me, I don't know her.'

'My son,' she'd boast to them, 'he's always joking.' Turning to me: 'Don't you know you can't joke with these people? These are very serious people. They own Ridley Road market. Where would we be without them? How could life go on . . .?' Our double-act of unsubtle sarcasm was not always appreciated.

'Who's next?'

But joy in shopping is something I learned from her. Not 'learned', you don't 'learn' how to shop, it's an illness, handed on, hereditary. That I inherited so much from her is recorded – where all is recorded – in the plays. *The Old Ones* was originally scored for oldies and three young males – cousins. John Dexter, who directed the play, suggested the character of the son, me, be turned into a daughter for the sake of tonal variety, a suggestion with which I could find no argument. Checking over the text it seemed that both the relationship and the dialogue worked just as well in female form. I still do think it works, and yet . . . For Rosa to have been Ronnie might have offered a mother/son relationship of greater veracity and dramatic edge. Nevertheless – here's the scene in which I acknowledge roots, repay debts, pay homage.

Act II Scene 5, Rosa, a careers advisory officer, is visiting her mother after a depressing encounter with school leavers. Sarah has been cleaning the flat and reassuring her. Rosa is replacing chairs from table to floor.

ROSA   One day, Sarah, we will die . . .

SARAH   *You*, silly girl? You're at the age when you'll never die.

ROSA   . . . It's the most terrible fact I know. Every lovely, lovely thing I cherish will, for me, one day, be ended. And I don't know when it will be, or how, or where. I try to think of it, imagine the circumstances, but I can't, there are too many possibilities. And it's such a pain, that loss, of you – and me. You can't imagine how much I dread it. Says Boswell: 'But is not the fear of death natural to man?' Says Johnson: 'So much so, sir, that the whole of life is but keeping away the thoughts of it.' [Pause] I won't ever die happily; no matter what splendid life I lead I can't see myself smiling sweetly with my last breath; I'll rage – that's for sure. But could I rage less? What could I do to make me rage less? I don't know. I ask myself but I don't know. I can't even recognise which is the real problem. Capital versus labour? Computer versus individual? Rich versus Third World? Affluence versus spiritual poverty? Which is it? One or all or something else? And if I find out, what can I do? And those cruel little cripples – who'll be the real victims, you know – they block me.

　　　　[SARAH breaks away from her and throws a big
　　　　white tablecloth over the extended table.]

SARAH   A white cloth!

　　　　[ROSA, her mood spent, takes the other end]
Nothing like a white cloth, fresh, clean, happy.

ROSA   Happy! Happeeeee!

　　　　[ROSA unpacks a box of drinks]

SARAH   What are you doing?

ROSA   Drinks! I've bought you a little arsenal of socialising equip-
        ment. All those thirsty tipplers you entertain.

SARAH   Take them back.

ROSA   It's a present. I got an income tax rebate.

SARAH   You got money? Keep it! You may need it one day.

ROSA   Cointreau! Your favourite! Cointreau, gin, Tia Maria,
        cherry brandy, brandy – only half-bottles. Indulge your-
        self.

SARAH   It makes me ashamed. Me, an old-aged pensioner in a
        block of flats for old-aged pensioners.

ROSA   A *few* bottles.

SARAH   It's immoral. A couple of pounds they've got to live on and
        I've got a brewery inside here.

ROSA   And why do I love to see full cupboards? You! Got it from
        you.

SARAH   Me! Me! Always me.

ROSA   You! You! Always you. I used to love unpacking your
        shopping bags, and now when I go shopping it's terrible, I
        can't stop. Biscuits from one shelf, tins from another, and
        cheeses – all those different cheeses. You never know
        who's coming and I feel so ashamed. The children see me,
        taking, taking, taking – in a fever. What will they grow
        into, I think. [Pause] Psst! I'll hide them under the bed.

SARAH   [Dusting chairs] You're a good daughter, not everyone's
        got good daughters, take them back.

ROSA   Mother, there's not a law against having good daughters.

SARAH   You mean well, I'm very grateful, don't argue with me and
        take them back.

ROSA   There's no logic in you.

SARAH   She's starting on me again. Something else wrong with me.

ROSA   I'm not starting on you, I'm criticising you.

SARAH   You're always criticising me.

ROSA   No, *you're* always criticising *me*.

SARAH   There! Another thing I've done wrong. I made a New Year's resolution – no more quarrelling with the children.

ROSA   Will you stop being paranoic.

SARAH   Don't be crude . . .

ROSA   I'm not really criticising you. How could I? Everything *you* are, *I* am . . .

SARAH   . . . calling me names.

        [ROSA stops her in her work, embraces her from behind]

ROSA   . . . everything! The little I respect in myself I've inherited from you.

SARAH   A terrible life I gave you . . .

ROSA   You!

SARAH   . . . terrible . . .

ROSA   Generosity, tolerance, intolerance, sanity, insanity. You!

SARAH   . . . leaving you alone to go out to work . . .

ROSA   The weather gets overcast – I'm depressed. You!

SARAH   . . . not caring enough for your education.

ROSA   When I lose my temper confronted by bloody-mindedness? You!

SARAH   You think it pleases me that you've inherited my faults?

ROSA   [Casually stepping up on to a chair] I read about the terrible things men do to each other – wars for gain or prestige, massacres for religious principles, cruelty to children, indifference to poverty – and then, one morning, one person, one, does something beautiful and I say 'See! People *are* good!' You!

[Jumps up on to the table. SARAH slaps her off]

SARAH   *I* was a fool? I brought *you* up to be a fool.

ROSA   [Stepping from chair to chair like stepping stones] The pompous action that makes me giggle. You! My laughter, my ups, my downs, my patience, my impatience, my love of music, mountains, flowers, knowledge – a reverence for all things living? You! You, you, you!

[Leaps into her mother's arms]

Flesh under canvas, and a visit to the poet

I think Doris Segal came into our family because my mother, while sitting under the hair dryer, persuaded her to join the Communist Party. A proselytiser, my mother, of the Salvation Army type. As God's captains might say to the shoppers listening to the band, 'God is love, God is everywhere', so my mother might say to her greengrocer, the woman in the bus queue, the postman, my visiting friends, our neighbours, the Bridgers whose sons were in and out of the nick, to her hairdresser – anyone at whom she might briefly glance: 'Politics is living, you can't live life without politics.' Doris joined, not that she had the most acute political mind but for friendship's sake. She liked my mother. Most people did. They felt in the presence of a woman of substance, to be reckoned with, relied upon. And the party branch numbered good-hearted, sociable women among its members who organised outings, socials, evening discussions led by London District luminaries, and local *Daily Worker* bazaars to herald which, for many years, I would dress up as Father Christmas and stand outside the school in Northwold

Road hired for the purpose, yodelling with actor's declaim at pass-
ers-by to come in and snatch bargains before they'd all be taken up.
'They want to know if you'll do Father Christmas again this year,'
my mother would ask. Pleasing her was often more important than
asserting political opposition.

Doris carried her heavy flesh like a sack of feathers, and made up
her pretty face exquisitely. The result was a highly sensuous lady
who presented herself to me as inexperienced in sexual matters,
coyly adding that she would be forever grateful if I could help.
Which I did on the occasions my mother was out shopping in
Ridley Road market without me, rare because, as can be seen, I
loved the market and helping her to shop.

The party attended to Doris's political enlightenment, but there
was nothing in Lenin to appease a twenty-year-old's sexual smouldering. I took it upon myself to supplement his teachings. We
became delightful friends and went camping by the hills and lakes
of Cumbria where all was damp and mist and fun for a few days
until – misery. The English climate. Soaked sex is not quite what
the eighteen-year-old Byron had in mind. We fled north to the
most famous Scottish poet of the day.

I am not certain how kindly I'd take to a young dramatist des-
cending unannounced upon me here, but Hugh MacDiarmid and
his patient wife, Valda, were kind and indulgent. We were fed, put
up for the night, perhaps it was two nights, and photographed. He
was being interviewed and a photographer got us to pose on the
lawn of the huge laundry house, set in a pine wood, belonging to
the Duke of Hamilton's Lanarkshire mansion in Dungavel. Doris
gave him a haircut and in the evening, after supper, he read to us
his latest poem. It was the first excruciating artistic experience of
my life. Not because the poem was bad. I don't *know* if the poem
was bad. That was the problem. I had sent MacDiarmid a batch of
poems and he had replied encouragingly, saying many of them
were a damn sight more poetic than some of the stuff he'd been
asked to comment on recently – his instinct more generous than
perhaps his judgement was honest – but I was no poet, and certainly no judge of poetry. What he read may have been

magnificent. I didn't hear it. My listening time was absorbed worrying what on earth I could say. Of course I listened to some of it – incomprehensible! Not like his earlier lyric poetry I'd read and admired. God knows what I *did* say. Whatever, it was a lie.

Doris married Ginger and they went off to Australia where, Ginger later told me on a trip back to England, her prettiness fell apart, she became embittered and destructive and brought ruin upon him. He didn't know where she was. Dead, he hoped.

Amateur nights

The hallucinatory seed of mummery was dropped into my blood while evacuated to Barnstaple. Aged about eleven. A school dramatisation of Alfred Lord Tennyson's *The Beggar Maid*. I'm seated on one throne next to another that's empty. Over my shoulders – a cloak. In my hand – a sceptre. On my head – a crown. A girl in rags is walking towards me through an aisle between parents and pupils. A bride with no father. Solitary. The Chorus intone:

> *Her arms across her breast she laid;*
> *She was more fair than words can say:*
> *Bare-footed came the beggar maid*
> *Before the king Cophetua.*

As she nears me I rise, very, very slowly and . . .

> *In robe and crown the king stept down,*
> *To meet and greet her on her way . . .*

hold out my hand which she takes . . .

> *'It is no wonder,' said the lords,*
> *'She is more beautiful than day.'*

and draw her with Arthurian grace to my side . . .

> *As shines the moon in clouded skies,*
> *She in her poor attire was seen:*
> *One praised her ankles, one her eyes,*
> *One her dark hair and lovesome mien.*
> *So sweet a face, such angel grace,*
> *In all that land had never been:*
> *Cophetua sware a royal oath:*

and I utter my first line on the stage before a public, loud and clear:

THIS BEGGAR MAID SHALL BE MY QUEEN!

and seat her by my side.

That slow rise accompanying the rhythmic beat of Tennyson's lines, that briefly borrowed regality, that moment of munificence – able to turn rags to riches, make of a beggar a queen, the power of it! Action without responsibility, control of an awed public, admiration for being who and what one was not – oh, the deeply satisfying, addictive power of it. Encouraged to be reader of the best roles during Bill Walsh's explorations of Shakespeare at Upton House, sharpened by Habonim's dramatic candlelit soirées, applauded for my performance (and singing talents) as King Ahasuerus in the Movement's *Purimspiel* – all was preparation to play, on 1 November 1947, three years later, 'A Robot' in Karel Čapek's futuristic drama, *R.U.R.* with the Query Players in Toynbee Hall's theatre, directed by Miss Patricia L. Burke. I was fourteen. (*Purimspiel* – a play for Purim. The Jewish Festival of Purim celebrates Esther's unearthing of Hamman's plot to have the Jews exterminated. He and his ten sons are hanged. The children enact a play about it every year though it doesn't seem to have stopped the attempt being repeated throughout history. Poor Jews! Still, as the United States' first black president said: 'They got rhythm.')

Patricia Burke directed and acted in the professional theatre where, because it was a struggle for a woman, she had to supplement her income running two amateur companies with LCC backing – the Islington Players, who performed at the Islington Town Hall, and the Query Players, who performed at the Toynbee Hall. Pat Burke was the god-daughter of G.K. Chesterton. In 1932 (the year I was born) he wrote a play for her called *The Surprise*. It was put aside for revision but he died before he could revise. Dorothy L. Sayers revised it and the Querys gave the only performance.

I was persuaded by cousin Doris – the cousin who wasn't really a cousin but the Kurtas, remember, were as close as any – to visit the Query Players at work in Daniel Street School which also housed other parts of the LCC Evening Institute in Shoreditch. Pat Burke took a liking to me and I was immediately accepted, given stage-management tasks, and, eventually, my first role on a real stage, the robot; though on reflection, King Cophetua must have been more satisfying – the stage to myself and all that kingly largesse, everyone's dream. (Why else would I have stood by the window flinging down hundreds of cigarette cards like alms to the poor and hungry?) Advancement was swift. From a Czech robot in 1947 to Launcelot Gobbo on roller-skates in 1948 – programmes priced 3d – a production where I learned how inspired accidents, which often make a production memorable, critics praise as evidence of directorial brilliance. During rehearsals of a scene, I don't remember which one, I had to skate on and off stage uttering a hasty gabbled line. Being merely a learner I fell arse over tit as they say in Iceland. 'Keep it in! Keep it in!' Burke cried. It was not easy to recreate the excitement of an accident.

The Query Players mounted two productions a year. I was fifteen when I played young Gobbo. By November 1948 I was sixteen and old enough to play Corporal Hodgson in Somerset Maugham's *Rain*. The role I coveted though was, who else, no – not Hamlet – Eugene Marchbanks, the poet in Shaw's *Candida*. It was not simply that I wanted to play a poet, I wanted to read one of my dreaded poems on stage! Awaiting the distribution of roles within an amateur company is a tense time, as with professionals. Who will get who? Allotting roles will always be an indication of what the director thinks of your talent and, to a degree, of your personality. Burke gave me the big break. *Candida* was scheduled for November 1949 with Patrick Corrigan playing Reverend Morrel, the striking Elizabeth Mills playing Candida, and the unworldly Arnold Wesker playing the eager, petulant, romantic, unworldly poet, Eugene Marchbanks. I would be seventeen and a half. Halves mattered at that age.

What kind of poetry was I writing? What would befit Shaw's passionate poet who fell in love with the Reverend's wife and forced her to choose between the two of them? What a glorious moment when she declares: 'I give myself to the weaker of the two' and it is the wise child-poet who knows at once she has given herself to the Reverend. The Reverend, 'great baby' that he was, imagined she had chosen the poet, after all everyone knows poets are weak and men of God strong. Oh, how I would love and learn that role of wise child. I couldn't wait to begin rehearsals. But which poems? As soon as I got home that evening I reached for my thickening file and tried to imagine the one I could best declaim seated at the feet of Candida.

I cannot remember which of the dreaded poems I read in the role, I only know that Burke didn't give me much time to establish my credentials as a poet at the feet of my beloved Candida, a couple of lines, no more. The performance was a nightmare. When the curtain came down on Act I and there was supposed to be a short but desperately needed interval Burke rushed into the wings in a state of high excitement and called out, 'No interval! No interval! Straight on! No interval!' I was shattered. The first scene ended with Morrel – Patrick Corrigan – shaking me vigorously and, added to the high tension of the moment and my nervousness, I was left trembling, my knees weak. The curtains parted within seconds. The scene had to begin with me standing. I couldn't. Legs betrayed me. I folded into a chair by the table from where I delivered my lines until I felt strong enough to stand again and play on play on MacDuff.

Why had Burke whipped out the interval from under our feet? We were the second half of a double-bill with Christopher Fry's *A Phoenix Too Frequent* – had the three actors playing it run over time? Reflecting now upon the reasons, and with hindsight knowledge of audience behaviour, I suspect that Burke, while out there among them, had sensed their restlessness and knew – like the pro she was – that given the escape route of a second interval the audience would take it. She wasn't having an audience walk out on her production.

The prize of that experience was not my performance, it was the card written to me by GBS. Six months before performing his poet, Eugene, I wrote asking for advice. No simple letter, no short note, but pages and pages – a mini-autobiography. Four months earlier I'd asked, remember, for a donation to help get me to Paris and had offered to come in person explaining myself. The old man had sent a pink and a blue card: 'He cannot engage in private correspondence, nor read long letters . . . He cannot discuss his published views in private letters . . .' None of which daunted me. I wrote not merely a long letter, but a long, long, long letter. Whether he read it all I cannot know. Something must have touched him for he replied by hand from his house in Ayot St Lawrence, on a buff card dated 10 June 1949, in his spidery handwriting – he was a man of ninety-three years – thirty succinct words:

> It is a curious part, clever experienced actors fail in it. Novices suc-
> ceed in it.
> Take care to make your lines heard. Leave the rest to luck.
> Advienne que pourra.
> GBS

Nine years later, after the opening of *Chicken Soup with Barley* on the stage of the Belgrade Theatre, I understood the playwright's concern that his lines should be heard.

The following year, 1950, brought me the roles in Thornton Wilder's play, and Taplow in the Rattigan. I seem to remember being brilliant as Taplow. The role in which I failed dismally was the swashbuckling lover, Captain Carvallo, by Denis Cannan, performed at Toynbee Hall in July 1953. Lover of long-standing though by now I imagined myself to be at the age of twenty-one – charming, debonair, courteous, chutzpadik, able to skip down stairs sidewise, raise my left eyebrow, dress with Byronic flamboyancy, yet was I not sophisticated enough to perform Cannan's officer. Not only did I not understand what I was talking about but I played alongside the sexy Miriam Barrett who, ten years my senior, was behaving on stage in ways utterly incomprehensible to me. I could deliver the lines, even with some feeling, but in those innocent days I really wanted to be a laid-back Spencer Tracy, instead here I was having to pull her bosom to my bosom, suave and velvety and confidently masculine, and it was beyond me. Give me the hopeless longing of Eugene Marchbanks any day. And how did I learn all those lines?

Actor I wanted to be nevertheless. Burke helped me through LAMDA and RADA examinations – one I took before going into the RAF, the other when I came out – but nothing could get me past the LCC examiners. Harold Pinter took his test at the same time and passed. Obviously he had what they thought actors should have. I applied as well, in the last months of the RAF, to get into the Oxford Playhouse School of Theatre run by Frank Shelley. Auditions were held in the theatre. Shelley and one or two others were there as I jauntily leapt on the stage and looked around with the air of one who did it all the time. My renderings earned me a place.

The Oxford Playhouse Company
April 12th 1952

Dear Sir

I most earnestly wish to recommend Arnold Wesker, (AC2, RAF Wethersfield, near Braintree, Essex – home address, 32 Weald Square, Upper Clapton, London E5) for an Educational Grant or Scholarship. During our entrance tests here, for the Oxford Playhouse School of Theatre, he came out with top marks in each department. In other words, he shows quite exceptional talent for the theatre. It would be a great pity if, through lack of private means, he was unable to follow this as his career. His sense of comedy, and his general dramatic imagination are absolutely first class: very rare material indeed!

Yours faithfully

` Frank Shelley

It didn't help.

I was able, however, to use the Playhouse offer of a place as a reason for extricating myself from His Majesty's Air Force two months ahead of demob date. Conscripts were released early to take up university places. Perhaps my speedy release was further helped by a record of good behaviour. I had created a drama society with officers and men at RAF Moreton-in-the-Marsh, and directed my second production, the first being a heroic play about the French Resistance written specially for a school arts festival which I organised. This one was a sci-fi one-acter about an encroaching green mass which I think was taking over the world, and was called *The Green Mass*, a chilling little work whose chillingness I heated to above zero by using the thumping beat of Holst's 'God of Mars' from his Planets suite. I felt quite proud of myself directing officers, people used to giving orders rather than receiving them. But I was posted on. I kept being posted on. A move every three months. Why? Officers and men protested and made representations that I be kept at Moreton-in-Marsh to continue running the drama group – so healthy for the spirits and wellbeing of the camp. Nothing helped. One day I found myself alone in the office where secret files were kept. I looked up mine. A note was attached saying something like: 'Gave a speech at a peace rally. Likely to be a troublemaker.' Strange logic.

After the Query Players I engaged in no more acting until moving to Norwich as kitchen porter at the Bell Hotel. The Norwich Film Society advertised for actors. I would take up a film career. Somewhere in the film archives of the city is footage of me playing in a film I wrote and directed about a murder on Mousehold Heath. My cousin Bryan, becoming soberer and soberer by the minute as he pursued law studies, had less and less patience with me.

> . . . for heaven's sake grow up. If you're set on working in the film world then you've got to start right at the bottom (handing slides to the cameraman's mate) – and work and study and work some more. Making a film isn't just pointing a camera at a rolling landscape and pressing a button – it's a skilled art – and skill is learned by practice. Use your loaf before you find that you've wasted the best part of your life and got nowhere . . .

My last acting role in this short career as actor was 1961 in Rome. A theatre club invited Dexter to bring over the cast of the Trilogy and perform excerpts. The actor playing Ronnie couldn't make it. I took over. I shone on the first night. Faded out on the second. An interesting experience. We played the excerpts in chronological order which meant jumping backwards and forwards between the three plays. (I've since written a film script of *The Trilogy* which takes on just such a chronological shape.)

The actor in me remains. I love reading, and read well. Since Rome my stage appearances, apart from lecturing, are as a performer reading from the plays and stories. Mostly readings of the *One Woman Plays*. On a number of occasions I've given a marathon reading of all of them lasting from 2.30 in the afternoon to around 9.45 in the evening, with intervals. Give me a bar stool, a table, a glass of water and an audience and I glow with that power I first experienced playing King Cophetua. Not a talent, more a facility to capture, hold, control an audience. It would give me pleasure to have a space where it was known I would be every Sunday for a year, reading something. And like a pop singer there would be favourites. The audience would call out: 'Give us *Betty Lemon* . . . the mother going on holiday . . . Beattie Bryant's last speech . . . Sonia's love letters . . .'

The first play

The first *full*-length play, *And After Today*, was written for the Query Players. There had been the scripts for Habonim candlelit soirées – scraps sewn together with music incorporating no doubt a dreaded poem or two; and there was the sketch about the French resistance – on which, aged thirteen, I was an expert – involving much shooting and dying and beautiful last utterances performed before embarrassed staff, the amazed pupils of Upton House, and my admiring parents. And at around sixteen an ambitious attempt called *The Trial of God*. Or was it *God on Trial*? No sheets exist, not in my possession anyhow, they may be among the papers swimming around somewhere in London, belonging to Alastair Sutherland who once told me he'd mislaid a chest full of his and my papers, so I recreate it from memory.

The play is set in heaven, crowded of course, full of rather grumpy people. Every day greets a new contingent of the newly dead – sad, bewildered, and angry. The first demand each new arrival makes is to see God. They have complaints. Where is he? When will they be brought into his presence? Weary angels explain – they have been doing so for some time now – God will see them in due course, at the appointed hour, but don't expect too much.

In a corner of the stage is a little old man trying to pretend he isn't there. He looks anxious, nail-biting, Jewish, as though each moment brings problems for which he was not born to cope. He's God. Every day he has to confront dead malcontents who hold him responsible for their death, the mess their lives were in, the misery of life in general down there on earth. He has to explain, endlessly; it's not his fault. He was playing around in the galaxy and one day – boom! He'd created earth! All the things he'd been trying to assemble for aeons – assembled! fell into place! He'd created earth and life thereon! But that was all. That was it. Having created life he had no control over it. Day after day he must tell his helpless story to each new chariot-load of arrivals. He's sorry, but there it is – a pain but what can he do? That's life! Or death! Or whatever – amen!

Up until this moment of stage-time all newcomers had accepted his explanations – reluctantly, sceptically, resigned. Heaven, rumbling with divine discontent, was not a happy place. On this day, however, heaven's chariots spew forth a new breed. God's explanations are, these newcomers insist, unacceptable: the timid, limp, whining of a conscienceless, culpable, irresponsible old Jew (for, as everyone knows, God is an old Jew). Something must be done. Meetings are held, speeches made, resolutions formulated and voted upon, culminating in the momentous, epoch-making, shattering decision to put God on trial for crimes against humanity.

A court is prepared, counsel for prosecution appointed – the loudest mouth, naturally – witnesses called from all walks of life, all classes, and the poor old man with a long white beard – of course a long white beard – takes his place on the stand. The accusations come thick and fast with overwhelming persuasiveness. God cowers, regrets, stutters apologies, tries explanations, is bludgeoned by damning evidence hammered home by witness after witness, and seems about to drop to his knees in a wail of lamentation and confessions of guilt when – something! A word too harsh, a recrimination too unjust, a conclusion too unreasonable, a self-righteousness too far. The old man can take no more. God has had enough. He turns the tables on them. Yes, he didn't know what he was doing when he created life; yes, he did set in motion something over which he had no control; yes, he could see that such a magnificent creation would mislead people into imagining a guiding hand must be in control somewhere. But what about them? Humans, themselves? Is no guilt to be attached to them? Thereafter, with mounting confidence, he marshals evidence of human cruelty and stupidity and becomes the accuser instead of the accused. I have no memory of the number of pages written, not many, a dozen perhaps. Ambition, I must intuitively have recognised, exceeded ability. The work was abandoned.

The play I did complete aspired to less giddy omniscience. *And After Today*, written some time in 1950 – unusually for me I didn't date it – was about aunts Ann and Sara. Sara – the trade union organiser, tiny, tough and widely read; Ann – dumpy, giggly, a reader too, but untogether. Three reasons excited me to write the play: the autobiographical one with myself and the aunts central to the drama, sister and parents existing in the background; a wish to explore why two women remained unmarried, and what it felt like to be without children and male companionship; and a wish to provide a play for my amateur drama group. They never performed it. Pat Burke was a maiden lady herself, the questions too raw for her to confront. Or so I explain it to myself. It is possible she didn't think the play was good enough. I certainly can't bring myself to read it and discover whether she was right, but a playwright was I not yet meant to be. When that time came seven years later I scavenged the maiden-aunt play and changed focus. *Chicken Soup with Barley* became a play about my parents, Della and me, with the maiden aunts in the background.

The characters of aunts Ann and Sara have never been fully realised. One of the *Four Portraits – of Mothers*, Naomi, is inspired by the character of Ann, but the full sadness of their two unfulfilled lives – both wanted to marry and have children – I have never explored. Sara's decline has been hinted at in the description of her death from 'A Time of Dying'. Ann's last years I've sketched into a lecture but never, apart from the fifteen minute *Portrait*, incorporated into a dramatic work. They were distressing years for her, as I've described. Occasionally it was possible to move her into spirited conversation. One day I asked her did she believe in an afterlife?

Her reply was: 'No I don't! When you're dead you're bloody dead! And that's that!'

Chapter Twelve

Friends and friendship

> . . . I'm tired of myself, Rosie, so tired of my thoughts, my habits,
> what's expected of me . . . I have this overwhelming desire to be dif-
> ferent. Change my skin, disappear from everyone I know,
> everything I am, everything I feel . . . Every time I catch up with
> myself I'm not there anyway . . .
>
> Stanton – *Lady Othello*, Act II Scene 6

A disturbing aspect of this self-imposed incarceration in the Black
Mountains is that I do not miss friends. It's frightening, as though I
had lost one of my senses – touch, hearing, sight. A gift for friendship is a rich human quality. Can you ever possess and lose it? You
are either blessed or not blessed with the gift; it can't be lost just as
the capacity to laugh can't be lost. Yet we know it can be; as sight
fails, appetites retreat and hair turns grey. The real question is –
since past evidence suggests I once possessed the gift – why do I
feel no sense of loss? Perhaps because I know friends are never lost
and when the time comes . . .

Perhaps this retreat is a phase. One morning I will wake up, the
need will come flooding back and I shall flee these hills, return to
the city. I don't know. I only know that for years there has been
upon me a need to slough off old skin, creep out of a personality I
no longer care about. Of course we can never change what we are,
but there are always untried, unexpected, surprising parts.

This need to surprise myself had grown over the years. I saw a
stale image reflected in those who had been close to me – except
my children, they occupied a unique, unassailable place, I felt fresh

with them. Even with you, Lindsay Joe, despite your harshly judge-mental recalcitrant mood of these last three years. And with grandchildren even fresher.

There is this, too: one small act disappoints, casts a shadow over how a friend has been viewed so that it becomes impossible to re-turn to a relationship that once had been.

This section is being written in November 1993. Recently I have attempted to renew a relationship with an old friend. I had stopped contacting him because he had done something I'd considered a betrayal of our trust. The betrayal was real enough but on re-flection, minor. I had overreacted. Should we not try to recapture what had once been? We met for dinner. A deeply depressing en-counter. And I understood: I had not overreacted. The broken trust, however minor, had been a last straw. The personality flaws, which in the past could be ignored because the friendship seemed worth it, had accumulated. When the minor betrayal took place all that I had suppressed rose to the surface. Now the years had passed, we were trying again. I wrote and thanked him for the even-ing. He replied that it had been a pleasant evening but not quite like old times. Oh, really? It had seemed to me *just* like old times. In our three hours together he informed me his house in France was better than another friend's house in France, that his Welsh cottage was better than my Welsh cottage, that financially he was now very well off, 'to put it mildly'; he corrected me in the use of a word (he'd missed the point but I was too mesmerised to explain, he was like a man possessed), and he insulted two very dear members of my family. There were other slips and utterances of a desperately com-petitive kind which I withhold in order not to reveal the person concerned. Perhaps I should have felt pity. These are his last years. All our last years. We should love one another. But the heart har-dens without one being able to do anything about it. The competitive, opportunistic spirit hurts, offends me – traits I most despise. Not grasping opportunity when it comes our way, not seiz-ing the day, more a grabbing of opportunity at the expense of another, stepping on them to achieve an end, attaching to oneself that which is in the air, of the moment, ephemeral. Power rather than substance becomes important. In the arts power is often found in the hands of the opportunist, which is perhaps another reason for staying in the hills – to be in his presence is deeply depressing. I stray.

This question of the hills, retreat, to be honest there are other reasons. I fear dependency. I'm not shy to request or accept help but if a situation threatens to render me helplessly dependent I bristle. I fear being controlled, I fear emotional blackmail, I fear loss of freedom. It is important that I know myself to be self-sufficient, and I know this to be a reaction against my father's total abdication of responsibility and his subsequent dependency upon others.

RONNIE Can't you see that I can't bear what you are. I don't want
        to hear your lies all my life. Your weakness frightens me,
        Harry – did you ever think about that? I watch you and I
        see myself and I'm terrified.

HARRY   What I am – I am. I will never alter. Neither you nor your
        mother will change me. It's too late now; I'm an old man
        and if I've been the same all my life so I will always be.
        You can't alter people, Ronnie. You can only give them
        some love and hope they'll take it. I'm sorry. It's too late
        now. I can't help you. Don't forget to have supper. Good-
        night.
                              Chicken Soup with Barley, Act II Scene 2

I read through the letters of old friends and immediately I'm a young man of eighteen, twenty, twenty-five. I see the faces and events to which they refer, names of those with whom I've spent nights in animated discussion, shared meals and movies, all-night poker games, long walks, passionate embraces. Gone. Some dead. From Habonim days – Ruth, Pauline, Bibi, Helena, Helen, the two Esthers, Shifra, Rhoda, Audrey, Dennis, Michael, Chaim, Bryan, Boris, Judith, Edit . . . Outside the movement – Robert, Alastair,

Stan, John, Beales, Jean, Barney, Pete, Squibbs, Maureen, Mavis, Doris, Ginger, Roy and Rita, Dai, David . . . As I list them I see a scene for each: Rhoda – lying with her on a carpet, kissing each other, out of breath to the exotic chords of de Falla; the girlfriend to whom I offered more than she wanted, who gave me up for a macho man of verbal violence who gambled and drank. Bryan – both of us in shorts folding blankets outside our tent in a weekend camp at Arkley. Mavis – madly in love with me for a few months, endless conversations for the price of three pennies from a telephone kiosk, some over an hour long, one lasted more than two hours. I was only fourteen years old – what on earth did we talk about? Chaim, a chiropodist, poker player, guitarist and folk dancer. He carved my feet and those of my mother, and he taught actors to dance a Yugoslav folk dance in my TV play, *Menace*. Doris – passionate lovemaking in a small tent by Lake Windermere. Alastair – listening with him to the Brandenburg Concerto No. 6 in his London flat in Grape Street, a flat full of large rooms sparsely furnished and frequently occupied by itinerant jazz musicians and their groupies. Roy and Rita – walking with them and Dusty over Pont Neuf in Paris, probably discussing philosophy. Boris – running from our room in Rue de L'Ancient Comedie chased by a man with a knife – that story comes later. Dennis – playing 'machenayim' on Hackney Downs, a game involving throwing a football at one of the other team who had either to catch it or jump out of the way. Dennis was a powerful thrower, I was a nimble catcher. Dai – walking him from Weald Square, E5, to his home in Homerton Road, E8, and him walking me back to Weald Square, and me walking him back and him walking me back . . . until in the early hours of the morning the conversation came to an end and we agreed to leave each other halfway, round about the Salvation Army Home on Lower Clapton Road.

It is through the letters of cousin Bryan (affectionately known as Lippy), Robert Copping, Squibbs (Sydney Greenspan), Alastair Sutherland and Dai Vaughan that I catch glimpses of myself and the life we all led. Weald Square was central to our relationships. I loved bringing friends home and lavishing upon them hospitality. Leah and Joe shared and encouraged the open house. Sarah to Ronnie:

> . . . Don't go away again. It's been so lonely without you and your friends. I don't mind not having any money, we can always eat, you know that, but I can't bear being on my own . . .

My mother's words. It was true. Whatever criticism she may have had of my friends – she certainly didn't approve of everyone – she relished them being around the flat. In one of his letters written to me while I was in the RAF and he was lodging in my room in Weald Square, Alastair exclaimed, 'I love Leah!' In a later letter he tempered this love. Still affectionate, but:

> . . . How her insistence on forcing the subject [communism] on her guests cuts into her hospitality. That was just a price one had to pay for Weald Square.

The poker school, where stakes rose as the young players grew into wealthy professionals, began in Weald Square. My mother and father were part of it with Bryan, Barney, Chaim, Rhoda, Squibbs and Ginger. Bill Carter, Ashley and others were added at a later date. But to begin with, as long as my mother was playing, there was a modest limit on the betting. A halfpenny kitty and never more than sixpence in any one round, the stakes usually rising by halfpennies. As the years passed the limit rose to half a crown. Then the school moved to other venues, Bryan got his law degree, Chaim opened his chiropodist's practice, Bill Carter became a surveyor – the stakes rose by tens to £10, £20, £30. Soon hundreds were passing hands. But the 'sixpenny limit school' began on the third floor of Weald Square – we'd provide the basic tea, bread and butter, others would bring frillier bits. Drink was not part of the event. Cider or shandy at most. It was a fun poker school to begin with, nothing hard-edged or desperate. And we played according to our personalities. I gambled, took risks, bluffed with bravado, and mostly lost. Fortunately gambling for money never became an obsession. I gambled with emotions and art. The results were rich and catastrophic and just as costly one way or another.

Bryan

Cousin Bryan and I were close. He was a good-looking baby and a handsome man with a precise mind and dry wit delivered in soft Welsh tones drawn from the Lipson side of the family who had settled in Swansea. A glorious sepia photo exists of him and me standing angelically either side of Della. From an early age he suffered night blindness, which has now developed miserably into total blindness – an affliction he carries with humour and fortitude, pursuing Open University studies as though the handicap didn't exist. We were affectionate cousins but he never held back from admonition. I've recorded one chastisement and select from others written in early 1954 when I fled London with a new girlfriend, Olive Gloyn, met while working in Stoneham's bookshop, to live in Norfolk.

> . . . From time to time I hear from Squibbs about your 'goings on below stairs'. I knew that you were a kitchen porter and that your affair with Olive was over. I'd also heard about this maid [Dusty] who has designs upon you, but for all my advance information I was glad to receive your letter.
>
> I still don't see your reasons for staying in Norwich . . . Come back to London – here there is scope and opportunity. You've chosen a hopelessly overcrowded almost bankrupt profession. You think you're good, you've got supreme self-confidence – good luck to you. I will do anything I can to help. But what chance can you have stuck over a pile of vegetables in a hotel?
>
> I know that you have no trade and that there is little that you can turn your hand to. I see that you regret this just a little. I don't say

that you should become a clerk in an insurance office . . . try to find something useful to do – if you carry on as you are the years will pass and you will be a complete failure . . .

. . . First you wanted to write a masterpiece of poetry and drama – then you wanted to act and now you want to film. You have failed to persevere at any goal for any length of time. You seem to drift as your fancy takes you.

These are harsh words – but kindly meant. I hope I may be wrong but I can see no vision of Arnold Wesker bursting upon the world as a film genius . . . I pray I am wrong.

Profession and domesticity took most of us up and away, but both Della and I used his legal services, for which he charged us at cost. In one instance, for me, it proved unwise: when I sued the Royal Shakespeare Company for loss of earnings resulting from them breaking their contract to mount *The Journalists*, a lawsuit affordable only because Bryan acted for me without payment until settlement. Over eight years he gave thousands of pounds worth of time coping with endless, prevaricating demands made by Messrs Harbottle and Lewes, solicitors to the RSC and many other theatrical institutions, who deliberately spun out proceedings hoping to wear me down, which those foxy manipulators of law succeeded, finally, in doing. Trevor 'Goliath' Nunn beat Arnold 'David' Wesker and went on to become a multimillionaire while 'David' scratched around for pennies knowing stones from slings don't always find their target and wishing he'd never read that particular biblical fable. It had been a mistake to involve my generous cousin. He was wise about the nature of the law in general and his field in particular, but his field was not 'show-biz'. Harbottle outmanoeuvred us and I settled out of court for a mere £4000 instead of the £25,000 I felt the RSC's treachery had robbed me of. Half went to Bryan. A fraction of his real costs, I'm sure, though he graciously made no mention of what they might have been.

Squibbs

It is when I read the letters of Squibbs and Alastair, both volumi-
nous, that I reflect with incredulity on the intensity of friendship
and the ease with which it can cease. Why should I be incredulous?
Don't we know love comes and goes? The twenty-four-hour day-by-
day living with adored children, about whom we were in a state of
constant anxiety fearing accident and death, over whom we pined if
separation was too long, all comes to an end. They're off! Abroad!
Into other loves, other milieus! Why am I then so amazed as I read
the letters of long-gone friends? It is because not only has the
friendship ceased but that person who was me, and to whom they
were a loving, concerned friend, no longer exists.

I have described, in an earlier chapter, the framework within
which Squibbs and I became friends. A laconic young man with
glasses and a dry ironic wit, who ached to become a writer, Squibbs
earned his living mainly as a pattern-cutter in the tailoring trade.
He performed in a couple of Query Players productions, attended
writers' classes here and in Canada, tried to learn to play the guitar
and to sing, bought himself a cine-camera and briefly romanticised
a future as film director. He was one of life's aspirers who never
took off, though at the time it seemed to me his pen flowed more
eloquently than mine. After national service in the RAF and three
years in Canada he met up with and had his pities-and-sympathies
hooked by the plaintive neurosis of an American student of architecture called Pat. He has since separated from her and lives with an
antique dealer in Northamptonshire.

His first letter was sent to me while I was stationed in Moreton-
in-Marsh. He writes from his brother's house in Loughton, 8
January 1952:

> . . . Having started on night work I should doubtless be supplement-
> ing my income as is the window cleaner across the way. Am I

envious to see the whipping wind punish his aristocratic blood (his dungarees are already blue).

It is certainly huddle by the fire weather, come cuddle me weather, I'm not tired but come to bed weather . . .

. . . It's about time I started work on my new thriller. I already have the vague outline, not for plot but for motive, very important, (must go to lunch, chop and chips).

The trouble lies in deciding the form, probably the best method is amble all over it in novel shape, then condense it very cleverly into a play and sell the film rights. Of course a first novel is a thing to be avoided like a pox, or as the critics say vice versa . . .

It has been my ambition to feature a female detective. I will have to fit her in somewhere. This insipid work is to be glorified with the title *Stuff Me, Stuff My Goose*. I think a cast of two men and four women will make a sizeable heap of corpses at the final curtain.

. . . With the passing of time (22 on Friday) I can no longer grovel in ecstasy over the poetic blank face of a cabbage knowing that I will soon be eating it.

I would like to print most of what Squibbs writes to me. His letters after all chart a life of the times, offer glimpses of family and friends, reveal the personality with whom I shared, and upon whom I sharpened, an intellectual life. There are too many. But some must find a place.

As a Weald Square lodger Squibbs becomes witness to the tensions between my ailing father and distraught mother.

You may judge Leah's agitated state when asking me to acknowledge your letter. Her upset was worse than I have [ever] witnessed. It must surely be about time her trouble and she were parted. I am no diviner of means and methods to be able to suggest the appropriate action without money, but the simplest solution would be to eradicate Joe. I am sure your doctor friend would certify him for half a crown.

The sandals have gone to the sandal maker the raincoat to the rain maker and the country to the dogs . . .

So anyway, if you don't come home send a photograph.

'Your doctor friend' was a quack doctor from whom conscripts could obtain a medical certificate justifying extension of leave due to illness. The doctor would ask what was wrong with you and write down on the certificate your chosen malaise. Price 5/–.

Squibbs keeps me informed about Weald Square's lives and the goings-on among old friends.

What ho the boy

Of course I miss you, how could it be otherwise, even be it only in brief snatches of remembrance. . . . It is inevitable that we listen to Brahms and Leah remarks about you . . . It dawns on me that Alastair and I have never discussed anything fundamental unless it be through the medium of discussing you which we do practically continuously. The formula we use, 'The trouble with Arnold is . . .'

The gang gathered at Fitzroy Street last week ostensibly to hear records à la Jack but really to glimpse the new sylph whom Hannah [Bryan's German-born wife to be] is flaunting namely one Ruth a virgin resident of Israel's state, born in a Germany of turbulent times . . . Is she not sloe-eyed, raven-haired, a creature of sensuous mystery? She is not.

Teutonic as a mug of beer, with flaxen hair and eyes of Aryan blue which set me thinking of Aryan milkmen . . .

Bryan has been the revealer of a pertinacious witticism. Namely the newly invented contraceptive with ink in the teat. The instructions are 'If you can't come – write'.

Keep writing, riting, righting, ryeting, wrighting, rahting, ritying, ratink, rioting. Love everly Squibbs.

But, like most people in those days, he doesn't always date his letters so I can't be certain where I'm receiving them. In August 1953, having failed again to obtain that elusive grant to pay my RADA fees, and having been hit once too many times by rejection slips for poems and stories, I fled with Olive to join Della and Ralph in Norfolk. Olive married her farmer and I became a kitchen porter in the Bell Hotel, Norwich, where I met Dusty.

Squibbs, like cousin Bryan, chides me for being a 'hermit'. Being a kitchen porter in a busy Trusthouse Forte hotel is hardly a hermitic existence, but he does point to something in my nature which is reclusive, or partly reclusive. A need not to run away but to go somewhere from which to gain a new perspective.

> . . . What degree of serenity do you find that is not possible here? I don't suppose that the situation is void of conflict, possible even with Olive. To the point of presumption how long can your intimacy last, unless her attitude has reversed to what I understand her requirements to be. Surely you are going to come off very much the worse . . .
>
> Leah has two sayings which are repeated . . . 'I wish Arnold was here, and I'm so glad I interfered when Alastair tried to embroil him' . . .

It is not easy to disentangle everything that drives one. A wish to withdraw, exercise willpower by not participating is evident at an early age. And yet my natural instinct was a social one, home-loving. The close warmth of Fashion Street fashioned my propensity for family, fires, and domesticity. I painted the walls and woodwork of Weald Square, bought heavy, warm-coloured curtains and matching furniture, creating a cosy place where I loved bringing friends. I make myself at home in rooms and enjoy making homes. Dusty shares this passion. People were drawn to Bishops Road as many are drawn to Ashley Road. And yet I had to leave London and my friends for Norfolk, and England for Paris. Squibbs' later letters remind me of plans contemplated for joining him in Canada with Dusty and a baby we nearly had, of meeting him in Mexico, working my way round the world on ships, emigrating to Israel. Plans to get up and go! As soon as Blaendigeddi was purchased I used it for refuge and writing. I could break the back of a new work here and read more in three weeks than six months in London. More than a place to write, it became a sanctuary where I learned to live with myself, become self-sufficient. I once stayed here for a six-week stretch and frightened myself because each time the farmer, off whom we had bought the cottage, dropped in for a chat I became irritable. Something unhealthy was happening to me, I thought. And yet, look, four years – with breaks, it's true – and I miss neither friends nor social gatherings. Does the spirit wrinkle like a prune?

One letter from Squibbs, rumbles with the spirit of Jimmy Porter. I'm in Norfolk. He continues to keep me informed about friends and family. The poker games flourish. Bill Carter continues to break hearts and cause emotional havoc. My beloved Esther drifts restlessly through unhappiness, no man pleases her, she too is destined for Israel. Squibbs wants to know about 'a certain Rusty'. He leaves Weald Square because tension has grown between him and Leah and Joe.

Leah gave me a wonderful feeling, one might say a warm smirk of the heart. I am sure she felt somehow guilty at my leaving in spite of the worry-lifting fact of my departure. She turned up next day with a cup and saucer, eggshell blue, which I shall not return. When I went to collect my toothbrush, looking perhaps as wanting to be patted on the head, she declared the house was always open and offered me the key. I cannot surmise what effort this cost but in humility it is a gesture I shall treasure.

Joe I am sure will miss me, he is a child for company, nagging argument, diverting talk, confidences and gossip. I kept thinking that he was prodding himself to see if he was sane, that he kept fear well in the background. I had an absurd urge to lock the door at night in case he went rash, but I could attribute that to the mounting tension in the house . . .

Then one day, shortly before he picks himself up and sets sail for Canada, he explodes:

. . . What we accept! To awake and hear the alarm clock, see the wash basin, to feel the cold water, to eat porridge, to open the door and set in motion the wheels of another monotonous day, drudging in uncongenial work, bitten by the virus of frustration, angry at such docile acceptance, fearful of change, demented by inadequacy, desiring peace with understanding, coitus without obligation, heaven without death.

I'm sick of this room without joy, this middle-class family with Jewish hypocrisies, adolescent sons, bloated daughters and the moral code of Zion.

I want a house to ring with laughter, echo with the crash of gigantic music, jokes and words to reel from the walls, and rooms to be rude with luscious colour.

So don't stagnate and meander, just leave and come to London. We'll find a place and wait till spring breathes a warm greeting and then jump into the willing arms of the world. I await.

I don't know whether he made his house ring with laughter and gigantic music. I hope he did.

Squibbs was disappointed when Dusty and I decided to go to Paris instead of sharing a flat and a new life with him in Montreal. He missed London and when, in December 1958, he made the big decision to return, his last letter bounced with anticipatory delight.

I gather that if you are still living in Norfolk you are out of touch with the London mob. I hear from Bill Carter that the poker school is still going strong. My God it is now more than three years. I suspect some of the faces have changed. I feel the excitement mounting in my throat and long to be with you all again and be caught in a surge of rising socialism, if there is such a thing, and develop and discuss and create a fucking uproar. It will be good. Write as soon as you can. I love you all.

Squibbs didn't know that a play called *Look Back in Anger* had been written ten months earlier.

Diary extract 1952

This is how I moved from my 20th into my 21st year:

The bastards! Not a penny extra for XMAS. A gesture of 10/– or so would have been the right thing to make after all the rush of those last few days, after they had taken almost £1000 on Monday. [I'm working in Stoneham's bookshop in Old Street] Olive received nothing as well and poked her head into the rest room and said, 'I feel like pinching a book!' with an annoyed tone that made me suspect she had done so already.

But at lunch time on Wednesday I went out into the Lane [Petticoat] and bought some cheese and chopped liver and a box of matzo, some tangerines, biscuits and cholas [plaited egg-bread] for Mrs Levy. From work to her basement to give them to her. I must have been knocking for about five minutes before she eventually appeared. Poor woman, asleep in her dirty bed of dirt, there because what else was there to do, no one to talk to, nowhere to go – and she must have been a little frightened as well. But when she saw me and what I had brought she bubbled with an irrepressible glee calling me 'ma mignon! ma mignon! – for me? you brought these things for me? Oh, ma mignon.' Her excitement was a great reward. Why do I talk of rewards I wonder? Did I want her to have some good food and the pleasure of knowing someone had thought of her, or did I want that satisfaction of power which one finds in the certain knowledge that they and they alone were the only people capable of committing such an act of goodness? The introspective mauling of a self-righteous conscience can turn good intentions sour in us.

What the hell! She had the food, a little happiness, a tiny taste of kindness – what matter to her my motives? This thought process is ridiculous. I never diabolically planned a cheap thrill of power.

But what abject poverty! Filthy walls hanging with God knows how many years of dirt, and dusty bits of furniture, broken furniture pushed away with no semblance of an inhabited room, and in the alcove an iron bedstead with rags to cover her, and on the chairs more rags, and on her body – what else but rags. A yellow, electrically dim room where little daylight penetrates and still less clean air. She babbled on about wanting to move perhaps on to the first or second flight of stairs up, she talked of having no one with whom to talk, nothing to do; she no longer goes to the soup kitchen, people asked about your affairs, she didn't want everyone to know about her, she was ashamed. Now she thought the police were watching her. She instructed me not to look out of the window or they would see and I must not give her money for two tins of herring (which she got from the soup kitchen and was going to sell) or they would see. Outside the one window was a blank wall the other side of which were the back yards of the houses from the next street. She asked was there going to be another war and I felt stupid trying to explain how there were little wars in other parts but no, I didn't think there would be another big war.

Funny how I sit here now – I've been reading for the last two and a half hours, it's now nearly midnight – and hope for someone to come. Squibbs is out, Joe and Leah in Norfolk. Audrey at a three-day party, Esther stubbornly at her sister's, Doris and Ginger at a party, Alastair in Birmingham, Barney in Derby. I don't mind being alone, I am almost completely contented, a wonderful peace, toute seul, but I still listen and think I hear a whistle there, a footstep here. Who do I expect?

I wait for vague visions of any woman to appear, in answer, through the door.

I shall wait a lifetime . . .

The diary records a dinner with aunts Ann and Sara and their friend Beatie Marx, secretary to Harry Politt, leader of the British Communist Party . . . Later I go to Pat Burke's house to rehearse my RADA pieces. I offer her my Chris Fry monologue for the first time. She does little to it or any of the pieces I've chosen for this leap into my future as a great actor. I take it as a good sign.

Chapter Thirteen

2496288 AC/2 Wesker

Call-up papers were awaited. It was an event. 'Have yours come through?' we would ask one another. In the signing-on office sat a tired sergeant asking the same questions of every nervous pimpled youth. Not all of us were nervous – just as I suppose not all of us were pimply – but a new regime was awaiting us; many shat themselves, others made certain their tongues were well in place.

SERGEANT	Name of father?
ME	Joseph.
SERGEANT	Profession?
ME	Tailor's machinist.
SERGEANT	Where was your father born?
ME	Russia.
SERGEANT	Russia?
ME	Yes, Russia.
SERGEANT	Whereabouts in Russia?
ME	Ukraine. Dnepropetrovsk.
SERGEANT	Could you spell that?
ME	D-N-E-P-R-O-P-E-T-R-O-V-S-K.
SERGEANT	[Less jaunty] Name of mother?
ME	Leah.

SERGEANT   Profession?

ME   Sometimes tailor's machinist, sometimes cook.

SERGEANT   [Slightly nervous] Where was *she* born?

ME   Transylvania.

            [He thinks I'm taking the piss, there's no such place]

            Honest, Sergeant. Transylvania.

SERGEANT   [Really nervous now] Whereabouts in Transylvania?

ME   Gyergószentmiklos.

SERGEANT   Look would you take this form home with you, fill it
            up and send it back? Next!

Some numbers have rhythms which rumble around constantly like arguments in your head – my wartime identity-card number for example: TCBG 864. Nine eleven fifty (9/11/50) was my intake number, the date of arrival at RAF Padgate, the kitting-out-sorting-out camp where dazed, lost conscripts, most of whom had never left their square mile of streets, were given uniforms, badges, kit for polishing boots and brass, blanco for belts. And numbers.

   '2496288 AC/2 Wesker, sah!'

   I was embarked upon eighteen months which one way or another through events and encounters turned my life around.

   I had not wanted to join. The idea of being part of an armed force appalled me. Me? Non-taker of orders? Hadn't they read Miss Webb's school report? 'He should realise though that people older than himself should be able to guide him.' Yet I made this surprising discovery: that I was able to take orders, *and* was competent at carrying them out. Paradoxically, good leaders can follow good leaders. Once I accept a secondary role, the follower's role, trust a superior skill, then I turn into a dependable fetch-and-carrier. It makes me a comfortable writer at rehearsals, and a director actors trust – I listen. I know what I want but can be shown other possibilities. Some imagine that if you listen you're weak; others become offended if you listen and then don't act on their advice. Sometimes I do, sometimes I don't.

Taking orders was not the only issue – there was killing. Wasn't I a pacifist? I don't think I can remember what I was – virginal and eager for experience! How could I have been a pacifist? All that hasty excitement during the war charting the Allied progress across a map of the world pinned on a wall in our Weald Square flat. No, my moral dilemma was not pacifism, more 'the military support of a capitalist, imperialist system'. I had need of my 'priest'. The general secretary of the YCL (Young Communist League) was a friendly young man called John Gross (not the writer and critic). An appointment was made and with heartfelt earnestness I outlined my problems. Those were delicious days when problems were simple and there was a catch in one's throat as one's depth of feeling was laid before elders for their admiration. Admiration was forthcoming. Advice was as obvious: my duty was to become a conscript and spread the gospel of peace, brotherhood and socialism among the working-class conscripts. I thanked him from the bottom of a heart swelling with mission and renewed purpose. There were times, I'm sorry to say, when my tongue slipped from my cheek, and, though there are times when it should, this was not one of them.

RAF Padgate was not only the dressing-up-equipping-and-dispersion-centre, it was also where your balls were held while you coughed hard, where huge tough men, who had jeered at those fearing inoculation, took their jabs, walked a few paces with cocky grins and passed out. It was where you filled in more forms listing your preferences for training and postings. I applied for air crew. A pilot. Or anything in an aeroplane except gunner. I failed the maths test. Nor did it help that I discussed literature during my interview. One bright young man named Pip with whom I struck up a friendship was upset to discover he was not accepted to train as a pilot because he couldn't go boss-eyed. We asked him to show us. It was true. When he tried squeezing both eyes to look down his nose his right eye wandered off on its own.

It was the strangest of experiences returning home to Weald Square in uniform. I felt not so much a stranger as – out of place. Awkward. Neighbours smiled at me as I crossed the playground dressed in RAF blue with overcoat and beret and blancoed shoulder-bag. I'd been absent only a couple of weeks but my smile back was coy. In the flat I wasn't certain where to place myself, how to arrange my body, what my role was. I felt disorientated. My home yet not my home. A visitor making a brief call. Soon I would be up and gone. After nine years Weald Square was not going to be my home for a long, long time. Was my girlfriend, Rhoda, there when I arrived, or other relatives? I can't remember. I remember only this sense of strangeness. An umbilical cord had been severed. Now as a parent bereft of his children I understand how my mother felt fussing around her son who sat at her table like a visitor.

During those couple of weeks a motley cross-section of the nation's swaggering, gawky, clueless youth rushed backwards and forwards between Padgate's huts collecting this that and the other: trousers the legs of which had to be altered, jackets the sleeves of which had to be shortened, berets angled as cockily as we dared. Brief relationships were formed to be mown down as everyone was posted apart, scattered all over the place for eight weeks' initial training – square-bashing!

> Out! I'll give you sixty seconds or you'll be on a charge, one, two, three, four – come on out of that hut, twenty-five, twenty-six, twenty-seven, twenty-eight. AT THE DOUBLE! Now get into a line and stop that talking, get into a line. A straight line you heaving nig-nogs, a straight line.
> This is a square. We call it a square-bashing square. I want to see you bash that square . . .
>
> Corporal Hill – *Chips with Everything*, Act I Scene 3

I was determined to get something out of that experience. A novel! I would write a novel about square-bashing. Every day of the eight weeks I wrote home to someone – mother, sister, Rhoda, Bryan – reporting on relationships, drawing character sketches, describing the routines of the day: the spitting and spooning of boot toecaps till they shone like black ice; walking around on skids to keep the floor highly polished; drinking tea round the coke-fired stove in the centre of the hut, singing to our corporal's mouth-organ. And I asked them all to keep the letters which I'd gather later as material for this landmark in English literature destined to make my fame and fortune. Eight weeks' worth of letters were collected, placed in chronological order and accompanied me on my first posting to RAF Spurn Point where I made friends with the lighthouse-keepers who allowed me to sit gazing out to sea while I wrote my exposé of military malevolence.

The novel was written between washing dishes and pots and pans in huge vats of greasy water which clung to my arms and put forth a sickly smell of rancid steam and rotting leftovers. At my second posting, to RAF Moreton-in-Marsh, I was assigned to the dustcart, collector of rubbish bins, a cushy number which began at nine and finished at eleven in the morning, leaving me the rest of the day to complete writing the novel and type it in the education centre where I was given free rein by Flying Officer Gordon Slynn, now Lord Slynn of the High Courts. Sometime in August 1951, a carbon copy of the typed manuscript was sent to cousin Bryan from 2496288 AC/2 Wesker c/o Salvage Section. His suggestions to improve it didn't help.

No one liked the novel sufficiently to publish it. Their judgement, like his, was correct. Not a good novel, but after the Trilogy had been successfully mounted, I was scouting around for my next play and remembered what lay in the bottom drawer and, on re-reading, it struck me: each chapter was the scene of a play. *Chips with Everything* was born – square-bashing as a metaphor for conformity, suppression of the individual spirit, the civilised defusion of protest.

It goes right through us, Thompson. Nothing you can do will

change that. We listen but we do not hear, we befriend but do not touch you, we applaud but do not act – to tolerate is to ignore.

Act II Scene 1

The experience of square-bashing was a complex one. Square-bashing – the period of learning how to march, dress, salute, parade, shoulder a rifle, fire one, use as a bayonet. A remarkable period which, despite my resistance, I ended enjoying. To watch a rabble of clumsy men slowly transform over the weeks into a disciplined, efficient unit is a mesmerising experience. As with everything in my life it aroused ambivalence. I despised the training of men to obey orders unquestioningly, and yet the forging of the group in this military furnace resulted in unexpected outcomes of an essentially human and seductive nature – camaraderie, shared purpose, group pride, challenge and achievement. Not an intellectual challenge, true, not even a challenge of artisan skill but a challenge to be part of a team. No matter a team for what, a team! Yes, it finally does matter what the team is trained for, but this was not a murderous team. It was more important to shoulder a rifle with precision than shoot a bullseye. *Chips with Everything* handles this ambivalence. The pass-out parade, after the brutality and cynicism, becomes a stirring moment. To the music of the RAF march past Corporal Hill inspires his squad, a heterogeneous paddle of ducks he's transformed into swans and with whom he's lived these last eight weeks:

Lift your heads, raise them, raise them high, raise them bravely, my boys. Eft-ite, eft-ite, eft-ite, eft. Slope that rifle, stiffen that arm – I want to see them all pointing one way, together – unity, unity. Slam those feet, slam, slam, you're men of the Queen, her own darlings. SLAM, SLAM! SLAM! Let her be proud. Lovely, that's lovely, that's poetry. No one'll be shot today, my boys. Forget the sweat, forget the cold, together in time. I want you to look beautiful, I want you to move as one man, as one ship, as one solid gliding ship. Proud! Proud! . . .

That was not the way life at RAF Innsworth began. Corporal Hall spoke very differently to his raw recruits on their arrival. From the file containing Bryan's letters I see it was to him I wrote recounting that first day's speech.

> That's better. In future, whenever an NCO comes into the hut, no matter who he is, the first person to see him will call out 'NCO! NCO!' like that. And whatever you're doing, even if you're stark bollock naked, you'll spring to attention as fast as the wind from a duck's arse, and by Christ that's fast. Is that understood? . . .
>
> Right, you're in the RAF now, you're not at home. This hut, this place here, this is going to be your home for the next eight fucking weeks. This billet here, you see it? This? It's in a state now, no one's been in it for the last four days so it's in a state now [Pause] but usually it's like a fucking palace! [Pause] That's the way I want it to be 'cos that's the way it's always been. Now you've got to get to know me. My name is Corporal Hill. I'm not a very happy man. I don't know why. I never smile and I never joke – you'll soon see that. Perhaps it's my nature, perhaps it's the way I've been brought up – I don't know. The RAF brought me up. You're going to go through hell while you're here, through fucking hell. Some of you will take it and some of you will break down. I'm warning you – some of you shall end up crying . . .

Rebellion

The central dramatic moment for me during training was the unacceptable order to snap a bayonet into the end of our rifles and run screaming at a hanging sack of straw. After the stupid bullying, after the pain of marching and marching and about-turning and smashing feet hard on tarmac (I wrote poems about all that, too) I found I couldn't take any more. My being was offended – body, soul, intelligence.

Even officers must go through this. Everyone, but everyone must know how to stick a man with a bayonet. The occasion may not arise to use the fucking thing but no man passes through this outfit till he's had practice. It's a horrible thing, this. A nasty weapon and a nasty way to kill a man. But it is you or him. A nasty choice, but you must choose. We had a bloke called Hamlet with us once and he had awful trouble in deciding. He got stuck! I don't want that to be your fate. So! Again, hold the butt and drop the muzzle – so. Lean forward, crouch, and let me see the horriblest leer your face can make. Then, when I call 'Attack' I want to see you rush towards that old straw dummy, pause, lunge, and twist your knife with all the hate you can. And one last thing – the scream. I want to hear you shout your lungs out, 'cos it helps. A horde of screaming men puts terror in the enemy and courage in themselves. It helps. Get fell in, two ranks. Front rank will assume the on-guard position – ON GUARD! Run, scream, lunge . . .

Without the letters in front of me I cannot say this was word for word what Corporal Hall (stage name Corporal Hill) said to us. It is certainly more so than less. I refused. Corporal Hall couldn't believe it. No one had ever refused such an order. Here I was back with Miss Webb again being told to go to my desk and start working. My new friends, the other conscripts, like the boys in the typing class, had mixed feelings about my actions.

ANDREW   Idiot.

PIP   You?

ANDREW   Who the hell is going to be impressed?

PIP   You, Andrew?

ANDREW   Yes, Andrew! I'm asking you – who the hell do you think is going to be impressed? Not me. The boys? Not them either. I've been watching you, Pip – I'm not impressed and neither are they.

PIP   You don't really think I'm interested in the public spec-
               tacle, Andy, you can't? No, no I can see you don't. Go
               off now. Leave me with it – I've got problems.

ANDREW   No one's asking you to make gestures on our behalf.

PIP   Go off now.

ANDREW   Don't go making heroic gestures and then expect grat-
               itude.

PIP   Don't lean on me, Andy – I've got problems.

ANDREW   I don't think I can bear your martyrdom – that's what it
               is; I don't think I can bear your look of suffering.

PIP   I'm not suffering.

ANDREW   I don't know why but your always-acting-right drives
               me round the bend.

PIP   I'm not a martyr.

ANDREW   It's your confident cockiness – I can't stand your con-
               fident cockiness. How do you know you're right? How
               can you act all the time as though you know all right
               from wrong, for God's sake?

PIP   Don't be a bastard, Jock.

ANDREW   I'm trying to help you, idiot. The boys will hate any
               heroic gesture you make.

PIP   Andy, you're a good, well-meaning, intelligent person.
               I will die of good, well-meaning, and intelligent people
               who have never made a decision in their life. Now go
               off and leave me and stop crippling me with your own
               guilt. If you're ineffectual in this world that's your look-
               out – just stay calm and no one will notice, but stop
               tampering with my decisions. Let *them* do the sabotag-
               ing, they don't need help from you as well. Now get the
               hell out – they wouldn't want you to see the way they
               work.

301

Something strange is going on here. I selected, compressed, shaped, extracted an essence hoping to recreate a truth about the experience of those square-bashing days. Not the whole truth, not the only truth – we've already accepted the impossibility of achieving that – but something, a flavour, a poetic moment with resonance; and now I'm using these extracted, highly stylised scenes as autobiographical stand-ins. I'm not even sure if such a scene took place between me and my Scottish hut-mate whose real name was Bill – or whether it was a conversation with myself. Art and experience – the boundaries become blurred.

The morning I refused to use the bayonet was a Saturday. A series of encounters ensued as I was drawn up the hierarchical ladder to see reason. First hauled before a sergeant who addressed me as though my action was a slight directed at him personally – my arguments were presented with a degree of intellectual reasoning, he felt challenged, and there came from him the most amazing claim. Something like this:

'You're not the only one who's read a lot. My father was a great reader too, and a writer. Wrote a book called *Seven Pillars of Wisdom*. Ever heard of it?'

The son of T.E. Lawrence? Had Lawrence ever married? Wasn't he homosexual? Not that being homosexual need have precluded him from fathering children. I didn't take Sergeant Lawrence seriously but have often wondered – did the Major of Arabia bequeath a son to the Royal Air Force which he had joined when it was known as the Royal Flying Corps? The sergeant dismissed me, warning of dire consequences; he would have to talk to 'the higher-ups'. I was shuttled from the sergeant to the warrant officer and on to the pilot officer. Again my reasons, again my arguments: I could not stick a bayonet into something representing a human being. What the pilot officer said to me on our first meeting is wiped from memory, but not what he said on our second meeting which, in a state of gloomy desperation, I later requested.

The major confrontation was with the squadron leader. By this time my adrenalin must have been pure, unadulterated high tension – partly thrilling to the experience, partly terrified of what I had embarked upon. The squadron leader was a civilised, intelligent, attractive personality. He was also a wily old handler of human baggage who, I now suspect, sized up me and my emotional state within minutes. The AC/2 sitting the other side of his desk was a very different kind of fish from those who swam constantly before his gaze, though National Service must have netted all sorts. Coming from no upper class I spoke like one – confident, articulate, well read. Confident except – when presented with a friendly relationship of equals he must have seen the utter relief that spread through me, and from it deduced my tense state. Perhaps, he surmised, this young man's resolution is not what it seems.

For about two hours or more he engaged me in intelligent conversation enquiring of my background, my plans for the future, slowly, slowly lowering my guard and lulling me into a false sense of security. Then came the 180° change. His tone stiffened. Stern shutters came down on that 'friendship of equals'. The man I presumed to be my new friend changed back into a squadron leader. This, more or less, is what he said:

'I must now warn you, that on Monday morning you will be called once more to the parade ground and you will again be given the order to use the bayonet. If you refuse you will be court-martialled and sentenced. When your sentence is completed you will be released and at the gate of the prison again given the order, and if again you refuse a new term of imprisonment will begin, and so on until you obey. Think about it. You have the weekend.'

He was lying. The RAF authorities would have considered long and hard before entering into the expense of a costly court-martial. Expense and unwelcome publicity, for what? – the offence wasn't that serious. Nor would the order have been given again after my sentence had been served. You can't be court-martialled twice for the same offence. But what did this unworldly confrontationalist know of RAF law, or even simple low-cunning human psychology? *That* well read he was not. He had been given the weekend to frighten himself and that is exactly what he did. For the rest of Saturday morning and all through Sunday I read. When concentration faltered I argued my action against their consequences, weighing them, imagining them. My past life of family, friends, and good times flashed through my mind, a swimmer cramped with indecision, drowning. I must have talked with fellow squaddies, argued with some, considered others, whipped myself round in circles until there was nowhere left to go. I needed someone trustworthy in authority.

The pilot officer, himself a National Service recruit, had seemed interesting and sympathetic. I requested an audience. It was granted. We talked for a couple of hours. Unwittingly he presented me at the end with an image upon which I latched my decision with huge relief.

'You can,' he put it to me, 'either stand in the wind like a stiff and brittle reed to be snapped, broken in two, or you can be like a reed that bends with the wind and when the storm has passed stand up straight again.' The ambiguity of the metaphor was suppressed – 'bending reed'? was I that? – and my sense of survival surfaced. Bending reed or not, the feverish image glowed like powerful poetry. I would indeed bend, and more than that I would usurp it as the title of my novel: *The Reed That Bent*. To me on that Sunday evening poetry and nobleness of spirit merged. I had been given a face-saving image of myself. Came Monday morning and our line-up on the killing field I lunged at that sack of straw with a bloodcurdling shriek like no one else. This actor who murdered straw sacks was no slouch. Not only did I scream and plunge my bayonet with expertise, I volunteered for guard duty, a chore involving alternate two-hour watches through cold nights. Let them see that this young man who'd made a weekend stand against the cruelties of war, who was a poet, was as efficient as any drilled airman passing through their gates. No stereotype wishy-washy artist, he. It became important to me that I surpassed their imaginings. Poets, Jews, and dissenters were not the flabby, unreliable layabouts of newspaper cartoons. They could snap to attention as smartly as any. War was abhorrent, but if evil was around we were not to be dismissed. From then on no part of square-bashing was unpleasing. We became a brilliant squad, one of the best in the pass-out parade. Corporal Hall was proud of us.

No irony – an aside

The play was initially turned down by the Royal Court who agreed to mount it only when the commercial producer, Bob Swash, offered to co-produce it with them. After a six-week season there it ran for a year at the Vaudeville Theatre in the West End and then six months on Broadway where a moment in the play caused a furore: Act II Scene 2, the hotting-up period of training, no longer a time for jokes and laughter, no room for mistakes. The clumsy recruit, Smiler, is mistake-prone and when he drops his rifle for a second time Corporal Hill viciously withers him:

> . . . Slob! Your buttons, your blanco, your shoes – look at them. They're dull. You're dull. You're like putty. What keeps you together, man? You're like an old Jew – you know what happens to Jews? They go to gas chambers!

New York's Jewish theatre-goers – feeling uncomfortable with irony, the nature of which seems to confuse or threaten them – and knowing nothing about the play's Jewish author, complained to B'nai Brith – an organisation set up to protect Jews against anti-semitism – and asked them to investigate the play. Which they did. B'nai Brith's representatives took me aside in the foyer of the Plymouth Theatre and said, '. . . Of course it's not an anti-semitic moment but listening to audiences in the foyer talking about the play it's obvious they don't understand what it's about anyway, they see it as a comedy about forces life, we advise you to cut the line.' I argued it was a play about training people to obey orders, which had been Eichman's excuse – he was just obeying orders. Besides, I added, the play was being performed in Israel. If it was understood and acceptable there it should be understood and accepted here in sophisticated New York. I refused to cut the line. Coach-loads cancelled their bookings. Later – irony of ironies – I learned from Shaike Weinberg, the director of Tel Aviv's Cameri Theatre, that they *had* cut the line.

I am indebted to the RAF and have this dark, heretical suspicion that conscription kept crime and violence to acceptable levels. Brutality was once ashamed of itself, furtive. All is changed. Brutality is now brazen. Like ignorance. 'Yeah! I'm ignorant and I'm proud of it.' As Toni Morrison wrote: '. . . nothing needs to be exposed since it is already barefaced . . .' It worries me deeply. Freedom is precious and what threatens it must be controlled. The old ambivalence is at work again. I don't hanker for disciplined days of saluting and cowering obedience, but there is an absence of respect for other people's lives and freedom. Conscription achieved something that did not have to do with war. It brought young people together from different classes, aspirations, cultural backgrounds. A kind of tolerance was forced upon them. They had to live together. The weak grew strong and the strong were chastened. Today the streets are ugly with frustrations and discontent. Natures are coarse. Something awful has seeped out of the bottle. This is not, as I write, a happy country.

RAF and friends

The most influential friendships of that period were with two young men who drew me into their worlds and added to me in ways for which I shall ever be grateful – John Lavrin and Alastair Sutherland. John was a fine painter. Indifference has frozen his hand for the moment. I prophesy he will be discovered. On a wall in Ashley Road hangs a painting of Dusty, me and you, Lindsay Joe, aged one year. John also painted a miniature of you in a red dressing gown waving a spoon. Somewhere exists his huge canvas of the young playwrights who began their careers in the sixties – Bernard Kops. Anne Jellicoe, N.F. Simpson, Harold Pinter, John Mortimer, myself and others. I look every day at three of his drawings in my Welsh study. One of me – not my favourite but a good drawing; one of 'an airman'; a third of Stan. Stan, John and I fused into a trio at Moreton-in-Marsh, became inseparable, of a closeness to arouse envy, causing sour tensions in hut 77A about which, of course, a story exists called 'Confusion', begun November 1951, finished 1 January 1952 at 1.15 a.m. I must have worked through New Year's Eve to complete it.

According to the story (written in the first person; Stan is called Chris, John is called Michael) I first met Stan, a large-muscled, bright-eyed young man of enviable handsomeness, as he was limping out of the camp cinema. I offered a helping shoulder. Through him I met John who told me about Stan's background. Born in the Potteries, Stan grew up believing life's supreme achievements were to do only with the body. His grandfather . . .

. . . was once famous on the stage for juggling with knives and swords, among other feats. He would fit twenty or thirty bayonets into each other forming a shape resembling the branch of a tree. Then he would balance the lot at the point of one of the knives on his chin, and flick them all in the air making sure he got out of the way as they fell and stuck in the floor. Occasionally a stray bayonet would stick in his back, but that was part of the game as Chris would say.

Chris's father was skilled in the art but settled down to the job of fireman. He was killed in the Second World War.

Chris himself was always a daredevil lured on both by the stories his grandfather told him and the things to which his father dared him.

When his father told him he'd once walked round the narrow ledge on the stack of a cotton mill Stan had to do the same. Having climbed to the top board of a swimming pool just to look down, he felt shame at the thought of climbing all the way down again, closed his eyes and dived.

Stan was in the grip of confused, raging appetites. He was one of life's volcanoes, erupting with a violent energy that had no sense of itself or its destructive propensities, a powerhouse of complexes both attractive and murderous. His zest for life magnified his actions, gestures, and utterances threefold. He revelled in excessive-ness, yearned for experience, but was constantly betrayed by intellectual limitations and fragile complexes. John was stronger but not without his own complexes: wealthy, intellectual, bohemian upper-class family, John looked to National Service as a means of breaking away from their claustrophobic pressures in order to see how the other half lived. His parents feared for his shyness. They need not have worried. John was a success among the conscripts. He possessed the facility of making himself one of the lads, mainly by agreeing with any nonsense they put forth. Coming from a milieu of strong opinions John rebelled and professed to no opinions, or rather he *did* have opinions but withdrew them in the face of what others said. Not for a quiet life or even out of in-tellectual cowardice, but in the name of a tolerance famously identified by George Eliot.

> Don't you think men overrrate the necessity for humouring every-body's nonsense, till they get despised by the very fools they humour?
>
> *Middlemarch*

I was not always comfortable with John's unfocused attitudinising. We argued. As a socialist I felt the need for at least a handful of political, cultural and human values. John perversely doubted the lasting value of anything. Nothing was permanent, all was shifting. He didn't promulgate those 'succulent doubts' of Shylock, doubts founded on a vague sense that other values were about just waiting to be identified; rather he aired, too breezily I thought, a brand of sterile negativism: 'What could ever be positive? . . . What is *really* desirable? . . . How do we know if we need Tolstoy more than Hank Janson?'

From such a background he was drawn to Stan's primitive ex-uberance. John introduced him to Benvenuto Cellini, the Renaissance artist who, to assuage his honour, murdered people. Stan thought that splendid, rather manly. Manliness and honour were important to him. Stan hero-worshipped John and saw a parallel between Cellini's attractive anarchic lawless style of living and John's bohemian personality, his artistic eccentricity. They were both slightly manic, though of the two John was the more careful and lived within a tight framework of behaviour, knowing where not to overstep the mark. Stan had no such benefits of cultural restrictions. John wound him up and set him off like a favourite toy whose erratic gyrations fascinated him. Though he bubbled and boiled, flirted with a kind of nihilism and talked Plato to an uncomprehending Stan, John himself lacked the courage of total commitment. He introduced Stan to his view of the world as a state of utter chaos about which nothing could be done to help those who lived within it, so why bother. The theatricality of such views excited the boy from the Potteries. He dared anything, a dare was a challenge to his masculinity. John had background and an inheritance to lose. Stan had nothing to lose. I was by comparison, though with my own brand of iconoclasm and courage for risks, a cool in-between, an observer, and finally a threat to Stan.

Stan prickled with resentments. He resented the speed with which John and I became friends, our outings to exhibitions and theatres, the ease with which we conversed on a level beyond him. John and I were drawn to one another immediately, became marvellously close. He was restless with enthusiasm and appetites, and one day, after a camp sports day, he pointed to a beautiful sun setting behind a Cotswold hill.

'I bet the view from the top will be superb,' I said. He needed no other prompt.

'Then let's see it from the top,' he cried. 'A wonderful cross-country run.'

We ran. For three miles solidly. Across fields, through hedges, over wire fences and ditches and railway tracks – to see a sunset. At the top of the hill we stood, arms over each other's shoulders, watching a pink glow spread to dusk across the valley before us. Which of us suggested we stand on our heads to look at the horizon upside down? I think it was me who suggested we climb the tree –

where we stayed till dark exchanging experiences, shaping our lives, sharing hopes.

I remember it as one of the happiest moments of my life – the fulfilment of a romantic impulse, my body pushed to an extreme, glowing with health, and the loveliness of it all shared with a soul mate. Oneself, nature, and another – a triumvirate of harmony. And still all my years before me.

Stan had made his first steps under John's tutelage but seemed unable to go further. Musically his tastes stopped with a little of Mozart, Haydn trumpet music, Beethoven's 5th. 'Oh the loudness and power and strength of it.' A little of Wagner, inevitably. But de Falla's *Three-cornered Hat* was 'confused and muddled', the Sibelius 2nd symphony 'has no tune or pattern'. *Pavane for a dead infanta* 'has no power'. Those fragile complexes led him to interpret most differences of opinion as a personal insult, an affront to his honour. Stan had trained to be a physical instructor, a post he lost due to a crash on his motorbike resulting in a smashed kneecap. Risks were a challenge to him as I discovered riding on his pillion to London during winter. The ice was a challenge. We skidded. No more than a few cuts and bruises, but close! He recovered from his big crash but was considered fit enough only to be an assistant PTI, which was galling.

Stan throbbed with an urge to 'create' but like many it was the throbbing of an engine that could never engage with a gear. The engine idled, he dabbled! Sketched a little, taught himself to play the trumpet – which drove us mad in hut 77A – worked in leather for a while, and was a natural mechanic who half built himself a motorbike he and John painted in bright colours and proudly decorated with French words. With Stan I found myself engaged in those endless debates which seem to have dogged my life, to do with standards and that maddening, hoary question of 'who's to judge?' Even now, as I write, the Culture section of *The Sunday Times* (14 November 1993) features on its front cover: 'High art and popular culture – can they ever live together?' Keats or Dylan? Mozart or Madonna? It's a curious debate – that everything is as good as everything else – which can keel over into bloody conflict between those gifted with a power to respond at a deep level and those who feel intimidated not possessing that power. It is why bullies in school beat up the clever ones, and why artists and academics are singled out for slaughter and gulags.

There was no holding back resentment once John left. Fragile complexes fluttered helplessly in the winds of barrack-room debate. We shared trips to London, our friendship continued, but I had to tread carefully. It is difficult to share a life of the mind with those whose minds are concerned only with an image they have of themselves.

John's father, Janko Lavrin, a Yugoslav – Slovene – intellectual, was professor of Slavonic studies at Nottingham University, author of books like *From Pushkin to Mayakovsky*. His mother, a Quaker from the Fry family of Liverpool, was renowned for her etchings; her sister's husband was adopted by the Tate and Lyle sugar family; her brother was the eminent architect, Maxwell Fry. John was an only son released from parental eyes and I soon understood that most of what he said was to do more with rebellion than conviction. Despite this, or perhaps because of it, he was stimulating company. On weekend leaves he introduced me to museums and talked about porcelain, painters, and sculpture as though about old friends, and in a manner that related art to life rather than art for art's sake. This was his appeal – we shared a perception of art as an expression of extraordinary human spirit, alongside which perception we measured what we loved: did it shine a light, echo a recognisable truth, revive flagging dreams and joys? It was not optimism to which we responded but truth. Even a depressing truth about human nature was somehow exhilarating. Only mediocrity and dishonesty were depressing. And this is what irritated me about John and why we argued: he *had* standards. He had a natural eye for what was true in art, a sense of excellence. It was he who first demonstrated to me how one comes to know excellence by comparisons: place two materials side by side, feel the textures, look closely at the differing depths of colour, the different quality of fibre and you know, you just know that some things are better, of more substance, value, durability, satisfaction than others. There *is* high and low class, in all things, from people's natures to people's artifacts. I learned this from a young man who it seemed, in certain company and against his innate instincts, denied what he knew was right. I couldn't understand this at the time, why he was so dismissive of his own views. Now I know it to be a kind of graciousness: you don't risk hurting or diminishing others by presenting tastes they had not the opportunity to cultivate. Yes, well, thank you for your graciousness, but how were those like myself, with limited opportunity to cultivate those tastes, ever going to become acquainted with them? Fortunately John behaved differently with me. He recognised fertile ground. He knew if he planted a thought it would take root, if he shared a taste, a judgement, it would not rock self-confidence, intimidate. John got on well with the lads, he knew how not to intimidate. From wisdom, generosity of spirit, or sheer self-protection he knew not to insult the fool. Because stupidity knows itself it is better not to inflame it by letting it know you know it knows. People must be allowed to be stupid, like dogs going off into corners to lick their wounds.

One of the most thrilling theatre experiences to come through John was Christopher Fry's play *A Sleep of Prisoners*, part of the 1951 Festival of Britain, performed in St Thomas's church in Regent's Street. A play in a church! *That* was a new horizon – as was the entire Festival of Britain, blasting new shapes, colours, design, creative energy, pride and confidence like a dynamic spring throughout the country. But it was the visual arts to which John most opened my eyes, not only to new painters and sculptors but to what one lived with daily. He personified the William Morris maxim 'Have nothing in your houses that you do not know to be useful, or believe to be beautiful'. The interior of 18 Addison Gardens was certainly beautiful to me, I had not entered a house of that size before with walls rich in hangings, rooms cramped with elegant furniture, arresting objets d'art.

Poor Stan! Work though I did at our friendship, it was doomed.

For him I was the usurper of his cherished place at John's side and I wonder now whether John did not in some way destroy the friend he wanted to build up. That's a harsh word 'destroy', unsettle, perhaps. Stan was possessed of a simple but desperate need to channel gargantuan energies out of control; John was possessed of an anarchic spirit controlled because his background endowed him with a fortifying sense of the past. You can question with ease if you're confidently knowledgeable about the civilisation that shaped you. Denied that knowledge, clothed with only scant notions of his human roots, Stan floundered. With each new thought heaped upon him, confusion deepened. John seemed not to understand this.

The story I wrote charts what led up to the evening when after a series of frustrations Stan went berserk in hut 77A and threw choppers at me – one of his party tricks, spinning small axes into wood. He'd signed on for five years and pined as friends left him one by one. He missed John most – their friendship was established long before I arrived at Moreton. But the truth was John had lured Stan out of his depth and when he was demobbed I was left with this sapling withering in eternal winter, its sun gone forever. Stan and I remained together but the foundations of our friendship were shaky – I did not possess the authority of John's background and when we clashed I was in no position to command respect as John could. However, worse was to come.

Enter a woman

One day before his demob John returned from a weekend leave to announce he'd met an extraordinary young woman. She was from Yugoslavia, the town of Split in Croatia. Her father was a famous sculptor, Marin Studin, and her uncle one of the illustrious sculptors of Europe – Ivan Meštrovic. They were going to be married. Her name was Sunćana, nicknamed Beba, and she was to have a profound effect on all our lives.

Beba, a student of art history at the Courtauld Institute, claimed friendship with Marshall Tito and, so her story went, had been a brave young messenger for the partisans. She married John in January 1952, had a son, took on an au pair from Croatia called Ivka, and accepted from an old admirer the gift of a pet monkey which John had to look after and I hated with a quality of hatred I enjoyed. Stan and I were contemptuous of John for this liaison we considered a betrayal – hadn't he always decried marriage and vowed to us that no woman would ever capture him for good? We mocked and teased him. 'Avowals,' he replied, enjoying our contempt, and happy further to demonstrate the unpredictability of human behaviour, 'avowals are made to be broken.' He described Beba in such vivid colours – she was obviously a match for his brand of perverse and playful sophistry – that we were curious and eager to meet her.

The opportunity came on John's twenty-first birthday party in his parent's house in Putney, a fancy-dress affair offering a prize for the most imaginative get-up. I'd never been to a fancy-dress event before, nor had Stan. We put together something, I can't remember what – a Roman toga for me made out of a curtain, I think. Whatever, I won the prize, though I suspect it was awarded more for pity's sake than imagination's. Stan and I had stayed up half the previous night writing in script on a scroll of 'parchment' – which we coloured and burned to make look ancient – a twenty-first birthday greeting full of advice. What wisdom had we wittily cobbled together, I wonder? Did John keep it? A hit, anyway. John's RAF working-class friends were graciously received in W11 and applauded. When we left, Beba said to John, as he later told me, something like: 'Keep your eye on Wizzie. He's special . . . Something is going to happen there . . .'

I must find a way of describing Beba in a paragraph or two or she will occupy a book. After all these years I've still not been able to make up my mind whether she was a brilliant talent never able to identify itself or whether, like Osborne's George Dillon, she had only the symptoms of talent but didn't suffer 'the pain, the ugly swellings' of the actual disease. Her frustration was fearsome, a strong and desperate spirit looking around for a body to inhabit. First she inhabited John's, then mine. John was helpless. She had no private income and was dependent upon him. Only his inborn caution acted as a kind of brake on her demands, and, I suspect, the cautioning of his mother who was never entirely comfortable with her son's courteous but acerbic young bride. Informed taste, sharp intelligence, warm, sympathetic, haughty – I learned from, enjoyed, but fought her. Her reasoning was amoral. She claimed a Jesuitical mind that could defend contradictory views. What was right on Monday was not necessarily so on Tuesday if it didn't achieve what she wanted. Some men, overanxious to be seen doing the right thing at all times, depend upon such a trait in their women. It helps survive in famished, oppressive times.

In June 1958, during the weeks I was waiting for my first play *Chicken Soup with Barley* to be mounted and had written anxiously to Dusty at Butlin's: '. . . I almost dread it going on now . . . That play is terribly personal and yet here I am throwing it to the wide world for their scrutiny . . .' I described a session I'd had with John and Beba:

> . . . Spent last night with them. They read the play and thought it was a good play of great despair. Despair! And I thought it was a play of exaltation. They suggested I was not aware of what I'd written. Talking with them is always stimulating and depressing at once. Beba delights in smashing all illusions, she sees nothing as being pure in intention. When I looked at a newspaper she said, 'Ah, he's looking to see if they've written anything about him.' Of course it was not seriously meant but it creates a level which I find hard to talk on . . .

Beba spoke with Slavic low-voiced charm, and a slow, seething determination as though fearing she inhabited a world of fools, or at least ill-wishers, against whom she must patiently protect herself. Somewhere within her, despite her famous patrimony, was a sense not of inferiority but fear that she might be thought inferior – after all she was both a woman and foreign. She was on guard against being upstaged, insulted, slighted, dismissed for being a savage Balkan peasant. At one level she was not an unfamiliar type. A type of foreigner can be identified who feels the need to assert their place in certain circles of English society, mainly intellectual or artistic ones, where they reply to simple questions with the phrase 'of course' rather than 'yes'.

'Have you read *The Brothers Karamazov*?'

'Of course.'

'Do you know Paris?'

'Of course.'

'Have you seen the recent exhibition of—?'

'Of course.' *Of course* sung to the melody of 'What do you take me for? Who do you imagine I am? How can you doubt it? Please understand to whom you're speaking . . .'

Some people found Beba sinister. Others adored her for her audacity, her ability to puncture pomposity, her courage to adopt unfashionable views. She enjoyed shocking – hence the ugly monkey on her shoulder, claiming to judge people by their response to the vicious thing. One of the reasons I became a favourite was that I didn't care that I might be judged for disliking her stupid pet, nor was I overly impressed with her obvious desire to shock. I saw *through* her Eastern European affectations which, as I kept reminding her, ran her the risk of being viewed as caricature. Rather I responded to a genuine intelligence, to her tastes. She admired courage and risk-takers, those who enacted the unexpected. My crazy actions impressed her, whether it was taking up the job of kitchen porter for which I was obviously not born, going off to Paris with a girlfriend with no prospect of work and only £100 between us, sinking my savings into a six-month course at film school, walking four days to Aldermaston, writing a play with thirty characters, spending a month in prison for membership of the Committee of 100, or offering Lionel Bart the rights in all my plays in return for £10,000 that I wanted to help pay for the Centre Fortytwo Festivals in 1962. (Fortunately he didn't accept!) John was both proud and perhaps a little anxious of this bride called Beba who could narrow her eyes dangerously and control everything but purse strings and his painting. He enjoyed watching the effect she had on people, and her tongue was a whip that respected no class and knew no mercy. She pitied the defenceless and scorned those who were pretentious, smug, of unearned or unmerited status – which was noble; but she also lashed at those who in some way threatened her – which was not so noble.

I quarrelled with her often needless maliciousness, her unjust scorn, her intellectual snobbery, but defended her courage and woman's common sense when male ineptitude tried to put her down. Sometimes I saw her as wasted energy – she may turn viper if threatened but she was herself a threat to men who, when not tingling with excitement at the way she castigated them, hated and feared her superior intelligence. At other times I sensed in her a destructive, almost evil spirit. She worked as my assistant at Centre Forty Two and though her judgement was often unerring I just as often had to guard against it. Her motives were not always pure. Beba was like no one else I had met, as I think I was for her, and she inspired Kate in *Their Very Own and Golden City*:

SCENE SIX

ANDY's bedsitter. KATE enters. ANDY is at work on his drawing board.
KATE nonchalantly sorts through his books.

KATE   Why did you run away from Jake's that night?

ANDY   You're a forward lass, coming upon me like this.

KATE   Were you afraid?

ANDY   How did you know I'd be in?

KATE   It's my nature to take chances. Were you afraid?

ANDY   I bet you smoke pipes.

KATE   No, cigars. Were you afraid?

ANDY   I try not to be feared of anything.

KATE   Why did you go so quickly then?

ANDY   How you do persist.

KATE   Persistence is a family trait. You turned on your heel
        because my mother is Lady Ramsay, didn't you? I want
        you to know, Mr Cobham, I'm a classless woman.

ANDY   Aye, I can see it.

KATE   I can't bear people who wear class on their hearts like an
        emblem.

ANDY   Seems to me you're more intent in denying it than I am in
        looking for it.

KATE   I want us to be friends.

ANDY   You sound desperate.

KATE   Passionate, not desperate. You must know certain things
        about me, Mr Cobham.

ANDY   I don't see as I must know anything. I was brought up to
        earn friendship.

KATE   That's our difference then, I don't have to earn anything, I
        was born with rights.

ANDY   Aye, of course, you're a classless woman.

KATE   [Attempting to fold his pile of unpressed clothes] You're a
        fool if you think I'm talking about class rights. [He
        snatches shirt from her hands. She gently retrieves it and
        continues folding] Human rights, Mr Cobham, from any
        class. There are certain people who are born with natures
        that naturally deserve love and respect. Yours, like mine, is
        one of them.

318

Beba challenged comfortable attitudes. I frequently met her challenge and was sharpened in the process, but alas, though a hard worker with a wicked wit who wickedly charmed others to work overtime, she was also wilful, stubborn, petulant, unpredictable and, in a strange way, corrupting. Kate/Beba identified the danger in the notion of 'participation': the inhibiting view of 'the common man' whose imagination can be limited and limiting, whose receptivity to the new and the different is stultified. Yet common sense is often found in 'the common man' on the factory floor. 'Experts' could have averted disasters had they listened. Kate/Beba's contempt had to be confronted but it was not easy.

In 1951 this striking, slightly plump young woman with red-tinted brunette hair and a penchant for suede and dark glasses became John's wife and I learned from her how to make Turkish coffee, thick and sweet, in a copper pot which we drank between puffs of Balkan Sobranie cigarettes. I loved their house with its dark blue velvet curtains and coverings, ochre ceramic plant stands, and dark mahogany furniture. The first room on the left was John's studio. The next a dramatically darkened lounge, one corner of which was lined with mahogany panelling. Tucked in there was a box divan convertible into a bed, where I frequently slept. We played chess, listened to music, talked away nights, and went on excursions together. One, to the Elizabethan mansion Knole in Kent, gave me a new perspective on living space. Never having seen the inside of an Elizabethan home I gazed in wonder at the huge central room and knew – this was the space I wanted to live in. The LCC had built Weald Square big enough for rabbits, Knole was built human size. When Dusty and I moved into Bishops Road, our first house, I made signing the contract conditional upon being able to knock the two ground-floor rooms into one. Not Elizabethan size but the largest space we'd ever lived in.

John and Beba visited me when I was a kitchen porter in Norwich – John drove an old Wolseley at the time. I felt they were keeping an eye on me, watching over my decisions, my movements. John, though he was tight-fisted – he could find no cash to lend us

when Dusty wanted an abortion, Beba was ashamed of his protestations of poverty – was nevertheless an encourager, generous
with spirit, he could distribute an abundance of soul-support. His
urgings were electric. When he talked he somehow curled his body
into a crouch, he physically crouched, like a boxer waiting to spring
his enthusiasms on you; he was a livewire, a practical man who
could construct things, a gardener who made beautiful roses grow.
In his company one felt a restlessness, a rumbling, he was impatient, wanted to be doing all the time. That same energy fuelled
others around him. I had my own energy source but was grateful
for the affectionate encouragement he fed into me as time and
again my poems, stories, hopes for this that and the other were
dashed. John and Beba knew I had retreated into the kitchen of the
Bell Hotel in despair of ever becoming a successful writer. They
were not going to leave me alone.

Ten years later I tried to repay my debt of gratitude. When in
1962 I'd acquired the Roundhouse in Chalk Farm as a possible base
for Centre Forty-two, I assembled twenty-four of John's huge canvases and brought them to the empty old Victorian engine shed,
leaned each up against one of the twenty-four pillars and asked the
Sunday Times art critic, John Russell, to come and offer a judgement. Here was a painter I thought highly of, could he help?
Russell obligingly came, walked round the vast dome looking in-
tently at the sculptured figures on canvas in browns and greens
against black backgrounds: Beba, Beba and the monkey, Beba's
mother, Beba and their son, some nudes, the painting of the playwrights . . . No lighting other than the electric lights with their
yellow hue, all too gloomy perhaps, the colours merging into the
brown pillars and the dirty grey of the unswept cobbled and concrete floors. Russell didn't respond. He was dismissive of all but the
portraits of the playwrights. I was disappointed and of course not in
agreement. As we walked away I asked what I realise in retrospect
was a typical Perlmutter unworldly question, bordering on the insult, though at the time I couldn't see it. Certainly no insult was
intended. It seemed to me a question an honest critic might consider: 'Are you sure,' I asked Russell, 'that you're not looking at

these paintings with contemporary eyes?' His denial was fierce though I thought, and still think, that's just what he *was* doing – it was 1962 and figurative painting had not yet returned in fashion. John's painting of Dusty, me and the young Lindsay Joe is the first canvas people ask about when they enter the lounge. Not that we possess a huge collection or because that painting is one of his best, but it is unmistakably like no one else's work – powerful, confident, respectful of its material and full of love for its subjects.

Beba and I became lovers. I remember exactly how it began. Kenneth Tynan had organised an international writers' conference at the 1961 Edinburgh Festival. It was the one where a nude young woman ran round the balcony of the conference building, and where a stunned Harold Pinter stood before his large, expectant audience and haltingly said he didn't know why he was there and doubted that he had anything to say to them. I had agreed to give a speech on 18 April 1961 at the Albert Hall for an anti-hanging rally organised by the publisher Victor Gollancz. The organisers flew me down and I stayed overnight at Addison Gardens before returning to Edinburgh. I was to sleep, where I'd frequently slept, on the mahogany box divan in the corner of the blue-velvet room. Beba sat by me and we talked through the night by candlelight until she said – and yes, these were her words and I had never heard them before – 'Wait, let me get into something more comfortable . . .' The moment was inevitable. It had hovered over us a long time.

Our relationship was tempestuous. She competed with me, unwisely attacked Dusty, and resented my attachment to family. When Centre Fortytwo's future looked gloomy, she began to establish contacts in other areas. When I took to my bed with toxic poisoning she played silly politics and attempted to get me dismissed as Fortytwo's artistic director. I rose from a sickbed and made an unexpected appearance at a crucial meeting. There was no alternative. I asked her to resign. She did so but not without sending a maligning letter to everyone with whom Fortytwo had established a relationship. The damage done will never be calculated. Who knows but that it contributed to our failure to raise the funds needed to convert and run the Roundhouse. In the background to all this were the mothers, mine and John's, unhappy and anxious, watching what was unfolding. Leah, especially, became distressed on behalf of Dusty, and intemperately rang Beba telling her to leave her son alone. John overheard the conversation, looked for evidence, found letters, and sued for divorce. I was named, along with others. The judge was asked to read *The Four Seasons* as evidence. He did so and, though he judged it a beautiful work, found it supported John's claim.

Leah in her diary dated 20 October 1964:

> If I would be the solicitor for Arnold's case . . . I would ask John how long ago did he notice that his wife is unfaithful . . . why then was he so friendly with his wife's lover . . .

She had no love for either John or Beba. Their politics offended her and they exuded the air of those who ruled. She suggests that John deliberately threw us together and suspected him of jealousy and even latent anti-semitism – totally unfounded.

> I did not like Johns paintings. He made a painting on Arnold Dusty and their little son Lindsay. He portrated Arnold as Shylock the Jew and made Dusty for St Mary, Lindsay as little Jesus . . .

I had never viewed the painting in such a light – it is a possible reading. Intemperate Leah, maybe, but not without her perceptions.

How long John was aware of our relationship I do not know. Somewhere I must have supposed that, having lost what once existed between him and his fierce Croatian, he gave us his blessing. His mother may have been less obliging. Would John have pressed for divorce without her behind him? Did she see an opportunity for disinheriting a woman she did not like? Only one person has answers to those questions.

For some time after the break-up I helped Beba financially. Her tastes may have been fine and subtle, they were also extravagant. I had to cry halt in the end. Stories came back to me over the years that she was trading in oil, armaments, drugs. She was a fantasist. Her end was mad. Beba gave and took, built and destroyed. I have recurring dreams about them both, always saturated with friendship, joy, and time past. I remember her with confused emotions of guilt, anger and sadness.

How I wish I could sing now. You're right, it is a kind of crippling when your voice can't make music. You know, I'm not really as treacherous as I sound, or cold or humourless. Sometimes a fever gets in me too and I don't know what I say. But I'm always honest, at least to myself, and good and really – very wise.

But I'm damaged, I blush for the creases in my skin. I'm ashamed of my worn limbs, second-hand. Third-hand to be precise; third-hand bruised and damaged – like a clock striking midnight when the hour is only six, and it wheezes and whirs.

But if we'd met each other before we'd met anyone else then the right hour would have sung clear and ringing at the right time, every time. If, if, if . . . Oh, Adam. And what wouldn't we have done together then? Raised storms among the dead – that's what we'd have done then. Do you know what my husband once said to me? 'You're like a queen,' he said, 'without her country. I hate queens,' he said, 'without their countries.'

And he was right. A queen without a country, or a king. No home and no man to pay me homage. All my life I've looked for peace and majesty, for a man who was unafraid and generous; generous and not petty. I can't bear little men: mean, apologetic, timid men, men who mock themselves and sneer at others, who delight in downfall and dare nothing. Peace, majesty and great courage – how I've longed for these things.

He once abandoned me in a fog, that man, that man I called 'God'; in a long, London fog, left me, to walk home alone.

Peace, majesty and great courage.

And once I ran through a storm and stood on a station platform, soaking and full of tears, pleading with him to take me, take me, take me with him. And he wanted to take me, I know it, because we loved walking through streets in strange towns discovering new shapes to the houses and breathing new airs, but he refused to show this need.

Peace, majesty and great courage – never. I've found none of these things. Such bitter disappointment. Bitter. Bitter, bitter, bitter. And out of such bitterness cruelty grows. You can't understand the cruelty that grows. And I meant none of it, not one cruel word of it. And he knew and I knew and we both knew that we knew, yet the cruelty went on.

But laments for what's done and past are not a way to cure an invalid are they? I should be making plans for tomorrow shouldn't I? For when you get up, and the day after, and the month after and all those long years we'll have together. What shall we do in those years, Adam? Eh? All those great long years ahead? Shall we set to right 'the silly world's intolerable pains'? I have plans, of children and travel and daring all those things you didn't dare before. We'll plot and build each moment like two brilliant lovers. And peace, above all – peace, and trust and majesty and all that great courage.

Get well my darling boy and you'll see. My voice may not sing but my love does. Get well.

The Four Seasons – Autumn

Beba died of cancer on 1 July 1988 in St Stephen's Hospital, Chelsea.

Chapter Fourteen

Oxford and friends

Ageing is dreadful and the dread of ending is heavy with regrets. We hanker for the return of youth and, hankering, memory becomes mischievous and spins us all sorts of yarns. My letters, stories, even the dreaded poems, are more reliable.

One of the editors who gave a lot of time reading and commenting on the dismal things I sent month after persistent month was the historical novelist, Jack Lindsay, who, together with the poet, Randall Swingler, ran an outfit called Fore Publications and a bi-monthly called *Arena*. Wishing to share the burden of relentlessly rejecting my unstoppable outpourings, Jack Lindsay recommended I write to a young Oxford student planning a quarterly to be called *Root and Branch*. Poems and a prose sketch went off immediately sometime in October 1951 – prompt even then. Blessed with an idea, set with a task, I have no *seitz fleich* (Yiddish for 'sitting flesh').

The student editor of *Root and Branch* replied on 15 November apologising for having kept my poems and sketch so long. He had been away in Spain and my letter 'got buried in the wrong file until recently'. Publication of the quarterly had been postponed but he liked my sketch 'The Hill' – a portrait of the Jewish area called Stamford Hill – and thought 'it should be published somewhere'. He also liked a poem called 'Tired' dedicated to Esther. But more significantly he wrote: 'I see you're stationed at Moreton-in-Marsh – if you're ever in Oxford do look me up – I'm living in Balliol College.' It was signed 'Alastair Sutherland'. He was a student of PPE – Politics, Philosophy, and Economics.

I did look him up, and discovered an exhilarating world completely unknown to me of architectural grace and intellectual vivacity such as I had never encountered. There on the lawns of Balliol young men lounged with comfortable confidence – reading. Reading! They had been paid grants to lie around and read! We developed an intense friendship. Perhaps he fell in love with me – his letters read like that, and certainly I remember basking in a quality of affection quite fresh and new.

I soon became involved with university life. Ate in halls, attended the May Ball, and met living poets like the American, Pearce Young, at Alastair's cider-and-Stilton-cheese-parties. I had never heard of Pearce Young, though we came to like one another, and I certainly had not heard of Stilton cheese! It was the generation of Stanley Myers, the composer; D.A.N. Jones, critic and writer; a young man who became a rabbi named Lionel Blue; another who became a publisher and whose father, Neville, was later to claim that, as chairman of the English Stage Company, he had 'discovered' me – Anthony Blond. I had to borrow his dinner suit to attend the May Ball. I'd never worn a dinner suit before nor heard of May Balls, let alone attended one. Anthony's father, Neville Blond, ran a flourishing enterprise called Emu Wool and was married into the Marks – of Marks and Spencer – family.

Reading Alastair's letters remind me I balked against some of the people, the goings-on, 'the architectural grace and intellectual vivacity'. Was that attributable to the envy that accompanies deprivation, or a wish to assert equal status? Somehow I must pick my way through and accurately identify what was vibrant and what was deathly. How confusing, dream-like, sometimes nightmarish, sometimes shaming, sometimes gorgeous the landscape of our past life.

The poems had been despatched around the time John Lavrin was preparing for demob. I accepted the invitation to look Alastair up, and took Stan with me. The intellectuals at Oxford were utterly different from the Jewish East End intellectuals of my family circle who were not really intellectuals, just autodidacts, the kind familiar to impecunious Jews – of whom there were many in those days. Alastair had red hair and spoke with a charming impediment. Not a lisp but a way of making his 's's sound like 'z's. He was born in Birmingham, middle class. Stan and I must have appeared to him exotic, as we were for John.

After the first visit I was constantly invited to events at the university. One little invitation I retain, 3½" by 2½", has on the front a drawing in red of a mandolin, cider bottle, glass and bowl of fruit:

LUNCH

Alastair Sutherland invites you to
a Sunday lunch on
Friday, 20 June
in the Cape of Good Hope
(The Plain, over Magdalene Bridge)
Opening with coffee at 11.15 a.m.
and followed by Stilton Cheese,
Ale and Cider
Price 3/–

MUSIC

I was so often in his rooms and visited with him the rooms of his friends that I felt part of student life, and even now – tongue in cheek – refer to it as my 'Oxford days'. The world I discovered was thrilling. Alfred Deller, I'd never heard of counter-tenors – discovery! The 1954 Arlem/Capote musical, *House of Flowers*, lasted only 165 performances at the Alvin Theatre, adding to the pleasure we took in the work – discovery! *Guys and Dolls*, most of the songs from which I could at one time sing by heart, went on to the record player again and again – discovery! And the Brandenberg Concertos – whenever I hear them the early years of the fifties surge back. All was discovery. On a number of occasions talk flowed so late that college was closed and the last bus to Moreton gone. A well-worn drainpipe escape route existed down which I clambered and felt myself the wildest of high-flyers, a romantic feeling which ebbed as I walked eight miles back to camp hoping for a lift that never came, arriving at seven in the morning just in time for reveille.

Balliol College
21st February 1952

Dear Arnold

I hope you got back OK on Monday night – I feel that I may have been misled by your optimism ... Did you find Hopkinson [ex-editor of *Picture Post*] worth staying for? – next Monday Mrs Nash, the widow of Paul Nash the painter, is coming to tea here, so if you're early enough you'll meet her.

Try to bring all you can next time – or better still could you drop anything in on Friday? I should like to have your writing together for a week or two.

I have read the Copping letters – I think they're comparatively sensible – a bit cranky, though. They give me an open mind on him. I think you're terrifically impressionable – a good thing really.

I've missed two nights sleep, and spent yesterday prospecting for paintings in the London galleries, so I'm almost too tired even to concentrate on letters. I have a vague feeling that I've forgotten what I wanted to write you about.

Best wishes.

Alastair

If you walked back to Moreton I trust you got a poem out of it.

I did. A not very good one.

The reference to 'prospecting for paintings': Alastair had the enviable task of purchasing works of art on behalf of the college. On one occasion he took me to Henry Moore's studio. I remember a conservatory full of maquettes and finished works large and small. Alastair purchased a tiny six-inch figure for what seemed to me an enormous sum of money. Could it have been £75? It was the only occasion I met Moore, a little man slowly moving from one to another, answering questions, quoting prices, a salesman at a sale! The thought that a famous artist might still need to be a hustler of his own work was slightly shocking to me. No longer!

The most bizarre and enraging occurrence in Balliol was the sconce. D.A.N. Jones, writer and journalist, was at Oxford at the time and a friend of Alastair's. Alastair had brought me to halls for dinner and I was without a tie. Not wearing a tie in those days was my defiance of convention, and Alastair, though knowing it was against rules to appear without one, bowed to my refusal, curious to see what would happen. Would it be passed over as I was a guest? Alastair sat on my right. To my left sat D.A.N. Jones. A college servant handed a note from another student, Alasdair Morrison (Hon. A.A.O. Morrison, the second son of the first Viscount Dunrossil who had been speaker in the House of Commons as W.S. Morrison). It was in Latin, a protest about his guest not wearing a tie. A reply was awaited. But I was not David's guest. Alastair asked to handle it. David was amused and indignant at the pomposity of the protest and insisted on taking on the challenge in my defence. In reply to a letter I wrote to him recently asking for my memory to be jogged, he replied:

> . . . Alasdair sconced Alastair for introducing a guest who was improperly dressed. Wasn't it a Sunday – a day for traditional ceremony? Were you not wearing an open-necked red checked shirt, revealing the hairs on your chest? . . .

Probably. David responded in Latin, and handed it to the college servant who took it back to the protesting Hon. Alasdair Morrison. A further response was written by Morrison in Latin and the three notes were handed to the high table where the Master of Balliol, Sir David Lindsay Keir, had to pass judgement on the rights and wrongs of the protest. Judgement was written in Latin. Right was awarded to the Right Honourable. David's letter adds:

> The Master must have replied: 'Fiat pena' ('Let the punishment stand'). He ought to have been allowed the appeal, on the grounds of courtesy to a guest, but that might have been difficult for him to express in Latin. We always fancied that Sir David was no good at Latin . . .

The process is called 'sconcing'. David Jones had been 'sconced'. To 'build a sconce' is to run up a debt, applied in the past to building up a debt in a tavern. Having lost the 'argument' David was now 'in debt' to Alasdair Morrison. It had to be paid in the following manner. Both parties to retire to the buttery accompanied by their friends. There a huge bowl was filled with two and a half pints of beer. David had to drink it in one go without the rim of the bowl leaving his lips. When achieved, Morrison had the choice of paying for the beer or drinking the same himself. He drank his bowlful. David could now either drink another or pay for the two. I think he got halfway through the second bowl and gave up, paying for the two. Had he succeeded then Morrison would either have had to pay for both bowls or drink a third. Had he got through the third (his second) then David would either have had to pay for three or drink *his* third bowl. And so on. It had in the past, the records tell, ended with the deaths of students. I deemed it a barbaric practice and felt hugely guilty, though I think David enjoyed the experience. He had no intention of dying.

. . . Alasdair was a good fellow to drink with: when we were both sober we disapproved of each other . . .

Alastair's file of letters is thick. They don't simply remind me of forgotten incidents and characters, they also carry a flavour of the times, and his too-sweet-to-be-stern personality. He's at odds with the Oxford Union Labour Club, and bubbles with his own dreams:

My own dreams – *Root and Branch* a focal point of like mind – enough money to have offices rooms a library etc. where interested people can come and meet and discuss our ideas and feel that they are taking part in a communal adventure – little groups of people spreading out from this – a free school – people getting together in their own neighbourhood to build locally the kind of society we want (it can be done, regardless of government and political parties) – people on the shop floor of factories getting together to work for what we want inside their factories – sympathetic artists, musicians etc. helping to raise money (from Robeson & Chaplin onwards) – a pub (I've always wanted to own a pub) . . . We can start our communism among ourselves – you & I and our friends, those who are sufficiently devoted now – until such time as we can reach other people through magazines – oh, and through health centres and countless things . . .

One thing, Arnold, I insist, and I am absolutely certain of it. I cannot say it too sincerely to you; you *must* believe this. You are not a communist [echoed later by John McGrath writing in *Black Dwarf*: 'He must . . . not confuse anybody . . . that he is in any way a socialist . . .'], you're a bloody anarchist! Everything, everything about you speaks this – your view of people, your interests, your idealism, your enthusiasm (e.g. Copping), your sympathies . . . your ideals and my ideals are not those of communism. (They have many ideals in common, but others which clash.) It may be presumptuous of me to speak for you. I'm sorry, but I know I'm not mistaken – I know because I've met you . . .

I suppose I had found in Alastair an older brother, someone to replace Ralph; nor could I resist the warmth of his enthusiasm for me.

. . . First, your letter. I loved your letter – what you wrote on Tuesday night is sheer delight. It reads wonderfully, with all the tones of your conversation conveyed. Oh, I loved what you said and I loved your way of saying it – inseparable here – the style breathes your enthusiasm.

A few comments on your political points. How I am with you in your dreams of selling poetry in Petticoat Lane and so on. Please, you needn't ask me, include me in all you say. You'll find I may differ from you on details – I may doubt the practicability of this, the expediency of that – but one can discuss details, weigh the pros and cons, trying to find what is best, knowing that we share a common purpose . . .

The letter continues full of criticism and advice, and he signs off: 'Sorry, Arnold, I will never let you rest until you're perfection!' To which end he extravagantly buys me books of poetry by Shelley, Burns, Pearce Young and some seventeenth-century lyrics.

Again, his letter reminds me of what I had forgotten: plans to stand in Petticoat Lane and sell my poems.

There are many parts of Alastair's letter I can't bring myself to quote, they throw up images too unbearably embarrassing. Just one example:

> Wizzie, you must accept that there is such a thing as maturity of outlook, and that you tend to overdramatise your proletarian Jewish background. You are so wonderfully happy, why do you need to luxuriate in the self-pity of 'Young Muddled Jew'? It is sheerly melodramatic ... I would not ever wish you to forget you are a proletarian Jew, but personal revolt may sometimes be an easy way out; acceptance and understanding may be harder ...

Did I ever seriously promote such an image of myself? And yet we put our imperfect selves together with whatever is to hand. Alastair's words sank in, nevertheless. In 1961, at the time of the first Fortytwo Festival in Wellingborough, I gave a lecture I was to give in many other cities around the world: 'Two Snarling Heads'. In it I attempted to pinpoint and explain the mistrust between artists and the working class: '... it should not matter where the hell artists come from, the fact that we come from where we do does not make us better artists ... a working-class background is not a halo he can wear with any privilege. One's background is an accident ...' A sentiment that confused my admirers.

Alastair thought he discerned latent homosexuality. This becomes clear in the long November 1953 exchange in which he urges me to

> ... adjust yourself to this, that our relationship was in its nature homosexual, and that all that was best in it came from that source ... we were walking to the bus stop to Manor House late one evening. This time you accept in a vague way that you might be

somewhat homosexual but that it didn't matter – and I let you believe this lie . . .

It wasn't a lie. Accepting it 'in a vague way' meant, I suppose – though God knows how we can ever know what we meant forty years ago – that I recognised a feminine side in myself. What he later quoted me as saying was, however, nearer the truth. 'I physically prefer a woman to a man. It is as simple as that.' But he wasn't convinced. Well, the years have passed and I have no sense of a suppressed secret life, no latent homosexuality. Not at all. My conflict was the conflict of a moral youth between lust and love: the body craved what the heart questioned.

It's obvious from the lengthy exchanges that I'm thrashing around in response to his criticism of both my writing and my personality. That was my life: buffeted between friends – Robert, cousin Bryan, Alastair, John and Beba, others to come, all concerned about me, feeling a nascent gift was there – crude, rough, worth taking my wild sometimes hurtful returns for, and I'm grateful. They force me to grow, drag me yelling and screaming into maturity. It is not an instant process. I resist, resent, and flail defensive angers at them, but slowly the criticisms and lessons sink in. I'm moulded into a better writer. The poems never become memorable but the prose improves, and then one day it's discovered – I'm neither poet nor prose writer, but dramatist!

Fascinating for me are his glimpses of family and friends to whom I've introduced him. I'm at RAF Wellesbourne Mountford. Alastair, having got his degree – not a desperately good one, he was more interested in a social/political life than in study – is staying at Weald Square while looking for a flat of his own in London. On 2 September 1952 he writes:

These letters get read, as they're typed, by Joe and it rather cramps my style. Now this sheet I keep to myself, I hope – otherwise it's going to shake someone . . .

God, I can't stop Joe talking, no wonder this gets incoherent.

Joe has just said that he won't speak to Squibbs any more. [Squibbs is lodging at Weald Square.] I guess that those two don't mix; but Squibbs at least keeps himself to himself.

Two days ago I rather disapproved of much of Joe. He wanted to know why he couldn't sleep and what he should do about it: I suggested that he should do some work. But I'm a bit more sympathetic now; Joe's a very sick man. It's all rather tragic. Leah is very snappy at Joe; Joe is very uncooperative. He's very trying. There is some liking between Joe and Leah, thank God. And some disliking. Squibbs has a sound protection against it all of just keeping himself to himself and withdrawing from it all. For all his faults, Joe is often intelligent and understanding. It is quite amazing how sensible and understanding he is on you – very rare for father on son. I can't think that 'Portrait of a Man' is a very full picture either of Joe or of the family set-up here. I want to say much more but I can't with just Joe and Leah sitting at the table. I love Leah.

He reports on a meeting with Esther, she said she needed a man of the world.

That was it! I was not a man of the world. They'd all seen it – Esther, Shifra, Rhoda. Not Audrey. Having no ambitions for herself she sensed . . . something.

I can't read *all* his letters to find myself. But just glancing through them throws up other scenes: he's looking for jobs . . . I want some money returned, he hasn't got it . . . he wants to borrow more money, I haven't got it to lend . . . In April 1953, a month before my twenty-first, he writes a densely typed, twenty-five-page letter, full of his own poetry and passages from other poets he wants me to know. He meets my friends and types in red type a letter packed with impressions, comments, requests. Of Shifra: '. . . so different from all the others . . . in a different class . . . just more outstanding . . .' Perceptive – she hadn't yet built the General Motors building in New York! They later row and fall out '. . . probably because we were both using each other so blatantly . . .' He dismisses Rhoda as spoilt, bemoans Barney, asks me to work for him . . . urges me to read *The Catcher in the Rye*. He thinks of me as Holden. In September 1955 he writes:

You are one of the unsettled of the earth, but for a different reason from me. You've never found your metier, but you believe it is there, like the Holy Grail.

And he quotes back at me something I said of him:

... no one has as much understanding and sympathy, so much tolerance for that which I want tolerated, dismissed so much that I want dismissed as you. All that I ever believed was good in me you found, and that which I have known to be objectionable you found too ...

I'm glad I once said such a thing to him. The ardour, the hopes of youth, filter away between the pages. He finally stumbles upon his idyll – a hut by a lake near Inverness where, among the rhododendrons, to the sound of seagulls, snow on the hills across the loch, a beautiful dog under his chair, he struggles to survive and write.

We correspond intermittently. He is critical right up to *Chicken Soup with Barley.*

I hope all this doesn't sound too harsh. I would honestly be surprised if the Royal Court took it – you might as well have that opinion now; I really feel bad at saying so, but I suppose it's better to say so if it corrects now the opinions others have given you to build upon ...

Well, he was right and wrong.

And then, leaping the years, he's involved in a handsome-looking magazine to do with Iraq and the Middle East. I remember we met and fell out over Israel and the Palestinians. The last letter I have from him is dated October 1972, twenty years after that first coming upon enchanted Balliol life. He had been trying to interest me in his latest project, a new magazine called *Resource.* His rough outline came to me here in Wales when I was on one of my writing retreats. Our roles are reversed. I'm having to make comments on something *he's* written. It is an irony that our first communication was about a magazine – *Root and Branch* – and that our last was about another. My mood is bleak because I'm reeling from confrontation with the RSC who have bowed to their actors' veto on *The Journalists* and broken their contract with me. I'm not enthusiastic about his proposed magazine's purpose or future, though I do advise, with bitter humour, that as I don't warm to its aims it might be a great success. He comes back at me and this time it's *my* reply which reveals the autobiographical moment.

My dear Al

I always loved receiving your letters and find that I still do. You are lucid, gentle and forgiving and it helped me through to my first success.

I'm sorry about my last letter. It was a bad moment. The first day here on my own, away from the family I adore, is always one of self-pity. It only lasts a day and then the confidence which comes with this wild and isolated landscape and being solitary in it washes it away. *Resource* might get off the ground if it struck the right note. Perhaps your pages went on for too long. The untapped resources in one *are* important. I want to write prose, to be sent, like Hemingway, a long way away on a journalistic assignment, to be asked to direct more plays, to direct a film, to paint, sketch, write lyrics for songs, to sing. Could *Resource* contribute to the fabled Renaissance Man? You argue well for it. My fears of it can, at least, sharpen your hopes for it.

Dear Alastair, your file contains at least a hundred letters about dreams and literature. Under your dry, sardonic and lisping affection my skill sharpened and thinking demisted. What these pages cannot carry are all my early letters to you. Just as well, for I fear they must have been badly thrown together and full of pompous self-defence and justification. Yours were better, thick with encouragement, attention to detail, knuckle-rapping. You gave unstintingly of your time, lavished great care on our friendship, and I thank you here for the love in them.

336

And the destruction. Taking over from Della and Ralph, you urged upon me books I *had* to read. One, more than any other, reduced to ruins my simplistic bolshevik views, a collection of essays – *The God That Failed*.

'The God That Failed'

And pricks of conscience are strong
My son
The days to come
Are long.
I wonder, when you are old like I
Will you too pause at the plough in the sky?
Spots in the dark
That look like a sickle
Or question mark?

'Query' – an early poem, October 1950

I'm not sure what it was about my writing or conversation that persuaded Alastair I was an anarchist. It's not a description I've ever boasted except when I was a seventy-eight-year-old woman named Betty Lemon. There had been much talk, and burning of midnight oil; argument, sparring, blows to the head and heart. Then came the collection of essays by ex-communists which Alastair insisted I read.

The God That Failed, published by Hamish Hamilton – edited and with an introduction by Richard Crossman, political theoretician and subsequent Labour cabinet minister – consisted of six essays: by the poet Stephen Spender; Ignazio Silone, Italian novelist and founder, in 1921, of the Italian Communist Party; Arthur Koestler, English novelist; Richard Wright, black American novelist; André Gide, French novelist; and Louis Fischer, journalist and writer. Koestler's essay gave the book its title. The experiences and arguments presented by the contributors have long since melted down into brain marrow. What remains are the memory of its impact and a file. The impact was the pain and anger of betrayal later fuelled by the Khrushchev revelations at the 20th Congress of the Party in February 1956, followed by the Soviet suppression of the Hungarian uprising, the novels of Solzhenitzyn, the memoirs of Nazdazia Mandelstam, Yevteshenko's poem 'Baba Yar', the Yiddish poet who named 'Stalin's Idiots' . . . others . . .

Though *The God That Failed* was my turning point in 1952, it was the Hungarian uprising of 1956 that I used as the catalyst for Ronnie's loss of faith in *Chicken Soup with Barley*. Spanning twenty years between 1936 – the year of the popular demonstrations against Mosley's fascism, and 1956 – the year of the uprising, suggested an arc beneath which the disintegration of a family could be poetically charted against the background of disintegrating ideology.

My file on *The God That Failed* consists of notes on, and quotations from, the book, and 'letters'. The quotations are powerful arguments which have stayed with me:

The intellectual in politics is always unbalanced in the estimation of his colleagues. He peers round the next corner while they keep their eyes on the road and he risks his faith on unrealised ideas, instead of confining it prudently to humdrum loyalties. He is in advance and in this sense, an extremist.

Richard Crossman

For I knew in my heart that I should never be able to write that way again, should never be able to feel with that simple sharpness about life, should never again express such passionate hope, should never again make so total a commitment of faith.

Richard Wright

The reformer is . . . apt to forget that hatred, even of the objectively hateful, does not produce that charity and justice on which a Utopian society must be based . . . that man is a reality, mankind an abstraction . . . that the end justifies the means only within very narrow limits; that ethics is not a function of social utility, and charity not a petty bourgeois sentiment but the gravitational force which keeps civilisation in its orbit . . .

Arthur Koestler

Liberty is the possibility of doubting, the possibility of making a mistake, the possibility of searching and experimenting, the possibility of saying no to any authority – literary, artistic, philosophic, religious, social, and even political.

. . . The distinction between theories and values is not sufficiently recognised, but it is fundamental. On a group of theories one can found a school; but in a group of values one can found a culture, a civilisation, a new way of living together among men.

Ignazio Silone

There can be no question of harmony when the whole choir sings in unison.

André Gide

Propaganda which paints friends entirely white and enemies entirely black persuades only those who are already convinced, to others it is humanly incredible.

Stephen Spender

Such reasoning, together with much else, marked me for life and set me on a road which ensured that almost everything I wrote would never be popular – much to my dismay; and led, I can now see, inevitably to the simplistically politicised actors of the RSC's 1971/72 season becoming enraged with *The Journalists*, a play in which I could not paint 'friends entirely white and enemies entirely black' and in which characters questioned literary, artistic, social and political 'authorities', or at least the cant in vogue whether of left or right.

The letters

I typed out letters in readiness to send and attempted to obtain addresses. I secured the home address of Spender in London and

Silone in Rome; for Louis Fischer his publisher's address in New York, and for Arthur Koestler his agent's, A.D. Peters, in London. My letters went off to them. Koestler and Silone replied, Fischer and Spender not.

I was left with top copies of letters waiting to go to Howard Fast, American novelist; Professor Blackette and Professor Joliot Curie, scientists; Mátyas Rákosi, Secretary General of the Hungarian Communist Party; Ilya Ehrenburg and André Gide, Soviet and French novelists. The addresses were never obtained, the letters never sent. This is the kind of angst-filled letter I wrote from Weald Square, E5:

Dear Mr Fast

I am writing to you as a young Communist on the point of losing faith. To go into details as to why would involve a long and tedious explanation. Suffice to say that in the same way as *Freedom Road* opened my eyes and helped me to understand the workings of American capitalism, so the book of essays *The God That Failed* have opened my eyes to the workings of Soviet communism.

But to read and accept is far too easy, and a friend of mine once told me that if I really cared for the truth then no efforts on my part would be too much to secure it.

Consequently this is one of many letters I am sending to various people in quest of the truth . . .

Questions followed, as did silence. Silone replied, in Italian (translated by my Italian friend, the film critic, Irene Bignardi) – to a different set of questions from those posed to Fast:

Rome, 19th November 1952

Dear Sir

I beg your pardon for being late in answering your letters. The question you posed to Togliatti is superseded by the fact that he has already answered publicly to what I stated in *The God That Failed* in a lengthy article published by the main organ of the Italian Communist Party, *L'Unità*, in the January 6, 1950 issue.

In the Italian edition of *The God That Failed* I have published in a footnote the section of Togliatti's article in which he explicitly confirms the truth of the episode about Trotsky which I related, as well as of the one about trade union tactics in England.

I enclose the relevant quotation.

Kindest regards.

Koestler replies, less friendly:

> c/o Messrs. Collins Publishers
> April 14th 1953
>
> Dear Mr Wesker
>
> Through an error in filing, your letter of August 21st has only just turned up on my desk.
>
> You will find the answers to your questions, with the exception of question no. 4, if you will take the trouble to look up the facts in a public library. The details concerning my late brother-in-law, Doctor Ascher, will be found in a forthcoming publication.
>
> Yours truly,

Koestler was right, I could have found answers to many of my questions by engaging in extensive research in the Hackney Library. But the concept of 'research' was foreign to me. I worked my way through the crisis of faith alone, lashing out at my parents, Uncle Harry, Aunt Sara and any other party member who came through Weald Square's door either to collect dues or hold meetings. I was not the obsessive diarist I am these days so no record exists of the unfolding anguish except reflected in a letter from Alastair – who had set the damned anguish in motion! I'm in Norfolk, in despair, he's trying to revive my spirits. The date is 23 May 1955, from Inverness. If his letter arrived next day it arrived on my twenty-third birthday!

> Dear Arnold
>
> I feel like replying to your letter, just read.
>
> You say you believe in nothing. This may be exaggerated by a

mood; but I suppose many people pass through a time when they are young when their beliefs are undermined and consequently they become so disillusioned for a time they do believe in nothing. At least this seems to be very common among Christians – I am thinking of fairly great ones who have left some autobiography. If it is of any consolation to you (it isn't much to me), they frequently go back to their first beliefs again, with all the fervour of the lover returning to his love after a quarrel, and with, admittedly, a rather firmer basis for them. My beliefs have changed, but I can't say that I have ever been through a *general* disillusionment. And certain fairly basic beliefs I have never for one moment discarded. But these are mainly simple ethical beliefs, and if you examine yourself you'll probably find that you still have held on to these as well . . .

You may feel disillusioned, but I do not think you will ever escape from certain things. You will never escape from socialism. I have known people who have been as devoted to socialism as you ever were, and who have worked in the movement for much longer, who have eventually given up politics. They have laid the political problem aside, and freed themselves to concentrate on a personal or a religious problem. But looking back, one can see that this was in their make-up. It is not in you to escape from socialism . . .

If you really see yourself as a hollow shell, it must be because you have temporarily lost your purpose. That will come back. But you exaggerate your view. It is necessary to try to strip things bare at times. Sincerity is about the most difficult of all things: it is much harder than leading a good life, having good taste, or anything: one has nothing to imitate. But soon you will see this period as a necessary development, as necessary as the period before. You may, in fact, discover that you have more to say, not less, as a consequence . . .

I have omitted huge sections. It was typed on two sheets of paper torn out, clumsily, from a blue lined exercise book. It was a loving letter directed at bolstering my flagging spirits. Two years later I began to write *Chicken Soup with Barley*.

Chapter Fifteen

The twenty-first year

The twenty-fourth of May 1953. I'm twenty-one years old. Demobbed seven months previously. The year has begun with me working as a bookseller's assistant in Stoneham's bookshop, Old Broad Street, EC1, where I fall in love with Olive Gloyn; in June my audition pieces gain me a place in RADA; in July they fail for a second time to earn me a grant from the LCC. In the same month I begin work as a plumber's mate in St Katherine's Dock, and play the role of Captain Carvello – for which I'm hopelessly ill-suited – in Pat Burke's production for the Query Players. Esther is one of the stage managers! By August I've joined Olive living with Della and Ralph in Norfolk.

On the Northwold Estate there is recently built between Wensdale House, Wentwood House, Pernhill House, Melton House and Weald Square, a new community hall – Northwold Community Hall. I hire it for my twenty-first birthday party and invite friends and family to bring not only food and drink but their talents.

Some brought their paintings, others their guitars. We danced Israeli dances, the twist, played party games, card games, and solved the world's problems with loud, animated confidence. We covered trestle tables with white lining paper and spread sandwiches of chopped egg and onion, cream cheese and salami, bagels and chopped liver, pickled cucumbers and the assorted cakes baked by my mother, my aunts, the mums of friends, friends themselves, swilled down with cider, soft drinks, and tea made in the kitchen downstairs. A tradition of large gatherings was begun. Olive wrote:

I also remembering refusing to clear off to Hackney Marshes with a party of your friends after your 21st birthday party [was *that* when

Barney and I stripped and dived into the river Lea?] but going home instead – such was your stuffy girlfriend!! . . . I always remember that white Broderie Anglaise dress you bought me to go to your 21st in – I bought you the Phaidon El Greco – Your cousin tidied my wild hair and I bought some red shoes and my father said it was the first time he'd seen me look like a real woman . . .

Four years later in the same community hall were gathered family and friends for another twenty-first – Dusty's. Another assembly of talents, more bagels and chopped liver, more Israeli dancing and perhaps some jazz boogieing. No hi-fis yet with loudspeakers thumping out rhythms, just an electric turntable turned up loud. By this time Olive had married a Norfolk farmer.

The river Lea story. One evening Barney, Rhoda, Esther, perhaps the Mond sisters, perhaps even the unpleasant Paddy for whom Rhoda had spurned me, all went 'over the Lea' in to the tall grass for cuddles and gropes. It was moonlight when we started back, slowly walking towards the river. Suddenly Barney began to trot away from us moving faster and faster towards the bank. As he moved he peeled off his clothes. I realised what he was going to do and followed suit, peeling off *my* clothes. The girls picked them up running behind these two naked young men, calling us madmen but loving it. Barney reached the bank. A barge was in the way. Somehow he knew where exactly to leap on to it, get to the other side and dive into the dark water. I leapt – Byron that I was – but missed solid wood, landed instead on the tarpaulin covering the hold, fell through, clambered out and hoped my dive into the dark waters was swallow enough to match Barney's romantic flight. Barney – wild, mad, Irish Barney who loved the Jews and ended marrying a Jewish French girl because he'd made her pregnant. We were all so close.

There were two additions to Dusty's twenty-first party on the estate: her paintings added to other local talent on the walls; and the dessert that was to become linked to her image – trifle. My mother used to make it – a simple assembly of jelly, sponge, tinned fruit and custard, an afters ordered every time I was taken to Lyons Corner House. Dusty's mother often made it for me – hence its appearance in the last scene of *Roots* when mother Bryant enters with a huge, oversized trifle to plonk in the middle of a table already laden with high-tea fare in preparation to greet Ronnie. 'He like trifle you say? Well he need to because there's plenty of it!' As there was on Dusty's twenty-first. From then on she became 'Queen of the Trifles', trifles which progressed in variety and sophistication. Her reputation spread, and when it was heard that she was coming to New York for the opening of *Chips with Everything*, a request for trifle was put in from Audrey Hepburn which Dusty brought over – against regulations – in a tall glass jar. Her secret was to soak the sponge in sherry or Marsala and to make her own custard.

I suppose if my friends were asked what was the feature that characterised a Wesker party they might point to the mixture of friends with family. Not simply a sister and mother but cousins and aunts and uncles and often my mother's crony friends – those waifs and strays who delighted to find themselves among young people. Throughout the sixties, once established in Bishops Road, not only did we make first-night parties and entertain entire visiting theatre companies – the Habimah from Israel, the Picolo Theatre of Milan, the Spanish troupe of Nuria Espert – we also instituted an annual Christmas party again mixing aunts, uncles and cousins with writers, actors, directors, musicians and painters. Dusty cooked for them all, a hundred at a time, offering a choice of three or four main dishes and sometimes as many as six different desserts. The centrepiece of these Christmas gatherings was the lucky dip, a moment our children loved. Throughout the year we would buy curios, antiquey objects: an old coffee cup that had lost its saucer, a saucer that had lost its cup, a discarded comb of bone, a shoe horn, a pretty tea plate that had lost its family. The criteria was that it had to possess age and – in the early days – cost no more than 25p. As the years passed the limit rose to 75p. The children would help us wrap them, and at a high point in the evening two of them would bring from the bedroom a blanket full of wrapped surprises and everyone would dip – children, the aged, the women, the men. Guests were allowed to exchange with one another if what they'd selected had an aspect of gender that was not theirs.

Parties! The gathering of friends and family. The sharing of talents. An unholy mix sometimes, but the instinct to feed and entertain is rooted deep in a character formed in Fashion Street where my parents gathered family and comrades to eat, and discussed how to make the world a just place for free men and women, and where there was singing:

> So comrades face the wind
> Salute the rising sun
> Our country turns towards the dawn
> New Life's begun.

Then came a day when Dusty said – enough! No more Christmas parties. She was tired, perhaps bored. I understood but knew a tie with an important tradition had been broken. The dinner parties continued but they were more intimate. In 1987 publishers Chatto and Windus invited her to write a cookbook. She wrote the diary of a year of feeding people, with delightful drawings by our youngest son's girlfriend, Jo Delafons. Dusty thought up a fine and appropriate title for the book: *Cooking in My Sleep*. The publisher, Carmen Callil, rejected it and replaced it with the dreariest of substitutes, *The Dusty Wesker Cookbook*. It was sourly reviewed – the English were uncomfortable with the spirit of abundance suffusing her entertaining.

There is no diary entry for 24 May 1953. All that exists are letters from my mother to her brother written around that date, a very bad, very long poem called 'Ten Stanzas to a 21st Birthday', and the brief diary crossing over from 1952 to 1953.

Monday, 1st January 1953
Well
I'm waiting now. The last test [RADA] taken and all one can do

346

is wait. I know it's not three weeks or three months to wait, merely three days. But with this test there is no way of assessing how one has done. Five will get through for the money out of – I estimate – fifty, and because one can't see or know how high were the standards of the other auditions one has no measure.

I did not do too badly, lost no nerve, made no mistake, had complete control over my voice and actions – but it might not be good enough . . .

I went to see *Miracle in Milan* myself . . .

. . . And the new year chiming in, like the uncertain thing it is, in the middle of the foggy night, in the middle of people sleeping for work – some of them.

I wonder how Robert's party went. Should have gone. Two years ago I would have run there.

Two years ago I would have still been writing.

I am beginning to worry. I have not written a thing since demob. I have lost the desire. I used to think in terms of poems and short stories, in terms of dialogue.

Now?

I am frightened a little. I was good while I wrote. Whether I wrote well or not I was fresh. I was living . . .

In my twenty-first year Leah is writing to her sister-in-law and niece – Perly's wife, Betty, and their daughter, June, who are on a long visit to relatives in the States. I am twenty-one years two months and four days old. After thanking them for their cards, complaining about the 'lousy weather', and hoping they're enjoying themselves, she sketches the domestic scene:

I am sure you will be pleased to hear that Joe is home, and improving, he regained his faculty just as he was when he first went into hospital which means that he remained as he was before and I doubt whether he will get better at all. Of course that remains to be seen. God knows how long. Still, he is going to Della's for a week or two. I get very nice letters from Della, they are all OK.

Arnold has just started as a plumber's mate – which I hope he will stick to as I am sure plumbing is a good trade to know. Still you know Arnold! I don't know how long he will stick to it.

I haven't phoned Perly now over two weeks but I will do so tonight. Both Perly and David [their son] are independent. I asked them if they need help and if they want to come to any of my kosher meals or weekends. However it's nice to be independent.

The next dated 2.9.53.

. . . Now for news this side of the world. We are all very well. I'm glad to say including Joe. He completely recovered from the stroke he had. But I don't think he will ever be able to work. Did you say 'he never did'? Well now I can't expect him to work. Anyway I am used to it. I am working now, I don't know how long for as our trade is so seasonal, 3 months work and 4 months slack. Still we get over everything.

Arnold is now in Wacton [Norfolk], he intends living there, that is if he can find work there. Not so easy to find anything there as it is in London. Myself I don't think he will stay long. I can't say anything as he is old enough to know what to do himself. I suppose he must learn the hard way. All I can say is that I hope he won't be sorry in later years.

Della and June – I meant to say Della and Ralph – and the children are very well. Della has now 76 livestock. Turkeys Ducks Geese Chickens. She will soon open a poultry farm. She has her head on the right shoulder.

Now about June. How are you? I do hope well. What are you intending to do, are you staying in America? It wouldn't surprise me if you found a very rich Prince Charming and you'll marry and stop there. However I trust you will let me know in good time so I can book my place in the aeroplane and order my dress! Joke aside, would you like to stay or come back home? I am eager to see you both so we can hear all the things you like and how you enjoyed yourself . . .

She cared about everybody. A brother's wife especially – to be respected, maintained contact with, reassured that everything was all right in her absence. Penniless, a sick husband to look after, she was in no position to hold the ship together but dutifully, lovingly, she wrote them letters from home.

Olive

Olive Gloyn had a voice that leapt around with dirty, deep-throated, slightly Cockney cadences; a fresh face, high cheekbones, green eyes that laughed in the way only women's eyes can, moving between mockery and a milky lust. She was youth at the brink, looking out on the world as though anything could happen.

We engage with eyes, don't we? They beguile with impishness, tremble with eagerness to learn, with vulnerability begging to be protected, sparkle with promise and eroticism. Protector, teacher, daredevil, sensuous – we engage. Not like with like but key with lock. Olive's appeal was a mixture – her eyes glowed with the promise she saw in all things, and I felt she looked upon me as one who might dare what her background rendered her too timid to contemplate. She read a lot, lived in her head and dreams. We were drawn to each other and fell passionately in love.

Olive's story is a special story, one deserving a volume to itself. Someone should ask her to write it. In part she's *told* it, spoken it into a trio of tapes which she sent me, from Norfolk where she now lives, and has given permission to quote from at length. Her voice is missing – a gentle, slow, alto sound, rich with amazement at the way life has taken shape around her, full of her personality trying to make sense of events. I want to shift over a little, to make room for her in this book, as in bed, a place to rest as it were.

Before me, Olive had another Jewish boyfriend, a student artist from the Slade School of Art. She was working at Foyle's bookshop nearby, in the section dealing with art, about which she knew nothing until the department manager, taking pity on her, sent her home with copies of Vasari's *Lives of the Artists*, and Gombrich's *The Story of Art*. This student came into the bookshop, 'a rather tall young man with a shock of curly, black hair and rather cheeky eyes' and asked her out to tea. Jewish, exciting, spontaneous, they became lovers. His name was Philip Sutton.

One day, it was in the Chelsea post office, he asked her to marry him. She declined. She told him she didn't think their relationship would work. He took it quietly, didn't say much, just left it to Olive to make the decision. She knew she couldn't deter him from what he wanted to do and that unless she moved in to his studio garret beginning her life from scratch, fifty-fifty, share alike, it wasn't on. There were tears. It wasn't on. She left Phil.

Olive's conflict was this: she had been evacuated during the war from Hoxton in London's East End, to the countryside where she developed a deep attachment to fields and fresh air. From that moment her personality was split. One half was the city girl – not for the city's streets and urban energy, but for its cultural life, its ability unexpectedly to thrust into view dynamic souls like Phil Sutton; the other half was the lover of rural landscapes. She dreamt of a country life, 'roses round the door', a settled life with a farmer-prince who would look after her along with the sheep and the cows and who she, in turn, could cook for, care for, and help harvest the corn and pull down the apples and gather in the plums for jam and fruit pies.

> . . . give me home-fires, happy husbands, kids who aren't too bad, and foolish dogs. I know these things. I know how to handle them . . . they content me . . .

Her tape tells of her beginnings – evacuated to Leicestershire where at school she was good at history, English lit., and religious studies. She left at fourteen despite being advised to go on to grammar school. She wanted to chance her luck in the world, begin earning her own living. 'I told them my ambition was to be a waitress!' Not true, but it stopped them applying pressure. First stop – evening classes to learn shorthand and typing – two pillars spanning the gateway to the world, but soon abandoned for classes in English literature where she won a prize for an essay on Macbeth 'which

AW (aged 4), Della
and Bryan.

Della and Ralph.

ABOVE AW and mother, Leah, in Rock Park, Barnstaple, circa 1941, aged 9.

LEFT AW outside 43 Fashion Street, with daughter, Tanya Jo.

MAIN PICTURE
Weald Square – X
marks flat.
FAR LEFT AW with
cousin, Bryan
(left), and second
cousin, Stan, circa
1950.
FAR BOTTOM LEFT
Leah, Joe,
Squibbs, 1952.

BELOW LEFT Joe,
1950.
BELOW AW and
Leah, circa 1950.

5th form at Upton House, 1948. Bill Walsh, left. AW kneeling left.
AW and Leah in playground of Rothschiuld Buildings, circa 1974/5.

LEFT Esther.
ABOVE Shifra.

BELOW LEFT Rhoda.
BELOW Olive.

Dusty outside Norwich Castle. 1953.

AW outside Norwich Castle. 1953.

Bell Hotel – window to left AW's room, other end Dusty's room.

boosted my ego'. It didn't help. A job as a filing clerk in the City bored her bosseyed and every lunchtime she raced up 365 steps to the top of the Monument where she remained reading Harrison Ainsworth's *Old St Paul's*. To escape a constricting family life she'd go for cycle rides to Victoria Park, lie on the grass, read, dream, row on the lake. She tells of a couple of Hindu boys with whom she became friendly, and their mother who pulled paste and made strudel and said all the time, 'Come, eat!' One of them had a name straight out of the Arabian Nights – Gayzar Boldizhar.

Olive's tapes

From filing clerk to book assistant in Foyle's to Philip Sutton and a Breconshire summer with him to Stoneham's bookshop in Old Broad Street where worked:

> . . . a huge, ungainly, kind-hearted spinster called Maude who'd often take off to Lowestoft to the fishing boats and come back radiant because she'd been to sea. I believe she lived somewhere in Islington and had a sort of quiet, select life with her parents but she was very dutiful and very kind and kept her eye on me in the shop and told me what to do.
>
> And there was also a delicious, delicious young man – I'd never met anyone like him before, with such culture. He was then going off to Cambridge to get a degree and his name was James Mossman, and he was huge. Very tall with a beautiful dark brown voice and a dark brown suit and I saw, one day when he was dressing the window and he took his coat off, that his trousers almost came up to his armpits. So I got a feeling he wasn't too well off and got his clothes from some stall or other. He used to tease Maude unmercifully. She used to have an office at the back of a small balcony above the shop and I'd be dusting the books and keeping my nose down and he'd lean over the balcony and say, 'Maude. Maude. Come into the garden, Maude. Do Maude come into the garden with Jim, Jim Boy.' And of course Maude would flush scarlet to her

hair roots, poor bugger . . . And the length of his lunch hour used to astound me. He was a bit of a goody-goody and kept strictly to time but when some of his friends turned up he left at one to go round the City pubs and came back at three! All couldn't-care-less-devilry and smelling of beer, eyes twinkling and full of fun . . . When Jim went the shop seemed empty and very dull without his banter. Later he became a journalist and worked on *Panorama* and went out to Vietnam. Later still he bought a lovely cottage at Gissing not too far from us here in Norfolk and even later still he killed himself. The rumour was he had cancer. But whether it was true I don't know. And when I heard the news I was really very low. I thought of the young man full of love, full of fun, and all his girlfriends with their exotic clothes wafting in the shop and out again and I thought oh God, whatever happened? Whatever happened to that young life? And I suppose life took him and used him and that was that.

Well I'd been at our bookshop I suppose about six months leading a quiet life downstairs in the basement among the children's books where we had a little switchboard, and I used to order theatre tickets for the people who came in from the offices. And one day I was over this switchboard in the basement and suddenly there was this great flying commotion coming down the stairs. And I looked up and there was this rather short chap with very very glowing eyes, in a sort of duffle coat, long black hair and a huge woollen scarf wrapped round his neck who introduced himself as Arnold Wesker. And I said hello I'm Olive Gloyn. And that demon, really . . . changed my life completely.

This Arnold had all the impish charm of Gayzar Boldizhar and the cultured pleasantry of Jim Mossman rolled into one. He seemed a very kind young man, and warm, and outgoing. The young girls at the shop thought a lot of him. He was a bit of a rogue, really, and led the manager a dance. I remember once – he used to ride a racing bike – and he dressed the window with it! It was quite a good display, but the best one of all was when he got a huge study of a nude, a Modigliani nude I believe, laid flat out, reclining, pubic hair rustling away, and all the City types, the office chaps and the girls, stopped transfixed at this nude and giggled. In those days, in the fifties, it was rather startling to see anything quite so naked, and he was asked to take it out and do something a bit more modest, perhaps a display of books on book-keeping, typewriting manuals,

Shorthand From A to Z, Pitman's System in Two Weeks, something safe and solid and city-like. And so the Modigliani nude came out and was put away in its wrappers. The book never did sell. A brave attempt, I think, to shock, but Arnold liked to shock. He liked to show life could be bright and shocking.

Anyway I went home to his little flat in Clapton and met his mother who was a dear little woman, tiny, a bit like Gayzar Boldizhar's mother. And she too would say, 'Come, eat, come have tea, come!' There was always food, always welcome, always warmth with Leah. She was lovely. His father was quite depressive, he'd sit by the fire and not say very much and not move. Occasionally he'd slap your thighs and say it was a nice shape or you've got a lovely behind or something like this, but I felt he was so much in Leah's shadow that he kind of lost his own drive. She was the overpowering drive in the family.

He – Arnold – had a sister, Della, who was in Norfolk and whom I was to meet later and I found her, too, overpowering, intellectually overpowering. In fact I'd never met a family quite like it. I was so English and rather sheltered, a tiny bit insecure of myself and where I was going. And the whole family seemed so overwhelmingly intellectual, overwhelmingly vital and virile. They rather swamped me. For a bit . . . In our family at home we didn't talk about socialism, revolution, Marx, Engels, William Morris, the socialist way of life, marches, counter-marches, politics. We didn't talk about anything much. We talked about each other. We'd talk about the price of food, we'd talk about what was on at the pictures, we had a laugh about life in general. But there was nothing philosophical or educational . . . Ours was just a free, very happy-go-lucky, lower-middle-class way of life. I suppose you'd call us conservatives . . . my father had his own business before the war. He was fairly self-reliant. He believed in keeping his nose out of trouble, earning the best living he could, sticking to one wife, going along happily, innocently, inadequately . . .

. . . One Easter I decided to go to Norfolk with Arnold to meet Della and Ralph and the children and see this socialism in practice, this life they were trying to lead, this self-sufficient life in the country away from the East End and all its noise and strife, in the peace and quiet of the Norfolk countryside. I'd never been to Norfolk. I'd heard it was terribly flat and dull and boring, and we hitch-hiked there in various cars and I remember that we sang all the way. Arnold had a great store of Jewish songs and we sang and we were happy. And when we got there, got to Long Stratton, we had to walk up this long road and again another long long walk up a country path to this cottage in the middle of fields, and he said – when you get there I want you to pretend you're very, very Cockney. And I thought, why pretend? I *am* bloody Cockney! Nevertheless I agreed to put on this real bleedin' rotten accent and smoke a fag and just see the reaction dear Della, dear cultured Della would have.

I was already intimidated at the thought of meeting Della. To me she seemed like a paragon of all virtues an intellectual woman could be. But underneath all this profound intellectualism was the quiet voice, the beautifully modulated, beautifully cadenced voice which made my Cockney stammerings a bit incoherent at times, and when I was trying to put my rather totally confused thoughts into words – it was very off-putting. Ralph I found more down to earth, more ordinary. I don't say that in any disparaging way but – I can't quite put it into words – he was a very lovable man. More approachable somehow.

Anyway, up this lane we went, and we came out to a kind of clearing, an old wrecked barn, and a square, stern-looking cottage with a nice Georgian front set in a wild uncultivated garden with a well, and a few chicken houses and chickens running about. And we went in. And there was this stone-flagged kitchen with brick walls painted white and a bucket under the sink to take the swill, and a wooden table and dresser and cups and this dark, rather beautiful woman in a smock and sandals with two little boys playing on the floor. And I had to put on this terrible voice to this woman with up-swept black hair, this motherly, this earth-mother-looking woman, and I had to say with my fag in my mouth, 'Watcha, Della, pleased ter meet yer I'm sure, 'ow are yer?' If Della felt any sense of shock and surprise she was pleasant enough not to show it. 'How do you do,' I believe she said, 'it's so nice of you to come and keep us company – hello Arnold,' and there was kisses and hugs and presents and food and tea and somehow I just couldn't keep up the pretence of the old Cockney slang any longer and I had to confess that it wasn't my normal voice and that it wasn't quite so dreadful as it sounded. But it *was* rather fun to greet this austere-looking woman with the upswept hair and this very cultured voice and to say, 'Watcha, Della, 'ow are yer?' It amused me for years afterwards.

After a few visits to Norfolk I asked Della if I could come and stay . . . I got so used to the bleak, barren fields, the outlook – you could see for miles. My life at home in Shoreditch seemed very compressed in comparison. Also with Della I was learning so many things about music, about art, and I loved the children.

Opposite there was a woman called Sybil Harket who ran kennels – I think of a dozen hounds – and I asked her to give me a job and she agreed and I went there as a kennel-maid at a pittance. But in a way I was happy walking these bloody dogs across the common, and creosoting her barns and sheds.

Once or twice Della and Ralph took me to the Maddermarket [famous amateur company in Norwich] to see plays, and, one day, walking across the common with Miss Harket who was very lame I turned to her brightly and asked, 'Do you enjoy the theatre, Miss Harket, do you like the Maddermarket?' And she turned her face aside and didn't answer and it was my first intimation in Norfolk what a gap there was between employer and employee – that we should know our place and keep quiet and be good, do our work and go home with our pittance and say nothing. And I was quite amazed and quite shocked and I went and told Della and she said that was the way it was in Norfolk and that was the way they were. But it was an eye-opener.

Arnold used to come up at weekends full of laughter and fun, kisses and presents. He was trying to write and he had to be in London to get established. One night I said to him look, we don't seem to see any locals do we, let's go out and find some fun. And he was typing away and seemed quite happy and didn't really want to come, but with his usual kind way he said yes, come on, and we got the bikes out and went through the back lanes to Hempnal and found this pub with a dance going on in a barn next door. This barn was painted blood-red and rather eerie, and there was a bar of sorts up in the corner full of young people and atmosphere and youth and gaiety and good fun. I looked round – and in another corner I saw this man who was very blond and very brown and very kind, a very kind-looking man, very solid. And I thought you look nice. And I

thought of how I liked . . . the farming dream. And this man asked
me to dance, and I introduced Arnold as my brother and we went
out many times together, many times after this, and gradually he
grew and – I married *him*.

'Him' that is instead of me! Kindness and solidity is what she
wanted and what she found. One important fact, however, was left
out – and it is a comment on the nature of autobiography, no doubt
one that many who knew me in those days will make about this
book: we omit that with which we feel uncomfortable. Olive
neglected to record that she had told me about wanting to marry a
farmer, that life between her and me held no prospects, and that
not only had I accepted this but had offered to help her find the
husband she wanted by pretending to be her brother! A plot between us! I would chaperon her in her search! Helping the woman
you love find a safe substitute to replace your own, conceded, barren promise was the zenith of unworldliness. But rage followed:

> *Take him, this farmer then,*
> *Over the fields in your arms.*
> *Spin him out on your skin*
> *About the moon in your lap till the pen*
> *In your tongue has worn him thin.*
>
> *Take him then, this fair-haired man,*
> *Burst your wonderful ways*
> *In the damp ricks of barley corn*
> *And there, lay, and love and plan*
> *The world again where we had shorn*
>
> *Apart. Take up where we lost touch*
> *And go, go dance with him*
> *This better boy. Soon the Spring*
> *And countryside will crouch*
> *To catch your love and laughing.*

Cover, comfort and cover
The man alive in you now.
Now you have him
You need not long for the last lover –
He has grown wild and lean

Anyhow. Then with your lips
Rise to him, reach. Open
Your loins and lay, lie
For him, turn him with your finger tips
And chain him to the sky.

Hold his hand, go run, go make
New sounds again. Bury
Bad bones and be his wife.
Living demands that you break
Your beautiful bodies on life.

Have him then, finger his ring
And keep him. Heavens! hide him
Away among blood and bone
And love, laugh, do anything –
But God! leave me alone.

Written on 20 January 1954. A bleak month.

The rage has long since passed. We became friendly soon after her marriage, though once her husband came to understand the nature of the restless, book-loving creature he'd married, he eyed me with wariness. He was everything she described him as – good, kind, solid, a man whose main passions, aside from his splendid sons lovingly guided through school and college, were cricket and farming. I hope he quenched her restless spirit, shared her intellectual curiosity, matched her dreamer's dreams.

Shifra, Rhoda, Esther, Olive – all were drawn to me but found me wanting. To be found wanting always causes pain but it is the right of lovers to cease loving. Hell may hath no fury like a woman scorned but there is a curious immodesty in raging against being turned from.

In 1989 when I gave a marathon reading of the *One Woman Plays* at the University of East Anglia Olive came with a friend and sat through from beginning to end. Her response is generous.

. . . And so we find our seats, and sit down in the front row, and there's this very bare blank stage with just the table and the chair, a mainly black and white setting, and a spotlight, and I've got this tape recorder I'm not quite used to, and we sit there all agog and I think oh come on get on with it, let's see what's going to happen. And – in he comes, with a burst of clapping, and sits on the chair, opens his papers and begins. And I can tell, I think, that he's quite nervous, his voice hasn't the full command which later it develops. And as I sit there watching him, watching all this richness unfold, I feel a sense of wonder almost, it's like knowing a tree in its acorn stage, you know, when it was very small and developing and groping. Now seeing it in its full maturity, full of richness, confidence and yet, I felt, not totally confident under*neath* the confidence. And this voice, this marvellously modulated voice, carrying all before it and the audience with it and these various gradual characters unfolding, very real, very true. In fact my friend whose husband had ditched her, well, *Yardsale* almost moved her to tears because it was so apt . . . I thought bloody hell where's he heard all that because it's so true, rings so true, one's had them said to oneself so many times . . . like a record with the needle stuck . . . which you recognise as being trite and overdone, as a signpost of the end of the relationship. You think where's he heard all these things? Where's he heard all these phrases and picked them up like a recorder?

And so the evening wound on and we . . . heard the last, and then I'm never quite sure what to do, whether to breeze off home or just say cheerio . . . I don't like hanging about, somehow I feel . . . I don't know. . . I feel a bit – demeaned, which is stupid but I still do. Anyway, my friend Bridget wanted some posters signed and so she said, 'Come on, you must stay,' so we did and we had our posters signed which was very sweet and said cheerio and got in the car and came home. And I thought well yes, that's it. That's over. He really is very very clever and he really is very very funny with terrific potential . . . that it's really . . . rather lovely. He's still accessible, a homely fruit cake really, nutty and fruity – cor!

Anyway, so home we came and it was all quiet in the old farm-house. My husband had gone to bed, and I sat and had a little think and I thought, gosh! I'm so – so pleased, so grateful somehow that all his effort and his faith in himself has paid off so well, so hand-somely, and his life appears to be so rich and fulfilled. And I went to bed very happy with this thought. I went to bed and thought well, in a way, although my life isn't like that, in fact it's the complete opposite really, a bit of a grope, but it's fulfilled in a woman's way, the children and gardens and animals and all the things that keep me ticking over, feet on the ground, keep me to earth really. And I thought of Ariel, Shelley: in life there's spirit of the mind, which is in us all, really, and in me surfaces like a whale coming up for air . . . Then somebody like Arnold, or some other poet or some play, will set it all in motion again, and for a few weeks you're living in an-other world, like a spirit world that's full of words and harmonies, and sometimes misery, which you can't quite fetch out. And it stirs you and moves you and wants you to be different. And this mood will last perhaps for two or three weeks and you don't want to let it go because it's quite creative and then – somehow life will overlay it. The busyness of life begins to overlay it, erodes it, till something else happens to spark it off. But it's such a tiny spark, it doesn't get fanned into anything flamelike, and it's often derided, denigrated by oneself anyway and so you shove it to one side and say well – it's the part of life that somehow in the village has no use.

And yet it does have a use 'cos when you go out and you meet various folk and you respond and they respond, you know that it has got a use: it's the life, the life in you that has to come out, that has to show, that has to come forward and does. And so when you see people like Arnold and other playwrights and see plays or read books or see a picture which moves you, this whole inner substance, or whatever it is, this world wakes up again and you become more alive, more receptive, you become more feeling, quieter, you want to sit and have time to think about things and not rush about so much. And it's funny how this always happens. And you feel richer. You *do* feel richer. And you really want to use this richness to create words or create something, a – a relationship or a feeling, a mood, a picture, a cake. You want to do something with it, anyway.

So, that's what happens. Time and again. It intrigues me. It sometimes perplexes me really, but I wouldn't be without it. Not for the world.

One section of the tape is unbearably moving for its honesty recording the agony of choice. She talks of her rich life with a good husband and four sons, but delicacy prevents quoting most of it in full, only that which touches on my life.

And when I think of my 40 years in Norfolk, of the still-carefree woman – mother of four beloved sons – standing in her garden looking out across the fields of corn to the ruined church restored at vast expense, and breathe deeply, I know I belong here amongst family and friends even though they think I'm mad, even though the lovely people who were part of early life in London moulded my nature so that I'm left a kind of half and half person. It's all fading now, besides: Phil striving with his painting, Arnold striving with his writing and poetry, young men who, apart from this artistic striving, were very human, happy-go-lucky, casual, loveable – especially Arnold who would roll about the floor with laughter and jump on a soapbox and pontificate; and Phil, often amazingly shy, you could shock him, you know, if you went too far with a joke or teasing or play. And they both had this loveable trait of boyishness and they really left you completely free to think, say, do as you like – which in my case was completely the wrong thing to do because I would do exactly that and perhaps bring down disaster. But looking back you realise that in this atmosphere of struggling artist – artists struggling with themselves, with their material, with their surroundings, with their thoughts, minds and emotions – somehow you lived at a high pitch, you felt deeper, you gave more of yourself, it moved you in many ways to be with them. You went to concerts – and I remember once going into Sadlers Wells with a group of Arnold's friend and I was very young and very impressionable and very emotional and quite virginal really, strangely enough, and I remember sitting behind Arnold and – I can see it even now – and they were playing, I think, a love duet from 'Madam Butterfly' which is highly,

highly emotional music, and I'd always been a loner being an only child, and Arnold was sitting among a whole bunch of his friends who were young communists [young Zionist, actually] and was very much in demand, and very popular, and I was very shy really – although I could make on the surface as much of a row – but I was sitting behind him and I remember watching his neck and hair, the thick, dark hair on the back of his neck, and his square shoulders, and I sat behind him and – I think for the first time – my playfulness gave way to a sense of possessiveness.

But the mad-cap London girl gave way instead to the country wife with London undertones – a shadowy hotchpotch personality who warms and revs up to any overtures of gaiety and gentleness and refuses to accept the kindly blandishments of old age. Forty years on village life is not the same. The small community of little farms is now a prosperous – and much burgled – Norwich suburb of mainly professional people. But it still feels like a village, homely, people caring for each other. And all I want, really, is to end my days here in old familiar haunts, scribbling my little letters to the press, and my odd short stories, keeping my hand in, reminding myself of that other girl 'mad as birds' who shared life with two of the most exciting and promising young men of our time and was happy and, in her own way, is happy still.

But it didn't stop her ruminating on how, incomprehensibly, she had in both cases, destroyed trust, intimacy and love – she had been so attuned, so happy, they had been unique, special relationships; how could she have so wilfully broken them down? Her reflections are heartbreaking. She searches for explanations: being an only child . . . marriage as a romantic, Barbara Cartlandish experience with roses round the door . . . dark, hairy young men in hairy jackets with patches on their elbows were fine to muck around with, and laugh with, and have fun with, but not to be taken seriously as marriage partners. Explanations such as these. Olive didn't enjoy this image of an immature self. Nor should she have done. With such fears and expectations she had undervalued herself. By the time Phil and I reached her the damage was deep, courage cracked, self-esteem ossified. But her tapes remain, touching gems of vivid self-honesty.

If we are as honest as Olive, Phil, we would admit that we responded to her as Pygmalion: a striking young woman vibrating with possibilities. Not simply sexually but as a force for action. Coming from a narrow background everything was amazing for her. Such wide-eyed enthusiasm is irresistible. But there was more. She was blessed with that poet's spirit which cherishes the remarkable in life, nature and art. It was the final courage to go with it that she lacked. Her background was against her. There was no tradition of risk-taking in it. I'm not even sure *I'd* have risked marrying you, Phil. Would you have married me?

Chapter Sixteen

Norfolk

I don't know at what stage in their marriage Della and Ralph decided to leave London in search of the rural dream. Perhaps it wasn't a rural dream they were in search of, more a wish to be quit of city life. Motives are mixed, the drive is multi-powered. Longings merge with discontent; books merge with conversations; other people's lives become role models; dreams jumble out of everywhere. Gradually a path shapes called 'the future'. Nothing precise. Something just comes into focus. We take it. The stern-looking Georgian cottage Olive saw at the end of the lane with its water supply from a well, its stone-flagged kitchen, a swill bucket beneath the sink, primus stove for cooking, tilly lamps for light, all set in a wilderness of uncultivated greenery, is now a beautifully cultivated country house with a swimming pool. The penniless couple from Stepney took a path they had no idea would end with a swimming pool. A pool is not, of course, the acme of their lives nor, had they been asked, would it have been within their stated goal; Ralph wanted to become an artist-craftsman, Della wanted to keep livestock, rear children in the fresh air, and be her husband's partner in all things.

Our mother didn't see it that way.

26.9.47
My daughter & son-in-law have gone to live far away. I will not be able to see them so often. Fare is £2-4. They have not spared my feelings although I was pleased that my boy Arnold who is 15 years of age, went with them to help them. Still he was very pleased to go without any thought of leaving me all alone. I'm somehow not able to keep my family. My Della as a child, never wanted to come home

straight from school, she was never very pleased to stay home, she married when she was 17 years of age with the first one she met. If she wouldn't have such a home as mine . . . she did not give me much of her self so that I can have pleasure from her, I could not make the home attractive enough that she could stay a little longer. I am sure if she hadn't such awful life with me, she would not have got married so young, although my son-in-law is a very nice young man, seems to like my daughter very much, I like him, but . . . I cannot give myself an explanation, why I feel that my daughter is not very happy, it seems to me that she became – morbid, her face has such cold expression, she is like ice, as if she has no feeling, so serious. If she would only laugh more joke more. But then that is all my fault, it is I who comes with my troubles to her, I am the one that makes them both miserable. There is no life in this house, there is nothing to hold them, I am an angry miserable old woman. They had to go far, far from me.

My sister was not like 'ice'. She felt deeply. The endless fighting of my parents forced her to withdraw into a protective shell. Besides, she was more of a Wesker than a Perlmutter. My mother knew there was a difference between the two families and of course preferred the soft, emotional, unworldly Perlmutters to the controlled, matter-of-fact Weskers, but it never occurred to her that her children could be one or the other or a mixture of both. Yet she sensed a difference between us without relating it to family genes.

Poor Leah. She possessed a kind of wisdom and sensitivity, but life in general, and the lives of her two children in particular, were not entirely comprehensible to her. When my father died she was thrown into labyrinthine confusions of guilt.

19.12.59
. . . In my heart there was love for Joe as well as there is love in my heart for Della. But unfortunately like Joe – may he rest, so Della – bless her. One can't come near. He did not let me. There was something in his manner that I could not say to him Joe, I love you, or

like you. I did not mind working, when I worked I used to feel happy. I even came home on Friday with wages and used to give him cigarette-money according how much I earned. £1. Or 10/-. Even less. But he used to borrow more anyway. My God, it was not always my fault.

It was not you Joe who died. You don't feel anything at all. It's I who died. I am a living death. My heart is aching. I am suffering from the shame that you made a fool of me. To take revenge from me you died a death that left me a living statue. The thought that I could not help you, and you did not let me . . . you really hated me. I am inclined to think that Della does not like me either. I only think so. It may not be. In fact it's more not so than yes. My dear Arnold shows out more emotion. He is like me. He shows what he thinks.

When will I really stop writing these morbid things.

My dearest children, you go on living and don't be sad. Life is too short for that. Tear and break up anything I write and remember that I am just an unhealthy woman, and I am just a mother like all other mothers when they get old. Only a highly socialist education and a peaceful world will keep men and women young and in- teresting until they die.

She is wonderfully all over the place, hitting right and wrong notes, making a kind of discordant sense. But in the early days it must have been distressing for Della. Not 'must have been' – it *was*. And in some degree, though Della might deny it, my mother was right – flight into Norfolk, September 1947, two years after the war, prob- ably had something to do with ' . . . such a home as mine . . . '

Their first move was to a village north of Norwich called Sloely, near North Walsham. My memory of it is dim. They called it 'The Shambles' and struggled there for eighteen months until they saw for rent this run-down cottage in the middle of fields near a com- mon called Wacton Common, a mile from the town of Long Stratton, twelve miles south of Norwich. No road led up to it, no running water, no drainage, no gas or electricity. From their bed- room window they looked out upon a field of wheat. The land was flat flat flat. Huge skies lorded over the landscape dictating what would be seen and not seen. But I suspect the feature that convinced them that the life they wanted could be lived here was an old barn resting on massive oak pillars. The workshop! Here the furniture-maker could hang the tools of his trade. They took it. Hill House Farm. Moved in 1 April 1949.

I loved the cosy isolation of Hill House, a hideaway just for us, and was there as often as possible, visiting with friends, cousins, girlfriends. Hard work for Della and Ralph, a fun place for me. Everything was a small thrill, a tiny game, a ritual: the ritual of undressing into pyjamas under the bedclothes because it was too cold to stand in the bedroom, sleeping in socks. The tilly-lamp ritual: pumping vapour into a spun asbestos mantle. The water-from-the-well ritual: winding up two buckets at a time. 'Arnold, it's your turn to fill the buckets . . . empty the swill pail . . . take the Elsan to the pit . . .' Ralph was always upbraiding us for leaving the Elsan to get too full before it could be emptied. Yeach!

Approaching the house was especially exciting; approaching at night – which I frequently did arriving on leave, or after an evening shift at the Bell Hotel in Norwich – the excitement was tinged with fear. Today that B road to Wacton is lined with houses – Long Stratton expands; then it was lined with trees through which the wind howled. I had no *real* fear but I did whistle loudly and sometimes sang with warning raucous tones to the stars. Arriving in the mellow glow of a tilly lamp was a moment.

'Anything to eat?'

'Bread and cheese.' It became a joke between Ralph and me, 'For your brother – bread and cheese!' The tilly lamp filled the house with lingering smells of paraffin and methylated spirits. And always food smells: baked flour, the hint of vanilla from cakes, herbs, vegetables from thick soups. And warm dog smells, Patch, one black eye, stupidly friendly. And at nights the smell of damp. It appalled my mother to begin with, though gradually she accepted the life and even found a way to enjoy her holidays there.

It was not simply that she was hurt, she found the cycle of events incomprehensible. Born into a rural backwater in Transylvania she had emigrated to one of the world's major cities, lived through gas to electricity, went from an attic flat in the slums to a spacious council flat in the suburbs; believed roads, buses, Underground trains, shops on the corner, milk at your doorstep, post through the letter box to be signs of progress, and here was her daughter stepping back to the muddy paths such as she, Leah, trod when a girl of thirteen. It made no sense to her. When her son left town and joined his sister the pain and bewilderment deepened. The burden, too; she was left alone to look after a sick husband.

I left the city, as I've explained, for a number of reasons: I had failed for a second time to secure a grant from the LCC which would have enabled me to take up the place awarded by RADA. I was not to be an actor. Poems and stories continued to attract rejection slips. I was not to be a writer. My stories about the building trade, the story about my homosexual friendship, the one about Stan and John, the crude novel about the RAF, the portrait of my father, and the dreaded poems with titles like 'Penny Quarrel', 'Spring Train', 'Once Upon Ago', 'Summer Streets', 'For My Babe Unborn', 'So it's Weeping I'm Doing' – for Olive, that one – all rejected. All deserving rejection. No misunderstood Chatterton, me, but demoralising none the less. I stood, as it were, at the top of Highgate Hill where once stood Dick Whittinghton, looked down on the fair city, no black cat promising me fame, fortune and thrice Lord Mayorship of London, and turned my back on it. And though fame and fortune could hardly have been what I expected to find in Wacton yet of some things I was assured – love, some indulgence, and a little cheese.

There were also my nephews – Miles and Adam. We are unbelievably distant now but then – I baby-sat endlessly, invented stories, played games, built Meccano sets, and indulged them beyond the wishes of their parents. In fact I was guilty of the unforgivable: arguing with my sister over certain of her attitudes towards bringing them up, in front of them. From one of my mother's letters to us in Paris in 1956:

Now . . . I must tell you about Adam's dream. I was up there one day & he said to me Grand Ma Grand Ma . . . Is Arnold married? I said no, why? He said in his lovely baby talk, I dreamed about Arnold that he came off the bus & Dusty came as well & she was holding a Baby. Della & I were astonished. Never expected him to dream about you in 'this way'. & also before that, he wanted to know where you are working, & what's the name of your workshop, & you should write a letter to them telling them all about your & Dusty's work, where & what & etc., etc. He says Miles will read it to me, I like to get a letter from Arnold. As for Miles he is out of this 'world', he is getting cleverer & cleverer every minute. He also talks about you very much & says Oh! I love Arnold & Dusty.

From an early age I was passionate about children and couldn't wait to have my own. The heartache at this time of writing is the family tension preventing me enjoying my grandchildren. There is a cruelty in it that I have difficulty understanding. My instinct is to nurture, make things grow, release potential, stroke people's self-confidence. It might even be an instinct stronger than the one to write; or to be charitable to myself it is perhaps the instinct that informs my writing.

Freelance journalist

At the beginning of this book I quoted Annabella Wharton, the novelist, from the *Annie Wobbler* triptych, who, in response to the question: 'When did you begin writing?' replies:

> I think I began writing when I wanted to affect others the way writers affected me.

Art, especially literature, shaped and nurtured me – layered over the genes that juggled for position. I too burned to affect others the way writers affected me. I couldn't. I had not the talent, it seemed. And so, turning away from the city was also turning away from a preoccupation with myself. Leave ambition behind! You are no artist! Look to your adored nephews. Tell them stories. Help Olive find whatever it was she wants in life. There's water to be drawn from the well, there will be jobs – on farms, roadworks, something! And in between, why, you could supplement your income with odd pieces of journalism – to which end I found money to pay for printing headed paper declaring myself:

Arnold Wesker, Hill House, Wacton, Long Stratton, Norfolk

freelance journalist

An aside. A sheet of this headed paper exists. On it is typed a poem of nine verses written during these flummoxed times. I quote one for a reason:

> *So there is left no language for my song,*
> *Only the soft vowels of a kiss.*
> *But love is not enough and I long*
> *To harbour the erupted music of my heart*
> *And unlearn all the lessons of my times*
> *And say that it shall come to this . . .*

At the end I wrote in pencil:

Why is this no good? The conclusion is whimsical? . . . the ringing is hollow? . . . The idea is there but the verses are too easy . . . Not rebels without causes but without tongues. There is *still* no language, or I cannot find it, or I have missed it, or I am looking in the wrong place. There *are* tongues, there *are* weapons, God knows where!

What strikes me is the concern about causes. *So there is left no language for my song.* The line echoes the title of a film made famous by the legendary James Dean: *Rebel Without a Cause*, but it also looked forward to the line made famous by Osborne's Jimmy Porter: 'There aren't any good brave causes left.' The film was a lament for an energy that couldn't find its cause; Osborne's anti-hero rages that there are no causes anyway; my pencilled note suggests both causes and energy exist but we possessed no tongue to shape them into form. Hearts are in the right place, but the tongue is a blunt weapon for want of learning, unsharpened by knowledge, unfashioned because uninformed. We had our causes but were tongueless.

The attempt to establish myself as a freelance journalist failed. Smart headed paper in blue typeface excited nobody. Two feeble articles – the first about Della and Ralph returning to the land, for the *Jewish Chronicle*, December 1953; the second about Ralph and the Windsor chair for *The Norfolk Magazine*, May 1954 – were all that appeared in print announcing to the world my arrival on the scene as a storming young writer. No writer, no job, no nothing. My poems my diary.

> *I walk the streets of Norwich*
> *Looking for a job*
> *And only a few bob*
> *In my pocket.*
> *And I look clean, and young*
> *And handsome*
> *And I look like any other man*
> *Walking the streets of Norwich.*
> *And I am like any other man.*
> *Only I can't earn a living . . .*

Labourer

Of course I could and, eventually, did. In the short space of time I lived with Della and Ralph – during which I said goodbye to Olive and before I answered an advert in the *Eastern Daily Press* for 'Kitchen porter, £3 10s. a week, live in, the Bell Hotel' – I had three jobs. The first working for a firm laying huge pipes in the road. I can't remember how I found the job, how long I stuck it, or why I quit. Too hard? Was I not muscular enough? The pay was good and I had fun working one of those machines that jumped up and down thumping the earth back into place and sometimes my feet.

I became a farm hand next and found myself back in the Middle Ages gathering with other farm hands in front of the farmer first thing in the early morning, 6.30, to be informed of the day's tasks. I shared sugar-beet fields with a couple of other old hands, and I mean old, who shamed me by the speed they could move along rows of beet which had been churned into view by a machine ahead of us, and stayed bent lifting two beet, knocking them together to displace the earth, putting one down, with a sharp knife slicing the end of the other, flipping it in the air, catching it to slice the other end, dropping it, picking up the second beet, slicing that, dropping it, lifting another two – knock, top and tail, knock, top and tail. They left me standing in pain. I wrote a story about it – 'Sugar Beet' – which I thought lyrical, capturing the expansive landscape, my misery, the dry mocking humour, the craggy personalities of the farm labourers, and the gorgeous Norfolk dialect with which I fell in love and was to use in four plays.

My third job was as a seed-sorter in the maltings of Pulham St Mary. I was, unawares, moving closer to Dusty. Her parents, Hilda and Edwin Bicker, and her brother, Sam, and his family lived in Harleston, a few miles further up the road; and a sister, Bridget, lived with her husband and children in Pulham itself. Bridget, who died young of leukaemia leaving a husband and two daughters, used to cycle to work in the Hill House Hospice for old people at Pulham Market (now a garden centre) every morning, passing me at the same time in the same spot as I cycled to sort seeds in the maltings. We got on smiling terms. An early flirtation. No word spoken except 'G'mornin'.' Once, on an icy road, I turned for an extra wave. My body swivelled to the right, my left hand automatically swivelled the handle bars to the left. The bike buckled and Lord Byron sprawled again, slithering with indignity over the iced tarmac surface. She laughed, did Bridgy, little realising she was laughing at her future brother-in-law.

Seed-sorting, though it involved hauling heavy sacks on my back, was a cushy job. The task was this: the seeds from oat, wheat, and barley had to be sorted from the chaff. Sackfulls arrived and were hauled up wooden steps to a wooden floor from which chutes dropped into 'shakers' – sieves which shook. Beneath were attached empty sacks to catch the shaken and sieved seeds. Along with a couple of others I hauled the heavy loads upstairs, poured the contents down the chutes, descended again to wait as the sacks filled, then dragged them to a section awaiting lorries. I describe the process roughly. To be honest the exact stages have gone from memory. I think there was a two-wheel fork truck which we slid under the sacks and wheeled to the lorry. But don't I also remember lifting a sack with one other who heaved it on to my back, leaving me to walk with it to the lorry? Whatever, I recall these things: the noise, the smell of sacking, cutting lengths of rough, hairy string to size for tying up the filled sacks, and the long periods when there was nothing to be sorted and I lay on top of seed sacks reading my current Penguin book or writing the dreaded poems.

The Barn

The barn is an important memory. It was what I surmised attracted Della and Ralph to Hill House. But the barn had to be pulled down. We also rebuilt it. Over thirty years lay between.

It was a two-hundred-year-old edifice. Ralph converted a small section but it was all collapsing – the brickwork had gone at the base and needed underpinning. He couldn't afford to repair it.

Ralph had a talent for turning the smallest chore into an event. 'Right, now, this is what needs to happen. We'll attack it this way. If Della does this, and you, Arnold, do that, I'll meanwhile . . . ' Bringing down the barn was not a small chore but a dramatic event.

Ralph had worked out the mechanics of the operation. The huge oak timber supports needed to be sawn through, heavy ropes slung and knotted round one of the bearers, and attached to the jeep. It was a spectacular sight. Centuries caved in upon themselves. Although there was an abundance of wood to make both fires and furniture, Ralph, in later years, regretted the deed. He came to see how the barn could have been saved. But another has taken its place. Well, not quite a barn, more a large workshop. Constructing that, too, became an event.

With retirement approaching, Ralph assembled the materials and began building a fully equipped joinery workshop where he could construct this and that in his own retired time. One weekend at the end of June 1985, a huge gathering of family and friends was brought together at Hill House for the raising of the roof. Once again Ralph had it all worked out, what each of us was to do. Della and Dusty laid on the meals, the rest of us heaved and hauled and laughed. Byron was there climbing dangerous heights, balancing on precarious edges, acting daft for the amusement of the crowds below. My diary records:

. . . It was a good weekend. We spent most of the time constructing the four central trusses and erecting two; and creosoting the lighter trusses. Ralph tired himself out and I too felt it in my bones, climbing ladders, hammering, sawing, lifting. It was very satisfying when, sitting by the fire on Sunday, we had erected the two heavy trusses. I wanted to be part of the construction because I'd played such a major role in bringing down the original barn – parts of which remained. One of the most impressive moments was when we had to tie a rope to the apex of the truss in order to pulley it up on to the shoulder of the wall, and Miles revealed that he knew the knot that was required – one that would hold and could be pulled undone at a tug without having to climb up to the unreachable apex. It was called a 'Billy-the-Kid knot'. We were all curious to know where he learned such a knot. 'From the *Eagle* annual,' he replied. 'I took one look at that knot and I knew the day would come when I had a use for it.' . . .

Part of the pleasure was being Ralph's help again and feeling like a young mate. And I *did* feel like one. There I was, 53 years old, taking his instructions, leaping up towers, precariously leaning on things in order to hammer. It came so naturally to me as though I'd spent my life doing it. The delight must have shone through because everyone remarked on it, and Ralph kept saying how agile I was which all seemed strange to me. Why should they be saying it? Did I look *so* old and therefore odd to be scampering about? . . . Later, as we were in the barn at work, Julie [Adam's wife] said: 'You ought to write a play about all this, the family erecting a barn, and the erection of the parts as a metaphor for the parts of the family . . . '

It was a striking idea. Fun days.

Chapter Seventeen

The Bell Hotel

The Bell Hotel
Norwich
Norfolk.
Saturday 12th Dec. 1953

Hello dad Joe,

I know it is not often that I write specially to you, but as I hear from mummy that you are not as well as you should be I thought that a few lines might cheer you up.

I think somehow that you would like my room. It is an attic over-looking what is almost the busiest part of Norwich, and today, Saturday, I can look out of my little window and see masses of people and cars in the streets. Christmas shopping! Thousands of people spending what must be millions of pounds. Actually it is quite exciting. Immediately across the square I can see Marks and Spencer and Woolworths. Not far away on the left are neon lights that burn into the night and keep my room in shadowed colours. And below is a car park and in it a gorgeous collection of cars.

You'd like it. The room is small, but is queerly shaped and must date back a few hundred years. The Bell itself is probably among the oldest hotels in the city. Norwich, as you will remember from that walk you took some time ago, is certainly a good thousand years old. The castle is Norman. Of course there is the inevitable hotel where Queen Bess stayed. I think every old city in England claims that the good Queen stayed there at some time or other.

Perhaps my biggest delight, and it would be yours as well, is to look around the bookshops. There are many here and you can pick up some classics very cheaply. Do you know I have bought five second-hand copies of Jack London's books. One a collection of short stories. 'The Abysmal Brute'. 'Before Adam'. 'Michael Brother

of Jerry'. And the classic which I have been trying to get for ages –
'The Iron Heel'. For sixpence each! 'The Iron Heel' I have read
before but I am reading it again. It is quite an inspiration.

I get a lot of time to read here. I can go to bed at about ten o'clock
and read on till twelve. In this way I have read the autobiography of
Jimmy Phealan, Gorki's *Decadence* (I confess that this is the first
book of his I have really read). He is brilliant. It is almost a lesson in
novel writing. And a few others. I have a hell of a lot to get through.
And do you know that it does not really take long to get used to
being by yourself. I even enjoy it. I organise my own time and I get
a lot of work done. I have not made friends with anybody here, not
to go out with – though the waitress Rene would go out with me I
know. The Cine group meet once a week and that is sufficient. I
hope. And then I can go and see Della and Ralph when I want to. I
have been pretty low in the past but it passes. And with Olive as
good as completely out of the picture I am pleased to be alone. She,
incidentally, is working for the meanwhile in Woolworth's.

Tonight for instance I am going to see the Norwich Players – the
Maddermarket (one of the oldest amateurs in the country) – their
production of Ibsen's *Ghosts*. And next week is the Annual dinner of
the Cine group which costs ten shillings to attend. I am almost
debating whether to go or not. It costs so much, and with the debts
to pay off my money does not go far. Still.

If you can manage it drop me a line and let me know how you are
daddy. What was the result of hospital tests about your diarreah (I
can never spell that bloody word) . . .

The manager's name was George Taylor, a fatherly and absent-
minded man. When he interviewed me for kitchen porter, the lowest of the kitchen's low, my demeanour confused him. Who was
this young man before him talking with a 'cultured', steady and
confident voice, wanting such a menial job? Two and two was not
making its reassuring four and he felt driven to ask a question
which, had he thought about it, made no sense: 'You're not a student running away from college or anything like that are you?' It
was the only way he could frame his confusion. I reassured him I

was not. Students don't run away from college, college is not an institution which binds. But I knew what he really meant to ask: 'Have you run away from public school?' My image must have appeared to him that of a rebellious rich kid who had escaped from the boarding school in which his wealthy parents had abandoned him. That's the impression I gave, rich and upper class. Though hardly 'abandoned' – no wild-eyed orphan look about *me*. Nor did my clear enunciation sound affected. I'd spoken that way from early childhood. Della spoke with a BBC voice. I picked it up from her. She'd correct my mispronunciations.

'Not "I can't draw a straight lion", Arnold. "I can't draw a straight *line!*" *Line*, not *li-on!*' Shop keepers would ask my mother: 'is he your son? He doesn't sound like your son.'

Mrs Taylor referred to her husband as 'Daddy', presumably continuing the way she spoke of him to their two daughters. Mr and Mrs Taylor were known, to the faintly scathing hotel staff, as 'Mummy and Daddy'. Mr Taylor usually wore grey flannel trousers with a blue blazer and metal buttons – an outfit that would instantly tell all on stage – at other times a brown golfing outfit. His 'best' was a grey suit. Medium height, grey-haired, he never seemed quite sure what was happening, hoping everyone else knew and could be relied upon. A sweet though characterless man who once announced with a weak, guilty smile that he was going to see a famous stripper called Jane – she became a *Daily Mirror* comic strip character – 'with one of the residents!' Just before Christmas I asked if he or the hotel till could lend me five pounds which I promised to return two weeks after the season. I offered him my watch as security. No, no, he couldn't, he couldn't, not with the firm's money, it was more than he would dare, no, no, sorry and all that, but you know how it is . . .

'Mummy' was an officious, domineering little woman who divided people into those with and without money, those with a place on the ladder, those with none. She rarely condescended to answer my 'good mornings'. I puzzled her. Some vague intelligence told her there was more to me than a slicer of spuds. That tone of confidence, I was not supposed to possess it! That air of equality, it was unnatural. It is for staff to air greetings, it is for management to ignore them. She kept her distance, looked right through me, nagged at others but left me alone. With me 'Mummy's' sixth sense sensed fear.

Before Forte took over there used to be staff Christmas parties. That year they ceased, and the Taylors gave us a choice of 3/6d for a Christmas box or we could put a penny towards a packet of twenty cigarettes which cost 3/7d! Nor was any gesture of recognition made of the overtime we all worked. My notes tell me:

> Last night they had a party for R [Rosemary, one of the daughters]. The chef stayed overtime making pies and jellies and so forth. My guess is that it came out of the normal supplies, not out of their pockets. No tip for the chef, as if his labour were taken for granted . . . small class, a small people. Yet we are called by our first names, they are even friendly in their address, but it is the patronising tone . . . I have no doubt that sooner or later I shall come to words with madam.

The pettiness, however, was not oppressive. My attic room was my castle, inviolate. They respected our privacy.

The dining room at the Bell was long and narrow, decor dating back to Edwardian times. Not regal but homely, the kind of atmosphere Trust House, in those days, liked to offer commercial travellers. The building, listed, is now a bank, but if you face its south wall and look up to the top row of small windows my one is still there, on the extreme left. On the extreme right is the window of the room that was soon to be occupied by a living-in waitress who became my wife.

Tom the chef

The large kitchen was set about six feet below ground level. Suppliers came in off the street to descend steps with their deliveries.

Chef was Tom Bullock, his wife, Mary, nick-named 'Boozey', handled the accounts. They fought, and he spent most of his time in his mother's house – of him, soon.

Tom soon realised I had potential for more than mere kitchen-portering and he taught me the rudiments of cooking – roux for sauces, pastry for sweet or meat pies, simple tasks. His skills were not *haute cuisine* though on occasions, for special functions, he rose to heights above the normal, travelling-salesman fare: *poulet au riz*, for example, or a more than basic sherry trifle. Staple menus consisted of roast beef and Yorkshire puddings, grilled chops, roast leg of lamb, roast pork, apple pies, bread and butter puddings, prunes and custard. And so my days in the kitchen were varied – not only scrubbing surfaces and mopping tiled floors, not merely shelling peas and peeling spuds, but whipping eggs for meringue, kneading dough for steak-and-kidney, letting out sauces with stock, stirring and sieving the custard smooth. Later, when Edie the breakfast cook went on holiday, I was trusted to make breakfasts on the upstairs servery facing the swing doors to the dining room.

And I had help. During the fourteen or so months I worked at the Bell there worked alongside me, at different times, two vivid personalities: Gordon and Harry. I can't remember who came first – Gordon, I think; second porters, as it were, to my first, though no such division was ever stated; longevity dictated the pecking orders. Harry was a charming scoundrel who could be relied upon for nothing. His wages were gone within twenty-four hours. For the rest of the week he scrounged. Gordon, dark-haired, short stature, vivacious, witty, very shaky some mornings over the kitchen sink peeling potatoes, often still with make-up smudged over his face, was gay, and earned extra money as a drag artist singing lewdly at a pub near Norwich station called the Blue Room. He possessed a modest talent but his penchant for 'rough trade' kept him earth-bound in a messy life; and although his toughness was of the street-corner kind he was really one of life's victims, craving love and conferring kindness unerringly upon those who then abused him. Of Gordon and Harry, more later.

It was Tom Bullock, the chef, who was the star personality – ebullient, egocentric, self-opinionated, bigoted, good-natured, not deeply interested in others. On first acquaintance his joviality charmed until it became apparent that his bounce and interest in your welfare was more to do with his wish to impress rather than his curiosity about you. He solicited admiration through ostentatious democracy. Hating subservience he was anxious to assure others he demanded none from them. Utter friendliness and informality was what he expected from relationships, and he let it be known from the start. But the informality he invited he soon resented. His hunger for instant affection left him exposed to that hearty, insensitive jollity that quietly degenerates into abuse. He never learned the old lesson about contempt shadowing familiarity; and suffered.

But he *did* bounce, like a young boy, full of pranks and jokes which he loved you loving him for. One way or another he was amusing. And restless. Constantly in motion, a little tap dance here, another there, a swift sidle up to a chambermaid's waist for a cuddle, a pinched bottom, the sort of action to invite stern winces in these confused times uncertain about what is high spirits to delight in, and what is lasciviousness to be shunned. In many workplaces the two go side by side but in those days most of us knew the difference. Men communicated, and women knew when touch was innocent, safety obtained, and affection – even a curious respect – resided in the manner. Tom certainly was courteous if loud – nothing coarse or brutal about him. Except with his wife.

He was never missing from a conversation, his assertive, opinionated tone bullying everyone with incontrovertible facts for – let no one be in any doubt – he knew anybody who was anybody, those who were top in their sphere of activity, their profession. He never knew 'runners-up', only leaders in the field. Richard Tauber was the greatest tenor that ever sang or ever will sing – Tom had not heard of Jussi Björling, but never mind: 'I don't care what you say, he's the greatest there ever was or ever will be.' His ex-boss was at one time the fastest cyclist in the world. American pictures were the best ever produced and he wouldn't give a snap of his fingers for what the British or French or Germans or Russians produced. 'And I'm representative of the man in the street,' he would beat his assertion out on the table round which we sat in the cramped staff room, 'and he's the judge of what's good or not. It's the money they pay that counts, you can't argue with what comes in at the box office.' The argument was old and endless and without resolution. Especially from Tom whose views, like the views of most people, were insistent proclamations of who he felt himself to be rather than reasoned, substantiated arguments. Ephemeral, too. Thrown at one then forgotten.

Not the man, though. The man was full of colour and contradictions, and was remembered, which I suppose is what he most wanted. On the one hand intolerant, on the other – just. A child had been murdered in Scotland, the case hit the headlines. The little woman who delivered the groceries came through the kitchen door, off the street, laden with cheeses and righteous indignation over the tragic event. 'I think,' she said, 'he ought to be put up on a tree where the public can get at him and tear him to pieces, I do! Nothing is too much for them.' To which Tom exploded: 'You're as bad as the murderer himself. A sadist, if you want that.'

Alongside Tom's absolutism was his power of exaggeration. I knew only one other like him – an LAC in the RAF called Paddy who always knew someone to beat your someone, who had done something more often than you had done, who could double what you could drink or eat or smoke or fuck. Or if he couldn't he knew someone who could, or had done, and always had a witness to prove the fact! 'Don't believe me? Write to so and so in Timbuktu, or ask whatshisnameyouknowwhoImean.' That was Tom. But behind the exuberant boy was the unhappily married man.

Mary – Boozey (why did she allow herself to be called Boozey?) was a dark and attractive little woman with a supercilious air, rather like the women in Paris shops whose haughtiness vainly attempts to convey they're made for better things than serving you. Most of the staff disliked her, and Jimmy – the dishwasher Tom had befriended

– told me they quarrelled with hatred and cruelty, while Irene – a chambermaid – called her a bitch and said she gave Tom a dog's life. Tom himself confessed he lived most of the time with his mother, who lived alone – he was a man with a high moral sensibility about the child's duty towards parents. Mary spent most of her time on her own. 'Better like that,' he said, 'avoids the inevitable clashes. Separation like that is a happy married life!' On another occasion he said: 'People think we quarrel, my wife and I. We don't. Not that I care what people think – nothing worries me less . . .' Of course nothing worried him more. That was Tom, full of little dogmas, axes to grind, contradictions, inconsistencies, a full bag of petty human weaknesses. Yet affable, for which you ignored the silly hypocrisies. Except one.

He frequently cried 'Justice!' but failed to defend *our* rights. Because he worked long hours overtime rarely demanding extra pay, he unreasonably expected the same of us. The kitchen was Tom's life. Nothing else engaged his attention except possibly his mother; for the rest of us the kitchen was not our life. He could have done something about overtime pay but remained silent. To which there was a flip side – he didn't nag. Nor chase. He expected of his kitchen staff only what they could do, or what was needed to be done. There was no fear of being told off for burning the cakes, peeling turnips instead of swedes, using up the last of the pears for fruit salad when they were needed for the *Belle-Hélène*. Consequently, there being no atmosphere of fear, little went wrong. When it did, Tom remained calm and efficient. The kitchen functioned smoothly because he knew what had to be done, in what sequence, and how long each action would take. He was moody but never panicked, and I'd only twice seen him in a fury. The first time when a customer asked for a bigger portion of his order (or was it a request for seconds?) and he raged. Tom was righteous about greed. The second occasion was when the apprentice fried the wrong fish. Tom flung them into a corner of the kitchen and swore in torrents. But he was no tyrant and never pulled rank. No little Caesar reigned in the kitchen of the Bell Hotel, which was a relief and blessing, for in those days little Caesars reigned nearly every-where, flaunting petty authority over their two-by-two fiefdoms in murky corners of murky workplaces. What it's like today I have no idea but unchanging human nature being unchanging . . .

At the heart of his restless, sprawling spirit was that old cancer – the inferiority complex. He was aware that intellect could be measured and that the level he respected was beyond his reach. He often floundered out of his depth, competing, hating someone else saying what he felt he ought to have said. He'd mock: 'Yes, yes, quite so, that's right, of course.' In the tranquillity of reflection I think of him more kindly than my notes suggest I experienced him. His loud, insistent bombast must have got on my nerves.

Yet, despite the banter, we liked each other, though violence was only a whisper away. Not between us, between him and his wife, Boozey. My notes continue:

> Tom never appears to go out with his wife. Boozey is a vicious woman; once, apparently, there was a girl, a waitress with whom Tom used to mess around with his usual flippancy. One day she came down into the kitchen to look for Tom, she did not see Boozey sitting in the office. Jimmy Moore saw the girl come down and the next thing was that he heard a crash. The poor waitress was stretched out cold on the floor and Boozey standing over her push-ing her sleeves up. 'Any more to come?' she said, with a sort of madness emanating from her black eyes. But Tom has done his share. One day they were quarrelling in the kitchen.
>
> 'Shut up,' said Tom, 'don't you tell me what to do.'
>
> 'I'll tell you how I please.'
>
> Tom, quick to temper, lifted his clenched fist and whistled her unconscious at the jaw. Her bag fell open on the floor and gaped like a surprised mouth as the money rolled out.
>
> 'And I'll give you more over the road too.'

The first story is obviously one I was told by Jimmy, and recorded. Perhaps a pinch of salt is needed, but not much. The second story seems as though I witnessed it though I can't remember having done so, nor do I know where 'whistled her unconscious' comes from. 'Whistled'? Boozey's face looms more vividly as I retell this, and I see what in innocence I knew nothing about: she was no battered wife. A hard, malevolent beauty shaped the contours of her features, and I have read since of the strange pleasures of sadomasochism.

The last note on Tom rounds off his personality with a familiar pattern. Alongside violent feelings towards his wife was his almost pathetic devotion to animals. The Taylors owned a tiny terrier called Phoebus who spent most of his time in our kitchen where, together with a black cat, Tom fussed over them in the way people do who have nothing else upon which to lavish affection. He would interrupt the most important of conversations in order to greet the dog as it entered the kitchen, nose to the ground, tail wagging with Pavlovian pleasure and anticipation, making straight for him.

'Ah, little manny. Eer's a good dog. You is! A good dog! Wadja say, eh? Oh little manny, little manny.' Tom's most ardently felt boast was how that dog went to him more than anyone else. 'He loves me that dog does.' And he descended into the rituals of overzealous petting while his pretty, hard-faced wife stood by, distantly smiling, used to it all and knowing, no doubt, much that we did not.

Others – Nick

Others hovered in the kitchen: a part-time assistant chef, Jimmy, a roly-poly, timid blubber of a man; the snapping little whippet, Jimmy Moore, who washed up, lived in and complained in the way those with demeaning jobs complain to assert threadbare dignity. He hero-worshipped Tom who looked after him fondly.

'Moore! Come here, Moore, blast you!'

'Yes, Bullock. I'm coming, Bullock.' It had been going on for fourteen years. Tom cared about underdogs.

Albert, another washer-upper, gay and also mother-bound,

attended to afternoon teas and fell passionately in love with me. The more good-humouredly I teased, the more he chased. Edie, the breakfast cook, a gypsy-looking, worn and married woman of lingering sensuousness with whom I think Tom was having an affair. Certainly he was covetous of her. She had a soft spot for me and we flirted – young man older woman. Tom grew jealous but couldn't be too overtly green for fear of revealing true feelings. One day an apprentice chef, Nick, was thrust on him. The boy had a criminal record and apprenticeship was part of his probation. Tom enjoyed this new image of protector, though Nick was thick – sweet but lugubrious. I became his surrogate older brother. Waitresses – Irene, Rene, Dolly, Winnie; an old-time waiter called Bob; and a head waiter, the most lecherous of young men who fucked all the female staff he could pin down in passages, storerooms, on the edge of dining room tables. Somewhere on the East Anglian coast he runs a country house of monstrous decor.

Nick, to whom I played long-lost brother, was a mentality of the type I wasted much time upon. 'Thick' is too easy a word to describe him. It may be distressing to experience limited mental powers but it is not a crime to have been born limited. Put positively, there are those with limited resources of intellect whose company may be infinitely more pleasant than those more generously endowed. Nick was other than that.

The conflict tormenting many of us whose hearts are generous is between a need, a wish, to see all humanity as equally good and sensible, and the experience of much of humanity as stupid and irrational, often cruel. The conflict between wanting everyone to be equal and the everyday experience which manifestly demonstrates that everyone is not equal. It hurts and confuses and leads many to adopt false attitudes, positions. We know that all are born with equal *rights* but this is not the same as declaring that all are born equal. Everyone is aware of this distinction because lives are conducted from morn till night, daily, on that basis: you do not request of people what you know they are incapable of providing; you do not employ those you feel unequal to the job required; you do not

make friends with those you feel intellectually above or below you –
unless you're prepared to be stretched and challenged by those of
greater intellect, or prepared to sacrifice intellectual stimulation for
stimulation of another kind.

My notes record Nick's utterances.

Apart from not liking classical music because it has no tune – but it
makes me think of things, you know, things that have happened or
might happen – it drives me crazy at times . . . It's a wonderful feeling to know you can order people, that someone is under you. The
feeling of power. I only use it over bullies – I hate bullies . . .

He was obviously a young person about whom I cared and who at
the same time I didn't really know how to handle. My notes continued.

. . . I'm sure he cannot understand more than is necessary to keep
him alive . . . yet he is a strange lad. Well intentioned but with the
smallest mind I've ever encountered. There is about him one re-
deeming feature: a sensitivity that confuses him, that he can't
express except through the odd remark. He has a brain one feels was
hit on the head aged four from which he has never recovered. His
sensitivity is manifested through an awareness of all his shortcomings. 'I'm not even as clever as your nephew, Miles – so there!'
[Miles was about six at the time.] Living is something he only just
manages to cope with. 'I don't think – I can't think. My mind is a
blank.' He hates to be alone. He runs after the slightest company if
only for a few minutes in the staff room where the waitresses are
changing, or with me up in my room even though I may be working, just to sit and be with somebody . . .

Interesting that I used the word 'working' instead of 'writing'.
Though not yet a professional I still considered writing to be my
work.

. . . He will sit, do nothing, stare or say a few things of no import at all. I feel as though he is never thinking, merely working out the images that reach his eyes. He will pass a remark on the thing in his hand, on his financial position, on his efforts to stop smoking. His conversation consists of remarks rather than thoughts. He has never deduced an idea for himself, simply seen it written or heard of it. Little is worked out other than what is based upon another's thought – Harry said this or Tom that, or Mr Taylor the other . . . The more I think about him the more pathetic and incredible this boy is. Tall, awkward, feeling for what is good though unable to support his feelings with any mentality.

When he left the Bell I never saw him again.

Irene and Shakespeare

Irene was a tiny, pretty shrimp of a thing who walked shaped like a letter S, her belly forward, coy, awkward; big, sleepy eyes; hair pinned loosely in the mornings but smartly dressed in the evenings. Unsubtle but with a generous heart – 'Don't believe anybody is wicked. There's always a reason . . .' – and a pert sense of humour – 'Oh, I must have a boyfriend – I couldn't do without it!' She was losing patience with her current one.

'Ray, he keeps asking me whether I love him and of course I say yes that I wouldn't go with any other man, just to keep him quiet. Then he asks me *why* I love him. I used to tell him he was different etc. but now he keeps asking I can't answer. I get fed up answering. I don't know why I do love him. Thinking about it – he's forced me to! . . . Habit I suppose. So I change and I tell him well I don't know, Ray, you're no different from anyone else. An' he keep talking about wanting to marry a virgin. Do all men want to? They seem to forget that women would also like men virgin.'

'Do they? Don't women want an experienced man?'

'Well I don't know. Sometimes. Would you want your woman to be virgin?'

'All I'd want is for her to love me. I have few prejudices!'

I took Irene to see a touring production of *The Merchant of Venice* at the Theatre Royal, directed by a man I'd never heard of, a certain Peter Hall, with Shylock played by an actor I came to hear of and subsequently cursed daily – Tony Church, one of the signatories of the letter written on behalf of the RSC actors who refused to perform *The Journalists*. I have no record of what I thought of his performance, I remember only that Irene, knowing nothing about the play, became agitated when it was Bassanio's turn to choose a casket. She gripped my arm with excitement, whispering, 'Will he choose the right one? Will he? Will he?' And was hugely delighted when he did. During the court scene she turned her eyes away when Shylock was about to cut his forfeit from Antonio's breast. It had never occurred to me that anyone could not know the story of Shylock, the merchant, and the pound of flesh. After such a night how could we not make love? My first time in an age. Next morning I leapt around the breakfast servery high on satiated hunger. Thank you, Mr Shakespeare, not you, though, Mr Church!

From the kitchen into The Kitchen

> There is no curtain . . . the kitchen is always there. It is semi-darkness . . . The night porter, MAGI, enters. He stretches, looks at his watch . . . it is seven in the morning . . . with a taper he lights the ovens. Into the first shoots a flame . . . MAX enters . . . then Bertha . . . one by one the waitresses . . .
>
> *The Kitchen* – stage directions

None of these memories found their way into the plays or published stories, but into that trilogy of stories *The Terrible Valley* which, though never published, were important for me. Only one incident found its way into *The Kitchen*. It took place during the first week Edie went on holiday and I was promoted to breakfast cook. Up at 6.30 to make porridge, fry bacon, sausages, and bread – eggs were done upstairs on the spot – and boil kippers all ready to be served by 7.30 from the heated serving cabinets. An empty hotel greeted me, I liked that. Empty except for Jack, the night porter, and Bob the old waiter who was always first there getting the tables ready – last to leave, too; and the one chambermaid who was up and about before the others.

It was a simple routine which I carried out with sleepy eyes, but exhilarating, awake just as everything is about to be set in motion. From the days of the building trade, I have loved early mornings, the slow awakening of life, the one by one, the bit by bit. Light the hot plate, load the dumbwaiter, pull the rope, go up to unload, stack food to keep warm, feel the still room heat up, fry eggs in preparation for the rush. It became hotter as activity increased. The first orders came slowly – the cups and saucers could be washed at an even pace – then with greater speed, heightened intensity, hum building to roar. Breakfast was on! Rhythm! Swing! Sweat! Temperament! Like the slow unfolding of work in the film musical *On the Town* – the first great musical I ever saw – with an opening sequence of dockers coming to work one by one, ending with the troopship bursting into life and spewing its rookies into bustling New York. *On the Town* is what I had believed to be the inspiration for the opening of *The Kitchen*. Not so. Such slow openings began in the kitchen of the Bell Hotel long before I saw the Bernstein musical.

Aside: from the beginning I had this fascination with beginnings! 'Once upon a time, when the world was young . . .' I made an 8mm film of Hill House, called *Morning*, using a camera borrowed from a member of the amateur cine group. A film about beginnings. I forced everyone awake before dawn, climbed a tree to film the sun rising over the horizon, drove Della and Ralph mad making them wake and stretch, lie back again, wake and stretch, lie back again, rehearsing and shooting until I got it right. Adam wakes, Miles wakes, Patch, the dog, jumps awake, breakfast is made, close-up of kettle boiling, milk being poured, bacon frying, Della calling . . .

Beginnings, unfolding, the reasons why, the process of growing, evolving – these things have captured my attention.

Among the first people I served with breakfast were the chambermaids. On the third day, Wednesday, Winnie and Dolly were waiting for their breakfasts. 'Don't give me any bacon, just an egg,' Winnie requested. 'Just do it fried.' She was a big woman, coarse, friendly, gossipy, sluttishly dressed, hair shaggy-grey and always uncombed, top teeth gone. At forty-five she was used, battered, unattractive but oozing with a faintly disgusting sensuousness. I had finished serving three breakfasts of bacon and eggs to Bob before laying out the breakfast for Dolly and Winnie. When I turned to give it to them they had disappeared. There on the counter was their tray of plates and toast and a pot of tea waiting for the eggs and bacon. Imagining them to have forgotten something I put their food away to keep warm, and continued serving the breakfast staff their dining room orders.

Twenty minutes passed, still Winnie and Dolly had not appeared. In the rush I didn't stop to work out what had happened, it didn't seem important. Waiters flew backwards and forwards throwing their orders at me. I ran out of bacon and rushed downstairs to find more. On the stairs the manager, Mr Taylor, passed me. He carried on up and beyond the hot plate and out of the other door, the direction Dolly and Winnie had gone. At the door I heard him pause.

'Hello. Who's been trying to kill themselves? What's this blood here?' I took no notice and continued down the stairs in search of bacon.

The morning's back had been broken, I was clearing up the greasy ruins of the day's first meal, Winnie and Dolly had not returned. When I asked Irene where they were she told me Dolly had taken Winnie home. I asked why.

'Tell you later,' she said in a manner that made me think Winnie had been caught with a bad period. The day's work continued.

It was Dolly who came with the news that Winnie had been rushed to hospital for an operation. She had attempted an abortion and was terribly successful. The baby was delivered amid a mess of blood, a stain from which now lay at the foot of the door near my breakfast counter. Later that day Irene drew me aside.

'I'm frightened,' she said. 'About the tablets.' Jacky had been giving them to her. And to Ann who was two and a half months gone.

'You, Jacky, Annie, and Winnie. How gone was she?'

'Four months.'

'She must be insane. Doesn't she know the facts of life?'

'She should do. She has seven children and been married for about twenty years.'

'Whose child was this?' I asked.

'Some soldier she's friendly with. But what about the tablets? Jacky has given them to me to mind. What if they find them on me?' I offered to hide them but she decided to return them to Jacky.

The news soon spread, and Chef Tom was not slow to enlighten the kitchen staff, because of course he was an authority on everything. His words are those I used in *The Kitchen* after a similar abortion incident is enacted.

Knew this would happen. It can't be done. What makes people think that by taking a tablet through the mouth it will affect the womb? Impossible. There's only one way, the way it went in. What happens? Nothing! Nothing can! All that happens is that the stomach is irritated, squeezed, see. And that forces on the womb, presses it. Oh I know about this all right. Only one drug is effective through the mouth. And you know what that is? Ergot. Heard of it? The only thing can do it. And that's rare. Oh yes, I studied this in the forces when I had nothing else to do. Very interesting this psychology. Complicated. I knew Winnie was pregnant soon as she started here . . .

Of course he did! Loud, vociferous, excited, gesticulating ostentatiously, and dogmatic beyond contradiction. I gave the speech to Max, the butcher in *The Kitchen*. A bigot.

That hotel seemed chosen by God as his playground, for in it things happened nonstop, the world was mirrored: emotional upheavals, psychological states, confrontations ranging from the ridiculous to the pathological. I had difficulty holding on to a sense of normality, in fact I didn't. My feelings ranged from bewilderment to lust, from anger to fascination, from amusement to guilt. The conflicting tensions which animated the assortment of personalities – and I haven't yet described them all – made me wonder whether *I* was the ridiculous, the crazy one.

For really I felt a stranger to it all though I craved to be at one.

I had forgotten those words written in 1954 when I wrote *The Prologue* to this book in 1993.

In such a state everyone I know becomes a stranger. It is a depressing sensation because I want to be here, to belong.

Albert in love

The most absurd situation I found myself in was with Albert whose infatuation was growing beyond a joke, but it was not until lunchtime on the day of blood that I realised how far it had gone. Lunch had been sent up to Tom on the dumbwaiter. Gordon and I – it was roly-poly Jim's day off – were clearing up the kitchen detritus after cooking done. I was preparing to attack the larder with mop and pail. Albert came down from his domain, the still room, and started up the coffee-grinder. Gordon, hovering outside, bounced in suddenly.

'Oh!' he cried. 'Sorry, dear, I didn't know you both were there. Shall I lock you in?'

'I wish you would,' said Albert, casting his insinuating eyes at me, 'nothing I would like more.'

'Do the larder!' I ordered Gordon, throwing the broom at him. 'I'll stick to the kitchen. The man frightens me.' They laughed and mumbled as I hurried away.

Later, Gordon to Albert on his way upstairs:

'Keep on trying, dear, you'll get it in the end.'

'Like hell!' I yelled. Albert disappeared and I collared Gordon. 'Will you stop egging him on.'

'I was only trying to help. Poor girl. You provoke him and then turn a cold shoulder.'

'Me?' I cried. 'That man doesn't need provoking, he's been living on love at first sight ever since he came. Tell me, do I look like a queer?' We laughed it off.

That there were three homosexuals among the staff I worked with, and that this kind of bantering took place, made kitchen life interesting, intense, varied and – odd. I enjoyed them, Gordon and I became friends, but there was a cautious edge to their tolerance. It was tolerance under sufferance. As though there was no alternative. They had to accept the little mockeries in a way I would never have accepted those 'ho-ho' innuendoes about Jews. Nor was I innocent of prissy moments.

'Don't you sense a madness about all this?' I asked Gordon.

'All what?'

'No one here seems normal. There are prostitutes, girls having abortions, unhappy marriages, queers, alcoholics – all here. Doesn't it seem a bit unreal, if you think about it, a bit?' I had not yet learned to accept the pleasures of a motley humanity. The romantic artist in me was drawn, the artist confronting chaos hankered to make order.

I have for a long time accepted the traditional function of art as the creation of order out of chaos. Not of course complete order out of total chaos; chaos is endless and all order is relative, besides. But art as the creation of a tiny corner of order out of a world of chaos, I have believed that. Today I'm not certain. Perhaps it is enough to *describe* the chaos, and the description is a contribution to its ordering, as identifying a problem is half its solution.

Whatever, strange things began happening. I began to write behind my back.

Chapter Eighteen

Writing behind my back

Fourteen months working at the Bell as a kitchen porter – a long time for a young man who till then had been thrashing clumsily in the waters of art. But I was happy working there. For many reasons. I had made a decision about my life which afforded me peace of mind: ambition dismantled! What a relief! The future was a kitchen, my role in life – a chef. Had not cooking always engaged me? Had not some of my most delightful memories been of the Weald Square kitchen, helping my mother with simple tasks, or just sitting on the board which covered the bath, soaking in the smells, the warmth from the oven – a small, cosy space, she and I talking, sharing a sardonic tongue-in-cheek view of life? Here at the Bell was just such a home. No mother of course but – a hotel, an institution! How comforting to be part of an institution where the major decisions are made by someone else and all that was required of me was to fit in, fulfil assigned tasks. I was learning a not unpleasant skill in a city architecturally pleasing for the way it combined new buildings with old. It offered all the arts I could afford: a cinema, the Norvic – screening foreign and classic films; a first-rate amateur theatre company, the Maddermarket; a museum, cobbled old streets, a lively and colourful market, churches, concert and dance hall, and an amateur cine group. Most important were the assortment of characters I worked with in the hotel whose variegated personalities engrossed me.

Here I come to an aspect of those months the most difficult to explain. I had made this momentous decision in my life: to abandon all ambition, to face what I thought an unarguable truth – I was not a writer. A weight lifted. No pretence, no shame, I was a kitchen porter en route to being a chef. Letters home were all I would write. But something happened. It was odd and eerie. A kind of second self rose out from me and seemed to be living another life. I retain this distinct sensation – I was writing behind my own back. It doesn't make sense, but as some people claim they have momentarily died and risen above themselves, able to look down and observe their own life being lived, so I too, having made a decision to write not another word aspiring to literature, seemed to be standing by, watching myself write. I began to make notes for a story. It was to be called 'The Diary of Jon Smith'. Later I wrote another story called 'Hal Scratch,' about Harry the other kitchen porter. Following on from 'Hal Scratch' came a third, about Robbie, an alcoholic waiter. All three were bound into a trilogy of stories under the overall title of the third story – 'The Terrible Valley.' And all were about me working at the Bell Hotel, my encounters with its characters, and – my meeting with Dusty. They were not good enough but I knew, when I had finished writing them, they were the best work I had ever done. A future had been signposted. The ability to develop, to mature, revealed itself. No gold medal yet. Not even a bronze. But with a little more training, thought, discipline, the possibility was there. How curious: having surrendered ambition, having told myself to quit vain dreams of literary fame, I had taken off the weight which lay heavily on the lid of my talent and the gift had sprung out. Or so it seemed to me at the time. Even before writing it I must have felt elative intimations for I wrote to my mother high and pregnant with something:

. . . I don't know, but I am beginning to feel that maybe I will get somewhere. I can't believe that I am barking up the wrong tree all the time. I must have something to offer . . . Something makes me go on, it is not conceit or insanity, it will happen, there will be a result. It needs so much patience and courage . . . Like love, the ways of creation are rarely smooth, or straight forward. I have a vision and aspirations, if I am wrong then I am mad, and nothing can be done about that.

'The Diary of Jon Smith' – extracts

July 3rd 1954

I am calm.

That is my first entry. Simply three words, solitary, on their own. There must be many such groups of three words which, on their own, contain a world of meaning.

I love you.

I hate you.

I need you.

I am calm . . . Perhaps that is why I begin. Once before I started a diary. It lasted six weeks and held a dozen entries. Experience makes me sceptical as to the likely length of this present one; but whether I make another entry or not is of no real consequence; that I feel like making one this evening, that I have even wished to do so and am now so doing is enough. I am unconcerned about the future and that is my calm . . .

. . . I have lost ambition, I have no desire to produce great works of art, no desire to be more than what I am. With ambition goes vanity, that is the real calm. I have rid myself of the vanity of ambition, and this means: I expect nothing of myself and no one else will expect anything of me either. I am free to be nothing. It is contentment absolute . . .

. . . I look back at the letter I thankfully did not send to O. At the poems, the stories. I cannot believe the madness of those days, the nightmare of having failed to hold her. She had not loved me. *She* had not loved *me*. Me, all that I imagined I was. And now that I know she did not I realise that my love was a vanity; my ambition, my art was a pretence. Aspirations to genius reduced themselves to human roots. I am made very human. That is all.

But now that it is passed I am happy. She comes in to see me, we are friends. She is satisfied with her engagement and I have developed a sort of detached, pleasant cynicism. The effort to be true lovers has become the effort to be real friends; it is as difficult.

The nature of my contentment is not in any way a despair. I enjoy working here, I feel very much down to earth; having lost some vanity I have suppressed my personality to be free to observe and understand the people around. Because *I* simply do not matter any longer everyone else comes into focus. Do they call this maturity I wonder? Having seen through and forgiven myself I can now understand and sympathise with the people around me. Sympathy means tolerance. I think they like me, they may even respect me. I have never worked in a place where I was so satisfied.

I do not object to the late hours nor dread the morning. Time flies and work as a kitchen porter is pleasant. I can remain alone. I am tied to no one, can disappoint no one, and no one is beside me to make demands of either my personality or my time. I can refuse the invitation to go out for a drink, I can read at my leisure knowing I am reading simply to please myself or increase my knowledge for none other than its own sake. I have solitude to contemplate.

When A spoke of being alone I could not appreciate what he meant. I always wanted to share my experiences. Share! I have changed. Once I wanted to be part of all groups and now – I wish to avoid any group at all. There is no one to pretend to, no one to impress. And it is strange, keeping to myself I am not in the least introspective. Quite the reverse. Ah well, there are no rules.

This is one of the first things I understand in maturity. And another, for the records: there is less in you than you imagine and far more than anyone else believes. But even that is a rule. I wonder if I shall ever become a platitudinous old sod!

Calmness, detachment, contemplation, and solitude.

I am enjoying writing this, I could go on for hours but I know I must not work my enthusiasm out, besides it is so late. We had a party of sixty tonight.

My current state of mind here in these hills first took shape in those days of the Bell Hotel. *'I can remain alone. I am tied to no one, can disappoint no one, and no one is beside me to make demands of either my personality or my time.'* It was this emotional state into which Dusty sunnily burst one day out of the dining room, gaily hurling breakfast orders at me for the hotel guests at her tables. But not yet.

Monday July 5th

Have just returned from seeing *Bicycle Thieves*. I would like to comment but am content instead with having seen.

I come back again, look around my room, think: what shall I do? I can read, answer some letters, listen to the radio – but of course I am eager to continue this diary . . .

. . . Jock is leaving next week. I wonder what the new kitchen porter will be like. One of the fascinations of hotel life is the people who seem to wander in and out, vaguely, like nobody's shadow. I think Irene will leave too.

Pathetic girl. She moves about with a vitality that one cannot believe in. Behind that caked, made-up grin there is a bitter unhappiness, and her ebullience is a manifestation of a despair. She has a baby boy she does not really want, a beautiful, blue-eyed bastard by a faraway American soldier. She has been pushed around from lodging to lodging. When she had Paul her sister drove her from the house. She took rooms with a woman whose daughter had cancer. Irene, the baby and daughter shared the same room. Then she rented another flat where the landlady took most of her wages in rent. Then on to another place where the husband had TB. Finally her sister took her back. With her sister lives their father, their brother, another sister, four children and the husband. That baby must go through hell. Irene professes a love for the child but I can see she feels it is a burden. She is always fed up. I feel like screaming she tells me with that mask of a grin. I feel like getting drunk. And she does. Too many times. What must happen to a girl like that in the end? She is only twenty-one. I am not sure who is the more tragically situated, she or the child. But the hall porter's wife has offered to look after Paul while Irene goes to the coast to work.

Must return to my reading. Am in the middle of Eisenstein's *Film Sense*. What a lot of books I have lined up to read: from Schweitzer to *Industrial Art*. Suddenly I realise the fantastic amount of knowledge that exists . . .

Thursday July 8th

'Mummy' asked the apprentice and me to wash some walls down this afternoon; we consented – at 2/- an hour – and spent two hours in the still room with bucket, soda, soap flakes and sugar soap. It was like a scene from *Alice in Wonderland*. She persisted in hanging around watching over us and ordered that we start from the bottom and work upwards! No amount of arguing would convince her that this was the wrong procedure. I've organised this sort of thing before, she told us. I told her that I had *worked* in the trade. Well, she retorted, it was considered that *I* was able to do the supervising and I know that you wash walls down from the bottom upwards. She thought me quite rude when I suggested that would be washing walls up! So we had to do as she said and I felt ridiculous.

. . . Jimmy is upset again. He is a strange little man, pathetic really. What is it to be like him? I try to project myself into his position. A tiny, anaemic little dishwasher who has washed dishes in the hotel for fourteen years. He is not a bitter man, not as he might be. He is obliging, merry, embarrassingly unfunny at times. Yet there are moments when he becomes acutely aware of his position, aware that he is disintegrating, aware of the dishes, of the pots and pans, of his ruptured walk and his diminutive body, of his utter sexlessness and the waste of years. And then he revolts, he picks a quarrel with anyone who is near at hand starting, as he always does, with the familiar phrase – you'll be doing this job next week, I'm leaving. Jimmy is leaving once a month. I shudder at his helpless dependence. At forty he has no home but the attic room next to mine. I think I am the one person he cannot quarrel with. I simply give in to him and do my best to make him forget who he is and where.

I cannot quarrel with anyone in this hotel. I refuse to. It is so easy to argue over the many petty issues people are prepared to bring up. There is no level here at which I *could* fall out! I remain detached. One of the staff tells me that my tolerance is a sort of myth – no one can pick a row with Smithy! And about what? Staff breakfasts, a missing tea-cloth, the football results, someone else's clothes! A strange crowd.

Perhaps that is why I remain content. I am part of them and yet I am not. I do not let myself become involved. It is a subtle game.

Forgive me, Kingsley, I don't compete – an aside

My lack of competitiveness, it is recorded here in the Jon Smith diaries. I don't compete, I don't quarrel, *'my tolerance is a sort of myth – no one can pick a row with Smithy'*.

I am reminded of Kingsley Amis's *Memoirs* in which he un-pleasantly recounts three encounters with me. The first was when, having read his none too complimentary articles on the Trilogy – which he had read and not seen – I invited him and his then wife, Elizabeth Jane Howard, to attend a performance of *Their Very Own and Golden City*, joining us for dinner afterwards at Bishops Road. Having admired *Lucky Jim* I wanted Kingsley to warm to some-thing of my work. I felt he had carelessly lumped me into a facile 'left-wing' category through which distorting prism he was mis-perceiving the plays. He and Jane accepted the invitation but remained unimpressed.

> The curtain rose. In my charitable way I had been secretly a little worried lest the play should turn out, against all the odds, to be some good, but the first few minutes put my mind firmly at rest about that.

It is of course gratifying not to disappoint colleagues but his tone bewilders me. He is a writer of some achievement, why this need to play to the gallery? How could he possibly know from the first moments what the play was about? 'The dialogue preserved in full that air of being hastily translated from some other tongue.' Nice turn of phrase that he had used in a review and obviously didn't want to lose in ephemeral newsprint. Did it *really* apply to my dialogue? He then attempts – and fails – to remember the theme. It's about compromise, and the sad difference between dreams of youth and realities of age. An old and honourable theme. Kinglsey invents the play's narrative, misnames Andy and Jessie, calling

them Gerald and Brenda – or was it deliberate, imagining Gerald
and Brenda to be derisory in that curious English tradition of laughing at names considered comic like Gerald, Bognor Regis,
Tunbridge Wells, Vladivostock. His little memoir is splattered with
hedging-bet phrases: 'it was some question like . . .', 'he said something like . . .', 'well, that was roughly what she said'. He claims: 'I
greatly took to Dusty' but later attempts to diminish her by reporting she had misused a word while telling someone 'The
Wesker holiday to Andalusia by train would be comfortable enough
because they had reserved courgettes . . .' I can imagine Dusty trying to utter the word 'couchette' with a French accent in such a way
that it came out sounding like 'courgette', but why should Kingsley
have wanted to shame a woman he 'greatly took to'?

We met again at a mutual friend's house where we played cha-
rades and I appalled Kingsley by not remembering which
Shakespeare play 'Oh what a rogue and peasant slave' came from. I
don't recall such a failure of memory but knowing how easily even a
friend's name slips from my head when I have to introduce them in
company, Kingsley could be right.

We were brought together on a third occasion by Penguin Books
to meet Japanese teachers of English. Kingsley remembers me 'now
wearing his hair down to his shoulders'. I once *did* wear hair down
to my shoulders but not then. Before me are the photographs taken
of the event. A mass of hair clusters round my neck – and what
wouldn't I give for that cluster back again, and those days, too – but
nothing reached my shoulders. Kingsley accuses me of talking for
forty minutes instead of ten – very unlikely since I become hugely
embarrassed at the thought of exceeding my time. No matter. His
memoirs record those three encounters with that peculiar brand of
English whippet nastiness parading as the truth of things. They
also contain a passage pointing to that absence of competitiveness
in my character that obviously distresses people. It certainly distressed Jane who, I fear, may have an aversion to hairy chests: those
photos of the Penguin event reveal I perhaps revealed an undone

button too much. In all fairness to Kingsley he attempts to be charitable and gracious but weakly succumbs to the insidious whisperings of his Lady Macbeth – a woman I'd met on a few occasions and had thought to be on amicable terms with; she came as a guest to this cottage on the occasion of Tom Maschler's marriage to Fay, a feast which Dusty and I cooked. I now understand her dark glances to have been a sly hatred of me. Strange these hatreds people form without really knowing us – though perhaps were they to know us better the hatred would run deeper!

> A few minutes into the food, feeling that someone had to start somewhere, I said, 'Arnold, I'm afraid I didn't like it.'
> 'Well, I didn't expect you to,' he said with a smile, rather negating the message of his letter. 'What didn't you like about it?'
> A full list of the attributes of any and every play was what I should have given him, but after a few lies about having thought the character of the old trade unionist was well done, I told him, 'I don't know anything about architects, but surely the first things they go on about are how much money they can spend, the position about water, practical stuff, not about it going to be a city for the young and for the old and, er, and things of that sort.'
> Before I had finished he was laughing and shaking his head. 'The trouble with you, Kingsley,' he said amicably, 'is that you don't know anything about the theatre. I tried it the way you're talking about, in fact I took six numbers of the *Architectural Review* to check, but it just didn't work *dramatically* like that.'

I don't remember reading the *Architectural Review* but I do remember reading the biographies of Mies van Der Rohe and Frank Lloyd Wright and books on the history of architecture and on town planning; and that I gave an original draft of the play to the eminent town planner, Graham Shankland, who advised me against just the kind of detail Kingsley was suggesting I should have used.

> It went on for a good half-hour, probably more, with [Frank] Marcus [theatre critic] coming in on my side with different arguments, me getting a bit heated, Dusty looking more anxious, and Arnold

altogether unshaken, in fact cool as a cucumber, rather disappointed of course with me and the others that we had kept missing his point, at no juncture taking the smallest offence.

'Pretty impressive, you have to admit,' I said to Jane as, in *New Yorker* style, we drove home discussing the party. 'I said some things back there that would have got me not far from throwing me out of my house, and he just sat there and took it all on the chin.'

'Impressive in what way?' [said Lady Macbeth]

'Well, for tolerance. Good temper. Grown-upness.'

'You're wrong. It was conceit. He's so sure he's marvellous that it wouldn't matter what anybody in the world said to him.'

'Not even someone he really respected?'

'He wouldn't respect anyone who didn't think he was marvellous.'

Well, that was roughly what she said.

Roughly or not it was a silly thing for the lady to have said. I respect all sorts of people who don't think I'm marvellous. Myself, for example. Nevertheless the careful lady had seen something. Not 'it wouldn't matter what anybody in the world said to him' – it so obviously does matter, I constantly feel hurt. But somewhere in me – despite all that goes wrong, all the failures, the incredibly foolish mistakes made emotionally, professionally, and with my craft – nevertheless a quiet core of confidence resides. It was there from the beginning. It had nothing to do with self-esteem but with a sense of balance between strengths and weaknesses, between my talent and its limitations. I seemed to know who and what I was and was not. No need to compete. That's what Elizabeth Jane Howard saw and, apparently ill-equipped to perceive at any level but that of the sour literary fringe, misread. Kingsley didn't like my writing – so what? I laughed helplessly at *Lucky Jim*, full of admiration for what I thought was a shared contempt for humbug, and I would have been proud to earn his respect. It wasn't to be. We were very different animals, it seemed. He wasn't Jewish for a start and, though, no doubt, some of his best friends were Jews, I must have given out a literary smell that curled his poor nostrils. Pity. But Tolstoy is reported not to have admired Dostoevsky, Benjamin Britten couldn't stand the music of William Walton, Thomas Carlyle dismissed Charles Lamb, Virginia Woolf was not crazy about James Joyce, Arnold Bennett considered Shaw incompetent, Blake declared Titian an idiot, Tchaikovsky called Brahms a scoundrel, Zola despaired of Cézanne, Monet of Renoir, Degas of Lautrec . . . We must live with such disappointments. I just wish Kingsley hadn't smudged his eminence amusing the baby whippets who prance and yap with glee at the feet of smug wags.

'The Diary of Jon Smith' – continued

July 24th 1954
At last I have been to the Blue Room. Gordon took me there this evening. A most irrelevant name for this public house, unless it be to describe the dense smoke that hangs in a sort of blue twilight on everyone's shoulder. The walls are a dirty, dull orange, greasy with so much breath and sweat.

The Blue Room commands an excellent position, just by the river. Outside, leaning over the bridge and huddled in the doorway, American servicemen in their easy, light-coloured clothes were talking to young women and girls dressed in tasteless costumes, sweaters and jeans; girls made up without care and smelling very strongly of too much scent. Gordon waved an airy hand at them, stepped on the last light of his cigarette and gaily entered like one about to face his audience. We pushed our way past crowds of service men and women into the thick atmosphere of talk and smoke. A soberly dressed woman of about forty-eight with one arm stopped us first. Gordon greeted her.

'Hello, Mary.'

'Hello, dear.' She sounded a little weary and indicated the crowd. 'Full again,' she said. Her Cockney dialect was familiar and I felt at home at once. Gordon introduced us and bought the first round of drinks.

We had not been standing long before a chant came up from a group of people sitting near the piano. WE WANT GORDON! WE WANT GORDON! WE WANT GORDON!

'You're in demand,' I shouted above the general din. I was in for a surprise for I had not guessed that he sang in public. He smiled and yelled for them to 'Bloody well wait till I've finished me drink!' Then, aside to me: 'My public!' Moving with deliberate slowness he laid his drink gently on the counter and then walked cheekily to the piano.

The moment he mounted the stage and took off his jacket there came a loud, raucous mixture of cheers, applause and whistles. The motley faces glaring bleary and weary-eyed would have daunted and silenced the best of singers. Gordon, though not being the best of singers, is nevertheless a performer. He stood a moment and glared at them, then he took off his blue tie, opened the collar of his black shirt, pulled up the cuffs of his sleeves and, confronting them like a Dietrich who expected any minute to see the establishment go up in flames because of her impact, began.

'Walk with baby she's got big feet. Tall and little lanky had nothing to eat but she's ma baby! (grunt) Love her just the same. Crazy 'bout that woman (grunt) 'cos Calidonia is her na – ame. Cal – donya! Cal – donya! WHAT MAKES YOUR BIG FEET SO HARD AAAAAAAAAAAAAAAAAAH!'

His voice was harsh and steel-pitched, like the scream it had to be above the voices of the many others who either talked, catcalled or sang in groups by themselves. His rendering was slow and clumsy but the sway of his hips, the twisting of his fingers towards the audience, the sweep of his scintillating eyes and the intrinsic rhythm of his voice amended for the failings in its qualities. He sang to everyone, looked at them, threw his personality at them and thrived on the gaze in their eyes, heedless as to their scorn, amusement or admiration. He seemed part of them, a figurehead.

Gordon finished amid the thunderous cacophony of shouts, whistles, comments and applause. Beads of perspiration on his fore-head trickled down his nostrils as he stepped down and introduced me to his own circle.

There was Anne, Marge, and their landlady, Beryl. Anne was slight, thin with long blonde hair. She had blue eyes, pale skin and her hair hung straight and plain, save for a slight wave to the front; she wore a man's red striped T-shirt with a light green windjammer over it. Her legs, that which showed beneath her short, blue jeans, were spindly. She hung closely to a young good-looking American in civilian clothes and sipped her gin. Marge was the more attractive of the three. An oval-shaped face, soft grey eyes and full lips, a fuller body too. She also had long hair, tidier than Anne's, which fell slightly over her face in the outdated style of Veronica Lake. She wore, in this smoke and heat, a coat buttoned at the neck and sat up erect and dignified, held her American's hand to her own and with the other sipped gin and smoked, alternately. Beryl who might have been the mother of them both and who was nearly the age of her two young lodgers combined was small, slight, with short, untidy, too obviously peroxide hair, and diminituve features, the most apparent a snub nose! One of her brown eyes was bloodshot, apparently from sticking a hair pin in it! She too wore a coat, unbuttoned and somewhat beer-stained. Her appearance was untidy, as though she had just rushed out from a house of chores. And she too hung on to and giggled with a short, gaudily dressed American with a scarred face, and sipped gin.

'Hey Gordon honey,' Anne cried to him. 'Give us "Gypsy Rose Lee" will ya?'

'Yeah, yeah, wait a minute, let me catch my breath,' he replied. Some soldiers from a parachute regiment sat near by. Apparently they had been coming down here for the last few nights and were friendly with Gordon. One of them pulled him down to his knee.

'Come and sit with me, Gordon, you haven't even said hello.' Gordon titterd a little exclamation of surprise.

'Darling! Please! Not in company. Have a little patience,' and flashing his black eyes he patted the soldier on the cheek and wriggled out of his grasp. Later he confided in me that this particular soldier had asked him to come home to live with him in Manchester. 'He's only got his mother and he's a lovely boy, so sweet and kind. I don't know what to do with him. Bought me all those drinks the other night and pleaded with me. I'd like to go. I don't know what to tell him. And he wants an answer because he's going back in a few days' time.'

The crowd had by now taken up the general demand for 'Gypsy Rose Lee' and unable to refuse them any longer Gordon returned to the stage leaving me to mind his drink. Pushing up the cuffs of his sleeves he lapsed on one hip, raised his bended arms to the level of his chest, sensuously arranged his fingers and commenced to recite, with appropriate gesture and glance, 'Gypsy Rose Lee'.

'I'm Gypsy Rose Lee, I'm the queen of them all. I strip for a living, but that isn't all. My body is lovely, though I don't wanna boast, I'm the pride of the nation, I'm the national toast. So girls watch your husbands, and keep their eyes off me, 'cos I do strange movements, with my – anatomy. I twist and I bend, I swirl and I sway, but if you wannit, ya gotta buy it, 'cos I ain't givin' nothin' away!' By this time the seething mass of people which had over-whelmed me when I first entered gradually came into focus. I could discern distinct groups standing in various corners. Gathered in an elegant set by the juke box were the Teddy Boys. Immaculate young men in the latest and most daring revival of Edwardian-cut suits. Were it not for the thick crêpe-soled shoes upon which they slowly revolved to the bop rhythms of the latest 'creep' record, and the un-dignified look of self-conscious bravado on their faces one would imagine that such a company was Oscar Wilde's. But these are Edwardians without the grace and wit of the time.

Elsewhere were American soldiers hanging on to girls who were unsuccessfully trying to appear uninterested. Scattered here and there, standing or sitting, were men and women in twos and threes who were eyeing each other and giggling. Everyone was high. Through the blue smoke, the haze and thickness of speech, the rooms seemed to rock. As I stared at them all very hard, observing each movement and glance, I was aware of the rocking; perhaps it was the quickness of my eye travelling around the bar, eager to see everything. Perhaps the drink was having an effect on me. Certainly I had caught the merriment of the place. I grinned at everyone and spoke with them as though I had known them a long time. It is easy to feel part of the Blue Room.

Gordon was called upon to sing again and again and when he did not sing solo he led the company in all the latest songs. And as we sang the excitement and noise grew. The drink swelled in my head. The singing became boozy and disintegrated among small rival groups trying to outsing each other, so that soon the air thundered with shouting.

Then suddenly Annie came to life.

'Hey! Where's my man?' she cried. 'He hasn't come back yet. He went to spend some coppers. Where's my Johnny?' She turned to one of the other Americans slobbering over Beryl.

'I ain't seen him,' he replied.

'He's gone for a piss,' said another.

'He ain't gone for no piss,' she said a little sadly. 'Hell! I been stood up.'

'Say, Annie,' Marge whispered. 'Didn't I warn you he was gettin' tired? I told you, but you kept nagging – Jesus, Annie!'

Annie then let out a torrent of abuse, a minor peroration on the merits and demerits of the members of the United States Forces who were stationed in Britain. The remaining Americans appeared to be unperturbed as though their experience attributed this hysteric outburst to an excess of gin.

'Aw gee, honey,' one commiserated, 'don't get sore. We'll find you some other guy. A regular guy.' And true to his word the one whose name was Hank disappeared and soon returned with a rather oversized, not too sober, pimple-faced companion.

'This is Butch. Butch this is Annie.' Annie looked at him a second, smiled sweetly, she had a rather exquisite smile becoming her fragile-featured face, and said: 'You'll do, brother.' Then turning to me, as if by way of excusing her promiscuity, she added: 'I gotta have someone to keep the bed warm!' It seemed perfectly reasonable. The American thought so too.

'Sure I'll do, sister,' he grinned. I heard Marge, who was nearest to me, whisper to her companion.

'Who is this guy you found for Annie?'

'I don't know. I ain't never seen him before. What's the matter, he no good?'

'Yeah,' replied Marge, 'yeah, sure, he'll do.'

The last drinks were called for and with much raving the chaos unravelled itself leaving the bar deserted. At the door the girls carted their men away and Gordon and I made our way to Eve's, a snack bar near the cathedral which was open till midnight and where they sold hamburgers, hot dogs and coffee. The soldiers accompanied us part of the way and then, as I stood some discreet yards away, Gordon bade his 'affair' a fond farewell, for the soldier would not be able to come into the city again. Some minutes later, sitting with cups of coffee in our hands in the overfull snack bar, I watched tears course down Gordon's face as he sat, staring in the distance thinking of his lost love.

I suppose this could be termed the underworld part of the city. It is the closest I have ever been to a prostitute. Curious, that after six months of living here I have only just come across this quarter.

Tuesday July 27th

Gordon has been relating the history of everyone we met in the Blue Room. Nearly all the women have one or two babies being looked after by somebody or some organisation. Half are married, either to husbands who have deserted them or do not care any longer. Most have had gonorrhoea at some time or other and Annie told Gordon on Sunday night that she picked up 'crabs' from a sailor. I was not sure what crabs were but I did not ask him. According to J.B. they are pubic lice.

I am tempted to write again. All day I have been evolving a story. How like a disease writing is, and what better material could I want . . .

The new waitress started yesterday. Have not had much contact with her. Chef passed his usual early judgement.

'Can see what she is, flinging herself about in the dining room!'

Dusty is about to burst on the scene. But not yet.

The Blue Room didn't always buzz and Gordon wasn't always high.

Went down to the Blue Room. Gordon was there. It was quite empty. No singing. He was on his own. For the first time I see him as a lonely man. Deprived of his audience, his soldiers, he sat on a stool sipping a light ale, his pale face was powdered and old. His shoulders sagged, his features drooped, his red corduroy jacket was beer-stained, how will he finish? I cannot help feeling that he does not want this. I seem to see in his eyes a distaste for it all, as if he had made a mistake. As he looked around the deserted bar he seemed to wonder what he was doing there . . .

'The Diary of Jon Smith' autobiographically records days at the Bell, including my relationship with Dusty – called Dee – from the beginning. It is written up as fiction, an 'invented diary', but my powers of imaginative invention being notoriously scant there is no reason to doubt the 'diary' accurately records the way our relationship evolved.

The denouement of the narrative of *The Diary of Jon Smith* is absurd, melodramatic, but its central point, simple and obvious, has remained pivotal to much that my writing strives to convey. The 'diary' was to paint a picture of the Bell Hotel; trace the burgeoning relationship between 'Jon Smith' and the new, eighteen-year-old waitress called Dee; establish the atmosphere within which the other two stories could exist; and finally to chart the transformation from a state of calm insouciance to a state of agitated distress. The prose attempts to echo the distress. Having begun with no contractions, an evenly paced-out prose, the structure becomes choppy, pronouns contract. Such careful finesse of style didn't help. The story ends heavily, wood upon wood. But though the *manifestation* of the distress is melodramatic; the *cause* has validity. I'll explain.

Jon Smith, alias A.W., finds himself a kitchen porter in a hotel full of characters with whom he imagines he can exist in a state of detachment. Smithy wanted to write. His calm derives from surrendering literary ambition in the belief that he has no talent nor anything to write about. (Bizarre, really: writing behind my back about a young man writing behind his back.) A vivacious country girl enters his life, falls in love with him. He resists her, feeling, as with literature, he has nothing to offer. But the characters in the hotel with their failed, impoverished lives, both agitate his calm and stir his creative juices, and the country girl begins to get under his skin. His equanimity is stormed, rocked, shaken. Through the storm shapes an image of life that fills him with despair: second best. Everyone's dream of a beautiful life cracks under pressure, driving them to choose second best. The triumphant outrage of Beatie Bryant in *Roots* has its seeds in this diary.

> . . . The whole stinkin' commercial world insults us and we don't care a damn. Well Ronnie's right – it's our own bloody fault. We want the third rate we got it!

While in the Bell Hotel, as the diary reveals, I contracted 'crabs', pubic lice. I had never heard of the damn creatures before and persuaded myself they had jumped up at me in the lavatory! The discovery shocked and disgusted. I tried to get rid of them by shaving and bathing in Dettol but finally had to face an embarrassing appointment with a doctor who helped by treating it as an everyday event, which it probably was, and prescribed an ointment. But the fearsome things added significance, they drew events together and became a symbol of 'second best'. Jon Smith writes in his diary:

> . . . This infection has made me think again about the Blue Room and a story. I have decided. It is no good taking pen to paper and declaiming the iniquity of human beings, on the other hand it is mere journalism to observe. There is nothing clever in reporting life, and something more than sympathy has to hold a story together.
>
> So I have evolved an attitude. Oddly enough it ties up with that discordance I had with the chef. In fact it fits in beautifully with everything around me. It is this: their living is second best. Almost everything they do from choosing a costume to a man is the acceptance of second best. Somewhere in their lives they have lost the ability to decide, the inclination to seek for that which is most satisfying. Let Anne, Marge and Beryl walk the streets, sell their sex if that is what they want, but let them dress well. If their body is their living let it also be their pride, retain a dignity about that. As it is they don't care. These are not so much fallen angels as apathetic children. They have a sublime indifference . . .

I resist rewriting that passage, though God knows I yearn for a more precise language and itch for the chance to rephrase, certainly rethink, some of the views expressed. However, a valid, central view is identified: that of human misery resulting from apathy, lives mangled from misjudged choices. It informs plays like *The Kitchen, Roots, Their Very Own and Golden City* and much else. For this reason I've spent so much time describing and quoting from it.

Before the days of Dusty begin there are two remaining Bell hotel characters to describe: one a kitchen porter, the other a waiter.

411

Harry is the subject of the middle story – 'Hal Scratch'. Robbie is central to the last story – 'The Terrible Valley'. Both attached themselves to me and were drunks living in fantasy worlds of inebriation. Not so much 'stories' as portraits of personalities. I had forgotten them until I raided these stories in search of life at the Bell.

Hal Scratch

Harry joined the Bell as a kitchen porter a year into my time there. I fell in a blink for his northern, yarn-spinning charm – young innocent for mature rogue. He'd been in the army, returned home to find his wife had deceived him, had hit the lover and abandoned the traitress. He claimed to have played professional football for Stockton, and to have worked thirteen years as a cloth dyer in a large factory. I was never certain of anything he said, though, true or false, he seemed able to distinguish between one weave of cloth and another. Before starting at the Bell he had been on the road, he said, for months, working here and there, sleeping in 'spikes' – reception centres.

It was the second day after Christmas, the fervent taste of goodwill still lingered in our mouths. I was at the furthest end of the kitchen, one foot up on the table, peeling the last sprout. The manager walked in with him at the other end, through the tradesmen's entrance, and introduced him to the chef.

'Hasn't done any kitchen work before.'

'Soon pick it up. Nothing to it. Smithy down there'll show you what to do.'

I put down the knife and waited as he came up. 'They call me Smithy, I don't want to call you Oi!'

'Well, 'Arry'll do.' He was from the north country.

'I suppose you can help me with the cabbage, here, like this.'

Harry made a quiet entry, having that quality of softly arriving. He wore no overcoat, simply a neat though ancient grey tweed suit, a shirt and tie. I could see through the gap made by a missing button on his shirt that he wore no vest. The winter was at its bleakest heights. He was quick, and by the time the morning was done I could see that he was adaptable.

A humble appearance was exaggerated by a fit of shivering which shook him quietly from the time he came in – just after breakfast, till the end of lunch. I watched him closely. The trembling hands cutting up the cabbage, the uncertain words from quivering lips, and a twitching face as if he were frightened of losing this too-good-to-be-true job. I did all I could to put him at his ease. I joked, made light of the work, introduced him to the rest of the staff. Then I offered him a cigarette and could tell, by the way he accepted, not overanxiously, but with a grateful dignity, that he was penniless. I went out and bought him a packet.

The morning soon passed, he shivered throughout. The food was sent up to the hot plate and he and I were left alone to clear away the debris of the morning's cooking. Then we chatted in earnest . . .

. . . I loaned him five shillings and a clean shirt. As the food came down I said cheerily:

'Well, I suppose you must be quite peckish now.'

'Ay, I am a bit,' he smiled coyly.

'What did you have for breakfast?'

'I didn't.'

'You didn't?' He seemed flattered at my concerned surprise. 'When did you last eat then?'

''Bout two days ago!'

'No Christmas dinner?'

'No Christmas dinner.'

I passed the word on to Chef and he put extra helpings on to Harry's plate. The agitation in his movements relaxed.

But if Harry was not quite fit when he first came to work with us it was not many days, with regular food, before he regained his strength.

The first Saturday evening he was off he went out to sort the city into shape, find his bearings as it were. His bearings, I later discovered, steered him a direct course from friendly public house to friendlier public house. He returned that first evening and came straight to my room, he had been drinking. The tale tumbled out and the evening's outing was told.

One of Harry's greatest assets it appeared was an ability to throw

413

a straight dart. This skill was a sort of passport to rounds of drinks and the pleasures of unlimited friends. He had strayed into one of the numerous public houses in the cathedral city – 'Said 'ow d'yer do t'landlord and ordered me drink. It were a small pub – forget the name – cosy like; and in the corner they were playing darts. I watched a while, said nothing, drank me beer, bought another, drank that, had a couple of pints – you know – chatted with one or two of the regulars, they said, "Yer new round here?" I said, "Ay," and told them where I worked, where I came from. And then they asked me for a game. I didn't like to, being new, I didn't know what they were like, see. Anyway I said, "Ay, I'll have a run round the board." . . . His grin, his eyes, the smoke coming out of his nose, the delight he took in telling me – 'Well, you should 'ave seen them. All round me. Begged me to join their team, bought me drinks, called me 'Arry. Had a grand time!'

The following Saturday was the same. He returned, slightly more intoxicated, made himself at home in my room and told me what he had been doing.

'Found a lovely lass. In't pub over the road. "Back's". The barman pointed her out after I'd treated him to a drink. "If she likes you you're in," he said. So I walked up, introduced myself and we were well away. Took 'er racing. Ay. Went racing and lost fourteen bob. Got two and a tanner left, but I 'ad a lovely time. She took me to her home. You should have seen it. Spotless. And the daughter. Eh, lad. She's just for you. I told her about you, wants to meet you. Well, anyway, I got rid of some dirty water. That's the main thing. A man's got to get rid o' the dirty water on his chest.' He rubbed his chest. 'It's all this rich food you know. And she's a clean woman, straight up, she's not a bloody old prostitute, she's – well – she's a *respectable* whore.'

No consistency in the writing of the dialect, and again I've had to resist pruning and honing, but coming across these pages re-evokes so much: I can *see* Harry, vividly, standing by me at the sink with that button missing on his shirt and his weak, undernourished, helpless smile. I would have remembered none of this. It was the beginning of a friendship that rose swiftly in intensity and as swiftly declined. The loving rise, and the ugly, messy decline captured my imagination. This portrait of a weak no-goodnik, as I think about it, with his charming limp nature and empty promises of good deeds which frothed like the beer he couldn't resist, resembled my father. The portrait fails because although Smithy, who is writing it, is aware of the need not to moralise, the moralising tone creeps in. The plea Smithy makes is for tolerance of human frailty – all great literature operates from a moral perspective – but even being moral about tolerance can jar if sung in the wrong melody. Tone and balance is all. I had failed to achieve the right balance, the right tone. What strength is in the story resides in detail of character, behaviour, and in the dialogue.

Harry – Hal – drinks away his week's wages by Sunday night, borrows from Monday on, accrues debts, has less money to drink with on payday, and sinks deeper into self-disgust and subsequent anger. He falls in love, lets the woman down, pinches money from Smithy's wallet, has a long quarrel with him oscillating between belligerent venom and maudlin apology throughout a drunken night following which, next day, they nearly come to blows. Inevitably Hal is sacked. Six months later he returns looking for references. Unworldly Smithy collects money from other members of the staff to help Harry make his way to London and salvation. He drinks the money away in a pub round the corner, returns to the kitchen when no one is there, thieves a set of knives, and disappears leaving Smithy uncertain whether he had done right to collect money for him. It is a story about betrayed friendship. The middle section, the long drunken quarrel, is a passage I'm not ashamed to have written and perhaps one day I'll rework 'Hal Scratch', or all three – eighteen months of my life in a Norfolk hotel: 1954/1955. For now, just a short scene.

Jimmy was the under-chef in the kitchen. A frightened, secondary man. Frightened of losing his job, of giving the staff too much to eat, of doing the wrong thing, saying the wrong thing; frightened in a way which Harry simply had not to be. A lonely man, perhaps.

Old men are. He was married, no children, fat and puffing, humourless and sour, with small, ever-shifting and uncertain watery blue eyes; tired and terrified of age creeping too quickly, of the time when he would not be able to work, of the time when he would have to draw on the savings he had so avariciously accumulated; a fear of that security Harry so much despised and yet needed.

Where Harry drank whenever he could Jimmy smoked. He would sooner have done that than eat or drink or go to the pictures. He smoked between forty and sixty times a day. This was Jimmy's dilemma then, how to put by enough for old age and still indulge in this luxury. He rationed himself, but his rations invariably fell short of his requirements, so he borrowed, not money but 'a fag till I get some'. We could tell when Jimmy had no cigarettes, he would hover around, restlessly moving this, needlessly touching the other, casting sidelong looks at his victim. Having sorted out his benefactor for the day he would approach, remark on the weather or pronounce a feeble pleasantry, assume an air of intimate friendliness, so visibly different from the distance he normally kept, and then, bending low, whispering in his ear lest anyone might see him, he would ask: 'Lend us a fag till I get some, give it you back later.' Sometimes the cigarette was returned, most times not.

The most pathetic time was at the breakfast table when having eaten, one or other of us would draw out our cigarettes and smoke. Then he would sit, clutching his hands in front of him, rubbing his eyes or lips, the nerves in his face twitching, his mouth moving, his whole body restless. Had he any cigarettes he would take them out as soon as his meal was finished. If he did not do this, if he sat with furtive hands clasped, then Jimmy wanted a smoke.

On most occasions I could not bear to watch this performance (though the continual repetition, by its very obviousness, annoyed me at times) and, not waiting till he was forced to cadge, I offered him a cigarette to save his embarrassment. Yet, with a self-righteous twist of his mind, Harry connotated Jimmy a 'scrounger'.

One lunchtime, lunch itself having been served and the food put to rest awhile till dinner, we were all sitting down eating our own meal. It was Monday, the dark day following the lost weekend. I cannot recall exactly what it was that had upset Harry, doubtless something do to with the previous weekend; however, he was angry.

Jimmy finished first and sat, his hands clasped together, attempting vainly to appear unconcerned, awaiting as it were the will of the gods. Next to him sat Harry. I was completely unaware that anything was amiss until I had finished my own meal and rose to leave. Harry caught my eye and motioned me to remain seated. I had no idea why. Harry glanced fiercely at Jimmy once or twice. Jimmy twitched and shifted and looked from Harry to me, becoming increasingly uneasy as the moments passed, while I sat not knowing what to expect. Suddenly Harry smashed his knife and fork down on the table, reached into his pocket, withdrew a cigarette and slammed that down in front of Jimmy.

'Here, take it, for Jesus Christ's sake take the bastard!' Jimmy looked up pitifully pained and tried to appear surprised. Harry continued: 'You sit there twisting and turning, I knoa what you want, I knoa you want a fag, you been waiting there to ask me. There's the bleeder!' He spat bits of food out as he shouted. 'You're nowt but a tight-fisted old scrounger. And you knoa it. Well for Christ's sake man take it and stop looking at me. If only you'd ask. But you doan't, you sit there humming and hahing. I doan't knoa why. You're a bloody chef, but you've never got any money. I'm only the ruddy kitchen porter me, that's all. I doan't knoa what yer do with your cash. You've no children, you've no rent to pay, you get your grub here most o' the time. You make me f-ing sick!' And with that he left his meal half eaten and went upstairs. I looked at Jimmy's offended face, he had turned a blustering red and looked for support.

'Smoke it, Jimmy,' I said, and followed Harry upstairs. I found him in my room. We looked at each other and I smiled.

'Well the bloody man drives me to it,' he said.

'Got a nerve haven't you,' I told him.

'That's it, you side with – '

'For God's sake,' I interrupted. 'I can disagree with you can't I?'

'So we've got to give into his crave?'

'Not give in, just don't humiliate, don't you see that?'

Robbie

Robbie was a well-spoken, semi-cultured gambling alcoholic, who, like Hal, came to my attic room in the Bell to talk after a night's drinking. Where Hal, through his drunken haze, seemed not to know when to leave, when enough was enough, and would turn nasty if prompted, Robbie's natural, old-world courtesy clung to him, made him a more tolerable midnight companion. He'd knock at my door, lean forward to catch a sound of movement, more often than not waking me from exhausted sleep, I'd pull back the bolt and he'd enter conspiratorially and sit on the edge of my bed. Till now I've blatantly used chunks of early autobiographical writing, which recall with more certainty than I ever could, events and thoughts of the past, and have not tampered with them; but in 'The Terrible Valley' are passages of clumsy prose which have to be cleaned up for the reader's sake. What remains will still be a twenty-two-year-old's autobiography, no less authentic for having been pruned.

It reconstructs the portrait of Robbie, a middle-aged waiter, and weaves him into a story about a moment in his life when he vows to give up drinking and betting after just one last wild bet on the week's big race.

The story opens with a quote from Schopenhauer, the current philosopher with whom Smithy (A.W.) is grappling.

> . . . But the enterprise is vain. For in everything in nature there is something of which no ground can ever be given, of which no explanation is possible, no cause further is to be sought.

Robbie visits Smithy who invites him in and reads him the philosopher's words. Robbie is moved.

> . . . 'Beautiful words, what a mind, eh? How did he come to that thought? . . . The mysterious force . . . Life is a struggle, a battle from the cradle, and the mysterious force? – the result of billions of

years of conditioning . . . And when we die we are dead! Pah! No life after the grave. What are we? Go up thousands of feet and look down – we can't even be seen! Man is unimportant . . . Take the bee. Lovely, ordered life. Not uncouth, lustful, gaudy. Look at the work they put into living, get little from it . . .' He sucked on an empty pipe. 'Why do you think I drink? I don't know. Escape? Expression? Ever heard of AA? Alcoholics Anonymous and their twelve steps to salvation. The first step is an admission that I am an alcoholic. Powerless, dear boy. Beat. A power I can't overcome. And that's all. I – am an alcoholic! So? So what? Still I ask – what is it, this mysterious force? And you know, I used to be worse. Oh dear me. Oh dear. Without a penny, sold my last suit, lost jobs, everything. Even tried to commit suicide. Yes, dear boy. Silly, eh? And that was funny, you know, because I stuck my head in a gas oven – wonderful sensation, calm, restful, nothing, no agonies – and do you know what? My landlady comes in. Just then! She'd never returned at that time before but just that day, just then. Think of it? So what can we say? . . . Ah, dear boy. You're a good chap. You escape. You write. Expression!'

Robbie asks Smithy if he can read something he's written. Smithy is flattered and gives him four poems. The story continues:

Robbie was as ardent a gambler as he was drinker. Hardly a day passed without he staked between 10/- and £2 on a horse. Special occasions enticed him to stake £5 – such enticements resulting from a horse that stirred his strongest intuition. Needless to say his 'strong intuitions' were invariably wrong, as were most people's in the world of horse racing. But most habitual backers aspired to an understanding of form. Robbie aspired to no such pretence when placing his bets. He lost and did so without skill. One could count on his horse not winning. In fact, given a field of ten runners and asked which seven he thought would end nearest the post one could safely back the remaining three for a place. No one knew how he arrived at his choice. I suspect he simply chose the animal with the highest odds against it. The horses he backed were rarely 2-1, 7-2 or even 11-4; they had to be anything from 5-1 and usually they were in the region of 100-8.

Coupled with his uncanny skill for losing was the habitual gamblers knack of winning large sums once in a while. Every so often Robbie bet on a horse that won not shillings but pounds. Such jackpot days were his life's landmarks. The day he won £250. The day he won £160, £50, £90 . . . And each occasion was the signal for him to quit his job, go on a 'bender' and hit rock bottom harder than the time before.

Each time Robbie had one of these tips he became like a man inspired and the day on which he asked to see some of my work was such a day.

The coming Saturday was the day of the King George and Queen Elizabeth stakes. Every horse that had won a big race that year was entered, together with others of repute from afar. The winners of the Lincolnshire Handicap and of the 2000 and 1000 guineas were there; the Queen's horse – favourite, a beautiful animal – was there; Rowston Manor, a long though temperamental horse who had won two big races that season, was there. The Italian wonder, Da Vinci, had been brought over. And from the most renowned stables in France were sent D'Arcy, Caligula, and Montaigne. The distance was over 1½ miles for £25,000, the highest stakes offered in any race. The best beasts were there to compete.

Robbie had a tip.

On his day off in Yarmouth that week he had been shown a telegram that tipped a horse called Schwepps to win. A runner with little form but all the esoteric trappings which enticed the gambler betting on intuition. The race was the talk of the hotel. Robbie came down later that day to discuss prospects with Chef who humoured him with the air of one who 'really knew'.

Breakfast was over. 'Listen,' said Robbie. 'it's the only horse entered from Digby's stables. The owner is stacking all he has on it, and they're calling Rae Johnson over from France specially to ride it.'

'Of course they're calling Rae Johnson over from France,' the chef replied, looking round to make sure everyone caught his humour, 'the man lives there!'

'No, really,' persisted Robbie in his quiet, oddly cultured way. 'This is *it*, dear boy. It's the goods.'

'But it has no form,' the chef cried in despair. 'What's its price?'
'Forty to one.'

'Forty to one? It would be! Look, there's the Queen's horse came third in the Derby; then there's Darius won the 2000 guineas; Rowston Manor is placed in the same race; there's – oh hell! I could name six horses to beat Schwepps. What weight is he carrying?'

'Nine four. But it won the Queen Alexandra Stakes.'

'The Queen Alexandra Stakes is over two miles, this is a mile and a half. It won't stand the pace. Impossible!'

'Ah, dear boy!' was all Robbie could say, and he looked as one who has had a vision upon an unbeliever.

But if Chef was sceptical the rest of the hotel staff fell under the inspired spell of Robbie's tip. It had no form, too many better and proven horses in the field, the odds were against it, it couldn't possibly win but, they reasoned illogically as poor men do in search of easy money, for all those wrong reasons it would. Pathetic faith – like the million-to-one pools punter. This week! It will be this week!

A week before the race there is a drunken scene where Robbie passes judgement on the poems Smithy had given him to read.

That evening Robbie returned to my room again drunk. It was not far off midnight, I was in bed, my lights out. I heard his slow, unsteady, flat-footed climb up the narrow winding staircase. I was really too tired to entertain him and sleepily hoped he would walk past on seeing no lights through the crack under my door. Darkness and silence were no deterrent. He tapped softly. I imagined his big body inclining forward to catch movement. I hesitated a moment but then rose on one arm, switched on the light and slid back the bolt. He began his chatter as though he had been with me all evening.

'Remarkable!' he said, turning to close the door behind him. 'I've lost my pipe.' He sat down on my bed as I propped myself against a pillow showing my attention was complete. 'You know, the curved one. I can't remember where I left it. I think – I think it was stolen. Bloody, eh?' He looked at me and laughed, a drunk and hollow laugh. Then abruptly changing, his face became serious.

'You want material?' he asked, putting a cigarette to his lips and inhaling sharply. 'Well, here I am, though drunk I could give you lots of material. Often thought I'd write – and I could write, too. Ah, yes! You know your poems,' he switched with the inebriate's weakened powers of focus, from subject to subject. 'Now I don't want you to be offended old chap. You won't be will you? I must criticise.' He paused, looked at the floor, then raised just his eyes, almost disappearing into their lids. 'Trash! No, really – trash!' If I felt abashed I revealed no sign. In fact I laughed, there seemed nothing more sensible to do. 'But the foundations are there,' He continued as if to soften the blow, feeling he had been too rude, perhaps. 'Some good lines. That's what's important. Not offended are you? It's escapist, like me. I drink, I express myself in a drink, but I can appreciate the masters you know. Deeply, sincerely. In their brush strokes!' He moved his arm over an imaginary canvas. 'Violent! Browns! You can see it can't you? Beethoven, you know. Bang! Powerful! You don't mind do you old boy?' He patted my knee consolingly. 'You have the foundations, that's important. Build on it. You start off all right. The first line – lovely – then you go down. Don't! Stay on an even keel.' He rocked from side to side. 'It's infantile! Really! Shit!' There was a slight hint of viciousness in his tone as though he were tired of a lifetime of niceness and was grateful for this opportunity of high-voltage criticism. But it was soon spent, flash of murderous lightening that it was. 'But you have the makings. Some brilliant lines here and there. Follow the masters. You're a good chap. Well – good night.' He rose to go. 'You don't mind do you? I must criticise. I tell you about myself to stimulate you, you know.' I protested that he did, indeed he did. 'Jumble of lines – shake 'em up. You're working up to something. Even if you write a line a few months at a time.'

There was something so very sober about this unsober man that I could almost forget he was drunk. Only his staccato phrases reminded me. 'Steady keel. Be logical. Think. Inwardly digest. If I wanted – I could write. Material. Real life. I've known it, old boy. I *know* it. Rock bottom, right down. Into the valley. The terrible valley. It *is* terrible you know. No way out. None.' He spoke again as though to himself, and the terror of his valley must have reflected in my face for he looked at me, laughed and whispered. 'Terrible valley. But there, primroses grow, beautiful flowers.' He laughed again at his sort of madness. 'You don't mind do you? You're a good chap. Intelligent.' I did not feel it.

'Sometimes,' I said, depressed now.

'No!' he cried. 'All the time. Don't condemn yourself. You must be there. Go on. Break all the barriers. Not "sometimes". All the time!' He might have been a father scolding his son.

'The interesting thing,' I said, 'is tomorrow. What will you say tomorrow?'

'Ah yes! Tomorrow! I shall be lifeless, empty. Now, with booze, it rests my brain, soothes, soothes, eases. I feel comfortable. No more viciousness and nastiness. I've driven the animal out, right out. Know what I mean? Wonder why it is?' He dismissed his speculations. 'No questions. Mustn't question, you say. Funny isn't it? Ah well, dear boy, you're a good chap. Good night.'

He was by this time halfway through the door and I bade him good night. But he reappeared once more, poking half his body through the door.

'That horse, Schwepps, back it, it's a good thing. I'm going to back it and when I win – no more. Not another bet. Not another drink. In fact, win or lose – not another drink. Good night.'

I lay back on the pillow. Idle, drunken vows. I outed the light and nestled into sleep. What *would* he say tomorrow?

Tomorrow came and he repeated his determination to give up drink. Spurred by his euphoric belief that Schwepps would win, Robbie found the strength to go on the wagon. It was hard but Smithy helped him through the thirsty days with conversations and outings. Robbie declared he would buy a typewriter with his winnings and made Smithy promise to teach him how to type so that he would be able to write his memoirs. Smithy hovered over him watchfully, protectively. On the Friday before the big race, Robbie, his sunken eyes large with black rings, talks of suicide. Smithy coldly warns him suicide is a final surrender.

The rest of the morning was slow. I felt listless. Halfway through breakfast Robbie came down to the kitchen to ask if there was any cold bacon for a customer. Chef was sharp.

'Is it on the menu?' Robbie said it was. 'First I knew of it.' Chef hated being disturbed. 'Nothing pleases them. They want it all.' An unreasonable man at times, often grumbling at no one in particular just taking opportunities to express his distaste for working in the hotel.

'By the way,' Robbie added, 'have you a little raw tomato the customer could have?'

'Sure. The whole green salad if you like,' Chef replied testily. I watched Robbie's face. Petty clashes like this upset him, made him sick of life. Did he have to put up with all these silly people roaring over trivialities? I could see it in his face and it worried me for the rest of the morning.

When breakfast was over I ran upstairs to see him. He was sitting in a corner of his room smoking and reading a small printed yellow card. He showed it to me. It was headed 'Just for Today', a leaflet for the alcoholic to help him get through a day well and sober.

'Just for today,' it began, 'I will try to live through this day only, and not tackle my whole life problem at once . . . I will not show anyone that my feelings are hurt; they may be hurt, but today I will not show it . . . Just for today I will be agreeable . . . I will be un-afraid . . . to believe that as I give to the world so the world will give to me.'

Words like that sounded to me brave but somewhat useless. Still, they had helped many, perhaps they might help Robbie. I encouraged him to believe it, and believed it myself. He laughed at the card.

'Just for today,' he said.

'Only today and tomorrow,' I added, grinning back. His face was pale and sad but he moved off back to his work, singing. At the swing doors he turned to me, went boss-eyed, hung his tongue out and toppled crazily through the door in mock drunkenness. I heard his laughter from the dining room and returned, less worried, to my work below stairs.

Schwepps wins the race. Robbie wins £200. He disappears claiming he's going to buy clothes for himself, clothes for his girlfriend, and a typewriter. That night the slow flat feet mount the winding stair-case.

424

'Dear boy,' he called, his whisper sounding sober enough through the door. I opened it. He was more drunk than I had ever known. He stumbled in and with difficulty closed the door behind him.

'The terrible valley,' he whispered, placing something heavy on my desk. 'Ah the terrible valley. With primroses!' He laughed. 'Too late to buy clothes,' he said sitting on my bed. He fumbled in his jacket and took out a wad of notes. 'A hundred and forty-nine pounds eight shillings less thirty three pounds ten and six. It's a beauty, dear boy.' I looked to my desk and saw a bright, black typewriter. He got up and placed the notes on it, then toppled over the chair and staggered to the bed again. He fumbled once more in his jacket and drew out some cigarettes, one of which he gave to me. Then, unsteadily striking a match and lighting his own cigarette, forgetting mine, he said:

'I say, dear boy. Do you touch-type or with one finger?'

The story ends there. Confession: I now cannot remember if that ending is part of the reality or owes itself to imagination. The characters, personality, the horse race, the clash with the chef, the outsider winning – I remember all taking place. But that typewriter. I cannot see that typewriter. I fear the typewriter is wish-fulfilment and is what weakens the story.

Robbie, Hal Scratch, Irene, Tom the chef, Jimmy the second chef, Gordon, Albert, 'Mummy and Daddy', little Jimmy Moore – all these characters during my fourteen months at the Bell Hotel made an impression on me that I only now realise, gathering these pages together to make a life, was deep and seminal. I concluded: the world was too vast to fit into a single comprehensible scheme of things; too many people chose second best too often; their perplexity, fear, and frustration rendered them naked, exposed; they were bereft of the wherewithal to defend themselves against grubby exploitation – from the world of commerce and politics, the media, the workplace, and perhaps most bruising and debilitating of all, exploitation from one another. Their understanding came in tabloids; their greatest dreams lay in the hopeless columns of a football-pools coupon. War might have been an escape, created a purpose in life. There were no wars. Two had decimated the first half of the century. They had only each other, a neighbour to bash. The hotel, where I came to find peace, escape from messy entanglements, whose doors I'd entered with ambition dried up in the heat of self-castigation, hoping for a life beyond the firing line, beyond the condemnations of friends and relatives, where I would be called upon to prove nothing, to be neither judge nor prosecutor, drew me slowly into a vortex of lives abounding with petty intrigues, short tempers, self-righteous moralising, and sudden tempestuous hilarity. An existence of intense extremes, an emotional hothouse where one minute you might be laughing with the man you insulted an hour ago and not know why. Relationships mixed and boiled. Each individual struggled to assert and protect himself. I was fascinated and it was upsetting. But I had stumbled upon some of the themes for a lifetime of writing: lives wasted accepting second best; lives vulnerable from inadequate nourishment – spiritual, emotional, intellectual; lives stultified from the wrong choice based on chimeric dreams, self-delusion. All began in the Bell Hotel and found their first voice in these three stories.

Chapter Nineteen

Dusty

> Dusty pottered around clearing out the case, re-ordering the ward-robe, and glanced through my notes and an old diary (she is reading that at the moment) and some miscellaneous MSS. Some minutes ago she looked up and said – 'You know, I don't think I could ever really be happy all the time with you.' When I asked why, she replied: 'Because every so often I stop and think that I wormed my way into you, that you did not want me in the beginning, and I feel that I haven't got you all, that some of you you keep back.' I said perhaps she was right but that did not mean I did not love her . . .
>
> Paris diary, 28 June 1956

I come now to that part of this old life where I must put together facts and impressions more carefully than any other, for I am about to deal with the days of Dusty – wife, mother of our three children, companion of forty years, the central character of two plays and a story, aspects of her etched in here, there and all over the place, viewed as an anchor within my family, loved and depended upon by friends, a woman who – as you, Lindsay Joe, so vehemently declared to me on the phone a few weeks before Christmas 1993 – 'hasn't a bad bone in her body'. We have lived apart for three years, and though it seems to me that I have simply been away at the Welsh desk working on a new play for a few weeks, as I have frequently done over the past twenty years we have owned this house, I do not know if we could ever live together again as we once did. (By the time this book is published it will have been four years, and during the fourth we are attempting to build a *modus vivendi* leading who knows where.)

It has been a strange experience this separation. Unreal, intangible, a time of suspended animation, a limbo-life. There are two explanations: the first, though I fell heavily in love, it never seemed I was separated from Dusty. We met on family occasions – weddings, birthdays, at John Dexter's cremation in Golders Green; and now and then shared a cinema, a theatre. Hers was – is – a personality, no matter how I fault it, that impresses itself with energy. (I'm even confused what tense to use!) She radiates a unique aura, one not easily surrendered. The second: I had spent so many intense, writing hours sitting at the Welsh study desk, looking out across fields at the creviced Twmpa, registering the changing light on that mountain's side, the restless weather, the ravaging winds, the seasons' colouring – all those distractions of landscape – that, looking out upon the same majestic panorama during these three years (with breaks of course) it seemed as though no upheaval had taken place. I was simply here at my desk writing *Blood Libel, Three Women Talking, Letter to a Daughter, Wild Spring*, this autobiography . . . just as years previously I had been here writing *Love Letters on Blue Paper, Shylock, Caritas, Lady Othello* . . .

The story of my life with Dusty is another book. Or two. Most of it would be found in letters from the Bell Hotel to friends and family; in the diary I kept of our time in Paris; in letters written to her from Norfolk and London while she was working in Butlin's Skegness holiday camp; in letters exchanged while I was directing abroad. A hint of our life together, a taste of it, moves through the pages of *The Dusty Wesker Cookbook* – a year of feeding people, with recipes after each diary entry. But the greater part would be found in the forty or so journals kept from 1966 up to the present day. Though I was whirlpooled into other relationships none of them, finally, offered what had been built with her. Whatever inadequacies we saw in each other, no matter those aspects of character which disappointed us, on balance – and with the added bonus of three children we were devoted to – ours was a relationship we could mine for ourselves and in it find riches for others. A full life, one in which I matured as a writer, Dusty grew to become a powerful individual, and we meshed like God's chosen.

But we were not God's chosen. Though something in each of us and *about* each of us wanted to make the relationship work, though aware we had somehow stumbled upon a gold mine, yet ours was not a marriage of soul mates blessed in heaven. The mine had shaky props, explosions burst from hidden gases; landslides, subsidence, cave-ins. The mine was rich but disasters inevitable. We evolved a rhythm of working, sang as we hacked happily at the seams, but it was impossible to avoid hacking the relationship. Not each other – we were not quarrellers. I especially harboured this dread of family fights. Dusty lashed out but quickly forgot; I suppressed and became icy silent. Then bounced back, and the relationship continued to be mined – until the next lashing, the next cave-in.

It is asked: how many ever find partners they're 'made for'? Few. What seems to happen is that we bond with the possible. We cling to, nurture, devote overtime to those aspects of character we love, and ignore the rest. As much as we can. For as long as we are able. Until, toleration worn thin, there emerges an image of ourselves that becomes insupportable. (Say that word with a French accent and its full impact is felt.) By which time history accumulates, cartloads of emotional baggage – it becomes impossible to pull apart. A force tries to heave us asunder like those logs we slog to axe in two, but, cement-like, a knot holds. It can't be split. We can hack and bleed chips off but in the end we either abandon it to rot down or throw the whole into the fire and watch it burn, slowly.

Gold mines, tree logs, blessings from heaven – we reach for and mix our metaphors, frantically hoping they'll do the work of establishing the truth of things *for* us. John Osborne, when I shared with him my fears for this autobiography, advised: 'Facts are secondary, feelings are all.' Tempting, especially for a Perlmutter. But I'm not sure. An honest juxtapositioning of facts like stepping stones conveys feelings which often surpass with impact the mere expression of them.

From the first days I was both powerfully drawn to Dusty and as powerfully resisted. Letter to Squibbs, 10 December 1954:

. . . I cannot describe Dusty to you. She is a simple country girl of eighteen who has been working as a waitress for four years. She is so blithe it is incredible, so impetuous I find it difficult to keep up with her, so unsubtle that I cannot even insult her (not that I have the least desire to – but you follow), so full of joy that she thinks I am depressed when I'm serious, so uneducated that she has neither awe nor scepticism at the fact that I write – she simply cannot make it out – and above it all, she carries the sincerity of a Thomas Hardy milkmaid and she loves me so much that I feel like a wretched rake. I made the mistake of vanity in imagining she would tire of me, she has done no such thing and oddly enough neither have I of her – despite that her lack of subtlety leaves me speechless and even somewhat terrified. She is a natural blonde and has a full attractive figure and when I finally leave she will hate me with every ounce of feeling she can muster up. But there is nothing I can do, she would have hated me had I not returned any sort of affection – which I attempted to do for some time believe me. The tragedy is that I can understand exactly what would, has and will happen and she cannot. Shock and despair is her lot and I remain the guilty one. I have only one vain consolation: the hope that knowing me might have been of some use when her hatred has died down. I have not abused her affections, I simply cannot fulfil them. My one weakness, dear Squibbs, is that I cannot bear to be hated – not on the spot. For that weakness I shall suffer sore tribulations – unless greater maturity sets in. It might – you know, like rigor mortis.

Beginnings

Dusty was born Doreen Cecile (my mother was Leah Cecile) on 30 May 1936, our daughter, Tanya Jo, was born 25 May 1960. I was born 24 May 1932. Three Geminis in the family! In fact we were surrounded by Geminis. My ex-secretary, now close friend (and researcher for this book), Mikki Groom, shares Dusty's birth date; another of our close friends, Vera Elyashiv, was born on 29 May. And there were others – like the late and lovely Jill Tweedie – sufficient to give Dusty an excuse to create the Gemini party. I was allowed to cook for it only sometimes. An abandoned ritual now of course.

Dusty's nephew, Keith, a tyre-dealer with a penchant for history, lives with his wife and family of four in the house in Starston, Norfolk, where she was born fifty-eight years ago. Her father, Edwin Bicker, Eddie, known as Poppy to his children, bred dray horses for the local farmer, rose to cowman, and at the time I was introduced to the family was a pigman. He lived with his energetic wife, Hilda Florence, ex land-army girl, in a tied cottage near the church of St Mary's, Redenhall, where, aged eighty-five, Mother Bicker still lives, alone for the last twenty years or so, doing her own shopping, house cleaning, cooking, fiercely independent and on the lookout to do as many good and neighbourly deeds as she can before quitting this earth.

When I was first courting there was no bathroom or running water. Water was heated in the coal-fired boiler – similar to the system we encountered in Weald Square – filled with rain water from a huge tank outside the cottage. I frequently had baths in the front room in a long tin bathtub which Mother Bicker filled and kept replenishing; cosy in front of the coal fire where towels were warming, reminding me of a time even further back when I was bathed by my mother in a tin tub on the table in front of a coal fire in Fashion Street beneath the yellow glow of a gas mantle. No prudery about nudity either in Fashion Street or Beck Farm. You, Lindsay Joe, adore your granny and know only too well that your mother inherits the old lady's strength and bustling vitality. Her stubbornness, too! As have you?

I don't think Hilda Florence and Edwin's marriage was the happiest of unions. Poppy had given up interest in almost everything but his vast garden – which Mother Bicker took over when he died. A man smaller in size than his wife, he bowed out into silence before his steamrollering, endlessly loquacious spouse who dominated the household and made the major decisions. She was, is, a good woman, but one cluttered with simple, immutable opinions. It was easier for Poppy to let her spin on. Sometimes her views are unconventional – she was, for example, sympathetic to the plight of one of Harleston's homosexuals, caring more for the man than his supposed immoral deviancy long before it was acceptable to knight a self-declared homosexual actor. Mother Bicker's father was drowned in the First World War, her brother drowned at sea in the Second World War, and she developed a fear of water so powerful that she handed it on to her daughter. Dusty to this day cannot swim.

Hilda and Eddie Bicker gave birth to four children. Joy, the oldest, mother of Keith by an American airman (who Keith came to discover was Jewish), married a generously spirited man, Charlie Keeble, garage-mechanic, who took on Keith and fathered three of his own. Sam, Dusty's brother, a farm labourer, married Cis and had two sons and a daughter. Bridget, who I used to wave at cycling to my job as seed-sorter, married John Adcock, farm labourer, and died young of leukaemia, leaving him with two daughters. In the background, till she died at a very old age, was Granny Loombe, Hilda's mother, a kindly old lady with an Audenesque-lined face of whom I became fond. There exists a history of quarrels, resentments, and on-off-on-off bouts of silence and non-communication between mother, grandmother, daughters, sisters too complicated to detail, nor are they relevant except to observe in passing that these, my in-laws for whom I have an abiding affection (though it may not be shared by them these days), form the background and inspiration for *Roots*.

Dusty's education was little less than mine. She attended Redenhall Secondary School in Harleston, enjoyed sports but not much else, and left aged fifteen to work as chambermaid in the Annersley Hotel on the road south into Norwich. From chambermaid she rose to waitress, her second job, for the Townhouse hotel in Thorpe St Andrews, a leafy suburb east of Norwich. Her third job, where she developed the skill of handling silver service, was in the Royal Hotel. Then came the Bell.

Dusty was talked about before she was seen: 'Can see what *she* is, flinging herself about in the dining room!' chef Tom Bullock had sourly remarked, confusing high spirits with lewdness. She was described as a young woman who enjoyed kicking her legs up high with excessive tomboyish energy and no shame. One morning she appeared. I was serving breakfast. An effervescent personality burst through the swing doors, the sunniest young woman I had ever seen. I can't remember what she ordered but her voice dared one to refuse her.

Dee

The new waitress's name is Dee. Young, slightly plump, and a real blonde; seems extremely efficient, sounds jolly. The head waiter is after her. What a promiscuous man that is. Married, has two children and beds every waitress who enters the hotel. She seems to have attached herself to him . . .

So I record Dusty's arrival in 'The Diary of Jon Smith'.

. . . Dee and I are taking notice of each other now. I see gay glances and note the loose compliments. The air is pregnant with signs of infatuation. What do I do? Ignore her and reap the rewards of coldness? Instead we carry on little flirtations during the day. I suppose she is pretty. I do not want to become involved again, this much I must make clear at the first opportunity . . .

. . . Dee and I have become an odd pair. I confess her youthful exuberance attracts me. We are continually joking together but I resist the temptation to go out with her. She is constantly asking me to come for a drink and she finds every conceivable excuse for talking to me. She is infatuated and now I have to break her of it as tenderly as possible . . .

I remember attempting this with Dusty, break her of what I thought was simply an infatuation, an 'office romance'. It was not easy. A quality of careless innocence seemed unable to take my protestations seriously, as Dee was unable to take Smithy's seriously.

. . . Dee is going to live in next week. She will occupy the room at the end of the corridor, ten seconds away! The child is not in the least reticent about her infatuation. I am the object of much buffoonery. It will take all my time and willpower to keep her at bay. I stand waiting as it were, watching the enemy mount and wondering how to defend myself against the mad charge he is bound to make, only he is a she and that is worse. I have already made the first tactical error in fancying her as a companion for a cycle ride . . .

. . . Dee and I went for a cycle ride this evening. Out of the city into the black countryside. There is an excitement about riding at night, it is like not riding at all, only the occasional bumps to remind one of the road beneath . . . We cycled in silence a great deal of the way, and because the road was black it was not an awkward silence.

Dee is a happy individual. Quite unsophisticated and not in the least pretentious – simply unsubtle. She wanted to know about me. What did I do every time I locked myself in my room? Apparently the rest of the staff imagine me quite a shady character. It is so unusual not to want to go out every evening. I was tempted to invent a fantasy about having left a wife and two children and that I was studying to be a doctor. But I laughed instead and assured her that there was nothing unusual about me, certainly nothing mysterious, unless reading be considered a form of witchcraft.

We lost our way, I wanted to cycle on but she insisted that she had to be back at her lodging. It is a long time since I have been out for a ride with anyone. I kissed her good night. It is a long time since I have kissed a girl too . . .

All this is an accurate record of the first encounters I had with the woman who was to be my wife for thirty-five years. And as I read them, typed extracts from this not very good story about a certain Jon Smith, I live them again. I see the young Dusty, the attic room, recall her voice outside asking me to come for a drink, me declining. I remember details like the ashtray I had brought back from the first World Peace Congress in Paris, March 1949 – a Notre Dame gargoyle, wings cracked with the years, hovered over the stained cup. I can see the cover of the book I was reading: yellow and red –

Irving Stone's biography of Van Gogh, *Lust For Life*. It is all there in the Smith diary.

. . . Went to the Blue Room with Dee this evening. Really I should not spend so much time with that girl, yet her happy disposition appeals to me, I like her company and, I suppose, her attentions flatter me. She would do almost anything I asked her and a great deal more. Each day now as she goes out to morning break she asks me if I want anything in the shops. I dare not let her buy things for me, she refuses to take payment. She constantly asks if I have any washing to be done, any mending or ironing. Most of my energy is spent in declining her offers, I refuse to let her skivvy for me. It was quite embarrassing when for no reason at all she bought me a small book of Van Gogh paintings, she had seen me reading a biography of him . . .

. . . Dee has now moved her belongings. She is officially 'living in' . . .

Those Sunday bells which were to drive Jimmy Porter mad a couple of years on were haranguing me too:

It is a Sunday of bell-ringing discouragement
When ideas sleep in the lullaby of church rings.
There is a hatefulness in their ringing despair
That you want to scream for the silence to wake.

Screams Jimmy Porter:

Oh, hell! Now the bloody bells have started! Wrap it up, will you? Stop ringing those bells! There's somebody going crazy in here! I don't want to hear them!

And Smithy records their impact:

. . . Sunday is dying in its own quiet way, with its bell-ringing and

best suit, its groups of young women and young men walking aimlessly in the mild air . . . Sunday. My day off . . .

The aimlessness induced in the godless by God's bell-ringing Sunday leads to lovemaking. It is the first time. For Smithy and Dee.
Me and Dusty.

I woke very early. Breakfast. Dee woke early too. I do not know
where she is now. I think she said she was going to church. I am
afraid I avoided her this evening. The temptation to take the papers
up to the castle and read, to be alone, was too great. Yet being alone
on a Sunday, especially here in Norwich, one is caught up and dan-
gled by the emptiness of the day. I am not sure what to do now. I
wanted to come back and work on the story; instead I come back
again to the diary. And I see I have not made a single entry for the
last month. It would be hopeless to attempt a summary. Evenings
out with Dee, nights in the Blue Room, the calm going perhaps . . .

The next twelve pages recount a tortuous, strung-out Sunday afternoon spent in the attic room of the Bell Hotel. The writing is not
good enough to sustain all twelve pages, but some. Smithy, though
he has set up the conditions for Dee to seduce him, resists at first. A
reversal of roles! The woman is expected to seduce and resist! Dee
is patient, open, winning. Smithy is torn. He wants to be able to
claim doubt and uncertainty while succumbing to her irrepressible
and finally irresistible nature.

I sat for some minutes on my bed trying to focus my mind on something tangible; the early darkness closed over the windows and I
could not. All I could do was surrender to my lethargy and stretch
out on the bed. She watched me for some seconds, then pulled off
my shoes and . . . stretched out at my side resting her head in the
crook of my arm . . . Half an hour later a tiny voice roused me.
  'Let's get under the covering, I'm cold.'

In that twilight between sleep and waking I obeyed and we resumed our positions beneath the red eiderdown and counterpane . . .

. . . But sleep I could not. Neither, it appeared, could she, for I felt her undo her skirt and let it slip to the floor. Why, I again asked myself, do you not want to make love to this girl? And again I answered – because she has said she is in love with me. I was simply attempting to cling hold of a principle. It is curious how one reaches that state of mind where one wants desperately to behave in a certain way and one observes, objectively and with some shame, that one does not and is powerless to do otherwise.

Under the eiderdown, with our clothes on, near to each other, the heat swelled. I pushed down the coverings a little and muttered that I was hot. Cautiously but surely her hand moved to my shirt and began undoing the buttons. It was a cool hand. I was aware that this was a sort of game. At first I toyed half-heartedly, but within ten minutes we shyly slipped under the blankets half dressed. In the half-light I turned to look at her. Her eyes were helplessly soft and enquiring. For a second our breasts touched, then she sat up, stretched her arm to the door, locked the latch and returned to my arms . . .

In this case the dots signify not passages skipped but the lovemaking I felt could not be described in literature. It was the first time between Smithy and Dee, Dusty and me. How many husbands and wives, forty years on, can remember such details?

And then?

We parted and sank very slowly on our backs. I lay on her arm which, after a few seconds, she withdrew from under me.

'Now I'm damp,' she said.

'Me too.'

'I wish some of it had gone into me.'

'And then you would have had my child.'

'Yes,' she sulked. 'But if anything like that would happen you would take fright and run.'

'I'd run as far away as possible taking you with me. To the Shetland Isles to keep goats.' She laughed. 'How do you suppose I could support a wife and child?' I asked.

'Oh we'd manage somehow.' There was no point explaining what she would come to understand herself in time; there really was no point.

Inside the little attic room it was hot and with a weary movement I pushed the muddled blankets down to my thighs. The lights from the night street outside cast window-frame shadows on the slanting ceiling that rose a foot away from my right side. I looked absent-mindedly at them, not having much else to do, and lay motionless, in a very careless frame of mind.

Lying thus a thought came to me. This was the kind of careless mind that chose second best. But I did not harbour the thought long. It glanced in at me, that was all; the only actual words I formed for myself were – well? what now? And as I did I rolled slightly to my right and gazed at a gargoyle that presided in miniature over an ashtray. It is a replica of one of the Notre Dame devils and it leans there, forward on two hands with its head resting in them; the ears are pointed, sticking up with a brown nicotine stain in between where I had once laid the last breath of a cigarette. His alabaster wings are broken but that does not seem to upset him. Nothing seems to disturb the hooked nose, the wide mouth and pointed chin, the half-smile that stays, imperturbably on his face, as he leans, so terribly at ease, gazing; the placid observer of all that goes on in my room. Somehow that devilish face inspired a calm as if to say – I know it all and one day you will too . . .

This is an awful – in the sense of awesome – confession. Forty years ago I was describing the slow tumbling into a relationship with my future wife as a careless choice of second best. I only dare recall this now because, whatever those qualities we each came to feel the other deficient in, she has since grown into a kind of magnificence. The instinct that drew me towards her, the qualities I sensed, were well founded. That my doubts and hesitancies were just as well founded is more to do with the complex knot of foolish decisions into which I had entangled my head and heart, as will become clear.

Poor Smithy! If you run away to strange country places and apply for strange jobs then you run the risk of a strange, unexpected life.

. . . What was I doing lying there with a country girl? There is so little we have in common, our minds separated by religion, culture, experience . . . Why do I allow her to dig her affections deeper into me? She knows we cannot marry, that we are miles apart, she in a country village and I? Nowhere in particular. The blame, and yet no blame, lies with me. I have not lied nor misled; but it is the half-lie of accepting. Again the thought – second best – came to me, and as easily slipped away . . . No human turning is without conflict. I want simplicity where there is none. Love without love. Living without life. Am I part of the life I have been criticising? It is becoming more and more difficult to understand.

'I have failed,' I said portentously. Feeling that at this point she should be offended she turned right over on to her left side and answered with her back, finishing my thought:

'Because you've been with me, I know.'

'I've only ever tried to be honest.' I ignored her comment. 'Well, I've failed.' Somehow this did not upset me as much as the words implied.

'How about me?' She returned to her former position on her back.

'Oh you're all right, you're in love.'

'I know. I'm crazy. It's because I throw myself at you that you feel like that, that's what the others say, they warned me. But I don't care.' She laid her head on my chest. I remained motionless.

We lay there silent for many more minutes and I recalled the words I had spoken only two weeks before, probably less. I had said: 'We shall be friends, not lovers.' Now it was as though I were thinking one way and my body behaving in another. I reached for a cigarette and puffed easily.

'Look at him, I could go on for another two hours and he lies there exhausted already, a young man like that!' Her bravado amused me, but she was quite right. Lust is soon spent. She laid her head on my chest once more.

'I could sleep with you every night,' she cooed.

'I doubt it.'

'Would the charm wear off?'

'For us both.'

'Do you hate me that much?'

'I don't hate,' I answered with a laugh. 'I'm simply not in love.'

'Huh! Not in love!' she repeated. It was as though she accepted the idea. She raised her head from off my chest and stretched, sensuously, slowly, clutching her fist in mid-air. Then I too stretched, arching my back. We stretched together and, with the confidence of familiarity, having breathed deeply, we eased down, gradually, falling into each other's arms ...

Mixed emotions, conflicting, unresolved feelings – Smithy and his young waitress make love for the second time in their relationship. Two so very disparate beings seeking, perhaps, nothing more than comfort from each other.

... She nestled into my arms again and, running her hand over the length of my body, sighed, satisfied, and said: 'I couldn't sleep with a fat man to save my life.' Suddenly I felt that I wanted to be very much alone, without the presence of another human being. But I hated to offend her by asking her to leave. She appeared so peaceful and the noise of her hate on being asked to dress and leave would echo in my mind and not allow me to feel alone anyway. Instead I said: 'I don't think I shall ever marry.'

'You will,' she replied lazily. 'And you'll make a good husband.'

'But I like being alone, I like –' I was becoming angry ... The girl with short blonde hair like dust at my side breathed contentedly into my left breast. I played with the light in her hair.

'You're wasting your time,' I said.

'But I'm not wasting my time. I like your company, you let me go out with you, I enjoy myself. It's not a waste of time.'

'And when I've gone?'

'Why don't you stay here, you're happy working in the kitchen, aren't you?'

I turned abruptly on to my stomach and mumbled into the pillow: 'Jesus Christ! ... '

She had failed a test. That's how relationships could be described: as an ambush of tests. Unexpectedly – a situation demands a response. And when we respond in a way that disappoints our partner, it's chalked up. Failings accumulate. We forgive, but a little less each time. Though Smithy had made the momentous decision to surrender ambition to life in the kitchen, he couldn't accommodate anyone else agreeing it was a right decision. *He* could underestimate his talent, not others. Dee had failed to see how unsuited he was to kitchen life. She had failed to perceive the incongruity. She had imagined him happy! Such was the limitation of her horizon, the paucity of expectation she had of him. Jesus Christ! Later, they go for a meal. She tells him: '*I think that I shall try to hate you a little, little more each day.*'

The following Monday morning she attempts just that: a perfunctory 'good mornin' and cold glances.

> . . . At first I smiled to myself: the inane defence of a cynic. Then I was fascinated. Her movements and expressions were diabolic, cold and calculated; and then the cold seeped into me. I was being hurt. The cynical smile turned sour on my lips that way it does when a smile is ignored.
>
> It occurs to me that I do not want to be hated; though I know were she to cease hating I would not want her to love . . .

Smithy doesn't at first know how to behave. He becomes annoyed, then cold. Which confuses him because he is not in love and has no cause to respond in an aggrieved manner. He reasons:

> . . . She is in love with me. It will be some time before the impact of unrequited love reduces her to an emotional reaction. She has started however. The next time her hate will last a little longer and be deeper. Hatred is part of our defensive equipment . . . Next time will be worse and I will watch that hate grow and dissolve me in itself. It will hurt not because I love but because I feel nothing. This is curious, it is sad as well . . .

But love is a river that changes with the changing terrain – gently between gentle banks, gaily over pebbles, fiercely through harsh rock, sadly through days of drought, mysteriously through moonlit nights, fearfully when no moon shines. Smithy records in his diary:

. . . She found me washing potatoes in the larder, annoyed with something the head waiter had said. She asked me to make some tomato juice, said: 'Kiss?' I replied it would not be a very good one, that I was not in the mood to do her justice. 'And I'm not in the mood to do *you* justice either,' she retorted, and sulkily moved away.

Just now she lies on my bed listening to a concert on the radio. As I write she waits, patiently, unmoved by my preoccupation with writing. A poem holds no significance for her. Being a writer is not being anybody at all. The gulf between us is fantastic, yet I sleep with her and these two facts I cannot reconcile . . . I console myself with the hope that she is acquiring a taste for music. She listens with me to concerts on the radio. Out of love? I think there is every chance she may come to enjoy good music . . . one should be able to pass on to others something of worth . . . to be able to say this was more than lust . . .

Four years later Beatie Bryant tells her mother:

Listen Mother, let me see if I can explain something to you. Ronnie always says that's the point of knowing people. 'It's no good having friends who scratch each other's back,' he say. 'The excitement in knowing people is to hand on what you know and to learn what you don't know. Learn from me,' he say, 'I don't know much but learn what I know.' So let me try and explain to you what he explained to me.

Ronnie – Smithy – Smithy – Ronnie. They are interchangeable. Beatie goes on to demonstrate what she/they mean. She puts on a record of Bizet's *L'Arlésienne* suite and urges her mother to sit and listen to the two tunes:

. . . It's simple isn't it? . . . You don't have to frown, because it's alive
. . . See the way the other tune comes in? Hear it? Two simple tunes,
one after the other . . . it goes together, the two tunes together, they
knit, they're perfect. Don't it make you want to dance? . . . It's light.
It makes me feel light and confident and happy. God, Mother, we
could all be so much more happy and alive . . .

Beatie – Dee – Dee – Beatie. They are interchangeable.

Smithy's relationship with Dee inevitably convolutes. Tensions
set in, as they did between Dusty and me. Her life was becoming
schizophrenic. Part of her hung back in the familiar world of
dining-room flirtations with waiters and commercial travellers, a
new part was discovered able to respond to opera and paintings.
My rhythms were, though by now familiar, still alien to her. I, on
the other hand, stubbornly refused to allow myself to fall in love –
too many bruises lingered, some self-disgust – but I was caring
about her. Smithy's diary tries to recreate the confused states of
both our minds.

. . . I wanted to stay in this evening, Dee wanted to go out. She said
she would get one of the commercial travellers to take her out for a
drink. Why will she not understand that I wish to be alone sometimes? I am furious. Not because she is going out with someone else
but because she imagines it will upset me. We quarrelled . . .

. . . Dee and I become more involved as the days pass. And this is
the most horrifying aspect. I do not love her, I know I cannot, yet
our relationship has developed to that extent where I am jealous of a
man she may contemplate.

And I am aware of the process, this, this is what stupefies me . . .

It is from here on that 'The Diary of Jon Smith' enters melodrama.
Until now the diary, with more accuracy and detail than ever I
would have been able to recall, recreates the first months of my relationship with Dusty. Once again I don't enjoy the picture of
myself that emerges. Do most writers self-denigrate themselves by
projecting the most pompous image possible? I was conscious of

deliberately doing this in *Roots* and *I'm Talking about Jerusalem* where the character of Ronnie is put down to allow those I believed to be the real heroes and heroines to shine. Beatie grows under the shock of Ronnie ditching her, though in reality Ronnie (A.W.) married Beatie (Dusty). Similarly, in 'The Diary' it is Smithy who goes to pieces while Dee grows and glows with blithe innocence.

She had fallen in love with a young man who had been rejected by a series of young women he had declared himself in love with – Esther, Shifra, Rhoda, Olive. A young man who'd persuaded himself he had talent for nothing but the stirring of sauces and the patting of pastry, and who wanted to be left alone to live a simple life of reading, listening to drama and music on radio, baby-sitting for his beloved nephews. Something, so this young man had concluded, must be wrong with him. He was not equipped for either the world of art or the world of love. The young, blonde, ardent waitress had chosen the wrong man upon whom to lavish, unashamedly, her generous affections. In such a way did I, the young man, arrange and organise my thoughts and feelings as I had organised and arranged printed slips in a file called 'Rejections'. I even committed the most extraordinary folly of going to the barber's one day to have my hair shorn 'army-short' in the absurd belief that my lovely locks were a false attraction. Without them Dusty would find me less appealing. She was shocked but laughed at me. Rightly so. What had love to do with long or short hair?

Baldy – an aside

Like father like son, eh, Lindsay? Remember that time when Dusty and I went abroad for a first night of one of the plays and we returned to a horror story? We came in through the front door of Bishops Road to discover as usual the house full, buzzing with your friends, only this time the buzz had a strange quality: you were not downstairs to greet us. And as we turned our backs to the stairs to unload presents on the hall table the children called up: 'Lindsay!

Lindsay! Your mum and dad are back.' We heard you come down the stairs and turned to embrace you. You stood, halfway down, looking at us, waiting for our response. I froze, gaped, understood everything in an instant, and wanted to weep with the sadness of what I saw. Your mother gave a scream and instantly turned away unable to look at what you had done.

You had been worried that your hair was falling out. Your hair your pride! As it is for many of us foolish men. In our absence you had made an appointment with a doctor seeking advice. The idiot man had told you, with brutal insensitivity, that there was no hope, your hair was going, as once in Paris the barber had sent shivers down me with the words: *Monsieur, vos cheveux sont malades.* And with that quality of impatient extremism, which you've got from I wonder who, you had shaved your head bald. It's going, you thought, let it go. Now! At once! Why waste time! Let me face the inevitable right away! That's what we saw on our return, and had made me want to weep. Such desperate honesty, such unnecessary courage. And you'd cut yourself in the process. There were globules of blood on your young head.

We were lovers

Just as I had been writing behind my back, so loving slipped in behind my back. I didn't possess the talent for either literature or love, I reasoned, therefore neither love nor literature could be happening. We possess ourselves of delusions and tangle our head and heart into such absurd, impossible knots.

Nothing could hide it though. We were lovers – me and the blonde bombshell who I told: your hair is like gold dust, I will call you Dusty. We were a couple. Everyone at the Bell watched it growing and talked among themselves. We made love in the attic room, held hands in the streets, snogged in corridors, shopped together, the cinema constantly, theatre and concerts occasionally, she accompanied me on location to Mousehold Heath when I acted in a film for the Norwich Amateur Cine Group, and we moved in and out of tense times. Of course I wanted to introduce her to Della, Ralph and the nephews at Hill House, and she wanted to take me home to Beck Farm to meet Mother and Poppy Bicker. 'He looks like a gypsy,' her mother said. 'Is he a gypsy?' They had never met a Jew before. Not surprising, there were only a quarter of a million in the country. I was welcomed with kindness and, being a sociable fellow, was at home as soon as the Bickers made me feel it.

One particular memory locked and remained. I came from a tradition where you always took something to a house you visited – a flower, a packet of tea, a box of biscuits, of chocolates, anything as a greeting, a recognition that somebody was opening their home and you were not taking hospitality for granted. The first time Dusty took me to meet her parents I wanted to buy a box of chocolates. She was surprised and told me not to bother. 'They'll think it strange.' Which in turn surprised me. How could anyone think it strange to be brought a house gift? Was it a cultural difference between town and country, Jew and gentile? Our family were constantly on the move in and out of each other's homes (and lives!), Norfolk farm labourers hardly ever. They met in pubs and at whist drives. But Dusty had been wrong. My box of chocolates was graciously received. It was the first time I experienced Dusty misrepresenting people, one of her failings: a strange mixture of animal perception about some, an utter misreading of others. The girl who left school at fifteen to live away from home had little experience of such social courtesies, though she learned quickly and exploded into a generosity – with material things if not always of the spirit – for which she is now famous.

Della and Ralph received her with open house though wondered at the relationship. They responded, as everyone did, to her vibrancy; Adam and Miles loved her. But modest though our cultural framework was Dusty had none. For me that was part of her attraction, for Della and Ralph it was bewildering. They could see no future for us and imagined our relationship would be soon over and done. Certainly they wouldn't allow us to sleep together, and

Dusty – when everyone was asleep – crept through dark corridors over squeaky floorboards to share my bed. Yes, *I* should have been the one creeping over squeaky floorboards to share her bed. I know it. But that was our relationship – she was the pursuer. I had frozen myself into an icy, nonsensical belief that I could make no one a happy partner, for which belief I took myself out of love's arena. A part of me has always remained there. I fear it has played havoc with my emotional life.

Last months at the Bell

The time was approaching to leave the Bell. Two letters home spell our plans and fears: to my mother, 25 November 1954:

> . . . I hope to leave the last week in January, that is just over two months from now. The only thing that can delay that date is if the film the group is making is not finished by then. But we are rushing to get it done in time. I don't like to let them down, because it involves money, and as I have the lead my presence is required . . .
>
> The only other thing, which I know you will not like, is that I want to take a flat. I have written to Squibbs asking him if he will share one with me, I have told him I want it to be a private place where I will get no interruptions from people; I do not know whether he will agree to that. If he does not then I will get one on my own . . .

This Garbo urge to be alone – I had forgotten. My reputation among friends and family is one of gregariousness. Not unfounded – I've been good with, and enjoyed, company. But that little worm of secretiveness, wanting to burrow out of sight, be locked away in dark clay – I possessed it, from the beginning, hiding under the caverned duvet making radio dramas for myself.

It worries my mother. She has written a letter urging me to come home and 'face the consequences'. I'm confused.

447

I simply do not know what you are talking about when you say that I should 'come home and face the consequences'. The consequences of what? I am not ashamed of having been born of poor parents. It is not that I wish to avoid. It is simply that I find too close a contact with people depresses me, it is like living in a hot room . . . There is nothing odd or peculiar in wanting a room of one's own, and it is unfair of you to say that I am irresponsible. I am quite capable of looking after myself. You taught me how to keep house, you made me independent, that is what you wanted; and I have learned one or two things about cooking. But the real point lies beyond all this, and the real point I cannot explain. It is just necessary for me to have a place on my own where the way I want to live does not interfere with anyone else, I have no right to ask anyone, let alone you, to conduct the running of a house according to my whims and fancies . . .

I've always understood people's need for their space. In my mother's case other anxieties operated: her fear of loneliness.

But as far as you are concerned it is a question of company. I shall be seeing quite a bit of you, that goes without saying. Friday night suppers.

Mother, I am nearly 23. I do not want to depend on anyone . . . You say Della is not like you. She is, so am I. We are all three of us stubborn, or rather I should say – determined . . .

. . . I am not sure what job I shall be going to, but I hope to have enough money to enable me to look around for a week. I might even get a job with Trans Atlantic Airways as a steward, or I might take advantage of Uncle Perly's connection with the Hungaria, I am writing to him. But whatever I get I will not stay in London all the time. I hope to go to Israel for a little while, or somewhere abroad. I want to travel.

The other letter is to Squibbs, 10 December 1954. We're planning to go to Israel together, working our passage on an orange-boat. By this time I've decided not to take a flat on my own.

. . . Instead I am going home to Weald Square where I feel it my duty to be for at least some time before I move off again. I cannot explain this sense of duty. I have always felt guilty at not being able to do anything for Leah and Joe. The problem has always been – can I do anything by being with them? The answer is no. But if it gives Leah some pleasure that will be something . . .

I inform him I'm coming to London with Dusty and that we're going to the Festival Hall, perhaps he could accompany us; but I urge him not to discuss our plans for travel in front of Dusty.

You see she does not like to face the idea that I am leaving and pre-fers that no word is said until the last day and then – I should just disappear . . ..! This is a very sad case dear Squibbs and one which I shall inform you of at some later date. No woman has ever been so in love with me. That does sound a little dramatic, but then you know, there is a certain amount of drama in life and though I have been trying to avoid it since being here, or rather since the affair with Olive ended, I'm afraid I have not succeeded. I find things hap-pen around me. Without looking . . .

In that earlier letter to my mother is a story about Dusty's mother which illustrates a striking Bicker trait:

Ralph . . . told me you had a very bad cough . . . Why don't you go to a doctor? . . . Dusty's mother has done what you should have done. She has been troubled with gall stones and has had to go into hospital for an operation. Her family said that she would not go in before Xmas. So yesterday morning, after her husband had gone to work, she left the house and came into hospital not having told anyone excepting Dusty, who met her and took her in. She left a note for her husband – gone to hospital for an operation, see you in three weeks' time. Neither her son nor other daughter knew any-thing about it! What a way to carry on, but she is in, and it will soon be over. You should do something like that.

Decisive, stubborn, independent. Like mother like daughter. Like mother like son, too: Leah was full of doubt, guilt, self-criticism. Mother Bicker never discussed anything. She talked, endless stories, but no exchange of ideas or opinions; Mother Leah imagined that talking solved all problems, she believed that if you listened to others they would listen to you. My father's refusal to talk aggravated her sorely, though of course as time went on he became silent because unable to counter anything she said. A vicious circle: expectation, failure, chastisement, silence. But between her and me argument flowed hot and relentlessly. We both believed, in our unworldly ways, that people could be reasoned with. My letter to her continues, reasoning:

> ... You ask me to be a man and face the facts. Suppose I were to believe you were right. Look what it would mean. You say I should not dream, that I am irresponsible. So I say to myself, 'Arnold, you are quite a child, you cannot roam around on your own because you cannot look after yourself. Arnold, there is no other future for you than to go into a trade like the rest of your cousins and friends. Do what your mother wants and go home to her and let her look after you, she knows better. Her experience is good enough for you.' Is that what you want? ... But what kind of man would that make me? Wasn't Daddy continually going home to Boba? ... Now I do not suggest that the alternative is to ignore and completely lose contact with one's parent, but I do believe that there is a time in a man's life when it is healthy for him to break away and live life on his own. And that is what I am doing. And it does not mean that I have deserted you or lost my love for you, on the contrary it means that you have given me confidence and I am extremely grateful ...

A lot of living was being done: Della, Ralph and the boys in their rural retreat; me in the kitchen surrounded by quirky personalities living quirky lives; and in London my mother and father, locked in that eternal wrestle of the sexes, each wondering what had gone wrong, when precisely, and who was to blame; and around them a cluster of other lives – relatives and friends – all, all doing a lot of living. But for Leah the two most important people in her life were her children, the source of endless guilt. She needed constant re-assurance. Sometimes I could offer it.

One night last week as I lay in bed listening to music, I think it was Elgar, I suddenly felt a longing to see you. I have not felt like that since I was evacuated. It was very strong, I think I know why it was. I sometimes feel your loneliness so much, I know so very well your every feeling, that you feel failure and emptiness. As if I were there with you when you think about us, as if we were the same. We both know loneliness, you and I, we are the same. I shall always be your son . . . it will be a combined effort to success even though we are apart. It's no use telling anyone else that, it is no use explaining. What kind of laughter would the Uncles and Aunts and cousins raise? . . . I cannot believe a struggle will prove nothing in the end. And if it does then God! we have at least tried . . . I have my life three times to live over, and there is still room for your happiness. But you must look after yourself, you must not do silly things. Not even genius can live on ill health . . . body *and* soul must be kept together . . .

Both Della and I were the outsiders in the family. We were close to cousins and loved by aunts and uncles – many paid visits to 'the country estate' in Wacton – but we were the unconventional ones. There was something of risk-taking in the lives we lived. My mother frequently had to face them, her brothers and their children – my uncles my cousins. They asked questions, made observations, did not withhold judgement and warning. Leah defended me to them, I know. A son could not have wanted for a more loyal mother. There was less need to defend Della. Living in the country might be viewed odd but she had done conventional things like marry and have children. I was the problem. It wasn't always easy to explain me to relatives and friends. Some of her distress came through in her letters to which I responded with heat and passion, if slightly illogically.

. . . I say I want to write and make films, but what does that mean to friends and relatives? They are so practical and experienced that they lack the enthusiasm to live . . . I can feel their scepticism even at this distance and in their silence, their doubt and warnings. And because I can feel it I know what it must be like each time you face them. At the age of twenty-one your son has no bank balance to show, no fine clothes, no wife and children, and he is chasing nothing nowhere. That is all you can say to anyone who asks you how your son is. My darling little mother, this is your agony isn't it? Not because you want to boast of him, I don't mean that, but you feel it is a reflection on you, that you could give him nothing. But you can tell them this, that my dearest possessions are what you gave me, that if there is any integrity, any nobleness, any goodness and kindness, any sensitivity – it is yours. If I love music it is because you love it, if I am tender with children, if I appreciate beauty, it is inherited from you. If I am prepared to go without luxuries to achieve my ends it is because you went without them to bring up your children. Any guts I have you had. That is what you gave him, and you can tell them all that, and when you have told them that you can tell them to go to Hell!

I was in a state of guilt and confusion over my relationship with Dusty. I returned to London. She vowed she would join me and find a job. I warned her against following me. We had no future together. In June 1955 the letter I wrote urging her to stay in Norfolk and finish with me was prophetic.

. . . Despite an immense affection for you, despite some gloriously happy times we have together, despite that at times I pine for your company yet still . . . I am not nor will allow myself to be in love . . . My relationship with you – though easy for the most part – is that little dishonest as to cause me utter misery, and this feeling every so often touches you, and then you too become unhappy. If it does not end now it will become more complicated and worsen. I see that so clearly that it is almost a vision.

She ignored me as she frequently did and found herself a job working and living in at the National Hotel near Russell Square. It was a period of being together and not being together. Hazy, actually, until Uncle Perly found me a job at the Hungaria restaurant at 16 Lower Regent Street, and then life settled down into another kind of rhythm. I learned how to bake pastries and concoct desserts, Dusty became 'my woman', and the tendrils of our lives began their slow, embracing twist and curl, each around the other.

Chapter Twenty

The Hungaria

It not only made sense, having spent fourteen months working in a kitchen, that I should continue working in one, I wanted to as well. Kitchen life appealed to me. Though I had not yet been introduced to the sensuous pleasures of kneading dough, slicing out segments of orange, tossing pancakes, whipping egg yolks, and pulling sugar, I knew I would be happy in a kitchen. Uncle Perly came to my rescue. He had made a friend of Louis Vechi, the Hungarian who created and ran the Hungaria restaurant, and through him secured me a job as a trainee pastry cook. I began in September 1955.

The restaurant was in decline, its glory passed – if the subdued-lighted rooms with their decor of Magyar emblems, faded panels of green, red and ochre-coloured flowers, and the pseudo tzygane band of violinist and accordionist could ever be called 'glory'. Once upon a time three rooms throbbed nightly with hundreds of patrons desperately gay between the wars; now the evening atmosphere gasped like a dying age, only one room served at most a hundred and twenty-five mainly old patrons remembering their youth, businessmen entertaining mistresses, tourists seeking the grandeur that was Rome.

Not long after I began, Louis Vechi sold out to an enormous Italian with sad saucer eyes, Andy Mazzula. Vechi had the *maître d'hôtel*'s supreme virtue of making his guests feel they and only they were his specials. He became their friend, their confidant, and attracted that affection he would bestow. He was an unhappy man for reasons I knew nothing about.

Mazzula, a pale impersonator of Vechi's charm, one minute mournfully pleaded for a customer's happiness and patronage and the next raged at chef's incompetence. Exaggeratedly pleasant with his guests upon whom he beamed a disarming charm and childlike smiles, he could storm down upon the kitchen in a loud Italian or French rage to complain of a raw steak or a burnt chop. I experienced both – pleasant salutations and angry barks. He spoke a Cockney English and castigated me for offering up a clumsily laid-out peach melba, a crime I was not guilty of and told him so. The temperament of culinary folk at fever pitch tended to be childish. Naughtily, I was aloof and amused. It would have been easier, more in keeping with the place, to shout and be angry, but, as at the Bell, I had this damn angel who rendered me sweet and observing. Not an angel of goodness, more a literary guardian angel who cautioned: stay calm, smile, make notes!

We clocked in by the doorkeeper's office and descended steps into the murky womb of iron and steam where the *chefs du monde* bubbled, fried and screamed their culinary births to life. We lived an isolated, privileged life away from the prima donnas who cooked and sweated out their furies.

The pastry cabin – and cabin it was, if you were more than 5ft 4ins you were too tall – was hidden round the corner from the main kitchen off a low passage, leading up to the restaurant, above which rumbled generators and the intermittent quake of our fridge sounding like the depths of a ship. Here we worked undisturbed by the distant feverish screech of crazy chefs and the harsh bark of the clerk ordering meals through the loudspeaker. No need for a tannoy in our cabin; commis waiters came with special papers for desserts. Poor devils, mainly Cypriots, they had to run up and down two flights of stairs balancing trays laden with food in silver dishes. Occasionally one would trip throwing chips, chops, peas and silver service in all directions, escaping injury perhaps but never the shock or scolding for lost profits.

When I started, three other people worked in the pastry section: Victor, the first pastry chef; Sylvester, the second pastry chef; and Michael, the young apprentice. Six weeks later, having worked four years from five in the evening till one o'clock at night, Sylvester left to take a course in ladies' hairdressing. He had been an officer in the

Polish air force – why were all the Poles officers? He left triumphantly as though he were at last leaving the rabble for a higher level of social occupation. Michael didn't stay much longer. At seventeen he was a restless suburban youth, full of romantic tales about 'incidents' that befell him. He seemed hardly able to live a day without 'a very funny thing' happening to him, usually involving a girl in St James's Park, where he spent his three-hour break in the afternoon; or on his train home, or in the district of Barnet where home was. Victor never believd his stories, and would smile his slight smile of mocking incredulity at me while Michael bumbled heedlessly on in that north London accent that was trying hard to forget its Cockney origins. There was the girl who smiled at him day after day and one day – winked. Michael told his stories as though he could hardly believe all that life offered. Though not every day winked at him – one girl he met in St James's Park didn't turn up for the second date. Imagine! Some days bewildered him. Which perhaps is why he should have been believed. He told us a long story about a girl who walked by in the street and responded to his pass; they went to a dance, got very drunk – 'Her blouse was wide open,' he assured us, 'but I didn't touch her.' Instead he carried her half a mile in his arms to get her safely home. 'Honest!' Gallant boy. I don't think they make them like Michael any longer. He broke off his apprenticeship and went to work in a factory canteen. Conscription hovered. Do Michaels ever find the woman they deserve?

I was left alone with Victor in the cabin where he taught me how to toss and stack a supply of crêpes, roll butter between layers of pastry for '*mille-feuilles*', drop dates, marzipan and grapes into boiling sugar, toffee, which I tested for 'soft' or 'brittle' by dipping my fingers and quickly cooling them in cold water. Brittle was time to dip. I learned about meringues, and how easy it was over a bain-marie to slowly stir yolks into zabaglione for which the earth was charged. Some recipes I asked Victor to repeat for me to write down. Like most chefs he left out an ingredient or gave me the wrong measurement. Efforts at home never matched what he achieved. Only by stealth and cunning I built up a black book of recipes which is still somewhere around in the house.

I enjoyed pulling the paper-thin paste for strudel but the most satisfying activity in the kitchen was pulling toffee for *petits fours*. When brittle, the boiling water and sugar would be poured and spread like molten lava over a well-oiled marble slab. A spatula would be slid underneath it from time to time while it cooled. Then, when cooled sufficiently to handle but still hot enough to be pliable – and that was very hot – it was shaped into a length of sugared piping, pulled arm's-length long, the ends brought together, the length gripped in the oiled palm of a hand and squeezed and slid down to the end which was raised to meet the other end, brought together again, squeezed, pulled, the ends brought together, squeezed, pulled, brought together and so on. Each time the ends were brought together a thin tunnel of space was formed. So the first bringing together created one long tunnel, the second, two long tunnels, the third, four long tunnels, eight, sixteen, thirty-two . . . The aim was to create a length of aerated toffee which could be cut into crunchy sweets, usually minted. The hotter you could stand, the more pulling you could do, and the more holes create before it became brittle and unpliable – more holes, more crunchiness! Skin hardened, inevitably. It was satisfying, a touch dangerous, and fun.

My pastry chef, Victor, was born in Tunis of parents descended from Sicilian grandparents. He spoke French, Arabic, Italian and perfect English. At the outbreak of the Second World War he had escaped to English lines, grew in the ranks to sergeant because of his command of languages, and – probably because he had made her pregnant – married an Irish lass in the Women's Royal Army Corps. Victor complained tirelessly in soft sarcastic tones of not being suited to family life, confessing he was a bad father, wishing he could return to Tunis. His moans were more than the habitual regrets of a married man with responsibilities, they were the bitter complaints of one who viewed his life as wasted upon an alien family. Yet he was entirely responsible. In addition to working at the Hungaria from 9 a.m. to 2.30 p.m. and from 7 p.m. to midnight he worked at Le Caprice between 2.30 p.m. and 7 p.m. His family wanted for nothing.

Victor had attended night school to study the science behind his culinary craft. But studies on top of work and family became too much and were never completed. Though something remained. With great pride, if occasional boring pedantry, he enjoyed explaining to me such dazzling phenomena as the chemical process taking place while sugar, glucose, and water were boiling. Intelligent linguist, a kindly, first-class chef who baked with craft, decorated with artistry, looked at the week's orders and efficiently planned and coordinated both his and my work – why then did he speak like a man crippled with a shame? Why with arrogance, facetiousness, and abuse did he hide behind a flow of caustic comments about other pastry cooks and, like most chefs, whisper snidely about colleagues behind their backs? I suspected that either his mother or father was Arab and he was ashamed, he felt foreign. A pity, for it led him to squander his intelligence trying to convince everybody he was the best. In Victor's view all the other pastry cooks baked 'shit'. 'Mind you,' he would temper his condemnations guiltily, 'he was a nice fellow, a very nice fellow – but – he used to make the most funny macaroons, no, honestly, don't laugh, all over the place. Loved his wife, nice to the children, but those macaroons, I'm telling you – shit!'

At the other end of the spectrum was Rosie, the cleaner who helped Miss Razin, keeper of the stores. Rosie was like no one I had ever met, though there must have been countless such chars whose 'Daily Mirror Charlady Ball' she once attended at the Savoy Hotel. Widowed for twenty-five years, proud of her three fine daughters, faithful to the memory of her sailor husband whose virility she constantly reminded us satisfied her 'even up to this very day', Rosie was the most gloriously smutty person I knew, whose vulgarity was as delightful as she was good-natured.

I could always tell it was Rosie trying to surpise me from behind because she invariably placed her middle finger deep into my young

bum and moved it gently around, asking: 'Like it? Nice, eh? Not
spiteful am I? Got a nice touch 'aven't I? That's what me 'usband
always used to say – "You got a nice touch, Rosie love."' Bashful, in
case someone thought I enjoyed being touched up by an old
woman, which I did, I would turn and hasten to ask what she
wanted. A dessert, usually, for Miss Razin and herself. 'Watcha got
for two nice little gals?' I would dish out some of yesterday's fruit
salad, knowing she would push her glasses up her nose and complain: "Ere, what the fuckin' 'ell is this?' It was a ritual. I would
pacify her, assure her the salad had been covered in the fridge, was
still crisp enough to enjoy, and she would relent her ferocity and
move up to me in search of other parts. 'All right darlin', now don't
get angry. Ooooah! That's nice! Gotta nice little bunch there 'e 'as.'
When I backed away she complained: 'Gertcha yer miserable sod,
won't let me 'ave a feel.'

Somehow everything was – innocent. Round, plump, and pleasant, Rosie never offended. Her eagerness to share intimate details
of her past was warm rather than prurient. 'My 'usband, a real sailor
'e was, 'ad a weapon like this,' she bent her arm, slapped her
muscle, and clenched her fist, 'a weapon to be proud of. You don't
need a bed for it . . . Best place is on the rug in front of the fire. On
a Sunday afternoon we'd pack the kids off to Sunday school an' then
me an' my ole man would get down on the rug an' 'is little ole bottom would go up and down an' I'd pat it an' say "Good ole boy,
keep goin'", an' 'e'd get roasted an' then me, I'd get roasted an'
ooooah!' Rosie sighed and cooed over memory and loss. A lonely
woman despite the heartily shared confidences – all those years,
and three daughters to handle. But she swore she had never lain
with another man. 'Never wanted to. Me 'ubby give me all I
wanted. Now? I've got another one growin' now, all new and virgin
. . . ooooah.'

While Rosie was sexually teasing me, Victor teased Annie, a
sweet Irish waitress who cooed her way into our hearts and seemed
not to mind Victor stroking her bum while she waited for me to
ladle out a fruit salad or sprinkle with icing sugar a crêpe Suzette to

grill and douse with lemon. She'd mind now, no doubt, and Victor would not dare, as he did in those days, to lay a mirror at her feet that would show him what her skirts hid, and his hands would freeze before sidling her curves. I have no memory of patient forbearance on the part of Annie, though; she passed the time of day with him. They exchanged matrimonial problems and professional grouses. It was a tolerable lechery for the work-worn. It was part of the play. And Annie was not shy to stroke a thigh or two. Limits were understood.

Fire! Fire!

It was the day of the 'great fire'. Victor and I were at work in our cabin off the passageway away from the main cooking area. We heard the rumblings of commotion and the muttering of 'Fire, fire,' repeated again and again. Bodies ran backwards and forwards. Victor poked his head round the corner and reported, laconically, 'I think there's a fire in the kitchen, I'm not sure, a lot of running around, something.' He returned to piping his *langues de chat* or macaroons or cutting out pastry for piroshkis, or whatever. His cool demeanour was appealing. Nothing agitated him. He was the Spencer Tracy of the tarts and strudels.

What was happening was this: over the ovens hung huge extractor fans which sucked the smoke and smells along metal channels out from the kitchen into the street. No one ever cleaned them and they accumulated an inflammable mixture of grease and dust. Frying pans often flew afire and flared for split seconds, flames shooting up to disappear in air. One flame, refusing to disappear, had attached itself to the dust and grease. The greedy fan had sucked it into the dark tunnels thick with combustiles, and a happy fire was en route wherever the tunnels ran. They ran outside our cabin.

Victor, to begin with, was not worried – the fire seemed to be playing only in the kitchen area. We were safe. Young Byron continued to work alongside Spencer Tracy. Until. Until suddenly smoke was creeping towards our cabin. Without moving, Spencer said: 'Perhaps we'd better move.' Young Byron shrugged his shoulders and remained. He enjoyed the image of himself not panicking. The smoke thickened, the light dimmed, the scurrying appeared more urgent. 'Come,' said Spencer Tracy, picking up his pouch of tobacco from which he rolled his cigarettes. But Young Byron felt he ought to make a stand and fight the fire. A few yards along the passageway towards the restaurant stood a huge red fire extinguisher with its brass button on the top and a small hose dangling at its side. Young Lord Byron reached for it, stood bravely in the passageway facing the oncoming flames and banged down upon the brass button with his right hand, the little hose in his left. Nothing happened. He banged again. Nothing. He kept banging but the button failed to plunge. No extinguishing fluid ejaculated; too old, too rusted, obviously. The smoke became overwhelming. Young Byron fled. He'd not been taught that to operate the contraption it had to be turned upside down and the brass button smashed against the floor. Had he a tail it would sheepishly have drooped between his legs.

One day Victor announced he was leaving the Hungaria for Le Caprice. They had offered more money. 'Better class of people,' I remember him saying. 'Be appreciated, too. Not like this place. They treat you like shit in this place.' An Italian pastry chef took over. His hame was Raymond. I have no memory of mannerisms or incidents with Raymond, though I see him clearly. Where Victor was taciturn Raymond was open and friendly, more homely. He was still there when we moved to Paris.

While I worked at the Hungaria Dusty worked at the National Hotel. During break between lunch and dinner she'd meet me at the back door and we'd either sit in the Harmony Inn, a small Italian restaurant nearby, visit galleries, window-shop, or walk across to St James's Park, spending hours in the grass snogging, exchanging news, talking about our lives, the future and what was to be done about her pregnancy. Dusty's pregnancy – I'll come to that. There was rarely enough time to go home to Weald Square during the short break, though I remember doing so when it seemed crazy to wander around the West End for wandering's sake.

Uneasy returns

However much I craved a flat of my own, living at home was more convenient and, though I contributed generously to the running of Weald Square, cheaper. Contributing to family finances was one of the factors deciding me to return. It gave me pleasure to help put a home together. A last letter to Leah from Norwich before returning:

> I can imagine the rush and arrangements that are taking place at Weald Square just now. Big furniture rearrangements, large bakings and midnight polishing sessions. Ah, the children are coming, the children! The children! And the dog no doubt . . .
> When I say I like quiet I do really mean just that. Oh not all the time of course, but I think you will find that I shall spend a lot of time in my own room, that is if the job I find does not call me elsewhere. I am a son, but I am also an individual with my own likes and dislikes which you cannot expect will conform to your own. Another thing is that I cannot possibly hope to get a suite of furniture and pay off for it. I do not intend to hang around for two years unless I get the job I want. There are other plans for furniture afoot which you will know of in due course! Meanwhile a lot of patience and understanding is going to be needed from us both. We are very good people, you and I, but we are difficult to get on with . . .

It was not easy returning to Weald Square. Love them though I did, Mother and I quarrelled over politics, and I became impatient with Joe.

Two letters written by Squibbs from Toronto remind me what was happening. He wants us to join him in Canada. It was one of the ventures, along with other ideas for travelling the world, which Dusty and I discussed lying on our backs in St James's Park. Two months later I write informing him Dusty is pregnant – a factor bearing upon deliberations to join him or not in Canada. By the end of March 1956 we decide Dusty should have an abortion. Canada is out, Paris in. Squibb's had offered to help with our fares. He is sad and disappointed. Canada, he felt, offered more financial rewards than Paris.

> . . . Paris in the spring will surely be beautiful but hunger knows no frontiers . . .

I can't remember how we found the money to pay for Dusty's abortion. It wasn't a Harley Street job and so couldn't have been a Harley Street fee. Which means we took risks. It was not pleasant, I was full of guilt, Dusty full of pain. I accompanied her to wherever it was, and have only the haziest memory of a woman greeting us at a door and taking Dusty into the doctor's room. We returned to 523 Finchley Road, the huge Victorian house which Della and Ralph had by then taken over as wardens of the Primrose Jewish Youth Club. It was the venue where, two years later, we gathered 150 guests to celebrate our marriage, but sometime in March or April 1956 a small top room in that large, rambling house was where, under Della's watchful concern, Dusty lay down to cry, sleep and recover from her ordeal. Neither of our parents were informed that they nearly had a grandchild.

The notebook

In the little buff notebook, 4″ × 6″, are diary sheets which not only record events but reveal a state of mind memory might have romanticised. We are approaching Christmas 1955.

This morning he must have risen with mother. Usually he is asleep till I leave for work about 10 a.m. The first sounds I heard were of them shouting at each other, or rather he was shouting. There is a difference in their quarrels nowadays. They do not scream, and the harangue lasts only a few minutes. As this morning. The shouting done, their voices subsided into low, intimate – even friendly – mumbles. This was around 7.30 a.m.

At 8 their voices rose again and this time mother was urging him to go down and buy cigarettes for himself insted of waiting till I was awake and smoking mine. I knew he would soon be in to ask me. Each morning he asks me for a cigarette. There is no reason why he should not, nor is there a reason why I should not give it to him. Yet each time he asks I feel a tightening of my nerve ends. This routine of asking me for a cigarette wears upon me, as the perpetual drop of water upon a certain place. So that when on some mornings he has cigarettes of his own I feel a relief, a relaxation. It's a pleasant feeling.

This morning, as soon as mother brought me some tea in bed, he came in and asked for his cigarette. I had only one left and told him so. He then asked for my matches, and as I lay in bed I could hear him striking match after match puffing at his pipe which could only have been filled with ash. This annoyed me and I wanted to tell him not to waste my matches. I controlled the impulse. What is a match? What, for that matter, is a cigarette? I could have given my last one.

Then I heard mother complain to him about his shirt which must have been sticking out of his trousers displaying brown stains – the result of a recent attack of diarrhoea. He does not keep himself clean.

When mother had gone to work he asked me who it was that I had invited for Sunday.

'Heinze,' I replied.

'Who?'

'Heinze,' I said louder.

'Oh, Chaim.'

'No! Heinze, HEINZE – a cook I work with. You don't know him so why do you ask?' I had shouted.

'Oh, oh!' he said, and shuffled away. I was suddenly reminded that this was how my aunts, his sisters, had behaved with their mother, who had been bedridden. She used to aggravate them no end with her nagging questions. It seemed to me that he too was becoming like his mother. As though he *wanted* to be like her, to do nothing, to be attended to. The cycle completes itself. He can't help but grope towards that existence which was his mother's. My grandmother's.

Christmas Day 1955

The table is laid prettily. Dusty has set it in style upon a clean, white tablecloth. Two glasses are set, one each for the white and red Chianti, another for the Cointreau or Kummel. All three rest on the table suggesting not the ostentation of an un-Christ-like Christmas, but the simple layout of a family unused to the luxuries of wines with meals. Four of us wait. The table is set for five. We await Ann Gould [a friend of Leah's].

But He, my father, sits by the fire where he has sat most of the day and most of yesterday. We have been trying to infuse him with some spirit. We asked him to wash, change into a clean shirt, comb his hair. 'Ach! Leave me alone.' But finally he moved to change his shirt.

Last night he sat as Leah, having spent most of the day cleaning out the house, was finishing the floor. In fact it was about one in the morning. She turned to him and asked:

'Joe, do you remember what you promised me last night when we went to the pictures? Remember? Eh, Joe? What did you say? That you would help me today. Well? You've sat like this all day, and watched me. All your life you've done this. Sat and watched me.'

What does he feel when such words are said to him? He sat, and looked away, as he always looked away. Leah was not shouting, nor did she nag. Rather it was a sort of lament. Then silence.

Leah finished work and we sat down for a last cup of tea. Again she turned to him, again it was neither nagging nor shouting.

'In all seriousness, answer me, why? Why did you not help me do the house all day? Answer me.'

He shrugged his shoulders, looked away and said: 'I don't know. I don't know.'

Leah turns to me. 'He doesn't know.' And she too shrugs her shoulders in acceptance.

And so all day long he sat. What is in the mind of the man that he can sit and watch his – not all that healthy – wife work, and he be content? His illness may slow up his activity but the cause of such complete inertia must have its roots elsewhere. And where is that 'else'? There is something in moving to make an effort for anything that seems to have great significance for him. To move means – but what? Why should all effort be so repugnant to him?

At last he has changed his shirt. His hair is combed.

'I could fall in love with you all over again,' says Leah.

19th March 1956
Dreams
Last night I dreamt that Dusty accompanied me on a journey into what appeared to be a sort of jungle. We carried rucksacks. It was not a dense jungle, more like an English forest. We had pieces of meat which I said we must eat at once or else they will go off, and that we must buy more tinned stuff further on, like black beans and such because that is what we will need to eat as we go deeper into the jungle.

Then the scene changed, not as abruptly as usual. There was a reason. A friend of Dusty's, God knows who, said she must come to her house first, before continuing on. So we find ourselves wandering along streets that are vaguely familiar. Now events do become hazy and I know that I am looking at prostitutes in the street. A taxi comes along and one prostitute stumbles out after having been with a man. She is ill. I see the others go to her and lay her down on the pavement. This is not wrong, it is like laying her in a hospital bed.

Then I am with Dusty in a taxi. She tells me with half a smile, as though it were only a joke and she 'only merely did it to see what it was like'. She tells me, or I guess, that she has been with a man. I am astounded. Then she says, 'Oh Wizzie, I don't feel like I want to do it any more.'

I don't know what happens next but it seems that Dusty has taken to prostitution, only the woman I now see is not Dusty but someone else, a woman we both have seen in the Harmony Inn on occasions, a woman heavily made-up, tall, long face, looking as though she was once either a chorus girl or a prostitute. This is the face we see but somehow I know it is really Dusty.

I find myself chasing her along the street. She darts into a passageway that leads to her room. It is a place where other women stay.

She is one of a syndicate. I push my way past people who are ineffectually attempting to stop me. She tries to close her door on me. I push it, force it open, and confront her. Then I slap her face, once, twice, back and forth. I seem unable to stop. I can only keep slapping. Then I stop and fall to her feet in uncontrollable tears. She says, oddly: 'All I have to do is hoover three times a day, and I've only seen three men. What *is* it?'

I am horrified. I say: 'What was it, what happened, where was the mistake, what did I do? Because it's me! It's because of me you're like this.' And she nods her head very knowingly. Of course she knows.

That dream was full of such despair it remains with me this morning. Two feelings are uppermost – how I slapped her and how I cried.

There was a sequel to this dream, I mean in reality. The dream affected me the rest of the day. By the time Dusty came home I was in the most distant of moods, moved and angered. I had been waiting to see her, to be with her, and when she came I was one minute holding her close and the next minute turning away. The dream had unsettled me. We ate, I bathed and changed ready to go to the Festival Hall. God knows what was going on inside me (though I did know – her pregnancy was affecting me more than I imagined it would). She told me she had been to the Lyceum dancing in her new dress. She was not wearing it that day for me to see, and that upset me. We waited for time to pass and as she sat on my knee I murmured, almost as though it were another man talking: 'You're not really a tart like the other dance-hall girls are you?' She didn't take my tone too seriously and replied: 'No, of course not.'

Victor Sylvester's music came on the radio. She has a passion for him and started swaying to his rhythms. This unnerved me. Her levity, her youthful joy twisted itself into me. I stood up. A rumba, her favourite, was playing. 'You don't want me to dance it with you, do you?' I pleaded. She said no. I moved swiftly into the bedroom. I was trembling and on the verge of tears. She followed me and hugged me from behind as I stared out of the window.

'Don't be like this,' she said. We remained in silence for some minutes, she holding me, not knowing what was wrong. 'When you're like this I feel I want to do something,' she said.

'Do what?'

'Anything to please you.'

More silence. We men never cry. We fight for our damned manhood. Then I told her:

'I dreamt last night you were a prostitute.'

'But nothing has happened to give you that idea.' I did not reply. Instead I turned and embraced her passionately. She took me to the bed and we lay down together. I wanted to bury myself in her. Disappear. I told her the whole dream.

'But we're not like that.' She spoke of herself and the other girls.

'You all are,' I said in madness. 'You are all capable of becoming prostitutes. What would happen to you if you did not know me?' I asked. 'You would have nothing to hold you back.'

She was silent. Then she muttered:

'Oh dear! I am disgusted – with you!' And she began crying. I could not bear that and felt unutterably mean. I kissed her and tried to soothe her.

'It was a dream about me,' I said, 'not you. I feel guilty for despoiling you, hurting you. It was about me.'

Children that we are. I wiped her tears with my cheeks and held her close. We are rarely masters of ourselves which is why we are dangerous to each other, but at such moments we come so close.

31st March 1956

The incredible turn of events in the history of communism cannot pass without I recall it, briefly, here.

Stalin died only a few years ago. Beria – head of security police – was shot for betraying the principles of socialism and being the cause of many innocent people's death.

Burgess and Maclean, from the Foreign Office, defected to Moscow . . . Khrushchev and Malenkov have stepped forward with large, childlike smiles, into the Western world, and renewed relations with Jugoslavia . . . The *Daily Worker* now praises Bertrand Russell and Sartre – whom I once remember them damning as reactionaries . . . The CPs of the world and especially of Britain suddenly found that Stalin and his policy which they once praised was now in disgrace; that the men they once criticised as reactionaries and traitors were not so; that the men whose death they once condoned were in fact innocent.

There has been an enormous spate of letters in the *Daily Worker*
from party members who are virtually in tears for having been so
lacking in courage, approving the policy of 'the Russian brides', 'the
ten doctors', 'anti-titoism' etc. Many are confessing that at the time
they did indeed feel uneasy, and now – now that the new Soviet
leadership has given them the lead – a great weight seems lifted
from their shoulders. They can look people in the eye. It is as
though they had all gone to a mass confessional and now, with the
terrible secrets in their heart out in the open, they feel like new
people . . .

And yet – despite the horror and implications of these confessions – there is a superb naivety, an amazing childlike appearance
to their new attitudes. These are children, at once guilty and innocent. Personally I am torn between a righteous accusation and
absolute forgiveness.

But Leah cannot understand what has happened, what to say or
feel or think. She is at once defensive and doubtful. She does not
know who is right. To her the people who once criticised the party
and were called traitors are still, to her, traitors . . . For her there is
either black or white, communist or fascist. There are no shades.
Perhaps it's unfair to judge all communists alongside her, for she is
an extreme case. Her politics are intricately bound up with her
psychological dilemma, a dilemma which sees everything as a
capitalist conspiracy not merely against progress but against her.
She has quarrelled with almost every shopkeeper in the district and
now goes as far afield as Petticoat Lane in order to shop. She feels
estranged from a greater part of her family because she imagines
that a criticism of her politics is a criticism of her.

'If you are not with me,' she cries, 'then you must be against me!'
If she admits that the party has been wrong, that Stalin committed
grave offences, then she must admit *she* has been wrong; all those
she mistrusted she must now have second thoughts about, and this
she cannot do because having bound her politics so closely to her
personality she would then have to mistrust her personality. You
can admit the error of an idea but not the conduct of an entire life.

For you see, the conduct of her life has been as chaotic as her
politics were vague. To live with her, to shop with her, is to be conscious of a strong personality not knowing the right thing to do.

(Minor, yet indicative, is the number of times she asks me to go down to the shops to buy something she has forgotten.)

The most important observation to be made of her is that she never wanted to do the wrong thing but never knew what was the right thing. Because she was a woman of action she had to do something, and it was usually the wrong something! Different from Joe, who, though he too never wished ill, never did the right thing simply because he did nothing. These are the two extremes between which I've lived – indolence degenerated to morbid apathy, and dynamic ill-chosen action now become neurotic activity.

Collapse is inevitable, tragically. I can foresee it, and feel powerless. There is nothing more depressing than the sight of two exellent human beings moving towards destruction without knowing why and without the ability to avert it.

Sometime later – undated
Such times are depressing. The day is dull. My mother is ill. Not only has that active spark lost its drive but the machine itself is puffed out and short of breath. Her face has a deathly pallor and the house itself, despite that I redecorate and brighten it up, seems to fall to pieces. She seems no longer able to keep ends together. There is always washing and ironing to do, surfaces to dust, dishes to be washed. All that was the energy of the Wesker household is now ashes in time. And in the midst of it all, perhaps top of the pile, sits Joe. Silent and immobile, guilty and listless. She and I still feel he could make the effort, we shall always feel that, yet know he will not. He remains unshaven, smoking, in trousers that are dirty and smell with urine he could not contain, and I want to sit at his feet and weep and ask him to take up the responsibility of our lives which he has never done. He has pulled her down, held her back, and I feel he does the same to me. There he sits like an immovable mountain blocking the view. I do not seem able to see beyond him. I know Leah cannot.

Oh to be able to gather everything up and move to a new place.

Sometime later – undated
Consider the things he does not care to do. He told the doctor that he no longer cares. At night he does not care to undress. He removes only his shoes, socks and trousers, and sleeps in his vest,

pants, and shirt. But this he has always done. In the morning he does not care to wash – simply to smoke a cigarette, as soon as his eyes open. He does not care to do up his shoelaces or his fly buttons so that his shirt hangs out from the front. Nor does he care to shave or comb his hair or change a dirty shirt or reach for an ashtray which is an arm's length away, instead he uses the cup or the carpet. He does not care to go down for cigarettes but remains seated puffing at a pipeful of dog-ends, and once seated cares not to move, but will sit, slumped and fitted into the chair, with his legs outstretched, his hands in his pockets and his chin upon his chest. Sunken, within himself.

Somehow I understand his state of mind so well.

He does not care to wash up or clear up, to make himself food. A cup of tea, some bread, an egg perhaps. One might say that his ill-health does not allow him to do anything more. Partly correct of course – but it is the spirit that is dead, the will. It is the unavoidable end of a man who has watched his own disintegration, knew it even, knew also that nothing could be done. That is what the death of a spirit is – the resignation with which one accepts what one knows to be inevitable.

Primrose

Shortly before the war ended, the official Jewish community in Great Britain formed 'The Committee for the Care of Children from Concentration Camps'. A clumsy name deliberately formulated to avoid equivocation about purpose. The committee requested permission from the Home Office to scour Europe for young survivors. Permission was granted for a thousand to be brought into the country. Only 732 children under sixteen could be found. Little wonder. The records list a million and a half children slaughtered in the camps. Had my mother remained in Transylvania, Della and I – or a variant of us – could have been among them. Many of us feel 'there but for the grace of God . . . '

The youngsters were filtered through Britain's country lanes into hostels specially set up for the purpose. Sam Braun must have been one of them. They recovered, more or less, from their traumas, grew up, found jobs and professions, wives and husbands, and must have wondered – why them? One group felt the need to stay in touch with each other. Primrose Jewish Youth Club was born, Thelma and Solly its first club leaders. Jewish club life began in a Christian church hall – where else! St Peter's Church in Belsize Park. Number 523 Finchley Road was found two years later, the top rooms converted into a flat for Thelma and Solly and their daughter, Deana. They opened up the club to take in other Jewish youngsters.

The original members, the camp survivors, moved on into other cities, other countries and a variety of occupations, but determined to maintain regular contact, to be there for each other in times of financial or emotional distress. The Nazi 'final solution' had tried to exterminate them, now nothing and no one else would again be permitted to achieve such a murderous goal. Few of them, as it turned out, needed financial or emotional help. Most flourished. Life is a conflict between destroyers and survivors; I believe both are born, not made. The responsibility of government is to create a society in which the one flourishes and the other cannot. Germany created an environment in which the destroyers flourished; Britain had an environment in which survivors flourished. Why? Economics never seems to me an entirely satisfactory explanation.

The Primrose group found itself with energies and resources which, because there was scant internal need, could be diverted elsewhere – worldwide to other children in distress. The '45 Aid Society' was established; 1945 was the year they came into the country; 'Primrose' was Finchley's telephone exchange. The group, now old men and women, continue to meet regularly. 1995 celebrates their fiftieth anniversary. This is the background of the club Della and Ralph took over in January 1956 some five months after I'd been working in the Hungaria. The Norfolk rural experiment appeared to have failed. But had it?

Arnold Wesker

Rural anti-semitism – an aside

Ralph had moved his workshop out of the barn into a loft over a garage in Long Stratton. Working with him there was another of my jobs before moving to the Bell. He had obtained some handsome commissions to make individual pieces of furniture, especially through the Royal Norfolk Show, for which high prices had to be charged as costs were so labour-intensive. He took pleasure in, and was gratified by, the work he produced but insufficient orders came through and he found himself making ladders and wheelbarrows and fitting out kitchens. 'It was a process of retreating from what I wanted to do to what I *had* to do,' he told me recently. 'The only way to have made it work would have been to combine it with a private income – which I didn't have, or teach – which I didn't want to do . . . Della was working as a schoolteacher but still we were not earning enough money to attend to the house.'

Even so they might have struggled on until his reputation had grown but for two other circumstances which affected Della. The first was our father's deepening illness. She felt, dutifully, a need to return to London and be near our mother. The second was confrontation with anti-semitism. Her teaching job was with infants in a church school in the nearby village of Morningthorpe. Adam was three years old and she was able to take him with her. There was no problem until a second headmistress took over and wanted Della to convert! Out of the question, of course. Tension developed and the headmistress took it out on Adam who eventually bit her. Perfectly reasonable! But it didn't advance the cause of education as Della saw it. Her real crime was her intelligence. The headmistress was intimidated. She went out of her way to make Della feel an alien in their midst. 'It was the first time I knew what it was like to be an only Jew in a community. It wasn't an atmosphere I wanted the kids to grow up in.'

A combination of all these things plus, I suspect, a sense of cultural isolation, drew them back to London. Running Primrose provided everything in one swoop: a salary, a place to live, time enough for Ralph to develop a small joinery business, good schools, and an interesting district to live in – Swiss Cottage to the south, Hampstead to the east.

He found a basement workshop in Winchester Road behind Swiss Cottage Underground, below a shop that sold chocolates handmade on the premises so that a cocoa-sweet smell drifted down to mix with the smells of glue and wood-shavings. They sell brass and ironmongery there now. I not only helped Ralph shift machinery down the narrow staircase, and install it – which he had no permission to do – I worked there to help myself through the six-month course at the London School of Film Technique. I was never convinced that Ralph found me of much use but was grateful for the pounds which saw me through the week. It was an uncertain start. The two of them worked all God's hours running the club and the business. They wrote dozens of letters by hand to designers, knocked on the door of Heal's the furnishers, 'but they didn't pay for three months', and slowly built up a reputation for quality joinery, reliability and good nature. Ralph's first commission was to fit out a pub. Then came restaurants, banks and hotels, with luck in later years they found themselves occupying premises in Hampstead which turned out to be valuable during the property boom. The joinery business flourished and they moved it three times, selling each time at a profit which now allows them a modestly untroubled retirement.

But their return from Norfolk to London upset me. I shared with them a sense of defeat, though with hindsight I think it possible they felt defeat less than my romantic youthfulness construed. The distress, as I recreated it in The Trilogy's third play, *I'm Talking about Jerusalem*, was not in reality so acute; but my admiration for the kind of people they were and the quality of life they pursued through those eight years in the Fens was deeply felt. They had put their beliefs into practice. They were my heroes.

Ralph and I were coming away from work in the basement workshop, walking back to 523 Finchley Road past the row of shops on the right before the Finchley Road Underground on the left. I seem to remember there was, perhaps still is, a toy model shop. We must have been talking about the Norfolk perod, its significance for them, for me. Whatever – he stopped and pulled me aside into one of the shop doorways to tell me something that was obviously burning within him. He was in an emotional state, I recall he was on the verge of tears. What he told me made a deep impression, though it was a strange setting for a confessional. Somewhere, perhaps, there are sheets on which I recorded his exact words. They're not to hand. Only this speech from *Jerusalem*:

DAVE   What do you think I am, Ronnie? You think I'm an artist's craftsman? Nothing of the sort. A designer? Not even that. Designers are ten a penny. I don't mind, Ronnie, believe me I don't. [But he does] I've reached the point where I can face the fact that I'm not a prophet. Once I had – I don't know – a ... a moment of vision, and I yelled at your Aunty Esther that I was a prophet. A prophet! Poor woman, I don't think she understood. All I meant was I was a sort of spokesman. That's all. But it passed. Look, I'm a bright boy. There aren't many flies on me and when I was younger I was even brighter. I was interested and alive to everything – history, anthropology, philosophy, architecture. I had ideas. But not now. Not now, Ronnie. I don't know – it's sort of sad this what I'm saying, it's a sad time for both of us, Ada and me, sad, yet – you know – it's not all that bad. We came here, we worked hard, we've loved every minute of it and we're still young. Did you expect anything else? You wanted us to grow to be giants, didn't you? 'The mighty artist-craftsman!' Well, now the only things that seem to matter to me are the day-to-day problems of my wife, my kids and my work. Face it – as an essential member of society I don't really count. I'm not saying I'm useless, but machinery and modern techniques have come about to make me the odd man out. Here I've been, 'comrade citizen', presenting my offerings, and the world's rejected them. I don't count, Ronnie, and if I'm not sad about it you mustn't be either. Maybe Sarah's right, maybe you can't build on your own.

Careless rudeness that poisons the pleasure of writing

This is a horrible profession which has never been held in such contempt; it is awful.

John Osborne, on receiving the
Writers' Guild of Great Britain Award for a lifetime achievement,
27 September 1993

While working at the Hungaria I wrote my first publishable story – 'Pools'. The date on the front page is 16 October 1955 (not, as the published version states, 1956). The story waited three years to be printed in the *Jewish Quarterly* (winter 1958/9), and then became part of the collection *Six Sundays in January*, published by Cape in 1971. It is not yet time to describe the tiny steps up towards recognition. I mention 'Pools' now because it occasioned my first encounter with the careless rudeness that poisons the pleasure of writing.

'Pools', as described elsewhere, is a story inspired by my mother's eccentric pursuit of fortune: weekly marking O's down columns of a Littlewoods football coupon. The story describes how she – thinly disguised as a Mrs Hyams – had taken over the task from her deceased husband and then her son. My father was still alive when I wrote the story, I have no memory of him filling out the coupons. Could the story be more accurate than memory?

When her husband was alive nothing used to irritate Mrs Hyams more than Wednesday night, pools night. Every week he would ask

476

her to write it out for him because he was afraid of making a mistake; every week he asked her whether or not he should change the numbers he used. 'Will Stockport and Wolves draw, do you know?' he would ask. 'If I knew,' she replied, 'I'd tell you, fool!'

Nor do *I* remember ever filling in the pools coupon other than at my mother's request – she too feared blotting the sheet with her unpredictable, scratchy nib and ink. Perhaps memory fails me there, too.

She never won, as did not Mrs Hyams. Not winners, either of them.

(My mother-in-law won. Before I came on the scene Mother Bicker won £100, a vast sum in those days. Not my poor mother.)

It was a good story, 'Pools'. Short, tight, with a bitter ending. Nicely ironic, self-deprecating. 'The Bespoke Overcoat', a short story by Wolf Mankowitz based on a tale by Gogol, had been made into – what seemed to me at the time – a touching film. Its length was between seventy-five and ninety minutes, an odd length in those days. The director was Jack Clayton. Surely 'Pools' could be made into such a film? I wrote to Mr Clayton who replied agreeing to read it. I did not expect a response within a fortnight, nor even within four weeks, but weeks into months and months and months struck me as rude, and insensitive to the growing pains of an anxious young writer. After repeated requests for a response or the return of manuscript were ignored I engaged, on a cousinly basis, the legal skills of cousin Bryan who, still early in his career, his legal spirits young and cheeky, constructed a letter of mild legal threats. Mr Clayton returned the manuscript promptly with no comment other than a sulk: well, if that's the way you're going to behave!

Such insouciance is incomprehensible to me. I reply to all correspondence on the same day, usually before I start work. My mind feels cluttered if I know letters remain unanswered, promises unfulfilled, requests unattended – even if to decline them. My character is tattered with many flaws but the courtesy of acknowledging the effort someone has made to contact me is inviolate.

Most writers have horror stories of the way they have been treated in the profession: manuscripts lost, unacknowledged, ignored; actors taking months to decline parts offered them; directors ignoring polite enquiries as to whether they would read a new play; producers who make promises which are forgotten or broken; contacts broken; enthusiasms which raise hopes then inexplicably evaporate; betrayals by colleagues who gossip poisonously, carelessly condemn. Not many weeks ago a bright young director returned the script of *Lady Othello*, after holding on to it for seven months, crumpled and coffee-stained. Even an august public body like the BBC, through the action of one of its producers, Michael Waring, behaved in such a way that I felt cheated out of a year's work on a four-part adaptation of Doris Lessing's fine novel, *The Diary of Jane Somers*. I don't fantasise vitriolic exchanges with him though I have contemplated employing the services of a witch to fashion me a pincushion in his likeness. Knowing no witch, I instead imagine him strapped between bee hives with honey spread from toe to crutch. Trevor Nunn alongside, perhaps. And Tony Church a third while I'm about it.

John Osborne wrote to me in June 1993:

> The 'production' of *Inadmissible* has been the most bitter, ignominious experience of my life. Director (nice woman, but . . .) feeble. No authority and full of fashionable 'expressionist' shit. Leading actor a TV star of monumental ego and *minuscule* talent – a familiar combination. I was *banned* from the theatre and never spoken to – not by *anyone*. When I asked the 'director' of the National: wd he have treated Noël, Beckett, Miller, or indeed Harold with such open, public contempt, he just apologised most perfunctory, adding that he thought the actor was 'convincing' (like the butler and the housemaid in Act One!). It's accepted that writers are treated like shit.

I, too, couldn't bear the screaming actor who ranted and raged without pause. No real pain. I had to leave after the interval, something I do rarely.

A litany of betrayals offers reading as sour as the nature which prompted them. They will not be documented here, I wished only to refer to their existence and chronologise the first one that happened to me: 'Pools', my initiation into the careless rudeness which poisons the pleasure of writing. I was aged twenty-three.

But of course, not everyone was rude or careless or poisonous. I owe my launching to the prompt and generous spirit of Lindsay Anderson, which was only eighteen months away from the 'Pools' misery.

Chapter Twenty-one

Paris – an introduction

We left for Paris by train and boat on 27 May 1956, three days after my twenty-fourth birthday, three days before Dusty's twentieth (nineteen days after the first night of *Look Back in Anger* which we were oblivious of), with just over £100 between us. I promised her adventure. She had never before left England. She was nervous, even a little afraid. We had not arranged for anywhere to live or work.

An exchange system operated within the catering trade arranged by the appointments bureau of the Hotel and Catering Institution – chefs wanting to work in London were exchanged for British chefs wanting to work on the Continent. My plan was to find a position for myself and then apply for a work permit. An instinct for taking control of my life asserted itself from an early age. Sometimes it works, sometimes not. Our contacts were Barney who married Monique and lived outside Paris in Mantes-la-Jolie, and a waiter from the Hungaria with whom Dusty and I became friends, a tall, good-looking, shy young man, Gerry Simpson, who worked in what we had been told was the most expensive restaurant in Paris – Tour d'Argent. I had no doubts it would be a simple task finding somewhere cheap to stay for a couple of nights while we looked for a permanent flat. All would be well. No problem was insurmountable. We were young.

It was quite a send-off. Only Leah to wave. A tiny figure on the platform. More goodbyes. Her children leaving her again. We took our seats rather than hang fondly from the door. She waved blindly at the train as it curved out of the station. She couldn't possibly have seen us through the window.

We are dazed by our own bravado and sit silent with shock. We have done it. We are actually leaving the country for foreign parts. Only Paris, it's true – not Shanghai, Katmandu, Tierra del Fuego, just Paris, a few miles beyond a narrow channel, but still – foreign parts! At first the intense state of our spirits permits nothing more than to gaze out of the window. Gradually we come down from our high – not too far down – read our papers, picnic off homemade sandwiches, have difficulty with, and giggle over, the pouring of tea from a thermos flask as the train shakes and the 'lovely South Downs' hurtle past. Nor does the boat fail to excite us. There's something dramatic about its slow easing away from harbour – the engines roll, gain momentum, the boat hisses through water, gulls screech, the driving throb increases, human voices relax and babble. The swell is light, we take in colours of sea and spray, sit in the sun till it moves out of reach, talk with a spirited young woman who is making for Naples and relates tales of travel through Europe hitching lifts with Turks.

Three cases had been sent directly to Saint-Lazare station in Paris leaving us to disembark with merely a typewriter, a holdall and Dusty's make-up case. A porter offered to show us to our seat on the train. That meant a tip. We could find our own seats 'merci beaucoup'. Another porter rudely brooked no refusal. He snatched from my grasp typewriter and holdall and fiercely led the way. Nothing was going to stop him earning *his* tip – service required or not. I offered him twenty francs – about 4½d. in those days. He shrugged his shoulders and sullenly hung about for more. I gave him another twenty francs but really wanted to kick his arse.

Finally – Paris! No surly porter could spoil our arrival into this most fabled of cities. Oh, I was going to have great thrills introducing its sights – the few I knew – to Dusty. And there were all those we would discover together. More than anything I wanted her to experience that unique street life; just sitting with a *café au lait*, dunking a croissant and watching the flow. Cousin Doris who had given me introductions to friends had also written down the address of a hotel in Rue de L'Ancienne Comédie facing Odéon Metro. Tired, hungry, grubby, it was the first place we made for.

Full! We walked in search of somewhere else and within ten minutes found a tiny room at the top of a shabby hotel in the back streets of Saint-Germain des Prés. It was eight feet by ten feet, white ceiling, walls panelled with green wallpaper – oddly contemporary; a bed, tiny bureau, small table, one chair, one midget wardrobe, basin hot and cold, no door, just a curtain for privacy – price per night 450 francs, roughly 7/9d. The weather was hot, close. First thing – strip and wash. Then – out into the streets again in quest for a permanent flat. Youth wastes no time! But we were hungry and couldn't resist beefsteak and chips in a cheap, students', steak-tough restaurant. Nor the wine. Dusty didn't like it so I drank it all and we took to the narrow streets with me dazed and tipsy. I was not yet a wine drinker.

No digs that day which ended walking by the Seine in search of the Tour d'Argent and our waiter friend from the Hungaria, Gerry. The restaurant was closed. We bought milk and biscuits and returned to a disturbed night in the tiny cubicle – our first home in Paris, our first night in Paris – where little air reached us and we kept waking to the drumming of heavy rain. Thank God for the view next morning from our balcony – sloping roofs at different heights, haphazard and endearingly human.

Gerry proved a great help when, next day, we found him. He too had experienced difficulties when he arrived. He directed us to a bureau for au pairs who told Dusty it would take at least a week to get her fixed up; then he made contact with a restaurant who were always in need of chefs, called Le Rallye on the Boulevard des Capucines. My hope had been to find work in a first-class kitchen and learn more of pastry cooking, perhaps other culinary skills. My dilemma was this: Le Rallye was not a first-class kitchen, I would learn little but – the pay was roughly six or seven times what I would earn as an *haute cuisinier*! (A pay slip dated Décembre 1956 reveals an hourly *salaire fixe* of 259 francs which for a sixty-hour week earned me £15. A fortune! Added to which were three meals a day and the odd veal cutlet or chicken breast I took home for Dusty. Towards Christmas the hourly rate increased and with it the hours we worked.) We searched on. Gerry phoned a friend who said a job was on offer in a first-class restaurant for a mere £6 a week. Commence next day! So – £6 a week or £15 rising? Fortunately the dilemma did not confront me at once. I had no permit to work first, second or third class anywhere. The people from the £6 per week restaurant, anxious to start me as soon as possible, sent me to an address where they thought I would get an instant permit. A cigar-smoking official listened patiently but informed me permits took time.

Then – a moment never to be forgotten. We had been nineteen hours without solid food and found a cheap restaurant to eat – Paris catered for students and the young. It had been a long day. Dazed, sweaty, dispirited, we returned 'home' to strip and wash. But no clean clothes. Our three trunks were still at the station, we were making no move to retrieve them until we had found a permanent residence. It was Tuesday, 29 May. Next day was Dusty's twentieth birthday. I lamented: 'I can't even send you a card,' the pathos of which made her burst into tears. My heart went out to her. All was alien. She was feeling lonely and homesick. I turned on her the full force of my confidence and high spirits. We were not stranded! We were not orphans! We were not criminals on the run from justice or naughty children absconding parental control. We could return any time, we're rich! don't worry, don't cry, we're rich! we're rich! And to prove it I grabbed our hundred English pound notes and threw them into the air to rain down on her like confetti.

Not very consoled!! But she now sleeps, naked, on the bed, and I write – naked – at the small table. Perhaps when she wakes we will go to pictures or for a walk, or to contact some contacts to help us find a place.

Next day, her birthday.

We did neither. Dusty fell asleep after I had started reading an Irish story to her – at about 7.30. I lay down at her side to wait for her to wake up. We both woke up at midnight and then slept on to 7.30 a.m. Roughly twelve hours' sleep.

D feels better, is now washing herself after having just bitten my bottom as I lay admiring its curve in the wardrobe mirror. Today we look for digs and I shall give D a birthday treat by having a slap-up meal somewhere.

No records exists of where we ate, nor does any image linger. Throwing money in the air, only that lingers. I hope we were generous to ourselves on her twentieth birthday.

Fruitlessly we followed up adverts in *France Soir* and walked and walked until we found an agency run by a woman who demanded £5 to find us somewhere to stay. The first room she found was too small, the second available for only six weeks. We took it, six weeks was better than forty-eight hours, but I stormed back to her angrily and she promised to find us somewhere more permanent for no extra fee. We rushed to retrieve our cases from Saint-Lazare and hit another moment of mercenary misery when the proprietor of the hotel we were quitting insisted on payment for the night we were not going to spend there.

Neither was I happy with the district we were now in. It was not Saint-Germain des Prés on the Seine where there was life. We were 'abroad', dammit! in search of fresh experiences, new impressions. Like a child determined on compensation I dragged poor Dusty against her will to the risqué life and bustle of Pigalle. It was late. Raining. Selfish of me. I regretted it. But it was good to be able to change into fresh clothes.

Next day we awoke to discover our hotel was close by a busy market near République. Paris after all! A breakfast of bacon and eggs for Dusty, sausage and eggs for me, bread, butter, coffee – price 10/–, then the Metro, with its famous smell of hot leather and Gauloises about which every writer writes, to Madeleine to secure a postal address, 'poste restante', and back again to our local market for a shopping spree.

Bought: camper's boiling pot, tea strainer, spoon and fork, plastic plates and cups, potatoes, onions, sugar, pot scourer and cloth; found shop where you help yourself and pay afterwards – frankfurters, pork chops, marg, baguette, bottle of wine (85 francs – 1/6), lavatory paper, salt, eggs and cheese. Came home, had wonderful time cooking first meal. Wrote letters. Went to see Elianne [friend of cousin Doris] – not there. On way back bought tube of concentrated NESTLES milk. Returned and made first cup of tea. Magnificent. Will read now – or make love. Raining still. Dusty looks well and keeps mumbling 'à ce soir' and 'poisson' and 'à demain' and 'merci beaucoup'.

Diary letters diary letters

My Paris diary – 21 June 1956 to 17 January 1957 – consists of over 30,000 words; my mother's remarkable letters to us take up more than 29,000. We were grateful for them. A lifeline. A source of encouragement reflecting our time in Paris, life at home, her humour and her indomitable spirit.

3.6.56
My dear Arnold

I was so glad to receive your letter & first of all a card, that you both arrived safely, & am glad you're having a nice time. Enjoy yourself while you are young. By now I hope you found a decent place to live in, & permit for your job.

Arnold I rather think that the place where you had two days for pastry & 4 days for cooking I should think it's good experience to learn & see French cooking, it wouldn't harm if you know the both don't you think? However by now you must be in one of the jobs, or aren't you? How long does a permit take getting? & the way accommodation is so dear I don't think you can hold out without working very soon.

How about Dusty. Dear Dusty it seems that you like Paris. Make the best of it while you are there. You've not said anything about liking it but I assume so. Why Dear Arnold do you get depressing moments? What can you lose more than a few pounds? When you'll start working you'll find you will feel more settled. Don't worry about us home at all, we are alright. I am not working yet, heard nothing about Daddy going away. But everything is going well. Daddy washed his head today without telling him, & he is just now in the kitchen having a wash. He told me he misses you for a cigarette, & many a times I want to put the kettle on for you when you come home . . .

Paris threw up lifelong friends – Sami and Lisa Dorra and their son, Francis, for whom Dusty was au pair. And six months working in Restaurant Le Rallye gave me my first play which despite its large cast of thirty is the one most performed – sixty cities, twenty-five countries, eighteen languages – and is called, not surprisingly, *The Kitchen, La Cuisine, La Cocina, Die Küche, De Keuken, Köket, Kuchnia, A Cozinha, A Konyha, Kjøkkenet, Mutfak,*   ,

   . . . Work in Le Rallye, it could be said, paid well!

4.6.56

Dear two

Here I am just back from the Hungaria. Saw bellman &, I believe it must have been, the Hungarian chef, as he happened to be upstairs speaking to the porter in Hungarian but the porter said he can't understand Hungarian. So I said I do & I told him Arnold is my son. You ought to see how he ran back as he was nearly downstairs again, & he shook my hands & said how pleased he was· to know me, & asked me how you are & whether you are working or not yet. He said nice boy, send him my best wishes & regards, & the same from the porter at the door.

Anyway your washing is not ready yet. Raymond took my address & said he will let me know when it comes back from laundry. So I can't send you the parcel yet. I haven't got your trousers from the cleaners . . .

It's a miserable day today, it has been raining all day. I hope it will clear up soon. I found daddy in bed, I don't blame him. Only I am going out today & get a job. I must earn a little more, you know what I'll do, I'll work here & there a day & so make up my money.

Don't worry about home everything is OK just write & let me know what I asked you . . .

Bless you both.

Dusty, who had never left English shores, landed her job with the Dorras through an agency. It saved us. She went for an interview. Sami, a Syrian Jew, was a travelling salesman in women's swimwear; Lisa was his American-born, gentile wife, working for American Red Cross. There was instant rapport. They judged Dusty and me sufficiently trustworthy to offer us their flat to live in for three weeks while they went on holiday to London, after which everything fell into place: my work permit came through, Le Rallye engaged me, and we found our long-stay apartment in Rue de L'Ancienne Comédie.

5.6.56

Dear Arnold

. . . I was out today rather this morning to see Norma & baby. Lovely baby, & she had a lot of cards, & I had a letter from Uncle Perly to phone him, & he said that the Home where Daddy's supposed to go, can't have him because he was under psychiatrist. Anyway I am going to try & get him to convalescent for a while one or two weeks. We here are all well. I still haven't got your washing . . .

Dear Dusty don't worry if you don't like Paris. There is still 32 Weald Squ. London England very welcome.

Only try to enjoy yourself while you are there . . .

15.6.56

My Dear Arnold & Dusty

. . . I will not have time to write until about Monday night, & hoping to get a letter from you tomorrow so I will have this letter ready to answer. I'll send it even if I don't get a letter from you tomorrow Saturday, as I know how 'anxious' you are to get a letter from 'me'. I do miss you very much. I have been for your clothes & I have to pay 9/6 for it. I am sure you paid there, but they are robbers swindlers. I asked him why I have to pay him that much. He says well we keep an office & people & we got to live. Anyway of course I'll pay it, but I don't know what you sent back. He wants to know where the receipts are of the clothes? & when you bought them? & what's in it, haven't you declared there what you are sending back? Anyway I have a letter from Raymond saying that your laundry is done & I should come & collect it. I will go on Monday. I asked you in the last letter whether you want me to send on the trousers & that washing now? . . .

I still am not working, getting pretty low myself. Only don't worry about me, I still manage, I have done half day work at furs but it's no good. I'll soon find work. Daddy is all right, heard nothing yet about going away. Still he is alright, still sitting outside & getting brown . . .

Thursday 21st June 1956

. . . It was about 10.30 in the morning. Found myself in rue Montmartre. This, I romanticised, was the famous district. Here I should like to live. Yet despite that everything is new and interesting. I felt this couldn't have been the haunt of the red-haired Vincent, or Lautrec, or the absinthe drinkers. Still, it was all fascinating. A long foreign street. I was content being a foreigner. In this city I was going to work.

Crossed Boulevard Montmartre northwards, vaguely in the direction of Pigalle through Fauborg rue Montmartre. Here was one of the many Paris markets. How could we ever imagine Petticoat Lane was a market? We have nothing to compare with the way they dress their salads, lay out their fruit and vegetables and cheeses. But it's all expensive and after twenty-four days I'm still not working. Money is ridiculously low.

I looked down one of the side streets and there – the Folies Bergère! Nude women! Paris! though I'd seen photos like this in London. On an impulse I turned into another street hoping to get back en route when suddenly I found myself surrounded by kosher delicatessen stores. Vorsht [salami] hung in the windows. Soft cream cheese and halva lay on shelves. Peering inside I could see brown and black bread, boxes of matzos, basins of olives, pletzels [kind of rolls], and there – oh God! laying in thick recluse, like tired baby whales, were 'oogerkers' – pickled cucumbers!

That morning I had eaten only baguette with margarine, some cheese, a cup of tea. I was hungry. I stared. I sighed. And, dazed, passed from one shop to another as though each offered something new and different; but in each was soft cream cheese and halva and pletzels and black bread and olives and rye bread and – oh God! oogerkers.

I thought I had lost my love of markets. Was a time I loved walking through the Lane and the stalls of Ridley Road. Then the excitement went. The shouting became offensive and faces unfriendly. But here again in Paris I was rediscovering the old pleasure of aimlessly ambling among stalls and hidden, covered bazaars, where the dealers sing in a sort of plainchant fashion about what they have to sell and what they have already sold. They sing your bill: 'And a kilo of potatoes, madam, and your carrots, madam, that makes 135 francs, madam – voilà! Voilà!'

And on up to Pigalle. What exactly I wanted from Pigalle I'm not certain. The tourist's cheap thrill? In daylight? There was nothing interestingly mysterious or sinister or stimulating. Then something most curious happened. In the way writers do, I imagined myself writing about this walk, and a sentence came to me: '. . . So I turned off the main street and walked up into the little back alleys . . .' And as if to fulfil the sentence I did just that, thinking I might come to Sacré Coeur. It was a steep climb. Passed more shops looking, as Dusty and I do constantly, into every patisserie at the rich oozing pastries on display. I knew what I'd find yet time and again I stopped and stared, dying to rush in and buy any one of the cakes to eat. Each seemed the most glorious meal I could ever have. With astonishing willpower I passed on satisfying only hungry eyes.

It was uphill all the way but – where was I coming to? The streets began to resemble the photographs and paintings of cobbled alleys I seemed to know so well – here were Utrillo's canvases! At last! *This* was Paris! Montmartre down below was not as exciting as this. Here must have been where the painters came and, sure enough, round a corner, I am upon half a dozen of them busily tracing the outlines of the cobbled road, the cracked houses, the chaotically slanting roofs and behind them all – the white dome of the Sacré Coeur.

I glanced at their canvases and observed the noticeable absence of cubism, dadaism, surrealism, or anything that could be described as influenced by abstract art. Here were sincere little artists, mainly elderly, doing their best to do precisely what Utrillo had already done. Painting what was pleasing if not exciting.

Outwardly calm nevertheless I was tingling to have discovered this quarter, unlike any encountered so far, and with greater eagerness continued up along other streets. It did not seem to matter which one I took. Climbed some stairs and headed for what appeared to be a cul-de-sac, a small square surrounded by houses on one side and a low wall on the other. Slowly I climbed and reached the wall.

Over it and before me stretched Paris. It was a shock and a surprise. I seemed to be on a mountain looking down. So surprised that I turned to look back where I had just come from and then it dawned on me, of course – this was really Montmartre. *These* were the streets where the little laundry girls ran, and painters roamed, the cafés where they drank and raged at each other, here were the histories and the paintings. Alive! And I was actually among it all. I lit a cigarette and told myself to be adult, for what were stones anyway? I stared down at Paris and rolled the great names around in my head – Van Gogh, sweet Theo, poor Lautrec, the little Jew Pisarro – but there was nothing little or poor about them, they were each and every one magnificent and I swam, romantically, among their shadows and their memories. No painter should have dared follow them. The people who came after, seeking the leftovers, were slightly foolish.

I glanced around, not many people about, some kids with a scooter, a couple on holiday, an American in light grey clothes and a shirt with no tie – at least I think he was American. And to complete the atmosphere, from one of the windows came the sound of someone playing an accordion. It was all very peaceful, quiet, sacred. And not quite a cul-de-sac. A door led into a garden café. I asked could I pass through and was told, yes. I walked through and turned left. It was like stepping into a Hollywood film set of what they imagined *should* be Montmartre.

In a small square were chairs, tables and coloured umbrellas shading them. Waiters, dozens of them, stood around waiting for customers. Shops surrounded them all, little art shops and cave-like cafés. And filtering in and out were the sightseers. A wizened, well-dressed man, speaking American with a French accent, was conducting a party of Americans on a tour.

'Now come here,' he was saying urgently as though to a lot of schoolchildren, 'now come here and see this. I want you to see this place. Now this place is actually where they all came and ate and drank. Renoir, Lautrec, the lot. Now come along, come inside, inside now.' And they disappeared into a tiny, heavily decorated café which I imagined could not take them all. I smiled a little superciliously to myself. Yet why not? It was a common heritage. Why should I be aloof and annoyed? They had every right to be there. Why should they not come and breathe the air, touch the walls, walk the streets where once roamed the now mighty heroes of Impressionism?

I descended. This time through different streets, just as quaint, not so crowded, back down into Paris. I thought: I am annoyed because far from being the lone discoverer of this quarter, of 'the real place', it was *too* well known, it was the common vomiting ground of all those seekers after romantic shadows. I thought: I am also annoyed because I know that these very same people, the eager, admiring sightseers, these paying tourists, had they lived in those times, would, along with the others, have rejected Van Gogh and called him crazy. Then, more urgently, I thought: I must bring Dusty here, as soon as possible, surprise her in the same way I was surprised. And if we walk blindfolded perhaps we will not see the other people.

Saturday 23.6.56
I did take Dusty there. Two nights later. A lovely, warm evening. And we climbed the same route and saw the same people. Everyone was cashing in on a good thing. I can think of no reason why they should not except that it is vulgar. But who am I to accuse them of vulgarity.

This time we walked right round and came suddenly upon the front of the Sacré Coeur. Now, *there* really was a view, a cinemascopic view of Paris. Impressive but not, curiously, exciting. The city stretched just like a view of London from the top of a dock warehouse. There was nothing beautiful about it. Paris is lovely at close quarters where you're actually touching the boulevard or la place, its shops, its walls.

I would not like to live in Montmartre, it is phoney now and very sad.

Still no work. I asked Le Rallye if they would start me before the permit came through. They replied they could not in case I had an accident. Dusty and I return to the hotel. It is her half-day. We bought some frankfurter sausages, eggs, butter, orangeade, soap, something we thought was parazone, and a yoghurt for me. Now realise we simply cannot move out of the hotel. We cannot afford it. For tea we had bread and an egg, some frankfurters and orangeade. It is a dull, cool evening. I shall soon settle down to read. We don't mind staying in. It's a lazy life. Dusty at the moment is on the bed leaning against the wall and hemming her red skirt. She hums and is in a mad, amiable mood; every so often she attacks and fondles me and then jumps back to her work. She has decorated the walls with some cut-outs of animals from a magazine, and six Rembrandt paintings. How a room changes with something on the wall. Near the bed I have pinned up that lovely sepia photograph of Della.

With only 7000 francs left and next week's rent to pay we're still calm. No money for fare home, it's desperate, yet we do not panic. I am not worried. Why do I imagine it will be all right? Have written to Barney asking him for a loan of 10,000 francs. God knows if it's forthcoming.

Dusty says she is tired. It's only 5.30 p.m.!! She complains she wants to go to the toilet but cannot be bothered to move. I am constipated – it must be the irregular and scant food I digest.

A motor car tunes up outside. I write on a table covered by our blue towel. The gargoyle ashtray with its broken wings is with me. Alongside are some spoons, glasses, a salt cellar, a tube of concentrated Nestles milk. Shirts hang against the wall. A washing line stretches from corner to corner. Somehow this is not like Paris. We only *know* we are here, we do not feel it. This is not a complaint.

Dusty is away to the toilet. I turned and caught her taking toilet paper with her. 'I tried not to let you see me,' she said. 'I tried not to make you envious.' And she flies to the door – then pokes her head round again. '*Don't* sit on the bed, there's my skirt there, and somewhere in that is a needle. Now that would make you go!' I shall make tea and then read.

The big disappointment today was not finding a parcel at our poste restante. The two of us traipsed to Madeleine to see if our biscuits had arrived. Dusty has sent 10/- home to her sister with instructions to buy some biscuits, in particular the chocolate-coated ones with orange flavouring inside. We have been looking forward to these for the last week. Slowly these chocolate biscuits with orange flavouring are becoming an obsession. We think about them continuously and imagine how we shall have a feast when they arrive. Decent biscuits and sweets are so expensive here. It was a great sorrow for us not to have received them, but now I look at Dusty's stockings with a big hole in the heel and think of our longing for the biscuits and our general predicament and it seems hilariously funny.

Wednesday 27th June 1956

This evening we paid 4200 francs for rent; we also bought six eggs, a tin of pilchards, two yoghurts (vanille and citron), some shampoo and one and a half baguettes. Supper was pilchards and bread, followed by bread and jam, followed by yoghurt with bread, followed by a cup of tea. I have just washed Dusty's hair and she has washed mine. At the moment she is bathing herself and we both parade around without any clothes. We have been generally fooling around. There exists a wonderfully free air. I feel healthy, clean, happy and perturbed – for all we have left in the world is 700 francs plus some hundred or so to get back on yoghurt bottles. Dusty has 3000 to come for this week's wages – of that, 2000 must be saved for next week's rent to go with the next 3000. That means, roughly, that we have 1800 frs to exist on for the next two weeks.

I wonder what will happen.

Last Saturday, not having enough money, we had decided to stay in for the whole weekend. That evening Barney rang and asked us to visit and stay overnight. So they had not gone on holiday after all.

Of course both of us were longing to go, to get out of Paris into the country. Dusty in particular wanted to see the baby. We explained we simply could not afford it and told him we had in fact written asking for a loan. After much humming and costly hahing he offered to pay the fare there and we could hitchhike back. We were delighted and promptly made an early night in order to catch the 10 a.m. bus from Port Maillot.

Due to some odd, early morning, sleepy lovemaking, we managed by two minutes to miss the bus. This meant an hour and a half's wait for the 11.30. We sat on a bench for half an hour deciding whether to have a coffee, lamenting our inability to be on time, and chewing some awful, cheap biscuits we had bought in the market that morning. We spent the next forty minutes drinking one cup of coffee watching the traffic on the wide road leading up to the Arc de Triomphe. People were boarding the bus.

Started off with Dusty sulking because we did not sit on the front seat near the door and inside was rather stuffy. Eventually I asked the woman in front of me if she would kindly ask the man in front of her if he would mind opening the window. So began a slow, bumpy, crowded ride through the French countryside to Mantes-la-Jolie arriving two hours later – roughly as long as it takes from London to Norwich! For some odd reason the fields of France seem bigger than those in England.

Barney was waiting for us on his bike and after some banter we moved off in the direction of his house. A girl dressed in black sweater and trousers approached. I remarked that she looked like Monique – it was! We exchanged salutations. She shook with hard, firm hand and spoke as though really she had not wanted us to come. I said of Dusty – this is my wife, to which Monique replied, pointing to Barney: 'Hello! And I'm *his* wife!' Barney went off to buy some cake leaving us to proceed home.

Home was two rooms, a kitchen and a bathroom. The rest of the house belongs to Monique but is tenanted. On entering, one's first impression is of an overcrowded Victorian room. On closer inspection one is aware of Louis-the-someteenth chest and wardrobe and chairs all closely packed together. There was not much room on the walls either for they were covered with old, heavily framed paintings, prints, and plates. The baby whimpered and Dusty rushed to see him. Oh how she sighed and heaved over his beauty. When he eventually awoke she soon made friends with him which they told us is normally impossible. This of course increased Dusty's admiration of him but I found the unfortunate child a bundle of nervous energy. He was continuously moving about and throwing things, and occasionally howling.

It became obvious why this was so.

We sat down to eat and soon discovered it was Monique who wore the trousers. She spoke loudly and heavily and gruffly, every so often barking and complaining of Barney. This was mainly a show-ing-off in company, for really she was most friendly and generous even if thickly so. She would complain how lazy he was, how little he did in the house and: '. . . When I look at him sometimes and he needs a two-day shave, I think oh God is this what I'm with for the rest of my life?' Barney meanwhile sits quietly, attempting to sit it out with nonchalant calm, but really he is embarrassed for her and I am embarrassed for him. Some of the things she said to him I would not have stood for two seconds. Jesus! I said I would tame Monique in a year, not as a boast, more a hint that she needed taming. She caught the hint and later asked: 'So you think I'm a bad wife for Bar-ney, eh?' By this time I could answer that I was capable of seeing deeper than the surface show.

For indeed Monique has a heart of gold, a good head on her shoulders, a sense of duty, and the energy of two; but when a woman is like that it is fatal. She expects her husband to be two of her, and then makes sure he is not because she couldn't possibly stand living with two of herself. With Barney especially such a situa-tion is worsened. He's responsible but in his own time, no one else's. If pushed to move he will slow down to be still. If shouted at he will say nothing. Only when he's goaded past endurance will he smash five cups at your head, which is just what he did with Monique one day. Barney is the type of person I would pay to do nothing except be around. I could have wept when I realised the marriage he'd made. Already such things happen and he's only twenty-three and she twenty-one or twenty-two. They have three times as many years to live together!! And yet, one wonders, perhaps Barney wants a woman like Monique? That night Dusty and I lay in one bed and re-garded Barney and Monique in the other. She was propped up under a bedside light, in a white nightgown, with glasses on, read-ing. It was 3 a.m. Barney lay asleep curled up in her arms, his head upon her breast. It was a very human picture, only Monique looked more like a granny with a child in her bosom.

The day had been pleasant. We had turns each on the motorbike and ended up at an auction sale where Monique bought a cotton blanket for 1000 francs, a set of windows for 500 francs, and six small and six large wine glasses along with two decanters of pure crystal for 500 francs. 10/-!!

That evening she gave us a jar of preserved peaches, another of plum, and one of apple jam to take home. She said we must contact them as soon as we had need to.

At 5 in the morning we awoke and Barney drove Dusty to Paris on his motorbike. I returned to sleep. At 10 a.m. Monique's mother and I hitched into Paris. Her mother was around all the time, a kindly woman, highly educated who has travelled all over the world and who is swelling in various places due to a cancer which, so Monique says, will allow her only two or three more years of life.

Needless to say we have received, as yet, no money from Barney. I think he is afraid to ask his wife for it.

28 June 1956
Bought tonight's supper: a baguette and a half and two yoghurts. I've also bought a box of fresh cream as a surprise for Dusty to eat with the peaches. The peaches had been left open and some flies had boldly entered and thereupon died, but we boiled them in sugar and will eat them later. For supper we ate the remainder of the pilchards with sliced onions, and an egg with the baguette and marg, followed by a yoghurt – with more baguette and marg, and tea.

It has been another early return home. Finished supper and sat in our chairs – unhurried. Dusty squeezed a few specks first out of her right breast and then her left. I smoked and watched her. She asked me to brush her hair. It is beautiful and speckled as if with gold dust and it shone and crackled and rose to its own electricity. I fiddled with her hair arranging it this way and then that.

We begin to feel despondent. We can read, write, Dusty can wash one or two things but here we must sit. To do this out of choice one does not mind, to remain bound by the invisible law of impecunity [think I meant 'impecuniosity'] tends to deaden the spirits. Dusty begins to be chagrined by our uncertain future. We must move out of here soon and continuously move until we find a permanent room, which means we shall not buy cleaning utensils till then, so our room remains dirty. We don't exist in filth – though the cracks in the wall no doubt harbour bugs, and flies drone around – but the room is not as clean as we would want, and we can't afford to buy sprays.

Afford! With money back on some bottles we have today spent only 62 francs! [Less than 10p.]

Friday 29th June 1956
Have just tried to ring Barney to tell him our position is desperate, but in Paris – from public telephone booths – one cannot ring outside the city. It will have to wait till tomorrow. We have left only 197 frs – roughly 3/11½d. i.e. 1/11¾d. each. Tomorrow Dusty gets 3000. 2000 of this must go towards next week's rent. That leaves 1000 francs – £1! For next week!

This evening we ate egg and chips. Dusty had a yoghurt and I had some soft cheese and bread.

Now we *feel* desperate. That is to say we feel a little unreal; the situation seems unreal and somehow an atmosphere of madness is around. We have been making funny faces at each other and erupting queer sounds. Suddenly we pounce and rag each other, dig ribs and laugh hilariously. We seem unable to settle, be calm, know what to do with ourselves. It is now 10 to 10 p.m. Dusty is in bed reading de Maupassant. Soon I shall join her. She cannot really concentrate and asks me to come to bed. She coos – it is a crazy coo – or do I see it as a crazy coo? I think on one or two occasions this evening she would sooner have wept than laughed.

She has been hoping Barney would come this evening, and at the sound of each motorbike she has jumped to the window – poor kid.

We must not lament –

Saturday 30th June 1956
Let us write day by day.

Let us observe us. If I can't create a poem, if I can't write a story then let me fill in the little details of living. Paint the predicament.

It is a warm, close evening. The day has been summer and hot. Soon a storm will break in our ears, it hides for the moment. The time 23.00 hrs. We have just come out of the pictures. It was a luxury we gave ourselves. I lie across the bottom of our bed; lying lengthways, her feet stretched over me, Dusty has surrendered, naked, to the heat, and reads restlessly on top of the blankets. Her Renoir body reclining with the ease of an animal at home. Scattered on the bed is a Bible (I want to read the gospels – I am working on an idea about Christ coming to Hyde Park Corner); a camera which

497

we tried, but failed, to sell; a book of Salinger Short Stories and another of Modern Poems we bought at an English bookshop by the Seine near Saint-Michel; and my gargoyle ashtray.

I have been sneezing. I feel not merely warm from the weather, but hot – perhaps I have a cold.

We rang Barney today to ask again for a loan. Now they really have gone on holiday. We contacted Gerry who promised to loan 5000 francs though he, poor devil, is still moving around from hotel to hotel, paying exorbitant rents.

Our supper was egg and chips again. Dusty was paid her 3000 frs wages of which a 1000 or so has already gone. We should not have strayed out of the house this afternoon but it was such a fine day, we could not stay in. We bought eggs and milk, and D was going to buy a tin of fruit and some condensed milk. She asked me which fruit I like. I felt it too much of an extravagance and hesitated to choose. Eventually I had to tell her that I thought we could not afford it. I hate having to tell her this. It makes me feel mean, I want her to realise these things. It upset me for a time and we spoke little until we went out again.

We strode to the Seine. The quays looked colourful with people promenading, men fishing and a couple of painters easily daubing at their canvases. On to the English bookshop where we were tempted to buy a Salinger. The proprietor – a young American – tried to tell me I was a journalist. He did not guess I was a pastry cook. When finally I revealed what I did he said that, ah! when he first saw D he thought now there is a pastry cook's wife!! We almost organised a lemon meringue pie on the spot.

Then, an incident leading to a nasty row between D and I. I pointed out to her a book of bawdy ballads at which she glanced but quickly laid down in disgust. Oh, that's really dirty, she moaned. I picked it up and became engrossed in an old RAF favourite called 'Eskimo Nell'. She badgered me in a nauseating, prim manner saying – lay that down, don't read it, how dirty you are – the kind of annoying phrases one would only expect to hear from a stupid, narrow-minded, self-righteous old dame. Her attitude embarrassed me and her demands irritated. I said: as soon as I can afford it I shall buy this. She said she would not have such a book in her house! I replied: Right! We'd separate, and tried to laugh it off. She left the shop in a haughty disdain that was out of proportion to the moment. I stayed behind, more to assert independence than from inclination. When we sat over a coffee I was furious, and, I'm afraid, barked at her that I wanted my actions allowed me, and would not be embarrassed in such a manner in public. I tried to reason how ridiculous it was to be disgusted by such things. Sane argument collapsed in petulance when I asked how dare she, and she answered who did I think I was – that sort of silly exchange.

I can't bear scenes in public, and if I feel my freedom of action threatened I stiffen. I hate false dignity and hysteria over harmless and trifling things when there is so much cause for real anger. Nor will I be treated as a child. [Oh, Wizzie!] My tone of voice upset her more than my words. When we finished drinking she walked on ahead of me. This was unwise for within a few seconds an Algerian lecherously smiled and accosted her. I rushed up angrily crying, 'Dites! C'est ma femme!' I could cheerfully have hit him but as it is something I've never done I did not know how! It happened again in the Metro when, still in anger, she moved away from me to find our direction on the map and another North African came up and accosted her. This time she came back to me and took my arm. He melted away in shame.

Yet a third time. In the market near our hotel she strode ahead. I saw a man look at her and begin to follow her. I caught up and told her to hold my hand. He soon dropped behind. Then, as if to distract us from our own fight we came across a real one. A crowd had assembled around some type of Teddy boys. Something had already been happening, for one of them had a bad cut round his eye and by his lip. What it was about and what had happened I do not know. But suddenly the injured young man, rather burly, caught hold of his opponent – a tall, handsome and well-dressed individual – by the collar, pulled him down and banged his face with his head. There followed a series of fistal exchanges and suddenly the tall fellow broke away from the crowd and ran off down the street. The crowd returned into the market throng and we continued home to eat our familiar supper. At the table D could stand it no longer and released some very sad and pitiful tears. I took her in my arms, kissed her eyes, her cheeks, her lips, her hands and apologised for barking at her.

We hurried our meal and went to pictures to drown our sorrow. *Laurel and Hardy in Oxford* – a film about an expedition down the Amazon.

Now I shall undress and read my book of poems. A strange thought has come to me.

I have known my face for many years – sometimes it is ugly with self-pity, sometimes it is very beautiful. Tonight it is beautiful. I must not be afraid to use this word, I must not be shy to admit this fact; for because of this it occurs to me that I am not living in my time; that the potential grace of my personality shall cut itself to a jagged shape in an attempt to fit. I feel I want to stand still and never move, to remain as I am, going no ways, to be looked at and thought about – as one does of a flower, or a painting, or a twilight night.

I read that now as of a young man who is writing down what comes to him without reflection, without wondering if it is what he means. It is a thought of total exposure, of the kind crude minds play merciless havoc with. I have considered carefully before releasing it. Perhaps in the end I will strike it out.

1.7.56

My dear Arnold & Dusty

There was no letter this week. I hope that you are both well. It will make you happy to hear that Daddy is really worried because no letter from you this week. I am really sorry My dear Arnold that it takes such long time to send the parcel off to you, anyway you will receive this letter before your parcel as there is forms to fill out & you know that I don't understand them. So I have to wait until Della is coming tomorrow, with the children, as Miles has no school Monday. By the way Miles hasn't been very well lately, he stopped away almost all last week, still, I hope he will soon get over whatever it is. Anyway they are coming tomorrow, Monday for lunch, are you coming home this afternoon?! I wish you were, Arnold my dear I do long to see you & I miss you but I don't fret. I know you will soon be back even if it's 6 months, that's not a life time . . .

. . . what can I do more than keep telling you that you should make a stand in your life & know where you are going to & stop fiddling about with your life, just live & live in decent way for a future & happiness to yourself & all that is around you connected. That's all. Don't go searching for the unknown & emptiness. There is such a lot for everyone in this world, to work on & live happily. Otherwise I am quite well thank you.

I was going to finish off but I had something more to add on. No really Arnold my dear I am quite fortunate to have two children like you & Della & the Laws, & my sweet two Grand Sons. Bless you all. There is only one other thing. I don't like to be left alone. Don't ever leave me either of you alone, that is the worst thing that can happen to anyone to be left alone. I never left my children alone, I never left them & I don't like leaving anyone alone. That is the reason I don't leave daddy, as I know what it means, more in next letter [she means next page]. Together we stand, divided we fall . . .

. . . Do you think you'll keep it up until the 14.7.57? I hope you will. That is your heart desire. Do write please . . . look after yourself. Remember your stomach, & how is your stomach? I do hope well, & remember you got to eat little but often & you mustn't starve yourself, look after your stomach. You only got that only one!

That's all for now. Keep well & Bless you both
all my Love Mummy xxxxxx

Monday 2 July 1956
Yesterday morning, Sunday, opened our eyes at about 10 a.m. Read a little, I made tea, and then we lost ourselves in some complicated love-play. When we had finished D jumped, and bounced, and pranced on the bed to show her delight with living, and we went shopping.

I made a not very nice milk pudding – 50% water – with what was left of the spaghetti. D fried potatoes and frankfurters, and this with tea sufficed. Again we lay down to read and – it was now about 3.30 p.m. – soon dozed. A dull, heavy day. D woke up feeling slightly sick and weak in the knees. I suggested we needed fresh air. Proceeded to our little chip café for a drink and to see if our kind friend had any good news. It seems almost certain that we shall have this room in Belville but we must call in again on Tuesday night.

Dusty complained of wanting to be sick and could not stand up. We came home and at once she crept into bed. For some reason she started to cry. I thought she was in pain but she said no. I thought perhaps she suddenly felt upset because of our miserable position – but no, this too she denied. I guessed however that her morale was generally low but still could not think why she felt ill.

I ironed her dress and for about 90 minutes she remained in this tearful state. Not crying but her eyes watering, and a stray tear betraying her heart every now and then.

She stopped and tried to read. Then, at about 9 p.m. I went into bed beside her and to my horror found her skin burning. I made her put on my pyjamas and tried to keep her covered as much as possible. It was a restless and hot night. I kept as close to her as I could to keep any stray draught out and in the morning she was cooler, a little better but with a bad headache. It was I, on the other hand, who now felt weak in the joints, a little achy.

A rather sad pair this morning. We had both been feverish in the night. D woke up at about 3 a.m. and asked me what I was laughing for. It so happened I had been dreaming about laughter. She told me that she had heard someone say, three times: 'Psst – Dusty! Psst – Dusty! Psst – Dusty!'

D went to work and I to meet Gerry who had promised to loan me 5000 frs. He was there with the money, and together we went to see the Bureau in charge of permits. Mine is due in 8 days.

Bloody bureaucrats!

Gerry works 72 hours a week for 6000!!

On hearing from M. Dorra that one pays between 1000-1500 frs for a doctor's visit we decided that the money was better spent on staying well. So we bought butter and pork chops!

D seems a lot better, cheerful. I feel weak. We both feel a little dopey however and now await the arrival of Barney!

6.7.56

My Dearest Arnold & Dusty

. . . How are you? any luck with work? By the way I only worked 2

days at Dressmaking, then I stopped for a week & now I am working again at my own work, linings. Still I will be earning £8 per
week, only the governor is closing down the first two weeks in
August & he told me that he will open again after August & he
assured me there will be plenty of work then, so I needn't worry. I'll
have work after August that is when the season starts & it's busy
until Easter.

Well there is really nothing more to write about. Daddy & I are
keeping fine, it's a terrible state to come down to not to have a
stamp to send a letter. I know what it feels like myself, & there [was]
just such time that I could not send you even the parcel before now,
because I didn't have the postage. I am saying this with 'impunity'
because I have got it now & it will go off tomorrow & do take the
money from Monty Goldman [a party member, Leah's friend], only
I would wish that you won't tell him that you live together with
Dusty. Tell him Dusty sleeps where she works, he [will] be none the
wiser. I hope you don't mind? . . .

Monday 9 July 1956
So much has happened in the last week. Most important is that I
started work this morning! Last Friday before the Dorras left for
London my permit arrived. To be frank, although I'm much re-
lieved, I did not greet it with enthusiasm. Had I some other place to
work than in the kitchen of Le Rallye I might have been happier.

At nine o'clock I went into the restaurant with my few knives and
my recipe book. The book proved unnecessary! It is a large kitchen
which starts off clean and then becomes dirty and greasy – and desperately slippery – until the kitchen porters throw sawdust and
sweep up which they do at regular intervals during the day.

I looked about me, spoke to the pastry cook, and waited for
someone to show me around. A German boy eventually did (there
are four of them here, all exceedingly kind and helpful). They
showed me where to change, where I was to work for the day, and
attempted to give me an idea what I was supposed to do.

New places at first seem cloudy and things people say sound
vague, for one is attempting to take it all in at once and of course
never succeeds. I was presented with lemons to peel and slice; some
onions, eggs and gherkins to chop and put into a tin of vinegar and

oil; I was shown how to cook and serve Cervelle – some poor animal's brains – and 'pied de veau' – a ghastly, evil-smelling meat which I think we give to dogs in England. These and some sausages and spaghetti marked my station. I had to have it ready, to serve it and watch that I was constantly stocked up.

The chef nearest me offered a bowl of white wine. Unheeding, and not wishing to appear unable, I swallowed the basinful. I was very thirsty. Then we ate. I cooked myself a steak with some chips, and helped myself to flan and yoghurt and red wine and pink wine and blue wine and all sorts of water and then – then I started cooking and serving. I had only the vaguest idea of what I was doing and what was expected of me. Rows of pretty French waitresses began forming patient queues for what I was cooking. People appeared out of nowhere and yelled for Cervelle – Saucisse – pied de veau – single, together, without potatoes, with them . . .

The heat was hell's specially sent up. My face poured sweat; my back felt small streams course down its centre; my feet became heavy, my face stung and sizzled with the intense oven-heat. I drank and drank and drank, anything I could lay my hands on.

Everyone was the same. Every so often someone emerged as though from a shower to lend me a helping hand. My 'brains' soon ran out, and the next lot were burnt; sometimes I served too much, sometimes not enough. There was no finesse to our labour – it had to go out quickly and hot.

Soon the smell mixed with heat, the wine mixed with the steak. I felt violently sick. I wanted badly to faint, to pass away, to run from this nightmare. It is impossible to believe human beings work like this. Once I went to the lavatory and nearly decided not to return – I have never encountered such work. It would be cruelty to an animal.

All this went on in my mind, yet my conduct was calm. I decided from the start both clients and waitresses could go to hell! I was not going to panic or rush. This was wise. I had managed to involve myself in an understandable mess due to it being my first day – to panic would have been fatal.

Suddenly it was all over. A German boy came up to me and said he would organise my station for this evening, and somehow I staggered out or up to wash and change.

The evening was better. I had got over the mental shock; the

German had indeed organised my station and explained more about the rhythm and routine of the place; we were not so busy; and I did not drink any wine – merely water.

It is a great relief to return from work to Wagram – the Dorras' flat. The Dorras are in London and have given us the use of the flat in their absence. D is on her own and passes her time cleaning out the apartment. We are very lucky, very fortunate. But now we must find a room . . . Barney eventually turned up with five thousand francs [approximately £4.5s. pre-decimalisation]. This is all we have. It will be enough – soon I shall be paid.

Thursday 12th July 1956

There is a dull thunder, a long sound, drawn out, and soon you lose it in the general roar that is surrounding you. But when you pause and perhaps are not thinking of anything in particular the sound catches you, as it does me, and I realise it is the gas jets shooting an ugly, long flame into the ovens, five of them. The heat is unbearable for too long at a time. Sometimes I have to stand with my back to it cutting onions or lemons and I feel it burning my white jacket so that I cannot have the jacket touch my skin. What happens is that I sweat and soak everything I am wearing, and the fire steams the garment!

Once the rush has reached its height and is sustained I have not time to wipe my face which pours salt liquid. Now and again it gathers to my nose and drips into whatever I am cooking or serving. Here it does not matter, no one cares. If only the customers could see! I can feel the rivulets course down my back into the crevice of my backside and down my legs. This I cannot dry up.

What I really must have are two sets of clothes, for when I return in the afternoon my trousers and jacket are still soaking wet. It is uncomfortable at first but within seconds in the kitchen I am sweating again.

Sooner or later one dies, or has a bad accident.

Sunday 15th July

It is like working in a large room with an enormous blast of hot air buffeting you about. Work at high pressure. Occasionally one has to scream. I do. I cry out aloud: 'Shoot the bastards don't serve them!' In English, no one understands; so much noise hardly anyone hears!

Five flames thrusting themselves with venom among the stones in iron ovens. Sometimes I feel they must explode – force and fire cannot happen like that without something giving away. And eight of us stand among them serving 2000 customers a day.

It is insanity. For us to work like that, for any man to work like that, for people to expect a man to work like that, that there should be such work – is wrong. No ifs or buts. No saying it is only a job. No saying someone must do it – it should not be. I do not care about people needing to eat a meal out – there must be other ways. No one should work like this to produce anything – anything! Nothing is more important than the man. Nothing in this world is more important than a man's humanity, his dignity. I do not care if you have to alter the whole world – alter it! If all the comforts we have in life – our cars, our food, our water supply, our electricity, our ease of communication – need a man to work in this manner then do without it. I love a car, I enjoy our radios, I want a house fully equipped with gadgets but I do not want a man to suffer indignities for it. Break the machines, smash mechanical values – raise the man, for God's sake raise him or we shall all fall with our luxuries tumbling after.

12.7.56
My Dear Arnold & Dusty
received your letters thank you. & I am really happy to hear that you are working & also I hope that you are well. As from the way you must have been living I don't suppose you could have got fat on it, on the contrary you must both be skinny, & I asked you my dear Arnold how your stomach is? You haven't answered me, & before I forget do let me know if you received the parcel? . . . & by the way have you been one of those people who sleep on the pavement? Did you? Where do you sleep? & if you have a place to sleep why can't you give me an address? It just dawns on me the more I think of it the more I am sure you must have been sleeping in the streets. Do please tell me.

It's funny that I should tell you the same thing about me starting to work & I could not afford to send that parcel, & now I can tell you that without hesitation I am better off. I am working & earning £8 per week only I haven't worked full week yet. As it is still slack in our trade. I haven't given up insurance & etc., you know what I mean, yet, as I am not sure how long I will be working. So far so good. I was able to clear off my debts which was £4 from Della. It just came together, by borrowing one pound, & 10/- shillings, & 5 shillings until it was £4 . . . still I only got £2/10 to pay off Uncle Harry & £7 more pounds to Smarts [a never-never furniture shop] & that will be a load off my head. Anyway it's going towards the busy season, & so I hope to work for a few months . . .

The Paris diary continues

Having reread the diary, Paris, I now realise, turns out to have been not only an adventure in travel – sights seen, people encountered – but a trial of our, Dusty and my, compatability. Pointers are there: incidents that reveal our different personalities, boorish moods, mostly mine, and guilt heavy guilt; young people wriggling in a relationship that confuses and frightens them both. I squirm at what of myself comes through in a desperate attempt to be honest.

And yet, a kind of human rhythm is going on in those Paris pages. We fail tests and take measure of one another, clumsily, informed by threadbare wisdom, heavily stamped by a parental personality that characterises us rather more than it offers role models to guide and caution us. We make it up as we go along. My political head – barely rooted in theory at the best of times – is all over the place, and, though prickly alert to humbugs, my judgements are not the most reliable. And yet, and yet . . . thumbnail sketches emerge, two lives are taking shape. We make love, we quarrel, we decide to part, we come together again. Dusty falls in love with one of Le Rallye's German chefs called Knut; I yearn for a waitress who emigrates to Canada. We neither of us consummate our longings. At least – I don't think she did. Did she? Could she have done? The thought is new to me.

And along the way are characters: Dolores and José – flamenco dancers. John – their pianist who also played for a Paris-based ballet company. Sarah – the mean American for whom Dusty was au pair, her second job. Friends and relatives visit us: cousin June and her new husband, Graeme. Cousin Bryan who falls for Dusty's friend, Marianne. Boris – later Bryan's partner in law – who also falls for Marianne but not before we play upon him the most spectacular of practical jokes. Dusty takes up painting, I continue to write bad poetry. The workers in Le Rallye become my community. The summer passes. I'm at work there when Christmas and New Year comes . . .

I can't remember how we came to take up permanent residence in Hotel Windsor at number 8 Rue de L'Ancienne Comédie. I think – it comes to me as I'm writing – that a chef who worked at Le Rallye was leaving and I was told we could secure his room if we moved swiftly. It must have been a coincidence that the first hotel we aimed for, alerted by cousin Doris, was in that same street. The room was ideal. Large enough for a double bed, a table on which to write, space to cook and hang clothes, sufficient floor area on which to lay a mattress for visitors – after arranging for a little extra on the rent with Madame who ran the establishment. Two tall windows opened out on to the street a floor below, constantly seething with people and traffic making their way from Odéon to Pont Neuf – beautiful, gently curved Point Neuf with its graceful small alcoves into which loving couples tucked themselves to gaze upon and feel the Seine was theirs and theirs alone. Every shop a wink away, and the market on Rue de Seine round the corner. Because Sartre, his circle, and his existential philosophy had not impinged upon me the proximity of Les Deux Margots held no especial thrill. All Paris was a thrill.

It's an erratically kept diary. Huge gaps exist. There's no record of the practical joke, for example, probably because, as with much else that happened to us, I spent hours describing it in a long letter! That would account for the diary consisting mainly of character sketches, records of exchanges between Dusty and me, tortuous reflections on my ineptitude, how without promise the future, and how like a wilderness the prospects for love everlasting between us. Hardly substance I would want, in those days, to share with friends.

Here they are then. The prose has been rendered simple country fare, better by far than the glutinous pottage of the original, but faithful, I hope, for better or worse, to the head and heart of the original's twenty-four-year-old author.

Sunday 15th July

Yesterday, Bastille Day, Dusty met me from work, a cherry pie in her hand. We were going to George's American bookshop, on the Seine in the vicinity of Notre Dame, for a party. He was opening it up to one and all. We hoped to meet interesting people. Paused on the way to mingle with crowds at Saint-Michel watching fireworks shooting up one at a time. Clever, exciting lights. The crowd gasped oooooh as the firework burst into its pattern and aaaaah as the sparks descended.

At George's were all the types I feared would be there, except George. He'd had a motorbike accident and broken his collar bone. A gaily drunk plump blonde was welcoming everybody in a nauseating English accent sounding like Julie Harris playing Sally Bowles. She gushed, was simply terribly pleased to see us, was in a friiiiiightful muddle but doooooo come in. We moved to the end room. Two Americans and their girlfriends sat drinking, idly waiting for things to happen. Hi, one man greeted, where's your drink? Replied we'd brought food instead. One of the girls nastily squeaked how terribly kind of you. We soon moved out of shot and after glancing at the pony-tailed women and bearded men decided to throw the pie in their faces and return home. The sight of people being inartistically 'artistic' reduces me to venomous, cynical loathing. Their pretentiousness is scary, makes me feel superior.

We went back into the end room and said here is the cherry pie for you, we are . . . But could get no further. Their manner changed. One of the Americans jumped up and said we must have a drink; a girlfriend went into ecstasies about the pie, and being hungry devoured it with good humour. How could we not now stay? Introductions were exchanged. We sat down. People wandered in and out looking for people.

Suddenly a large, bearded, Jewish-looking American leapt in, threw himself on the bed and cried out: Hi everybody make way I just got in from Spain, haven't slept for three nights. We enquired what Spain was like and he said wonderful, everybody buys you a drink and you drink all the time. But he was not really tired and called for drink and food and in a loud voice called for his girlfriend. Come in and meet these terrible people, don't know who they are, my girl – he added – is an English type, hope nobody minds. The girl appeared, smiled gaily, but could not match his bounding energy though she did attempt some feeble English efforts. No stopping *him* however. He seemed to know everyone, greeting them in a loud voice and announcing to each that he'd just got in from Spain and hadn't slept for three nights.

Suddenly he cried out: Hi Desmond you old Irish bastard, come in here man and meet all these lousy people. Desmond – he told us – was a real Irishman with a real Irish accent who made sure you heard the Irishness of his accent. Desmond O'Connor, with fair hair, appeared with a large beer bottle at his lips. He looked Irish and spoke softly – between gulps. His tie was askew and though his general appearance was not of one debauched his act with the large bottle in the middle of the room seemed calculated to let everyone know he had already written his greatest plays and was now drinking himself to death because this was a lousy world. Pity, I had been expecting Baudelaire to walk in.

The tall bearded traveller loudly encouraged him on like a circus trainer. Go on, man, kill it, that's it, kill it! He was of course referring to the bottle. Right, said the bearded man, had enough of this party let's go on to the next one, come on man, great conversation here. He pushed his way out. We, the four Americans, D and I, had been watching his antics and those of his friend and had been unable to get a word in edgeways. We could hear him greet someone else on the way out. Hi somebody or other, you rotten something or other – delighted giggles and exclamations – just got in from Spain, haven't slept for three nights. Oh, he *was* witty. . . .

22nd July 1956 – Bastille Day continued
Next Sunday night the Dorras return. We must leave here in two days' time, find a place to live. God knows where.

This lunchtime Dusty met me and from the questions she asked I guessed immediately that she was excited about something. She had found a flat! Hurriedly she told me all the details: 20,000 francs a month, one room, two beds in a luxurious block, two stops away from Wagram, seventh floor up but there's a lift. She'd seen it in the papers, belongs to an artist and his wife, all his paintings on the walls, lots of rooms. His paintings are colourful, quite unusual, she said, never seen anything like them before. He spoke English well, had lived there for 5 years, in the house of Lord Harewood for a year and a half, their son is in Blackheath, London . . . D passed on her enthusiasm to me. Instead of shopping we went straight to view it.

The woman opened the door to us. It was a long, rambling apartment and there, true enough, were his paintings on the wall. We were immediately shown the room on offer. Not very large, simply furnished, a cupboard turned out to be a wash place. I can't remember precisely what pieces of furniture were about but my impression was one of dullness, an unimaginative layout. Not what one would expect of an artist. Nevertheless it would have done. It would have done nicely. Excitingly. We were shown the kitchen, we could have the run of it. Details were discussed. She wanted 25,000 francs for two people. I had to point out we couldn't afford it and had been under the impression the rent was 20,000. The woman had taken a liking to Dusty and confessed her delight on seeing that I was dark and Italian-looking and not blonde like Dusty. So she said all right we could have it for 20,000 a month. I had to explain that if they wanted money in advance we could only pay 5000 down and 15,000 the following week, and after that we we're not certain we could pay 20,000 all at once in advance – though we probably could. This seemed to rock them a bit but she was keen on having us and said this arrangement would be all right. At a certain point in the proceedings he took us on a tour of his paintings. But of that later.

We were offered grapefruit juice to drink. The woman, we discovered, accompanied herself on the piano singing, mostly negro spirituals, in an alto voice. Pleasant, shabbily – or rather carelessly – dressed. She sat down like an excited child, hoisting her skirts absent-mindedly too high – but it was so warm! The idea of a young couple around the place appealed to her. She dreaded the idea of an old couple. The painter was a nondescript-looking man, fiftyish, far from artistic-looking, more like an old bank clerk on his day off, humble and apologetic – but pleasant.

It was all pleasant. No, not pleasant – friendly. And yet – I was unaccountably oppressed in that apartment. This sense of oppression grew and finally became so strong that I had to risk disappointing D and offending them by saying – after all their concessions we'd let them know. When we had left and were alone I sensed that Dusty sensed I was not enthusiastic and was waiting for me to say something. I did. Told her I felt bad about it but, though pressed for digs, there was one reason I could not take to that flat. Ridiculous when I think back over it, nor can I even recapture the most peculiar effect they had on me but – his paintings! It was that!

They were to my mind so atrocious as to affect me emotionally. The idea of this man hanging them all over his walls, of him being associated with Lord Harewood who owned an art collection more fabulous than the Tate Gallery [that could hardly be], of him being commissioned by Princess Mary to paint some canvases illustrating Conrad's *Typhoon*, the fact that he could not see why his paintings were so bad – all this depressed me beyond reason. [There followed a lengthy description of the paintings.] I persuaded Dusty we should not take the flat.

Tuesday 18 September 1956
MAX is a German boy working in the kitchen of Le Rallye. His father owns a restaurant in Germany. Max is doing the rounds of 'abroad'. Nineteen, a pimply youth, blue eyes, fair hair, stoops a little, works hard though hysterically in the manner of a young man trying to be in control of things. We struggle to communicate in French, a language we can neither of us speak fluently. He even less than I. He talks mainly about three things; his future as cuisinier, for of course he intends one day to have his own restaurant, something like Le Rallye God help us! about how bad a cuisine is Le Rallye; or about the time he worked on a ship and went to New York. He can never cease acclaiming the magnificence of the ship and the splendour of Manhattan. He is very proud to have been there. Minor topics are girls – being still awkward and pimply he has some difficulty in finding companionship; the last war – he acknowledges the stupidity of Hitler and Nazism though he's too young to understand their awful seriousness; and the current political situation – Egypt in particular. And he's worried about Russia! Max is characterised for me by his constant habit of rubbing his thumb over his other four fingers – money! Though most people have the habit, in one his age

it is sad. Nor can he understand – especially coming from a Jew – when I suggest to him that to have achieved Le Rallye or a big chain of Waldorf Hotels is to have worked hard and achieved nothing.

PIERRE is another of the Germans. He's working in Le Rallye for over two years. He knew Max in Germany and Max tells me he was entirely different there. Pierre is 23 and the reason for his continuing stay in Paris is his passionate love for Marcelle, a young Parisienne blonde, slim and attractive and, I hear, married. Pierre has no parents and it seems to me his love is obsessive. Nothing exists for him except Marcelle and he guards her image like a child afraid of losing its teddy bear. When I first came to Le Rallye (he speaks good English) he bent over and whispered in my ear, 'That's my wife, almost anyway, we are waiting to get married.' He has an odd habit of bending over and talking into everybody's ear as if either they were deaf or everything he had to say was a great secret. Marcelle is a waitress. He watches her come and go. Sometimes they quarrel and she snubs him in front of all. It is distressing to wit ness a person so obsessed. I don't think she is in love with him. I may be wrong but I feel she is compromised by his persistent declaration of their relationship. Once a week the hostess at the head of the stairs is off and Marcelle takes her place. The kitchen is so placed that, at one part of it, one can see into a mirror which reflects where the hostess stands. On the day Marcelle is hostess Pierre is constantly gazing into the mirror, watching her. It's embarrassing. He seems to be asking everyone to see how much in love he is. When Marcelle was on holiday – he was due to join her in the South of France – he was continually showing us cards and letters from her on which were written, 'I love you and will not be happy until you arrive.' Sometimes he showed off the imprint of lipstick made by a kiss on paper. Very few like Pierre. He is aggressive and excitable, though of late he seems remote and quiet, as if certain now of his love. But I don't know, he loves too much to make anyone happy. And having lost his parents he has too much to make up for. Blond and blue-eyed, heavily built, almost fat. Youth protects him from corpulence. I suppose his face is red from the intense heat in which we all work. His eyes are watery and, because he is living on such high-pitch emotions, they're intense and anaemic at the same time. He has a lovely smile. I think he's good-looking, Dusty disagrees. I would very much like to be friends with him but I'm afraid we seem not to get on. He's a sad young man.

RAOUL plays and sings in cafés. Calm, sweet, not angelic though sufficiently innocent to command my respect. Perhaps what more commands my respect is that he can play the guitar, read music and sing. He is 19 and has just finished school. He hands out a little printed slip of paper which says on it: 'I am a student. I am leaving for a tour of the world. Grace à vous. Thank you. Raoul . . . Citizen of the World.' And then he stands in front of them and sings in Spanish, French, Russian and English. He makes a lot of money. £3 to £5 for more or less a four-hour day. The most arresting thing about him is he has no beard or moustache, no bright-coloured clothes, or jeans, or sweaters. Simply a suit, a shirt and tie. He could be an office boy. His appearance is as modest as himself. Of his ideas I know nothing. We have spoken together at no great length. I only know that the spirit that will take him round the world, and the way he sings – standing with trousers that seem almost too long and wide for him – is worth any number of hotels Max may one day open . . .

Tuesday 25th September 1956
An event occurred in Le Rallye's kitchen last week, the outcome resulting in the most ironic statement ever. It began with a remark made to Max by the pastry cook: 'Tous les allemands sont dégueulasse!' Quite what 'dégueulasse'means (or how it's spelt!) I'm not sure. Certainly not a nice word. And Max, like so many young Germans, is sensitive about being part of a twice-defeated nation. Not that they regret being losers but are weary of accusing fingers and hateful eyes asking them to account for that which they were too young even to remember. I like neither their shame nor their aggressiveness. Nor should the French, nor any other nation, provoke such feelings. In his worst possible French Max said to me: it is an unhappy thing that I am in France now! and bitterly continued frying his omelette. The incident didn't dampen his spirited efforts to address me in a few words of English. I try to teach him, he picks up quickly.

Working alongside of us was a young Frenchman engaged as an extra. French hatred of the Germans goes deep. Most countries mistrust foreigners. I talk of any man-in-the-street's fear, confused by everything in this enormous world. Foreigners are scapegoats. The young extra could not bear to be surrounded by people talking in English and German, and suddenly pounced on Max crying: 'You're in France now, speak French!' Max's spirits fell to zero. He drank and drank and became drunk and full of self-pity and hatred and confusion. Add all this to his dislike of working in Le Rallye. That's how little boys are made to fight wars. The following day I suggested that as he would not want us to judge him by the actions of a Hitler or Goering so he must not judge France by the pastry cook and the extra. My French was probably as futile as my reasoning. Max, that evening, worked himself into tears. Poor kid, he struggled but they came into his eyes, and not even the sweat of his red face could hide them. I told him to go home but he stayed, and on a couple of occasions disappeared into the lavatory to dry his eyes.

All of which, set in the rush and the heat, confirmed the insanity of a place like Le Rallye. How do we tolerate such lunacy? God knows! We produce our little excuses, reasons: we shall not be here long, we need the money, it's a job, a job is a job!

And in the middle of it all Max turned to me and said: 'Tu sais, tu es un Juif et moi, je suis un Allemand. Nous souffrons ensemble!' The irony of which contained too much innocence for me not to smile.

The Practical Joke

Cousin Bryan had by this time spent his holiday with us in Paris, sleeping on a spare mattress on the floor of our room in Rue de L'Ancienne Comédie. We'd given him a good time, shown him the sights, partnered him off with Dusty's friend, Marianne. Boris, Bryan's friend from college, had just finished law exams and was soon to become a lawyer in partnership with him. He had heard from Bryan about his exotic days in Paris and asked could he too share our room for exotic days in Paris – the rent sounded most reasonable. We extended an invitation to the city about which we were becoming proprietarily proud, and he wrote back heady with expectations: would we not only reveal the world's most exciting city but also – find him 'a woman'? We promised him hospitality, exotic days and – a woman.

Boris was an affable young man in the tradition of Jewish humanism, declaring his love of the Sunday *Observer* and the week-end *Statesman and Nation*. With a degree of self-serving self-deprecation he claimed that we – he included us in his 'we' – belonged to that new group of ineffectual young intellectuals characterised in books we'd not yet heard of like *Lucky Jim* by a new novelist called Kingsley Amis, and plays like – he named another we'd not yet caught up with – *Look Back in Anger* by a young play-wright called somebody Osborne. Boris's view of human behaviour in those days was that there was a reason for all things whether that reason was known or not – not a view with which I had sympathy. Art and music, he said, meant a lot to him, but although I could see he was alive to them I was never certain he was alive *through* them. Widely read, intelligent, witty – I felt he worked at himself too much. He must be a very different person today, but in his eager days – well, the lad wanted a woman? Then he should have one.

The plot involved our friends and neighbours in Hotel Windsor – Dolores and José, the fiery flamenco dancers. He was Mexican, she from the States. A dark, handsome couple, looking their parts. As soon as Boris arrived we were agog with news of a beautiful Spanish woman married to a Spanish man of violence who fortu-nately was never there since he travelled the world conducting nefarious deals, leaving his wife to seek tenderness and kindness where she could, when she could, from whomsoever she could during his long absences. Which agogged Boris! His gullible, hand-some eyes shone with masculine protectiveness and tumescent promise.

With our black-haired, dark-eyed bohemian friends we arranged that shortly after introducing Dolores to Boris – a tryst planned for our room – 'the husband' would burst through the door, utter bloodcurdling summonses and threats, Dolores would scream, swoon away upon our bed, leaving Dusty and me to freeze with horror.

Boris couldn't wait for rendezvous hour. During the minutes leading up to it we stirred his blood and expectations with a mixture of Latin promise and descriptions of her Latin lover's uncontrollably jealous rages which, fortunately, were many miles away. The appointed moment ticked into place. Dolores entered. She was breathtakingly bizarre. She had put together a personality we had never seen, theatrical and stereotypical beyond our imaginings. High heels, black stockings, flamenco-style black dress, mantilla complete with veil, the longest eyelashes in the world and a cigarette plunged into a cigarette holder you could play billiards with. Dusty and I gaped and swallowed our laughter, but Boris fluttered and shook with excitement like a small puppy about to be fed, or stroked, or shown a playmate. He barely knew what to do with himself, what to say, where to place his limbs, how to address her. Nothing so exotic had ever entered his life. Nor ours, come to that. Dolores played her role a touch over the par of subtlety, talking to him about God knows what while we tiptoed around making tea or coffee or something. I seem to remember that she spoke to him pathetically, seeking his sympathy, his pity for her plight of abandoned, brutalised wife. Boris was all sympathy and Anglo-Jewish gallantry until, on cue, came a loud and frightening banging on our door and the voice of violent Spanish spousedom thundered through the thin wood.

Dolores screamed and assumed a look of fear and terror. I said something like 'Oh my God it's him!' and urged Boris to flee in danger of his life. Poor Boris, flee to where? His murderer was the other side of the only exit available. All that was left were the windows. Even if he could get to them in time he'd break his legs from the drop. Sliced jugular or splintered limbs – a harsh choice for a young man who had psyched himself up to experience life's darker passions rather than its bloody ones, to clutch breasts not drainpipes. The only place he could think to hide was along the wall against which the door would almost certainly be crashed open by the jealous husband with no regard for what might stand behind it. Boris might be bruised by the slam but – briefly he'd be hidden. Or

was it me who grabbed and thrust him there? The door was cata-
pulted open and the most ferocious-looking José strode three paces
into the room brandishing a long knife. Dolores swooned. Boris,
seeing the two Spaniards engrossed by one another, sidled round
the door and fled. I rushed to close it after him and we all waited,
with breath held, before collapsing into uncontrollable laughter. I
found him some time later hiding in the lavatory under the staircase. He was hurt and angry when told the truth.

His protestations of injustice were, I have to confess, justified: he
had not been given the opportunity to be so brave since I had told
him to flee for his life. Besides, he didn't see the point in dying for a
pleasure he'd not achieved. And what, he asked, would *we* have
done in the circumstances? What would anyone else have done? I
suggested that even though *I* might not have thrown myself in front
of the woman to defend her, others, braver than either of us, might
have done. Or attempted to disarm the assailant. Or at least cried
'Help!' Boris was not persuaded. Though he was finally amused.
Sheepishly.

The diary continues

Wednesday 26 September 1956
Le quartier becomes ours. Boris was right when he said 'I bet you
love that walk to and from the Metro across Pont Neuf bridge.' And
so we do. To come from work, my blood still hot from the kitchen,
and emerge from the underground into the wide expanse the bridge
spans, is indeed a pleasurable feeling. On either side the river moves
between what is perhaps the loveliest stretch of Paris. Behind on the
right is the Louvre. Ahead is the tip of island in the Seine. To the
left Notre Dame, and nearer still, Châtelet. The banks are lined with
trees. In the morning men are fishing, at nights the symmetrical reflections of bridges and lamps in the still river. We walk into a maze
of back streets around the rue de Seine, people loitering in the
shadows or at café tables, dim lights, crazy houses, garbage bins on
the pavement – and home.

The room is warm and friendly because in the short time a lot has happened in it. Bryan has stayed, and Boris. Raoul has played and sung to us. I was drunk one night and Dusty put me to bed. We played that magnificent practical joke on Boris. Six people have eaten at our small table. We are familiar with the walls and ourselves.

The same evening
The salient feature of the CHEF DE RALLYE is that he does not really care. A large man, incapable of smiling, who goes out of his way not to be friendly. Not that he is unfriendly but that he fears conversation might involve him in complicated relationships. When le Patron complains to him that something is not cooked properly he will chide the offender not so much for having done something wrong as for causing him to be disturbed. When I caught the oil on fire and the maintenance men were rushing to extingush it he simply looked on from a distance to see what was happening and then vanished! He holds both Le Rallye and the catering trade in contempt as I discovered when I complained about not having Sunday for my day off. I told him I never see my wife. 'Moi non plus,' he complained back. If I wanted Sundays I should change my job, this was not my 'metier'. 'Work in an office or be an interpreter then you can have Sundays and evenings and Christmas, but not in this trade. How old are you?' When I told him I was twenty-four he said: 'If I was twenty-four I would rip off my jacket and go – whisht!'

LE PATRON is an odd person. A stout, white-haired old man with a soft, kindly face, pleasant blue eyes, a gentle manner, as one might imagine the original Father Christmas to be. He walks around the kitchen glancing at this and that, sympathising with the difficulties one has encountered – 'C'est chaud, mon petit, eh?' – and wearing a look on his face as if to say – Oh, God! I am responsible for having created this monster of a kitchen, but I cannot stop it now! Yet the profits roll in and his management is steady and sure and shrewd. No regrets whatever his 'kind' eyes may say.

How I nearly burned down Le Rallye

As follows.
After scattering me around the kitchen to sweat over this and

that, they finally settled me among the fish and chips. The routine was simple. I prepared layers of fish by dipping them in water and milk and slapping them around a tray of flour to coat – a high-class restaurant would have dipped the fish in egg and coated them with a fine matzo-meal. The 'frites' were ready sliced – a huge machine spun the potatoes clean of their skins and they were then, end up, levered through a sharp grill to fall into a tall vat of water as fingers ready for frying. I'd pull a vat full of raw slices to my station and blanch them.

Blanching. My station consisted of two deep-fry pans of oil each with a metal basket and handle. Above were two heated spaces to be stocked up with blanched chips on one side, hot ready-to-serve chips the other. In one trough of oil, kept moderately hot, I would blanch – that is, cook the potatoes soft but kept white; in the other I'd raise the temperature of the oil until pale blue smoke rose, signifying it was hot enough to dip my blanched chips which instantly turned brown and crisp ready for eating.

Occasionally one of my oils would become too hot, the smoke too blue. The 'wrinkle' for cooling was to fill a basket full of wet chips and dip them in out in out quickly. It always worked. On one condition: that the oil was not too hot, the smoke not too blue, and the raw potatoes not too wet. Whyso I was to learn.

One day I had stayed away too long from my vats of oil, perhaps I lingered in conversation with someone or other. When I returned, the left-hand vat was smoking heavy blue. No one seemed concerned. Why should they? I'd soon attend to it. In the usual manner. Pas de problème. A pannier of wet chips – in out in out. Mais, pas de personne in the kitchen had told me, nor had I learned at school, that when you put water to very hot fat it ignites. My vat ignited. Diaphanous, seemingly harmless blue flames danced like genies released on the surface of frying oil. I was amazed. Worse, I was intrigued. Worse still, I was mesmerised. How on earth did it happen? Because there was no panic around me I was not filled with a sense of danger. Surely the dancing flames would dance away? Burn themselves out? Within seconds of course the dancing flames danced higher. Chefs around me laughed and I laughed with them. But I had no idea what to do. Wait! Wasn't I England's young Lord Byron? Here was my second fire to handle. I moved in and huffed and puffed and waved my tall chef's hat around but to no avail. Fire is fire and I was not Lord Byron. Suddenly, out of nowhere there appeared maintenance men with fire extinguishers. Squirt, squirt and squirt again! It was soon over. I have no idea what happened next. Someone must have renewed the vat of oil. But what happened to me? Was I put on to a different station? Allowed to carry on frying fish and frites? Who, I wonder, which friend or relative possesses a letter that tells the full story? Whatever happened I was not endeared to le Patron, and especially not to le Patron's son. As will be seen.

The diary continues

17 October 1956

Winter approaches. The mad summer months have passed and with them the laxity of procedure that comes with pressure. Closer attention is being paid to the way work is conducted. Hats must now be worn. Le Patron's son stands on guard between the salon and the kitchen, hands behind his back, legs astride, his sleepy eyes watching what's happening in the kitchen and the food that is coming from it, always immaculately dressed, always a white shirt and cuff links showing. Every now and then he takes out a little notebook and pencil and ticks, erases, or notes something. God knows what. Like his father he's becoming bald.

Le Rallye is a community of workers. Despite the monstrosity of the place there exists a homely atmosphere – when work has ceased, that is. As the oven fires subside so the noise and rush. The last waitresses clear away then settle down in the empty restaurant. No point in returning home for the few hours between lunch and supper. Some sit gazing out of the large windows, others idly gossip in groups round a table, some knit, some sleep. The 'plongeurs' – dishwashers mainly from North Africa – return upstairs to the dressing rooms to sleep on the floors or the benches. Others sit in groups and listen to one of the more educated ones translating the news from a French newspaper into Arabic. Occasionally one plays a sort of guitar, I don't know its name, it has four sets of two closely arranged strings which give it that sort of oriental, double-note, whining effect. Another sings. One of them, a very large, fat boy, dances, wiggling with rhythm and great ease.

In the mornings the waitresses, as they are numerous, help peel the vegetables and fruit while the others dust and polish the vast rooms. All use is made of them. And the plongeurs, too, who gut and clean the fish. Even the laundry is filled with waitresses. At 10.30 they eat.

Only the cooks go home in the afternoon break. A strange lot. I think they must be that the world over. Three of them drink steadily throughout the day and by nightfall are contentedly oblivious to all that they wish to be oblivious to. Fernand, the sous-chef, resembling a dark-haired Jean Gabin, a sardonic smile continuously on his face. A good man. The butcher, Rolain, fat and red-faced, screwed-up eyes, slowly working, slowly drinking, slowly moving. And young Raymond, an Arab who claims Spanish descent and sings Spanish flamencos, married to one of the waitresses, a large, heavily made-up girl, ill-matched. Day after day these three drink, their eyes becoming heavier and heavier. Yet they work.

Alfred, a cook, is rumoured to be a communist. I think he is. A first-class worker. In the mornings he arrives, never late, walks slowly up the steps. He attacks his work with method, gathering all the pots he knows he will need and the vegetables. Rarely a word to anyone. His station is always ready on time, often before time. He eats 15 minutes before any of us, and finishes 15 minutes before us, too. He is ready for the first client, no last-minute dash or panic. During the service he forbids anyone to help him and no matter how long the queue of waitresses he serves them all in good time turning backwards and forwards from the stove to the counter, sweating but never panicking. Everything is prepared. Regularly each day he takes home something – veal cutlets, a chicken, onions, green beans, lemons, pork chops, unperturbed, pushing the food behind his apron, in his pockets, everywhere possible in his clothes. He bulges when he leaves, and always leaves on the minute. As soon as it is 2.10 or 9.10 Alfred is away. No word to anyone, no matter how many waitresses need serving. Slowly he walks up the stairs to change. His clothes are typically French, typically a worker's, I might almost say typically a communist's! Woollen vest, shirt, no tie, trousers and braces, boots, a corduroy jacket and beret. Medium-sized, well built but fat now, his humour is dry, never smiles at his wit, and my French being shaky he can easily get one over on me. Or perhaps it can be said he does not, since the meaning eludes me. In that he does not care what happens around him he is French. I have been at a loss to know how to cook something at times and, on asking him, have been met with a shrug. 'Ask the chef.' I do not know whether to like him or not. I respect him. He is a good worker, a calm personality. Once a tin of his gravy with a lot of fat in it boiled over and large flames flew at the ceiling. He was eating. Everyone rushed to it. He got up, stuck his hand in the midst of the flames, withdrew the tin, ousted the oven, and returned to eat.

Most are good cooks, even the German boys. They are at Le Rallye for the money – that is all.

18 October 1956

The fight between Gaston and Pierre. Gaston is an 'extra' working at Le Rallye. A thin, spidery man, born in Marseilles, full of apparent good nature except that he started to bully the apprentices. Young Michael dislikes him intensely and will not work with him.

Pierre we know about: arrogant, parentless, in love, at times good-natured and friendly but so uncertain of himself that he does not know whether to be thoughtful and silent or shouting and boisterous. The other day he was talking of all the good things Hitler did for Germany – and France as well!

Yesterday he and Gaston started to argue. I am not sure over what. Knut tells me Gaston was starting on the boys and Pierre told him to leave them alone. Both are fiery and they continued to shout – Gaston raising a metal vegetable spoon to strike Pierre. But it was only a threat. All seemed to die down. I went to get my dessert. Heard the sound of glass smashing. Looked through the glass panel separating the cash desk from the kitchen, saw these two fighting. Pierre the bigger of the two had Gaston pushed over the stove. I did not stop to think but rushed in between to stop them. A blow from

Pierre in the face left me with a headache for the rest of the evening but with others to help they were eventually separated. Gaston grabbed the pallet knife to attack but Pierre snatched it from him and somehow Gaston ended up with a large lump under his right eye and a long scratch.

Tempers smouldered all that evening. Pierre explained to Knut the cause of the fight: he had been looking for a ladle and found it in Gaston's vicinity and said 'Ah-ha!' Gaston had heard 'Ar-ab'. The fight began. In the course of service Gaston told me it was not over. Marcelle treacherously withdrew support from and quarrelled with Pierre. How one can count on a woman! But then what fools men are!

We finished service and I dashed upstairs to change and have a shower. On coming out from the shower I found the argument in full swing – this time Pierre was surrounded by all the other Arabs while he and Gaston quarrelled it out. Pierre looked reduced and frightened, red-flushed and young, explaining he had only said 'Aaha' and not 'Arab'. 'To me all people are the same – French, English, Polish – all the same . . .' Gaston told him he was lucky – all the young Arabs were dying to punch him. He, Gaston, was 42, Pierre – 23. He pitied him. Had not Knut and I been there they would have murdered him. Michael tried to say something against Gaston and one of the Arabs brutally pushed him aside. Again Knut and I had to intervene.

Pierre is a fool when he could be pleasant. I feel sorry that he has no parents and is besotted but I can't help feeling at the same time – he'd have been made a good Gauleiter. Poor boy, he's already had one beating from the North Africans. As for them, they walk around like victims. Being a Jew I understand that, but when one of them complained of being a victim of racial discrimination I thought – yes, but set them all around a Jew! These are not young men with a cause, they just enjoy a fight. They have a blood-lust given authority by ignorance. How good they must have felt surrounding Pierre. And it will go on and on. Reason shall take long reaching these parts. Among dirty saucepans and dishes what else is left but to take offence and fight like pretend he-men. Perhaps this is the significance of Le Rallye, it takes dignity from a man leaving him with only his basest instincts.

Went with Dolores and José to a two-hour rehearsal. José, run down by a cold, seems old, weary and unenthusiastic. Yet sparks of the fine dancer remain. He would be a great teacher. I contributed to his dinner afterwards but, fool that I am, handled it badly. Dolores had whispered to me that he would not eat from her money so I asked him if I could invite him. Of course he refused but then had to sit down and eat with us. It made him feel how he had come down in the world, though being a gentleman he finally accepted with grace and went on, mumbling, to explain the story behind the dance, attempting to appear unconcerned with the meal he could not afford to buy. Had he known that Dolores had paid for half he would certainly not have eaten it.

Dolores herself is a strange lady, with two dachshunds instead of children – Cyndie and Mitzi whom she worships. She lives on black coffee, bread and jam, but buys expensive steaks for them. Poor Mitzi is paralysed in her back legs. They live like human beings. Lovely, small creatures, tucked up in blankets in a basket though more often under sheets in Dolores' bed, their heads poking out.

José has been going mad with boredom as they've hung around waiting for engagements. They either read or play themselves silly with solitaire. Dolores, a girl from an American backwoods town, is educating herself on such as Bertrand Russell's *History of Western Philosophy, Poetic Criticism Through the Ages, The Stories of Philosophies*, thick books on art. When she was twelve she thought she could fly and to prove it jumped from a barn twenty feet high crying: 'Look, mummy, I can fly!' and broke her ankle. She is friendly, kindly, modest about past success, fussy, childish, naive, high-spirited and optimistic . . .

Having discovered they were sexually incompatible they occupy different rooms . . . Dusty and I are immensely fond of them. God knows where they will end up.

2nd November 1956
Revolts in Poland, Hungary, and Rumania. Israel attacks Egypt. Fortunately the Arabs working in Le Rallye, though they know I am Jewish, are friendly towards me – so far.

Nearly sacked on Wednesday. I was in the middle of making a ratatouille, cutting up tomatoes and peppers, when a waitress came in and ordered five eggs. I was certain she did not order them à la coq so I fried them. She wanted them à la coq! I had to wait for the water to boil but by now the customer had been waiting too long and the son of le Patron stormed through screaming his immaculate head off and, without waiting for explanations, cried at me: 'Dress yourself – get out of the house.' I did my best to remain unperturbed and continued cutting tomatoes. He ranted on about much else that I could not follow, leaving and returning again to repeat: 'Sortie, monsieur – habillez-vous!' Three times he cried out to me, and all the time I continued cutting tomatoes, hoping, I suppose, he wold burn himself out. His fit of temper remained with him, however, and he took the knife from my hand and laid it on the table. 'And the contract?' I asked. He made a violently rude sign about the future of that! I tried to offer explanations at various points and once or twice requested him not to shout, the calm of which angered him more till he shouted me down. So, with deliberate and continued calm I collected together my tools – a knife, fork and lemon cutter – wrapped them in my white cloth, said 'Bonjour' to which he was forced to make reply and, mumbling something about 'politesse', went up to change. I felt expelled from school all over again.

Of course the paying office knew nothing of my dismissal when I went to collect my money, and told me to wait. While waiting, went in to see M. Roberts [manager?]. What a hypocritical little sod he is. I asked could I be thrown out like this. He said I could and told me to return for my money at midday. I may have behaved calmly but felt deeply humiliated to have been shouted at.

M. Courtequisse is in charge of 'stagiaires' in France. Went to see him for advice. Roberts had rung him to say I did not want to work. Courtequisse spoke English and when I explained what had happened he said: 'Well look here, they can't do this. It has to be done through the proper channels . . .' He seemed eager to help. 'I like to see the justice,' he said. He rang Roberts and told him it couldn't be done and would he send the old man over. Over came the old man with his kind face I do not like. He brought up two other incidents, one to prove I did not want to work, the other as evidence that I spoiled merchandise . . . We nattered backwards and forwards, God help me, about poached eggs and hamburger steaks!

Dusty aged 17.

Dusty aged 18.

Dusty aged 18, at the well in
Hill House.

AW in Hungaria with Victor,
pastry chef. 1954.

ABOVE AW in Le Rallye, Paris,
1956.

LEFT AW in Paris, two gen-
darmes and two friends –
Marie-Anne and Nova.

TOP Dusty at Butlins, 1958.

ABOVE AW in Beck Farm with Mother and Poppy Bicker and young Lindsay Joe, circa 1962.

LEFT Granny Loombe and Tanya Jo.

ABOVE Top l to r: Nurse Lottie (looked after Joe), Aunty Ray, Mrs Kieve, Della, cousin Norma. Middle l to r: Aunty Anne, AW, Aunty Billie, cousin Bryan, Dusty, Aunty Sara. Bottom l to r: Leah, Adam, Miles (off frame).

LEFT AW and Dusty driven off in Ralph's Jeep

BELOW l to r: Lindsay Joe, Daniel, Dusty, Tanya Jo, AW by climbing frame in garden of Bishops Road. Circa 1979. (Two photos joined).

... and had three children
Lindsay Joe, Tanya Jo and Daniel.

1979

AW and Leah – 1960.

ABOVE AW and Leah backstage Belgrade Theatre, Coventry, 1959, with Dusty, Joan Plowright and Mary Ure.

LEFT Joan Plowright *Roots*.

BELOW From John Dexter's production of *The Kitchen*, 1959.

LEFT AW and first born, Lindsay Joe.

BELOW Blaendigeddi. Tanya Jo in foreground. Circa 1968.

BOTTOM Aldermaston 1959 – Peter Gill, AW, Dusty, Della, Miriam Brickman, and Nobel Prize winner, Wole Sojinka.

Leah 1977 – two months before she died.

AW in Rome. 1992.

3rd November 1956

M. Courtequisse did not translate exactly what I said, he took the sharp edges off my words with great tact. The old man sat at the desk with his hands clasped before him and nodded and hummed, rather like a schoolboy being told off. An odd situation, which ended in him agreeing to take me back. Said, trying to be friendly, I hoped this decision would not cause friction between father and son. The old man huffed, O dear no, they had more important things to think about. But I knew . . . How I hated having to return next morning, needing the money . . .

In our flat I asked Dusty if she could take some bad news. As soon as I began she turned on me as I knew she would: 'I suppose you were cheeky and did what your mother is always talking about – fighting for your rights. You can't be humble like everyone else . . .' I told her to go to hell and postponed explaining what happened. Later she relented. I asked why she never sticks by me. Such incidents are likely to happen again and again, she must be prepared. She told me not to go back if I didn't want to, but of course I had to.

The following day I worked in the pastry section. As soon as the son arrived to work he stormed down shouting at me: 'You have won twice but the third time . . . my father is an old man, you can do what you like with him but not me!' He threatened me with a shaking finger and said many other things I didn't quite understand but guessed were rude because he kept pointing to his penis and the door. The other chefs were rather impressed though. 'Ah, comme les Anglais sont flegmatique!' a bit of a hero.

The following day, yesterday, was my day off. Dusty worked in the morning, I struggled with some letters. A depressing day. Both of us lethargic and hostile to each other.

I suggested she start another painting using the seven-pronged Jewish candlestick and the star of David and some Hebrew lettering as symbols. Her first attempt failed. I urged her to make it a study in black and white. She ignored that suggestion and any other I made, and introduced yellow and blue. Today, while I was out, she finished it. It's excellent. I had said she would not be able to infuse it with the atmosphere of Jewish life because she was unfamiliar with it. It didn't matter. Somehow she has made it seem – ancient. Egyptian-like. It's a biblical study of Jewishness rather than a ghetto one. Curious and effective. Beneath the candles are the Hebrew letters for God which José had written out for her. Not the known ones, not 'Adonai' or 'Jehovah', but one of the seven names from the Cabala. José explained to me that ש is there to represent the 'manifestation', whatever that means. It is a mystical painting, then?

What can I say about Dusty's recent creations? They are arresting and naive and colourful. Perhaps she has talent – a country girl! Who knows! I know only that I cannot forbid her to spend money on tools and paints. She must have what she wants. At the moment she uses gouache. She's not yet sure how to handle the brushes and I was foolish to try to tell her how. What do I know! And besides, she should be left to do what she likes how she likes. Yet it does annoy me that she can't bear to be told anything. She's happy as a lark when I admire a painting, but when I told her the other day that her painting of fields, sky, tree, house and windmill could have been done by a child of five she sulked and angrily declared she did not ever want to hear me criticise, she would do what she wanted how she wanted.

These are the contradictions in her character: at times loving and thoughtful, generous and frantically happy; at others quite selfish. Example: when I had to post my story off to John Lehman costing 300 francs for postage she said: 'I get so annoyed when we spend money like this,' forgetting we spend much more on her paints and papers. And again, this evening, she had to baby-sit for Sarah. Before she left I announced that I'd like to return to England and start at the school of film technique. She pulled a face and asked: 'What about Stockholm? You know I've always wanted to go to Stockholm.' I pointed out that if we went I'd not have enough money left for the school. Somehow this did not mean much to her. Am I right to expect it to? Yes! After all, it has to do with my future and so our future. She suggested we split the money, she'd go on to Sweden and I to England. Again I had to point out – this would not leave me enough for the school. She left in a huff.

Have I the right to expect her to live her life to suit my plans? Not really. In which case we should not be together!!

12 November 1956
Life becomes unbearable at Le Rallye. A strong word that. And not really true. I can bear it but hate it. The sacking incident – could I be

developing a persecution complex over it? Seems to me I am being especially badly treated. The chef no longer allows me to work in the pastry section. 'With the eggs, until he goes!' The other day, during the rush, I failed to salvage some eggs which could have been used. Then old Mr Marangold, le Patron, came along, excavated them, laid them before me and said: 'You can't make use of these? These are no good I suppose.' I was about to offer an explanation but was pressed by orders. At the same time he turned his face away uninterested in anything I might have said. 'No stories, give me no stories.' I gave him instead my 'you-bloody-old-fool' look and continued working. He continued talking. 'In France we call this sabotage. Sabotage is the word.' There was such a pathetic look on his face, of double strife: to keep this monster going, and defend himself against workers secretly depriving him of his profits. The kind look evaporates with the falling of the leaves, and in its place comes the haggard countenance. The heavy, white-haired head rests among drooping jowls, slumps forward, worried.

I watch myself working. There I am before the red-hot stove. An order for 'oeuf-jambon'. I put fat in the timbale, place a slice of ham and over it crack an egg. Sometimes the egg breaks. I lay it aside. An order for gratiné – I ladle soup into a bowl, throw in bread, sprinkle with cheese, then under the grill. Some escargots are placed before me, I bend down to open the oven, place them inside to heat. An omelette is ordered. I turn to make that. Continually the orders come. I'm up and down, turning left and right, moving backwards and forwards and sweating all the time. I watch myself doing all this. And the waitresses rush here and there, hurrying with ten to fifteen plates cradled in their arms. And I can hear the hum of the furnaces, the clatter of dishes, the crying of orders, the sizzle of fat. And among it all the old man strolls, or the son stands watching the food go out, his sleepy, vicious eyes the only part of him that moves. It is theirs! The rushing, the heat, the hum, the activity – it's all for them. Not to provide people with good food but to earn them money. What makes us do this for others? What is our state of mind that we accept this as life, as right? How has this come to be sanity, and smashing it – madness? It is the negation of life. It is anti-life. It is not the hum, the grand busy hum of people living. It is the blind state of just going on and on because we cannot take time off to work it out.

Yet no one seems to be suffering. Not in the medieval sense of wretchedness. The waitresses still laugh and joke on the way, stop to talk of such and such a customer. They all dress smartly. The cooks enjoy playing practical jokes on each other. They have families and cars, they have money and fine clothes, they eat well and have homes. Who can say this is anti-life? How could one tell them this kitchen is insane, that they are men happily living upside down? Except for the chef. No rush for him, not even the full brunt of responsibility. When I pointed out that the blackboard had omelette Savoyard marked up and that the menu was marked with omelette parmentier he said: 'Je ne sais rien. Je n'étais pas là hier, demandez le sous-chef!' When I pressed and asked him were there any more eggs he opened his apron and said: 'Ils ne sont pas dans ma poche.' He wanders around, sucking his teeth, appearing to be interested and involved but never looking one in the face, never saying 'bonjour'. Mostly only talks with the sous-chef, or old M. Alfred. He can chalk squares on the onion board and escargot board – where the waitresses mark up what they've ordered – and make pretty designs when he chalks up the menu, otherwise he doesn't care. His habit is to shrug his shoulders. Not a spark of human contact, as though fearful that talking would invite a questioning of his status.

I vaguely believe people have little choice in what they become – their make-up has contours. Yet they can choose to resist a tendency to inhumanity. If I believe that what men call evil is a sickness then I cannot hate sick men. I don't hate what they are so much as their lack of fight, their surrender to nasty elements in society. We are all inexorably bound by our contours, beyond them we cannot go, but we have choice within those contours. Evil is the absence of fight.

20 November 1956

Strange things are happening to John the pianist. It began two weeks ago when he failed to turn up for dance rehearsals. Nina came to see him, and her mother – Madame Piankova – and Evelyn the young millionairess who is financing the company. He was ill. He had taken, in two doses, eighty tablets of some sort in a half-hearted attempt to get rid of himself. Dusty and Dolores were also up there in his tiny room. Dusty reported: he sobbed and moaned, 'Nobody loves or cares for me. And I love you all, all of you. You love me don't you, Nina? And you, Evelyn, and you, Baba (Mme Piankova)? But all the students, I felt they hated me, that's all it was, and . . .' And so on. Everyone humoured him and assured him that they loved him.

He is a tall, tall gawky man. Loose-limbed, thin, wrinkled skin and sunken cheeks, with front teeth missing and the remainder rather black. I didn't join them, the scene disgusted me somewhat, not only his wailing but the pandering of others. John is really far too intelligent not to see through himself. And them. He insults his own intelligence . . .

Once, he had to play for a well-known impresario who had suddenly dropped in on the ballet group. John was tight and after fifteen minutes had to excuse himself and leave. It was the second time he had let down the company. He has few chances left.

28 November 1956
Three weeks ago I burned my foot. After two weeks it had not healed. Went to the hospital and was granted seven days off – with pay! It has been an easy, calm seven days. Spent them reading and making notes on Dostoevsky's *Brothers Karamazov*. Read Herbert Read's *The Meaning of Art*, and Silone's *Bread and Wine*. And been struggling with an idea for a novel. I can see the last part more clearly than the beginning. Somewhere I have made notes for it.

Have an uneasy feeling about not working. Feel I'm not entitled to the money I shall receive. Feel I shall have to put on an act when I return, apologise for my absence. Like I was playing truant from school again.

Six weeks left before we return to London. Dusty and I walked this morning to Les Invalides to find out the cost of flying home. 8000 francs each. Too much. We'll have to return by boat in winter seas. Paris has become stark. Cold winds, bare trees. Today an almost empty blue sky across which fast winds are blowing high, white clouds. The pavements are wet from last night's rain. But the air is fresh, made walking feel healthy.

Most of these days off I have eaten bread and jam in the morning, bread and cheese in the afternoon, a little later some bread and cheese again, each with black coffee. In the evenings D returns and we go either to the Auberge in rue d'École de Médecine, or Chez

Jean round the corner for a cheap meal. God knows I can survive on it. Fortunately D has been doing a few hours' overtime and so have not needed to break into the kitty. Now she is more careful than I am in holding on to money to pay for my school. She buys no paper or paint, and her enthusiasm is down to Zero. Last night we had a restless night and she seemed in bits and pieces today. Yet between us we are very easy and satisfied. Love seems to grow if left alone. She remarks now and then on how well we get on together, and we do. I don't make the demands on a woman I imagined I would. Or perhaps I do and it's just that Dusty complies. I'm not sure. Best not to probe too deeply. We shall miss Paris. Just knowing we will soon be leaving for London has disrupted our existence . . .

The sad story of José and Dolores comes to light. For the last hour and a half José has been pouring out his history like a long walk in the rain . . . There were long pauses between his 'confession'.

'We were married in Mexico, it was a church wedding, everyone knows us.'

Pause.

'But I know, as sure, Wizzie, as anything, it just wouldn't work. I know it, you know that? Now we just don't love each other any more. I used to but we aren't suited. She hampers me, she will not listen to what I tell her to do. She knows. I work out steps and numbers just for her, that I think will make a good dance, but she argues. "I also studied in Spain," she says, "that is not my step." So I give in. She is so cocky, so stubborn, and even now when Nina asked whose number is that, she will say "José's and mine," and Nina knows damn well it's mine.

'So what shall I do? I feel I cannot leave her. Not like this. Though she has always been able to look after herself. I feel responsible for her. I'd like to get her back to New York or Mexico where I took her from. All this is getting me down. I feel cold inside . . . But we do not fight, not now. I've learned to take it and be quiet. I used to, we used to have – oh, ridiculous scenes – and one day she said something and I beat her up. That's the first and last time I ever laid hands on her. I beat her. And since then I've been quiet. She treads on me, Wizzie. I take it all and it seems as though I agree because I'm silent, in front of my friends even, I say nothing. So-'

Rather recklessly and not too seriously I interrupted: 'Why don't you give her a baby?' The moment he paused I knew exactly what had happened. She'd had an operation. She can't have babies any more.

'She had an operation and they messed up her inside and took away half an ovary and part of her womb . . . If only I were sure it had been mine. Although I think it was. Let me explain. At that time I was living in Hollywood. I had a beautiful apartment, beautiful. And I led two sorts of lives. There were the kids – I used to go around with them, we had fun, we had money, and Hollywood in those days was free. There was nothing to stop us from being free. And there was loose living. Girls galore. As many as one wanted, and you know, there was a little bit extra about me, a little bit more than the others. I could talk intelligently on serious subjects, I had money, I had influence. Everybody used to come in and out of my flat. Haefetz, Pola Negri, this conductor, that musician. In those days I didn't have to look for work, it came to me. Oh God, I was a member of every damn musical society going. In fact I nearly married the daughter of the conductor of the Los Angeles Philmarmonic. We listened to all the concerts and, you know, I had my wireless hooked up to all the European capitals – Paris, London, Berlin. And we could get the concert just as it was played. So we had drinks, and sandwiches, and everyone came in and listened. That was the other kind of life I led . . . I was a big person at that time, a teacher. Xavier Cugat had told me he had this kid whom he wanted to dance for him – his own dancer had signed a movie contract, she became quite famous – and he wanted me to teach this kid some dances, he would pay for it. The kid was Dolores and the idea of skipping appealed to her – she would marry her teacher . . . Now – I can't do anything. I have the offer of a school in Mexico, and Dolores of a job in the Bahamas. But . . . I don't know . . . I've got ideas. At night I lie in bed and I see dances, I hear music, I see new creations, and I can't sleep. I have to take up a detective story. Sometimes I have whole white nights when I don't sleep at all. I feel beaten.' . . .

He left the room, wrote a letter to his daughter, and now he is playing patience on his bed. I shall go in and play some card game with him for a little while.

29 November 1956

This is the kind of incident distances me from Dusty – to do with mean spirits, yet God knows I can still love her. Last night we'd missed the last train and had to catch a night bus the cost of which was 100 francs each. 200 francs down the drain, phst! When we're calculating franc by franc this kind of expense becomes an annoying setback. Dusty reckoned she had 1000 francs for today out of which she could easily buy paints and paper. The urge to do some more painting had returned. I had to be at the hospital this morning before nine o'clock. These last mornings we've been rising late, about 10 or so, which has had the effect of making Dusty lifeless for the day. She made me promise to force her to get up the same time as me.

No need to force. She was up and dressed in time to accompany me to the hospital. First thing – breakfast. Four croissants and a demi-baguette which came to about 82 francs. though tired we took a pleasant stroll to Hôtel Dieu where we had to wait 3½ hours before being attended to. Three and a half hours! I could have waited and cursed, but for Dusty it was a complete waste of time. She could have been painting. On the way home we bought 125 grs of butter – 100 francs; some macédoines de légumes, spinach, a baguette, two portions of chips at 35 frs each, and coffee for 245 frs. Quietly the 1000 frs was disappearing but as yet we had not noticed. It was bad enough to be peeved by a wasted morning even though we'd been humorously diverted in the hospital by the antics of three drunks who appeared one after the other turning the waiting room into a kind of stage – a comedy.

A bass player had moved into the hotel a few nights ago and when we returned wanted to change £5 into francs. It was a good exchange. He was talking to Dolores as we made the exchange. Dusty was making coffee. I had noticed that she was acting cold and unfriendly towards Dolores. When they'd gone and we sat down to eat I remarked on the fact.

'I think I'm entitled to decide for myself,' she replied. Indeed she is, but she has no reason to be unfriendly. Dolores might be a 'doom' woman, a bad wife, an uncooperative dancing partner but that had nothing to do with us. She had been nice to us in the past, friendly, good company. To cold-shoulder her now was mean.

'Do you have to behave so meanly? We can't cut ourselves off from people. We have to be friendly. We're not sacrificing our fortune, just offering a cup of coffee. You sometimes behave like one of the herd. Every other Tom, Dick and Mary behaves meanly, but I want a real human being at my side.' I asked was there enough coffee on the boil because I wanted to call them in to have some with us. Being chastised upsets Dusty. She hit back.

'Two out of every seven days you accuse me of being part of the herd,' she cried. 'When I do what you want I'm all right and when I don't then you tell me I'm one of the herd.'

Nevertheless she went into the passage and meekly – Oh God, like a child being told to say 'sorry' – she asked the young man, 'Would you like a cup of coffee with us, and you too, Dolores.' It was my turn to feel mean. Such a hideous task-master, such a lousy schoolteacher. What right have I to force her to be nice to people she does not like, to do anything against her will? And yet – it is not simply that. I too don't want to idle my hours away with people such as Dolores, nor present a false face to people I've no respect for. But I was not asking Dusty to do that. I was asking her to be big, not to let little natures disturb her. Was asking her not to descend to the herd where people are frightened of each other, mean to each other. I was asking her to be tolerant and sympathetic, to be big big big! I cannot bear the nastiness of small minds. It doesn't matter about culture and education and whether one can say witty things, only have a warm nature, get rid of the cold shells that make a man distrust his neighbour, that makes a man unbeautiful.

Yet what right have I? I believe so much in her freedom (if only as a means of establishing my own) that I've no right to ask her to be anything. It is this: she has elected to partner me for life, and life is a long time and only for once, and I am not going to live a long life of fear and meanness like the mass of people. The seeds of meanness are in me, as in all, I know. And that is part of the challenge – to overcome this inherent flaw. If I'm going to fight it then she has to as well. I make no other demands – a sense of value for life and all that goes with it, that is all. It is not an end, not an ideal, it is the first essential step. Then comes the ideal. What that ideal is, each man chooses for himself, but first he must reach for his humanity.

Our clash did not end there. It reached the high point as she was about to leave when she suddenly realised 360 francs was all that was left, and there were still envelopes and stamps to buy as well as painting materials. In the presence of Dolores and the young man – Dave somebody – she bemoaned the state of affairs. I felt defensive and reasoned that it could not be helped if I had burned my foot and so had to eat up the overtime she had earned. We would draw from the kitty only for God's sake let's not become angry over money. She continued to moan and when I repeated that we would draw from the kitty she cried no! she would not do any painting! and threw a little dictionary at me.

There is one good psychological reason why such a scene depresses me: I hated it when a public quarrel took place between Leah and Joe. Now I laughed and tried to make light of it in front of our guests but I was left with the horrible feeling: how could I love a woman who behaved like this? Then I realised she is not a woman, she is still immature. Maturity means you can behave calmly in times of crisis. Then again, experience teaches me that as a person behaves now so they will behave, more or less, in the future. And our future is going to be one where I shall be broke and at school and Dusty will be going out to work to earn our necessities and crises will be inevitable. Dare I trust myself to the sacrifice of an immature person? I dare, albeit with some trepidation.

It might nicely have ended there, but some 20 minutes ago Dusty rang from work, completely changed, no trace of smallness and immaturity left.

'I have never thrown anything before,' she said, 'I must have lost my senses. But I'm not mean, Wizzie. I don't think I'm a mean person.' She laughed.

'But sometimes,' I replied, 'you're like an animal. It wasn't a question of inviting them in for coffee, that was nothing. It was something beyond that, we've just got to rise above things.'

'But I've given enough,' she protested, 'now I want to save, to economise.'

'Of course we have to. We will do. But when one economises to the point where one becomes an animal then one should stop economising,' I replied. Or some such words. [I seem to have had a predilection for this word, using it in the sense of conforming, as animals do. Today's connotations are more crude, sound more offensive than was intended.]

She said she had been mad at the time but that she really wanted to laugh at the way the two of them stood there. 'I would have left at the sign of someone else beginning to row,' she said. 'Not them! I had a good laugh when I reached Sarah's. I mean – what must Dolores be thinking? She must be disliking me more and more. It's funny . . .' On the other hand she was amused at the way I was serious and distressed. What must I think, for Christ's sake? What am I to think when her moods change so quickly.

25 December 1956
Merry Xmas!

Walking home from Le Rallye I passed an Xmas tree in a box which had been either knocked down or had fallen down. I was just about to walk past it when I thought – what the hell, must I not care for anything? So I returned and set it right, in place.

As I approached Pont Neuf I saw a man lying over the hot grille on the pavement. It was bitterly cold but I didn't stand him on his end and set him in place!

The other day an old woman came to the back door of Le Rallye begging for food. Le Patron told one of the dishwashers to clean an empty apricot tin and fill it with potage for her.

Merry Xmas!

29 December 1956
José and his daughter have left for Mexico. On Sunday Dolores leaves for Oklahoma. In 12 days' time we depart for London. On the 26th January in the new year John goes with the ballet company to Monte Carlo. Something breaks up. One never knows what. José mumbled about wishing he had got to know us better. Dusty says she was near to tears when they said goodbye to her. I had said my au revoir just as I left for work, some fifteen minutes after getting out of bed, when my head was still sleeping and I could not find sadness only embarrassed confusion . . .

30 December 1956
And now Dolores has gone. She bequeathed her cooking utensils and leftover tinned food. José left me his Mexican sandals and Mexican hat. All the petty jealousies are forgotten. We know Dolores is OK, we know José is OK, we know that together they lose control of themselves. The dogs won't bark any more. Cyndie

won't rush in here after mice she has already scared away with her barking.

. . . precious friendships, routine, familiarity, chatter, loans for this and that, gossip – all ending.

How many more times shall I pack up a little home, I wonder, and kiss goodbye to walls we made our own?

1st January 1957
Happy New Year!

I saw it in as I saw Christmas – working.

It is the afternoon after the long night, a lovely feeling of tiredness, that tiredness that seems to snap bonds. A tired but a clearer head. Not eager, or unhappy, or depressed. More – languorous. A good languor is upon me. The kind that excuses all that one may now do, not that there is anything one is going to do, but the excuse is there in case.

Slept one and a half hours last night. At around two in the morning Pierre said – he was a little drunk by this time: 'Arnold, I want to tell you something. I want to tell you you are my best friend in Le Rallye!' His words made me happy.

Knut took Dusty out to see in the New Year. With others they went from café to café, a sort of café-crawl. They returned at six-thirty in the morning, Dusty rather under the weather though not incapable. Something vindictive in her manner. She kept laughing with Knut, squeezing his arm and saying what a wonderful time she'd had and how happy she was. Good! But I felt she was getting her own back on me because of the card we'd heard had arrived in Weald Square from my old RAF girlfriend, Jean, and because I persist in friendships with Olive, Shifra, Audrey and Rhoda. Not that I go out of my way to see them but I refuse to make enemies of them. It makes her feel insecure.

So I can't be surprised that she becomes vindictive, I never make her feel as though I need her. Yet I think so much of her. I just refuse to become oppressed with love, to feel restricted. I cannot – must not – ever be dependent upon a woman. However much I love her the fact is that were she to leave me I would survive. A woman cannot bear the thought of that. Secretly I despise women as women. I can enjoy them superficially and respect them on an intimate level yet, in the end, a woman is a woman and cannot overcome that. The same applies to men and to me; men are pretty lousy creatures in general and I am not offering myself as a good proposition. That's what upsets Dusty, I do not offer myself. She has had to come to me – though I've never taken advantage of that – and I guess she's now tired of making the running.

The boys who were with them on their night out kept saying to Knut – watch it – she's married. When the moment came they were alone together she told him we were not married!

Six months have passed, we've lived together, love has burned and now passion flickers. She's satisfied the appetites of adolescence, and approaches guarded maturity. Now she wonders, what is left? Who is this on her hands that she no longer lusts after? She is having difficulty assessing the ruins of her dreams. She can survive, that's not the problem. The last test of her love, now that she's had her fill of me, is whether to take on the risks and uncertainties I warned her of. I should really make the decision for her – but I was never strong in my dealings with women.

2nd January 1957·

All that I intuitively knew would happen has happened sooner than I anticipated.

Dusty went to pictures with John last night and bounced in upon my sleep with a loud hello. She started to chatter straight away and was soon in bed. After some moments of silence she asked whether she could have money from the kitty to go with her 1000 francs to buy a pair of shoes. Of course. Later she said: 'Oh, Wizzie, there's another thing. I'm going to have a little party on Sunday . . .' And then she told me about two boys she'd met at the Auberge with John. One, a Hungarian, one from Leeds. Terrible funny types it seems they were. One plays an accordion, the other a guitar, I think. She's asked them up for six in the evening and wanted to know how to get hold of Knut. I told her he would be working. Little more was said on the subject. I don't mind what she does as long as she's happy. I was very tired.

Some seconds later she said: 'Wizzie, when we go to London I must have a bed of my own. I must be independent or else I shall get to be relying on you all the time.'

'Good,' I said. 'As you wish.' She'd been thinking hard. After a while I said: 'I think we'd better agree that it's finished, isn't it?'

'Oui!' she replied.

'And once we get to London we'll make a definite break.'

'But I need you to help me get a bed.'

'Don't worry, you can sleep at Weald Square until such time as you want to. We shall always help you.' Again, some sort of sad silence. 'Dusty, only one thing. You're very easily taken in by people. I only hope you'll be careful who you go with in London.'

'But I shan't go with anyone,' she replied.

'You'll make friends, you'll see.' And then a little later I added: 'One last thing, the hardest, I think we'd better stop being intimate.'

'But why?'

'It doesn't mean anything any more.'

'You don't love me then?'

'I can't talk about love now.'

'Why?'

'I don't know. Love means sacrifice.'

'But I haven't asked you to sacrifice anything!'

'I know. I don't mean love forces one to sacrifice, I mean in love one is prepared to make sacrifices, and it's been you who's done all the giving.'

Not a great deal more was said but what I said was crude and cruel, everything at once. If she wanted independence then she had to understand fully the implications. But she hadn't realised independence would be as cold as I now was. She asked to lie in my arms, and began to cry. I told her she must guard against such moments, wait for mornings when thinking will be clearer. 'Tears don't last long. You'll survive.'

'Love me,' was her reply. 'I do need you, you are my precious one, I don't want anyone else but you.' Gratifying to hear, but the night was sad and there was no one else; but what about when familiarity breeds the contempt it deserves? It is to my shame that when she made love I responded. No longer than minutes, and soon we were asleep.

It is through such incidents we learn to despise ourselves.

4 January 1957

Ah, yes, it is surely over. She took my advice and guarded against that sad, night-time moment. Daylight renewed her determination.

She has felt like a crab clinging where it was not wanted. Not possible to do that for a lifetime. It only needed her to say such a thing once to herself and she would soon accept the fact. Though it is not a fact. 'Crab' is the lousiest of words. Nor is it true to say she has not been wanted. But it is true to say I have not been able to hide my doubts of love lasting, that I've not been able to hide the scepticism, the cynicism behind my idealism, and I've communicated those horrible things to her rather than what is of value.

And now it is over. Having said it to herself once makes it easier to say again and again and again and soon it will become a fact. 'I do not love him'. That sweetness shall be abandoned, that tenderness and playfulness she lavished upon me shall dry up because she feels it is neither reciprocated nor wanted. And it's sad because it is only a half-truth. Withdraw it all, I shall miss it all. When I asked her yesterday did she love me or not she hesitated, which was an answer.

I have known nothing sweeter nor more passionate than her love. Nothing more genuine. I knew no one more natural and uninhibited. She was a poem. She was lovely. The one thing I was terrified would happen is about to happen – sweetness turning sour.

Not that she is bitter or cold. 'I feel you are like my brother now,' she said, 'we must stay friends, you know.' And then an absolutely priceless question. 'Wizzie, if I came back would you have me? If after I've looked around and found no one I really liked and wanted you again?' What could I do but laugh. Kind laughter, though. How do I know? I shall prize and hate my isolation once she has gone. Who knows what new barriers I shall erect against her or how strong they'll be. 'All I know is – I shall never say "if you go do not come back again".'

She seemed happy and cheeky with her renewed determination. She sang and laughed and bounced around and I watched her and cried:

'You're bluffing. You're joking. I do not believe you, you're putting on a brave act.'

'Oh no! this is me now, my boy.' But I teased her more and we laughed and joked before I returned to work. And as I left I went on my knees and kissed her hand and said:

'You are a very fine person.'

'Bless you,' she replied.

In the evening she met me from work and we made our way to the Dorras, she saying all the time how she dreaded seeing them. But once there, and seeing Mrs D pregnant, and talking lightly, joking with Mr Dorra and eating a succulent fruit salad prepared specially by Mrs D, she repented. When we kissed them goodbye, leaving them with thanks, Dusty confessed how mean she felt about what she had said of them, how kind they were, and she must send them a large parcel when we return.

In the Metro we larked and bounced around, and I teased her again about her new feelings.

'Missed your chance, boy,' she exclaimed. 'I thought I'd have a little Wesker – still.' Back in our room we told each other how dead we felt.

'Like this afternoon,' she said. 'I felt I needed somebody. But it soon passed and I'm all right now.' Shrug of the shoulders, humming aloud while making tea-de-da-de-dum.

'Me too, but all right now.' I hopped into bed. 'Good night, girl,' I said, as though to my sister, and stretched out with my back to her. She jumped in alongside and began doing her nails. I turned and leaned on my elbow, watching her.

'Lie here,' she said, uncovering herself. 'On my breast.' I laid there, and soon the light was out and she lay in my arms and a gentle finger stroked my face. She kissed me and I kissed her and we loved. Just like that. No words. Like lost people mad in a maze, racing among passionate shadows. It ended around four in the morning. I can only remember her saying:

'Wizzie, I do not love you.' But it meant nothing to me at that moment.

This morning she rose late for work. My day off. Making tea she murmured:

'What happened last night was very bad. Mustn't happen again.'

'No. Agreed. Terrible. Mustn't happen again.'

'We were getting over it so well.'

'Yes. Must finish with that.'

'Yes.' And we laughed and joked and she kissed me goodbye off to work. I wonder what thoughts cross her mind this morning. Such playfulness will happen less and less. She'll win. She'll go to Sweden as she has decided. She will survive, probably with less trouble than me. How will I feel without her? All that's good about her has always by far far far outweighed what has been annoying about her. I shall miss her. I can feel it even now – myself missing her.

I'm going to get what I want and I shall hate it.

But this morning I did what I have been meaning to do for some time. I called up into the room the man from the art shop next door to show him Dusty's paintings and ask for criticism. He liked a number of them but it was a bad way to show them, laying them out on the bed, and to someone who hasn't really the time. Nevertheless he suggested we select some and take them to a gallery for an opinion. To be honest I was so nervous I could hardly understand what he was saying. I think he was impressed. Just a little, little bit. A young man. I was not sure whether he owned or merely worked in the shop. We must get John Lavrin's opinion.

An important point I'd forgotten to mention. Her 'revolt' was not simply against me but against her own torpor into which she had sunk.

'I'm going to live,' she said. 'Here I've been doing nothing in the evenings, going to bed early, not caring how I looked, dressed shabbily. No more!' This was a reference to my complaints that as soon as she got home from work she'd get out of her clothes and wander around in a dressing gown, already like an old, uncaring woman. How strange, I'd said, that before marriage men and women dressed up to greet each other; after marriage neither cared whether they looked nice or not. Perhaps these remarks have played on her mind.

6 January 1957
These last days have been a sort of crisis. I think it began when Dusty and I visited the memorial of the Unknown Jewish Martyr last month. An emotional excursion to a museum of photographs of Jews in concentration camps and other terrible and humiliating scenes. It left me cold and unresponsive to her, estranged me in some way. For weeks in fact. And I said some very harsh things at which she complained: 'You expect so much of me.' It was true. I had been unreasonable. She was only twenty. I expected the wisdom of a mature woman. And it all came to a head, as we now know . . .

The diary peters out as time and energy are taken up with preparations to depart, and we become entangled in a messy farewell party. We leave Paris in a state of confused emotions. Eleven days later we're in the home of Dusty's parents where I attempt to reconstruct what happened.

17 January 1957
England now [Beck Farm, Norfolk, in fact].

I've had no chance to write about those last few days in Paris. Pity. They were packed full of incident. Not even that last entry is complete. It ended very strangely. I talked and talked I remember, and talked Dusty into tears again. Unsettling days, those. She managed to hate, I think.

But the 'night of events' was the Monday night. We gave a party. Roy and Rita were there, Gerry and Knut. Barney and Monique came later. I was given special permission to leave work early. By the time I arrived Roy and Gerry were already a little tight, merry. Knut was dressed immaculately in his check suit and cuffs. When Barney and Monique arrived I went out to buy some frites to go with a pork chop Dusty fried for them. Not enough wine. Monique and I ran out to the shop for a bottle of brandy. We opened champagne. Roy was flirting with Dusty, making all sorts of licentious remarks. We tried to sing but our efforts collapsed because Barney insisted on singing a different song and others perversely sang out of tune. Drunk, we all lose control, disintegrate, go separate ways, unable to meet, not even desiring to come together. I lamented to Roy how everyone wanted to sing a different song.

Hostility grew between D and I. I remember – she cooed and fussed around Knut. Then a strange sequence: Knut and Barney went out to buy some more brandy; while they were gone Roy and Rita went home; then Knut and Barney returned. No one became sufficiently mellow to be interesting and happy, frivolous merely, Barney mainly the cause. Nothing happened. We sprawled around, chattering. Barney and Monique missed their train. We decided to lie down and sleep. Dusty changed into her dressing gown, the top mattress was taken off the bed, three on each. Dusty took command.

'You, Knut, lie here with Wizzie and I. Barney, Monique and Gerry down there. You don't want your trousers on, boy . . .' Knut took off his trousers. Likewise Barney and Gerry. There was something so eager and loose in Dusty's voice, and I felt so helpless, with no right to interfere, and the atmosphere became so puerile and empty, I grabbed my jacket, some cigarettes, said I was gong to the lavatory, flew down the stairs and ran, wanting to scream, all the way to Pont Neuf.

I looked for some of the hot railings the tramps sleep on, but they were either occupied or not warm enough. It was two or more in the morning. Lorries and activity around Samaritaine and Les Halles. I walked along the Seine. It was cold. Over the next bridge and back again into the back streets down to Saint-Germain, across that boulevard, into more back streets.

I came to a door with a long, empty passage. At first I was too shy to push it open. Found a cardboard box and sat on that huddled up against the wall. Dozed a little and became braver. The door pushed open easily and I sat me inside the passage out of the wind and the cold. It was not long before I dozed in fits and starts for about half an hour or more – then walked home.

Voices were coming from the room. I heard Dusty saying: '. . . I tried all I could. I can't help him.' I settled in an armchair in the hall in the darkness. Some ten minutes later I heard them coming from somewhere walking right past me to John's room and back again. Barney. He knelt before me. I was shivering. 'What happened, Wizzie?' How could I explain? We sat and smoked and talked – loving, friendly words. Monique and Knut passed by. We hid, like children, behind the table. But Knut came back and found us. He dragged Barney out and sent him upstairs. Me he dragged and pulled outside again.

'You come with me. I want to know what's wrong.' I protested that I was shivering. He took off his overcoat and, tall that he is, put his arm around me and marched me to some late bar. For 500 francs he bought us a brandy each and began.

'I know what's wrong but I want you to tell me. I want it from you. I've been waiting to talk to you ever since New Year's Eve.'

We had a foolish conversation but it was a touching scene. He told me he knew Dusty had fallen in love with him – I would not have put it as strongly as that – but that he had done nothing to encourage it. He was sorry, he did not want a friendship broken – and so on. I loved him at that moment despite all that was sentimental about it; and he, no doubt, enjoyed the mad stage-drama of it all.

Betweeen the reality and the theatricality was the dream-like quality of events.

The more so as I write about it in the home of Dusty's parents in Norfolk. The family is in bed and I'm alone in the large, low-ceilinged room, frost outside – all very unreal. The speed of getting from one place to another gives our lives a kind of unreality –

So, we returned to Windsor Hotel, Knut and I. Gerry and Barney had talked at length until Gerry decided to go home, at which point Barney went out looking for Knut and me. Dusty and Monique were at the table, drinking coffee. The bed was in order. Sobriety. Dusty had poured her heart out to Monique. Monique had been gentle and sympathetic. Crazily, Knut now went looking for Barney. At four in the morning we asked them to leave and let us have at least two hours' sleep. So quickly our moods change. We finished up in each other's arms.

So, Paris ended. A few more days at work, an incident I shall keep to myself, goodbyes along the Seine to Paul, Roy and Rita. Coffee and rolls with Knut on the morning of leaving, he the last person to wave to us from the platform of Gare Saint-Lazare, a calm sea voyage . . .

Epilogue to Paris

I don't know who Paul was, nor can I remember Nina and her mother, Madame Piankova. Lisa Dorra lost her second baby. We never heard again from Dolores, José, John or anyone from Le Rallye. Roy, who had been lecturing at École Normale Supérieure in Paris, became Emeritus Professor of General Linguistics and Fellow of Worcester College, Oxford, with nearly a dozen books to his name as either originator or editor. Boris left law and took a degree in psychiatry which he now practices. Barney divorced Monique and faded in and out of our lives, losing his boyish charm, and thickening with food and drink before disappearing completely from view. Dusty gave up painting though I bought her an easel, brushes and paints – perhaps *because* I bought her an easel, brushes and paints! She took to a camera instead and gave us all a splendid collection of portraits. I had a dark-room built for her while she was abroad somewhere. She learned how to develop and print her own negatives but when our youngest son, Dan, showed interest in photography she gave that up, too. Family and cooking took over her life.

I resist launching into lengthy commentary on those Paris days. Much speaks for itself. As with every other time and place I attempt to resurrect they refocus vividly, I have felt as if in a time capsule. I see that room in Hotel Windsor at number 8 Rue de L'Ancienne Comédie; I see where the stove was, and the table, and the postcards of Blake, Dufy, Picasso, Turner and Braque which we pinned or glued on walls. I had forgotten about Mitzi and Cyndie, and John the inebriate pianist. And that huge, stiff Mexican hat that hung around the house for so many years, I now know where it came from. The incident I vowed to keep to myself was not an amorous encounter – though it did involve the waitress I lusted after – more an embarrassing encounter, one of those Samuel Johnson warned a man should not tell lest 'they will be remembered and brought out against him upon some subsequent occasion.'

Did I *really* 'despise women as women'? It shocked me to read that, it is so far from what I have felt and claimed since. Yet at the time perhaps it was true. I had gone through rough relationships in the on-going battle of the sexes. The uncharitable will sneer that I invited wounds; the more generous will recognise the scenes of battle. How young and bewildered we were, what expectations, what impulsiveness. But among the foolishness was an innocent bravado, a reaching out for good things and butterflies.

The kitty grew. I seem to remember a certain week's pay packet, high from overtime, of 54,000 francs. £54! We saved enough to pay for my six-month course at the embryonic London School of Film Technique during which time Dusty cleaned out company telephones for a firm called Phonatas, and worked in a café in Mare Street, Hackney, serving such as Cliff Richard who was performing at the Hackney Empire. Soon I would write *Chicken Soup with Barley*, Lindsay Anderson would write his letter telling me I was really a playwright wasn't I, rehearsals would begin on my first play and I would walk into a theatre's workshop to see carpenters assembling a set for something I'd written in a small room in an LCC flat, and Dusty would temporarily fade out of my life to work as a waitress for Billy Butlin's Holiday Camp in Skegness where I would write informing her of those preparations for that first ever staging. All that was to come. Meanwhile, what awaited our return?

3.1.57

Dear Arnold & Dusty

While I am waiting for Ambulance for Daddy to go to Hospital once more I thought I might as well do something & I couldn't think anything better to do than write a letter to you. I am sure that I am going to miss this letter-writing when you come home. Anyway how are you? I hope you enjoyed New Year's Eve & if I haven't wished you a happy new year I do so now wish you both Happy New Year. As usually I was with my old Man & we both heard the old year out & the New Year in & so went to bed & at this moment I am just getting over a heavy cold I had.

I was supposed to take the children to a circus at Harringay. Through this cold I had I couldn't go so I phoned Della & she or Thelma took them as Deanna went too. By the way I hope you weren't in the cafe where all that shooting was going on? Shocking shocking situation. What a world to live in?

Is there anywhere I could meet you when you arrive home? Do let me know the exact time you arriving in London. Actually I haven't much to write except I don't know whether I told you that I was trying to get Daddy in a Jewish home again but they said it would cost £10.10/- to pay per week, but they would help me & offered me some old slips & worn shoes. Of couse I refused & am raging with anger & will send them a letter just as I feel about them. Only I am waiting until you'll come home to write a letter for me. You know you can write. Anyway I thought they would help me out with a little money. Still you know they are bastards. They won't help people like us, they will only help those that need for bankruptcy or £1000 for business. I doubt whether they will help you. [They didn't!] I do hope so but they will connect you with your parents. They honestly think that children should help parents.

I don't see wrong in that but the only thing they differ from me is that if children could be helped to get to the position they want that would be the happiness both to parents & themselves & to society. However you still go on with what you want to ask them for the money you want & we'll see what they say to you.

Whatever all will turn out good I am sure.

My mother's view that only bankrupts were helped is, of course, not true. The Jewish Board of Guardians – now called the Jewish Board of Deputies – like the representatives of Jewish communities all over the world, established charitable organisations for most aspects of community life, and my mother did on occasions receive help from them though nowhere near what her extreme case merited. Nor, I imagine, did her combative personality help. She spoke her mind, asserted her dignity and doubtless was not as supplicant as required. Even Jews produce the petty bureaucratic mentality that delights in humiliating victims of misfortune.

I am looking forward to your homecoming. I will start on the flat your room & the best room. Everything looks & is the same as you left it excepting that it's dusty everywere still you know me about my children coming so I must be busy I will probably be up [abrupt stop]

Here I am My Dear Arnold back from the hospital. I was going to say 'up all night the night before you'll come' when the ambulance came. Well the doctor has examined him & said that he is perfectly alright physically. He can move his hands & legs & he isn't mental either & that is the truth. There is however psychologically wrong with him that he just don't want to help himself. He is obstinate & lazy & I have to go with him again next Wednesday to see another Doctor & they will probably send him to a rehabilitation centre again & this time for a longer period. The doctor feels sure that he can & will be able to improve. So he might not be here when you come home. I am sure too that he will be able to be better off for at least 3 months away. I hope & maybe it will give me a chance to get back even if not for long or full time at least sometime to work. I nearly forgot how to work. I haven't been working for nearly a year. But never mind I feel sure something better for the best will turn out for me as well. As for you too . . .

I don't know if we returned on the 12th or 14th of January, or perhaps even earlier. Whenever, we were in Beck Farm with Dusty's parents by the 17th which is the day I wrote the last entry of the Paris diary. Dusty must have been eager to visit the Norfolk crowd, longing to tell tales of foreign parts, which accounts for spending a few days in Weald Square with Leah and Joe.

Following the last Paris entry are two pages of diary relating to Norfolk Life. *Roots* is taking shape.

. . . With Mrs B [Bicker] all that she talks about becomes a little story. '. . . Now I'll tell you what happened. Now this is the truth, you listen . . .' Each incident protracted: about how Sally, her son Sam's dog, had a pup, 'no one expected it!' About the time she was sleeping at her daughter, Joy's, and Joy's son, Derrick, had kicked her out of his bed . . . And about that beautiful huge dog that had followed her all the way home from Harleston . . . All delivered in this lovely accent, no, not lovely, rather – a fascinating one. And delightful sayings;

'He called him everything but a Christian.'

'Now hold you on! Half you a minute!'

And God! How I'm fed here. They pickle their own onions and their own cabbage. Jam too. The table is full of food, and no sooner have we finished one meal than I'm asked what I want for the next one.

18 January 1957

Ma came in from Harleston just now and said:

'Bit of a hold-up in the village. Accident there. Woman knocked

off her bike.' A slight hint of having witnessed something very important, but very matter-of-fact.

'Fatal?' I asked.

'Oh no, that weren't fatal. I could 'ave gi'en evidence, I saw it,
that I did, but I weren't goin' a get mixed up in that.'

'Don't you, mother,' said D.

'That were his fault, the driver's fault, oh yes. I could 'a gi'en evidence at another accident I saw in Harleston. But there were
another man there an' he reckoned that were the driver's fault, too,
so I let him be a gettin' on wi' it. But thaas none o' my business that
it ent.'

'Badly hurt?'

'Well you'd think it wouldn't you? A lorry knocked a woman
clean off her bike on hard ground you'd reckon she were hurt. They
called the doctors to her 'an that.'

'Who was she?'

'I don't know who it were. I see her around many times but I
don't know her to talk to.'

Mother Bicker, Mother Wesker: the one becoming an intrinsic part
of me as the other had been these last twenty-four years –
approaching twenty-five.

Chapter Twenty-two

The London School of Film Technique

I am in great need of the novelist's skill. All must now be drawn together – lives, endings, new beginnings. There can be no rushing. I must proceed carefully, not panic. Though it could be over in a paragraph:

> With savings from Le Rallye I paid for six months of 'study' at the London School of Film Technique; Lindsay Anderson read my play; the Belgrade Theatre in Coventry performed it and brought it to the Royal Court Theatre in London; I was awarded a grant of £300 by the Arts Council of Great Britain which Dusty and I spent on getting married; a year later, on the first night of *The Kitchen*, my father died; along with others of my generation I was made, overnight, an international writer which I was utterly ill-equipped to understand or cope with and probably didn't deserve but I worked hard, behaved responsibly, shared all I could of this new-found fame and fortune, had three children within the next four years and continued writing and living off my writing up until this very very very same day. There it was. That was it. So it became. Sugar and spice, heaven and hell, praise and envy, glory and decline, friends and enemies, decline and glory. It's not over yet. Anything can happen and probably will. Good night and God bless you all.

But we will resist gabbled summings-up, impatient last chords. Bear with me.

I had always wanted to be a student. It was my shame to be born with a head that could not retain knowledge. Perhaps it was a genetic impediment – memory-blind. Is there such a thing? The deficiency comes with age, they say. I seemed to have been born with it. I couldn't retain facts, names, a vocabulary. A dictionary had passed through me yet I struggled to find the right word in a discussion. It is a disability that affected my schooling, it is why I failed exams, it is my curse and torment: a memory so afflicted, I forget my opinions!

Le Rallye, with hard work and long hours, had earned fees for a six-month course at a newly established 'school' to study film technique. In the 1950s the Heatherly School of Art, an Edwardian school for middle-class girls, developed a film unit under the guidance of Gilmore Roberts whose experience in film extended to assisting set designers. Together with a Dan Burt as joint director he turned the unit into a school of film technique shortly after the inauguration of which Mr Burt died. The school became bankrupt and reopened in Beehive Place, Brixton. When I joined, at the end of January 1957, my first four weeks were spent laying concrete floors in the new premises together with students David Naden and Dai Vaughan. A wasted effort. Roberts moved us to a new address in Brixton – 33/35 Electric Avenue, premises above a builder's and decorator's shop – where part of our tuition involved editing a film, keyshots of which we discovered were missing. Dai possessed a Bell & Howel camera. We decided to shoot our own, a documentary of Brixton market – up before the sun to capture empty streets, the first solitary bodies, traders arriving, stalls emerging from garages beneath railway arches, the slow motion of setting up 'shop' . . . [*Morning* at Hill House all over again, precursor to *the Kitchen*?] Our frames were beautiful, lyrical. It was a documentary in the classic tradition – from sunrise and clean streets through to garbage-strewn gutters and the dustbin men; flowing, motley humanity between. The most exciting part of the work was editing, for me a major lesson in the poetic power of juxtapositioning. It has informed most of my plays. Successfully or not I have employed, consciously, the editor's skill of laying alongside each other scenes which did not necessarily make narrative, but poetic sense. In *The Journalists* above all.

There were few other students. Keith Waller began with ambitions to be a cameraman. He shot a sequence of scenes with my mother which we hoped would be the beginning of a short film based on my story 'Pools'. We didn't get far. A short opening sequence. But a record of Leah aged around fifty-five, and a couple of East End streets which no longer exist, including Flower and Dean Street where my grandparents lived. Keith and I pursued the idea of setting up as documentary film producers.

WESKER and WALLER
Film Producers
of
Social and Industrial events
A record in film is an exciting way to remember the most important events in your life . . .

At its most useful level the industrial film is a convenient way of informing foreign firms of the nature of your product . . .

I was forever attempting to set up enterprises, plotting and planning ways of making money. It didn't work, as most of my planned plots and enterprises didn't work. Keith has recently retired as head of lighting for Central TV.

The toughest of our bunch was Maurice Stanton who raised £450 to be used as security for the school's bank overdraft, which earned him a place as one of the managing directors of this Fred Karno outfit. There was now a triumvirate: Roberts, Stanton, and a TV film producer, John Dunbar, who had made a number of *Panorama* documentaries. Roberts faded in ignominy. David Naden somehow became the chief lecturer, staying awake all night to read up on what he had to lecture about next day. 'I got away with it most of the time.' One day, looking through the drawers of Roberts' desk, he came across some pornographic photos of a girl student. Others were of couples who had apparently asked Roberts to photograph their sexual prowess. It became an excuse for the businesslike Stanton to dismiss the poor old film school's founder for conduct unbecoming a college principal. Nevertheless, somehow, the school flourished, mainly from deposits from Nigerian students, and is now the London International Film School based in Shelton Street in the heart of London's West End. Stanton went on to organise Nigerian Television.

Little was learned. The benefits were in new friendships, long discussions, and a feast of films. David reminded me that we used to retire at lunchtimes to a Greek café where I'd loudly exclaim at the excessive number of sandwiches my mother prepared for me and beg him to help me eat them. Day after day she cut more than I actually needed. David, Dai and I became close friends, addicted to screenings at the National Film Theatre and the British Film Institute's little cinema off Tottenham Court Road. I wish I had kept a record of the films seen. My strongest memory is of the Japanese season – *Tokyo Story, The Four Chimneys, Living*, remembered because when *Roots* came to be written, a play that inches forward very, very slowly, with lots of pauses, I felt confident it could work having been mesmerised by the slow unfolding of *Tokyo Story*.

Declaration

Much was coming together to excite and help shape my thinking. Dai and I in particular, in our long walks to fro to fro and to again between our homes in Hackney, talked and talked and talked and talked. Now a film editor he had the mind of an intellectual. He read and argued philosophy. In the wake of his enthusiasm I bought a copy of Sartre's slim volume on existentialism but don't remember ever getting to the end. What I *do* remember is an observation about human nature which he handed on to me: when you criticise a person's opinions, he wrote in a letter, you do more than challenge their views, you challenge their very being since most consider their views to be an extension of who they are. Dai should have gone to university. As did many of the friends I've been blessed with, he gave generously of his time to read the early plays.

His first comment on *Chicken Soup with Barely* was 'You surely mean *Chicken Soup with Barley?*'

Not only were Dai and I sparking off each other but a new generation of socialists was attempting to redefine socialist values. Out of the universities came the *University and Left Review* which established headquarters off Dean Street from where the magazine was edited, an eating/meeting place set up, and a series of lectures programmed for what transpired to be packed audiences. In a letter – dated 6.5.58 – to Dusty at home in Norfolk preparing herself for work as a waitress in Butlin's Skegness holiday camp, I wrote about one such lecture. It was the year of a long-drawn-out bus strike.

At ULR there was a most amusing occasion. R.H. Crossman MP and Raymond Williams were talking on the press ('The Mass Persuaders'). Williams gave an analysis and an outline of development of the press since the 18th century. Very scholarly and interesting. But Crossman, he writes for the *Statesman* and the *Daily Mirror* – what a pair – he gave a brilliant, witty talk on absolutely nothing. Boy! He just did not know where he had come. He thought he could toss a few humorous crumbs to the crowd and a couple of observations and they would be satisfied. He didn't even prepare anything. Beside Williams he was a loud showman. And when the discussion came – Jesus! he didn't know what hit him. The boys stood up and lambasted him in clear, precise terms. How could he, as a socialist, support a paper which, for its vulgarity, was an insult to the mind of the working class; a paper which painted a glossy, film-star world. The smugness left his face, he evaded every direct question and even in winding up said nothing except 'Well, you high-class people are just as easily lead up the garden path in your papers!' Which may be true – but that does not justify him leading the working class up the garden path in their papers!

Seven years after *The God That Failed* – the collection of essays shattering dreams and hopes – came another collection to rekindle them. In 1957 a young, dynamic, good-looking, self-taught only son

of a German-Jewish emigrant couple, Rita and Kurt Maschler, became an editor for the publishing house of McGibbon and Kee.
The young man, Tom Maschler, blossomed as the maverick
publisher of the sixties and seventies, becoming one of the directors
of a venerable old publishing house, Jonathan Cape, which he built
up from gentlemanly modesty to aggressive majesty. His risk-
taking was rewarded with millionairedom when Random House
bought them up. Tom was to publish my first play and later
volumes of essays and stories he knew would show scant returns;
we became close friends, each of us taking on the role of godfather,
he to my daughter, Tanya Jo, me to his daughter, Hannah. Nineteen fifty-seven was my year as impecunious student of film
technique and Tom's year of opportunity. Then, he was lean and
hungry, an entrepreneur with a nose for what was in the air. New
writers were in the air. Tom plucked them out and edited a collection of their essays – *Declaration*. It was his break, his golden
opportunity. The essays captured the attention of reviewers and the
imagination of would-be new-world-makers like Dai and myself in
search of just such fresh thinking about old notions. We pooled
spare shillings to buy the book between us and pored for hours over
its pages arguing its arguments. I think Dai possesses that copy.
The one on my shelves was bought years later in a secondhand
bookshop in Hay on Wye. I'm told a reasonably preserved first
edition is worth about £300.

The contributors were opinion moulders of the day. Novelists
Doris Lessing, Bill Hopkins, and John Wain; a flamboyantly
dressed wordsmith who stuttered and smoked nonstop, holding his
cigarette between his third and fourth fingers, forging new criteria
for theatre criticism – Kenneth Tynan; the young Turk of British
theatre from Fulham – playwright, John Osborne; the precocious
twenty-five-year-old author of a first book of criticism, *The Outsider*, written while working in espresso bars, who had eminent
critics on their knees in homage to his brilliance and originality –
Colin Wilson. (The blurb claims his first book to have been written
aged thirteen, 'six volumes attempting to summarise the world's

scientific knowledge, including psychology and philosophy'.) And film-maker/film critic, Lindsay Anderson. An eclectic grouping and by no means complete. Novelists Kingsley Amis and Alan Sillitoe were missing, for example; poets, painters and musicians were not represented. Nor did there exist a common set of beliefs or values between contributors. Tom Maschler's introduction explains:

> A number of young and widely opposed writers have burst upon the scene and are striving to change many of the values which have held good in recent years. No critic has yet succeeded in assessing them or correlating them *objectively* one to another. This volume aims at helping the public to understand what is happening while it is actually happening – at uncovering a certain pattern taking shape in British thought and literature.

The book was immediately translated into about six languages and reprinted three times within a short period. Not everyone loved everyone. At a publication party held at the Royal Court Theatre, legend has it, a sack (or was it a bag) of flour was dropped from the balcony upon Colin Wilson who was thought by many to be oppressively arrogant. Whether he was or not I have no idea. No doubt he suffered, as many of us were to do, from the heavy mantle of excessive and instantaneous celebrity – not easy to wear when it hadn't hung there yesterday.

'Get Out and Push'

Of all the essays it was Lindsay Anderson's 'Get Out and Push' that captured the spirit exciting young hopefuls like Dai and myself. Its intelligence was fierce and lucid, linked poetry with ideas, and appeared to be rescuing the bruised from despair. It is so part of the time that I will quote from it at length.

First an acknowledgment. The title for my most commercially

successful play comes from the essay's opening paragraph.

> Let's face it; coming back to Britain is always something of an
> ordeal. It ought not to be, but it is. And you don't have to be a snob
> to feel it. It isn't just the food, the sauce bottles on the café tables,
> and the chips with everything. It isn't just saying goodbye to wine,
> goodbye to sunshine. After all, there are things that matter even
> more than these; and returning from the continent, today in 1957,
> we feel these strongly too. A certain, civilised (as opposed to cul-
> tured) quality in everyday life: a certain humour: an atmosphere of
> tolerance, decency and relaxation. A solidity, even a warmth. We
> have come home. But the price we pay is high.

Anderson, born in 1923 in Bangalore, southern India, had been a
classical scholar at Oxford with a number of documentary films to
his credit, the most moving being the Venice Grand Prix winner,
Everyday Except Christmas, about Covent Garden market long
before the fruit and flower men moved out and the Victorian edifice
was imaginatively converted into its present bazaar of shops and
restaurants. Let me confess, before recreating his essay – which I
believe to be one of the latch keys that unlocked my first successful
writing – that I have always been a little in awe of Lindsay's incisive
intelligence, though not unaware of an intellectual perversity occasionally blemishing it. The relationship, though we've hardly
shared time together during our long lives, will always be one of
confident upper-class scholar-artist and hesitant East End Jewish
autodidact-artist – whether the reality is precisely that or not. In
addition to being an eminent film-maker, Lindsay has been a spot-
ter of talent. He alerted me to the talents of a young actor working
for Joan Littlewood's pyrotechnic Theatre Workshop ensemble at
Stratford East's Theatre Royal: 'His name is Albert Finney'; he introduced British cineastes to the films of the Polish director, André
Wajda. And for better or worse he spotted me.

Significantly, his first paragraph – the title *Chips with Everything*
aside – identified thoughts and attitudes we could at once latch on

to – notions both critical and affirmative. Returning to Britain may be an ordeal but, he adds, it was a country of civilised virtues, a certain humour, tolerance, decency, relaxation and 'even a warmth'. Anyone who could recognise these qualities had earned the right to be critical, and commanded our attention.

Anderson, first and foremost a film-maker – though an original critical mind belonging, as I now see, in the tradition of Ruskin – had just returned from the tenth International Film Festival in Cannes and was ruminating on the plight of the British film industry. He'd seen films from thirty-five countries; prizes had gone 'to Poland, Sweden, France, America, Russia, Rumania, Japan, Yugoslavia . . .'

Britain did not figure in the list. It is six years since a British feature won a prize at Cannes. And this is not the result of political or economic intrigue, it is a fair reflection of the way our films have fallen out of the running. The cinema reflects, much more immediately than most of the arts, the climate and spirit of a nation.

What categorised British cinema?

The snobbery of our films is not aristocratic. In British films the aristocracy is generally represented by Mr A.E. Matthews, and is treated, though respectfully, as a fine old figure of fun. Similarly, the functions of working-class characters are chiefly comic, where they are not villianous. They make excellent servants, good tradesmen, and first-class soldiers. On the march, in slit trenches, below deck, they crack their funny Cockney jokes or think about the mountains of Wales. They die well, often with a last, mumbled message on their lips to the girl they left behind them in the Old Kent Road, but it is up there on the bridge that the game is really played, as the officers raise binoculars repeatedly to their eyes, converse in clipped monosyllables (the British cinema has never recovered from Noël Coward as Captain 'D'), and win the battles. A young actor with a regional or a Cockey accent had better lose it quick . . .

The number of British films that have ever made a genuine try at a story in a popular milieu, with working-class characters all through, can be counted on the fingers of one hand; and they have become rarer, not more frequent, since the war. Carol Reed's film of *The Stars Look Down*, made in 1939, looks somewhat factitious today; but compared with his *A Kid for Two Farthings* two years ago, it is a triumph of neo-realism. The real objection, though, is not so much that 'popular' subjects are falsified, as that they are not made at all. Quite recently a friend of mine took a story to a distributor to find out if he would agree to handle the film if it were made. (It is these middlemen, incidentally, who decide what reaches the screen in Britain, not the producers or the public.) The reaction was illuminating. It was a story of working-class people and it opened in a garage yard, with the men sitting in the sun, eating their lunch-hour sandwiches. One of them, a boy of sixteen, had a cold and needs to wipe his nose. 'For pity's sake, get your snot rag out,' grumbles one of his mates. The distributors' decision was unequivocal and its grounds clearly expressed, 'It starts on that social level, and it never rises above it. Audiences just don't want to see that sort of thing.' And this is why – even if the talent to make them were around – equivalents of *Marty* and *The Grapes of Wrath*, *Two Pennyworth of Hope* and *The Childhood of Maxim Gorky* cannot be produced in this England.

The essay struck note after note to which our spirits warmed. The climate of course did subsequently change, due – as is fully documented – to persuasive polemics such as these.

Perhaps the most exhilarating aspect of Anderson's blast was his attack in both directions, upon right and left. This section of my autobiography is being written at a time when the country is engaged in a debate about the need for 'a return to basics'. The following, written thirty-seven years earlier, is remarkably contemporaneous. Turning first to the right.

'It is vitally important that words like Duty and Service should come back into fashion . . .' So Lord Hailsham told the nation in a recent broadcast. But questions prompt themselves: Duty to whom, and why? Service to what ideal? . . . And when Mr Macmillan, making

561

his first broadcast as Prime Minister, talks about 'dreary equality', we recognise the concept of society that inspires him. We are back with the hierarchy, the self-idealised èlite of class and wealth, the docile middle classes, and the industrious, devoted army of workers. 'All Things Bright and Beautiful', 'The Rich Man in his Castle, the Poor Man at his Gate . . .' 'Wider still and wider Shall thy Bounds be set . . .' These are the songs Mr Macmillan will lead us in, with additional verses by Sir Arthur Bryant and A.L. Rowse . . .

Turning next to the left.

Fundamentally, our problems today are all problems of adjustment: we have somehow to evolve new social relationships within the nation, and a new relationship altogether with the world outside. Britain – an industrial, imperialist country that has lost its economic superiority and its empire, has yet to find, or to accept its new identity. The irresolution expresses itself widely, and in many different ways; in discontent or opportunism among young people, in nostalgic complaints and futile bombast from the established Right, and in a weary shrugging of the shoulders from those who were Pink, or even Red, twenty years ago. But the real question remains unanswered. If 'Land of Hope and Glory' is to be decently shelved, what song are we to sing?

In literal as well as metaphorical terms, the answer of the Left is so far inadequate. I have rarely heard a more depressing sound than the singing of those few, indomitable, old-fashioned Leftists who raised their voices in chorus at the end of the Suez demonstration in Trafalgar Square:

> *Let cowards flinch and traitors sneer*
> *We'll keep the Red Flag flying here . . .*

It was more a moan than a song; and no wonder. For how could a tired old vision like this expect to win new allegiances today?

Anderson went on to ask what kind of Britain did we want, pointing out that socialism

> . . . has yet to present its solution dynamically, to shake off its com-
> plexes of inferiority and opposition, to speak with confidence, and
> from the heart. We are still between Arnold's two worlds, one dead,
> the other powerless to be born . . .

at which point he welcomes Osborne and *Look Back in Anger*.

> . . . This was the heartening thing: that here at last was a young
> writer, using the language of today, giving passionate expression to
> his uncertainty and his frustrated idealism – and being received by
> his contemporaries, at least, with understanding and enthusiasm.
>   It is not really Osborne's anger that is significant, so much as the
> complement of it: his baffled aspiration, his insistent plea for a
> human commitment.

Note: 'a human commitment' not 'a political commitment'. From
the start Anderson had recognised that Osborne was talking 'feeling
humanity' not 'doctrinaire politics'.

I've quoted at length from the Anderson essay – and there's a
little more to come – because it not only contains contemporary
glimpses, it also captures the restless, intellectual climate of the
time. To illuminate Osborne's voice Anderson continues by criti-
cally comparing that voice with those of John Wain and Kingsley
Amis, writers erroneously linked journalistically to Osborne as
'angry young men' despite that 'they express the directly opposite
attitude'. His analysis of what he described as their 'anti-idealist,
anti-emotional, and tepid' views is sharp. They conjure up, he
writes, 'the quaint spirit of British "liberalism"'.

What did Anderson go on to affirm?

> A socialism that cannot express itself in emotional, human, poetic
> terms is one that will never capture the imagination of the people –
> who are poets even if they don't know it.

In the final pages of his essay Anderson catches up with where I am
chronologically in this autobiography.

I have a feeling – and I hope that it is more than a hope – that it is no longer seriousness that is felt to be a bore (particularly among younger people), so much as obsessional flippancy and the weary cult of the 'amusing'. When the *University and Left Review* appeared, in the spring of 1957, it was reviewed neither in the *New Statesman*, the *Observer*, the *Sunday Times*, nor *The Times*. Yet it sold out its first edition, reprinted, and sold out again. I take this as a portent. Perhaps people are beginning to understand that we can no longer afford the luxury of scepticism, that we must start again believing in belief. 'Only connect . . .' said Forster, a long time ago; and it was a marvellously wise thing to say . . .

Of course Lord Hailsham is right, and we must start being able to use words like duty, service, obligation and hope again without blushing – and community, and conscience, and love. But it is more than just a matter of bringing such terms back into fashion by using them in a party political broadcast. It is going to take a revolution to make these words clean, to revitalise the ideals they stand for, after their long debasement at the hands of journalists, politicians and copy-writers. And only a revolution of this kind can save us.

Making words clean. The challenge was thrilling. Ronnie cries to his mother in *Chicken Soup with Barley*:

> What has happened to all the comrades, Sarah? I even blush when I use that word. Comrade! Why do I blush? Why do I feel ashamed to use words like democracy and freedom and brotherhood? They don't have meaning any more . . .

It is important to understand this: I was a disillusioned socialist not one who had come to believe socialist principles were unworkable, rather one who felt those principles had been betrayed, never allowed to show if they *could* work. Making words clean implied rescuing the principles those words embodied. But how? Party politics were not for me. The University and Left Review Club of which I became a member was not a political party, it was a meeting point where old dogmas were challenged and young intellectuals were fashioning dazzling aspirations not of perfection, but ones which could accommodate imperfection, ambivalence, and cautious affirmation. The attraction was in the perceived 'newness' of the left. The dreary, discredited certitudes were abandoned. Gaiety replaced flippancy, and a humane seriousness informed debate rather than omnipotent solemnity.

I was not a theoretician. My pleasure in, and capacity for, social action was limited. Human relationships mattered more. The disintegration of my family resonated with meaning, as did the life led by Della and Ralph in Norfolk, as appeared to be doing the burgeoning relationship between Dusty and myself. All three became relationships around which was written the Trilogy. And the one line repeated in each of the three plays represented not a 'cleansed word' so much as a tenet through which I believed the words might come to be cleansed:

You can't change people, you can only give them some love and hope they'll take it.

1957

Much was happening in the world because much is always happening in the world – scientific as well as political. Innovations like the cathode-ray tube and the microchip – and now fibre-optic cabling – reshaped the world as much a declarations of independence, twentieth party congresses, and the fall of the Berlin Wall. Suez, Hungary, the Khruschev revelations, the University and Left Review Club, Aldermaston – these impinged on my life, but it was a life absorbed just as a much by a dying father, a rudderless love-life, an uncertain future, a tense matriarchal home.

Sometime in the week beginning April a group of us from the London School of Film Technique paid a visit to the Streatham Hill Theatre not far from the school's premises in Brixton to catch up on the play everyone had been talking about. It was on tour. I have a photocopy of the programme in front of me. *Look Back in Anger* had shed Kenneth Haig as Jimmy Porter, Alan Bates as Cliff, and Mary Ure as Alison. It was still Tony Richardson's production and Alan Tagg's design, but the actors were unknown: Alan Dobie, Michael Bryant, Jocelyn Britton, Pamela Thomas and Michael Kent. The assistant director was certainly no one anyone had heard of – John Dexter.

The impact cannot be understated. I have no record of a front-line reaction, perhaps it exists in a letter to someone, but I remember four things: the energy of the dialogue and the way it fused to the personality of Jimmy Porter who uttered it; the image of those dead Sunday bells ringing as they had rung emptily for me in Norwich and for countless others around the country; the ending which I thought at the time to be weak, betraying this powerful play not with a bang but a whimper – I've changed my mind since; and an exhilarated feeling that not only was theatre an activity where important things were happening but one where I could add to what was happening. Six months later, on 8 October, I began to write *Chicken Soup with Barley* – original title *When the Wind Blows* – finished six weeks later.

Scribbled diary sheets exist from 1957, odd days recorded between May and September, painful days interleaved with days of intoxication. I was a student at last but still a disappointing son to a bitter, overtaxed mother burdened with a sick husband who had not cared for her when he was well so she could not care as lovingly as her nature wanted. And yet when he was dead she was riven by remorse. Her diaries record it.

21.12.59
So I cry & cry & cry. Of course no one knows. I wonder how long I'll be punished by my torturing myself for Joe's death? I can't get used or accept that he died because he had to die as a result of not one but 3 strokes. The question is would he not die if he had married someone else? But it's my conscience that are worrying me, and true enough he did not have a happy life. Neither did I, & yet we used to

enjoy ourselves in many ways. Although I feel so broken-hearted I'm sure would he still have lived we would still have quarrelled. We simply could not understand one another. Only he should not have died yet. I was happier in my strife with him than now without him. I cannot bring him back to life again but if I could I am sure I would still not be satisfied with every way he wanted, or done. Never the less he should have lived whatever misunderstanding we had. One thing my mind is clear of, & that is I never never wanted him to die. No, not die. But the end is such, & leaves those alive with regrets & memories in every case, & I just don't know how to live at present. I am still not settled. I go to my children not willingly. I don't know what I want of them & they don't know what they want of me. They are certainly very upset about their father & they are upset about me. I don't know though whether because I am alone or because they thought that maybe one day I'll get helpless like their father . . .

Nor was it easy between Dusty and me. The Paris experience had ended with a confusion of emotions and now, in the midst of Wesker family traumas and the demands of my 'student life', she was plunged into confusion. The 'student life' was a vigorous one – lectures, films, concerts – she enjoyed it, but within her were more years of Norfolk than of London. In time she would become attached to the Jewish milieu and claim it as her own, but for the moment a family whirlpool was throwing her all over the place. She had scant sympathy for, or understanding of, the toll life had taken of my mother and the consequent eruptions of bitterness. It was so alien to her. Leah, too, had difficulty accepting Dusty. For all her 'progressive' notions she would have preferred my girlfriend to be Jewish.

One observation in these diary sheets puzzles me. Leah had always accepted my sleeping in the same bed with girlfriends – she'd bring us tea in the mornings! According to these notes, sharing a bed with Dusty seemed to have pained her more than sharing a bed with others. Perhaps because Dusty was looming as the most serious of them all. This time it was for real. Leah was frightened, perhaps. The notes take over, honed, as usual, for readability, though this time not much; notes which transmuted into dialogue for *Chicken Soup with Barley*.

25 May 1957
The situation at home becomes worse, almost unbearable at moments. How helpless we are in our dilemmas. Joe has been incontinent four times since returning home. I can see Leah taking the strain with hatred in her eyes. She hates me for not going out to work and helping financially. Thinks I am wasting my time studying.

On all sides it is a battle for her. She has to face the battery of questions from the National Assistance men who also can't understand why her son does not keep her. She has to quarrel with the hospital authorities, fill in the National Health forms, wash Joe's clothes, feed us. And in addition she must suffer the indignity of allowing her son to sleep with his girlfriend in her home.

And all the time, questions: where do we go, what do we do? She feels I don't care about her and is terrified I shall abandon her to poverty and loneliness. Indeed, she feels this has already happened. And I feel that she doesn't care what I do as long as I keep her, provide her with grandchildren and a family she can boast of. I'm not taken seriously, have never been allowed to do what I want without conflict. I have always done it in the end but not without a fight and bitterness.

And on my other side is Dusty, without sensitive understanding of the situation, urging me with inane phrases like: 'mother's boy . . . *your* life comes first, they've had theirs . . . mothers-in-law are the same'. From the woman one is supposed to love one would like more intelligent and constructive comments than that.

Today's flare-up arose from me blowing back a tea leaf into the cup and Leah saying, 'Don't do that!' She has the right to say 'don't do that' but being still at home and told what to do struck open the crack through which an argument flowed.

And sitting around is sick Joe, smelling, unshaven, large eyes and drooping cheeks, mumbling and shuffling, smoking, breathing heavily. And I want to rush up to him and bang him against the wall becuase he is the cause of it all. How neither my mother nor I have managed not to injure him I cannot say.

So the private, vicious circle goes round among the four of us. We all hate and distrust each other, quarrel and shout at each other and yet – we each want to do the other good and show love. At what point do we loose that thin thread of understanding and sympathy that should keep us together? Dusty never had it. Her values are in the end the selfish ones of self-preservation, not merely before anyone else but, if necessary, at the expense of anyone else. I suppose Leah's too is one of self-preservation. Yet at her time of life it is valid. She is old enough to be frightened. And because of this fear, this hurt feeling at not being kept by her children – which she interprets as not being loved – she is stubborn and will not work. When she goes to look for work she must wander around like the bony mare who thought to be turned loose to pasture.

It is even more complicated and involved. Somewhere, mixed up in all this, is her tangled, woolly communism – everything is a kind of capitalist plot against her. All my friends are fascists or terrible intellectuals and are the reason I am what I am. So I say harsh things to her like: 'You poor, poor demented woman . . . You don't know who to blame . . . Always someone else . . .' I tell her to leave me alone, leave me alone, go out of my room. And she mimics me.

'"Leave me alone, leave me alone". That's all he can say. A communist talks things over, discusses. you've never listened to what anybody has had to say . . .'

At this moment she is in the other room. I can hear her washing up and clearing away, and every so often she screams at Joe who has not had a cigarette yet this morning. 'Don't you dare call anyone up –' meaning children from the playground he sometimes asks to go and buy him cigarettes. 'Don't you DARE! . . . And don't touch the kettle. Don't touch anything!' Because with his hands he dirties everything, he hardly washes unless we fight with him to do so. 'You are the cause of this,' she screams at him. 'You made this mess of our lives. You don't do this in the hospital, why do you do it here. I CAN'T LOOK AFTER YOU! You must go to the hospital, it's a better home for you, you must ask them to take you. We'll come and see you, it's better for you.'

What does he know? A wreck of a human being, hardly ever been one, drifting around the rooms like an old dog mourning its gone master, breathing like old bellows, dead to anything that matters.

Yet alive all the same, terribly alive and scared therefore. Now he is shouting to me from the other room, loudly. And why? Simply to tell me that there is a cup of tea on the table and that I should come and have it. There is nothing more important in life, nothing more worth shouting to me for than a cup of tea on the table.

Yesterday I was 25 years old!

PS. But the telling point – to show how the circle begins – was last night when I told Dusty mummy had borrowed another £1. She suggested I was being taken advantage of, that I was supposed to be leading my own life, that mothers came third – to wives. I told her I would face truth my own way and would she stop talking to me like that or leave me. Having last night denied her allegations I never the less behaved this morning as though they were true, shouting harsh words at my mother. Dusty was not here to witness it of course but in this way the mood was passed from one to the other . . .

I was trying to describe cause and effect; Dusty had taunted me, I'd snapped at Leah, she'd screamed at Joe. [It was not to be the only time I allowed Dusty to wind me up against my natural instincts.] I do not enjoy recounting such moments, no one comes out well.

30 May 1957

This morning I am home, not at school. The ambulance is supposed to come to take Joe to occupational therapy. He now sits waiting. Probably the ambulance will not come. Mum has just gone down with the washing. [To hang on the line in the playground.] She had urged him to change his pants. He maintained he had done so. Despite the fact that we cannot find the old ones he maintains he has changed them. Of course he has not. She asked him to get ready for the ambulance, to polish his shoes. 'The doctor told you to move your hands and limbs. To help yourself.' But how long can she talk to him like that? Instead she rushed out. He has no cigarettes. He asked her to get some. 'Never! You sit there and the whole world goes round you.'

So he collects his dog-ends, strikes matches and puts the dog-end to the flame and then puffs to catch a few whirls of smoke into his lungs. The matches fall about him and he throws the empty box down at his feet just missing the waste-paper basket, not able to make that little extra effort to reach it. The dirt gathers round him. He asks me to go down for a packet of cigarettes as I have none. 'No one,' I say, 'will do anything for you if you don't do anything for yourself.'

Still he sits and he will not move to change his pants unless I manhandle him and bribe him with a packet of fags.

'You would sooner go without cigarettes than change your pants?'

'I don't know where my pants are, what are you talking about!'

'Excuses always.'

'How do you know I haven't looked for pants?'

'How does one know *anything* about you – because we've lived with you for so long!'

Where does this kind of talk get either of us? Always this sort of argument. Snatches of defiance and spite in the air: I will not change my pants. I will not get you cigarettes.

11 June 1957

Yesterday I cleaned and washed up Joe, and washed his shirt and pants and part of the mattress. Fought with him not to smoke until he ate. He ate well. This afternoon I washed his hair. We have all – Leah and Dusty too – washed our hair. As I redressed him and dried his hair, he patted me – as though to say 'good boy', a response to my care. I felt like a conspirator then as I remembered that we are trying to get him into the permanent care and attention of an invalid's home.

20 June 1957

Have just now shaved about five days' growth off Joe's face. It was a good shave. 'Go and wash your face now,' I told him. I went into the kitchen to wash up the shaving tackle and said to mum: 'It's a good shave, isn't it?' Joe came in from the bedroom full of emotion and struggled towards me, reaching out to pat me. 'He's a good boy, my boy,' he stammered, and hugged Leah, stammering a sort of laugh, while Leah laughed to hide some tears. Then he washed his face.

Sometimes I recorded amusing exchanges that took place between my mother and her friends. She never lost her sense of humour. The bizarre aspect of human behaviour continued grabbing her attention to the end. Even my father's behaviour. She might rage at him and accuse him of destroying her one and only life yet she could never resist the moments he caused her to laugh. This following exchange between two Leahs provided one of the stories in *Chicken Soup with Barley*.

8 July 1957

An old friend of my mother's was round this evening. Her name is also Leah, a woman whom we discovered is the stepmother of Esther Lander. Much talk of how small the world is when what they mean is how small is London, or the East End even. It turned out that this Leah also knew my sister's in-laws. [Ralph's parents who had the stall in Petticoat Lane.]

'He used to sell corn in Norwich market. *She* used to dress up as a nurse and *he* would put corn on her feet – you know, to take away corns on the feet.' It took some time for me to work out what she was talking about. 'And all round the stall he'd hang letters – letters he used to knock up himself . . .'

'And pearl barley,' my mother interrupted, talking also of the in-laws, 'pearl barley, the pearl barley they used to sell to cure diseases – threepence each!'

'*Such* things the boys used to get up to. I had a house in Norwich,' the other Leah continued, 'And they all used to come up to me. And you know what else I'll tell you? Those haricot beans? the ones you put in soup? you buy them for threepence a pound? Well one of the boys used to dye them in my place, all sorts of colours, and sell them for sixpence each to the farmers as lucky charms. "All the way from the East this lucky charm, it came to bring good fortune." He also used to hang up letters from people who made their fortune. "Isn't that right, guvnor?" he used to say to a bloke. "Yers," the bloke would say. "Make a fortune!" And they would all buy. A bean! An ordinary bean!'

So my mother began.

'I'll tell you something. One day, I was shopping in Ridley Road market, and I see a man with an accordion and another man walking on the ground like as if he had no legs. So I go up and I drop a penny in and I'm standing there watching when suddenly a woman says to me, "You know, I bet he can walk as good as you or me, his legs are all right." So I says to her, "Look," I says, "so tell me what's the matter if he can walk? He's pretending! He's acting! He's an actor!" After all I only give him a penny. "Look," I says, "can you blame him in a society like this? There's lots of big people in big business and they swindle also." So – I'm not joking – she says to me: "Believe me, you're right! You say that because you've got a nice mind. I'm pleased to know you with a nice mind. You're intelligent," she says. So anyway, we talk a little and she goes off and I go home and forget all about her. And then the next time I see her is in Holloway Road and she's outside Woolworth's and she's singing with an accordionist!'

'I know, I know! I see her myself,' says the other Leah, but she can't get a word in yet. My mother continues.

'It's like I once saw a young girl and an old man in Heneage Street in the East End, you know? I'm talking about years ago now. They used to go as father and daughter and he would sing, and this time he was singing some song about "my little love and dreaming of you" and so on. It was just after the First World War – and as I walk by I just heard her mutter: "You rotten liar, you!" Just as he was singing!'

'I'll also tell you something,' the other Leah got in. 'Now listen. My daughter lives in Edgware and I go there every Tuesday – it's Tuesday tomorrow and I'm going there – and one night I was there and it was pouring with rain and there's a knock at the door. So I goes and answers it and there in the rain standing there in old rags, only plimsolls on her feet and big holes in them, a tall woman, Jewish, you know, and a story she tells me about "I married a yock [gentile] and he beats me and he's beaten my son so that he's in a mental hospital and he drinks and please I'm a poor woman, lady, can you give me something?" A long fairy she spins me out I tell you, I was in tears myself and I calls up to Jeanie, "Jeanie have a look in the wardrobe and see what there is to give away." So Jeanie looks and calls back, "Mother, I haven't got anything to give away." So I say, "Well bring something for God's sake!" I mean you couldn't let the woman go. So I brought her in and made some tea and "Look," she says to me, "look where he beats me," and she shows me all up and down her arm – bruises.'

'I also got bruises,' my mother says. 'Some mornings I wake up and I got bruises for no reason at all.'

'So anyway, Jeanie comes down with some clothes and on top of it I gave her four-and-six. Four-and-six! So next week she comes back again. All the way from the East End to Edgware she walks. I wasn't there. Four bob my daughter says she gave her. And she came back another week! Three times! So I says to my daughter, Jean! if she comes again you turn her out. She's nothing but a professional schnorer [cadger]. You get rid of her! Oh yes! You know my son-in-law he nearly murdered her he did . . .'

'I know, I know them . . .' But my mother couldn't get in now. The other Leah continued.

'It's like the yiddle [little Jew] who comes up to my husband one day and begs for something, so my husband gives him a sixpence. And next week he doesn't come – so listen – so the third week he comes and my husband gives him another sixpence so the yiddle turns to him and says in Yiddish, "But you didn't give me for last week!"'

By this time I felt that fact was becoming difficult to separate from fiction.

Did I record such conversations to help develop an ear for dialogue? As I read it now I can hear my mother's voice, I can hear her melodies. Even those of the other Leah. I have no memory for facts, I often forget names, events, and – as I've confessed – my own opinions. But mention a name and I hear the cadences of their voice, the way they structured their sentences.

31 August 1957
Mr Burke was taken away in the coffin today. Three long, black cars drove into the paper-spat playground. The women leaned over the railings and stood in groups in the yard. The children stood watching, propped by their bicycles, paused in their games. Mrs Burke came out trying to smother her face with a handkerchief. Nora was creased, Patrick was upset. Billy Gammer refused to come out till the last second, saying it was sightseeing. It is I suppose. My mother shed a few tears. She said:

'He used to stand out in the rain in order to catch cold. He didn't want to live as a sick man.' He and Joe and Mr Bridger, all sick men, used to stand around in the same way, stooping, lean, and ill.

Flowers were laid in the hearse – 'The Gates of Heaven' placed in the rear window, 'from his loving wife'.

Chapter Twenty-three

The thin trickle

Aside from the lost and forgotten poem published in 1948 in Habonim magazine, the years from 1944 – the year of 'The Breeze' – to 1952, when *Plan* magazine printed a poem of mine that was the first ever, were years of rejection. Justified rejection but painful. Tempering years when expectations froze and skin thickened – though never enough. A routine established itself: offering, rejection, offering, rejection, offering . . . Simple! Eight years of dismissal until March 1952 when 'The Poor' was printed and the thin trickle began.

My file labelled 'Rejection Slips' is full of small printed sheets from such as *'The London Magazine'* and 'Anthony Blond (London) Ltd – Literary, Film and Dramatic Agents'. The earliest offering is dated 20 July 1949. I'd sent a poem 'Listen – Peace' to *Challenge*, the weekly journal of the Young Communist League. A 'critique', handwritten and unsigned, revealed it was not the first time I had offered poems to my 'comrades'.

Some years later, in the last years of conscription, I engaged in a brief but intense exchange of letters with a new assistant editor of *Challenge*, George MacDougall, who addressed me as Comrade Weskler. Our theme: 'the working-class poet'. I did not believe the concept of 'working-class art' to be viable or useful to consider. There was only art or non-art.

A working-class poet. What is he I wonder? A poet risen from the working classes – such as myself? Or a poet who writes so that the mass of the people can understand him? Or a poet who writes about the working classes? But then what is there in life that does not affect the masses? Very little – which cuts out the last one. And if it is the second one then Shakespeare, Whitman, Kipling, Shelley, Keats, Auden, Pudney etc. are all working-class poets – in some way or other. If it is the first then we stand a chance of being uncritical and taking all poets from the working class to be good and worthwhile . . .

. . . the important thing is to get people to appreciate poetry as a medium of expression anyway. Even our so-called bourgeois poets have good things to utter. I read out Kipling's 'Gungadin' to two hundred lads and lasses in our NAAFI recently. It went down well. They liked it, could understand it. But Kipling is not exactly a working-class poet is he – or is he!? . . .

He responded simplistically, employing Marxist analysis:

. . . I think you have concentrated too much on style and not enough on content . . . I am doing my best to help the birth of a new, working-class, democratic literature in Britain. Content is the most important aspect of this new literature: it must deal with the problems of the working people, especially with their struggle for something better . . .

I was 'too introspective' for Mr MacDougall. Four pages of tightly scripted argument were hurled back within days from RAF Wellesbourne in Warwickshire.

. . . the poet is an individual apart from being a member of his society, therefore he must be allowed to sing his own hopes and ideas, his own depressions and doubts, his own joy and love . . .

Don't be narrow-minded, George, there is poetry in a beautiful woman as well as in people shopping in Stoke Newington, there are personal problems as well as the wage question. All are equally important . . . don't sneer at introspection . . . If we cannot sort ourselves out and define our own character we cannot possibly hope to help others. Invariably we are helped to understand others by what we truthfully know of ourselves.

After the first encounter with *Challenge* I reached out to more sophisticated pages. On 25 August 1949, aged seventeen, I typed an illiterate letter to John Lehman, then editor of Penguin New Writing, keeping a carbon copy, errors and all:

> Dear Mr Lehman
>   Enclosed you will find four poems. Poems after the Chinese are experiments.
>   I should like to see them published. It would be a great change from the long worded conglomerations you have managed to pick up in recent issues.
>   I have published no other thing before. As you know it is hard to be recognised.
>   Yours faithfully.

Seventeen days later, impatient and eager, poor Mr Lehman was pelted at Henrietta Street WC1 from Weald Square E5 with another four poems.

> Dear Mr Lehman
>   I refuse to let you have only four poems from which to take your choice.
>   Therefore you will find four more poems which I would like published.
>   Furthermore, if I don't hear from you within the next three weeks I shall send on to you yet four more poems. Do not please let this threaten you into a hasty decision.

Ask me – do I blush? I blush. But then I remember the photograph of the boy in the front row, tongue in cheek. This letter *must* have been intended to amuse. A smile is there. And to prove it, as threatened, I sent four more.

> Dear Mr Lehman
>   Following the four poems I sent, on September 11th, are four others. I said, you will remember, that if I did not hear from you

within three weeks I would forward these. At this rate you will have quite a collection.

Of course your silence can mean either you are too busy or that you want to see the poems. Frankly I just have no idea.

Even if you do not publish them – and I could so do with the money – I hope you enjoy reading them.

'False Memory of a Love' is thus called because of course no such picture ever happened.

These are comparatively later poems.

I am thinking of trying to publish a collection before conscription ropes me in.

Arnold Wesker

I can find no response from Lehman though on one of his 'The editor regrets . . .' slips is a handwritten PS: 'Sorry I don't think I can find room for these poems though I like the feeling in them.' This was to be the tone and sentiment of many.

I offered stories and poems in batches of four. The list of magazines and small publishers which turned me down reads like a litany of those who fell in battle: *Modern Reading . . . Arena . . . Outposts . . . Poetry . . . Poetry and Poverty . . . Editions Poetry . . . World Review . . . Argosy . . . New Writing . . . The Wind and the Rain . . . Lilliput . . . John O'London's Weekly . . . Here and Now Quarterly . . . Hand and Flower Press . . . Fore Publications . . . Chance . . . The Adelphi . . .* Most of the rejections are printed slips. Some have scribbled PS's. It was the scribbled PS which became my drip feed over the years.

We liked the story better . . . Oliver Coburn, Assistant Ed., *Modern Reading.*

You get to the heart of your subject . . . Reginald Moore, Editor, *Modern Reading.*

Sorry I have to return these, but I am interested in your work and shall be glad to see more from you. Good wishes. Howard Sergeant, *Outposts.*

Like any patient on his back, helpless and dependent upon a lifeline from elsewhere, I became combative, and got into trouble with Reginald Moore after an exchange with his assistant. Both had really responded with saintly if stern patience.

14/11/51
Dear Mr Wesker

I'm afraid the MSS you relentlessly send will have to be returned. It's not a question of lacking courage to publish your work, and if I gave that impression I'm sorry. Subjects like that of the enclosed story are exceedingly trite, they have almost been worn out by being written about so many times. If with our very limited space we were to publish such a story in *Modern Reading*, it would have to be exceptionally well written. Your stories are not yet that, despite the good and sincere feeling behind them. Your technique (which *does* include spelling correctly – your business not an editor's to see to this, unless it's accepted) can still be improved a good deal; partly by practice and partly by reading the 'masters' (including modern masters). That applies to your verse too, although that is possibly a more individual matter; this sort of verse isn't really our cup of tea anyhow.

Sorry to be so negative, good luck with your writing all the same.
Yours sincerely
Oliver Coburn
Assistant Editor

My intemperate gene surfaced. I must have replied with bitter sarcasm. Moore wrote on the back of a rejection slip:

You describe one of your characters as having 'a pleasant humility'. Don't you think it would be a good idea to acquire a little of this yourself? No one 'accused' you of being trite. Mr Coburn has given much time and consideration to your work. But if you think we are nitwits – then don't send us anything more.

'The Plan in Life' has the germ of a very good story – but is too hastily written as it is.

Despite his irritation he could still find generosity enough to say something encouraging about a story.

Poverty is out

I briefly met Anthony Blond – 'Literary, Film and Dramatic Agent' – through Alistair in Oxford. To him in 1953 I sent among much else the play written for the Query Players – *And After Today*. he responded:

> You are probably bored of people patting you on the back and saying 'Yes yes you have talent but . . .' However that is what substantially I should like to say. This play seems to me a play of personal exclamations. Your pot has boiled over again and again and in your anxiety to be outspoken and even shocking you have I think lost the possibility, so well exploited by Shaw, of convincing your audience by irony and witty device. Moreover, the plot itself is convincing but too slight . . .
>
> . . . You must pay attention to whether or not a theme is obsolete. You must beware of saying things that no longer surprise people. I think if there is any current vogue in this matter it is for plays which deal with problems of conscience, conflicting loyalties and perhaps perversion. In other words, poverty is out.

I replied:

> Thank you for your criticism. I of course must agree with almost all of it . . .
>
> But forgive me if I point out that the theme of the play was not poverty. This was incidental, the reason being that my characters did not come from a wealthy class . . .
>
> . . . one point put my back up. 'Poverty is out.' Nonsense. I might not be able to handle the theme well, but as long as there is poverty it will always be a subject for drama and literature in general.

I hope therefore you will not be too offended with the enclosed poem, my only attempt at satirical poetry . . .

Thank you again for your courtesy and I hope you will not consider the poem as being discourteous.

Good wishes.

Sincerely

For Anthony Blond Esq.

Poverty is Out

It seems there are subjects no writer should pen,
The worker has passions alright,
And he might be the backbone of living
But to dramatise him is trite;
You can be quite a wit
And produce some s—
For the soft intellectual
Who's parked in the pit,
But please not on poverty
Don't dare mention poverty
It just doesn't pay and it's quite ineffectual.

And so on.

By 3 December we were on first-name terms. I had sent him 'Pools', hoping he could find someone to buy the film rights, and when that failed I sent him the synopsis of an original film script called *The Rainbow* about a group of children who built their own adventure playground which the authorities made them pull down. After a storm the children search for the end of a rainbow. A small group grows into a horde. The police mistake them for a riot. Some years later adventure playgrounds were conceived and built but Blond could find no one to buy this prophetic story at the time.

Christy and Moore Limited – Literary Agents

The correspondence which by far was the longest, most detailed and generous – those with friends aside – was that with John Smith of the Literary agents Christy and Moore Ltd., 11 Suffolk Street, Pall Mall, London SW1. John Smith, when we were first in contact, had published one book of verse, *Gates of Beauty and Death*, under a pseudonym – C. Busby Smith. One of his letters refers to a new volume about to be published by the Hogarth Press called *The Dark Side of Love*, under his real name.

The correspondence began in September 1951 when I was living in hut 77A. I had sent him two stories: 'The Boy Who Was Always Wrong' and 'The Two Friends'. Though not good enough to place he had, like others, seen something in them.

> . . . I would, however, like to make clear that this should not be taken as the conventional rejection because your writing has a very distinct quality and I have little doubt that you will make a success of your literary career.

He thought 'The Boy Who Was Always Wrong'

> . . . not a story proper but a sketch . . . in a sense . . . an essay rather than a story, but that does not alter the fact that it shows considerable literary ability . . .

The second he thought 'more of a proper story' though

> . . . one must take into consideration the homosexual nature of the story which would make it impossible to find a place in a magazine other than the small highbrow magazines, and I'm not sure that the writing is sufficiently outstanding to find a place in the pages of the latter . . .

I had told him about the novel I'd written, *The Reed That Bent*. He asked to read it and hoped I would look him up one day. In a note dated 4 October 1951 he acknowledged receipt of more short stories and expressed pleasure

> that you found our meeting of some use and I should be delighted if I should be able to write to say that I would like to try to handle one or two of this new batch of works.

He couldn't! Two weeks later he wrote, 'I am going to disappoint you again, I'm afraid.'

> . . . Of course, your book had its good points. Believe me, I am not trying to soften the blow, because that would be unfair to you and it would be wasting my time. I have declined a number of novels this week and although I am declining yours, I do so with a certain amount of reluctance because it does possess a quality that was lacking in the others. If I say again that I do not doubt that you will, at some time, write successful and publishable prose – and possibly poetry – I am not merely putting off telling you that you can't write. I believe you can, and I think that as a production from a person of your age, this book shows considerable ability.

And with faith and generosity added: 'Don't forget to send me some of your poems.' Which of course I did. Probably by return post. Another two weeks later, with courteous promptness, and by now we were on 'Dear John, Dear Arnold' terms, he sent them back. The one he liked most was 'I Bought a Ship' though he described it as 'a slight lyric'. I reproduce his central paragraph both to record a nineteen-year-old's literary flaws and as possible advice for other nineteen-year-olds.

> As in your prose works, I maintain that you need discipline. You have a considerable amount of passion, but you do not control it, and you seem to be at all costs determined not to write in any accepted traditional form. This is a pity, I think, because while I am all for progress, the restriction that classical form puts on artists is

very often an excellent thing. Somewhere in *Remembrance of Things Past* Proust remarks that sometimes a poet's finest flight comes through having to wrestle with some difficult problem of rhyme or metre. I am confident that you won't think that I make this remark because I am a diehard traditionalist. Quite the reverse, in fact, for in music I am a lover of Bartok and Alban Berg; in the visual arts of Henry Moore and Paul Klee, while in poetry I enjoy Eliot and Herbert Read. Nevertheless, all these artists have, I am sure, mastered traditional technique thoroughly and it is because of that that they break the rule with such authority. I wonder which classical writers you read? I would suggest that you read Donne, Crashaw, James Thomson (*The City of Dreadful Night*) Hopkins, and among the moderns, John Crowe Ransom and Robert Graves, who all combine passion with discipline.

Passion and discipline, poetry and ideas – the four cornerstones of art. I was raw, ill-equipped, half-formed, a mixture of charming and pugnacious, confident and self-lacerating, cocky and fearful, but instinct drove me to do the right thing – expose my work to the hammer and forge of criticism. The battering was coming at me from all sides. My literary life was a siege. Alastair's sweet indulgence turning into steely analysis; polite lobs of gunpowdery judgement from John C. Smith . . .

And then Robert

Writing is one thing; the moment you pack and post it off the work shifts out of your gaze into the gaze of someone else. Your eyes become the eyes of the person you're sending it to. Suddenly its imperfections gape open. Confidence crumbles. I recall that in the early years of rehearsing plays I felt fine until sitting among the audience on the first night. Even then I remained calm until that moment the lights went down and I became part of an alien group who had come to see what I now felt had been written by someone else.

The most severe battering – for 'Portrait of a Man' – came from Robert Copping.

. . . Because you write about things that are personal to you, you seem utterly out of touch with reality and completely devoid of humour.

No humour? I was born laughing. But pain is pain. The English, I have found, become seriously angry if you don't share in life what they consider humour when it's often mere mockery; as others consider you 'difficult' if, simply, you disagree with them.

Don't you realise that if you say a man joined the Communist Party you have to be utterly dispassionate (assuming that you don't use the device to show the man a worthless knave) and analytic? To imply that it's quite an ordinary thing for a man to join the Communist Party, a thing that the reader might do himself if he had a mind to – is shocking. Communism shocks in the same sort of way that incest does: you just can't chat about it . . .

He was right and wrong. 'Portrait of a Man' was not 'chat'. Being more to do with personality than ideology it couldn't engage with the wretched collapse of communist faith as *Chicken Soup with Barley* did. I felt deeply attached to Robert and battled ferociously. The exchange is too lengthy and convoluted to recreate, especially after so many other samples of the way this street-corner entrant into the literary ring took his early lefts, rights, and body blows. But even Robert signed off with generosity.

. . . If you can find anything of use to you in what I've said then use it: I've said all I'm likely to say for some months to come. About the things that annoy you most – such as being called a self-righteous rascal – I suggest you get others in sincere and truthful mood, and see if you don't impress them in the same way.

Just keep on writing. Don't do anything that feels to you wrong. Don't accept intellectually any idea from me or from anyone else until you have completey accepted it emotionally. Preserve your integrity. What more is there to say.

Was I *really* self-righteous? I was too full of doubt to be self-righteous. Inevitably at that age I would defend my darlings, terrier-like. But to be self-righteous is to feel in possession of truths. I simply felt in possession of talent. Not the same thing.

I survived the battering. Not because I was strong-willed – that I was – but because material kept thrusting itself at me. 'Handle me,' it seemed to say, brazen-woman-like, 'take me, shape me, look how interesting I could become if you treat me right.' And, as with brazen women, I found the material irresistible. I survived, wrote on, and learned. *The Terrible Valley* trilogy of stories was carved out with slowly hardening and deft strokes, I felt a growing confidence. Letters began to supplant 'Editor regrets . . . ' slips. John Lehman was taking notice.

22.2.55

I read your story 'The Bath' with great interest. I think there are some very good things in it; but it seems to me just to miss the target all the same . . .

12.1.56

I liked the feeling in your poem very much, but I don't think you have succeeded in making it quite individually enough your own.

After some thought I'm afraid I finally decided I shall not be able to find room for it. I'm so sorry. I'm sending it back to you now, but with regrets.

14.12.56

We read your new MSS with considerable interest, especially the prose, and liked many things in them. I'm afraid however . . . I am so sorry . . . thank you for the pleasure it gave us to read them.

Three months later I wrote *The Kitchen*.

In the 'Rejection Slip' file from which this chapter draws its material is a last letter from John Lehman. It is dated 3 March 1960.

The first two plays of the Trilogy have appeared, and *The Kitchen* has received its two Sunday night 'productions without décor'. Lehman has asked me to write an article for him assessing the work of the English Stage Company. I have declined. His letter, as any good editor's letter, urges me to rethink.

> I do understand what you feel, and I know you have appeared on television at various times recently and may therefore want to stop making 'pronouncements' for a bit.
>
> However, I don't really agree with the view you express in your last paragraph. It is, of course, far too early to make a grand assessment, we need at least another ten years; but a great deal has happened during the five years since the Royal Court got its new management, and quite enough in my opinion for interesting soundings to be taken. You mention John Osborne; he has written three plays and a musical, sufficent surely to establish a playwriting personality.
>
> What I really was hoping from you was either a piece of autobiography on the lines of that series *Coming to London* I ran a few years back, or a 'thinking aloud' piece about the relationship between what you want to say, your material, and the way you have chosen to say it – in the theatre.
>
> If you change your mind, no one will be more delighted than I.

Thus fortune's wheels turn and turn and we should both beware and take heart.

Uncle Solly

I keep hinting at a story to be told surrounding my first ever published poem – 'The Poor'. I delay the telling a little longer to relate another, one of the last events of 1957. It carved itself so deeply into memory that a quarter of a century later it is regurgitated as an anecdote by Annabella Wharton in *Annie Wobbler*. The encounter – it was with Uncle Solly, known in the family as Shortie – took place on the morning of 1 October. Two days later I typed an account of it, peaty-rich in autobiography. First, though, a little about him.

No reader will remember, though it was spelt out in the beginning of this book, that my father had four sisters, two of whom, Billie and Rae, married their cousins, brothers Sammy and Solly. Sammy was the taxi driver, father of cousin Bryan. Solly, a man under five feet tall – hence his nickname – was a sub-editor on the *Daily Mirror* who aspired to be a writer. He had published a few short stories in newspapers and magazines; radio had accepted a couple of his half-hour plays. The sisters, and the cousins they married, all had warm Welsh accents and hospitable natures. Unhappily, Aunty Rae and Uncle Solly couldn't have children. They adopted a baby girl I grew to love and care for over the years, Freyda. Freyda became an unmanageable handful, married a young man who died on her, then an American airman with whom she had children, and moved to Arizona. We visited in 1974 which is the last time we saw her. She didn't maintain contact and is lost to us. It broke the hearts of Rae and Solly. Solly adopted Jewish orthodoxy and then converted to the temple of psychoanalysis.

3rd October 1957
Two days ago I received a letter from Uncle S. It ran thus:

> Dear A.
>
> I should like to see you to discuss something that may be of interest and of use to you. It's too long to go into a letter or by phone. I shall be out all day tomorrow but will be home by Friday. Could you come up in the morning? Aunty Rae will be having a Turkish. If you can't can you ring me? If I don't hear from you I'll expect you on Friday as early as you like. PTO It might be better if you kept this under your hat until you've seen me.

On Friday I reached Uncle S just on 8 a.m. That would give us an hour. Aunty Rae opened the door with a rather surprised Oh hello

Arnold. I was ushered into the bedroom. Uncle S was still in bed. He could not have guessed that I would turn up so early.

'Come in Arnold, come in, come in.' He sat up, dazed, a little sheepish. I asked him what it was. 'No, no,' he said. 'I can't. It's no good. I can't.'

'Have I not left us enough time?' I asked. 'Perhaps I could come some other day.'

'No, no. I can't, it's no good. I've got cold feet.'

'Literally or metaphorically?'

'Metaphorically!'

We were interrupted every few minutes for the first ten minutes by cups of tea, enquiries as to whether I'd had breakfast, Freyda coming in to say hello and then again to say goodbye as she went off to school, after which he began.

'Look, Arnold, what are you doing now? Are you still in the school? What's the position?' I told him: I was lingering on at school to finish a documentary on the Brixton market, this I would present to the BFI in the hope that they would finance another film; a trilogy of stories was at the publishers; ACT Film Productions was considering a script which they had liked; I was directing a musical for Primrose Jewish Youth Club which I had written; I was working on other scripts and a play.

This had given him pause to regain consciousness and gather courage to tell me what he probably felt he ought not to tell me.

'Arnold I'm worried about you. I am. No one else in the family is, no one else in the family understands your position, but I do. I know exactly what you're going through at this moment and it's not your fault.' He had a lovely Welsh accent which sang all the more because he was becoming emotional. Uncle S is not an emotional man. He's witty, controlled, cynical. I can remember him when he was a disillusioned man, I can remember him when at the height of his cynicism, and now I saw in him all that was left for him to become – passionate. Passionately concerned and anxious that someone near to him should not go through the same cold, unfriendly stages he had experienced. He continued.

'Everyone else in the family thinks that you are a lazy, drifting oaf – well, not oaf, but anyhow lazy. Now *I* know that's not true. You have an intelligence well above average, you have a good standard of self-education, you have good looks – whatever that may mean – and you have lots of energy, bags of energy, more energy than I ever had when I was your age. And how old are you now? Twenty-five? From time to time I hear of what you've been doing, nobody ever tells me anything these days, I have to ask, people in the family tell me what you're doing and I'm horrified! I'm absolutely pained and horrifed.' It was 8.20 in the morning. He continued:

'I probably have no right to say this, Aunty Rae thinks I ought to mind my own business but – I don't know. I was the same! You see that's it, I was exactly the same! At your age I wanted to – no, earlier – at *nineteen* I wanted to write! I was filled with the idea of becoming a big man. And that's all it is, Arnold, you want to be a big shot, you want to feel that you matter, that you're great. But you're not! You're not now and you never will be. It just isn't possible. You haven't got it in you and you must realise that before it's too late.'

As he spoke he beat his hand on the bed and shifted up and down, turning to the left and right, now lying down as though going back to sleep and then springing up again to renew the attack. At this point I felt I had to make some attempts at defence. Of course I could not become annoyed because he was obviously very concerned. He was not being insulting just terribly frank about a situation he felt was so desperate and pathetic and tragic that talking to me was a necessity.

'This is unfair,' I suggested. 'You don't really know my ability, you haven't read any of my work – though I've been meaning to show it to you for ages – and I don't think you're giving me a chance.'

'Why haven't you brought up your work?'

'I suppose because I felt you were not really interested.'

'Oh yes I am, of course I am. But you haven't shown it to me and do you know why? Because you feel it's no good.' I protested, to no avail. 'Yes, yes! That's why – because you feel it's no good. You can't make the grade, Arnold, and you know it. You yourself, in your own mind, know in all honesty that you haven't got it and that you never will have.'

I said something about all writers having doubts and that I was no exception.

'I know all writers have doubts, I know about that. But at your age you should begin to be getting somewhere, you should have produced volumes and volumes of stuff, novels, short stories, plays – volumes! from which you could say I know that here I have got some good stuff.'

I mentioned something about John Osborne being twenty-seven before he was discovered.

'John Osborne! You'll never write half a play like John Osborne. I'd give my right arm to have written *The Entertainer*. But I just can't. I've tried and tried but I cannot produce dialogue. I have a very good brain, I can think it all out, I just cannot write it. But that's my problem and I've got over that. I'm forty-seven and I'm content to have money put into my bank every month. I have responsibilities and my only fear now is that I should die. But you're twenty-five. And what have you achieved? Nothing! Absolutely nothing. You wanted to act – OK, so that gave you up. You wanted to write – well, that can't give you up because you can do that in your kitchen – but you haven't written anything that's successful. You want to be a film man but you'll never do it. It's just against the law of averages that you'll ever get in. You haven't got the capital and you haven't got the talent. And supposing you do publish a novel, or supposing you do get your script accepted, what will you get? £70? All right £170! And then what? So they give you a job in that production for three months, for six months, then what? But you won't even get that far. There are hundreds of people writing scripts and stories, hundreds and hundreds. Take John Mortimer. He's published six novels and he still has to be a barrister – though what he spends in a day could keep you for a week.

'Arnold, I don't want you to feel hostile about this but if you want I shall tell you what is wrong with you. You have illusions of grandeur and I'll tell you why. Your parents have never got on and it has left you feeling insecure. You have developed an inferiority complex and you feel you've got to show that you're somebody. It might have been a boxer or weightlifter but as you come from our family it's natural that you wanted achievement in the intellectual world. It happens every time in a house where parents don't get on, time and time and time again. It can't fail! It never misses! The child develops a feeling of insecurity and inferiority, and – I was the same! Only in my case it was due to the fact that I was small. I couldn't bear the fact that I was small and developed an inferiority complex about it. Now look, I'm telling you this because I know that once you know the cause of it you can go on and do something. And I feel that someone ought to tell you.' And so he carried on, obviously very worked up about it all.

And it was so very strange, at 8.30 in the morning, from an uncle I rarely saw but who felt that he was closer to me than anyone else in the family because I wanted to write and he too, when he was young, had wanted to write. He felt that I would understand him and that he, and no one else in the family, could understand me.

'It's not your fault. And your sister is exactly the same. She, like you, is suffering from exactly the same psyche and for the same reasons. And I'll tell you her picture. She has the fantasy of a grand Englishwoman with a house in the country surrounded by beautiful pictures and antique furniture. Why has she this revulsion from Jewish people? Why does she think that everybody in the Primrose Club is no good? That all Jewish people are vulgar? Simply – because she projects her own experience of East End life on to the Jewish race. This in her mind is associated with Leah and Joe and the quarrels they had.'

His view of Della was fantasy. She has told me of her wish to be buried in a Jewish cemetery. 'I want to do anything that affirms my Jewishness,' she said. It was Uncle Solly who, on the contrary, was displaying a familiar Jewish trait of philistine scorn. He possessed no aesthetic sense and felt threatened by those who did. In addition, there exists within the Jewish personality a seam, thin but unmistakable, of contemptuousness. We invented God, you understand, who else, therefore, could be taken seriously? An attitude of mind which bled itself into our genes and flowed through generations, making us the most argumentative race on earth, especially with each other. A Jew will diminish Mendelssohn as though he himself were Beethoven, Beethoven as though he were Mozart, Dostoevsky as though he were Tolstoy, and everyone as though he were God, which doesn't stop me loving them for their innate sense of social justice and their respect for talent and scholarship. Most of them. And all of them for at least some of those qualities. Uncle

Solly lacked a sense of visual beauty. How could he not comprehend that, married to a furniture-maker, of course there would be a
few antique items in the Wacton house. Not many, they could
barely afford to buy me the cheddar cheese I consumed. Della recalls that Uncle Solly was also scornful of her wish to go to
university – impossible for lack of funds; women were for making
meals anyway. He continued:

'Look, let me tell you, and this is really between us, but I'll tell you
. . .' And he proceeded to tell me how Freyda started off by being
happy.
   'But she was never any good at school. Suddenly we found she
was not getting anywhere in her work. And not only that, she began
to make friends with all the morons in the school. All the people she
brought up here were so obviously out of place and nowhere near
our level of living. She felt that she was not good enough, you see.
She felt that she could not make friends with anyone better. And I
felt . . . something must be wrong. So I moved her to a new school,
a more progressive school, and there she loathed everything. The
people, the teachers, the lessons – everything, and so she lowered
the tone of the whole place. She tried to bring everything down to
her level. Well I talked to her headmistress who happens to be a
bitch, she knows her job well enough but she's a bitch, and we
decided that she needed treatment. Freyda needed something more
than we could give her; her headmistress said she had a psychological block. So I took her to a psychiatrist. For the last eighteen
months she has been attending this psychoanalyst and it's costing
me a fortune. It's costing me an absolute fortune and it's worth
every penny. I have seen that girl visibly change before my eyes. I
can see it! Day by day I can see it – and I tell you what, by the time
Freyda leaves that school she'll be passing her exams with flying
colours, you'll see.'
   So that was it. Uncle Solly thought I would do well to have similar treatment. I tried to respond with the same sincerity that he had
shown.
   'Let me be frank, Uncle Sol. I'm aware of all this. It's natural that
I should be, and for that reason I've taken on no responsibilities. I

shall not get married . . . If I do not reach fulfilment then I am prepared to drift away until it's all over. I shall be satisfied with no other achievement.' [What did that mean? Fulfilment as a writer – I understand. Prepared to drift away to where? until all *what* is over?]

'But it doesn't matter,' he cried. 'This achievement – to fail – it's nothing. Do you think I like going to work and reading all that crap I have to? My culture is not my work. My culture is my private life, it's what I·do afterwards. The work I do is to earn me a living, and I *have* to do that. And that is achievment. This stinking little hole here is an achievement. I pay to keep it going, I have kept a wife and given a home to an orphaned child – that is achievement. That is just as important as any novel. I've known my limitations and I've fulfilled them, a man cannot achieve any more. And you have got to realise that or you know who you will be following don't you?'

He was referring to my father. I was aware of it all. I did not need my uncle's passionate talk to convince me. The only thing he overlooked is that out of all the unhappy childhoods (though mine was a glorious one, it's just that home life was insecure) there is a million to one chance that the attendant neurosis can feed talent – just as Turgenev was a genius with a domineering mother – and that was the chance I was taking.

It was only left to make the effort to show him some work and until then leave the final judgement – as far as he was concerned – in abeyance.

What that chronicle does not record is the bet Uncle Solly made with me: 'For £5! I'll bet you 100-1, your shilling to my hundred, that you won't ever get anything of value published.' Seven days later I began to write *Chicken Soup with Barley*. Three days after the play opened at the Royal Court, I wrote to Dusty at Butlins in Skegness:

This morning I received a cheque for £5 from Uncle Solly with a note saying: 'I've never been so happy to be wrong or to lose a fiver!' Very sweet and courageous of him . . .

That was 1958. Six years earlier, March 1952 (four years before the appearance of 'Look Back in Anger'), one of my dreaded poems, 'The Poor', had been published in the slim paper magazine of The Progressive League, PLAN. It was the first thing of mine ever to be published. In that same March issue appeared a review of a second volume of autobiography by Leslie Paul, founder of a youth organisation called The Woodcraft Folk. Its title: *Angry Young Man*.

Chapter Twenty-four

The Observer *Play Competition*

Excitement and interest was galvanised around not only the new theatre shaping at the extreme ends of London – Stratford East and Sloane Square – but the new cinema which, to begin with, was a documentary cinema called 'Free Cinema'. Free because – and here is an example of the delightful paradoxes of the time – the films had none of the normal commercial constraints laid upon them. The young film-makers could shoot and edit as they wanted because patronage came both from the state – through the funds of the British Film Institute – and commerce. Ford Motors sponsored Lindsay Anderson's *Everyday Except Christmas*, for example.

One day in the middle of 1957 – I wish it had been recorded precisely when, it's neither here nor there but I care and am intrigued by chronology – I was standing outside the National Film Theatre queueing probably with Dusty, Dai, and David Naden to see a programme of Free Cinema documentaries. Along with *Everyday Except Christmas* it might have included Anderson's acerbic *Nice Time*, about the shabby offerings of a seaside resort; and *Mama Don't Allow*, Karel Reisz's film about how some diverse working-class youths engaged their leisure time. Anderson was hanging around outside appearing to clock up the level of applause from an earlier viewing. He seemed amused, content, and pleasantly approachable. I approached. And introduced myself: a student at the London School of Film Technique who had admired his essay in *Declaration* and his review of Kazan's *On the Waterfront* in *Sight and Sound* which completely reversed the way I had viewed the film, and would he please read a story I had written which I thought would make a good film similar to Jack Clayton's *The Bespoke Overcoat*. It was my own script, I wanted to direct it, and if he liked the story would he please recommend it for a grant to the committee distributing the BFI's experimental film fund? His response was generous. Yes, he would. I sent him 'Pools', he read it, liked it, and recommended it for a grant. Karel Reisz and the committee he headed turned it down on the grounds that I had not sufficient of even the most rudimentary film-making experience. Anderson was consoling and asked did I have anything else he could read.

In June of that year he had directed a play called *The Waiting of Lester Abbs* by a novelist he knew and admired called Kathleen Sully, as a Sunday night 'production without décor'. Perhaps that helps date when I talked to him outside the NFT. I think I had seen his production by then. Or was his friendliness the *spur* to see it, which means I waylaid him before 30 June? Whatever, I told him about a play called *The Kitchen* entered for the *Observer* Play Competition. Would he read it? Of course. When the top copy came back – no photocopiers in those days – I'd post it. It came back, but having won none of the prizes I assumed it had no merit and did not want to burden Mr Anderson with a dud play – though God knows why since I had burdened so many poor others with dud everythings.

The competition was first announced in the *Observer* issue of 14 October 1956, offering a prize of £500 'with the likelihood of a West End production, for a full-length play in a post-war setting'; second and third prizes: £200 and £100. Judges were Alec Guinness, Peter Ustinov, Michael Barry (head of BBC TV drama), a young director called Peter Hall, and Kenneth Tynan. On 16 June 1957 the *Observer*'s theatre page informed its readers that there had been some two thousand entrants, narrowed down to fifty. The winners were announced on 18 August: first prize, Errol John for *Moon on Rainbow Shawl*; second prize, Guernsey Campbell and Daphne Athas for *Sit on the Earth*; three prizes of £100 each to Ann Jellicoe for *The Sport of My Mad Mother*, N.F. Simpson for *A Resounding Tinkle*, and Richard Beynon for *The Shifting Heart*. There were two honorary mentions accompanied by £50 each for Romilly Cavan, *All My Own Work*, and Andrew Davis, *Four Men*.

Meanwhile creative juices were churning from the effect of having seen *Look Back in Anger* in April. I had committed myself to writing a musical for the Primrose Youth Club drama group, but once out of the way I was able to begin writing *Chicken Soup with Barley*.

Birth of a play

My memory of how and why I wrote the play is clear. I had quarrelled with my mother over politics, raging at her continuing adherence to communism. We quarrelled constantly. I'm ashamed to remember how I rarely missed an opportunity to make a sarcastic observation about the misdemeanours of the Soviet Union or its satellites. 'There!' she'd say. 'He's attacking me again. Always criticising me.' 'No!' I'd say. 'I'm criticising the Soviet Union, not you.' 'You're criticising the Soviet Union because you want to upset me, to get at me. Don't I know you by now?' Sometimes even she would see how absurd our exchanges were and we'd both end up laughing. It was not easy to handle a mother who never seriously believed the Americans had landed on the moon; the films and photos had been faked, she asserted, to divert the attention of the proletariat away from their exploitation. 'What, you think they're not capable of such a thing? They're capable! And of much worse.' It went on, in varying degrees of absurdity and acrimony, until she died.

On two memorable occasions, after bitter exchanges, I wrote down what she had said, feeling them to be remarkable and moving declarations of faith. Unfortunately they are not dated. Written on different types of paper in different inks they must have come at me on two different occasions. I fused them into one speech but it's the second part I recorded first, knowing with certainty when I heard it that it would become the speech to end this play turning over and over in my mind.

Prior to that had taken place a fierce quarrel. I'd screamed at her: how could she still remain a communist?

All right, so I'm still a communist! Shoot me then! I'm a communist! I've always been one – since the time when all the world
was a communist. You know that? When you were a baby and there
was unemployment and anybody you talked to who was thinking –
was a communist. But it's different now. Now the people have forgotten. I sometimes think they're not worth fighting for because
they forget so easily. You give them a few shillings in the bank and
they can buy a television so they think it's all over, there's nothing
more, they don't have to think anymore. Is that what you want? A
world where people don't think any more? Is that what you want me
to be satisfied with, a television set? Look at him. He wants to die.
My son! You think it doesn't hurt me? The news about Hungary?
You think I know what happened what didn't happen? Who do I
know who to trust now? God! who is my friend now? All my life I
fought. With your father and the rotten system that couldn't help
him. All my life I worked with a party that meant glory and freedom and equality. You want me to give it up now? If the electrician
who comes to mend my fuse he blows it instead so I should stop
having electricity then? I should cut off my light? Socialism is my
light, can you understand that? A way of life. A man *can* be beautiful. I hate ugly people, I can't bear meanness and fighting and
jealousy – I've got to have light. I'm a simple person, Ronnie, and
I've got to have light and love.

It's difficult to be certain. Which are her lines which are mine? I
know she said things like: 'You give them a few shillings in the bank
and they can buy a television so they think it's all over, there's
nothing more. . . I hate ugly people, I can't bear meanness and
fighting and jealousy – I've got to have light.' But did she use the
metaphor of the electrician? Although it's on a separate sheet of
paper, numbered side one and two, thus indicating it was written
outside the flow of the play, yet the name Ronnie appears, suggesting the play had already been started. She could have uttered those
lines during the weeks I was writing and, realising they belonged to
the play, I noted them down.

The second part, although subsequently fused as I've said to the
lines just quoted, is pure diary written on a sheet of paper that has

nothing to do with the ledger book in which the play is written. This came first: the story which persuaded me I had an ending to a play. The play in my head had to lead to the moment when this story could be told. My mother had come into my room, driven there by guilt she produced within herself like bile, needing to explain her fury with my father. It was as much a pitiful attempt to put me at peace with him as it was self-vindication.

And now I'm going to tell you one thing; there's no reason why you shouldn't know, I couldn't tell you while daddy was here. But I tell you now because you wonder why I don't feel full of love – though this was a long time ago and now I've forgotten it. But when Della had diphtheria I was pregnant with Mervin and I asked daddy to carry Della to the hospital and he wouldn't. It was Mrs Bernstein's soup that saved her, she still has that taste in her mouth, today, it was chicken soup with barley. In those days I didn't know, not that I didn't ask, but I didn't know who to turn to for help and one of the relief officers told me to go to the Hungarians for help. But I didn't know. Now I know – that all the money is there for us, what's its use otherwise? And in those days the Board of Guardians knew my position with daddy and so on, but they didn't come round, not once, to see how the children were, not once. And not even Perly had a half crown to lend me, nor Uncle Harry. All the milk I had went to Della, and there were days I went without food. I found a bit of dry bread with a cup of tea, it was – ah! It was wonderful. But daddy, he had the relief money, and people told me afterwards they saw him eating salt beef sandwiches in Bloom's, you remember the shop. I don't know what was wrong with him. Could you do that? I tell you this now not to pull you down, but you should know, on the contrary you should fight for a better life; say – it won't happen to me. Never go down, always pull yourself up – never, never, never give in. From us you should learn. We got through. Well, there you are, it won't hurt you to know. Now you can get on with your writing. My only wish now in my lifetime is that he shouldn't mess in his trousers.

If these two speeches were the end, where was the beginning? I had learned from the huges sagas of Howard Spring and A.J. Cronin that for the impact of decline to be felt a story had to begin when the world was young and all things possible; the days of hope had to be chronicled first. Loss of faith could not be understood unless that faith was recreated in all its innocence. And when *were* those days of innocence? Which crisis more than any other in recent history presented itself as black and white? The days of the Spanish Civil War and the anti-fascist demonstrations in the East End, of course, when Jews and gentiles for an incandescent moment respected one another, held hands, shared angers, threw barricades across the intersection of Whitechapel Road and Commercial Road and rolled thousands of marbles into the paths of mounted policemen with batons, toppling their ferocious steeds; that thrilling day when Sir Oswald Mosley's blackshirts were thrown off their provocative route through the Jewish streets of London and many were lured to believe the end of capitalism was imminent, the millennium just across the road at Aldgate Pump. The year was 1936. I was four, aware of nothing; but so electrifying had the riots been for my family, so full of anecdote, of little braveries and farce, of colourful personalities, that it was talked and talked about into my teens until I felt I had lived those days with them. I made notes. Scraps, typed and scribbled, accumulated. And I thought so long and intensely about the play that it came out in a rush, with ease, a swift if imperfect delivery. Pain, a little, but not for long. Only one other of my plays had such an effortless birth – *Caritas* – written in ten days, though I'd been preparing for it with months of research; ten days in a state of near delirium, intoxicated, like one drugged, driven. It shows in the work. The strangest of my plays, I feel.

The completion of *Chicken Soup with Barley* whirled me into a high like a dervish dancer and I came out of my room bursting to read the play to my mother. She was in the front room with her friend, Mrs Harris. I made them stop whatever it was they were doing to listen. These two women were the first audience for my first play, a family saga covering twenty years from 1936 to 1956, read to them by its author sitting at a heavy mahogany table (the kind into which could be slid an extra panel to make it longer for family feasts by winding it open with an iron handle), there in the front room of an LCC flat off the Upper Clapton Road, E5, sometime in mid November 1957.

When I had finished, my mother smiled her faintly sardonic smile and said something like:

'It's very good, no, really, I mean it, it's a big work, a lot of work, but who's going to be interested in any of it, silly boy? It's about us, it's between us. It won't mean anything to anyone else . . . '

But I was elated and she could see I was elated, and though I can't remember her actually saying it – it was the 'silly boy, who's going to be interested in any of that' I remember more – yet I know she wished me well. As I write this down it seems to me I can hear Mrs Harris defending the play against my mother's hesitancies and doubts.

Whatever, I knew that at last I had written a work worthy of presenting to a public. It had substance, thrust, rich texture. There is no vanity in this. Artists know when the elements come together. Singers, actors, musicians – when every instrument in their body, every pulse, every nerve end functions as it was ordained to and they and their audience know it – come off stage glowing, dazed sometimes. So it was with me having written the first play of the Trilogy. I wrote at once to Lindsay Anderson asking would he read it. Without hesitation he agreed, and at the same time enquired about that other play I'd promised to send him. He'd not forgotten *The Kitchen*. That was impressive. I explained why he had not received it. This one, besides, was more important to me. He read it promptly and on 18 December wrote that letter which changed my life.

Dear Arnold

Thank you very much for letting me read the play, which I enjoyed very much, and think is important as well as very *good*. Obviously it needs reading again; but at a first go, it held me, convinced me, and presented its problems as well as its people in a complete, *undeniable* way. Can I send it to George Devine to read for the Court? It seems to me exactly the sort of play they should be searching for – much better, for instance, than one by Doris Lessing which they planned to put on, and which I read and didn't like. [But Doris, who subsequently became a good friend, is a great novelist instead!] Of course I haven't any idea what their reaction will be: they are rather incalculable people. . . and of course one can't be sure that the play, being as real as it is, would be a 'success' . . . but surely they have had enough of that recently to make them ready to put on something as good as this. You really are a playwright aren't you? I mean there it is, with characters as solid as I can imagine, and a whole way of life to them, and the necessary perspective, and a much more mature grasp of the whole thing than John Osborne (for instance) can provide. [Lindsay may not think this now, thirty-six years later, and I certainly view Osborne's work as inspirational.] I am sure it would act, and stage, most excitingly. The 20 years time-scheme presents its difficulties, of course, but *they* aren't insoluble. Congratulations, as I say, again, and thank you.

Oddly enough I have also been reading an interesting play from Poland, sent to the Court after it has been kept in the drawer for the last five years. Even more disillusioned than yours – I suppose you'll allow that yours *is* disillusioned? – and similarly obsessed with the Cause that failed. But of course they actually *lived* (and so to some extent no doubt still live) under the perversion of Socialism. . .

Let's meet some time anyway, if you have a moment. I am at home at least until 9.30 in the mornings – MAI 4719.

All best wishes – Lindsay.

Imagine, after all those printed editors' slips and letters of rejection, after the epistolic battles defending banal verse and rough-hewn prose; post-Sutherland, Copping, Smith and timorous, fearful Uncle Sol, imagine! The effect upon me. The swelling heart. The blood, warmed like mulled wine against the effects of a long bleak winter's day – imagine! And of course I rushed down to the red phone box on Upper Clapton Road alongside Lee's sweet shop to phone Lindsay my gratitude, and grant permission for him to offer the play to George Devine or whoever he liked. It was not an acceptance, I understood that. Lindsay was not the artistic director of the

Court, not even – at that time – an assistant artistic director; that invitation to pale power came in 1959 after his successful production of Willis Hall's *The Long and the Short and the Tall* (incidentally, a title Lindsay had suggested in place of *The Disciplines of War*). But I had a champion! Not a father figure, more an elder brother figure. Someone who was going to argue *for* me instead of me having to argue for myself. His letter lit candles. I glowed. We named our first born son after him.

The English Stage Company

In 1978 the playwright, Brian Clark, struck gold with an award-winning play *Whose Life is it Anyway.* Despite its phenomenal success no publishing house would print it. He established his own! The Amber Lane Press. In 1981 the Press published an excellent, well-documented book – *At the Royal Court* – full of evocative photographs, celebrating '25 Years of the English Stage Company'. Short essays and memoirs are written by directors, actors and playwrights tracing the company's unique style and achievement and their relationship or debt to it. The opening passage of Lindsay's contribution recreates the atmosphere into which he was plunging my play.

> I remember very well the English Stage Company's first production at the Royal Court in 1956. Or rather I remember very well the impression it made on me, for strangely enough the impression is much stronger than my memory of the play, which was *The Mulberry Bush* by Angus Wilson. At that time I had no professional connection with the English Stage Company. I was not even a professional of the theatre: I had been a documentary film-maker for some years, and I had been a film critic (not a reviewer) in various specialised magazines. I was a friend of Tony Richardson . . . It was a confident, hopeful time . . .
> . . . the aims of the Royal Court enterprise. These went far

beyond the simple encouragement of new work or of new writers
that seems now to be the accepted lore. Indeed, no account of why
the theatre started – at least as far as George Devine and Tony
Richardson were concerned – can be complete without some appre-
ciation of the historical context, and of the state of the London
theatre and of British cultural morale generally in the mid 1950s.
We were still in the post-war doldrums. Nothing that was done in
the theatre related in any stimulating or significant way to what was
happening in Britain or in the rest of the world. Non-commercial
drama was generally 'poetic' drama, represented most successfully
and most reputably by T.S. Eliot and Christopher Fry. The Royal
Court impulse was a 'realist' impulse, and its ambitions extended to
the representation on the London stage of 20th-century European
classics, and even classical revivals. Style, it was understood, was
just as important a part of the theatrical experience as theme or content. George was no sentimentalist, and nor was Tony. They had no
favourable predisposition towards writing just because it was 'new'.

George Devine

I possess, wrapped in cellophane to protect it, a press cutting from
The Times (*circa* early February 1950) reporting on the Festival of
Contemporary Plays which was taking place in Toynbee Hall. The
Query Players had offered Thornton Wilder's *The Skin of Our
Teeth* in which I played the Telegraph Boy and the Doctor. I re-
ceived my first-ever review:

Arnold Wesker gave a neat little study as the telegraph boy,
although he again could have used his lines to greater effect. . .

The Times review reported that our entry to the festival was adjud-
icated by the actor who had played the role of Mr Antrobus in
Laurence Olivier's 1946 production of *The Skin of Our Teeth*,

George Devine. I had forgotten. Nor did I come across this reference until after George died. We could never smile at the coincidence.

The personality of George Devine is central to an understanding of what gave the English Stage Company lift-off. As different as were writers like Arden, Osborne, Jellicoe and myself, so our experience with and perception of George was different. My mother was in awe of him. He was both the ruling class and a gentleman. He had warmth and grace, qualities my mother would forgive most things for, even being an intellectual and coming from an élite! She knew a 'mensch' when she saw one. George was a 'mensch'. Integrity saturated his being. His only blemish was – he didn't warm to my plays! Neither George nor his young co-director, Tony Richardson, shared Lindsay's enthusiasm for *Chicken Soup with Barley*. They did however share an enthusiasm for Lindsay – all from the same college in Oxford, it must help. Was it that I seemed an incomprehensibly foreign personality to George? He made every effort to understand. He visited us in our LCC flat – had he ever been in one before? – and he willingly agreed to let us take him to the awful Yiddish theatre with its overused threadbare sets, its tear-jerking sentimentality and shameless folksiness, playing out its last years in the Grand Palais on the Commercial Road to its endearingly, appalling, noisy peanut-cracking audience of argumentative old Jews. I remember that George watched with a mixture of bewilderment, incredulity and great courtesy. The only Jews he knew were the wealthy Ashkenazi ones surrounding the beneficent Neville Blond – who would never have been seen dead in the Grand Palais; and the deeply anglicised ones of the old Sephardic bankers, the Lousadas – who would never have known of the existence of the Grand Palais, and to one of whose sons Jocelyn Herbert, the designer, was married. Jocelyn was to design my first five plays, and George was to fall in love with her and both were to leave their respective families and live a short life together. George died a few years later in 1965.

John Osborne, by supreme contrast, was both a personality

George could relate to and a writer whose marvellous old-fashioned English bile of moral outrage George was more comfortable with. Quarrelling Jewish couples from East End ghettos, incontinent old men, earnest young idealists – these were hazy, unfamiliar, and perhaps implausible characters to him. In that same twenty-fifth anniversary book John Osborne's contribution begins with a eulogy.

> Nobody else but George Devine would ever have put on that old play of mine: that's the absolute truth. It had already been sent back by about twenty-five managers and agents when I answered the advertisement in *The Stage* and posted it to the English Stage Company. And nobody else but George would have supported it, to the hilt, in spite of a lukewarm reception by most critics; in spite of a slow box office; and in spite of being attacked – and hurt – by a lot of people he respected in the conventional theatre, including personal friends. History very soon began to be rewritten, and nowadays it isn't realised how much hostility George had to face in 1956 . . .
>
> When George and I first met in 1955 he didn't say a great deal but he did make me feel immediately that something very special was about to happen and that *I* was going to take part in it . . .

George's great virtue for me was his humility. He was prepared to risk being proven wrong about *Chicken Soup with Barley*. In this way: the English Stage Company had decided to celebrate fifty years of British repertory by inviting four provincial theatres to present for a week one of the plays they were mounting in their season of fortnightly rep. Devine and Richardson, trusting the instincts of their intelligent, talented and trenchantly persuasive colleague, suggested to Brian Bailey, artistic director of the recently built theatre in Coventry, the Belgrade, that he should take on my play instead of the one he was proposing, of which they were not enamoured! Bailey read *Chicken Soup*, admired it and agreed Lindsay should direct it. Only one problem: Bailey could not afford to give Lindsay more than two weeks of rehearsal. Lindsay felt himself too inexperienced to tackle, in so short a rehearsal time, such a difficult play spanning twenty years of contemporary history. He needed three weeks. And here's the magnanimity of the man: rather than ask me to hang around until more propitious conditions obtained, until perhaps he could try again and persuade George to let him mount it at the Court – as a more opportunistic director might have done – he advised me to take the bird in hand and allow another director to direct it in Coventry. This other director – young, lean and hungry – was, in his opinion, more experienced, apparently talented and, to the point, had waxed lyrical about my play. Meet and talk with him said Lindsay, he has some very interesting things to say, he appears to understand it and has ideas for mounting it. I was disappointed not to be working with Lindsay – by a quirk of fate I was never to work with Lindsay – but I too was lean and hungry and it was, after all, an alien world to me. If that was his advice I would take it, and would meet with this young man whose name was John Dexter.

Dexter

> . . . my career seems to have been, to a very large extent, a confidence trick executed by a very uncomfortable trickster whose aim was sometimes to be a magician . . .
>
> from *The Honourable Beast* by John Dexter – a
> posthumous autobiography

The first march from London to the nuclear weapons research station at Aldermaston took place over four days in Easter between 2 and 6 April 1958. It was initiated not – as is commonly supposed – by the newly formed Campaign for Nuclear Disarmament set up only seven weeks earlier, but by the smaller and more radical organisation: Direct Action Committee Against Nuclear War, which had been formed the previous year. CND, with its subsequent wider appeal, later appropriated the event. CND was a phenomenon. Not only because by 1961 the Aldermaston marches grew to 50,000 but because most large towns and many smaller ones had a CND committee. But in April 1958 it was only a few hundred of us, including Dusty and Dai, who set off from London, growing to four thousand on arrival. It was exhilarating to experience our small numbers swell as the word spread and we neared our goal.

For the first three days it rained. Dexter, the same height as me, seven years older, animated from head to toe by a demonic, black-eyed, crackling enthusiasm that was as quirkily unpredictable as it could be thrillingly infectious – who hated rain and marches and any public spectacle other than theatrical – joined us on about the first or second day, suppressing his loathing of street politics in order to woo my confidence in him. If protesting against nuclear weaponry was what it took to land his first major production then he would rub shoulders with types he despised, and tolerate whatever drenching the indignity cost. He walked alongside me sharing our packed food of Jewish deli-filled sandwiches, cold chicken, cold fried fish (that was new for him), hating the political rowdies who chanted brave slogans at the handful of disinterested bystanders, getting soaked, talking talking talking nonstop to me about how marvellous he thought the play and what changes he felt would help it work even better. Those were the days when, to quote Lindsay again:

> The text always came first, and writers were to be cherished and encouraged. But they were not to be mollycoddled. There was never any suggestion that a director should *use* a text in order to show off his own prowess or personality; at the same time he was expected to work with his author, guiding him where necessary and where possible, through revisions and rewrites. . .

Lindsay adds, mournfully, that 'as the years have passed, of course, this equilibrium has been lost'. It is so. But in those first Aldermaston days, in the rain, collecting blisters, and singing Blake's 'Jerusalem', John was concerned only to help me make better that which I perceived to be the drama of my family and their times.

As related, we lived in Fashion Street in an attic flat of two rooms where the kitchen was on the landing. Unsurprisingly, therefore, the first draft of *Chicken Soup with Barley* sets the first scene in the top rooms of a house in an East End street. John's first suggestion was: does it have to be an attic room, couldn't they live in the basement? I said they could because, it so happens, that row of houses in Fashion Street was built with basements. Iron railings protected the glass windows at ground level, it was common in many streets, I loved walking past them and looking down into other lives. Though not all were occupied as flats. In our basement worked a furrier whose premises one evening caught fire. Not a real fire. A smouldering, merely. The smell of smoke hung around for ages afterwards. So, yes, the Kahns *could* live in a basement. But why? Dexter explained. Living in a basement would permit two stage managers to run backwards and forwards again and again, only their legs showing, giving the impression that crowds were running to the barricades to join their comrades assembling against Mosley and his blackshirts. Dexter, in his posthumous autobiography, assembled from scattered papers by his lifelong companion, Riggs O'Hara, wrote:

> By setting it in a basement we helped to convey some sort of submerged society. It intensified the family feeling, and the constant coming and going of people, coming from one home to visit another, something which doesn't happen any more.

Creating the possibility for space not called for in the text but where contributory action could take place – that was the kind of inspired idea John offered a writer. Insisting thirty actors could re-enact on stage the work of a restaurant kitchen – that was a stretching of the stage's possibilities a writer could hand on to a director.

He was born in Derby in 1925 and, like me, lacked – and pined the lack of – a formal education. The posthumous autobiography is, curiously, not very detailed or interesting about his childhood, youth, growing up – what formed him; nor about our work together on the early plays. It offers no description of our first meeting, dismisses in a page and a half the first five plays we worked on together, devotes only half a page to *The Old Ones* which he directed ten years later, and – most incomprehensible of all – tells absolutely nothing about the tense and exhilarating days of rehearsing, five years later still, *Shylock* (then called *The Merchant*) in New York, ending in the heart-breaking death of one of New York's beloved sons, the huge (in every sense) actor, Zero Mostel. This play was going to be a crowning glory for all three of us – Zero, Dexter and myself. We rehearsed four weeks in New York, opened out of town in Philadelphia where Zero gave one performance, fell ill, and four days later died of an aneurism of the heart, taking with him the most golden of opportunities any of my plays had ever been blessed with and my chance to establish a financial nest such as I had never had, nor – to date – have had. A 250-page diary of the extraordinary rehearsals charts the daily progress of the thrills and despondency of those days; a copious file of our letters charts the pained and wretched aftermath. John's autobiography tells nothing. The play is mentioned only twice, in passing.

I confess – I'm hurt. We never shared a social life but in some way we were first loves. My first five plays were his first major productions. We were celebrated together, jumping off the high board hand in hand. There is only one tender reference in his autobiography which hints at much more.

16th November 1985
Arnold and John [Osborne] supported me at a time when I could not possibly support myself, mentally and financially. The work was the only happy return, and were either of them to ask me to direct a play which no one wanted to do, I believe we would find a wooden hut somewhere.

I'm grateful for the sentiment but it wasn't true. It might have been in 1985 when the emotionally charged memory returned to him but it wasn't true when everyone was turning down *The Four Seasons* and *Their Very Own and Golden City* in the mid-sixties and John, too, turned his face away.

Before directing *Chicken Soup with Barley* he had only mounted two 'productions without décor': *Yes – And After* by Michael Hastings and *Each His Own Wilderness* by Doris Lessing; a Yeats play called *Purgatory* for the Devon Festival brought subsequently to the Court; and a revival of *Look Back in Anger. Chicken Soup with Barley* offered him his first full-scale world première.

I can't believe John is dead. In a way it frightens me. If *he* is dead then it really means *I* am going to die. Don't ask me why the same conviction doesn't come into play remembering my parents are dead, it doesn't. To do with parents being part of an inevitable cycle, I think. John's death is different. He was an outrageous, cruel, and opportunistic old queen who could switch his abrasive warmth on and off with alarming, confusing and unpredictable rapidity. Incomprehensibly, too; and his most deplorable characteristic was his bullying. There was always a whipping boy (or girl) in the company whom he'd select to exercise his scorn upon, vaunt his reductive wit, vent his ill-temper for what had gone wrong the night before with his love life, annihilate with mockery for a foolish decision he had made that offended his sense of perfection and burned him with shame. But when he was high on his cleverness, his skill, his imagination, when he buzzed with elation from an inspired day's work, he was electrifying in a way that few other directors I know have been, and it communicated itself to the cast who would then give him their all. I despise bullying tantrums, I'm quick to detect the absurdity or petulance of ill-considered moments, and I can see through emotional blackmail. John went cold and silent with tangible fury at times, and it was best, then, to keep away; but something about both my ability to X-ray humbug, and our relationship rooted in shared beginnings, earned me his respect, caution, and, I think, a certain fear. John couldn't mess with me. I knew him. And so he listened to my notes on his production as carefully as I listened to his on my script.

Something about our family attracted him too. He loved my mother and Dusty, and admired Della and Ralph. Perhaps they echoed his background, or perhaps he felt comfortable in an atmosphere neither intimidatingly claustrophobic with university minds, nor sour with working-class resentments, nor judgemental with discontent. There was discontent, but my family maintained a generosity of spirit. Part of him hated theatrical camp. He was impatient with fools, weak, hesitant personalities and heartiness of any kind – especially that hearty intimacy which certain actors assume on first meeting. Having no education he warmed to intelligent wit, scholarship, and brilliant spirits. When I arrived in New York for casting *Shylock* (he was director of the Metropolitan Opera House at the time) he was ablaze with his research into the history of Renaissance Italy, and made me a present of two volumes of Fernand Braudel's *The Mediterranean and the Mediterranean World in the Age of Philip II*, excited by the historian's new method of building history through understanding the relationship between geography and climate and the socio-political personality of Mediterranean communities. He couldn't wait to begin rehearsals on a play which made of him the kind of intellectual and emotional demands he luxuriated in.

But he was treacherous, too, as this extract from my New York diary conveys – it also offers another glimpse of our love/hate relationship.

11 October 1977

. . . went to dinner a couple nights ago with Nick [Surovy, playing Bassanio], and Susan [Schulman] and Merle [Dubusky] of the press and publicity department. Heard something which shocked me. Susan and Merle, whom I like and respect, felt great bitterness about John's treatment of them and had comments to make. Although they hated some of the performances it was with John's production they were mostly unhappy: certain questions were being answered in the text but not, they thought, in the way he was directing it. I told them of my battles with the producers who seemed not to have appreciated how extensively I'd cut and re-written. Merle said something about them having been misled. On our return to the hotel I took him aside and asked him to clarify. He reported John had said to Marvin [Krauss, the manager], 'Get the producers down, the fucker isn't changing a line.'

Suddenly a lot fell into place. John must have said that *after* the confrontation we'd had earlier in the week. We had just arrived in Washington, met together with Jocelyn [Herbert, the designer] and because I'd accepted most but not all his suggested cuts he'd raged to the producers giving them the impression I'd adamantly refused to cut *any* thing, in this way canvassing their pressure to add to his. Since that confrontation, however, we had the long talk walking round the Kennedy Center and I'd also talked with Peter Shaffer (whom John had invited to see and comment) and as a result I'd re-written more. The fierce threats to me from Bernie Jacobs [head of the Shubert organisation] were ill-timed because the cause prompting them had passed. But more distressing was the sense of John's betrayal. He'd thrown me to the lions after a rehearsal period in which I'd cooperated in so many cuts and changes. It seems every-one, from management to cast, have this image of our relation-ship as something uniquely and immensely creative. The cast in particu-lar keep a wary eye on us, watching our moods, the way we talk to one another or don't . . .

All that was the future. Walking with me to Aldermaston in the re-lentless rain those flushed-out Easter days of 1958 we knew nothing of our lives to come. I had written my first admired play, John was presenting credentials for directing it and who knows but that it was the promise of fame and fulfilment rather than this four-day mission to save the world from a nuclear holocaust that made the squelch, the damp discomfort, the hard floors of schools and churches upon which we slept at nights, more bearable.

I agreed to let John direct the play, and plans were set in motion to design and cast it. Rehearsals began on 23 June, it ran for a week in Coventry from 7 July, and a second week at the Royal Court from 14 July. After which I was awarded a £300 Arts Council grant which, we know, Dusty and I spent on our wedding for 150 guests, and John went to prison for six months. It was a full year was 1958.

Committee of 100

You take protest. Nothing wrong with protest. Sign of a healthy society. What goes wrong? I'll tell you what goes wrong. People! They fuck it up. Start off wanting more democratic rights, end up wanting to overthrow democratic institutions.

You take commerce. People rage against capitalism. Nothing wrong with trading. Healthy instinct. What goes wrong? I'll tell you what goes wrong. People! They fuck it up. Get greedy. Produce cheap goods. Form totalitarian monopolies which become a law unto themselves.

You take politics. Nothing wrong with politics. It's the art of government. We have to be governed. Since Adam! So what goes wrong? I'll tell you what goes wrong. People! They become politicians, fuck up politics. Ambitious! Dishonest! Opportunist!

You take religion. Nothing wrong believing in a God. Jesus! Buddha! Muhammad! They're all saying the same thing – be good, love one another, look after the kids! So what goes wrong? I'll tell you what goes wrong. People! they become fanatics. Scream at one another. 'I'm holier than thou and all must be as holy as me!'

Rosie – *Lady Othello*

If one spirit characterised the fifties/sixties it was the anything-was-possible spirit. Something happened to provide a new generation with a mirror, as though one had never existed before, and reveal a mixture of surprising – if uncoordinated, even unrelated – energies and talents. Look, the mirror showed, you don't need a university education to be an artist – Osborne, Arden, Pinter, Lessing, O'Brien, Behan, Delaney, Kopps, Colin Wilson – none of us had been to university (though many of us might have regretted it);

look, the mirror showed, you don't need to come from a privileged, well-connected class to be given opportunity – Devine gave Osborne and Dexter a hand, Anderson offered me his; look, said the mirror, you can make music in the streets with tea chests, a broom handle and old rope, skiffle was born and groups sprang up on street corners strumming the fifties sound which led to a blaze of melody from those piss-taking Liverpool mockers-and-charmers – the balladeering Beatles; and look, said the mirror, people banding together and dropping party politics can focus the world's attention on one of the great threats to the world's survival – a hundred thousand marched into Trafalgar Square and gave courage to the students of America showing them that peaceful demonstrations could make an impact, produce results. CND inspired the civil rights movement which succoured the anti-Vietnam War campaign which surely must have taught Solidarity something about collective action which led to the toppled Berlin Wall and brought about the collapse of Soviet tyranny. From four hundred marchers to Aldermaston to the end of an empire.

Do I make extravagant claims for those years? Perhaps. But I offer them tempered by a sense of frayed triumph, and in the knowledge of how human cycles shift disturbingly between dream and reality, achievement and loss, steps forward steps backward, hopes betrayed, notions of the good and the brave and the beautiful transpiring to have been chimeras. The fervourists, those who fall in love with themselves as martyrs, took over. Energies became misspent, diverted.

Just as the old British Peace Committee march from Hyde Park to Trafalgar Square outwore its effectiveness and the four-day Aldermaston march seemed revitalising, so the four-day march itself, after three years, seemed to have run out of theatrical impact. Something more dramatic was needed. I became one of a committee of one hundred people who, with Bertrand Russell at its head and such as the Reverend Michael Scott, the poet, Christopher Logue, and playwright, Robert Bolt, among the hundred, advocated acts of civil disobedience unknown since the suffragettes.

A sit-down was planned for 17 September 1961 in Trafalgar Square.
Russell argued in his autobiography that it was:

> . . . a profound and inescapable duty to make the facts known and
> thereby save at least a thousand million human lives. We cannot
> escape this duty by submitting to orders which, we are convinced,
> would not be issued if the likelihood and the horror of nuclear war
> were more generally understood.
>
> Non-violent civil disobedience was forced upon us by the fact
> that it was more fully reported than other methods of making the
> facts known, and that caused people to ask what had induced us to
> adopt such a course of action.

I'm glad to have made the gesture but not especially proud of that
month during which I read more books in open prison than in the
previous six months of the year; and besides, it was such an utterly
puny incarceration when measured alongside the imprisonment of
a Mandela or a Solzhenitzen, to say nothing of the millions who
languished whole lives away and died in the gulags of the world.
And we could all have signed an order to keep the peace and been
released on the spot at any time during that month. Osip Mandelstam, I think, might have been grateful for such an option.

Robert Bolt was in the middle of scripting *Lawrence of Arabia*.
The film's producer, Sam Spiegel, drove up to our open prison,
Drake Hall in Staffordshire, and told Bob that hundreds of technicians were out of work because he wasn't around to complete the
script. Bob signed on the spot and was driven away from us to
London in Spiegel's car. Later he told me how ashamed he was of
his action. No one was out of work. Spiegel had lied. Bob, an ex-
history teacher, had once confessed to me his fear that he didn't expect to see his children live beyond thirty years of age. All history
taught, he explained, that given a conflict of interests which could
be resolved either by war or negotiated compromise, war had been
chosen. Old-fashioned human stupidity in a nuclear age promised
nothing but Armageddon.

I retain vivid images of my days as a criminal. The first was lining up to hand in our personal belongings on arrival at Brixton Prison where we spent our first weekend. Bertrand Russell, tiny-framed, old, frail with illness but bristling with intellectual eminence, stood before a row of prison officers, the smallest of whom – emaciated with ignorance, eyes red-rimmed with fury at his own stupidity – mocked this venerable old man with the viciously rude question (I recall the drift not the exact words): 'So you're a professor are you? Won't do you much good in here. You'll soon be sorted out in this place.' I knew then there would be those in this lovely isle would happily, unquestioningly, guard gas chambers.

To counter the action of the cruel little prison officer was that of the one who came out of nowhere and thrust some books in my hand saying: 'Here, you'll need these.' Literature, not pulp, and so welcome to help pass the seventy-two hours we were locked behind bars before being drafted to Drake Hall's spacious RAF-like huts, cosy beds, and gardening. That was a memory: the chill of horror on entering my cell and hearing the cold echo of steel bolts being drawn. The first thing I did was stand on the edge of my bed, tiptoe, and peer out of the high window to establish eye contact with the world outside. From then on I meticulously divided the hours between reading, eating, sleeping, and regularly pacing the cell for exercise hoping time would pass quickly. It didn't.

Sidney Bernstein, founder and paternalistic head of Granada TV, had sent Dusty a cheque for £100 to help her through any hardship she might be enduring. There was none really. In fact the most sobering observation which put in perspective the highly emotional scenes in the court room, was made by Dusty. The charges were read out – incitement to disorder – and we were asked did we plead guilty. Our replies were dramatically defiant and each and every one the same. We did not recognise, we said one by one, the jurisdiction of this court to pass judgement on our moral stand. Photographed sitting on the window ledge of our Finsbury Park flat with you, Lindsay Joe, in her arms, and thinking about all the tearing around I had been doing to get Centre Fortytwo off the ground, she replied, when interviewed and asked what she felt on hearing her husband was sentenced to a month in prison: 'The rest will do him good.'

Drake Hall, the open prison, was a relief from the cramped iron cell of Brixton, but boring. The high point of that month was the romantic Logue's leap on to the table one day in the dining room after dinner, from which he announced in his loud, gravelly, upper-class voice:

'Good evening, gentlemen. My name is Christopher Logue. I'm a poet. And this evening at 7.30 in the library I shall be reading some of my poetry and you are all invited and welcome to come. Thank you.' He had a packed house.

I wrote awesomely stupid epic poetry in code about life in Drake Hall. Some days before our release all written papers had to be submitted for vetting. Christopher Logue gave in his sheets containing work in progress on his splendid modern version of Homer's *Odyssey* – parts of which I felt honoured he had recited to me as we lay bed by bed in the evenings before sleep. Handing back our papers before leaving, the prison governor, a civilised, humane, and obviously cultured man who'd read what we'd written, advised me in gentle terms to stick to writing plays and leave the poetry to Mr Logue, 'if you don't mind me saying so'.

Chris taught me something about the confidence that comes from being born into the ruling class. We sat next to each other in court and when our sentences were to be delivered by the magistrate we all rose. Chris whispered something loudly to me. Two police commissioners in front of us turned to sternly shush him. 'Don't you shush me, my good man,' Chis rebuked them with confident authority, 'just remember *I* pay *you*.' I was mortified. It would never ever have occurred to me that the police could be spoken to like that. I tried it once in the state of New Mexico with deeply embarrassing consequences.

At the month's end cousin Maurice picked us up and drove us to London, but not before we'd called in at the nearest sweet shop, bought pounds and pounds' worth of sweets and chocolates, and driven back to a prearranged part of the surrounding wall over which we threw the goodies to be retrieved by those who had received the longer two-month sentence, like George Clark and Ralph Schoenman – Russell's secretary who some thought to be an evil genius goading the old philosopher into political actions he might otherwise not have taken. Some even thought Ralph to be an *agent provocateur* from the CIA. I don't know the facts. I liked him. He seemed at the time deserving of the wide variety of chocolate bars we threw over the wall.

After the month in jail I resigned from the Committee of 100 and urged everyone who'd been in jail to resign with me. I reasoned thus: if civil disobedience is to make its mark it should be carried out by fresh waves of law-breakers for each event. I warned against the martyr complex and predicted that if the same people remained on the Committee the next jail sentence would be longer. The movement would fracture. To feed it with new blood each time would have the additional virtue of demonstrating how widespread such deep feeling against nuclear weapons was. It was not simply that I was more pragmatist than hero, which I am, but I was suspicious of and had a profound aversion to 'sufferers'. Not those who pass through and need comfort during their pain or grief but those who seek suffering, ensure all around are aware of it, parade it at strategic moments for scrutiny and admiration, exploit it for mournful blackmail. I am perhaps sentient to such demonstrations of heroic endurance because they are not unknown in certain Jewish women. My aversion is a Wesker trait. The Wesker aunts stood sternly against sentimental displays. The Perlmutters were more prone to them.

No other member of the Committee of 100 shared my reasoning (perhaps not my experience of Jewish women either!). Not that they were 'professional sufferers'. Honourable, highly intelligent, most; like Michael Randle, secretary of the Committee who had helped organise the first Aldermaston march, and served a month with us. But as I predicted, he and others were again jailed, this time for sentences of up to eighteen months. Helen Anagransa, the only woman, after eight months in Holloway Jail, cut off from her comrades, suffered after-effects which exacerbated an unhappy personal life and hanged herself. In January 1963 Bertrand Russell resigned. The Committee faded. But I race ahead.

Chapter Twenty-five

Preparations

Giddy times were gathering on the horizon. The wisest can lose hold and spin off lost into space; many of the best-schooled and disciplined, those born into milieus where giddy times were in the genes, and where eminence, authority, cultural sophistication came with mother's milk, have lost control of their lives. I possessed none of those things. How could I not lose control?

Not that I became rich and squandered, not that I became famous and unbearably arrogant – though possibly that's how my new-found confidence appeared to some; rather I felt myself capable of taking on the world, possessed of abilities which were nonexistent, or crudely formed, or mistakenly perceived, or unripened as yet. My wildness lay in risks rather than abandon. Everything terrified me but I would not surrender to the fear. Posting *Chicken Soup with Barley* to Lindsay Anderson terrified me, the curtain rising for the first time in my life terrified me, getting married, having children, buying a house, launching a national organisation for the arts – all terrified me. Yet I hesitated at no point. The terror produced defiance and a kind of courage.

More than that – much more than that – was the image of my father. I loved him but would let nothing and no one frighten me as it did him (just as you, Lindsay Joe, have vowed that you will never spend money you haven't got, as *your* father did). I would be lovely and loyal as a friend, but move to enslave me and I would shake free. Weakness was a kind of enslavement, it fettered poor old Joe. I would not be like him. Within us all is the parent who nurtures us, to whom we cling, embrace; and the parent we despise who is in us trying to get out. The strong Wesker women overwhelmed and awed my sensitive, roguish, weak-spirited old man, and his Perlmutter wife pitied and foolishly hoped to change him as she foolishly hoped to change the world. This was the mish-mash I inherited and had to make sense of. I seem not to have done so, except now and then with him and her and this and that. But those days, when the giddy times gathered on the horizon, I felt able to walk with the gods, blessed by them who – if I worked hard and desired only the good – would now look after me for all times.

New personalities

New personalities entered my life. Each one interesting. Miriam Brickman, casting director; small, dumpy, clever. Being Jewish she understood *Chicken Soup with Barley* in a way the others didn't, it drew us close, she felt protective of me and the play. Miriam went on to cast films and was described by Lindsay as being 'responsible for a whole new style and class of actor'. Dead. Cancer.

Ann Jellicoe, a riot of high spirits, good nature, and a frank sexiness I'd not encountered before, smothered me with encouragement like a thoroughbred bitch who'd come across a sparky mongrel, new, odd, unfamiliar; she had the gift of making one feel interesting. *The Sport of My Mad Mother* and *The Knack*, together with the plays of a writer like N.F. Simpson, formed the genuine theatre of the absurd. Pinter, on the other hand, seemed to me a naturalist who wrote *about* the absurd.

And there was Keith Johnstone who lived for three years together with Pat, a woman seven years older, madly in love with him but he no longer with her. They shared a house in a leafy kind of commune in Cockfosters, at the end of the Piccadilly line. He too wrote strange plays. Keith hated the Church and doodled evil bishops all over his scripts. Pat desperately wanted a baby and was anxious about losing Keith for fear she'd not find another man. Both ignored this hovering fear. Keith said unpleasant things which Pat pretended didn't upset her and Keith pretended he didn't mean. It was the theatre of 'marriage' which some couples conduct in public to amuse us. For 30/- a week they rented one of a number of huts clustered round a big house. I spent a lot of time with them, eating out on the lawn, listening to Bach and Bartók. One sunny Sunday afternoon Keith taught me how to listen to Bartók's *Music For Strings, Percussion, and Celesta*, how to laugh at it. I had never laughed at classical music before; or perhaps I mean laugh *with* it. Listening with him I understood how one could, how one could smile at the audacity – an important component of art. Audacity, daring, courage, chutzpah. It makes you laugh to encounter brave spirits. They get things right in a way you had not thought possible – making the unimaginable work. I think of that high note Barbara Streisand reaches in a little-known ballad: 'Never, Never Will I Marry'. Up she goes from 'I' to 'marry'. Jumping an octave and two notes from bottom C to E. Unexpected. Unimagined. Impossible.

I think of the moment Richard Dreyfus first sees the mountain he's been drawing again and again out of his fevered, nagging imagination in Stephen Spielberg's film *Close Encounters of the Third Kind*, the laugh he gives, of recognition. It's there! The mountain *does* exist. He was not mad after all.

Learning to laugh at Bartók, friends who taught me new ways of listening and looking – all fed into me. Ann Jellicoe joined us that afternoon and it became one of the halcyon days, one of the memorables. Idyllic afternoons of youth like that were a long way from the vicissitudes of disappointed later life. These days when we meet a chilly embarrassment takes over. Then, it was days of love. Full of gaiety and laughter.

The Writers' Group

'George Devine cherished writers: it is really as simple as that . . .' wrote Ann Jellicoe in the twenty-fifth anniversary book. As soon as my play was accepted I was invited to join, and entered with enthusiasm, the Writers' Group. It was George's baby and with it came the idea of free writers' passes to the Court's productions. We met in the house of Anne and Peter Piper, two doors away from

George's house, in number 7 Lower Mall, Hammersmith. A huge Georgian mansion, cosy and relaxing, full of children, nicely scruffy, both children and mansion. Anne wrote plays, subsequently novels. Peter, who had languished in a Japanese prisoner-of-war camp, became an eminent art historian. Ann Jellicoe, Keith Johnstone, John Arden, Miriam Brickman, Edward Bond and many others passed through, tested ideas on each other, played games of mime and theatre: Ann Jellicoe is clearer than I am about the group's history and scope. Her twenty-fifty anniversary book piece continues:

> What he wanted from the Writers' Group was to make people feel that the Court was interested in them and thought them worthy of effort and attention . . . Very quickly Devine withdrew. He probably felt, rightly, that he overawed us. Dexter dropped out: it was not his scene. William Gaskill took over . . .
>
> There were some obvious absences: N.F. Simpson, a personal friend of Gaskill, Johnson and myself, would have been welcome. Harold Pinter always kept aloof from the Court, though they did two of his plays in 1960. Both probably disliked the idea of 'groups', and I know what they mean. John Osborne never came – was probably never invited – maybe he was too grand for us: we were on the brink of acceptance, but had not yet arrived.
>
> The group had strength and cohesion because we were all much of an age, of the same calibre of personality and at the same time not too egotistical. We recognized each other's talent and supported it. This is said to be rare among writers. We were extremely careful whom we invited into the group – not from exclusiveness, but because we were aware that anyone too argumentative or destructive would upset the balance.

The rest of Ann's memoir is fascinating. It's difficult to resist quoting it all – but the last paragraph dots and crosses. (I recommend the whole twenty-fifth anniversary book.)

The Writers' Group remained strong and lively for about two years. While preparing this article I spoke to Arnold Wesker and asked him what he found most valuable about it. He agreed with me that it was 'the ritual of going and seeing one's friends'. The meetings had all the fun of a party and none of the boredom . . . Perhaps we reassured each other – the support of professional friends meant much to me after the critical disaster of *The Sport of My Mad Mother*. But within two years we had become more successful and so more self-assured. The Writers' Group began to meet less often and then stopped altogether. There were attempts to revive it, but they never took. The need had passed.

John Osborne in *his* twenty-fifth anniversary article is, unsurprisingly, contrariwise interesting; another glimpse of George comes through.

We disagreed about many things, after we'd started at the Royal Court. George knew, for instance, that I despised the Writers' Group. I thought it was committee wanking and refused to take part. George went along with it because he thought there was some value in it, but he also went along with my opposition to it. We used to have running skirmishes about Ionesco's plays and other French work. I used to say, 'George, we're not going to do *another* of those, are we?' And he'd say, 'Yes, dear friend, I'm afraid we *are.*' He thought they were good. I couldn't abide them. But he could contain my reaction patiently, even though he was not a patient man. He could contain and comprehend many different things; that was one of his strengths. It wasn't that he was weak and compromising; he could be brutal and dismissive, and he went for what he wanted. But he had a special kind of tolerance. He suffered talent gladly.

I will later be able to confirm that with another story, one I'm not proud of.

Giddy giddy days

To be taken up, involved in the mounting of one's play is an exhilarating experience – to do with 'making things': launching an

ocean liner, designing, drawing up plans, assembling parts, then –
smash and away! That must thrill. Sketching, cutting, stitching, and
finally wearing a dress; planning a political campaign; building a
house; landscaping a wilderness – concept, plan, assembly, adrenalin, buzz! We are fortunate, those of us permitted to realise our
gifts.

Following the Aldermaston decision John went into action. The
months of May and June leading up to the opening in Coventry
were animated like few other times had been, till then, in my life.
The final decision to go ahead was made on 8 May – or rather that's
when I was informed that *Chicken Soup* was definitely scheduled in
a season of four plays from the reps. Settled! Second week in July.
We could plot, plan, and cast. John read and reread and reread
again the play, and talked to me about rewrites. To Dusty, 30 May:

> . . . work on *Chicken Soup* – one or two alterations and additions
> suggested by John Dexter. I had to work out the 'solo' game. Re-
> member there's a scene where they play a game of solo, it is a
> complete hand and so I had to work out a real hand, giving special
> cards to each character so that it fitted in with the dialogue . . . in-
> triguing.

A letter from John indicates the way we worked. It's undated so I'm
unable to identify which set of rewrites he was referring to – the
first, the second, the third?

> Thank you for the rewrites, Yes, Yes, Yes, very good, just what we
> need. I'll show them to GD when he comes out of the Shaw cloud
> which envelops him at the moment.
> *Matters arising:*
> ONE: I still think Ada ought to come in *before* the end of the act, so
> that we don't have to register her in a climax. What about bringing
> her on after Hymie and the boys have gone and *before* Sarah comes
> in (page 12) . . . [I don't quote all of it, the references will mean
> nothing.]

All the rest of the rewrites are I think very good indeed. Especially those affecting Sarah and Harry.

I am at the moment living with Doris [Lessing] so 58 Warwick Road will find me. FRE 4097.

Tony [Valentine, who played Ronnie] is well and sends love, so does Doris, so do I.

After the first production we agreed on further rewrites. We also agreed on the need to recast. John was busy, busy (another letter, also undated):

Again, dead centre. I see what you mean about the Triptych at the end of act one, but – don't see how, unless Ronnie means SOMETHING, he will make any effect at all on the scene. I have had a chat to Tom Maschler, he wants to have a copy of the rewrites. I have had four copies done, one of which has gone to George, the rest I am holding.

Now bloody awful news. Bill Gaskill is trying to take Frank Finlay to New York to play dad in Dillon [Osborne's *Epitaph for George Dillon*], that is, I think, a dirty trick, but no one else seems to mind. Nor has anyone asked me my opinion which is that he is completely wrong for the part. Frank has a generosity of spirit which no amount of acting can hide. This as you know is the last thing needed for Percy. However it is not settled yet and I am having a word with John O to try and put him off the idea. But I can't bring myself to speak to him, sorry to be so childish, but I have not your endless capacity for forgiveness. I'll give you further news as it breaks.

Now as for Sarah – I have made half a dozen lists and scrapped them. At the moment I am working on Frances Cuka, we are going to rehearse her audition together, and then let George see it and see what he thinks. Will you be back in time to talk to her and help with the audition? She is, I think, very possible. She has all the warmth and capacity for love, the question is one of strength. But we shall see.

The complications to which George was referring were about

America and possible dates, but after a week of frantic cabling, I discover that the Scotts still have no definite plans and so I am free to
do our play (it is ours isn't it?). America can come later. The real
bother is that because of keeping myself free for the Scotts, I am
now out of work, when I need not have been. Not to worry . . .

Throughout his career John was to manifest this characteristic – he
made things happen. At a certain level he was a wheeler-dealer, a
manipulator in the marketplace setting up a dozen productions at
once.

London was – as it is today – the metropolis. No doubt about
that. A cultural centre unlike any other. To be perfomed in London
is to perform before the world. Plays which have achieved local successes in Paris, Moscow, Johannesburg become international
successes if applauded by London audiences. I was excited to know
that my first play would be performed in London's Royal Court
Theatre – a theatre built in 1888 where a season under Harley
Granville Barker (1904-7) included productions of Galsworthy,
Ibsen, Maeterlinck and Shaw (eleven of his plays) – but it was as exciting to be launched in Coventry. To Dusty, 21 May:

> . . . letter arrived from Coventry from Brian Bailey the director of
> the Belgrade . . . I really am proud to be able to start off in Coven-
> try. You know about this city don't you? In the war it was almost
> completely destroyed by bombs. When the war was over the
> citizens said: not again! They elected a strong Labour council, re-
> built the whole city with a new cathedral and theatre and shopping
> centre, said we're not going to carry out any civil defence because in
> the next war it would be useless, and disbanded CD [Civil Defence]
> . . . Bailey says the play 'has so many real qualities . . . tremendous
> possibilities'. Encouraging!

The hot seats are the major institutions – the Tate Gallery, the
South Bank, the Royal Opera House, the Royal National Theatre,
the Royal Shakespeare Company (all 'royals'). Those who run them
are in the firing line. George Devine was no exception, even in

those early days. It bewildered me – though I was soon to have anxieties and criticisms of my own – that after only two years of its existence the English Stage Company, resident in the Royal Court, was coming under fire. To Dusty, 11 June:

> . . . University and Left Review Club last Monday was fabulous. Ken Tynan, Chris Logue, Bernard Kops and Bill Gaskill were on the platform, and people kept coming in and in and in . . . standing in the aisle and sitting all over the floor. Doris Lessing was in the audience. Lindsay Anderson was the chairman – a very good one too. He stopped people from speaking unless they were to the point. I spoke twice – confidence floods me now . . . Chris Logue was very despairing about the state of the theatre and suggested that the Royal Court had achieved nothing and that we should withdraw our support – at which I jumped up and protested that my play was due to come on soon and they should not withdraw their support yet, and anyway what other theatre was there to support apart from Theatre Workshop.

Our future plans were these: Dusty – home to Beck Farm before taking off for Butlin's to earn money, perhaps gain some perspective on our relationship. Me – remain in London, work on rewrites, complete rehearsals for Primrose Club play – earn my fee as 'club drama instructor'. Then, while Dusty was in Butlin's, I would live at Beck Farm soaking up atmosphere for, and thinking about, 'the Norfolk play'. Though not for long: rehearsals were due to begin in Coventry for *Chicken Soup* – which was also scheduled for the Theatre Royal in Brighton. London, Redenhall, Coventry, London, Brighton, Redenhall, London – not quite London, Paris, Rome, New York, still – giddy, giddy days.

But giddy dread was around as well and lived in me alongside excitement. A month before the London opening the Court were arranging block bookings for the ULR Club together with trade unionists, mayors and councillors of Stepney and Hackney. A discussion would follow. The political events surrounding 1936, 1945, and 1956, and my handling of them in personal terms, would come under scrutiny. Plans were afoot, chopping blocks loomed, I was going to be called to account, found out! Every artist's dread. To Dusty, 16 June:

> . . . A most depressing experience was attending the last-night party of Barry Reckord's play *Flesh to a Tiger*. It was a miserable affair with all sorts of hangers-on around in the bar. Some stupid débutante type girl in a sac – no, not a sac, the other style, what's it called? – anyway she was running backwards and forwards playing 'bulls' with her lean-faced boyfriend . . . The English girl going 'madly gay' sort of thing . . . And then came the break-up of the party and Barry shook my hand and said, 'O boy how excited you must be feeling – I know that feeling, I know it, man!' And all of a sudden I could see the terrible pattern: one playwright coming in, having his brief spell of excitement, followed by the next playwright greeted as though *he* was the revolution in the theatre and feeling on top of the world. Then the production, the critics, the half-empty houses, and it is all over, and the next one comes along . . .

Remember this fear, 'the terrible pattern, one playwright coming in, having his brief spell of excitement, followed by the next playwright': it contributes to that intemperate outburst which so angered George Devine and I've promised to relate. Soon.

And so the day approached. I left Beck Farm on Monday, 23 June. Bus to Norwich, train from Norwich Thorpe station to Coventry, arrival on Coventry platform. And there, on a billboard carrying the theatre's logo of a dove of peace, a red and white poster – so large I felt embarrassed, coy, like a young girl – announcing my play. *My* play.

CHICKEN SOUP WITH BARLEY
by
Arnold Wesker

The features of my face, my legs, my general demeanour took the bold announcement in its cool stride, as though a poster hung round whichever corner I turned in the world, but my spirits took a leap and a skip. Hop, hop, hop!

Did I take a taxi to the theatre? A bus? Walk with my case? Who did I see first? All I remember is the utter amazement of walking into the workshops where carpenters sawed, machinery spun and hummed, nails hammered, and joints were being tapped into place. A busyness of construction for a play I had written once upon a short time ago, nine months to be precise, in a Clapton council flat and had read out to two old ladies. All that activity! *I* was responsible! The thrill of that moment remains. Thrill, pride, fear, disbelief – the usual riot of conflicting emotions, a sense of unreality. Me? This is all to do with me? No! Not really. And yet – yes, yes, yes.

Letter to Dusty, 24 June:

. . . You will love this place . . . you will rave . . . the theatre is like a small Festival Hall . . . it is wonderful that my play should begin here, just wait till you see it. The centre of Coventry is modern and interesting, building going on all the time. Come early on Monday and we'll be together – Della and Ralph and mum and probably Roy and Rita. You will be staying the night here with us in this house. You'll love the setup. John, Tony and three girls and four boys, me too, are sharing it. We have a financial kitty and cook for ourselves. There is a television in the front room, two record players with a vast selection of records from Bach to Frank Sinatra. I've just come away from the chatter of my room – a room I'm sharing with Tony Valentine. There is a couch and a bed in the room, we take turns on it. Last night, our first night here, we had a fit of giggles and laughed till three in the morning – at which time we rose and made ourselves a pot of tea. Fell asleep as dawn came up to us – about 5.30 a.m.

The Midlands newspapers are beginning to buzz with news of the play – I've to meet the press sometime this week. There is talk of it probably going on in Brighton – and Tony Richardson has suggested we might have a run at the Court. 'It's the best thing in the festival' [Fifty years of Repertory], he told John Dexter. Still, we know about Tony Richardson and his wild statements.

John is a very good director – a hard worker and a keen one who knows what he's doing. I wish you were here to see these rehearsals, it really is an experience.

There were flats attached to the theatre for actors and technicians on a semi-permanent basis, but our lot lived in 43 King Richard Street, owned by a butcher, Mr Allen, who owned other houses, other butcher shops and a taxi service; a sort of godfather to the theatre's personnel. On one occasion he gave us a joint of lamb which we roasted for a glorious Sunday lunch. I remember John proudly taking me on a tour of the city's new shopping centre as though he'd built it, and buying a record of music completely unknown to me that he thought ought to become part of my musical experience: *Carmina Burana* by Carl Orff. As the years passed I came to understand his mischievous motive for wanting me to enjoy its lecherous syncopations.

I kept Dusty as much involved as possible with all that was happening. I didn't trust the bleak gaiety of happy Skegness campers to keep her blood at boiling point. When the first week of rehearsals was over I described in a 'despatch' how interesting it had been to watch John conduct them. The play, I wrote, was definitely moving on to Brighton after its week at the Court: '. . . Should get at least £100 for that . . .' We had met Tony Richardson in Stratford-upon-Avon and had a drink with him. His was the inspired idea to cast Paul Robeson as Othello (Vanessa Redgrave and Diana Rigg as Citizens of Venice and Cyprus) and he was now rehearsing Michael Redgrave as Hamlet. Tony – the brilliant and successful young star before whom John and I were a little in awe. Well, I was, cheeky and confident though I might have appeared. John was perhaps too streetwise and more experienced to be overly impressed. Both were ambitious young men with hidden reserves of treachery and no doubt they smelt each other out. I was the innocent between. But their skills were different. John was the more talented stage director and Tony, finally, the film-maker (*The Entertainer, Tom Jones,*

Charge of the Light Brigade . . .) which John secretly hankered to be but had failed after three unhappy attempts. Tony told us (I told Dusty):

> 'we are all hoping *Chicken Soup* will go for a run at the Court – we are *relying* on it to go for a run at the Court, there is nothing else!' But this is just Tony being charming.

All the ingredients that go into the baking of a production, all that can go wrong, all the tensions that rise like pressurised steam from a boiling kettle and were to be repeated during the next thirty-five years, one way or another, in part, variations of, were there in that two-week rehearsal period of my first play. The set designer, Michael Richardson, was beaten up at a friend's house by thugs, one of the actors was knocked down on his bike and had to rehearse with his arm in a sling, Tony Valentine had a nervous breakdown – he'd never played such a demanding role. John worked everyone hard, rehearsing all day and evenings too. And of course we had the first of our disagreements. Over what I don't record, but finally, 'I think he has sort of come round to my way of seeing it.' I experienced the first tech – the fun of staying up half the night – fortified by wine and sandwiches, sweets and cigarettes – to light the set, pull all the technical elements together. Rumours flew between London and Coventry on the state of the bookings – heavy in Coventry but finally only 26% of box office capacity for the week's run at the Court. (Though more than 82% on its return in 1960!) So intense are the emotions invested in a production that dreams are dreamt of impossible futures.

Friends and colleagues were planning to make special journeys to see the play – George Devine and Tony Richardson, of course, and Doris Lessing, Lindsay Anderson, Dai and David, Roy and Rita, my mother, Dusty . . . Apart from family, in the end it was only Lindsay who made it. Ann Jellicoe and Keith Johnstone came down after the first night, both to see the new theatre and to support a friend. To Dusty I sent clear instructions how to find King Richard Street and what to do on arrival.

Then came the first night, the night before which I had the first of my first-night-mares. I dreamt that the play was being performed at Toynbee Hall Theatre where I once acted, hopefully, ardently, and with more panache than talent. Not only had all the audience walked out but they had taken their seats with them. The auditorium was stark, empty except for three remaining red plush seats: one each for the women in my life – my mother, my sister, my girlfriend.

I have neither memory nor record of that first ever performance. Nor can I recall what we did afterwards. I think we went to a restaurant – what else? It was long before the days when Dusty made huge first-night parties. Records tell me she was dressed in blue. I don't know what anyone else wore, or said, or did. There was only the aftermath. Dusty returned to Skegness the next day and I wrote to her that though her stay had been wonderful it was unsatisfactory and that as the day of her leaving dragged on I became 'duller and duller' and that

> the performance at the theatre was terrible and the audience laughed in all the wrong places, and displayed such stupidity it was unbelievable. They are so used to seeing corny films and drawing-room comedies that when they come up against a little real-life drama it embarrasses them and they have to treat it as a joke. And to cap it all I had a row with John over certain points in production and he went to bed in a huff.

Nevertheless the reviews had been good and George had rung John to congratulate him, which meant that something was in the wind. What? *Roots* was not yet written; could it be that they were going to let John direct *The Kitchen*? No, it turned out to be plans for a possible revival October/November time with a better cast and longer rehearsals. It didn't take place. John's saga had to be lived through and *Roots* had to be a success for that to happen.

If the second performance on the 8th had depressed me, the one on the 9th hadn't: 'wonderful performance . . . cast on top form and audience a good one'. But poor Dusty, wanting to share the new experience of a thrilling first night, returned high and proud to a dreary rabble of Butlin's colleagues who at once put her down and whose vacuity depressed her spirits. I had to write consolingly:

Sweetheart, I can imagine what happened back at the camp. You bounced in full of enthusiasm showing them the reviews and the telegrams and they none of them responded or felt it important enough or interesting, so you became deflated and upset. But darling they didn't see what you did, and they have not seen my picture in the *Mirror* or any other paper – what do you expect of them? You feel sorry for them? That's a dangerous feeling . . .

The first night at the Court was, inevitably, something quite, quite different, though again – not without sloughs and desponds. On the day of opening, 14 July, I wrote to Dusty:

. . . They have just broken from the dress rehearsal for a cup of tea. I haven't been watching much of it. I'm sort of wandering around aimlessly not quite certain what to do. The Mayor of Coventry and the Jugoslav ambassador are coming tonight – and all the critics. It looks like being a full house – the rumours are warm and everyone is talking about the Court taking it up for a run. But I don't know – I'm not feeling terribly enthusiastic about anything just now and wish to hell you were here. The *Jewish Quarterly* have just contacted me on the phone for an interview, they are doing an article on Kops and myself – we were both in the kitchen it appears! . . .

. . . God in heaven – I sit here and I'm not quite sure what is happening. Bill [Gaskill] has just told me how marvellous he thinks *The Kitchen* is – though like Lindsay he feels it is slight – not big enough – he wanted more to happen. I have this terrible feeling that I'm not very interested any more, that I don't care if they put the play on or not, that I don't want to write another word – that I couldn't in fact. I just want to lie in your arms and let you caress me and fuss me . . .

But the mood of the day shifted. When Uncle Harry, my mother's favourite brother, stepped out of the taxi in Sloane Square and looked up at his nephew's name in lights, he wept. When the house lights went down after we'd stood for the National Anthem, and the stage lights went up on a very rep set before London critics and a sophisticated London audience, my heart started thumping. Next day I hand-wrote a rushed letter to Dusty – no date, no address – the hottest of hot despatches from the front.

My darling

We're in – I think. The first night audience in London was won – the press is favourable and Tony and George are already talking about a run at the Court. We had supper with the Jugoslav Ambassador in the club-room above the Court Theatre – cigars and champagne with a meal of chicken soup with barley – sole – steak, and fruit salad all beautifully done. Thank God John Dexter was with me. The Ambassador wants a copy of the play, and Tom Maschler has invited me out to lunch to discuss publishing the play in Penguin's. Brian Bailey would like to employ me as the resident dramatist at the Belgrade but they can't afford it yet. Elspeth, my agent, is trying to persuade a millionaire to give money to promising playwrights with me being the first one. John and I stayed up all night walking from Sloane Street in order to get the papers as they came out. The *Daily Mail* calls me a playwright of 'rare ability and even rarer promise . . .' The *Standard* says I have 'rare understanding . . . passion and urgency . . .' Even *The Times* and *Telegraph* are favourable. Now we wait for the *Sunday Times*, the *Observer*, the *Statesman*, the *Tribune*, the *Sunday Dispatch* and perhaps the *Reynolds*. But I think we are there – I mean we have reached the point where we can begin –

O Christ I'm tired and dopey – I must go off to meet the cast now so that I can take them to 523 where Della has invited them to tea. Sweetheart, it's going to be hectic for the next week or so – I'll probably arrive in Norfolk the same time as you. Please forgive me for this mad note – wait to hear from me more.

I LOVE YOU

Wiz

The note is bursting at the seams with relief and excitement. The most memorable part was not the meal in the restaurant upstairs (now the Theatre Upstairs) – run at that time by Clement Freud whose idea it was to lay on chicken soup with barley and who, sad-faced, told sad Jewish jokes – it was the walk to Fleet Street. John knew exactly where to go to get the first editions – a courtyard somewhere off the main street. I remember he bought all the available papers and we sat down on a kerb, the pile on his right side, me on his left, to read them. He opened them simply to look at first paragraphs, and having read all that he needed to read uttered in his clipped hard tones: 'Well, that one's all right . . . And that one's all right . . . And that one's all right . . .' and then threw them over to me. With each 'that one's all right' his elation grew.

What happened next? Did we go to an all-night café, somewhere frequented by the journalistic fraternity? Did we each return to our separate homes as the first light faded up over the city? I can't ask John. He's dead.

And then it all began to happen – though not everything as we had imagined. Tom Maschler launched *New English Dramatists*, the first volume of which contained *Chicken Soup with Barley*, Bernard Kops' *Hamlet of Stepney Green*, Doris Lessing's *Each His Own Wilderness*, and which is by now a collector's series; Wolf Mankowitz wined and dined me and expressed a fervent desire to see my plays in the West End – he was particularly interested in the musical. I had found myself an agent, Elspeth Cochrane of Theatrework; pretty, chubby, obliging and constantly worried on behalf of her clients, one of whom was John Dexter and another, John Arden. Elspeth negotiated my first contract. Money was trickling in: odd pounds drawn from my patient, obliging brother-in-law, Ralph; some quids working as drama instructor for Primrose Jewish Youth Club; 10 shillings a script read for The Court. I was at last able to sign off the dole. Hallelujah! How I hated those dreary, shabby, degrading Labour Exchanges, the queues, the questions, the hanging around, the indignity. I walked into my bank manager's office, the Westminster Bank, 98 Upper Clapton Road –

threw my reviews on his desk and said, 'My play's a success, can I have a £10 overdraft, please?' So fresh was the possession of a bank account – novel, and working in mysterious ways – that I had to explain to Dusty what an 'overdraft' was: permission to draw out £10 that wasn't there, a permission I have had to request all of my career up until this day.

Sunday reviews. Off went my news despatch immediately to Skegness:

> Sweetheart
>
> You have no doubt read Ken Tynan in the *Observer*, and it is most likely that you have seen the photo and article in the *Reynolds News*. Ken has done me very well – 'potentially a very important playwright', now I have to write a play and confirm that I am not merely 'potentially'. The *Sunday Times* dismisses me in 6 sentences – but the critic [Harold Hobson] walked out after the first two acts and consequently called it 'a Jewish comedy'! There are other favourable pieces in the *People* and *Sunday Dispatch*. In all I have been well received. The Court have bought up the option on it – though the battle now is to get them to put it on as soon as possible. An Australian broadcasting company has asked to read the script, the Assistant Drama Chief of ATV has asked me to lunch, the Belgrade wants to commission another play, and my agent is madly negotiating with some wealthy trust fund to finance me with a travel grant – which could mean a European or world tour of all the big cities and their theatres – FOR US. Still, this is all uncertain. My main worry is to write another play – just to prove I can do it – this terrifies me. What if I cannot write it?

The rest of the letter describes the discussion that took place with the public on the evening of the ULR/trade unionist/mayors and councillors block booking, full of just the kind of people who would understand what the play was about, who recognised the characters. It could almost have been written with them in mind – widely read, articulate, politically conscious, concerned about art and its role in their lives.

. . . people standing (Kay Kendal sat in the front row), half of them stayed behind for the discussion. I sat on the front of the stage along with Lindsay, Chris Logue, John, and Stuart Hall (Alex Jacobs [film scriptwriter] was in the chair) and questions were fired at me. I must confess that I left a great number of them to the others to answer. Some were quite stupid. One chap said he thought that the really interesting character was the unseen grandmother and he wanted to know more about her! What could I say to that? But the really funny thing was – do you remember the line in the play (which got a big laugh) 'Two Jews in the Cotswolds! They had to get a rabbi from Cheltenham to circumcise the baby. A rabbi from Cheltenham! Who'd ever think there were rabbis in Cheltenham!' Well after the discussion a girl came up to me and said: 'I must tell you this, I hope you don't mind, but my father was the Chief Rabbi in Cheltenham!' . . .

Even Uncle Perly, the sweet rich one in the family, was so thrilled by the play's success he sent me a cheque for £25 as 'a gesture of my esteem'. The sweet and less successful Uncle Harry who had wept at my name in lights was, on the other hand, displeased. He was still an ardent communist. For him the play misrepresented the truth.

Plans were afoot for productions abroad. I was commissioned by film producer, Leon Clore, to write a documentary film for the NSPCC – £100 when written, another £200 when made. I met with battered children, and fathers who had battered their children – one of them gave me a canvas, his painting of black and white trees closely packed. The film was never made. The option to bring back *Chicken Soup with Barley* in October/November could not be picked up but 'the Norfolk play' was now eagerly awaited. Expectations were terrifying, but – giddy times, giddy times.

In the middle of the excitement my father came out of hospital for a break. It couldn't be for long because Leah was unable to cope with his paralysis and incontinence. He was never well enough to see any of my plays – in his unhappy, struck-down state it is perhaps as well that he did not have to sit through the emotionally distressing *Chicken Soup with Barley* – though he understood what was happening and stuttered out his pleasure, pleased like a child. All good news or any act of kindness brought tears to his eyes. He seemed grateful for each breath he was able to draw out of this world.

The terrible pattern – an aside

. . . Barry shook my hand and said, 'O boy how excited you must be feeling – I know that feeling, I know it, man!' And all of a sudden I could see the terrible pattern: one playwright coming in, having his brief spell of excitement, followed by the next playwright greeted as though *he* was the revolution in the theatre and feeling on top of the world. Then the production, the critics, the half-empty houses, and it is all over, and the next one comes along . . .

In an earlier chapter I wrote of my debt to the writer, Wiliam Goldman, whose novel, *East End My Cradle*, confirmed that my own experiences and milieu might provide material for writing. I worried about the literary establishment's brief flurry of enthusiasm for the exotic aspect of his Jewishness and feared they had dropped him too soon and cruelly. His fate remained with me as a cautionary tale of rise and decline. And then came the encounter with Barry Reckord. I was an anxious young playwright with slippery-soled shoes on a ladder treacherously smeared with grease.

Two moments combined to ignite my saltpetre impatience: a chance remark George Devine had uttered during a car journey from somewhere to somewhere wishing middle-class writers could be found to handle their problems with as much vigour as we were handling ours; and a review by the *Statesman*'s theatre critic, T.C. Worsley, of Shelagh Delaney's play *Taste of Honey* when it transferred from Joan Littlewood's Stratford East Theatre to the Wyndham's in February 1959, suggesting that it would

... have been better left at Stratford E., or, if moved, moved to somewhere like the Arts. Still, its transfer to the West End is something of a portent, and a portent worth, perhaps, a moment's thought. The reserch begun at the Royal Court – four years ago was it? – has finally been perfected. The English play can now break through the class barrier at will. That objective has been achieved. Now the question is, what is going to be done with the ability? Those who were young in the thirties will remember much the same thing happening with prose writing. What a sense of liberation we felt when the 'proletarian' writers seemed to have burst through the class barrier of the sensitive novel! And, doubtless, young writers for the theatre now feel the same thing. It is an exhilarating sensation, but they had better make the most of it, for it is, as Wordsworth found and history shows, short-lived . . .

I replied with a mixture of petulance, panic and fear:

Sir, So, we 'prole' playwrights must make the most of it must we? We've been given our little say and now the hierarchy is a bit tired and we must finish amusing them is it? Mr Worsley's tone would not be so sinister if it were not for the fact that the same note is being struck in other theatrical quarters. 'We've had enough working-class plays' is the cry of one bright young director and now we so-called working-class writers must return to our proper stations of life. But let's get this straight, what the bloody hell do they think we do? Sit down and say, 'It's time for the primitive fashion – let's cash in'? Kops, Delaney, Behan, myself and others have written out of our own experience. Here we are, having just started, most of us with only one play performed, we are just getting into our stride and beginning to learn about it all, and now some 'fashion-conscious' young smoothy comes along and declares with a bored yawn that 'We've really had enough darling!' But out of fifty-odd plays in the West End there is still only *Taste of Honey* running – apart for the work of the court and Theatre Workshop. We didn't set out to break down class barriers – no need to be frightened – we set out as artists and we haven't half started yet!

Now, listen to me, Mr TCW and Mr GD [George Devine] and

643

Mr TR [Tony Richardson], I've been writing for twelve years and it's only in the last year that I've been given my chance. I didn't write *Chicken Soup with Barley* simply because I wanted to amuse you with 'working-class types' but because I saw my characters within the compass of a personal vision. I *have* a personal vision you know, and I will not be tolerated as a passing phase. You are going to see my next play soon, and I am going to write many more and you are going to see them as well, *not* because I'm a young 'primitive' writer out on a leash for a bit of airing but because I'm a *good* writer with a voice of my own!

George was furious and wrote demanding that I produce some definite evidence 'for your implication in the *NSN*'. I replied apologising, and attributing my outburst to 'intuition'. George wrote back:

. . . You really are a very silly man. you should tell that intuition of yours to grow up a bit. You have worked up a situation over all this which is based on wrong premises and nearly wrecked our relationship. I don't care what you say or write to me in private, but if you insult me in public I lose patience with you.

The depths or heights of absurdity to which your famous intuition pushes you is shown by your second paragraph. Why should I not mean that our association is of mutual benefit? You are a young writer of promise with whom we are glad and proud to be associated. The fact that you are adds to the credit of our work. Don't be so ready to invent conclusions that are not there . . .

I repeat what I said to you in the car. I wish I could find some plays about other levels of society written with vigour, feeling and sensitiveness. We could all learn a lot from them.

This does NOT, you idiot, mean that I don't want more and better 'working-class plays'.

Yours

George

I have no record of my reply but I do have a note from George, written by hand, saying: 'Dear Arnold, Forget it! Yours, George.'

The relationship recovered but I regret having locked George Devine into my spleen. He was a kindly man to whom I owed a lot, and who had merely made a legitimate observation about a future theatre it was his right to hope for. I regret, too, using a lazy and meaningless adjective like 'smoothy' and have since come to despise such cosy short cuts to nowhere: 'smoothy', 'trendy', 'arty', 'egghead', 'pinkos', 'do-gooders', 'chattering classes', 'armchair philosophers', 'pseudos', 'whingers' . . .

Those who use them, mistrust them.

The saga

It was this, and it tested loyalty.

The first hint came in a letter from John, undated, on English Stage company paper. It must have been written early May 1958 (what surprises me is that no reference to the 'saga' appears in any of my letters to Dusty):

> Dear Arnold
>
> I haven't seen you for far too long. I haven't even thanked you for the present which I treasure very much. I long to see you again. I'm in the midst of deep trouble about which I will tell you when we meet again, let it be soon.
>
> How are the rewrites going, do let me see them when they are done and before the others.
>
> Tony sends his love, he is off to Brussels today, for a few days, are you in Norfolk or London? Drop me a line care of the above.
>
> Much love

Sometime in the autumn of 1958 John was summoned to Bow Street Magistrates' Court on a charge of molesting a minor – a young boy in a play he'd been directing who had told his parents who had told the police. He was sentenced to six months in Wormwood Scrubs which put paid to any plans for reviving *Chicken Soup*.

Wolf Mankowitz offered to remount with a new director. I declined, saying I wanted to wait for John. Mankowitz's enthusiasm subsided in that quiet ebbing way that occurs so frequently in the theatre.

Plans for our wedding were made before John was hauled off behind bars. Dates couldn't be changed. By the time he was released we were living in our first flat, a rented basement at 15 Clapton Common, spacious and full of ugly but useful 1930s furniture which we had to buy for £100 (not bad for a complete home) from Mrs Wilton, the neurotic, red-haired, heavily made-up landlady who seemed to live in a dressing gown and was constantly upbraiding us for something or other while plying us with dishes she'd cooked that day. Her speciality, like mother Bicker, was trifle. She meticulously put together layer upon layer of jelly, sponge, cream, chocolate, blancmange, custard, nuts . . . and she had a tiny husband upon whom she heaped the contempt of her betrayed womanhood.

When John came out I met him at the prison gates and brought him back to live with us for six weeks. I can find only one letter from him written to us from the Scrubs. Dated 16 December 1958. But, before I quote it, there's the *Roots* front to sketch in.

Roots *and rejection*

Tony Richardson, assistant artistic director to George Devine, took me to lunch in the restaurant used by the Court's crowd – Au Père de Nico. Dexter mentions it in his autobiography. The first time, possibly, I was taken to a 'posh' eating place of the 'artistic' kind. Tony enjoyed introducing me to one of the corners of Chelsea's sophisticated life. Surprising, now I come to think of it, that having worked in restaurants I'd not heard of or tasted an avocado pear, but I hadn't. He recommended I try it. I did. I think he thought he was corrupting me.

We talked about a future. *Chicken Soup* had been accepted for a

July week at the Court in their 'Festival of Repertory Theatres' and now Tony wanted to know if I was planning another play. I was, about a farm labourer's daughter who returns home after living in London with her Jewish boyfriend. In a letter dated 30 May to Dusty on her twenty-second birthday, I had given more thought to it:

> In the Norfolk play . . . I'm spoken about all the time but I never appear. In the play I fail to turn up – ever, and after some terrible misery and 'There I told you so' from the family you turn round and say, 'So what! I do not need him now! I'm better than I thought I was and I do not need him now!' And the triumph of the play is not my triumph but yours. The intellectual has betrayed but the ordinary girl has found her own voice, her own language. Funny that, the triumph of *Chicken Soup* is also not my triumph but my mother's. I wonder why . . .

On 20 March 1958 Tony wrote offering a £25 option 'for your next play – the Norfolk one you outlined to me . . . a minimum amount but standard for all the plays we have commissioned . . .' Commission! Production! Bursary! and ten days later George Devine wrote to invite me to join the next Writers' Discussion Group. Giddy, giddy times.

Unlike many writers who complain they dread writing, that they must drag themselves to the desk, that it is all sweat and tears, blood and pain, it is not so for me. Or rather, yes, all those things, but as with the pleasures of sex they are part of the giddy times. Through the letters from Beck Farm looms the hazy shape of the play that was to become *Roots*.

5th June
. . . In ten days time I am leaving for Beck Farm. I must write to Mother [Bicker] and send her some money and instructions for newspapers. I'll send her £20 I think. That will be £10 for my board for four weeks and £10 I'll ask her to keep aside for me . . .

13th June

. . . I have only £5 left in the bank – still it was fun while it lasted. I think I shall pay Maurice 25/- to take me all the way to Beck Farm. With buses still on strike and having to get me a taxi from Diss it will be worth it. From door to door . . .

16th June

. . . I am still in London waiting for Maurice to take me early in the morning when I am mentally geared up to be in Norfolk. I feel as though I should not be here. Strange feeling, and to add to that feeling is a sort of dread of going to Norfolk and staying there without you – the thought of it makes me feel lost and somewhat lonely. Suppose I shall be all right once I am there. I don't really want to write this play – I'm a little terrified to start. Still, they say that all artists approach their new work like that . . . I have not written for so long – a year. But Lindsay tells me he has not shot a film for the last two and a half years! . . .

17th June [from Beck Farm]

I'm here. Maurice and I got up at 6 this morning and left London by seven. At 9.30 we had arrived in the house to be greeted by Ma Bicker and Joy with little Susan . . . Mother cooked us a breakfast of bacon and eggs and Maurice left by 10.45 . . .

It does not seem so strange me sitting here, in the front room, typing. Mother is laying the table for dinner in the kitchen and it is only 12 o'clock . . .

. . . I brought three of your paintings here for the family to· see. The copy.of the Van Gogh – which Joy and Ma like, the jazz band one in red, blue and white, and the two standing figures in green, red and blue. They didn't quite know what to say but I know they liked them – if only for the colours. I just asked Ma if she could live with a couple of them in the room and she said 'That would make no difference to me.' . . .

You know what we have for dinner? Pheasant! 'You write and tell Doreen that you're having pheasant, she could do things with that now I bet . . . that'll make her mouth water if that don' do anything else!' Of course *I* can hardly move – we had it with boiled potatoes and runner beans and Yorkshire pudding – followed by trifle . . .

18th June

Up at six this morning, had breakfast and joined Father Bicker down on the farm, fed the pigs – the pigs! – mucked them out and loaded fifty pigs on to a van to be shifted. Should have seen us. Home now for lunch and when I have typed this I'm away again to Gaudy Hall. [Name of the farm where Father Bicker worked.] The sun is shining and hot and slowly slowly I'm turning brown . . .

. . . I have just called Mother in to look at the typewriter and she is standing over me to see how the contraption works, so I am putting on my best speed and trying to make something up – anything, so that I can type for her and show how it goes . . .

19th June

Good morning good morning good morning – darling

I won 1/3d and a few queer looks at the whist drive last night. My number was 156 to Mother's 137 – I could play the game all right, it is simple enough, but what buggered me was remembering what to do, where to move, what to write down, who deals first and who leads out. My, that was a quaint collection of old dears in the parish hall wasn't it? There was a fellow there called Arthur Bryant, I sat alongside of him for the knock-out. He started talking to me in a manner that was faintly familiar, and then we went for a drink before going home and I went to the toilet first. He followed me and spoke about when I was coming again and that he and I should go to the pictures together and – Christ! I knew, he was a queer. When we sat in the taxi that old bugger ran his finger down my back and I couldn't do anything. I didn't want to say anything to Mother at first because I thought she might be his special friend and might be offended. But she happened to say in passing that she knew he was a cissy so I told her right out he was a homosexual and was gunning for me. She laughed. And Pop laughed. It'll be the standing joke of the family now . . .

. . . Father Bicker was up most of the night helping two old sows give birth. He'll be tired today. He does work hard. The funny thing was how Mother was telling how some people don't think he works so hard and she was adding how he had offered to swap places with them. And then when I was discussing this with Joy she told me how Mother don't think he work hard! Your mother is a strange woman, she talks to you as though she were making a political speech. And when she tells a story she acts all the parts with such gusto that I feel sure she would have made a good dramatic actress. I find her stories entertaining though, except when she repeats them. And how she hops from one anecdote to another . . .

20th June

The Norfolk play is beginning to take shape in my mind. I can see it a little more clearly now, I think I would like to start on the first act – perhaps I shall this afternoon when your mother goes into Harleston to post these letters. That would be wonderful if I managed to get the outline down of the first act . . .

. . . This morning she (Mother) asked Gully [Poppy Bicker] if he wanted a bath and he said yes, so she said to him he could have one after me. 'I don't mind that,' he said to me, 'as long as you don't shit in it so's it stick to me and I can't get it off.' That's a sign I am being treated as one of the family, isn't it? I couldn't quite make out whether Mother Bicker was embarrassed for me or not. He doesn't swear any more than Ann Jellicoe or Miriam or any of the other Court people do. That is something you shall have to get used to when we meet them – Lindsay too, they swear like troopers. I think it is slightly affectation with them though . . .

I started to write, as hoped, the play first entitled *Not Only the Corn* and fortunately renamed *Roots*. From the start it was to be about a girl whose boyfriend never turned up, for certain, that. And just as certain – the shock would lead to self-discovery. But what I was as excitedly eager to capture as much as anything was the slow pace of pause and silence in Norfolk rural life. Stage directions read:

This is a silence that needs organising. Throughout the play there is no sign of intense living from any of the characters – Beatie's bursts are the exception. They continue in a routine rural manner. The day comes, one sleeps at night, there is always the winter, the spring, the autumn, and the summer – little amazes them. They talk in fits and starts mainly as a sort of gossip, and they talk quickly too, enacting as though for an audience what they say. Their sense of

humour is keen and dry. They show no affection for each other –
though this does not mean they would not be upset were one of
them to die. The silences are important, as important as the way
they speak, if we are to know them.

Many moments would have to be concocted – like the intimate conversations between Beatie and her sister Jenny; the quarrel between
Beatie and Jenny's husband, Jimmy; Beatie's dance to Bizet's *L'Arlésienne* suite at the end of Act II. But the stories told by Mrs Bryant
would, I knew, be those I'd heard and noted down from Mother
Bicker, while other moments would come from my relationship
with Dusty. One of her dreams became the dream in Act II. The
lovely moment when Beatie looks at herself in the mirror after her
bath and observes:

> Isn't your nose a funny thing, and your ears. And your arms and
> your legs, aren't they funny things – sticking out of a lump –

is a Dusty moment. But the denouement is concocted. The tea
party, the family's confusion, the mother's wrath and Beatie's last
hosanna speech are pure imagination, except for one element: I *did*
write a letter to Dusty saying our relationship should end, but she
ignored it and replied asking me to pack and post a parcel of
selected Jewish deli foods. I think that response of cheerful insouciance as much as any other aspect of her character suggested to
me we could be lifelong partners. But cheerful insouciance is
charming not dramatic. Lindsay Anderson once said, or wrote, that
art is not only about what is, but what could be. This ending was to
be about what could be, and, with sad irony, in the way life frequently follows art, the split between the real-life Beatie Bryant and
Ronnie Kahn took place more than thirty years later. Dusty and I
are apart. The shock did not release her voice as it did for Beatie in
Roots – she had found that gradually through the years of our marriage. What has happened now, it could be said, is that her 'voice'
has gone into high gear!

I seem to remember *Roots* taking about three months to complete. By the end of August 1958 it must have been in the hands of Devine and Richardson. I was excited by its structure – a collection of moments juxtaposed in a way I thought added up to poetic impact. It was not a play of action, drama did not reside in the Aristotelian tradition of cause and effect, but in expectation. An event of great importance – not social or political importance, but personal importance – was about to take place: Beatie's lover was coming to meet the family. He was described, imitated, quoted, talked about, made fun of – and eagerly awaited. He stayed away. Instead a letter arrived saying he didn't think the relationship would work. The effect upon Beatie and her family is at first numbing then humiliating. They are incensed to have been left standing like fools. The ensuing anger with which they turn on her, her self-defence, her halting, hesitant stumble upon fluency, deliriously reaching high C, all take up the last fifteen minutes of the play. George and Tony turned it down.

Was I told over a lunch at Au Père de Nico's in between an avocado and zabaglione? Across a desk in Tony's office? I can't remember. I remember only the gist of what was explained: they were disappointed. Disappointed but – they had suggestions. They felt, quite rightly, that nothing really happened in the first two acts and their suggestion was: combine the first and second act into one act; make Act III into Act II; and write a new third act in which the London lover, Ronnie, appeared. After all, they reasoned most reasonably, everyone in the audience would by now be so keyed up and curious about this boy they would want to see him, witness his impact upon the family who had been driven mad about the proclaimed virtues of his, to them, quite odd personality.

I said I would think about it, and did, though not for long nor, I suspect, seriously. I knew the value of what I'd written. These brilliant men of the theatre had missed the point. Their suggestions had shocked me with their banality. I rejected them and prepared to face the end of my career as a playwright.

Arnold Wesker

Roots – *the performance*

Something of the English Stage Company's chain of decision-making needs to be described, at least as it was described to me. The decision about which plays to mount belonged to the artistic direction: George and Tony. It might be a play either of them wanted to direct, or one they wanted to see directed because a reader or an associate director like Keith Johnstone or Bill Gaskill had argued for it. A play under consideration was given to council members to read. They had to approve, no decision to go ahead was taken without them. But the artistic direction didn't have to seek approval to turn down a play they considered of no merit.

Roots was turned down while still being read by council members, one of whom was Dame Peggy Ashcroft. She not only admired the play but recognised it immediately as a role for Joan Plowright. Joan read it and announced she would play the role any where. George advised that the role would not enhance her career and attempted to dissuade her. The council's chairman, Neville Blond, argued that George should let Joan follow her own instincts. Brian Bailey of the Belgrade had by now read the play and was clamouring for the rights. What did John think? Poor John was languishing in Wormwood Scrubs out of it all. His letter, the only one I have from the wormy hole, pulls many things together.

From 2953 Dexter,

HM Prison
Wormwood Scrubs
16th December 1958

Both dears,

So you are joining the long procession of people who are going to write a musical that Jock Addison is doing the music for and which Tony is going to direct.

John O and Mike Hastings both fell victims to Tony's 'you must write a marvellous musical'. The scripts are still unproduced. John O fortunately had enough backing to put it on his own, Mike is lumbered with a script called *Fairy Story* – another victim in Tony's quest for new worlds to conquer! It isn't a question of your being able to 'handle' Tony, but of the thing going on at all!

As far as *Chicken Soup* is concerned GD has got to be told to either piss or get off the pot! I never really thought they intended to do it. It was, like the promise of the musical, a sop to keep you happy. They are as wily as a couple of conmen and they ought to be doing time. As people I am devoted to them both, as professionals I'd like to blast them out of the theatre.

Look here, I want to direct *Roots* [and] – *Home is Where You Live* [my musical]. I don't have to read it, I know you, I know the subject. If I had a cheque book I'd reach for it. Let's go to Coventry and use our kind of actors – (Alfie [Lynch] and Patsy Byrne for instance). I have more pleasure in remembering *Chicken Soup* than in anything I have ever done in my life . . . one of those absolutely enchanted times, when time and place perfectly cohered. If Bryan wants it, try to wait for me.

Now then, my return to life. Half of me wants and wants to come to you and Dusty for shelter, the other half thinks I ought to be strong. Give me a little more time (God how I get tears in my eyes if I remember those weeks in Coventry, your cooking, the swimming, the arguments, the demented lady visitor and that perfect play . . .) . . . John Osborne wanted to know if it was worth going into the nick to find out that people cared. My answer is – for *me*: yes . . .

I love you very much, and in you – Dusty, your mother, Ralph and Della. For the first time in my life there are twenty-six people I love to a point just this side of distraction. Write again if you can.

A sharp contrast to the last letter he wrote me twenty-two years later at the end of an acrimonious exchange which began with me begging him to redirect my new version of *Shylock* (still called *The Merchant* in those days) at the National Theatre.

Dear Arnold

I have received what I presume to be a photocopy of your letter of 22nd May. The delay in answering is explained by the fact that I have been in England for the last 4 weeks [I'd written to him at the Met in New York], and my secretary has been on holiday.

I signed my letter 'sincerely' and I meant sincerely. Since I no longer read your letters accurately any more than you can read mine with understanding, I think the correspondence should come to an end. For reasons so complex that, lacking your facility with words, I find it impossible to explain them, I do not wish to direct THE MERCHANT. Please let us leave it at that.

Yours, with as much sincerity as I can summon up,

John

Between those two letters had been done a lot of living, 95% of it apart but 5% very very close and intense.

Prison was the only time John allowed himself to be at the mercy of anyone or any institution. He learned a lesson early which, as I'd hinted, I learned too late: secure a power base. It's easier for a director to do this than a writer. Only five come to mind – Shakespeare, Molière, Brecht, Neil Simon, Alan Ayckbourn. The power base he always longed for was the Royal Court. He would have made of it something extraordinary. On 18 January 1977 he wrote to me:

> . . . I have learned that to direct plays is not enough. One must, in order to achieve anything approaching perfection, control all of the elements: promotion, building, budget, even the choice of carpenter and costume workshop, and become, in effect, producer as well as director. The results of this have always been, if not perfection, at least on-budget and efficient and sometimes original.

The Court was denied him. He was instrumental in creating the company at the National Theatre – for which, reading between the lines of his autobiography, he got little thanks – and became artistic director of the Metropolitan Opera Company, a position fraught with conflicts. Wherever he alighted he made his mark but perhaps – playing on his autobiography's title, *The Honourable Beast* – there was more beast in him than honour and so, little was entrusted him.

Sometime in the middle of March, it must have been, I met John out of prison with our first car, a second-hand Hillman Minx, convertible, and took him home to Clapton Common where, as we know, he was fussed over and looked after for six weeks till his spirits recovered and he began sorting out his life. Dusty was working behind the counter at Sainsbury's in Mare Street, Hackney, for £3 10s. a week, and I was still having to help Ralph in his basement workshop to top up our weekly earnings. John couldn't wait to read *Roots*. I have the sharpest memory returning from work – it must have been the evening of the same day – to an excited ex-con who leapt into my arms declaring how wonderful the play was, that it didn't need changing as Tony and George had suggested and that he knew exactly how to handle it.

He at once began assembling the elements to make *Roots* work. The Court didn't want it? Right, Brian Bailey did – we'd go to Coventry, this time to enjoy the luxury of three weeks' rehearsal instead of two. Joan Plowright said she would do it anywhere? Splendid – we'll get her to Coventry. And there was this clever designer, a woman, tall, lean and beautiful – the daughter of the eminent writer and independent member of parliament, Sir Alan Herbert, 'Herbert' a name with ancient lineage – who had been a scene painter at the Court and had just been given her first chance by George to design Tony Richardson's production of *The Chairs* by one of John Osborne's dreaded French writers – Ionesco. Her second design project was John Dexter's production of the Yeats play *Purgatory*. They had obviously worked well together and, like Joan Plowright, Jocelyn Herbert was a star in the making. From *The Honourable Beast*:

> When I joined the Royal Court, Jocelyn Herbert was one of the staff painters and our conversations were largely practical; she talked my language, which was more than most people there did. I saw Ionesco's *The Chairs* which she designed, and had watched her in the workshop, and then I asked her to do *Purgatory*.
>
> I came from weekly rep where you had a limited number of flats which are painted and overpainted until the paint flakes off, so the design ideas at the Court were new to me. I wanted to get away from naturalism and realism. I did two Sunday night productions without décor: *Yes and After*, with a stripped-down stage, and *The*

Kitchen, and these pointed me in the direction of provoking the audience to think for themselves and use their imagination.

The difference between working with Jocelyn and another designer is the 'rightness' of everything. One never has the feeling that she is trying to impose her design personality on a play – that, of course, comes through anyway – nor is she trying to make a design statement. The design is always at the service of the play. If Jocelyn likes what I'm doing, it's reassuring. If she doesn't, I question what I've done.

But I knew nothing of such things. I had only just been spotted, was still hovering on the fringes, unworldly as ever and, compared to John, an outsider to the theatre in general, and to the coming, goings, and politics of the Royal Court in particular. John was political in the real sense – he calculated, weighed reputations, smelt the wind. His energy like mine was boundless. We were a match. We complemented one another. I was talented but innocent, he was skilful and wily. I suspect had I been gay we would have become lovers.

This is what I remember. Dusty and I took Jocelyn to Norfolk. She wanted to see the settings on which I had based the play. John did *not*! Joan Plowright pointed to half a page in one act and suggested it really belonged to another. She was right. John decided that real liver and onions had to be fried on stage. 'It was,' he recorded, 'a practical problem of how long it needed to cook and serve and eat it . . .' The front rows gasped at the smell that wafted towards them as soon as the curtain went up. The major problem was pace. John's instructions to the cast were firm and clear: 'Don't be rushed. You'll hear shuffling, coughing – ignore it. *Dictate* the pace, they will accept it . . .' There may have been disagreements here and there between us, none stick in memory. We shared, and communicated it to the cast, a sense of being involved in something special. It was partly to do with the outrageousness of the play's rhythm but also to do with high points. For example: a long, delicate, incredible curve had to be carefully stretched from that very very slow beginning across three scenes to the end of Act II and the exultant Bizet dance. We felt ourselves in possession of an experience in the theatre which, if we could pull it off, would be unique, dynamic.

What I see as plainly as yesterday is that first night – 25 May, the day after my twenty-seventh birthday, five days before Dusty's twenty-third – John on my left, Dusty on my right, sitting dead centre in the front row of the balcony at the Belgrade. The opening was breathtakingly slow. Patsy Byrne, solid, experienced, intelligent, trusting utterly in the play and John's direction, called to her child offstage, waited, went into her, moved slowly back into the room, returned to her frying pan, and cooked. Charlie Kay took his time coming in from work, placing his bike in the front room, arching his back with pain. Patsy looked at him for a long time, watching, before asking: 'Waas matter wi' you then?' Slowly they built up the exchange that was to become the running joke in the play about Mother Bryant saying the pain in his back was due to indigestion.

JIMMY   Don't be daft.

JENNY   That's what I say. Blast, Mother, I say, you don't git indigestion in the back. Don't you tell me, she say, I hed it!

JIMMY   What heven't she hed?

On which line the audience laughed. As we had hoped, planned, plotted, schemed, rehearsed day after intense day! The actors had captured and held them. John's hand reached to clutch mine. 'They've done it,' he whispered. When I turned to nod and share the moment, I saw – he had tears in his eyes.

The applause, after Beatie's dance – scattily and touchingly danced by Joan in a mixture of hornpipe and impromptu nothing-steps sending shivers down our backs – was a great whoop of joy. By the end – after Gwen Nelson's poignant defence of Mother Bryant, and Joan's amazed, triumphant discovery that she was no longer quoting someone else but using her own words – we knew we had brought it off.

The next morning disparate groups of actors, friends, theatre staff assembled in the Belgrade's restaurant upstairs to pore over enthusiastic reviews. The buzz of excitement flew from table to table and as I sat with my family I could see George Devine and Brian Bailey, their heads down and huddled, negotiating a deal to transfer our production to the Royal Court. Brian Bailey was killed not long afterwards in a motor accident on the first of the nation's motorways – the M1 from London to Coventry, a development rendering the city an industrial base of huge value. It just cost them one of their newest sons. Brian fell asleep at the wheel. Overworked. Overenthusiastic.

The London reviews were even more ecstatic. Milton Shulman in the *Evening Standard* begged audiences to see the play. Ken Tynan, unprecedented for a critic, came out of the theatre in a state of such euphoria that he had to telephone and congratulate me. Giddy, giddy times, Mother, until –

The play opened at the Royal Court on 30 June. A month later, 30 July, it transferred to the Duke of York on St Martin's Lane during one of the hottest summers on record. Bernard Levin writing in the *Daily Express* claimed: 'I have now seen this great, shining play three times, and it seems to have grown visibly in stature each time . . .' It didn't help. Audiences stayed away. The play had to be taken off long before anticipated. It was the first of the gods' mean sports with me.

When the play was first published at the end of 1959, a volume on its own, by Penguin Books, I signed and placed a copy in a plastic wrapping and gave it to Mother Bicker, who by then was my mother-in-law. It remained in its wrapping for years. She left it lying around on the window ledge for neighbours to see. I don't think she ever read it.

Harold – an aside

Harold Pinter and I have this curious parallel career: our schools were round the corner from each other in Hackney – Grocers

Grammar and Upton House Central. When I was fifteen I had watched him perform Macbeth in his school production. We had applied at the same time for RADA – which we both gained entrance to – and then for LCC grants – which he obtained and I didn't. In February 1960 I was asked to review the first publication of *The Birthday Party* in the theatre magazine *Encore*. I defended the play but worried over its coy avoidance of the Jewish milieu against which it made most sense; as I'd worried over Peter Shaffer's similar veiling of a family so obviously Jewish in *Five Finger Exercise*. Arthur Miller and Neil Simon do it, too, disavow their sources – unlike the Irish, the Russians, the French, the Asians. Curious to me.

One day, as I was coming away from a rehearsal of the Trilogy at the Court which Pinter had been watching from the back of the stalls, he stopped me to express admiration of the plays and remind me that, as an actor who was Jewish, mine were just the sort of plays he enjoyed performing in. Two years later, 1962, recognition had come to him after a scathing launch. In July of that year I had a photographic session with Cecil Beaton in which he made me jump up and down against a white backcloth. As I left, the next 'personality' was waiting his turn to be done over. It was Harold. I warned him of the antics he was about to be put through.

My diary records encounters with him. I found him a touching mixture of warm, bewildered, astute and familiarly Jewish, of a type: streetwise, on the attack before attacked, slightly lumpen and steam-rollering, but on the side of the angels without quite knowing how to handle them. One encounter, over the Zlotnick affair, confirmed my view of him as a naturalist writer of what is absurd in reality. I had been asked to assist a campaign to get a Soviet sculptor out of prison and had written to Pinter, Graham Greene, John Mortimer, and David Mercer for signatures to a protesting letter to the Soviet Embassy.

14th December 1971
The Zlotnick affair continues. I sent off the final letter to Graham Greene in France, it came back very creased, so I ironed it out over

brown paper transferring, in the process, some light brown stains which added 'antiquity' to the 'dignity' of vellum-type paper. Then posted it to Osborne – Mikki [my secretary] sent it to the wrong address which delayed it by about ten days so I decided to take it round personally to the other three. Rang Pinter, Mercer and Mortimer last night to make dates for 10 a.m., 10.30 and 11 a.m. this morning.

Arrived at Pinter's beautiful terrace house in Regent's Park at about 9.50. Outside was a laundry bag. I was dressed in jeans, white aran sweater and Swedish snow boots. Rang the bell and a female voice came down the electric chute. 'Is that Vivien?' I asked. No, they said. Vivien is coming down, at which second Vivien opened the door. She was dressed in a black blouse and long black skirt. Her face looked worn, eyes pouchy; powdered and startled – but through the mad staring eyes was a Jewish beauty. [Discovered since that she isn't Jewish!] I had a feeling this woman would go mad one day, or very eccentric and wild. She obviously didn't recognise me at once, but I moved into the house with the authority of one expected and said:

'Oh, they said you were coming down.

'No,' she replied in confusion. 'I'm down.'

Once I pointed out I'd come to collect Harold's signature she registered me and glided into the kitchen. I followed into the front room, alongside the kitchen, and Harold soon came down. We shook warmly and he said how nice it was to see me, but he too didn't seem quite used to the world – though I guess he'd been at work with his secretary. I showed him the letter which he read through while I watched the odd Vivien wiping down the kitchen table and muttering:

'I never know what goes on in this house, no one tells me anything. I nearly gave him the laundry.'

It was extraordinary how uneasy I felt. No sense of welcome, no offer of a cup of coffee, no pen to sign with. Then a few words about how was my new play coming on – was I going to direct it?

'No,' I said. 'I was rather put off by my last production [*The Friends*]. Don't really like the theatre. I wish I could do something else.' No laughter or query, just a faint, uncertain smile. At the door he looked at the grey day and said he was off to see his mother and father in Brighton.

'That should be bracing,' I said.

A most anxious encounter of which I have the clearest impression of having no clear, full-blooded impression, simply a series of disjointed images: Harold turning around to ask for a pen, looking for somewhere to lean, Vivien's wide, uncomprehending eyes, her bending over the table, Harold seeming not in the world, Vivien seeming quite out of it.

The years passed and our separate images appeared to merge into a composite singular one of 'the Jewish playwright from Hackney' – I once received a letter addressed to Harold Wesker. Or was it Arnold Pinter? It was not for me. I forwarded it with instructions I thought would help the post office find him.

Harold doesn't live here. Hasn't for years. Arnold does. Not Harold. In fact, I don't think he ever has. Lived here. Harold.

On a certain first night, I can't remember of whose play, a now deceased theatre critic sat in front of me and turned to ask:

'Hello, Bernard, anything new on the stocks?' I was being confused for Bernard Kops on this occasion – Jews! they all look alike. I stammered a correction.

'I think you're confusing me for –'

The critic interrupted to offer an embarrassed apology. 'Oh, Harold, I'm so sorry.'

It was when, at a British Council function in Italy, someone asked me was I still married to Lady Antonia Fraser that I considered it time to write to Harold, list the years' confusions, and ask: 'What am I doing wrong?' He didn't respond. I hope he smiled.

Dusty's ferment

We shift back a little in time.

Dusty's abortion was traumatic for us both. I felt guilty and responsible; Dusty felt torn between an inborn restlessness,

Arnold Wesker

wanderlust, a devilish curiosity about what else lived out there apart
from emotional Jews, yackety-yak young students endlessly discussing she knew not what, a boyfriend overexcited by a lick and a
promise made on a four-day march from Aldermaston to London;
and her wish to settle and have babies. There were tensions. My
letters to her remind me. They also, to an extent, must have created
them, filled as they were with reports of a new life.

The range of interests, the level of articulation, the intellectual
ferment surrounding me – rough and deficient by rigorous academic standards though they were – intimidated her, unnerved her
with a sense of inadequacy she had never before encountered. Dusty's world had been pleasantly small and manageable. She had
excelled in it. An old schoolfriend of hers told me in later years that
she was nicknamed 'Bossy Boots' (or was it 'Bossy Pants'?), used to
having her own way. Now, in self-defence against this gold rush of
lively youth with strange intellectual appetites, she substituted sarcasm, stubbornness, and sourness for participation. She was as yet
outside that 'shared cultural framework'. It would be entered in
time; in time she would develop a sharp and critical intelligence of
her own, rich curiosities, informed tastes, and a perception of
people I was frequently to depend upon. But in those rough'n'raw
days we quarrelled with antagonistic impatience. Beatie Bryant explains to her sister, Jenny:

> I sit with Ronnie and his friends sometimes and I listen to them talk
> about things and you know I've never heard half of the words before
> . . . I get annoyed when he keep tellin' me what they mean – an' he
> want me to ask. 'Always ask, people love to tell you what they know,
> always ask and people will respect you' . . . I don't! An' you know
> why? Because I'm stubborn, I'm like Mother, I'm stubborn. Some-
> how I just can't bring myself to ask, and you know what? I go mad
> when I listen to them. As soon as they start to talk about things I
> don't know about or I can't understand I get mad. They sit there,
> casually talking, and suddenly they turn on you, abrupt. 'Don't you
> think?' they say. Like at school, pick on you and ask a question you
> ent ready for. Sometimes I don't say anything, sometimes I go to

663

bed or leave the room . . . An' he get mad. 'Why don't you ask me woman, for God's sake why don't you ask me? Aren't I dying to tell you about things? Only ask?'

The Dusty of today is another person. Though some of the sour stubbornness remains she is sophisticated, confident, capable, with a vast range of cultural appetites all her own. But in those days she was at war with herself. And me. It clouded the future which, being so uncertain, she opted not to confront, and for this reason went to work a season as a waitress in Billy Butlin's holiday camp in Skegness, away from it all. Of course, once gone, only the best memories remained. We missed one another acutely. Parting distressed us.

I wrote as soon as I returned to Weald Square from seeing her off at King's Cross coach station. It had been a bleak Sunday send-off.

4 May '58 7.45 p.m.
Darling
    Just back – Jesus! We must not do this too often. What a face you had as the bus passed me. You held your hand to your mouth as tho' you were going to be sick. And now I'm back and I look at the room we shared . . .
    . . . What a ridiculous situation this is. The dog [Patch, belonging to Della and Ralph] is curled up at my side. Mother has started sweeping the house out – now! at 8 in the evening! And you're on your way home. If I keep on writing I don't think of you, as soon as I stop I shall brood . . .

I wrote again on the 6th, the 9th, 11th, 15th . . . Nine letters in May, seventeen in June, nine in July, interrupted by a brief coming together for the first night of *Chicken Soup*. And she replied, as copiously.

Before going to Skegness Dusty spent a month at Beck Farm. It was an unsettling time for her there – wrenched out of one milieu, not fully in to another. After life in London and Paris, however much she balked against those emotional Jews, the energy crackling from new young friends – incomprehensible though much of it was – she was nevertheless slowly becoming part of it; films, plays, concerts – all set her alight, got under her skin, was making her sparkle. She didn't know it – how could she – but she was writhing and stretching in the throes of a cultural metamorphosis: demanding, aggravating, exhilarating, frustrating, stimulating, infuriating. Of *course* Norfolk and her good family must now have seemed unsatisfying. 'These people,' she wrote, 'mean less and less to me', though with the passing of the years and a growing confidence in herself they came to mean more and more, especially her mother, a battler, fiercely independent, whom she increasingly comes to resemble and for whom Dusty is now the apple of her eye. 'The apple,' said Mrs Bryant, 'don't fall far from the tree – that it don't.' Once again life moves helplessly behind art.

One of the curious memories I have of the early Dusty is her reluctance to call me 'darling' – not a common form of endearment in her family. From me to Dusty on my twenty-sixth birthday:

> . . . The food is in us, we relaxed round the table while the children [Della's children, Adam and Miles] climbed acrobatically over cousin Ralph. We talked about my article, and now Della has Ralph stripped to the waist on the divan and is massaging him while Mum washes up and talks to old Annie [one of her friends]. Suddenly I imagine you coming in. What would happen? This: I would be all over you hoping to get a large greeting, but you would probably offer me your cheek and look flustered and say hello to everyone and ignore me. And I would go all cold because you had come in so tight and frightened . . . Or would you bounce in and straight into my arms and ignore everyone else? That would embarrass you too much wouldn't it, you would be frightened of looking silly. Fear! We would have had less quarrels had it not been for your fear and obstinacy.

The emotionalism she encountered among the Weskers and Perlmutters was not easy for her to accommodate – though once she did, she became more Catholic than the Pope. *Love Letters on Blue Paper* contains a portrait of Dusty as an older woman, Sonia, written long before she'd aged. Sonia writes letters to a husband she knows is dying but who doesn't know she knows. In them she reminds him of their life together. It is a way of helping him face death.

When we first met I was really plain. Plain-minded I mean, not looking. I was pretty-looking but I felt daft saying darling and sweetheart and those things. Took me about two years before I could bring myself to call you any but your name. And I only gave in because you bullied me. Got proper annoyed in fact. You *made* me say the word, forced me. Remember? I do. It was after we'd been to have tea with my grandmother. A Sunday afternoon. One of those big spreads. Everything thrown on the table, you know, from home-made pickled onions to thick old crusty rhubarb pies. And she was making her usual fuss of me. Adored me she did and I did her too, and she was teasing me and saying 'She's a little darling, *isn't* she a little darling? She's *my* little darling.' And when we walked home you turned on me and said, 'She can say the word why can't you?' 'What word?' I asked. 'Darling!' you yelled. 'Go on, say it!' You *did* look funny, your face all angry while your mouth was saying words of loving. Didn't go together somehow. '*Say darling*,' you shouted at me and made me giggle. And the more I giggled the more angry you got. But you won, you made me say it. 'Darling!', 'Sweetheart Victor', 'dearest Victor', 'darling Victor', 'darling, darling' and 'my heart'. I was remembering. Just today. For no reason. While I was outside cleaning the windows.

Dusty had a mixed time in Skegness. My letters, as I've suggested, couldn't have helped, making her restless and aware of all that was going on in the big city. On 20 May thousands were called to the House of Commons by CND for a mass lobbying of MPs against nuclear weapons.

. . . Dai and I were two of hundreds of stewards and marshals. What a set-up . . . My job was to go to Pioneer House and pick up a wreath to be taken to St Martin-in-the-Fields where forty-two clergymen – including two rabbis, one friar and an RC bishop among others – were waiting to take it to the Cenotaph. The place was covered by press photographers and cameramen. The clergy walked in twos on the pavement dressed in full regalia. You know the rule – that there must be no procession or march within a mile of Parliament. Unfortunately I had to leave at 7.30 in order to get back for rehearsals [for the play I was directing at Primrose Youth Club] so I do not know how many eventually turned up . . .

2nd June 1958

. . . in the evening went to theatre workshop to see *Taste of Honey* by the young girl from Salford (nineteen years old). I'm still under the blow of it. Not that it's a great play but – I don't know – it's about ordinary poeple from the north talking in everyday language. The mother is a tart who goes off with a drunkard, the girl becomes pregnant by a coloured sailor and later sets up house with an art student who is a homosexual and who later leaves to make room for the mother who returns. It sounds gory and nasty but all these characters are treated as real human beings who laugh, have a little wisdom, like living, are warm and friendly but who somehow can't really cope with their problems. They shout at each other, interrupt each other, talk to the audience – this seems on the way to be real theatre, not quite there but an eye-opener. A brilliant performance by a girl called Frances Cuka who is halfway between Julie Harris and (as Tynan says) Anne Mangnani . . .

. . . Sunday evening there was a special performance of *Flesh to a Tiger* for the Moscow Arts Theatre people followed by a party. The party lasted till 4.30 a.m. I met John Osborne and had a long chat with Doris Lessing who would like one day to open a restaurant. The coloured boys set to on the drums and Johnny Dankworth blew his tenor sax. Everyone danced and limboed – everyone that is except me. I tried to get Doris to limbo with me but she cannot dance and was too shy to try even with a novice like me. But Osborne is a lad. He had his eye on a coloured woman and my God he moved in and had her by the time the night was out. Ken Tynan and his wife [Elaine Dundy] were there – he left about one but his wife stayed to get plastered. At one point she was dancing with Osborne who had to spend most of his time stopping her from falling down. It was all a little obscene because she nearly raped him on the stage. She was sick in the toilet and finally John Dexter took her in hand and took her home where he left her in the throes of a large row with Ken. It was too late for me to get home so I spent the night in Bob Stephen's house – remember he was the actor who played the lead in *Epitaph for George Dillon*. They have a lovely house in Chelsea. I had spent most of my time in the stalls watching them all dance and thinking why the hell you weren't with me. When Ann Jellicoe looked at me inquiringly to ask why I was not dancing I said: 'It's me upbringing.' But she replied: 'I think it's because you haven't got a girl with you.' She was partly right of course but I also find that with so many people around nothing much happens except in a large loud way. Much sooner an intimate party of a dozen or so. There was a magnificent coloured singer there called Bertice [Reading] . . . with a shock of blonde dyed hair. She let rip on 'St Louis Blues' and was tremendous with zest and personality.

Reading about such experiences in which she was not sharing must have set up tensions between her and the other girls on the camp. Before the play had opened she was writing sour congratulations on my 'success'. What success? Nothing had yet happened! What was she saying? I understood perfectly well. She was feeling out of it.

14 June 1958
Hey, Dusty – darling . . .

   a letter came this morning – I suppose it was from you, it had love from Dusty written at the bottom. But it was a subdued letter, no sign of love or affection – not even a 'darling' to head the thing. Do you find it difficult to write the word, or difficult to feel it? Can Butlin's be murdering such a deep love so easily and so quickly and so thoroughly? Is it that or did one of the campers kiss you suddenly and you are ashamed about it . . . hey . . .

   I had supper with Bill Gaskill and Miriam and Tony Page in a wonderful Greek dive in Soho with a bottle of wine on the table – that was a different world – wasn't it? – but I immediately thought how you would love it there and do justice to a splendidly cooked meal, and what a pity it was that, now I had a little money in my pocket and did not worry about how much I was spending, you could not be with me. Is it such a different world there? But I accept what you say, and can only hope you are not too damaged – or are you discovering that you are happier? . . .

. . . We must handle our meeting in Coventry very carefully – I shan't be able to concentrate on rehearsals while waiting for you. Perhaps we should not write about our feelings to each other, just about what is happening to us, and leave the feelings to look after themselves when we meet. What do you think? Though I should want to know what and how you are feeling. I don't know, this letter is falling to pieces a bit. I'll write better from Norfolk . . .

On 5 June – a most momentous event:

> . . . I must tell you – as the first cheque for £25 arrived [commission for the 'Norfolk' play] so I've opened up a banking account complete with cheque book!! Big thrill! There's only £5 left – I have sent your mother £10 – still, I'm expecting another cheque this week . . . leaving on Monday for Norfolk.

Such 'thrills' didn't stop our relationship from wobbling. I struggled, with difficulty, to remain celibate, she – and who can blame her – took on some boyfriends. I was not aware of it at the time. Though my reason for going to Norfolk was to live with the characters of my Norfolk play, it was strange being in Dusty's home without her. I felt lonely to begin with.

> Sorry about the tips – I hate that you should be living a life that re-lies on other people's tips. I hope to God when we are married that you shall not have to work as a waitress. You shall stay at home and look after me and paint and entertain – or doesn't that picture appeal to you any more?
>
> Write to me, darling – don't let Butlin's swamp me out too much. Butlin's is everybody else's holiday, one cannot live a whole life in everybody else's holiday . . .

She too was feeling lonely and depressed. I'm not sure from this distance what we thought we were doing enduring such a separation. Yes, she had to earn money, yes, she was restless, yes, she wanted to travel, even if only up north; we'd also calculated that I was going to be tied up with preparations for rehearsing *Chicken Soup*, and those were the days before she had carved out her role as organiser of a playwright's hectic life full of first-night parties for the world and his wife. But so far? For so long?

After spending the first night together in Coventry and witnessing the success of my first play, life got into a gallop and my letters to her became more intense. On 20 July I wrote a long letter, from which I've already quoted, about *Chicken Soup with Barley* at the Court:

. . . the [ULR] audience responded in just the way I thought they would, in fact I must have written it with this audience in mind! I have not seen Uncle Perly yet, but speaking to Mum on the phone she tells me he is very thrilled – I'm surprised. I've letters from all sorts of odd and unexpected people – a man in Dublin who read the *Standard* critic [Milton Shulman] and now desperately wants to read the play: from Esther Lander's sister . . . from Judith's mother. The magazine *ENCORE* wants me to pose for a photograph for their front cover [with many of the other contemporary playwrights].

But – I still do not feel famous, or excited or anything, except terror that my next play will be no good or will never be written. All I want is you right now . . .

. . . if we meet in Norfolk, where shall we be able to devour each other? I suppose we shall have to rely on midnight strolls and the tall haystacks. Not very comfortable, but it will be a long time since we have made love by moonlight . . .

. . . I have been reading over your letters of the last few days – I do enjoy them and you say some wonderful things even though you have odd judgements. Dust – do you really think you will be able to cope with our married life? I mean all the people that may come or whom we may have to visit? And the times when I shall have to be doing things on my own, leaving you behind – staying away some

days. Christ I hope so – or it will be Hell for us both. We must try.
You shall have to be so much more tolerant than you have been –
I'm sure you will be – even with my family . . .

On 23 July I write expressing surprise that she didn't make the
effort to buy any Sunday papers to read the reviews, but I'm still
eager to fill her in with what's happening: an hour and a half session
with Wolf Mankowitz dazzles me with what he wants to do with
my work (but never gets around to doing). Meeting with Leon
Clore the film producer (and brother of Charles Clore who made
millions and paid for the Turner wing to the Tate Gallery). Doris
Lessing, Tom Maschler, Alex Jacobs and I are planning a Christmas revue for the Court. The talk thickens about bringing back
Chicken Soup some time in October/November. *Vogue* magazine
want an interview but can't reach me, as no one can because there's
no bloody phone in Weald Square! And I have to organise myself
to get to Norfolk to write the Norfolk play.

. . . Darling, I don't know what this means as regards us meeting
where. If by August 3rd I am still in London you must join me here
– if I am in Norfolk then you must join me *there*. OK? . . .
. . . Doris Lessing wants to know why we want to marry, why
don't we just live together she says. I tried to explain.
I have had a long letter from Uncle Perly who is very moved and
thrilled by the play and has sent me £25 as a token of esteem . . .

A card, 25 July:

. . . Will you be mine? I can't wait till you come back. I think about
you and love you and pray we make a go of it. We will. Forgive this
shabby card – but my love is not shabby.

On 29 July I sent a telegram from Upper Clapton post office to
'Dusty Bicker, Staff 460, Butlin's Holiday Camp, Skegness, Lincs.'

asking will she marry me. There was no immediate response, and she didn't keep the telegram. On 31 July I sent another asking:

Well will you marry me for Christ's sake. Wizzie.

She kept that one. It's before me now – covered in red lipstick kisses. She must have replied with a telegram because my next letter was written the following day.

Weald Square, 1 August 1958
My darling Mrs Wesker
    Thank you for having me. I promise to do my utmost to make you happy and see your life full and rich. Dates and details we shall discuss when you return – meanwhile here is an outline of what we are doing: you return on Wednesday 6th (don't forget to tell me what time). On the following Sunday we are going down to Beck Farm – the 10th. On 20th – ten days later – we shall be moving to Wacton where until the 6th September we shall be living and having full charge of the kids. Ralph will be in London and Della in Spain. After that we shall return to Beck Farm.
    Now the work I have to do is as follows. Before leaving London I must gather as many details as I can about the work of the NSPCC. In Norfolk I shall be working on the film script, some alterations to *Chicken Soup*, and the new play. What happens to *us* in that time is our first problem and we must work it out . . .

PS When I sent the telegram the boy in the post office smiled, and now keeps asking me 'Did she accept?'

What was happening to my doubts about marrying? What of the June 1955 letter?

    . . . If it does not end now it will become more and more complicated and worsen. I see that so clearly that it is a vision . . .

There is no answer, only Dusty's personality and an accumulation of events. The 'stubbornness, sarcasm, and sourness' were out-weighed by her ebullient nature. Her sunny disposition dimmed that vision and she flung her lust for life like a shroud over doubts of incompatibility. Emotions had engaged in high gear, she endured abortion – such an investment of trust had to be honoured, my responsibility had to be fulfilled. And a need for her was growing in me. To all this add a burgeoning new world and a sweep of events crying out to be shared. There was no one else I wanted to share it with. And this: I was passionate about and eager for children. Dusty shared that passion. We talked of a family of six at least.

We were married on 14 November 1958 in the registry office of Hackney Town Hall from which we were driven away in Ralph's jeep. Food, drink and Entertainment were laid on in the premises of the Primrose Jewish Youth Club on the Finchley Road, I designed the wedding dress – Empire line! Don't ask me why. Don't ask me why the Empire line, that is. I know why I designed it – because I had ideas about everything! No sense of my limitations. Like the wedding celebration – it was to be different. We wanted to entertain our guests as well as feed them, do more than just invite them to dance to music played on an electric record player. Richard Williams, the film animator, ran a jazz band which we hired. Lottie, the nurse from Germany who looked after my father, sang songs by Kurt Weill and Brecht. We hired Irish dancers and their fiddles – I'd seen them perform somewhere and had asked would they dance at my wedding! A projector was organised to show cartoons and animated films including Richard's celebrated prizewinner, *The Little Island*. Caterers made the food in the club's kitchen for one hundred and fifty guests – relatives and friends. The Norfolk crowd drove through fog to get to London and entered the front door just as our wedding cake, a three-tiered thing standing on a wobbly table in the hall to be admired, collapsed like a detonated old monument because Adam and Miles were rushing excitedly up and down and around the stairs. We laughed when it fell, which horrified the Norfolk crowd. The iced columns were put back but now nothing could prevent them looking like Roman ruins.

Leah's last had gone. The youngster moved from Weald Square with his wife into their first flat – 15 Clapton Common, E5, and only now I understand the loneliness my mother must have felt. Sick husband, daughter long gone, her spirited, noisy son wedded and off. We had quarrelled but had loved one another, alive from fingertip to toe. Gone! All that argument, that liveliness – off in a jeep! I feel her sorrow more now as we feel most things too late. You hear me, Lindsay Joe?

Three months later John Dexter came out of prison. Seven months later *Roots* opened in Coventry. It was 1959. In April my father was admitted to the Jewish Home for Incurables, Tottenham, N16.

Chapter Twenty-six

Leah nursed her Joe

My father had three strokes. The first struck when I was fifteen. My mother's first diary entry reveals her filled with dread. In addition to their quarrels and the burden on my mother of earning money and running the house came the responsibility of a sick husband.

> 3.11.47
>
> I have not come to complain about my husband, all I want to know, after all the years of hardship with him, and now that he is ill, is it up to me to tolerate from him? I can see a terrible future for me with him as regarding my health and his. I think he will be better off without me, he will not have such a lot of responsibility.

Each stroke debilitated him pathetically more and more. It was his incontinence that most distressed my mother. She had to clean him and clean up after him. I helped when I could but she bore the brunt. She tore out many pages from her diaries. The discarded sheets must have been entries of great pain from which she wanted to protect us. Much though remains, painful enough.

> 4.3.59
>
> I feel much better to day, not so depressed, but never the less very sad. Joe is sitting in front of me. He looks ill to me, his face is yellow. I haven't washed him for the last two days. I cannot manage him very well. As time goes on he gets more and more difficult. He just won't get up, I have to struggle and now I'm losing energy. I don't feel so well myself. I don't know where and how all this will lead to? There is no end of struggle. You think you're finished struggling, then it takes a different form and you have to begin all over again . . .

If that is the quality of what she felt could be left behind without fear of causing too much distress, what was jettisoned? By December 1961 she could write:

Today I have torn out all the pages I wrote during this last year nearly. If I can't write better things I must not write at all. I have torn out 10 pages, it nearly broke 'my heart' but I feel much better now and I am going to sleep peacefully. Good night all.

That silent salutation to us, written words in an empty flat.

From the years of his first stroke I began the weary battle with the LCC to get us transferred from Weald Square to a more convenient flat. A thick file is before me. The battle seems to have begun in 1954 but the first letter on record is dated 8 March 1955.

Dear Sir
Re-transfer to other accommodation
I feel compelled to write a letter to accompany this certificate about my father because though Dr Roodyn affirms his disability he does not realise the full implications. We, my mother and I, as his relations do.

That we are on the third floor not only makes it difficult for my father when he has to move out but in addition discourages him from so doing. This means he does not get as much fresh air and exercise in the summer as he needs and in the winter cannot get to a public bath as often as he needs.

This brings me to the second point. There is no hot water laid on, the bath is in the kitchen (my father's slowness interferes with kitchen management) and anyway there is no direct hot water for the bath. If we decide to have one it means heating water in a basin on the electric stove. With an invalid in the house you must realise this is impractical.

The net result is that my father remains in the house on his own all day while we are out at work, the effect is depressing. Neither can he maintain an adequate standard of cleanliness; all this is encouraged by the inconvenience of the flat. It is a matter of urgency that we find a ground or first-floor flat with better convenience or I fear my father will suffer more than he need with his malady.

I now await your reply.

A reply came back fourteen days later from the Eastern District Office of the Housing Management Department in Bethnal Green signed R.J. Allerton F.R.I.C.S., A.M.I.MUN.E., P.P.I.HSE., The Director of Housing, who seemed too weighted down by degrees to be much concerned with my father's 'malady':

Dear Sir
Housing
With reference to the further medical evidence recently submitted in support of your transfer application, this has now been carefully considered, but it has been decided that the degree of preference already awarded to your application cannot be increased at present.

Over fourteen years I wrote, argued, pleaded, and sent medical evidence to support our case. Around the time *Declaration* was published, a month before breakfast with Uncle Solly, five weeks before starting to write *Chicken Soup with Barley*, I was still embroiled with Mr Allerton. 'I need you to write a letter for me' is how my mother would begin. I spent hours with her arguing over what to say and how it should be said.

'Quarrelling! He's always quarrelling with me.'

'No! *You're* quarrelling with *me!*'

'All right, don't write it then. I'll write it myself. I always have to do everything myself anyway.'

'I'm your son. I don't take things lying down.'

'Who's telling you to take things lying down? I need a letter written. It's such a difficult thing to do?'

'For no one else, only for you!'

'He gets at me. He's always getting at me.' Nothing was easy with her, but somehow we mostly ended laughing.

The letters went back and forth, back and forth.

> . . . to persist in sending us printed refusal forms is surely to disregard your own organisation. Is there nothing that can persuade you of the urgency of our case? If we remain in this flat then my father shall have to return to a hospital and will not receive the personal attention his condition requires. I beg you to reconsider your last printed form and to take notice of the enclosed doctor's letter. With all the new building going on there must be something for us . . .

The fag-smoking functionaries of the Eastern District housing Department inhaled nicotine to sooth their battered sensibilities and sent another typed letter of regret, and another and another, year after year.

> Your transfer application is already receiving the full preference on health grounds to which it is entitled and consequently no additional preference can be given in respect of the new medical certificate.
>
> I regret I cannot say when I shall be able to offer you accommodation, but you may be sure that I understand your needs and will help you as soon as I can.

In May 1959 the Housing Department insultingly offered her a prefab, a post-war edifice assembled in mere weeks and designed to last ten years though many lingered in them for up to thirty. Three weeks before *Roots* opened in Coventry my mother phoned: 'Arnold. I need you to write a letter.'

> *May 5th 1959*
> Your ref: D1/T.2757/3'A'
> Dear Sir
> I thank you for offering me the bungalow in No. 4 Lower Millfields which I viwed yesterday. I am afraid I cannot accept it because I want to feel that any move I make with my husband now should be a permanent one. We are too old and ill to take up temporary

accommodation in prefabs which should have come down two years ago . . .

Two years later Mr Allerton, addressing my mother as 'Dear Mrs Webster' was still requesting

> . . . up-to-date medical evidence in your case . . . The form should then be returned to this office and further consideration will be given to your application . . .

In later years I gathered well-known public and political figures to my cause. Mr Allerton's language improved –

> I fully appreciate your concern in this matter . . . I should also like to be able to offer her a transfer [that] she would like . . .

– but offers were not improved. Another seven years had to pass.

Jewish joke – an aside

In a village in the heart of Poland lived Hymie Lieberwitz and Mendel Moskowitz. Hymie was rich, flourished, neglected his prayers – his family adored him. Mendel was poor, depressed, virtuously devout – his family despised him. Day after day Mendel begged G-d to improve his lot, day after day he pleaded for a little good fortune to come his way, now and then. 'Not too much, Lord, just enough to relieve the suffering of my family.' Day after day. To no avail. The years of misery persisted like an eternal storm flooding his life with grief and despair. One day, the weight of misfortune by now unbearable, Mendel cried out his most dire lamentations to G-d.

'Lord! Lord! Explain it to me. I've got to know, I want to understand. Leiberwitz eats unkosher food, offers prayers only once a year on Yom Kippur, sleeps with other women, and rides to town on the Sabbath. Neighbours respect him, gentiles seek his advice, his family hang on his every word. And on top of it, Lord – him you make rich.

'Me, I offer prayers morning, noon and night, study the sacred books, observe the festivals, teach my children your laws, remain faithful to my wife, attend synagogue on the Sabbath. My neighbours spurn me, my family are ashamed of me, the gentiles beat me. And on top of it, Lord – you make me poor. Him wealthy, me destitute. The reprobate prosperous, the honest man despairs. The unholy one thrives, your most devoted servant – reduced, wretched, penniless, piteous, desolate, dejected, deserted, abandoned. Abandoned! Abandoned! Why, Lord, tell me. Why, why, why?'

'Because,' the Lord's voice boomed back with profound irritation, 'you nag!'

Meanwhile –

Leah nursed her Joe; cleaning him, hauling him around the flat she lived in for seventeen years, walking up and down six steep flights of steps with shopping – though she frequently phoned and requested: 'Arnold, I need you to do some shopping for me.' When he was in hospital she visited him almost daily. After the second stroke we were told a third would kill him. It didn't. The most horrendous period was when the ambling clot of blood that kept striking him struck his brain and he became briefly demented, throwing things in the ward, a danger to himself and other patients. He had to be placed in a padded cell. What tears that drew from us all. He looked so bewildered, frightened, cowering away in the corner. He knew this was not him. Nor was it. A gentle man, my father, eager to please, welcome, engage in conversation. I sat with him in the cell once, cradling him and weeping. The clot shifted and the madness passed but it left him more paralysed than before.

His sojourns in Hackney Hospital multiplied and lengthened. I made notes:

. . . they have taken him in partly to relieve my mother of the strain and partly to give him the attention and regular food our sad finances do not permit. He is in hospital now and has been for the last two weeks or so, happily smoking himself nearer death without restraint and in the kind of irresponsible idleness he has all his life wanted . . .

When I first went to visit him there were three other men along the same wall. An old man in the corner who had asthma, the one next to him who'd had a stroke and was also under observation – he was a countryman of my father and they spoke in Russian. Both these patients were Jewish. To his right was a third lean-faced man dying from the effects of a stroke. My father lay among them. It's a curious world the world of sick people . . . My father is used to it. When we visit him we say little but he lies contentedly back watching the other patients and their visitors. One could say he was at home in this world.

When he first started attending hospitals, eight years ago, he enjoyed getting up early in the morning and making tea for the others, or helping with the washing-up. He was more coherent and in control of his mental faculties then and related the personal history of each patient as he'd gleaned it from them during the day. Now he was content simply to smoke his cigarettes and watch them.

The years, the pain, and the struggling had mellowed my fiery mother, and a touching sweetness suffused my father. We all quarrelled less. A sense of arrival made me more tolerant of her political naivety; my achievements filled her with a mixture of pride and anxiety. Her diaries were full of unsent letters. One dated 15.7.59 records her confusion.

> Arnold, my son
> Don't let your head swell with all this fuss about your two plays. Only, you must remember that you are still a working-class man, and your mother still has to live on assistance. I am really very worried about you, I still wish you had a trade . . .

Eight days later she read over what she had written in her diary, and reflected on it.

Why, my dear Arnold, should I want you to have a trade when you are a writer? You are after all giving so many hundreds of people pleasure. What does it matter what you do? Of course you have made the world know you are alive, why should they not pay for all the hardship you suffered?

She viewed my life as hardship because she felt guilty having been unable to support me financially. It was not how *I* justified earnings from my plays. Royalties were for work done, not hardship suffered. She continues:

I, your mother, have not yet awoken to your ability. I have not given you encouragement. Why did I want you to slave for them [by taking up a trade I suppose she meant]? Good luck, my son. Go on showing them that there is life in all of us if only given a chance.

The memory of her evinces only a deep love and sense of loss and of guilt for not having been the son I would like to have been. Yet as with many such lingering memories the evidence tempers them. *She* was not without fault, and *I* was more loving than my guilt implies. Her sweetness was distorted by a bitterness which drove her into extreme states of hatred for those she imagined were the perpetrators of her misfortune, or at best had abandoned her; which bitterness in turn, when it was spent, left her troubled with remorse.

For my part, though I frequently lost patience with them and remonstrated with a man who was beyond change or recovery; and though I applied angry reason in the course of political exchanges with a woman who by now could not distinguish between intellectual exchange and criticism of character, yet I was attentive and loving, and in a battered way we all took pleasure in and were dependent upon one another.

But nothing could stop the decline of my father's health. After more urging of doctor, specialists, the Jewish Welfare Board – and not a little unaided by my public success – Joe was admitted in

April 1959 into the Jewish Home for Incurables. The care and attention he received there was infinitely more than my mother or we could give him, but no parent is consigned to a home without feelings of guilt, and guilt we felt, entangled messily with relief.

One of the most comical entries in her diary was written on 11 May some week after my father had entered the Tottenham home, and a few days after I had left to attend rehearsals for *Roots* in Coventry, it's a gem, and I'm happy to have unearthed it among all her not-so-easy-to-read scribblings, an example of a wit she possessed which so often cut through the tragic and the absurd.

I do wonder why Dusty should cry like this because Arnold will be away for two weeks to see his play rehearse. It's after all for his work. I didn't know she would take it so badly. Wonders never cease. She came up for dinner. I will not leave her by herself. She is expecting a child. My grandchild. Who more than a lonely person should know what loneliness means? I do. Three times my Arnold left home, not because he was unhappy, only because he wanted to get experiences elsewhere. He first left for Norfolk [she misses out the RAF]. Then he came home with a girlfriend who is his wife now. Namely Dusty. Then they both went away to Paris. My Joe used to leave me, I was always alone. Most times even if when they were here I was alone. Who really cares that I am alone now, and in such circumstances where I had to let Joe go into an incurable home. However, Dusty made me cry as well. I only wish that that was my trouble, that my husband went to have his play rehearsed . . .

So, Lindsay Joe, from such an entry in your grandmother's diary I'm reminded that your mother was carrying you when she sat on my right that first night of *Roots* in Coventry.

My mother twice attempted to rewrite my plays in her diary. On 18 November 1958 she ends the first act of a play that seems to be post-*Chicken Soup* and *Roots*, merging both, mixing art with reality, calling Dusty by her real name and me by the name used in the Trilogy, Ronnie.

> Sits down to wait for Ronnie and Dusty.
> She is just getting better from the flu. The
> decorators were in the same week that
> Ronnie was getting married. What with
> the work after they have gone and the
> worry of how Ronnie's wedding will go
> off, she looks ill and wearied.
>   She can hear Ronnie opening the door.
> She gets up to take the cups for tea.
> Ronnie rushes in.

Mummy, mummy, don't make us tea. We are not staying. We are going to see a film. Dusty is waiting at home for me. See you in the morning.

> Kisses her and goes out. She sits down
> again. A little forlorn and miserable – and
> says to herself –

Once more I'll have to get used to him not to be at home. I do feel lonely.

> Curtain falls.

She rewrote the ending of *Their Very Own and Golden City*, and in a manner that it is conceivable a young Turk-of-a-director today might adopt. The play and her reworked ending are worth recording. Synopsis:

Andrew Cobham, an apprentice draughtsman, and his young friends from Durham spend a Sunday sketching in Durham Cathedral. On entering, Andrew is overwhelmed. As though by osmosis he knows that one day he will become an architect. The year is 1926. He and his friends talk about the future which is all before them to do with, they think, as they please. As they plan it, the future unfolds. They will build six beautiful cities which will be owned by the people who live in them.

In the beginning all happens as they plan. But, as they continue plotting the future, still in the cathedral, we see their future swerve away in a different direction. Hope and reality conflict. Only one city is built, and not as they had envisioned it. Andrew is knighted and ends his life feeling he's compromised, failed. Although the final image of the play is of the youth in the cathedral, ever hopeful and oblivious to the future they cannot know will shape, nevertheless alongside is an image, just as strong, of the old Sir Andrew Cobham sitting feeble and defeated, his teeth clenched, in an armchair. He talks to himself.

I must stop clenching my teeth, I really must try and prevent my teeth from clenching. Howl, that's what I'd do if I opened my mouth – howl. Unclench your teeth, you old fool you. But why is it that I don't want to talk? Because I don't, you know, not a word. One day – I know it – one day I shan't even see people and then what'll happen? I shall stay just still-like, petrified, because I won't be able to find a single reason why I should make one word follow another, one thought follow another . . .

. . . They let us build the odd Golden City or two, even help us, and in the end – look at me! I don't suppose there's such a thing as democracy, really, only a democratic way of manipulating power. And equality? None of that, either, only a gracious way of accepting inequality.

Look, again, they were clenched again. Unclench them. Silly old fool, you. Unclench them.

You shouldn't force people to dirty themselves. A man loves the world only when he loves himself, and what love do you have left for yourself, Andrew Cobham?

My mother saw in that image of a defeated old man with no love or respect for himself, sitting in that armchair, attended by his wife, the image of my father sitting and sitting in his armchair in Weald Square. She wrote at length in her diary on 14 November 1964 about an early draft I gave her – the play went into fourteen drafts. I offer only a fragment:

. . . Your play, this Golden City, doesn't apply to your position at this moment. I have finished it, I mean reading your play. I have told you many a times My Arnold that you are a dreamer – not a persistent thinker. As for myself I cannot give any opinions on your play. There is a lot of truth in it but a lot of nonsense. I cannot point out to you, as you well know. At least until I have seen it in full play. Maybe after all if I did read the finished copy I could tell better. However for one I definitely don't like Andy finishing up in an armchair. Do you think all old people finish up in an armchair, or all disappointed politicians all end up ill like your Daddy? Your plays or some of your plays end up in armchairs. Fine [J.L.Fine, the founder and ex-general secretary of the Garment Workers' Union] is still a straight man and also active, not in the union but active, in his own personality. And the end should have been that if Andy could not achieve by the time he is old and disappointed, at the end the talk [the dialogue] should end by implying that Andy's work was is not in vain. The future youth will carry on and it will materialise. And then a youth should spring up from the audience and say I will continue to build the six cities and more, for the whole world Golden Cities. And old Andy should ask him – what is your name young man, and he should say, My name is Andy Cobham and curtain down.

An old-fashioned 'avant-garde' ending but I find it very moving. She got it wrong. Andrew Cobham was not an image of my father but a thirty-two-year-old's fearful image of his own eventuality. Well, wrong and right. As always.

The Kitchen

George and Tony were gracious about the overwhelmingly favourable response to the play, *Roots*, they had commissioned but turned down. John and I were now to be trusted. Not completely, with a full-scale production, but sufficiently. John was given the go-ahead to direct *The Kitchen* as a production without décor to be performed on two Sunday nights – 6 and 13 September.

Till then productions without décor were experiments using as many well-known actors as were available. They were paid £2 a day expenses while the entire budget was to be no more than £50 on two weeks' rehearsal. The play had to sink or swim on the evidence of one Sunday evening performance. An exception was made of *The Kitchen*, partly because it was a difficult play absurdly calling for a cast of thirty, partly because the success of *Roots* had earned us 'privileges': the budget was doubled to £100, still only fourteen days of rehearsal but at least the play was given two chances. *The Kitchen*'s structure is simply described. The huge kitchen of a restaurant serving two thousand customers a day has lain silent overnight like a slumbering monster. Early in the morning a night porter awakes it, lighting the ovens one by one. One by one the chefs and waitresses enter to prepare for the day's meals. Act I ends with the frenzied serving of lunch. An interlude followed. A few chefs and kitchen porters have lingered before leaving for their afternoon break. They talk about their dreams of a better life. The evening meal is never served because the central character, who is pursuing a hopeless relationship with a married waitress, is finally turned down by her and he goes berserk, smashing up the kitchen. Dreams die under the pressure of hell-holes.

The original version contained no interlude and was designed to be played straight through without an interval. My intention was to recreate the experience of working under high pressure, as I had worked in Le Rallye's kitchen in Paris, illustrating the dehumanising effects of the work processs. John saw at once that two parts devoted to demonstrating work would be overwhelming. A moment of contrast was needed. He instructed me to go away and write a quiet scene, he didn't care what it was about as long as it broke the intensity of the two 'work' parts. He was right. I wrote the dream sequence which, had it been part of what I'd submitted for the *Observer* Play Competition, might have secured for the play one of the prizes.

John, superb technician that he was, just as he had recognised that the card game in *Chicken Soup with Barley* needed to be precisely worked out – it was not enough to write a stage instruction 'they're playing a game of solo' – also recognised that 'the service' needed to be detailed more precisely than I'd outlined in the text. The full 'service' was painstakingly constructed during rehearsals which were manic but thrilling. Buoyed up by his success with *Roots* John was high on the difficult material he had to work with, rising to the challenge of choreographing thirty actors around a stage, goading each one to mime selected cooking actions, to concentrate, to be a constantly believable presence even though they had few lines. Round his neck hung a football referee's whistle which he would blow with huge delight when the hordes got out of control and he needed to call them to a halt and start again.

Central to the play's success was Jocelyn's design. A magnificent book has just been published on her work. In it she quotes John.

For Sunday night productions at the Court some of the responsibility and weight was taken off you. Everyone knew there wasn't going to be scenery so you could chance something like *The Kitchen*. You could risk doing with nothing. *The Kitchen* pointed me in the direction – not of minimalism, that's the wrong word – but of provoking the audience to think for themselves and use their imagination.

'Provoking the audience to think for themselves and use their imagination' is the kind of theatre rhetoric I've gradually, over the years, come to suspect and steer clear of – it sounds more liberating and heroic than it actually can be, using language in a mish-mash kind of way. To think for yourself and to imagine for yourself are two completely different processes. The claim for Jocelyn's set was misleading. Her marvellously bare and abstract structure didn't so much allow an audience to imagine a real kitchen as it left them free to concentrate on the text and enjoy John's choreography and the acting.

While the actors whirled round and round my father was dying.

20.4.59

I have fought that Joe should be taken into a home so that he can be with people and make him be better. At least so I imagined – seeing people and being dressed up in very nice clothes it would bring him back to think a bit. But on the contrary, doctor said that he has no more than six months to live. He doesn't look like that to me. Still how am I to feel about it? What can I do? I am very lonely. The older I get the less I'll feel to work. The less I'll be able to work. But pray to goodness that I'll never have to go to live with either of my children. I hope that if I have to die I should go to sleep and never get up.

I have no record of my father's weeks in the Jewish Home for Incurables. Only one last image. After the final run-through of *The Kitchen* in the church hall in Kensington we visited Joe who was failing. To be honest I can't remember if this scene took place on the Friday or the Saturday on which he died. They were the last moments my mother and I shared with him. The hospital had called us. He was going, they said. We sat either side of him watching him struggle for breath. My mother looked at me with a shrug as though saying 'Well, this is it, you must accept it.' I couldn't, and kept urging him:

'Come on, Joe, breathe, Joe, come on, keep breathing.'

'What, you think he can hear you, silly boy?' said Leah. We smiled.

Her diary entry that day was in pencil.

5.9.59

Joe died on this date. It's finished. I will not quarrel with him any more. I only hope that I too die as quickly and soon. My heart is empty. We did not live very happy. Joe had a rough deal from all sides since I remembered him as a girl. Why oh why did I not know how to live with him and not make such a mess of his life and mine.

The next entry was after his funeral.

> Joe was buried yesterday. He spent his first night there. I couldn't
> cry at the burial ground. I can only cry to myself. I always cry to
> myself. I blame myself for his early death. We had such a terrible
> life together. There were times when we both cried together and
> forgave one another the wrongs we done to one another. I know he
> did love me. I thought I didn't, but I must have done. Loved him
> for going through all these months of agony with him . . .

'Shiva' is the period of mourning. The immediate family – wife,
children, brothers and sisters, parents if any are alive – sit for seven
days on low stools while in-laws or friends attend to the running of
the house. Visitors come to share the mourning, help pass the time
in recollecting, bring food. Prayers are said each night. The men do
not shave. It is a ritual I scorned. Until I needed it. When I needed
it, I understood its value. Death stupefies, the spirit is in a state of
shock, you need release from the demands of daily life, time to
grieve and honour the dead. The ritual of 'shiva' recognises this. I
didn't sit 'shiva' all seven days. But some. I felt the need.

My mother continued for the remainder of her life to agonise
over her relationship with her husband. He entered her dreams.

> No one knows how bitter my life is. Yes, Joe, I have the loveliest of
> times with you in my dreams. It is always I who speaks to you. I am
> happy with you. So many happy things that I do for you and I feel
> so happy to see you. And I assure you with all my heart how happy
> we will be. You just never say a word and I don't see you happy.
> Friday night, the tenth October '64, I dreamed we were buying
> meat. I didn't have enough to pay. You said I have, there you are!
> You gave me a pound. When I gave it to the butcher it fell more
> than one. I kept counting and counting, more and more. And we
> came somewhere, we saw people in sort of glass cubicles. They had
> no air. A woman was taken out to be taken to hospital . . .
> You said something and I said: Oh yes, we will live happy and we
> can, you'll see. And I took you round and kissed you.

Yes, Joe, you were right. No one showed you that they did love you. You didn't think anyone cares. You were right. Although everyone did care but no one could do anything for you, including myself. I could not do anything for you. You were not the man to be able to talk to. You just wanted everyone to leave you alone. Just because you thought no one cares.

My dreams show me that I never had a bad heart to you. I always wanted to be happy with you. Somehow you provoked me. I needed a little stirring, a little life. Still, Joe, revenge is being taken on your behalf. I pay now. I am the loneliest woman. I have many people that I love and they love me but I am still alone, very much alone. Well, Joe, I don't mind. You can at least come to my dreams every night. If I could not be happy with you in life at least I will be in my dreams. I am sure it won't be long and I'll soon be a dream to other people. I don't mind at all. The sooner the better.

Curtain

I could not attend the first Sunday performance of *The Kitchen* which I was informed had been a success. The second Sunday performance was memorable. We sat, as we always did, in the front row of the circle. I could feel the sense of excited anticipation that moved through the audience. It was an audience that had been touched by *Chicken Soup with Barley* and *Roots* and had heard that with *The Kitchen*, a play for thirty characters, something unusual was about to happen. The atmosphere was palpable. There, before us, was that almost bare stage, only Jocelyn's orange-boxes, white sheets and the exposed walls of the theatre, revealed as they had never before been revealed. Something extraordinary was obviously going to take place in such a setting.

The lights went down. The audience hushed. The night porter came on, lit an oven, the first overhead light blazed down, the low oven hum burst into sound. With each oven struck into flame the intensity of light and the intensity of sound grew. One by one the chefs strolled into work, waitresses crossed the stage to change into black and white. The day's work was beginning.

My father had died, the first play I ever wrote – opened. Seventeen years later, on the first night of the world première of *Shylock* in Stockholm, my mother died. It is one of my deepest regrets that I was not with her.

On 4 October 1956 I wrote to my father in hospital from Paris.

> . . . I want you to read this letter yourself. Please do not ask any of the nurses to read it out to you, make an effort and sit up and smoke and read . . .

The letter describes our life in Paris and lists the friends and relatives who came to visit or stay; but the purpose of the letter was other.

> . . . Ever since your illness began to take a bad turn I have wanted to say something to you, something that you would at once grasp and realise was a great truth . . . Year by year you have grown to regard yourself as absolutely no good to yourself and those around you. You have been so aware of your weaknesses that you long ago gave up doing anything about them. You felt yourself not worth the trouble. Well there have been bitter and hopeless times but . . . I'm trying hard to remain simple and uncomplicated . . . I always wanted to say something to you that would pull you out of it all . . .
>
> Walking along the street the other day I began remembering some of the things we used to do together . . . The wrestling matches, the times I played truant from school and you from work and we went to pictures instead, the poker games . . . And I suddenly realised that out of it all I love you very much. From this I began to wonder why, and again, as quickly, the answer came – because you love me . . . It occurred to me that no matter what else you have done or not done you have loved Della and mum and me. It does not matter that you couldn't do anything about it, it doesn't matter at all – no event of the past matters. The important fact to you and to us is that you have always dearly loved us and have

shown it in lots of ways, ways that we have none of us acknowledged . . .

There is so much in life that is really tragic. Last night in our narrow street we saw three tramps sleeping on the pavement, a common sight. But now it is bitterly cold and they were lying over the hot gratings that cover the tube stations and – this is what was so pathetic – two of them were quarrelling about positions and one pushed the other over a bit. They had unkempt beards and dirty faces and rags for clothes and they were humanity at its lowest ebb. We have never reached such states. We have quarrelled and laughed, and had parties and friends, we have been very human and really most of the time very happy; and we have loved. Repeat that to yourself again and again. It is so important and so true. Whatever criticisms people have made of you no one has ever disliked you because always your kindliness and friendliness have come out. A person who is capable of love is always worthwhile. And that is you. That is the important thing I wanted to tell you . . . You must be happy because you deserve to be happy, because to be happy and to love and to be loved is essentially your nature.

Eight months before she died I sent a postcard from Wales to my mother.

March 27 1976
My dearest mother

I had a dream about you last night so I had to write and tell you. It was a crowded street, for some reason I seemed to think it was the other side of Commercial Street, near the Fruit Exchange. I was crossing from one side of a turning to the other along with multitudes . . . and you, aged as you are now, were waiting for me on the other side, looking very anxious. You'd come out from your flat (wherever *that* was) to look for me, and oddly you were waiting on that corner. I don't think I was a boy, but a grown man. You took my hand as though I'd been a naughty child. Well not quite, as though I'd been away and not let you know my whereabouts. But as with most dreams the atmosphere was more important than the details. What haunts me is how worried you looked, how very motherly you were. And sweet.

Editor's note: Arnold Wesker has since re-established his relationship with his son and begun one with his grandson.

List of written and mainly published works

1957	The Kitchen
1958	Chicken Soup with Barley
1959	Roots
1960	I'm Talking About Jerusalem
1962	Chips with Everything
1965	The Four Seasons
1966	Their Very Own and Golden City
1970	The Old Ones
1970	The Friends
1971	Fears of Fragmentation (essays)
1971	Six Sundays in January (Stories, TV Play 'Menace', diary for Stockholm)
1972	The Journalists
1974	The Wedding Feast
1974	Say Goodbye You May Never See Them Again (text to paintings by naive painter John Allin)
1974	Love Letters on Blue Paper (stories)
1976	Shylock (previously 'The Merchant')
1976	Words – as definitions of experience (essay)
1976	Love Letters on Blue Paper (the play)
1977	Journey into Journalism (record of two months spent in offices of The Sunday Times)
1978	One More Ride on the Merry-Go-Round
1978	Said The Old Man to The Young Man (stories)
1978	Fatlips (book for young people)
1979	The Wesker Trilogy (a film script)
1980	Fatlips (the play adapted from book)
1980	Caritas
1980	Lady Othello (original film script)
1981	Sullied Hand (one-act play)

1981   Breakfast (original play for TV)

1982   Annie Wobbler (One Woman Play cycle)

1982   Four Portraits – of Mothers (one-act One Woman Play cycle)

1983   Yardsale (one-act One Woman Play cycle)

1983   Cinders (play based on Paul Bailey's life of Cynthia Payne)

1984   Bluey (90-minute play for radio: The European Radio Commission)

1985   Distinctions (essays, lectures, etc.)

1984/85 Thieves in the Night (adaptation for German TV, four 90-minute parts of Koestler's novel)

1986   Whatever Happened To Betty Lemon (one-act One Woman Play cycle)

1986   When God Wanted A Son

1987   Badenheim 1939 (adapted from Aharon Appelfeld's novel)

1987   Shoeshine & Little Old Lady (two one-act plays for young people)

1987   Lady Othello (play adapted from film script)

1988   Caritas (libretto for opera, music by Robert Saxton)

1988   Beorhtel's Hill (community play to celebrate town of Basildon's 40th)

1988   The Mistress (one-act One Woman Play cycle)

1989   Diary of a Good Neighbour (adaptation in four parts for BBCTV of Doris Lessing novel)

1990   Three Women Talking

1990   Letter to a Daughter

1990/91 Homage to Catalonia (film script)

1991   Blood Libel (commissioned to open new theatre in Norwich, 1995)

1992   Wild Spring (play for Brenda Bruce)

1993   Bluey (adapted for stage from radio play)

1995   Maudie (film script of the Lessing novel: Diary of a Good Neighbour)

Index